THE LABORS OF IDRIMI

ANCIENT NEAR EAST MONOGRAPHS

General Editors
Jeffrey Stackert
Juan Manuel Tebes

Editorial Board
Angelika Berlejung
Abraham I. Fernández Pichel
Tova Ganzel
Daniel Justel Vicente
Lauren Monroe
Emanuel Pfoh
Madadh Richey
Stephen C. Russell
Andrea Seri

Number 33

SBL PRESS

THE LABORS OF IDRIMI

Inscribing the Past, Shaping the Present at Late Bronze Age Alalah

by
Jacob Lauinger

SBL PRESS

SBL PRESS

Atlanta

Library of Congress Control Number: 2024944355

For Marisa

Table of Contents

List of Figures and Tables ix
Acknowledgments xiii
Abbreviations xv
Note on Transliterations, Normalizations, and Translations xix
1. Introduction 1
  1.1. Alalah: The City and Its Excavations 11
  1.2. Circumstances of the Statue's Discovery 14
  1.3. Woolley's Description of the Archaeological Context of the Statue 16
  1.4. Introducing the Inscriptions 18
  1.5. Terminology 21
  1.6. Western Hybrid Akkadian 21
  1.7. Aims and Structure of the Book 25
2. Approaches 27
  2.1. Archaeology 27
  2.2. Destruction and Burial 35
  2.3. Dating and Historiography 37
  2.4. Art Historical Approaches 42
  2.5. Philological Approaches 46
  2.6. Linguistic Approaches 54
  2.7. Source-Critical Approaches 62
  2.8. Literary-Critical Approaches 69
  2.9. Approach of the Book 79
3. Ancestors 85
  3.1. Ancestor Veneration or Votive Installation? 85
  3.2. Textual Perspectives 88
  3.3. Material Perspectives 94
  3.4. A Middle Bronze Age Date for the Statue? 99
  3.5. From Collective Ancestor to Historical Ancestor 105

4. Arguments 109
 4.1. Paleography and Orthography: Making Sense of Variation 109
 4.2. The Idrimi Inscriptions and *Narû* Literature 116
 4.3. *Mānahtu* in the Political Siscourse of Anatolia and the Levant during the Late Bronze Age 121
 4.4. Arguments for Acknowledging the Hegemony of Mittani 131
5. Audiences 133
 5.1. Literacy and the *Maryannu* at Late Bronze Age Alalah 133
 5.2. Audience Identification: Idrimi as *Maryannu* 141
 5.3. Excursus: Audience Access to the Text 146
 5.4. The Political Influence of the *Maryannu* 148
6. Šarruwa and IM-nerari 157
 6.1. Šarruwa 158
 6.2. IM-nerari 162
 6.3. Addu-nerari, Ruler of Nuhašše 165
 6.4. Addu-nerari, Ruler of Qaṭna 171
7. Conclusion 175
Appendix: Commentaries on the Cheek Inscription and the Body Inscription 179
 A.1. Cheek Inscription 179
 A.2. Body Inscription 183
References 287
Plates 305
Indices 323
 Primary Texts 323
 Ancient Proper Nouns 334
 Ancient Roots, Words, and Phrases 341

List of Figures and Tables

Figures

1.1. The Statue of Idrimi on its throne on display in the British Museum.
1.2. Arrangement of the body inscription on the statue.
1.3. The inscription on the statue's cheek.
2.1. The feet of the statue in the sockets of the throne.
2.2. The vertical ruling between divisions 2 and 3.
2.3. The ends of lines 44–46, showing the extension of line 45 onto the right leg.
3.1. Signs read as *a-bi-i-ni* by Durand (2011, 147) in line 89.
3.2. Juxtaposition of the sign read as I or BI in line 89 (left) with NINDA_2 from Emar 538 (right).
3.3. Juxtaposition of the Statue of Idrimi (left) with statues from the Royal Hypogeum at Qaṭna (right).
3.4. Reconstructed plan of Level IB temple and annex showing the find-spots of the pit containing the Statue of Idrimi, the statue's throne and base, and the altar.
3.5. The altar, showing relief decoration.
3.6. The beginning of lines 10–12.
3.7. Composite image showing the extent of line 14 and space between NA and MA signs.
3.8. The end of lines 72–74.
3.9. The beginning of lines 90–91.
3.10. Niqmepa of Yamhad wearing a conical hat and robe with fringed hem.
4.1. The word *qa-qa-ri* (l. 61), showing paleographic variation of the QA sign.
4.2. The beginning of lines 41–42.
4.3. Forms of KI in line 38.
4.4. Forms of U_3 in lines 53–56.
4.5. The word *qa-qa-ri* in lines 61–62.

A.1. Comparison of ALAM signs in lines 92 (left) and 99 (right), with putative ALAM in line CI 2 (center).
A.2. Comparison of DUB signs in lines 98 (left) and 99 (right), with putative DUB in l. CI 2 (center).
A.3. Two examples of DUB in paleographic lists from Emar (Msk 74145+ on left, Msk 74193a+ on right).
A.4. Comparison of UGU signs in lines CI 3 (left) and 48 (right), with UGU in line CI 2 (center).
A.5. Damaged DAG in line CI 2.
A.6. Example of DAG in RS 14.128+.
A.7. End of lines 2–3.
A.8. Defective E! in line 5?
A.9. Three different forms of MA in line 10 (first = left; second = center; third = right).
A.10. The third, fourth, and fifth signs of line 11.
A.11. The third sign of line 11 (center) juxtaposed with attestations of I (l. 14, left) and DUMU (l. 12, right).
A.12. The second half of line 14, showing extent to the right.
A.13. The sign NA in line 14 (left) and Msk. 74193a+ (right).
A.14. IŠ (l. 16, left) juxtaposed to IŠ (l. 21, right).
A.15. The damaged sign at the beginning of line 17 (center) juxtaposed with KU signs in line 10 (left) and later in line 17 (right).
A.16. The second preserved sign in line 17 juxtaposed with an example of ZAG in RS 86.2222+.
A.17. Attestations of DUMU in lines 21–22.
A.18. D[UMU.M]EŠ, line 22.
A.19. RU in line 30 (left) juxtaposed with RU in line 99 (right).
A.20. Two attestations of UR in line 77 (left) and line 98 (right).
A.21. Juxtaposition of ŠU in line 31(left) with attestations of ŠU in line 34 (center) and line 96 (right).
A.22. Juxtaposition of E!? in line 33 (left) with E in line 34 (right).
A.23. The first, second, and third attestations of KI in line 37.
A.24. Juxtaposition of AZ in line 42 (left) with attestations of AZ in line 58 (center) and 69 (right).
A.25. Juxtaposition of AD in line 45 (left) with attestations of AD in RS 20.121 line 153 (center) and line 168 (right).
A.26. The signs *-ra-at-*, line 45 above *ad-bu-*, line 46.
A.27. The beginning of line 46.
A.28. Juxtaposition of *ub*!(TE) in line 46 (center) with attestations of UB in line 16 (left) and TE in line 47 (right).
A.29. The sign ⸢*pa*⸣, line 49.
A.30. The end of lines 49–51.
A.31. Second occurrence of NU, line 52.

A.32. Form of NU in line 65.
A.33. ME with check mark in line 52.
A.34. IB, line 53.
A.35. NU NU in line 55.
A.36. BU in line 62.
A.37. NU in line 69.
A.38. Second NU in line 51.
A.39. KAB in line 55.
A.40. RI in line 79.
A.41. The sign *gub*$_3$ (KAB) in line 59.
A.42. SI$^{!?}$ ŠUB, line 57.
A.43. The second half of line 59.
A.44. Juxtaposition of putative IL in line 59 (left) with IL in line 40 (right).
A.45. The first and second attestations of MA in line 60.
A.46. Juxtaposition of UM in line 11 (left) with UM in line 60 (right).
A.47. Attestations of UM in line 92 (left) with UM in line 96 (right).
A.48. Attestation of AL in line 19.
A.49. Juxtaposition of KU in line 62 (left) with KU(*qu*$_2$) in line 63 (center) and LU in line 69 (right).
A.50. DIDLI in line 65.
A.51. Smith's putative SI KI in line 67, better identified as LA.
A.52. AŠ$^{!}$ Followed by LU in line 73.
A.53. QA (*ka*$_4$) in line 76.
A.54. Juxtaposition of attestations of UB in lines 16 (left), 36 (center), and 78 (right).
A.55. UD$^{!?}$(*tu*$_2$) in line 79.
A.56. Defective I in line 79.
A.57. UZ Formed as UD + HU in lines 80 (left), 90 (first attestation in center, second attestation on right).
A.58. UZ in RS 14.128+.
A.59. U$_3$ in error for KI in line 83.
A.60. TUŠ (= KU) in lines 84 (left) and 85 (first attestation in center, second attestation on right).
A.61. The beginning of line 85.
A.62. Photo of *u*$_3^{!}$ (KI) (center) juxtaposed with Smith's (1949, Plate 12) copy (left) and Oller's (1977a, 236) copy (right).
A.63. The signs -*šu*-*u*$_2^{!}$-*šu*- in line 89.
A.64. The sign -*ṣe*- in lines 94 (left) and 97 (right).
A.65. The signs AN *u* KI in lines 95 (left), 97 (center), and 99 (right).
A.66. Determinative KI in line 95 (Smith's putative KU).
A.67. KI in line 57.
A.68. Attestation of ŠU in line 96 (left) juxtaposed with the second attestation of ŠU in line 95 (right).

A.69. Attestations of ŠU in lines 31 (left) and 34 (right).
A.70. The first attestation of MA in line 96.
A.71. The ends of lines 93–98.
A.72. Juxtaposition of a typical form of MEŠ in line 82 (left) with the form in line 97 (right).
A.73. The sign ⸢LU$_2^?$⸣ in line 98.
A.74. Two attestations of TUR/DUMU in lines 25 (left) and 91 (right).
A.75. Two cursive forms of LU$_2$ in lines 75 (left) and 99 (right).
A.76. INANNA in line 98.
A.77. Juxtaposition of LA in line 100 (center) with attestations of third LA in line 78 (left) and LA in 94 (right).

Tables

3.1. Statues of ancestors from Bronze Age Syro-Anatolia.
A.1. Various interpretations of line 55b.

Acknowledgments

As with any project of many years, I owe a tremendous debt to a number of different people and institutions, and it is a great pleasure to acknowledge them here.

In a sense, this project began when I first read the Statue of Idrimi text in the autumn of 2001 in an Akkadian seminar taught by Martha Roth at the University of Chicago's Oriental Institute (now Institute for the Study of Ancient Cultures). In the two decades since, I have had several opportunities to read it with students in my own Akkadian seminars at Johns Hopkins University. I am grateful to my former teacher and classmates in Chicago and to my past students in Baltimore for the conversations we had about Idrimi. A special acknowledgment needs to be made to Kathryn Medill in this regard.

Eleanor Robson helped me set up the Electronic Idrimi on the Oracc platform, and Steven Tinney has helped me to maintain it subsequently. James Fraser, then project curator for the ancient Levant at the British Museum, allowed me to study the Statue of Idrimi during a rare moment in 2017 when it came out from under its display case for a few days. Carole Roche-Hawley shared her at-the-time unpublished *Habilitation* (a revised version of which is now published as Roche-Hawley 2024) and has allowed me to reproduce some of her photographs that will appear in a forthcoming sign list.

Aspects of this book were presented as invited lectures at the British Museum and the Institute for the Study of the Ancient World at New York University in 2017, at the University of Pennsylvania's Art and Archaeology of the Mediterranean World Colloquium in 2018, at the University of Helsinki in 2019, and at Wheaton College (Illinois) in 2020, as well as in conference presentations at the annual meetings of the American School of Overseas Research in 2016 and 2017 and the Rencontre Assyriologique Internationale in 2018. I am grateful to the questions from audience members that I received at all of these presentations or in informal conversations afterward; one from Joshua Jeffers stands out in particular.

The translation of the Akkadian word *mānahtu* as "labors," which finds its way into the title of this book, derives from Andrew George's (2003) inspired translation of this same word in his critical edition of the Epic of Gilgamesh.

Murat Akar, Yoram Cohen, Alice Mandell, Adam Miglio, Mark Weeden, and Martin Worthington selflessly gave time and energy to read a draft of the book, which has benefited greatly from their comments. Of course, the responsibility for errors or omissions remains with me.

Michael Chapin helped to organize references to each line of the Idrimi text in the secondary literature; Ann Jacobson provided able copyediting; and Angela Roskop Erisman provided a final round of copyediting, typeset the text, and created the indices.

My past and present colleagues in the Department of Near Eastern Studies at the Johns Hopkins University continue to be the best one could hope for. Their kind regard for our community and their commitment to research make it easy to be excited about work each day.

Last, but certainly not least, I thank my wife Marisa and son Sammy for so many things but, most importantly, for just being there.

Jacob Lauinger
Baltimore, Maryland
January 27, 2024

Abbreviations

AASOR	Annual of the American Schools of Oriental Research
ÄAT	Ägypten und Altes Testament
ABL	*Assyrian and Babylonian Letters Belonging to the Kouyunjik Collections*
ABZ	*Assyrisch-babylonische Zeichenliste*. Rykele Borger. 3rd ed. Neukirchen-Vluyn: Neukirchener Verlag, 1986.
AeL	*Ägypten und Levante*
AfO	*Archiv für Orientforschung*
AHw	Soden, Wolfram von. *Akkadisches Handwörterbuch*. 3 vols. Wiesbaden: Harrassowitz, 1965–1981.
AION	*Annali dell'Istituto Orientale di Napoli*
AIPHOS	*Annuaire de l'Institut de philologie et d'histoire orientales et slaves*
AJ	*Antiquaries Journal*
AJA	*American Journal of Archaeology*
AlT	Wiseman, Donald. *The Alalakh Tablets*. Occasional Publications of the British Institute of Archaeology in Ankara 2. London: British Institute of Archaeology in Ankara, 1953.
ANESSup	Ancient Near Eastern Studies Supplement Series
AOAT	Alter Orient und Altes Testament
AoF	*Altorientalische Forschungen*
AuOr	*Aula Orientalis*
AuOrSup	Supplement to *Aula Orientalis*
BaghM	*Baghdader Mitteilungen*
BASOR	*Bulletin of the American Schools of Oriental Research*
BBVO	Berliner Beiträge zum Vorder Orient Texte
BeO	*Bibbia e Oriente*
BJS	Brown Judaic Studies
BO	*Bibliotheca Orientalis*
BSOAS	*Bulletin of the School of Oriental and African Studies*

BWL	Lambert, Wilfred G. *Babylonian Wisdom Literature*. Oxford: Clarendon, 1960.
CAD	*The Assyrian Dictionary of the Oriental Institute of the University of Chicago*. Chicago: The Oriental Institute of the University of Chicago, 1956–2006.
CDLI	Cuneiform Digital Library Initiative
CHANE	Culture and History of the Ancient Near East
CNIP	Carsten Niebuhr Institute Publications
CTH	Laroche, Emmanuel. *Catalogue des textes hittites*. Paris: Klincksieck, 1971.
CunMon	Cuneiform Monographs
CUSAS	Cornell University Studies in Assyriology and Sumerology
DULAT	Olmo Lete, Gregorio del, and Joaquín Sanmartín. *A Dictionary of the Ugaritic Language in the Alphabetic Tradition*. Translated and edited by W. G. E. Watson. 3rd ed. 2 vols. Leiden: Brill, 1995.
EA	El-Amarna tablets. According to the edition of Knudtzon, Jørgen A. *Die el-Amarna-Tafeln*. Leipzig: Hinrichs, 1908–1915. Repr., Aalen: Zeller, 1964. Continued in Rainey, Anson F. *El-Amarna Tablets, 359–379*. 2nd rev. ed. Kevelaer: Butzon & Bercker, 1978.
FM	Florilegium Marianum
GAG	Soden, Wolfram von. *Grundriss der akkadischen Grammatik*. 2nd ed. Rome: Pontifical Biblical Institute, 1969.
Gilg.	George, Andrew. *The Babylonian Gilgamesh Epic: Introduction, Critical Edition and Cuneiform Texts*. 2 vols. Oxford: Oxford University Press, 2003.
GMTR	Guides to the Mesopotamian Textual Record
HACL	History, Archaeology, and Culture of the Levant
HAM	Inventory number for an item in the Hatay Archaeological Museum
HdO	Handbuch der Orientalistik
HSM	Harvard Semitic Monographs
HSS	Harvard Semitic Series
HUCA	*Hebrew Union College Annual*
IOS	*Israel Oriental Studies*
JANESCU	*Journal of the Ancient Near Eastern Society of Columbia University*
JAOS	*Journal of the American Oriental Society*
JBL	*Journal of Biblical Literature*
JCS	*Journal of Cuneiform Studies*
JCSMS	*Journal for the Canadian Society of Mesopotamian Studies*
JHS	*Journal of Hellenic Studies*
JNES	*Journal of Near Eastern Studies*
JRAS	*Journal of the Royal Asiatic Society*

JSOTSup	Journal for the Study of the Old Testament Supplement Series
KAI	Donner, Herbert, and Wolfgang Röllig. *Kanaanäische und aramäische Inschriften*. 2nd ed. Wiesbaden: Harrassowitz, 1966–1969.
Kaskal	*Kaskal: Rivista di storia, ambiente e culture der Vicino Oriente Antico*
KAV	Keilschrifttexte aus Assur verschiedenen Inhalts
KBo	Keilschrifttexte aus Bogazköi. Leipzig: Hinrichs, 1916–1923; Berlin: Gebr. Mann, 1954–
KpT	Wilhelm, Gernot. "Die hurritischen Texte aus Šamuha." Pages 197–209 in *Textfunde aus den Jahren 1999–2017*. Vol. 1 of *Keilschrifttafeln aus Kayalipinar*. Edited by Elisabeth Riekne. Wiesbaden: Harrassowitz, 2019.
KTU	Dietrich, Manfried, Oswald Loretz, and Joaquín Sanmartín, eds. *Die keilalphabetischen Texte aus Ugarit*. Münster: Ugarit-Verlag, 2013. 3rd enl. ed. of Dietrich, Manfried, Oswald Loretz, and Joaquín Sanmartín, eds. *KTU: The Cuneiform Alphabetic Texts from Ugarit, Rad Ibn Hani, and Other Places*. Münster: Ugarit-Verlag, 1995.
KUB	Keilschrifturkunden aus Boghazköi. Berlin: Akademie, 1921–.
LANE	Languages of the Ancient Near East
LAPO	Litteratures ancienes du Proche-Orient
MARI	*Mari: Annales de recherches interdisciplinaires*
MC	Mesopotamian Civilizations
MSL	Materialen zum sumerischen Lexikon/Materials for the Sumerian Lexicon. 17 vols. Rome: Pontifical Biblical Institute, 1937–2004.
MZL	Borger, Rykle. *Mesopotamisches Zeichenlexikon*. Münster: Ugarit-Verlag, 2003.
NABU	*Nouvelles assyriologiques brèves et utilitaires*
NEA	*Near Eastern Archaeology*
OAC	Orientis Antiqui Collectio
OBO	Orbis Biblicus et Orientalis
OIP	Oriental Institute Publications
OIS	Oriental Institute Seminars
OLZ	*Orientalistische Literaturzeitung*
Or	*Orientalia (NS)*
Oracc	Open Richly Annotated Cuneiform Corpus
OrAnt	*Oriens Antiquuus*
PBS	University of Pennsylvania, Publications of the Babylonian Section
PEQ	*Palestine Exploration Quarterly*
PIHANS	Publications de l'Institut historique-archéologique néerlands de Stamboul

PRU	Le palais royal d'Ugarit
RA	*Revue d'assyriologie et d'archaeologie orientale*
RGTC	Repertoire géographique des textes cunéiformes
RHA	*Revue hittite et asianique*
RIMA	The Royal Inscriptions of Mesopotamia, Assyrian Periods
RINAP	Royal Inscriptions of the Neo-Assyrian Period
RS	Ras Shamra
RSOu	Ras Shamra-Ougarit
SAA	State Archives of Assyria
SAOC	Studies in Ancient Oriental Civilizations
SBA	Saarbrücker Beiträge zur Altertumskunde
SCCNH	Studies on the Civilization and Culture of Nuzi and the Hurrians
Sef	*Sefarad*
SJOT	*Scandinavian Journal of the Old Testament*
SMEA	*Studi Micenei ed Egeo-Anatolici*
SSAU 2	Dietrich, Manfried, and Oswald Loretz. "Die soziale Struktur von Alalah und Ugarit (II). Die sozialen Gruppen *hupše-namê*, *haniahhe-ekû*, *ehele-šūzubu* und *marjanne* nach Texten aus Alalah IV." *Die Welt des Orients* 5 (1969): 57–93.
SSAU 4	Dietrich, Manfred, and Oswald Loretz. "Die soziale Struktur von Alalah und Ugarit (IV). Die É = *bītu*-Listen aus Alalah IV aus Quelle für die Erforschung der geseilschaftlichen Schichtung von Alalah im 15 Jhr. V. Chr." *Zeitschrift für Assyriologie* 60 (1970): 88–23.
StCh	Studia Chaburensia
Syria	*Syria: Archéologie, art et histoire*
SyriaSup	Supplement to *Syria: Archéologie, art et histoire*
THeth	Texte der Hethiter
TT	Richter, Thomas, and Sarah Lange. *Das Archiv des Idadda: Die Keilschrifttexten aus den deutsch-syrischen Ausgrabungen 2001–2003 im Königspalast von Qatna.* Qaṭna Studien 3. Wiesbaden: Harrassowitz, 2012.
TUAT	*Texte aus der Umwelt des Alten Testaments*
UF	*Ugarit-Forschungen*
VT	*Vetus Testamentum*
WAW	Writings from the Ancient World
WO	*Die Welt des Orients*
WVDOG	Wissenschaftliche Veröffentlichungen der Deutsche Orient-Gesellschaft
WZKM	*Wiener Zeitschrift für die Kunde des Morgenlandes*
ZA	*Zeitschrift für Assyriologie*

Note on Transliterations, Normalizations, and Translations

The edition in this book originates from an online version of the Idrimi text that I created for the Open Richly Annotated Cuneiform Corpus (Oracc) platform, the Electronic Idrimi; see §2.9 for the URL. Because of these origins, I use h for ḫ, I do not indicate secondary lengthening or vowel length in proper nouns, and the lexical length of an Akkadian word follows the *Concise Dictionary of Akkadian*.

In line with Oracc protocol, the transliteration of cuneiform signs uses the sign values in MZL. For the confusion of sibilants (/s/ for expected /š/ or /š/ for expected /s/), if a value for the expected sibilant is in MZL, then that value is used; for example, *ma-si*$_{17}$*-ik-tu*$_{2}$ not *ma-ši-ik-tu*$_{2}$ for *masiktu*). But if the value for the expected sibilant is not in MZL, then the sign is transliterated with the unexpected sibilant; for example, *ah-šu-šu* not *ah-su*$_{x}$*-su*$_{x}$. I omit mimation in the case of final CVm signs; for example, *-ni*$_{7}$ not *-nim*. DA is transliterated as *ta*$_{2}$ if the consonant is expected to be voiceless, even in contexts where it is reasonable to suggest that it has subsequently become voiced; for example, via nasalization in the case of *im*-DA-*har* (l. 55). But other considerations, and not always obvious ones, for the choice of this sign exist, as the spelling DA-*ba-li*$_{3}$ for *tābali* (l. 34) makes clear. To transliterate *im*-DA-*har* as *im-da-har* would be, essentially, to make a possibility into a certainty, which is not justified on the basis of our current knowledge.

I do not normalize divine names. There are various possibilities, and the correct readings are unclear. It is not even clear that a logographically written divine name needs to be read the same way within the text; for example, in line 2, ^{d}IM could indicate Addu of Aleppo, since the deity is paired with Hebat (see the commentary to l. 2 in the appendix), while ^{d}IM in line 29 could indicate Teššub or Baʿlu since Idrimi's first act upon arriving at the shores of Mukiš is to climb to the top of Mount Hazzi (= Mount Ṣapunu), the traditional home of Teššub and Baʿlu, in order to make an offering (see the commentary to l. 34 in the appendix. The goddess written logographically as ^{d}*iš*$_{8}$*-tar*$_{2}$ or ^{d}INANNA could indicate Ištar,

Šaušga, Išhara, or even Aštarte. For similar reasons, I translate the divine names as just the Storm God, the Sun God, the Moon God, or, in the absence of any better option, IŠTAR.

I have intentionally tried to keep my translation of the Idrimi text more literal than idiomatic, with all the attendant advantages and disadvantages that come with this decision. The advantages are that it is easy for a reader to move from the Akkadian to the English and vice versa, and it will be transparent if anything has been dropped or added to the translation. The disadvantage is the danger of "Assyriologese." I follow the convention of putting the translation in italics when it is uncertain only when that uncertainty derives from epigraphic reasons. Otherwise, virtually the whole translation would be in italics.

1
Introduction

The Statue of Idrimi was excavated in or near a temple at Late Bronze Age Alalah in the modern-day Republic of Turkey and gets its name from the inscriptions carved on its body and cheek. These inscriptions are written in Akkadian cuneiform and, among other things, they tell the story of a young man named Idrimi who fled his home, spent time in exile, won a kingdom, and enjoyed a prosperous and successful reign. The essential question motivating this book is: Why was the story of Idrimi's life told at this particular time and place and in this particular way? This question, in turn, prompts some subsidiary questions about the statue's date, the significance of inscribing the text on a statue, the arrangement of the text on that statue, and who would have had access to the statue and the text, among others. The aim of this book is to try to answer these questions and explore how the answers inform our understanding of the social and historical context of the statue and the inscriptions.

The statue of the king, shown in figure 1.1 on the next page, is seated upon a throne. The statue is white, carved from magnesite, a soft stone; the throne is black, made of hard basalt and flanked by lions (or sphinxes?). Altogether, the king seated upon the throne measures about 1.67 m (5.5 ft) in height, so that the king's gaze meets the viewer's own. He is bearded and wearing a plain conical cap and an ankle-length robe, with his right hand open against his breast and his left hand lying in his lap. But little of the statue attempts mimesis. The king's robe is indicated only by the outline of its hem, his beard hangs as an undifferentiated mass that lacks any detail of its curls, and his lap has been left as a rectilinear block. Yet this representation is better understood as the sculptor's choice than as a lack of skill, for an interest in mimesis is evident in some parts of the statue's body. For instance, the king's right hand is depicted naturalistically, with his fingers the anatomically correct length so that the extension of his digits forms a crescent.

Alongside the tension between representation and mimesis, the second feature that catches the viewer's eye is that the statue is robed in writing. Its torso

Figure 1.1. The Statue of Idrimi on its throne
on display in the British Museum.

and legs are covered in a cuneiform inscription. A closer inspection of the statue's face reveals that another inscription of three lines extends along its right cheek, passing from the king's conical cap, between his eye and his ear, toward his chin. This inscription reads:

> $^{\mathrm{CI}\ 1}$ MU 30.K[AM.M]EŠ LUGAL-*ku* $^{\mathrm{CI}\ 2}$ *ma-na-ah-ti-ia* ⸢*a*⸣*-na* [U]GU-*ia aš-ṭu*$_{2}$*-ur li-*⸢*tak*$_{2}$⸣*-kal*$_{2}$*-šu-nu* $^{\mathrm{CI}\ 3}$ (erasure) *u*$_{3}$ *a-na* UGU-⸢*ia*⸣ *li-ik-ta-na-*⸢*ra-bu*⸣[1]

> I was king for thirty years. I inscribed my labors on [m]yself. May it (i.e, the inscription) encourage them (i.e., the descendants) so that they (the descendants) pray to me regularly.

If the inscription on the statue's cheek leaves the identity of the seated king a mystery, the inscription on the statue's body proclaims it in its very first words:

> ^{1} ⸢*a-na-ku*⸣ ^{m}*id-ri-mi* DUMU ^{m}DINGIR-*i-li*$_{3}$*-ma* ^{2} ARAD ⸢^{d}⸣[I]M ^{d}*he*$_{2}$*-bat u*$_{3}$ ^{d}*iš*$_{8}$*-tar*$_{2}$ NIN ^{uru}*a-la-la-ah* <<NIN>> / NIN-*ia*

> I am Idrimi, the son of Ilimi-ilima, a servant of the [Sto]rm god, Hebat, and IŠTAR, the lady of Alalah, my lady.

From here, the inscription on the statue's body plunges immediately into a tale of woe, narrating how, perhaps as a child, the seated king named Idrimi fled his ancestral seat of Halab, modern Aleppo, with his family for the city of Emar on the Middle Euphrates:

> ^{3} *i-*⸢*na*⸣ ^{uru}*ha-la-ab*^{ki} E$_{2}$ *a-bi-ia* ^{4} *ma-si*$_{17}$*-ik-tu*$_{2}$ *it-tab-ši u*$_{3}$ *hal-qa*$_{3}$*-nu* / IGI ^{5} ⸢LU$_{2}$⸣.HI.A ^{uru}*e*$^{!}$*-mar*^{ki} *a-ha-te*.HI.A ^{6} [*š*]*a um-mi-ia u*$_{3}$ *aš-ba-nu a-na* ^{uru}*e-mar*^{ki}

> In Halab, the household of my father, a criminal act occurred, so we fled before resident aliens at Emar, my mother's sisters, and stayed at Emar.

However, because the relatives from his maternal line with whom the family stayed at Emar were themselves resident aliens, they were not allowed to participate in the political life or collective decision making in the city. Idrimi, now identified as the family's youngest son and perhaps making a reference to a proverbial saying, alone realized the significance of how dramatically the family's opportunities had changed in their translocation from Halab to Emar:

> ^{7} *ah-he*$_{2}$.⸢HI.A⸣-*ia ša* UGU-*ia* GAL.GAL.HI.A ^{8} *it-ti-ia-ma aš-bu-u*$_{2}$ *u*$_{3}$ *ma-an-nu-um-ma* ^{9} ⸢*a*⸣*-wa-te*.MEŠ *ša ah-šu-šu u*$_{2}$*-ul ih-šu-uš* ^{10} *um-ma a-na-ku-ma ma-an-*⸢*nu*⸣*-um* E$_{2}$

[1] See §1.5 on the line numbering CI 1–CI 3.

a-bi-šu 11 *lu-u*$_2$ *i-*⸢*dag*$^?$⸣*-gal u*$_3$ *ma-an-nu-um* 12 *a-*[*n*]*a* DUMU.HI.A ^{uru}*e-mar*^{ki} *lu-u*$_2$ ARAD

While my brothers, who were older than me, stayed with me, myself, none of them mentioned the words that I mentioned. I said: 'Who can, indeed, see the household of his father, but (at the same time) is, indeed, a servant to the citizens of Emar?

Accordingly, Idrimi set out and traveled into the desert, where he joined some Suteans ("Southerners"), a term often used to describe seminomadic pastoralists. Although Idrimi's actions with them are now unfortunately lost, it is clear that he spent the night:

13 [AN]ŠE.KUR.RA-[*i*]*a* ⸢^{giš}GIGIR⸣*-ia u*$_3$ ^{lu_2}IŠ*-ia* 14 [*el*]*-te-*⸢*qe*$_2$⸣*-šu-nu u*$_3$ *i-na ma-at hu-ri-ib-te*^{ki} 15 ⸢*e-te-ti-iq*⸣ *u*$_3$ *li-bi* ERIN$_2$.MEŠ *su-tu-u*$_2$^{ki} 16 ⸢*e*⸣*-te-ru-ub* ⸢*iš*⸣*-ti-šu-*<*nu*> *a-na li-bi* 17a ⸢KU$^?$⸣-[x(-)x]x-*zak*$^?$*-kar bi-ta*$_2$*-ku*

[I] took [m]y [h]orse, my chariot, and my chariot-driver, crossed into the desert, and entered among Sutean people. I … -ed … with th<em>. I spent the night.

The very next day, Idrimi left the Suteans and traveled to Canaan. Specifically, he went to the city of Ammiya, probably located near modern-day Tripoli in Lebanon. Here the inscription has Idrimi depart from his narrative and provide the reader with a bit of background, informing us that "sons" (essentially citizens) of Halab and of three different, larger political units—Mukiš, Niya, and Ama'u—were present in the city of Ammiya; Mukiš is of particular significance because its capital was Alalah, the city where the historical Idrimi lived and the statue was found.

17b *i-na ša-ni u*$_4$*-*⸢*mi*⸣ 18 [*an*]*-mu-uš-ma u*$_3$ ⸢*a*⸣*-*[*n*]*a ma-at ki-in-a-ni*$_7$^{ki} 19 ⸢*al*⸣*-li-ik i-na ma-*⸢*at*⸣ *ki-in-a-ni*$_7$^{ki} 20 ^{uru}⸢*am*⸣*-mi-ia*^{ki} *aš-bu i-na* ^{uru}*am-mi-ia*^{ki} 21 [D]UMU.MEŠ ^{uru}*ha-la-ab*^{ki} DUMU.MEŠ *ma-at mu-ki-iš-he*^{ki} 22 DUMU.MEŠ *ma-at ni-hi*^{ki} *u*$_3$ D[UMU.M]EŠ *ma-at* 23 *a-ma-e*^{ki} *aš-bu*

The next day, [I] set out and went to the land of Canaan. In the land of Canaan, (the people of) Ammiya resided, and in Ammiya, [c]itizens of Halab, citizens of the land of Mukiš, citizens of the land of Niya, and c[itizen]s of the land of Ama'u resided.

When Idrimi entered Ammiya, these citizens of what the inscription implies were constituent elements of his father's former kingdom recognized him and collectively agreed to make him their leader:

24 *i-mu-ru-un-ni-ma* 25 *i-nu-ma* DUMU *be-li-šu-nu a-na-ku u*$_3$ *a-na* UGU*-ia* 26 *ip-hu-ru-ni*$_7$*-ma a-ka-a-na-ka ur-tab-bi-a-ku*

> They saw that I was a son of their lord, so they held an assembly concerning me, and in that way, I was elevated in rank.

The inscription narrates how Idrimi lived for a long time at Ammiya among the citizens of his father's former kingdom, whom it now identifies as *habiru*, a term, sometimes used pejoratively in antiquity, to designate displaced persons. After the clearly symbolic span of seven years, however, the Storm God communicated with Idrimi via ominous signs and gave him some indication that he should sail up the coast of the Mediterranean to the land of Mukiš, one of the lands that, according to the inscription, had formed part of his father's kingdom. Idrimi's ships made land near the southern border of the land of Mukiš at Mount Hazzi, the home of the Storm God.

> 27 *u2-ra-ak u3 a-na li-bi* ERIN2.MEŠ $^{\text{lu2}}$SA.GAZ 28 *a-na* MU 7.KAM.MEŠ *aš-ba-ku* MUŠEN.HI.A *u2-za-ki* 29 SILA4.HI.A *ab-ri-ma u3 še-eb-i ša-na-ti* ⌜^{d}⌝[I]M 30 ⌜*a*⌝*-na* SAG.DU-*ia it-tu-ru u3 e-te-pu-uš* ^{giš}MA2.⌜HI⌝.A 31 ERIN2.MEŠ *nu-ul-la a-*⌜*na*⌝ ^{giš}⌜MA2.HI⌝.A *u2-šar-ki-ib-šu-nu* 32 *u3* A.AB.BA *a-na* ⌜*ma*⌝*-[a]t m[u-k]i-iš-he2*^{ki} 33 *eṭ-he2-e*$^{\text{!?}}$*-ku u3 pa-*⌜*an*⌝ HUR.SAG *ha-zi* 34a ⌜*a*⌝*-na ta2-ba2-li3 ak-šu-ud*

> A long time passed; I resided among the displaced people for seven years. I released birds, and I inspected (the entrails of) lambs, and in the seventh of (those) years, the St[or]m God was looking favorably at me, so I built ships. I boarded troops, *nullu*-soldier(s), onto the ships, I approached the la[n]d of M[uk]iš by sea, and I reached dry ground before Mount Hazzi.

Although the mention of *nullu*-troops suggests that the expedition to the land of Mukiš was a military one, Idrimi's first action upon landing was to climb Mount Hazzi, presumably to make an offering to the Storm God.

> 34b *e-li-ia-ku* 35 *u3 ma-ti-ia iš-mu-un-ni-ma* GU4.HI.A *u3* UDU.HI.A 36 *a-na pa-ni-ia ub-lu-u2-ni7* ⌜*u3*⌝ *i-na* UD 1.KAM 37 *ki-ma* 1$^{\textit{en}}$ LU2 *ma-at ni-he*^{ki} *ma-at a-ma-e*^{ki} 38 *[m]a-at mu-ki-iš-he2*^{ki} *u3* ^{uru}*a-la-la-ah*^{ki} URU.KI-*ia* 39a ⌜*a*⌝*-na ia-ši2-im it-tu-ru-ni7*

> I went up (the mountain), and my land heard (about this), so they brought oxen and sheep before me, and in one day, as one man, the land of Niya, the land of Ama'u, the [l]and of Mukiš, and Alalah, my city, looked favorably at me.

When Idrimi's land heard about his arrival, it brought him its own offerings; possibly this land comprised the residents of Mukiš at the time, considered retroactively to belong to its future ruler. After this, the lands of Niya, Ama'u, Mukiš, and the city of Alalah acknowledged Idrimi as their ruler. Here the text seems to be engaging in a piece of legerdemain, whereby "it confuse[s] the seat of his father and his new submitted seat" (Márquez Rowe 1997, 184)—that is, with one exception, the list of lands together with one city enumerated in this passage is the same as the list of lands together with one city that collectively raised Idrimi to their leadership in Ammiya. The one exception is Alalah, which now takes the place of Halab, Idrimi's ancestral home. Furthermore, whereas the previous list had been careful to describe "the sons" of the lands, now this politically loaded term has been dropped, and it is simply "the lands" that acknowledge Idrimi's rule. The implication is that it is the actual collective political bodies of Niya, Ama'u, and Mukiš that are acknowledging Idrimi's rule, not just their scattered, displaced citizens.

Finally, as Idrimi assumes control of the lands of Niya, Ama'u, and Mukiš, this particular narrative arc comes to an end. The end of the narrative arc is marked by the sudden reappearance of his brothers, whom he had left to enjoy a second-tier status in Emar. Now they join him at Alalah, where they are explicitly described as his dependents:

> ^{39b} ⸢ŠEŠ.MEŠ⸣-*ia* ^{40} [*i*]*š-mu-u*$_2$*-ma u*$_3$ *a-na mah-ri-ia il-li-ku-u*$_2$ ^{41} [*a*]*h-he*.HI.A-*ia it-ti-ia-ma in-na-hu-u*$_2$ ^{42a} [*a*]*h-he*$_2$.HI.A-*ia aṣ-ṣur-šu-nu*
>
> My brothers [h]eard (about this), so they came into my presence. My [br]others were laboring for me, myself; I protected my [b]rothers.

At this point, the narrative widens its geopolitical perspective and begins a new and pivotal episode. This episode opens by describing how one of the great kings of the time, Parattarna I, the king of what was, or what would be, the Mittani Empire, was hostile to Idrimi. Accordingly, Idrimi sent an envoy to Parattarna I to describe his ancestors' allegiance to the Hurrian king's own ancestors and, presumably, to attempt to pledge his own fealty:

> ^{42b} *ap-pu-na* ^{43} [M]U 7.KAM.HI.A ^{m}*pa*$_2$*-ra-at-tar-na* LUGAL *dan-nu* ^{44} LUGAL ERIN$_2$.⸢MEŠ⸣ *hur-ri*^{ki} *u*$_2$*-na-kir-an-ni* ^{45} ⸢*i*⸣*-na š*[*e*]*-eb-*⸢*i*⸣ *ša-na-ti a-na* ^{m}*pa*$_2$*-ra-at-ar-na* LUGAL^{ri} ^{46} LUGAL ⸢ERIN$_2$⸣.MEŠ^{an}*-wa-an-da aš-ta*$_2$*-par*$_2$ *u*$_3$ *ad-bu-ub*$^{!}$(TE) ^{47} *ma-*⸢*na-ha*⸣-[*te*].HE$_2$ *ša a-bu-te*.HI.A-⸢*ia i*⸣*-nu-ma* ^{48} ⸢*a-bu*⸣*-te*.⸢HI⸣.A-*ia a-na* UGU-*šu-nu in-na-hu-u*$_2$ ^{49} ⸢*u*$_3$ *pa-nu-ti*⸣*-ni a-na* LUGAL.HI.A *ša* ⸢ERIN$_2$⸣.MEŠ *hur-*⸢*ri*⸣^{ki} *da-mi-iq* ^{50} [*u*$_3$] ⸢*a-na*⸣ *bi-ri-šu-nu* NAM.ERIM$_2$ *dan-na* ^{51a} ⸢*iš-ku*⸣*-nu-ni*$_7$*-na*
>
> Moreover, over seven [ye]ars, Parattarna (I), the mighty king, king of the armies of Hurri, turned hostile towards me. In the seventh of (those) years, I sent a message to Parattarna (I), the king, king of the Umman-manda, and I spoke of the tribut[e] of my forefathers, (namely) that my forefathers labored for them *and our ancestors* belonged to the kings of the Hurrian armies. This was pleasing (to the kings of Hurri), [so] they established a powerful oath between them.

Parattarna I was receptive to Idrimi's overtures. The text describes how he received Idrimi's peace offering and gives some details about a sacrifice that are obscure. The result, however, is clear: Idrimi formally acknowledges the Hurrian king's hegemony and, in turn, his rule over Alalah is formalized, his status now equal to the other rulers who belong to the Hurrian king's orbit.

> ^{51b} LUGAL *dan-nu ma-na-ha-te*.HI.A ^{52} *ša pa-nu-ti-ni u*$_3$ NAM.ERIM$_2$ *ša bi-ri-šu-nu*$^!$ *iš-me-ma* ^{53} *u*$_3$ *it-ti ma-mi-ti ip-ta-la-ah aš-šum a-wa-at* ^{54} *ma-mi-ti u*$_3$ *aš-šum ma-na-ha-te*.MEŠ-*ni šu-ul-mi-ia* ^{55} *im-ta*$_2$*-har u*$_3$ *ki-nu-*[*n*]*u*$^?$ *ša kab*$^?$*-tu*$_3$*-u*$_2$ *ša* SISKUR$_2$ ^{56} *u*$_2$*-šar-bi u*$_3$ E$_2$ *hal-qu*$_2$ *u*$_2$*-te-er-šu* ^{57} *i-na* LU$_2$*-ti-ia i-na ki-nu-ti-ia* SI$^?$ ŠUB *an-na-am* ^{58} *aṣ-bat-šu u*$_3$ LUGAL-*ku a-*⸢*na* ^{uru}⸣*a-la-la-ah*^{ki} ^{59} LUGAL.MEŠ *ša* ZAG-*ia u*$_3$ GUB$_3$-*ia il*$^?$*-lu-an-ni-ma* ^{60a} *u*$_3$ *ki-ma šu-nu-ti-ma um-ta*$_2$*-ši-la-ku*
>
> The mighty king heard about the tribute of our ancestors and the oath that was between them, and he respected the oath. Because of the words of the oath and because of our (former) tribute, he received my peace-offering. So *I made a brazier already heavy for sacrifice even greater*, and so I returned a household that was lost to him. In my status as a retainer, in my loyalty, I seized *this abandoned hem* for him, and so I was king. Kings from all around *came up to me* at Alalah, and I was their equal.

Significantly, Idrimi's statement "and so I was king" mirrors his statement "I was king" that is carved on his cheek in its use of a nominal predicate (LUGAL-*ku* = *šarrāku*; see §4.2 for more discussion). The implication is clear: although Idrimi had previously controlled a kingdom, only now, with Parattarna I's acknowledgment, was he actually its king.

With the conclusion of the Parattarna episode, the narrative portion of the body inscription moves into its third and final episode. The theme of this episode is kingship, as we see Idrimi perform acts that are associated with proper rule. His first acts are military: constructing defensive fortifications at home and then, once his people are secure in his absence, embarking on a military campaign. During the course of this campaign, Idrimi seized seven cities.

> ^{60b} *ki* BAD$_3$-*šu-nu* ^{61} *ša a-bu-te*.HI.A *i-na qa-qa-ri tab-ku-*⸢*u*$_2$⸣ ^{62} *u*$_3$ *a-na-ku i-na qa-qa-ri u*$_2$*-ša-at-bu-u*$_2$ ^{63} *u*$_3$ *a-na* AN.TA$_2$ *u*$_2$*-šaq-qu*$_2$*-u*$_2$*-šu-nu* ^{64} ERIN$_2$.MEŠ^{ba_2} *el-te-qe*$_2$ *u*$_3$ *a-na ma-at ha-at-te*^{ki} ^{65} *e-te-*[*l*]*i u*$_3$ 7 URU.DIDLI.HI.⸢A *aṣ*⸣*-bat-šu-nu* ^{66} ^{uru}*pa-aš-ša-he*$_2$^{ki} ^{uru}*ta*$_2$*-ma-ru-ut-la*^{ki} ^{67} ^{uru}*hu-luh-ha-an*^{ki} ^{uru}*zi-la*<^{ki} ^{uru}>*i-e*^{ki} ^{68} ^{uru}*u*$_2$*-lu-zi-la*^{ki} *u*$_3$ ^{uru}⸢*za*⸣*-ru-na*^{ki} ^{69} *an-mu-u*$_2$ URU.DIDLI.HI.A *aṣ-bat-šu-nu u*$_3$ *ul-lu-u*$_2$ ^{70a} *eh-te-pi*$_3$*-šu-nu-ti*
>
> Because the city wall of the forefathers had lain flat on the ground but I caused (it) to rise up from the ground and set (it) high up above for them (i.e., the people of Alalah), I took troops, went up to the land of Hatti, and captured seven cities: Paššahe, Tamarutla, Huluhhan, Zila, I'e, Uluzila, and Zaruna. These are the cities. I captured them, and I destroyed others.

To the extent that the seven cities mentioned by name can be localized, they seem to have been located around Mukiš's northern border in the land of Kizzuwatna (modern Cilicia). The narrative describes Idrimi's campaign as an unqualified success, as he moved unopposed in enemy territory, taking all sorts of plunder and distributing it among his soldiers before returning home:

> 70b *ma-at* ⸢*ha*⸣*-at-te*^{ki} 71 *u2-ul ip-hur u3 a-na* ⸢UGU-*ia*⸣ *u2-ul il-li-ku* 72 *ša* ŠA3^{bi}*-ia e-te-pu-*⸢*uš šal*⸣*-la-te.*HI.A*-šu-nu* 73 *aš*$^{!}$*-lu-ul-ma nam-ku-ri-šu-*⸢*nu bu*⸣*-še-šu-nu ba-ši-tu-*<*šu*>*-nu* 74 *el-te-qe2 u3 u2-za-iz a-n*[*a*] ⸢ERIN2⸣.MEŠ *til-la-ti-ia* 75 $^{lu2.meš}$*ah-he2.*ḪI.A*-ia* 76 *u3* $^{lu2.meš}$*ib-ru-te.*HI.A*-ia ka-ka4-šu-nu-ma* 77 *a-na-ku el-te-qe2 u3 a-na ma-at mu-ki-iš-he*^{ki} *at-tu-ur* 78a *u3 e-ru-ub a-na* ^{uru}*a-la-la-ah*^{ki} URU.KI*-ia*
>
> The land of Hatti did not gather and march against me. I did what I wanted. I carried off their prisoners, I took their valuables, their luxury goods, and <th>eir precious items, and I distributed (these) to my allies' troops, my brothers, and my comrades. I, myself, took their weapon, though, and returned to the land of Mukiš and entered Alalah, my city.

With the military campaign concluded, the narrative has Idrimi focus next on domestic concerns, another sphere of action associated with proper rule. Idrimi built himself a palace, ensured that his entourage and dependents had suitable status, and attended to the well-being of his kingdom's population, which now included some new inhabitants. Tellingly, the inscription explicitly states that the spoils of his military campaign provide the means for this domestic agenda:

> 78b *i-na šal-la-ti3* 79 *u3 i-na mar-ši-ti3 i-na nam-ku-ri i-na bu-ši2 u3 i*$^{!}$*-na ba-ši-tu2*$^{!?}$ 80 *ša iš-tu ma-at ha-at-te*^{ki} *u2-še-ri-du* E2 *uš10-te-pi2-iš* 81 ^{giš}GU.ZA*-ia ki-ma* GU.ZA.MEŠ *ša* LUGAL.MEŠ *u2-ma-ši-il* 82 $^{lu2.meš}$ŠEŠ.MEŠ*-ia ki-ma* ŠEŠ.MEŠ *ša* ⸢LUGAL⸣.MEŠ DUMU.MEŠ*-ia* 83 *ki-ma* DUMU.MEŠ*-šu-nu u3* $^{lu2.meš}$*tap-pu-te.*HI.A*-ia ki*$^{!}$(U3)*-*<*ma*> *tap-pu-te.*HI.A*-šu-*⸢*nu*⸣ 84 *u2-ma-ši-lu-u2-šu-nu* TUŠ.MEŠ *ša a-na* ŠA3^{bi} *ma-ti-ia*^{ki} 85 KI.TUŠ*-šu-*⸢*nu*$^{?}$ *ne2*$^{?}$⸣*-eh*$^{?}$*-ta5 u2-še-ši-ib-šu-nu ša* KI.TUŠ *la u2-uš-ša-bu* 86 *a-na-ku u2-še-ši-bu-šu-nu u3*$^{!}$(KI) *ma-ti*^{ki}*-ia u2-ki-in-nu* 87a *u3 u2-ma-ši-il* URU.DIDLI.HI.A*-ia ki-me-e pa-nu-ti-ni-ma*
>
> I had a house built with the prisoner(s) and livestock, the valuable(s), luxury good(s) and the precious item(s) that I brought down from the land Hatti. My throne was equal to the thrones of kings, my brothers were equal to the brothers of kings, my sons to their sons, and my companions to their companions. I caused the inhabitants who were (already) in my land to reside *in security*, and by means of those who did not reside in a dwelling, whom I, myself, caused to reside (in one), and with whom I stabilized my land, I made my cities equal to our earlier ones.

The final act demonstrating proper rule that is attributed by the narrative to Idrimi occurs in the sphere of religion. Significantly, Idrimi concerned himself with the veneration of a divinized ancestor. Having performed the necessary rites, he entrusted their future performance to his own son, a certain IM-nerari:

87b *ki-ma* A.A-*ni-ma* 88 A2^{te}.MEŠ *ša* DINGIR.MEŠ *ša* ^{uru}*a-la-lah3*^{ki} *u2-ki-in-nu-u2-ma* 89 *u3* SISKUR2.HI.A$^{ni\text{-}iq\text{-}qi2.\text{HI.A}}$ *ša a-bi* NINDA2-*ni ša uš-te-pi2-šu-u2*$^{!}$-*šu-nu* 90 *a-*⸢*na*⸣-*ku e-te-ne-pu-uš10-šu-nu an-mu-u2 e-te-pu-uš10-šu-nu* 91 *u3 a-na qa-ti* ^{md}IM-*ne2-ra-ri* DUMU-*ia ap-ta-qi2-id-šu-nu*

Just as our father, himself, attended to the signs of the "gods" (i.e., divinized ancestors) of Alalah, so I, myself, was regularly performing the offerings (Akk. gloss: the offerings) for our grandfather that he had regularly caused to be performed. I regularly performed these things, and then I entrusted them to the authority of IM-nerari, my son.

At this point, not just the third episode of the narrative but the narrative portion of the body inscription ends. But the body inscription continues with Idrimi's voice speaking a series of curses against anyone who harms his statue or, seemingly, the body inscription:

92 *ma-an-nu-um-me-e* ALAM-*ia an-ni-na-ti i-na-as-sah2-š*[*u*] 93 *u3* <<*pi2-ri-ih-šu li-il-qu2-ut*>> AN$^{ša\text{-}mu}$ *li-iz-zu-ur-šu* 94 *ša-ap-la-tu2*$^{er\text{-}ṣe\text{-}tu2}$ *pi2-ri-ih-šu li-il-qu2-ut* 95 DINGIR.MEŠ *ša* AN *u* KI LUGAL-*ut-šu u3 ma-at-šu*^{ki} *lim-du-du-šu* 96 *ma-an-nu-um-me-e u2-na-ak-kar3-šu i-ip-pa-aš2-ši-*<*iṭ?*> 97 ^{d}IM EN AN *u* KI$^{er\text{-}ṣe\text{-}ti}$ *u3* DINGIR.MEŠ GAL.GAL.E.NE ⸢*šu*⸣-*ma-šu* 98a *u3* NUMUN.MEŠ-*šu li-hal-liq* ⸢*i-na ma*⸣-*ti-šu*

(As for) anyone who might remove this statue of mine, may the Heavens (Akk. gloss: the Heavens) curse him! May the Underworld (Akk. gloss: the Underworld) gather up his offspring! May the gods of the Heavens and the Underworld measure out his kingship and his land for him! (As for) anyone who might alter it (i.e., the statue?) (so that) it is effac<ed>, may the Storm God, the lord of the Heavens and of the Underworld (Akk. gloss: the Underworld), and the great gods make his name and his seed disappear from his land.

After having Idrimi utter these curses, though, the body inscription suddenly shifts gears and drops the illusion of Idrimi speaking. In what is conventionally described as the inscription's colophon, the authorial voice belongs now to a certain Šarruwa, a scribe who claims to have inscribed the text on the statue (using the same word as Idrimi used in the inscription on the cheek; see §6.1) and who requests blessings for himself:

98b ^{m}*šar-ru-wa* DUB.SAR ⸢$^{\text{lu2?}}$⸣ARAD 10 20 30 *u3* ^{d}INANNA 99 ^{m}*šar-ru-wa* $^{\text{lu2}}$DUB.SAR ⸢*ša*⸣ ^{d}ALAM *an-ni-na-tiš iš-ṭu2-ru-šu* DINGIR.⸢MEŠ⸣ *ša* AN *u* KI 100 *li-bal-li-ṭu2-u2-šu li-na-ṣa-ru-šu lu-u2* SIG5^{u2}-*šu* ^{d}UTU EN *e-lu-ti* / : *u3 šap-li-ti* EN$^{lu\text{-}u2}$ *e-tim-mi* ⸢*lu-u2*⸣ TI.LA-*šu*

Šarruwa is the scribe, the servant of the Storm God, the Sun God, the Moon God and IŠTAR. Šarruwa is the scribe who inscribed this (divine) statue. May the gods of the Heavens and the Underworld keep him alive! May they protect

> him! May they favor him! May the Sun God, lord of the Upper World and the Lower World, lord of ghosts, keep him alive!

On this note—and in exactly one hundred lines (see §1.4)—the inscription on the statue's body ends.

As the guided reading that accompanies the translation above has tried to show, the inscriptions carved on what we can now call the Statue of Idrimi are remarkable. They are carefully structured and full of vivid detail. They have also provoked many questions for modern scholars—to name just a few: What is the relationship between the short inscription on the statue's cheek and the long inscription on its body? Why do two people, not only Idrimi but also a scribe named Šarruwa, claim to have made the inscriptions? Who is IM-nerari? Although he is Idrimi's son and successor according to the body inscription, other ancient texts from Alalah make it clear that the historical Idrimi was succeeded by a son of a different name, Niqmepa, and a son named IM-nerari is, in fact, otherwise unattested.

As the qualification to this last question makes clear, there is abundant evidence, archaeological and textual, from the site of Alalah, where the Statue of Idrimi was found. This evidence intersects with the inscriptions in exciting and suggestive ways. Among other points of intersection, cuneiform tablets from Alalah establish that there was a historical Idrimi who ruled Alalah and the kingdom of Mukiš around 1475–1450 BCE. This Idrimi and his descendants were in fact client kings of the Mittani Empire. And the historical Idrimi does seem to have fought a war with the ruler of Kizzuwatna, his northern neighbor and part of what can be described as "greater Hatti." Yet, despite these points of intersection, there is little consensus among scholars about the historical context of the statue and its inscriptions.

The variety of different approaches that these scholars have adopted in their work is the subject of chapter 2. The rest of this chapter is primarily concerned with providing the background necessary to follow those scholars' arguments and my own. I begin with the site at which the statue was found, Alalah, focusing first on providing an overview of the excavations and second on a sketch of the site's political history over its millennium-long occupation history. From there, I look at the circumstances of the statue's discovery and offer a brief discussion of the first reports of its archaeological context (a more critical discussion occurs in §2.1). Having introduced the statue properly, I continue by introducing its inscriptions, specifically the physical arrangement of the inscriptions upon the statue. Doing so raises, in turn, questions of terminology that need to be addressed at the outset of any sustained discussion.

1.1. ALALAH: THE CITY AND ITS EXCAVATIONS

The city of Alalah, modern Tell Atchana, is located near the great bend of the Orontes River in the Amuq Valley of what is now the Republic of Turkey's Hatay province. The city was inhabited for most of the second millennium BCE, during which time it was the dominant city in the Amuq. Assyriological interest in Alalah has focused on the site's cuneiform tablets, which were excavated predominantly from two different stratigraphic levels, Level VII and Level IV, and which date to the Middle Bronze Age and Late Bronze Age, respectively. While Alalah was itself never a major international power, its location at the southern end of a corridor in the Amanus Mountains placed it in "a conduit for the movement of people and goods" (von Dassow 2008, 1). Consequently, the city was exposed to Mesopotamian, Hurrian, Hittite, Levantine, Aegean, and Egyptian influences. In particular, during its best documented stratigraphic levels, the city was subordinate to the kingdoms of Yamhad and Mittani, two of the major geopolitical powers during the Middle Bronze Age and Late Bronze Age, respectively. The Alalah texts provide important windows into these two polities as we lack the archives of their central administrations.

Alalah was first excavated by the British archaeologist Sir Leonard Woolley between 1936 and 1949, with an interruption for World War II. Following the success of his excavations at Ur, Woolley began excavating at Tell Atchana in 1936 with the aim of exploring interconnections between the Aegean and the Near East.[2] The first cuneiform tablets were discovered the next year. He found the substantial archives of the Level IV palace in 1938 and both the Statue of Idrimi and also the archives of the Level VII palace the following year. The 1939 excavation season was the last before World War II forced the excavations to be postponed; following the war, they were resumed between 1946 and 1949.

In eight years of excavation, Woolley and his staff uncovered eighteen stratigraphic levels (Levels XVII-0) that span almost the entire second millennium.[3] Woolley concentrated the excavation's energies on the tell's northwestern summit, where he uncovered various city gates and palatial residences dated from Level VII to Level I. Two of these palaces, dating to Levels VII and IV, contained the majority of the cuneiform tablets discovered at Alalah. A deep sounding in this area revealed that monumental architecture went back to Level XVI (although

---

2 Von Dassow (2008, 2 n. 1) has traced succinctly the manner in which Woolley's interest in interconnections between the Aegean and the ancient Near East shifted its focus from the cultural to the chronological as excavations progressed.

3 Woolley (1955, 380–81) was of the opinion that the earliest levels at Alalah dated to ca. 3400–3300 BCE, but see Heinz 1992 for a redating of Levels XVII–VIII to the Middle Bronze Age. He also considered the last major occupation level to have been destroyed by the Sea Peoples, ca. 1200 BCE, but, as discussed immediately below, results from the new excavations at Alalah now suggest that the end of Level I dates to 1300 BCE.

see the revisions of Heinz 1992, 23–36). However, this earlier architecture was not further uncovered in order to preserve the Level VII and IV palaces. Slightly to the southeast of this excavation area, another deep sounding revealed that temples had been successively rebuilt on the same spot throughout Alalah's entire occupation; it was during this sounding that Woolley discovered the Statue of Idrimi (see §1.2). Further to the southeast and more toward the center of the tell, he discovered private houses dating to Levels VI–I along the remains of a city wall. Finally, he cut a series of trenches in the southwestern slope of the mound, one of which revealed another gate ("Site H").[4]

Excavations at Alalah resumed in 2003 under the direction of K. Aslıhan Yener and, subsequently, Murat Akar. Already, however, the preceding years had seen archaeological work on the site and in the region of the Amuq more generally within the framework of the Amuq Valley Regional Project (AVRP). In particular, between 2000 and 2002, the team paved the way for the resumption of full-scale excavations by conducting intensive surveys both on- and off-site, documenting the site with photographic records, correlating visible architectural remains with features recorded in the excavation reports, and, perhaps most importantly, creating the composite plans of the architectural features of Levels VII–0 excavated by Woolley that are mostly lacking from the preliminary and final reports; the results of much of these efforts appeared as an edited volume (Yener 2005).

Since 2003, the renewed excavations have concentrated on four different areas on the tell: the northwestern summit where Woolley excavated the palaces (Area 1); a more central part of the site near the cluster of private houses found by Woolley (Area 2); the slope on the site's eastern edge (Area 3); and, most recently, the southwestern part of the site (Area 4).[5] Among the most important developments to have come out of the new excavations so far is a revision of Alalah's stratigraphy showing that the Level I occupation "ended at the beginning of the 13th century BC.... There is simply no evidence for 13th century settlement in any area of Atchana yet excavated, with the exception of the Temple" (Yener, Akar, and Horowitz 2019a, 341).

With the vast majority of the textual data from Alalah coming from Levels VII and IV, we are naturally best informed about the history of the city during the late Middle Bronze Age and early Late Bronze Age. But some clues to the earlier history of the site and the region exist. Alalah, or at least a site with that

---

[4] The final excavation report is Woolley 1955. For a popular account of the excavations, see Woolley 1953. Woolley also published number of preliminary reports on individual seasons, mostly in the *Antiquaries Journal* (Woolley 1936, 1937, 1938, 1939b, 1948, and 1950). In addition, Woolley published many articles on the excavations, often with informative photographs not available elsewhere, in the *Times* (London) and the *Illustrated London News*; see, e.g., Woolley 1939a and 1939c.

[5] See Yener 2010 and Yener, Akar, and Horowitz 2019b for the final site reports of the 2003–2010 seasons.

name, may have been a dependency of Ebla in the third millennium (see Archi 2006, 4 and Archi 2020, 35). An entry in an administrative text, TM.75.G.10280: rev. iv 5–10, seems to indicate that Alalah rebelled and the two polities fought at least one battle, although it is unclear which side was victorious. Ultimately, however, it seems that Alalah rejoined Ebla's sphere of influence (Archi 2020, 35).[6] Mukiš, a region of the later Level IV kingdom ruled from the capital of Alalah,[7] appears in Ur III archival texts from Drehem.[8] During the Middle Bronze Age, the city formed part of the kingdom of Yamhad, the Amorite state that controlled northwestern Syria with its capital at Halab, modern Aleppo. Shortly before the period of time documented by the Level VII archives, Alalah appears in texts from Mari under the name Alahtum, where Zimri-Lim of Mari acquired it, with some difficulty, from Hammurabi, the king of Yamhad, and the queen mother Gašera (Durand 2002).[9]

After the fall of Mari, during the period of time documented by the Level VII texts, Alalah was an *appanage* for a junior line of the royal family of Yamhad. The first ruler of this line, Yarim-Lim, received the city in exchange for another that he had inherited from his father, and that was destroyed in a rebellion against the king of Yamhad. The Level VII archives document the economic concerns of this junior line and its attendant bureaucracy over four generations.[10] The end of Level VII is marked by a site-wide destruction level that is typically attributed to the Syrian campaigns of the Hittite king Hattušili I, although this attribution is not certain.

After Level VII, textual documentation is interrupted during Levels VI and V before resuming in the fifteenth century with the Level IV archives. These archives document that the city was ruled by three successive generations of the same ruling family: Idrimi, Niqmepa, and Ilimi-ilima, the first of these rulers being the same individual whose deeds are inscribed on the statue that is the subject of

---

6 Because Tell Atchana does not seem to have been occupied in the third millennium, but a third millennium settlement, including monumental architecture, has been discovered at nearby Tell Tayinat, "it is reasonable to suggest that the texts are referring to the EBA occupation at Tell Tayinat. When the settlement moved from one site to the other, so too did the ancient name" (Batiuk and Horowitz 2010, 168).

7 For Mukiš as "but one of several territories belonging to the realm of [Level IV] Alalah," see von Dassow 2008, 65.

8 See RGTC 2, s.v. "Mukiš," where the unpublished reference listed there is now published as OIP 121 575. For Mukiš as both the name of a region and a town within that region, see §6.3, citing previous literature.

9 For discussions of the identification of the toponym Alahtum with Alalah/Tell Atchana, see Lauinger 2015, 114–15 and Torrecilla 2021, 120–22.

10 I reviewed the question of whether the Level VII texts span two, three, or four generations in Lauinger 2015, 202–27.

this book.[11] The Level IV archives establish that Idrimi and his successors ruled a subject kingdom of the Mittani Empire during the period of time documented by the texts.[12] These texts date mostly to the reign of Niqmepa and generally concern matters of state administration, although several small assemblages record the personal affairs of nonroyal persons; see von Dassow 2005 for a reconstruction and analysis of the archives and Niedorf 2008, 31–1221 for an overview of the corpus. As with its Level VII counterpart, the Level IV palace suffered a violent destruction; here, too, the destruction is typically attributed to a Hittite campaign, this time perhaps of Tudhaliya I, although, again, this attribution is not certain (von Dassow 2020a, 201–2).

Following the destruction of the Level IV palace, our primary textual evidence for the history of Alalah derives not from Alalah but from Hittite texts or texts produced at other sites that were under Hittite hegemony. These sources, which have been gathered and reviewed by von Dassow (2020a), demonstrate that a ruler named Itur-Addu was part of a coalition that fought against Šuppiluliuma I during his campaigns in Syria, and that this coalition was defeated and Alalah conquered by Šuppiluliuma I, at which time the city became part of the Hittite Empire (see §6.3 for more discussion). Alalah would remain under Hittite rule, possibly punctuated by a local rebellion (von Dassow 2020a, 213), until shortly before the destruction of its last major level of occupation, Level I. While Wooley dated this destruction to ca. 1200 BCE and attributed it to the arrival of the Sea Peoples, as mentioned above, the end of the Level I occupation is now dated to 1300 BCE, with a subsequent occupation persisting only in the area of the temple.

1.2. CIRCUMSTANCES OF THE STATUE'S DISCOVERY

As mentioned in the preceding sketch of the excavations at Alalah, the Statue of Idrimi was found toward the end of Woolley's 1939 season. The season had already been busy, both locally and geopolitically. Locally, Woolley and his team were dealing with a very compressed season. Work had not begun at the site until the end of March due to late rains, while at the end of the season Woolley was hard pressed for workers because, as he wrote in the preliminary report (published almost nine years later), "the best harvest that the Hatay had known for many years called our workmen away at the beginning of June" (Woolley 1948, 1). Within this ten-week period, however, Woolley and his team of three (including his wife, Lady Katherine)—assisted, as was Woolley's custom, by his Syrian

[11] Following Sidney Smith, Woolley originally thought that Idrimi was Ilimi-ilima's son so that the sequence of Level IV rulers was Niqmepa–Ilimi-ilima–Idrimi. Accordingly, he attributed the Level IV palace to Niqmepa, the supposed first ruler of Level IV. For an unintended consequence of this sequence that has persisted in the literature, and on the historical Idrimi in general, see §2.3.

[12] For a comprehensive historical overview of the empire of Mittani, see von Dassow 2022.

foreman, Hamoudi, and Hamoudi's sons—employed four hundred men and made many important discoveries. Among the most important was the Level VII palace and the archives of cuneiform tablets therein.[13] Subsequently, the excavators had begun to dig the temple site, clearing what would be known as the Level 0 and Level I temples. It was at this point, shortly before the workmen left for the harvest in early June and the season ended, that Woolley wrote in a letter dated May 21. This letter is to my knowledge the first account of the discovery of the Statue of Idrimi:

> A rubbish-pit at the temple gave us great surprise. From it there came a white stone statue just over a metre high of a Hittite king, a seated figure; the head and feet were broken off but except for part of the foot the statue is complete and in wonderfully good condition and even the nose is only just chipped. The figure is covered literally from head to foot with cuneiform inscription which begins on one cheek, runs across the front and one side of the body and ends at the bottom of the skirt, rather more than fifty lines of text. Nothing like that has been found before.[14]

If Woolley's 1939 excavation season at Alalah was busy, to call the previous year "busy" from a regional perspective would be a profound understatement. The preceding months had seen the elections for the first (and what would be only) Assembly of the Sanjak of Alexendretta in July 1938, which had sat for the first time on September 2 of the same year and immediately proclaimed itself the State of Hatay, with Tayfur Sökmen elected to be the head of the new state (Khadduri 1945, 422–23). On June 29, 1939, only a little more than a month after Woolley wrote the letter quoted above that describes his discovery of the Statue of Idrimi, the Assembly of Hatay would meet again, and for the last time, as it voted to self-annex itself to Turkey (Khadduri 1945, 424; Fink 2010, 16).

In a penetrating article, Hélène Maloigne (2017) has detailed how the Statue of Idrimi became a pawn in the larger diplomatic negotiations between France,

---

13 In Lauinger 2011, 29–31, I traced the excavation of this structure through the testimony of the field cards for tablets.

14 The letter is quoted by Fink (2010, 16) and cited by him as *Sir Leonard Woolley's Excavations at Atchana: Extracts from Letters* in University College London Special Collections. As Fink remarks in a note (16 n. 1), there are, in fact, 104 (or, more accurately, 103; see §1.4) lines of cuneiform text, not 50. Interestingly, this same, incorrect line count is repeated in a caption in a newspaper article describing the season's excavations that was published in early December of the same year (Woolley 1939c, fig. 11). Since the final line of the body inscription carved on the statue's right leg is line 51, my guess is that Woolley initially thought that the lines inscribed on the right leg were a continuation of the lines written on the left leg. Note that in the same caption in the *Illustrated London News* Woolley dated the inscription to the fifteenth century BCE, whereas he had described the statue as representing "a Hittite king" in the letter from late May.

Turkey, and England concerning the status of the Sanjak of Alexandretta/State of Hatay. Such a role became possible because the State of Hatay adopted the antiquities law of the French Mandate of Syria when it came into being in 1938. In general, this antiquities law stipulated that "at the end of each excavation season the excavator was to divide the moveable finds into two lots, roughly equal in object category, materials and so forth. The country's Director of the Antiquities Service would choose one lot for the national collections, the other would go to the excavating institution as an indemnity" (Maloigne 2017, 207). Crucially, however, there was an important exception to the division of finds in that "the Director of the Antiquities Service … reserved the right to retain any exceptional items from the excavator's lot for the country and the division had to be approved by the head of state before an export license was granted" (207–8). At the end of the 1939 season, the Director of Antiquities for the new State of Hatay chose the lots of finds that did not include the Statue of Idrimi but then reserved the right to retain the statue on the basis of its quality as an exceptional find (208).

Woolley vigorously protested this action, and the matter went before the State of Hatay's Council of Ministers, which voted against Woolley on June 5 and once more, after appeal, on June 7, 1939. At this point, A. W. Davis, the British consul in Aleppo, "suggested Woolley, with the help of the British Ambassador, should involve Cevat Açıkalın, the Turkish Envoy Extraordinaire in the Hatay and head of negotiations with the French," after which "the Turkish Consul-General in the Hatay apparently forthwith received instructions from his government to 'tell the Hatay authorities that Sir Leonard's view must be accepted'" (Maloigne 2017, 208–9, quoting a letter of Hughe Knatchbull-Hugessen). Ultimately, then, Woolley's insistence that the Statue of Idrimi was *not* an exceptional find prevailed (see §2.4 for a ramification of this position) because a decision of the central Turkish government overruled the provincial government. However, the Turkish diplomats' interest in accommodating the request of their British counterparts seems to have had less to do with any strong feeling about the exceptional (or not) nature of the Statue of Idrimi and more to do with providing an easy concession to a potential treaty partner within the context of negotiations for the so-called Tripartite Treaty between France, England, and Turkey that was signed on October 19 of the same year (Maloigne 2017, 209, 211; Hale 2021).

1.3. WOOLLEY'S DESCRIPTION OF THE ARCHAEOLOGICAL CONTEXT OF THE STATUE

These diplomatic negotiations comprised, of course, only one small facet of the geopolitical tensions that were already exploding into World War II. To compare great things with small, this conflict had a profound impact on the modern understanding of the statue's archaeological context. The 1939 season would be Woolley's last at Alalah until 1946; he was recommissioned into the military in September 1939 and served in various capacities, beginning with the Intelligence

Division and culminating in his role as Archaeological Adviser to the Directorate of Civil Affairs, essentially functioning as a precursor to—and helping to establish—the famous division of Monuments Men (Winstone 1990, 221–42). Significantly, Woolley ceased not just the excavations but also all publications on Alalah with this refocusing on wartime activities. Indeed, the preliminary report on the 1939 season (Woolley 1948) did not appear until nine years after the season had concluded. (Interestingly, this report focuses on the Level VII palace and does not mention the statue at all.)

Accordingly, the only contemporary published descriptions of the statue's find-spot appeared in popular accounts in the *Times* of London (Woolley 1939a) and the *Illustrated London News* (Woolley 1939c); there is also the unpublished letter quoted above (see §1.2). Then, after the war, Woolley presented the statue's archaeological context in a series of venues over the space of about six years: his introduction to Smith's (1949) edition of the inscriptions, the preliminary report on the 1946 season (Woolley 1950), *A Forgotten Kingdom*, his popular account of excavations at Alalah (Woolley 1953), and the final excavation report (Woolley 1955).[15]

In general, these accounts agree in describing the statue as having been discovered in a pit that was dug into the floor of an annex to the Level I temple; the head and several smaller pieces of the statue lay next to the body in the pit. Furthermore, the basalt throne on which the statue originally sat is said to have been found on the surface of the floor of the same building. Woolley's description in *A Forgotten Kingdom* (Woolley 1953, 121) provides a representative if vivid account:

> When we excavated the Level I temple..., we found its forecourt littered with objects belonging to the final phase of the building; amongst them was a much defaced basalt throne, obviously that of a statue. In a room in the annexe of the temple proper, lying NE. of the court, we found a hole which had been dug into the floor and filled with earth and large stone (the largest weighing nearly a ton and a half) and smoothed over; under the stones there was a broken statue; the head, which had been knocked off, was set beside the body together with two smaller fragments, one of the beard, the other of a foot.... The statue belonged to the throne found on the temple floor, for it fitted exactly into the cut socket.... We can be sure that the statue was on its throne when the temple was destroyed because the breaking of the feet must have resulted from its being knocked violently off its base into which the feet were socketed.... After the sack of the temple someone must have crept back and piously collected all that he could find of the figure and hidden it in a hastily-dug hole in the hope of recovering it later.

Indeed, so vivid is this account that David Ussishkin (1970, 124–25) used it as his prime example of "the Syro-Hittite ritual burial of monuments," quoting it

[15] The statue is also briefly mentioned in the published summary of a lecture that Woolley gave on the 1946 season to the British School of Archaeology in Iraq (Woolley 1947).

word for word and saying that the description "speaks for itself." Yet, as mentioned above, a significant amount of time—and a world war—had passed since the statue's discovery and this or any other substantial published accounting of its archaeological context. It is perhaps not surprising, then, that differences can be found among Woolley's various accounts of the find-spot of the statue as well. These differences have profound implications and have prompted a substantial reevaluation of the statue's archaeological context, as discussed in detail in §2.1.

1.4. INTRODUCING THE INSCRIPTIONS

Up to this point, this introduction has said very little about the inscriptions carved on the statue other than to present their content. However, the inscriptions and, in particular, their material expression require some additional introduction, not least because a central contention of this study is that there are two distinct inscriptions carved onto the statue, whereas it is customary in the scholarship to speak of a single "Idrimi inscription"; see, for example, the Cuneiform Digital Library Initiative's list of the "100 Most Important Cuneiform Objects," which ranks the statue as number eighteen and reports that "the inscription [is] written all over the statue (even on the beard)."[16]

More accurately, we should speak of two inscriptions. One inscription of exactly one hundred lines is arranged in four units across Idrimi's chest and arms and down from his knees toward the hem of his robe,[17] while a second inscription

[16] The Statue of Idrimi of Alalakh, CDLI:wiki, https://cdli.ox.ac.uk/wiki/doku.php?id=statue_idrimi_alalakh.

[17] This inscription has traditionally been seen as comprising 101 lines. However, the putative line 101 is both indented and preceded by a *Glossenkeil*. These extralinguistic markers communicate that this "line" is to be understood as part of the previous line, which has run over; Mabie (2004, 171, 177) has described a *Glossenkeil* used this way as an "overflow marker." Indeed, Smith (1949, 23) acknowledges as much in his comment to the line, where he notes that the *Glossenkeil* "appears to mean that this line is an overlap"; see also "The single oblique [wedge] to indicate a run-over, 101, where this line given a separate number in the edition, is actually a continuation of 100" (29), citing parallels from the Amarna letters. However, perhaps because Smith nonetheless gave the run-over text its own distinct line number, the indentation has received no subsequent discussion, and the inscription on the statue's body is uniformly treated in the scholarship as if it were 101 and not exactly 100 lines in length.

of only three lines is carved on the statue's cheek. The inscription on the statue's body is arranged in four divisions. Described from the perspective of the viewer, not the statue, the first division contains twenty-three lines of text that are written on the statue's upper left chest and left arm. The second division, comprising lines 24–51, is inscribed on the statue's left leg, directly below the first section. Curiously, the third division of the inscription does not move to Idrimi's upper right chest and proceed downward from there, in which case we could describe the inscription on the body as having been conceptualized as two columns of text. Rather, the third division, comprising lines 52–74, is inscribed on the statue's right leg, proceeding downward from the lap toward the hem of the robe (although it terminates earlier than the parallel second unit; see §2.8). The fourth and final unit of this inscription is carved on the statue's upper right chest and proceeds downward to its lap. In other words, the inscription displays a counterclockwise arrangement on the statue, not a columnar one, as can be seen in figure 1.2. For a comparison of this physical arrangement of the inscription on the statue's body with its literary structure, see §2.8.

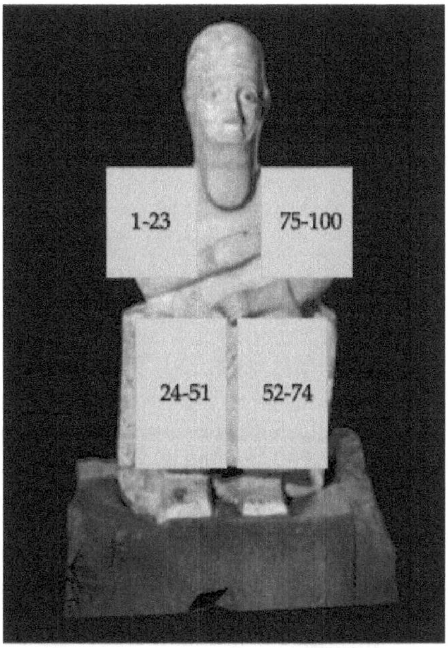

Figure 1.2. Arrangement of the body inscription on the statue.

As mentioned above, in addition to the inscription of one hundred lines carved on the body of the statue, there is a short inscription of only three lines carved on the statue's cheek; see figure 1.3 on the next page. In its vertical orientation, this inscription is clearly physically distinct from the inscription on the statue's body, which has a horizontal orientation. Indeed, Sidney Smith (1949, 10) considered that "these lines must have been inscribed while the figure was lying on its back." Nonetheless, this second inscription has traditionally been considered part of the same inscription as that on the statue's body. Smith assigned it lines 102–104 (on the basis of the body inscription being 101 lines), and this line numbering and placement is found in all subsequent treatments of the text.

To be sure, some dissenting opinions can be found in the scholarship. The earliest of these known to me was offered by Jean Nougayrol (1951, 154 n. 1), who

Figure 1.3. The inscription on the statue's cheek.

suggested that it was more likely that the cheek inscription functioned as a prologue to the body inscription than as a concluding epitaph. In a similar vein, Cory Crawford (2014, 256) remarked that the conventional line numbering puts the text on the statue's cheek at the end of the inscription on the body, "without noting that we have moved to the head of the statue, and back to the (spatial) beginning of the inscription." Jack Sasson (1981, 312–13) also considered that the cheek inscription "ought not to be regarded as an epilogue," but, instead of understanding it as a prologue, he argued that "these lines are comparable to the legends that are placed close to the bodies of protagonists." Writing the same year as Sasson, Manfried Dietrich and Oswald Loretz (1981, 245) occupied the more radical position that the cheek inscription was neither a prologue nor an epilogue to the inscription on the statue's body, despite referring to "Die Inschrift der Statue des

Königs Idrimi" and maintaining the traditional line numbering; for them, it was "a stand-alone text."[18]

1.5. TERMINOLOGY

I am in firm agreement with the argument that the inscription on the statue's cheek should be treated not as part of the inscription on the body but as a distinct inscription. Indeed, a central claim of chapter 4 is that intertextuality between these two inscriptions contributes greatly to the larger program of the statue and its inscriptions. In order to emphasize that these inscriptions are distinct, I depart from previous scholarship in distinguishing between the *body inscription* and the *cheek inscription*. I also give the cheek inscription distinct line numbers, *CI 1–3*; I maintain the numbering *lines 1–100* for the body inscription without an identifier such as "BI" in order to facilitate the consultation of previous literature; note that I consider line 100 of the body inscription to include the text traditionally numbered as line 101, as described in §1.4.

Because I understand there to be two inscriptions carved on the statue, I have tried to be consistent in this monograph in referring to the *Idrimi inscriptions* in the plural, following Jean-Marie Durand (2011, 130), who has spoken of "des textes d'Idrimi" in the plural (see the discussion in §2.7). However, on occasion, I do need to discuss the sum of the material inscribed on the statue as a whole, especially since, as mentioned above, I am arguing that both inscriptions are part of a larger program. On these occasions, I refer to the *Idrimi text*. Finally, in a number of different places, my focus is specifically on lines 1–91 of the body inscription, which encompasses Idrimi's self-introduction through his entrusting the cult to his son IM-nerari; when discussing this portion of the body inscription specifically, I refer to the *Idrimi narrative*. When discussing the nonnarrative remainder of the body inscription (ll. 92–100), I follow the scholarly convention in referring to the *curse formulae* (ll. 92–98) and the *colophon* (ll. 98–100).

1.6. WESTERN HYBRID AKKADIAN

One last piece of terminological housekeeping has less to do with the structure or content of the inscriptions and more to do with their language. The texts are written in an umbrella variety of the Akkadian language that is customarily referred to as "peripheral Akkadian" (German *Randgebiete des Akkadischen*). Krzysztof Baranowski (2016, 21 n. 2) has defined peripheral Akkadian as

> a cover term for the language(s) of the texts written by non-native speakers in various localities outside Mesopotamia.... The common characteristic of Peripheral Akkadian is the influence of the local languages on the grammar and lexicon

---

[18] Note that this position is fundamentally connected to their understanding of the redaction history of the inscriptions; see §2.7 for more discussion.

> that distinguishes it from the native varieties of Akkadian.... The use of the cover term Peripheral Akkadian does not imply its uniformity as a tradition or the homogeneity of its linguistic features.

As used in the scholarship, western peripheral Akkadian in particular encompasses corpora of cuneiform texts from a number of different sites in Anatolia, the Levant, and Egypt that date, usually but not always, to the Late Bronze Age. These sites include Alalah itself, as well as Hattuša, Ekalte, Emar, Ugarit, Taanach, and Tell el-Amarna, to name only some of the more prominent.[19] And, of course, even if certain texts have been found at one of these sites, sometimes they were written at and sent from other so-called western peripheral sites in Anatolia or the Levant. Again, to offer only a couple examples, texts from Carchemish have been found at both Emar and Ugarit, while the Amarna letters include texts from Amurru, Byblos, and many other locations.

On the one hand, then, the term "western peripheral Akkadian" can be considered relatively neutral in that it reflects the fact that texts written in this variety come from locations at the periphery of the core area where the Akkadian language was spoken (namely, Babylonia and Assyria) and that the general orientation of this particular periphery to the core was to the west. On the other hand, it is undeniable that value judgments are also at work with this terminology. As Baranowski emphasized, the various text corpora gathered under the umbrella term of "western peripheral Akkadian" can show as many differences from each other as they do from the standard Akkadian varieties, as a simple comparison of texts written at, for example, Qaṭna and Byblos makes abundantly clear. These differences derive in part from the fact that the relevant texts grouped under the term can often be separated from each other by hundreds of years and/or thousands of kilometers. What unites the texts is that their phonology, morphology, syntax, and lexicon is different, specifically from the standard Akkadian varieties.[20]

Because what unites so-called western peripheral texts is difference from a norm, a danger in placing these differences within a core-periphery model of Akkadian is that it facilitates a discourse in which the peripheral utterance is

---

[19] Vita (2021a, 1214–24) has provided an overview of the primary archives with relevant publication information. Sites producing texts considered by scholars to be peripheral Akkadian but not "western peripheral Akkadian" would include Middle Bronze Age Susa and Late Bronze Age Nuzi.

[20] For instance, in Akkadian texts from Ugarit, a construct noun in the nominative or accusative case can be marked with a case vowel before a noun in the genitive or a pronominal suffix. For instance, Vita (2021a, 1242) gives the example of the phrase *ni-id-nu* LUGAL, "a gift of the king" (see, e.g., PRU 3 65 [RS 16.247]: 14), where the corresponding form in nonliterary Old Babylonian is *nidin* (e.g., *aš-šum ni-di-in* ⸢*pi*⸣-[*i*]*m* ... *ir-šu-u*$_2$, "Because (PN) acquired an oral promise (literally, 'a gift of the mouth')," AbB 9 1: 9).

considered to be wrong instead of the product of a complex interaction of linguistic, material, and/or historical factors.[21] This pejorative attitude toward the language of the texts is reinforced by the fact that some linguistic differences may not be consistent even within corpora or are not currently explainable. The pejorative attitude is probably further compounded by the fact that Assyriologists are often also language teachers who communicate the standards especially of the classical Old Babylonian variety of Akkadian in the classroom.

But, as anyone who has worked deeply with these texts knows, the utterances that they embed are meaningful codes in their own right, and these codes are much more than a set of differences or deviations from a norm. Some may qualify as creoles or interlanguages; others seem never to have been spoken but only to have existed in written form. To be understood, these Akkadian cuneiform texts from Anatolia, the Levant, and Egypt need to be approached, first, on their own terms; second, in dialogue with each other; and third, in dialogue with other disciplines. Happily, such approaches have been adopted for over half a century now and have produced exciting and meaningful results.[22]

At the same time, the continuing habit in academic discourse of referring to all of these dialects under the umbrella term "peripheral" undermines this scholarly work.[23] Given the obvious difficulty with a core-periphery framework, why continue with it by referring to any text originating from Anatolia, the Levant, or Egypt as an example of "western peripheral Akkadian"? One ready answer is probably inertia.[24] But a second answer lies in the fact that it *is* sometimes necessary to have an umbrella term for the varieties of Akkadian written in these texts

---

21 To return to the example of PRU 3 65 [RS 16.247]: 14, the Akkadian construct form with a case vowel in the text from Ugarit cited in the previous note, it may come as no surprise that case vowels are preserved in this position in the indigenous Ugaritic language, even if positing direct substratum influence to explain the phenomenon is an oversimplification.

22 A pioneering example is Moran's (1950) dissertation on the dialect of Akkadian used in Amarna letters sent from Byblos. Vita (2021a, 1235–52) has exemplified this approach in his overview of the grammatical features found in the different text corpora from the Late Bronze Age Levant, conveniently gathering the relevant bibliography, as well.

23 The objection is not new; see, e.g., Boyes 2020, 12 n. 27: "The term 'Peripheral Akkadian' is often used as a catch-all for the various dialects spoken or written outside of Mesopotamia proper, but I avoid it here both for its Mesopotamia-centricness and because it risks obscuring rather than highlighting the linguistic diversity of the region." For a related critique of a core-periphery model of ancient Near Eastern cultural history, see Van De Mieroop 2016 and now Van De Mieroop 2023.

24 Cf. the continued use by scholars of the terms *Syrian* and *Syro-Hittite* to refer to tablet "types" from the Middle Euphrates despite the clear advantages of the alternate terms *Conventional* and *Free Format* that have been proposed by Sophie Démare-Lafont and Daniel Fleming; see Fleming and Démare-Lafont 2009 and Démare-Lafont and Fleming 2015.

in order to compare them with each other and with the standard Akkadian varieties, and no suitable alternative has yet, to my knowledge, been offered.

Here, looking at Near Eastern archaeology, which has long since moved past a core-periphery binary approach, may be helpful. For instance, world systems theory, in which the interaction of a geographic core with its periphery is foundational, was famously applied by Giullermo Algaze to the so-called Uruk expansion (see especially Algaze 2005). Assemblages of Mesopotamian material culture outside of Mesopotamia, whether these assemblages occur isolated at independent sites or mixed with indigenous wares at local settlements, are explained as different manifestations of the economic and political exploitation of the periphery by Mesopotamian colonists who resided there and extracted resources to send back to the Mesopotamian core. However, this analytic framework has rightly been criticized for "highly questionable assumptions [that] eliminate or minimize the roles of polities or groups in the periphery, local production and exchange, local agency, and internal dynamics of developmental change" (Stein 2014, 55, citing previous literature).

In one attempt to move past the limitations of the core-periphery approach, Anne Porter (2012) looked to the concept of hybridity that had emerged from scholarly conversations about contemporary globalism at the end of the last century (e.g., Bhabha 1994). For instance, she demonstrated that this term, which encompasses not "the mere melding of technical influences, differentiation, delineating differences in style" (Porter 2012, 79) but manifestations of identity, was useful in making sense of the complex distribution of Mesopotamian material culture outside of Mesopotamia that is attributed to the so-called Uruk expansion. In particular, she emphasized that "hybridity is not indicated by the mere *transference* of goods, symbols, and ideas from one group to another but by the *transformation* of those goods, symbols, and ideas through the intersection of different understandings of them" (142; emphasis mine).

A sustained application of theories of hybridity to the various corpora of Akkadian cuneiform texts from Late Bronze Age Anatolia, the Levant, and Egypt would be a valuable contribution, although it is unfortunately outside the scope of this study. However, given the degree to which the concepts of hybridity and hybridization have entered mainstream academic discourse over the past two decades, it also does not seem necessary. It is hard to imagine that an interlocutor still exists who would insist that the scribes of Anatolia, the Levant, and Egypt were merely receptacles for the knowledge of Akkadian cuneiform, which they received passively, partially, and imperfectly. Yet this vision of asymmetrical and exploitative core-periphery power relations is essentially the position that is implied when one speaks of "western peripheral Akkadian."

With its emphasis on identity and agentive transformation against these notions of (incomplete, incorrect) transference, I think that it is hard not to agree that the concept of hybridity is superior for talking about the similarities and differences in the varieties of Akkadian cuneiform in texts from Late Bronze Age

Anatolia, the Levant, and Egypt.[25] Furthermore, the concept of hybridity already has some foothold in these conversations whether it be in titles,[26] terminology,[27] or the simple use of hyphenation to differentiate Hurro-Akkadian from Canaano-Akkadian as varieties of Akkadian found in the Levant, which has the effect of creating a linguistic third space. Therefore, for the purposes of this study, when I have need of an umbrella term for the varieties of Akkadian from Late Bronze Age Anatolia, the Levant, and Egypt, I use the term *western hybrid Akkadian* in place of *western peripheral Akkadian*, where *hybrid* replaces *peripheral* in order to emphasize agentive transformation in place of asymmetrical power relations but *western* remains in order to communicate the broad geographical region in which similar linguistic developments may occur relative to the dialects of Akkadian spoken and/or written to the east in Mesopotamia.

1.7. AIMS AND STRUCTURE OF THE BOOK

One final reason why the concept of hybridity is appropriate for the linguistic code(s) studied in this book in particular is that this concept also captures the larger program of the Idrimi statue and its inscriptions. As stated in this chapter's opening paragraph, the question motivating this book is: Why was the story of Idrimi's life told at this particular time and place and in this particular way? Although I do not return to the language of hybridity to articulate it, the answers that I reach are very much informed by the concept. The vision of the statue and the inscriptions that I try to present in this book is more than simply a melding of Mesopotamian literary traditions with Syro-Anatolian practices of ancestor veneration. I see the Statue of Idrimi as a transformation of those traditions and practices and the creation of something entirely new.

The Idrimi inscriptions are obscure in many places. The statue's archaeological context is difficult to interpret, and its enigmatic representation of a robed

25 Similarly, in his study of writing at Ugarit, Boyes (2020) has stressed the analytical value of the concept of hybridity for understanding the writing of Akkadian cuneiform at the site; see, e.g., "we should be clear that we're thinking in terms of the emergence of a hybrid set of practices which, while on the face of it founded in extremely orthodox Mesopotamian traditions, are nevertheless distinct from them and specifically Ugaritian, even before alphabetic cuneiform arrived on the scene" (13) and esp. 103–4.

26 See, e.g., Rainey 2010 ("The Hybrid Language Written by Canaanite Scribes in the 14th Century BCE"); although cf. Izre'el 2012, 181 in reference to the term "Canaano-Akkadian": "One might also suggest the term 'hybrid language,' which is not usually associated with any specific type of language contact.... Therefore, I could resort to this solution. However, the use of this term would not be transparent enough for the actual split between linguistic components in Canaano-Akkadian."

27 See, e.g., the "suffix conjugation hybrid" forms like *irtīḫāti* (EA 196: 13 [Mušihuna]), which combine the suffixes of a perfective conjugation verb to a prefix conjugation base; see, in general, Rainey 1996, 2:317–46 and Medill 2019, 248.

human form—its style—is hard to contextualize. For these reasons, the history of scholarship on the Statue of Idrimi and its inscriptions is deep. In particular, this scholarship is characterized by a number of different approaches, and all of these approaches have informed my own particular attempts to answer the question I asked above. Accordingly, in chapter 2, I discuss the history of scholarship on the statue and its inscriptions from the perspective of these approaches before describing and illustrating my own approach in the book. I leave a more detailed description of the book's structure to the end of that chapter, where it can be informed by this discussion.

2
Approaches

Perhaps because it is a statue inscribed with cuneiform text as opposed to a cuneiform tablet or an anepigraphic figurine, the Statue of Idrimi has drawn attention from scholars working in a variety of disciplines, such as archaeologists, art historians, historians, and, of course, philologists. This chapter discusses some of the approaches to the statue and its inscriptions that scholars working in these different disciplines have taken and the conclusions that they have reached. To some extent, organizing the chapter by discipline or approach is arbitrary and potentially misleading because much of the scholarship discussed in this chapter crosses disciplinary boundaries. Nonetheless, as will be seen, the scholarship can generally be anchored in one discipline or approach.

I begin the chapter by revisiting the statue's archaeological context, reviewing what was reported by Sir Leonard Woolley, and summarizing an important reanalysis. From here, I introduce what evidence exists for the historical Idrimi, as well as the various scenarios that have been proposed for dating the statue and the inscriptions relative to him. I survey various art historical discussions, which, as will be seen, have also often had the aim of dating the statue. I describe some of the most important textual editions and translations of the inscriptions that have appeared over the last three quarters of a century, as well as the incorporation of the inscriptions into the two major Assyriological dictionaries. I consider some approaches to the inscriptions that have attempted to discern underlying source material, and I review various scholarly observations as to the literary nature of the inscriptions and how these observations affect our use of the inscriptions as sources for writing history. Finally, I conclude this chapter by further elaborating my own approach in this book.

2.1. ARCHAEOLOGY

In §1.3, I described when and how Woolley, the chief excavator of the Statue of Idrimi, reported the archaeological context of the statue. In particular, I noted that he reported the statue's location in a pit dug into the floor of the Level I temple, a structure that postdated the historical (Level IV) Idrimi by about two centuries. I also emphasized that a decade had passed between the statue's excavation in 1939 and Woolley's publication of its archaeological context. While some reports appeared as popular accounts in newspapers such as the *Illustrated London News* shortly after the statue's discovery in 1939, the first scholarly communication of the find was in the introduction to Smith's 1949 edition of the text. (See §1.3 for the references to these and other relevant publications by Woolley.) It is worth emphasizing that the decade between 1939 and 1949 was a period in which Woolley experienced many life changes, among them his active involvement in the British military during and after World War II and the death of his wife, Lady Katherine.

Significantly, Amir Fink (2010, 28–28, table 2) has assembled a valuable table that tracks eight different aspects of "Woolley's evolving records" concerning the statue's archaeological context across a contemporary unpublished letter and the near-contemporary newspaper articles, on the one hand, and the more in-depth articles and books that came out after the war, on the other. Here are a few representative differences between the two types of records:

- The statue's find-spot was identified as an in annex to the Level I temple in the postwar publications; in the near-contemporary newspaper articles, it was said to have been discovered just inside the Level I temple wall.
- In the unpublished letter written just after the statue's discovery, the hole in which the statue was found was characterized as "a rubbish pit"; in the summary of his 1946 lecture, however, Woolley characterized it as "a hole specially dug, as if for concealment" (Woolley 1947, 60).
- In the postwar publications, the broken head of the statue was described as "laid carefully by the side of the body" (Woolley 1947, 60), "set beside" the body (Woolley apud Smith 1949, 2), or "carefully assembled" at the bottom of the pit (Woolley 1955, 89); the prewar descriptions gave no sense of intentionality in the placement of broken pieces of the statue in relation to the body, speaking only, for example, of "a statue … prone on its face, the head broken off and lying beside it" (Woolley 1939a).

It is difficult to know what to make of many of these inconsistencies or discrepancies. Undoubtedly, the span of time that separated the discovery of the statue and Woolley's drafting of the postwar publications played an important role. On the one hand, this remove allowed for contemplation of the archaeological record, permitting Woolley to identify, for instance, the room in which the statue was found as an annex to the temple building and not the temple building proper. (On the question of which temple, see the discussion below.) On the other hand, one also has the sense that the intervening years allowed a narrative about the statue to take shape for Woolley, and that this narrative in some cases seems to have driven his description of the archaeological context, as opposed to the other way around. The question of the statue's feet vis-à-vis the throne is an excellent example of this conundrum. As figure 2.1 shows, Woolley's statement that the statue must have sat on the throne because the feet fit exactly into sockets on the latter is absolutely correct, but whether the damage to the statue's toes could have occurred only as a result of the statue's being violently knocked off of the throne, as opposed to sometime afterward, seems less certain.

Figure 2.1. The feet of the statue in the sockets of the throne.

Fink's (2010) reevaluation of the published and unpublished excavation materials also uncovered one profound issue with Woolley's presentation of the archaeological record—ironically, one about which Woolley was consistent in both the pre- and postwar accounts. While Woolley described the statue as having been discovered in an annex to the Level I temple, Fink's reanalysis led him to the conclusion that it was actually found in an annex to the Level IV/III temple.[1] This new date for the statue's find-spot would have important implications for its historical context, rendering some previous discussions out of date (see §2.3 and §6.1) and reinvigorating other long-discarded possibilities that would now need to be considered (see §6.3). Accordingly, we must look at Fink's claim in more detail.

The first step of Fink's argument lay in recognizing that the Level I temple was actually the topmost of the succession of such structures discovered in

---

[1] "Level IV/III" attempts to communicate that the find-spot postdates the destruction of the Level IV palace (Woolley's terminus for the end of the Level IV) but predates the construction of the Level III/II fortress (Woolley's terminus for the beginning of Level III); see §2.1 below for more detail.

Woolley's deep sounding of the temple area and not ten meters away from the other temples; in other words, the Level I temple was actually located ten meters to the south of its location as recorded in Woolley's published plans. Through a careful consideration of both published and unpublished records, Fink demonstrated a remarkable set of circumstances that allowed such an error to occur: inconsistencies in relabeling grid lines from architects' plans into squares in the published plans (Fink 2010, 17–21), the coexistence of grids displaying three distinct orientations (Fink 2010, 21–27), and the absence of physical evidence to which the stratigraphy of the temples could be attributed during excavation, as the surrounding area had already been dug down to at least Level IV and in some places to Level VII (Fink 2010, 40). Fink also identified unpublished photos of the temple in the course of excavation and noticed the reoccurrence of the same walls and the same gaps in the plans of structures that should be separated by ten meters according to Woolley. All of these observations taken together imply that such an error did in fact occur (Fink 2010, 31–33). The clear consistency of form that is visible when the plan of the Level I temple is superimposed upon those of the Level II–V temples (Fink 2010, Plans 15, 16, 18, and 20) provides still more confirmation.

This conclusion of course provokes the question of how Woolley could have recorded a temple that he himself dug ten meters away from its actual location. In fact, the error is more understandable than it appears because, with only two exceptions (the general plans of Levels VII and IV; see Woolley 1955, plates 14 and 22), Woolley's plans are limited to buildings or features of a given stratum isolated from their architectural surroundings (Yener 2005, 100; Batiuk and Burke 2005, 145; Fink 2010, 17). The misplacement in the grid of the Level I temple in Woolley 1955, 83 (fig. 34) thus was isolated synchronically from the rest of the features of Level I and diachronically from the features of previous levels so that the error created no "ripple effect," making it harder to observe, although it can be noticed where the narrative of Woolley's report contradicts his plans (see, e.g., Fink 2010, 44–47).

If the Level I temple was actually the topmost of a succession of superimposed temple structures, how can we be sure that the annex attributed to it actually belonged to the Level I temple and not an earlier one? One might assume that the attribution rested on a physical connection between the two structures. But because the temples were built on podia and the annexes were not, even when correctly associated, the floors of the two structures had different elevations, different states of preservation, and "a physical connection … was fragmentary or nonexistent" (Fink 2010, 40). Accordingly, if the attribution of the putative Level I annex to the Level I temple was not an issue when these structures were the only ones located ten meters to the south of the sequence of earlier temples, it became a question that Fink needed to ask after concluding that the annex was actually located ten meters to the north with the rest of the temples.

He began by reevaluating the findspot of the throne, which, according to the postwar publications, was found on floor of annex, and, as discussed above with figure 2.1, can be associated with the statue on the basis of the sockets, which are custom sized for the statue's feet. However, Woolley's various publications disagree as to where in the annex it was found. In the edition of the Idrimi inscriptions (Woolley *apud* Smith 1949, 2) it was in the annex's "north room," but in the final site report (Wooley 1955, 89) it was in the annex's "west room," while in the prewar popular account published in the *Illustrated London News* (Woolley 1939c) it was in a "long hall" distinct from these two rooms (Fink 2010, 56). These discrepancies suggest that, well after the fact, there was a good deal of subjective grappling by Woolley with an archaeological record that was already difficult to interpret. Indeed, one wonders whether the discrepancies reflect an instance of Woolley's tendency to allow narrative to drive analysis (see §1.3). This suggestion has a real basis in fact, because, among unpublished excavation records in University College London special collections, Fink (2010) identified the field card for the throne (now published as Fink 2010, photo 9). This field card was written at or around the time of the throne's discovery, and, significantly, it records that the throne was found on the surface of the Level II, not the Level I, annex!

However, it is far from certain that the Level II temple actually had a southeast annex. The existence of the so-called Level II southeast annex derives only from walls that "are heuristically and unconvincingly reconstructed" (Fink 2010, 44 with Plan 14). In fact, the thin remnants of walls attributed to this structure are more likely to be from the earlier Level III southeast annex. This annex was the best preserved of those found by Woolley, in part because it was destroyed by fire. Curiously, however, although this annex "was destroyed by fire (rather than being abandoned), no significant finds were reported from it" (Fink 2010, 44). But we should note that if finds like the throne (and altar; see §3.3), which were found on what Woolley thought was the Level II floor (per the field card), were retroactively assigned by him to Level I, and if a Level II annex is in fact an illusion whose remains are to be identified as Level III, then the throne was actually found on the floor of the Level III southeast annex, and the curious absence of any finds from this well-preserved structure destroyed by fire resolves itself.

We may now return to the association between throne and statue (and assuming no continued use of the throne; see Fink 2010, 56). Because the throne was found on the floor of Level III, not Level I, and because the pit containing the statue was dug into the same floor as the throne, this pit and the statue within it also date to Level III (Fink 2010, 57). This revised dating is further supported by photographs of pits such as the one in which the statue was found, which were taken during the course of their excavations (Fink 2010, Photo 11 and 12); as Fink (2010, 58) noted, "the observable pits … are extremely deep. …one can see a man standing, his head not even reaching the mouth of the pit." The depth of the pits makes it more likely that they were dug into a deeper stratigraphic level.[2]

To summarize, Fink's (2010) chain of inference essentially has four steps:

1. Move the Level I temple and annex ten meters to north so that it is above the other earlier temples.
2. Redate the floor on which the throne was found from Level I to Level II on basis of (a) conflicting published accounts, and (b) the field record.
3. Then redate this floor to Level III, because a Level II annex does not seem to have actually existed. Doing so receives circumstantial support by resolving the otherwise unexpected absence of small finds from the Level III structure.
4. Date the statue to Level III on the basis of its association with the throne.

To be sure, this chain of inference is relatively complicated, but I think it is ultimately convincing. In particular, Fink's arguments for relocating the Level I temple and annex seem sound, as does the association of the statue with the throne, wherever one places the throne. The steps in between—namely, the redating of the Level I floor to Level II and then, subsequently, to Level III—are a bit more difficult. I am inclined to accept redating the floor to Level II both because of the testimony of the field record and because Woolley did seem quite invested in the narrative of a pious devotee creeping back into a temple destroyed by the Sea Peoples to bury the broken statue, and this narrative required the statue to have been found in an annex to the Level I temple. With regard to subsequently redating the Level II floor to Level III, it hurts to essentially write off an entire structure, but in this instance the combination of the very poor remains of the putative Level II southeast annex with the robust preservation of the Level III annex immediately below it (as opposed to poor remains on their own) makes me comfortable assuming that Woolley interpreted the topmost remnants of the walls of the Level III annex as part of a later Level II annex.

Overall, then, Fink's reanalysis of Woolley's stratigraphic levels and, consequently, the Statue of Idrimi's archaeological context seems correct. At this point, we want to look a little more closely at these stratigraphic levels, especially what defines them and how they correlate to historical events and chronology. For Woolley, stratigraphic levels were often defined by their principal architectural monuments, which functioned for him as metonyms for important political

---

[2] Fink (2010, 58) also remarked on the fact that Woolley reported that the statue's pit was covered with slabs of large stones and a reused column, concluding that "the number of remarkably large and heavy building stones that Woolley removed on his way to the Statue of Idrimi increases the likelihood that the buried statue originated from a lower surface"; here, the logic of the inference is not entirely clear to me.

events.[3] This dubious principle means that Woolley's Level IV begins with the building of Niqmepa's palace (Woolley 1955, 156). However, it does not end with the destruction of this palace, "but Level IV continues until the Hittite conquest introduced a new political and cultural phrase in the history of Alalakh" (Woolley 1955, 156, 387). The evidence of said introduction is the construction of another architectural monument, the so-called Level III fortress, and "a new temple … built in the Hittite style. These must have been the work of Suppiluliuma, and they mark the beginning of our Level III" (Woolley 1955, 395).

Because Woolley's Level IV began with the construction of the Level IV palace but continued past its destruction to Šuppiluliuma I's conquest of the city, Fink (2010, 50) took the natural step of dividing Woolley's Level IV into two subphases: Level IVA^{F}, which spanned from the construction of the Level IV palace to its destruction, and Level IVB^{F}, which spanned from the destruction of the Level IV palace to Šuppiluliuma I's conquest of Alalah.[4] Furthermore, he argued that "not only was the Level IV^{W} palace destroyed … so too were the fortress … and all the buildings attributed by Woolley to Level IV^{W}" (Fink 2010, 50). To put it differently, while Woolley had assumed "that only the Level IV^{W} palace was destroyed and the rest of the Level IV^{W} buildings continued to exist during … the Level IVB^{F} period" (Fink 2010, 50–51), Fink's claim is that this was not the case, but that Woolley's Level IV fortress and temple were destroyed at the same time as the Level IV palace. This claim, in turn, results in an earlier date for the construction of Woolley's Level III temple during the period of time after the destruction of the Level IV palace (+Level IV temple) but before Šuppiluliuma I's conquest of Alalah—in other words, to Fink's Level IVB.

To be clear, from my reading of Fink 2010, this claim is more an argument that the Level III fortress and temple *could* date to his Level IVB than an assembling of evidence to support an argument that they *do*. For instance, he cited Eva von Dassow's (2005) conclusion that the Level IV archives end early in the reign of Ilimi-ilima; noting that these archives include tablets found in the Level IV fortress, Fink suggested that this archive "ceased to exist at the same time the palace archives did" (2010, 51). He also pointed out that Woolley described "the stratigraphy of this area" as "very complicated, episodic and inconsistent" (2010, 51). Probably the closest thing to positive evidence in this regard is his discussion

---

[3] Woolley 1955, 110: "There is a definite advantage in associating our archaeological levels with political events and thereby obtaining more or less positive dates for them." Woolley went on to stress that the transition from, in this instance, Level V to Level IV was "peaceful and gradual, so that both socially and culturally the actual dividing line between them is difficult to determine and, so far as the archaeological strata are concerned, is here drawn arbitrarily."

[4] The superscript F was used by Fink to designate stratigraphic levels that he determined; he designated Woolley's stratigraphic levels with a superscript W. I will generally omit these notations and refer instead to, e.g., "Fink's Level IVb."

of a lexical list that was found in Woolley's Level III/II fortress. According to Fink (2010, 114), this lexical list, which Woolley described as being of the "Boğazköy type" was "Woolley's main justification for dating the Levels III–II^{W} fort to the time of Šuppiluliuma I." Yet the tablet was actually found below the floor in the fill used in the fortress's foundation, so it could have been written prior to the fortress's construction—in other words, during Level IV (Lauinger 2005, 54). The lexical list, which is a unilingual (Sumerian only) exemplar of ur_5-ra = *hubullu*, can certainly be characterized as of the conventional (i.e., "Syrian") as opposed to the free format (i.e., "Syro-Hittite") type, following Yoram Cohen's (2009, 132) study of the scholarly material from Emar and so should date earlier in the Late Bronze Age.

As for Woolley's putative Level III temple, Fink (2010, 52) rejected the idea that there is anything "Hittite" about its plan, citing Machteld Mellink's (1957) review of Woolley ("a persistence of a basically Syrian ground-plan, although the entrance-system may vary" [398]) and Hermann Genz's (2006, 503) argument that the temple's plan does not resemble the plans of excavated Hittite temples. He then concluded that Woolley's Level III temple "was most likely built at the same time as the Levels III–II^{W} fortress; nonetheless, both building projects occurred during the Level IVB^{F} period." In sum, Fink's primary accomplishment in his reevaluation of the stratigraphy lies in demonstrating that "there are no archaeological, historical or philological reasons that stand in the way" of dating the Level III fortress and Level III temple to the beginning of his Level IVB ("the building, named by Woolley 'the Level III-II fort,' could, in fact, be the stronger, larger and higher palace of Itūr-Addu, king of the land of Mukiš" [51]), even if both continued to be used by Šuppiluliuma I after he conquered the city.

Aslıhan Yener, Murat Akar, and Mara Horowitz (2019a) interjected a note of caution into this revised date for Woolley's putative Level III temple and fortress. They disagreed strongly with Fink's redating of the Woolley Level III fortress to Level IVB because the Yener-Akar excavations discovered extensive rebuilding and reuse of the Level IV fortress during this time. With regard to the Level III temple, they did agree with Fink (2010) that the attribution of this temple to the Hittite conquest was not secure because it derived only from the temple's having "a very different inner configuration than its predecessor," and not from parallels with Hittite temples specifically (Yener, Akar, and Horowitz 2019a, 329). However, they were not as quick as Fink to assume that the destruction of the Level IV temple occurred at the same time as the destruction of the Level IV palace or that the construction of Woolley's Level III temple needed to have occurred immediately after. They warned that, "without a firm date for the founding of Temple III and knowing that Temple IV may well have survived the destruction of Palace IV, it becomes impossible to relate Temple III to any political order" (Yener, Akar, and Horowitz 2019a, 329–30).

This warning, while apt, still does not exclude Fink's hypothesis that the construction of the so-called Level III temple falls into that period of time between the Level IV palace's destruction and the beginning of Level III; in other words, the so-called Level III temple may antedate Woolley's Level III and Šuppiluliuma I's conquest of Alalah. There certainly seems to have been sufficient time for its construction. The Yener-Akar excavations have confirmed that the so-called Level IV fortress and gate were remodeled after the destruction of the Level IV palace and occupied for multiple decades; in particular, one excavation square in this area revealed three distinct local phases that represented rebuildings of the Level IV fortress during this interval (Akar 2019, 20–26; Yener, Akar, and Horowitz 2019a, 326), and Yener, Akar, and Horowitz suggested that Period 3, as the Yener-Akar excavations designate the time period between the destruction of the Level IV palace and the construction of the Level III/II fortress, may have comprised "at least 50 to 70 years" (Yener, Akar, and Horowitz 2019a, 329).

Although, to my knowledge, Yener, Akar, and Horowitz (2019a) did not suggest in the text of their contribution that the so-called Level III temple dates to Period 3 (nor did they state that it does not), tellingly, their "Temple III" is correlated precisely with Period 3—namely, the time span ca. 1400–1350 BCE—in a concluding synoptic table that correlates the excavation results from three areas of the Yener-Akar excavations with results from Woolley's excavations. As their Period 3 is essentially coterminous with Fink's Level IVB, on the basis of Fink's reanalysis of the statue's find-spot described above, the statue's deposition into the pit should date to sometime after the destruction of the Level IV palace, up to and including Šuppiluliuma I's conquest of Alalah.

2.2. DESTRUCTION AND BURIAL

Attention to the archaeological context of the statue's destruction and burial requires a few words about its deposition into a pit and the scholarly interpretations thereof. As has been noted several times already, the statue was found in a pit dug into the temple floor. Although much of the statue was intact, the head, a piece of the beard, and a foot (it seems) were broken off and found next to it in the pit. Large stones and, seemingly, a piece of a basalt column then filled the top of the pit. The surface of the pit was possibly overlaid with brickwork. (Again, Fink 2010, 28–29, Table 2 gathers the different descriptions of the statue's find-spot in Woolley's prewar and postwar publications.) Woolley's prewar descriptions stated only that the pieces broken from the statue were found next to it. However, the postwar publications stressed that the pieces were arranged carefully and intentionally.[5] These observations, in turn, played a crucial role in Woolley's reconstruction of the context for the statue's deposition, which, as quoted in §1.3, imagined a devotee creeping back to the temple after its destruction by the Sea Peoples, collecting

[5] The head was "broken off but laid carefully by the side of the body" (Woolley 1947, 60); although "knocked off," it had been "set beside the body with two smaller fragments" (Woolley 1953, 22), which were "carefully assembled" (Woolley 1955, 89).

the broken statue and its fragments and "piously" burying them in a "hastily-dug hole."

The difficult but necessary question to answer is whether the details about the care and attention to burying the statue fragments that appear in Woolley's postwar descriptions of the statue's find-spot but not the prewar descriptions formed the basis for Woolley's interpretation, or whether these details appeared because he had already settled on that interpretation. Unfortunately, I am inclined toward the latter opinion for two reasons. First, there is the evidence of the field card, discussed in §2.1, which clearly identified the statue's throne as having been found in Level II, not I, so it already seems that Woolley had made some adjustments to the record in order to accommodate his interpretation. Second, and relatedly, the description of the "hastily-dug hole" in which the statue is buried is contradicted by Woolley's other statements concerning the large slabs of stone that filled the pit above the statue; indeed, immediately prior to calling the pit "hastily-dug," Woolley claimed that the largest stone weighed one and a half tons! The effort required to cover the hole with stones of this size seems at odds with its description as "hastily-dug" and suggests that narrative drove description, not the other way around. Nonetheless, Woolley's analysis of the statue's find-spot as a burial has been accepted by many scholars; see, for example, Ussishkin 1970 (see §1.3), in which the same passage from Woolley 1953 is quoted and taken at face value.

On the other hand, Petra Goedegebuure (2012, 429–30) put forward the possibility that the statue was broken by the Hittites after Šuppiluliuma I's conquest (she accepted Fink's [2010] revised dating), considering that "probably, the Hittites toppled the statue of this venerated ruler as a political act to symbolize the demise of the city-state." Noting that "there is some evidence that burial of an image was considered very harmful by the Hittites," she suggested that the Hittites buried it as "a form of humiliation" or even, as she proposed earlier in the same contribution, "not out of vandalism" but as part of a larger project "to break the nexus between a ruler from the dynasty of deposed kings of Alalakh and its gods."

To my mind, Goedegebuure's proposal that the statue was buried by the Hittite occupiers of Alalah and not by local devotees is more likely, especially if we accept that the statue's deposition occurred at the end of Fink's Level IVB or the Yener-Akar excavation's Period 3—in other words, at around the time of Šuppiluliuma's conquest. The nature of the burial, with the pit filled in with very large stones, and its scale would seem to have required Hittite permission. If the Hittites were responsible for the statue's destruction, and if ritual burial of the statue was a good thing for the king whom it represented or his subjects, it seems unlikely that the Hittites would have allowed such a burial. Woolley's description of a "hastily-dug hole" was intended to respond to this logic but conveniently overlooked the large stones. On the other hand, a scenario in which the "nexus" between a deceased ruler and his gods is interfered with by toppling his statue and breaking off its head, and is then distorted further by sticking statue and head into a hole in the ground with large rocks piled on top of them—this is a scenario consistent with Hittite permission for such activity.

2.3. DATING AND HISTORIOGRAPHY

The various arguments about the Statue of Idrimi's archeological context presented here both inform and are driven by conclusions and assumptions concerning the statue's date of composition. The statue's inferred or assumed date of composition, in turn, has helped to define how the statue's inscriptions are used as historical sources. Accordingly, this section reviews some of the various dates of composition that have been proposed for the statue and its inscriptions and the historiographical approaches to the inscriptions that accompany these proposals. (For more discussion of the inscriptions' use as sources for writing history, see §2.8.)

In this regard, the first point to emphasize is that, as mentioned in §1.1, there is textual evidence outside of the statue itself for a historical ruler of Alalah named Idrimi. All of this evidence comes from the cuneiform archives found in the Level IV palace at Alalah, and it consists of:

- AlT 3 [1.2], a treaty between Idrimi and Pilliya, the ruler of Kizzuwatna
- AlT 71 [341.6], a contract for the purchase of a slave in which Idrimi is the purchaser
- AlT 99 [37.2], a legal text too damaged for its nature to be ascertained but that was drawn up before Idrimi
- AOAT 27, no. 189, the impressions from Idrimi's cylinder seal, identifying him by name in the inscription (*id-ri-mi* / IR_3 *ša* ^{d}IM, "Idrimi, the servant of the Storm God"), that is found on nine legal and administrative tablets dating to his reign and that of his son.[6]

On the basis of this evidence and its archival and architectural associations, von Dassow (2008, 33–37) argued that Idrimi must have inhabited the Level IV palace, and that at least part of his reign should be dated to the beginning of Level IV, since, as discussed in §2.1, the beginning of Level IV is defined by the construction of the Level IV palace, according to Woolley's stratigraphy.

---

[6] AlT 17 [31.3], 69 [341.4], 71 [341.6], 99 [37.2], 100 [38.3], 186 [412.3], 187 [412.4], 227 [412.19], 395 [47.4], and 401 [47.10]. AlT 71 [341.6] and 99 [37.2], as noted above, are securely dated to Idrimi by mention of him in the body of the text; so, too, AlT 17 [31.3] and 69 [341.4] can be dated to the reign of Niqmepa. The remaining texts do not mention either king by name but probably date to Niqmepa's reign on prosopographic grounds (AlT 100 [38.3]) or are administrative texts that should date to after Idrimi's reign. As discussed by Collon (1975, 169–70), the seal that produced the impression AOAT 27, no. 189 originally had caps, which were removed at some point during the reign of Niqmepa; see also von Dassow 2008, 24.

Von Dassow made this argument in explicit contrast to previous assertions that the Level IV palace was constructed by Idrimi's son, Niqmepa, with Idrimi therefore placed during the previous Level V; see the literature cited by von Dassow (2008, 36) and Jordi Vidal (2012, 78). As von Dassow pointed out, however, the Level IV palace was attributed to Niqmepa by Woolley on the basis of an incorrect reconstruction of the rulers of Level IV Alalah that put Niqmepa in the first position and Idrimi as his grandson; see §1.1. Accordingly, there is no reason to maintain the attribution, and scholars who wish to do so by arguing, for instance, that "the paucity of tablets from Idrimi's reign" is "proof that Idrimi did not reign during Level IV" do not take into account "the patterns of accumulation, storage, and discard through which archives are formed" (von Dassow 2008, 36). At the same time, von Dassow was careful to emphasize that Idrimi's reign probably began already in Level V, since the Level IV palace, the construction of which marks the end of Level V and the beginning of Level IV, probably did not inaugurate his reign. These arguments have received general acceptance by other scholars; see, for example, Christian Niedorf (2008, 14) and Akar (2012, 42), who further suggested that Idrimi might himself have been responsible for the destruction of the Level V fortress.[7] One dissenting voice was Fink (2010, 67–78), who continued to attribute the Level IV palace to Niqmepa and the Level IV fortress, which he called the Level VB^F palace, to Idrimi; see, however, the remarks of von Dassow 2020a, 197 n. 15 ("calling the Level IV fortress ... a palace does not demonstrate that it was one").

In terms of an absolute date for the historical Idrimi, the key pieces of evidence are a synchronism between the historical Idrimi and the Mittanian king Parattarna I that is attested in the treaty between Idrimi and Pilliya of Kizzuwatna (AlT 3 [1.2])[8] and ceramic evidence from Levels V and IV at Alalah. Unfortunately, neither of these pieces of evidence is too clear. As von Dassow (2008, 39) has observed, Parattarna I of Mittani is "virtually unknown except in relation to his vassal Idrimi, and the dates of both have therefore moved in tandem"; a good illustration of this point is the *Reallexikon der Assyriologie* article on Parattarna I and II (Wilhelm 2003–2005), where AlT 3 [1.2] and the Idrimi narrative comprise the entirety of the textual evidence that is cited.

Von Dassow (2008, 39–42) has also discussed Celia Bergoffen's (2005) analysis of the Cypriot pottery found at Alalah. Since imported Cypriot ware played an important role in dating Levels VI and V at Alalah despite its incomplete publication, Bergoffen aimed to publish this material completely and reevaluate the absolute chronology of Levels VI, V, and, by implication, IV. However, as von Dassow has explicated, the reevaluation is marred, on the one hand, by tautology

[7] Niedorf was responding to a similar argument that von Dassow (1997) advanced in her dissertation.

[8] The treaty stipulates that it goes into effect "on whatever day Parattarna (I) swore the oath of the gods with Idrimi" (ll. rev. 40–42).

(dates derived from the texts establish a chronological framework for the pottery, which is used in turn to date the architecture in which it and the tablets were found) and, on the other hand, by assigning quite specific dates to those structures on the basis of dates for that imported pottery found at other sites in the Levant, although those dates can provide only "broad and approximate date ranges within which individual finds may be variously situated" (von Dassow 2008, 41).

Extrapolating from Bergoffen's evidence, considered apart from the proposed historical framework, von Dassow (2008, 42) considered that

> the ceramic evidence seems to support dating the destruction of the [Level IV] palace to roughly 1400.... If the palace was destroyed c. 1400, working backwards from that point through three generations of rulers attested by the Level IV archives indicates a construction date 50–75 years earlier, sometime in the second quarter of the fifteenth century BCE.

Since Idrimi would have ruled for some period of time before the construction of the Level IV palace, von Dassow suggested that "his accession may therefore be dated early in [this] quarter century..., or perhaps a little earlier, i.e., roughly 1475 BCE" (von Dassow 2008, 42). Subsequently, she pushed this date forward, arguing that "on archival and archaeological grounds, Niqmepa's reign may be dated roughly around 1425 BC, and his father Idrimi's roughly around 1450 BC" (von Dassow 2022, 474).

Turning now to the date of the Idrimi inscriptions, the lifetime of the historical Idrimi has provided the basis for one school of thought. According to this school of thought, originally advanced by Woolley (see esp. Woolley 1953, 122–23), the Idrimi text was composed during the historical Idrimi's lifetime and inscribed on the statue then or immediately afterward, so that the inscribed statue should be dated to Level IV, when Alalah acknowledged the hegemony of Mittani. On this assumption, Šarruwa, the scribe named in the body inscription's colophon, can be readily identified with a well-attested Level IV scribe of the same name (see, e.g., Na'aman 1980a and the discussion in §6.1). After being inscribed, the statue was deposited in the Level IV temple at Alalah, where it remained on display in successive temples as they were rebuilt until the destruction of the Level I temple. According to Woolley, the statue was broken at this time as well, and its pieces were subsequently buried by a pious citizen of Alalah; see §2.2.

According to this school of thought, the statue was inscribed ca. 1450–1425 and broken and buried ca. 1200—or, better, ca. 1300 to use the updated date for the end of Level I; see §1.2. Therefore, it would have stood in the successive temples at Alalah for about 250 years (or, better, 150 years). However, for a good portion of this span, Alalah was under the control of the Hittites. Yet one of the major episodes of the text's narrative is an account of Idrimi's successful campaign against Hittite territory ("The land of Hatti did not gather and march because of me. I did what I wanted," ll. 70b–72a). Is it reasonable to assume that Hittite officials would have permitted a statue celebrating this accomplishment to remain standing in the temple?

Indeed, the interjection of "strong anti-Hittite sentiments" (Sasson 1981, 323) into the narrative is a key piece of the second school of thought as to the Statue of Idrimi's date of creation and inscription. Jack Sasson argued that the inscribed statue was better dated to the stratigraphic level in which Woolley reported having discovered it—namely, Level I. Sasson supported his claim with a variety of different strands of evidence: the narrative's similarity to a pseudo-autobiographical genre of Mesopotamian literature sometimes called *narû* literature (312–15); the documented existence of a certain *Šar*-[...], who is attested as the author of a Hittite letter from Level I—II Alalah, AlT 124 [ATH 1], and whom Sasson suggested as a candidate for the Šarruwa mentioned in the body inscription (318); an analysis provided by Marie-Henrietta Gates that found the closest stylistic parallels for the statue's throne at "the very end of the Late Bronze Age" (320); and parallels for statues of rulers inscribed with their (pseudo)autobiographies that date to the first millennium (320–21).

Tying together these various strands of evidence, Sasson (1981, 322) reconstructed a scenario in which "the fabrication of Idrimi's statue occurred during the last days of Alalah." Specifically, he suggested that a rebellion against Hittite hegemony occurred at Alalah in the final decades of Level I. Sasson was able, in fact, to cite Woolley himself for this suggestion. Woolley considered the burning of the Level IA temple and the rebuilding of another temple with a different plan, which incorporated the reuse of an orthostat of a Hittite official named Tudhaliya, as "the evidence of yet one more revolt against the Hittite suzerainty" (Woolley 1953, 163). For Sasson, the Statue of Idrimi and its inscriptions fit naturally into such a historical context:

> It is during this period, we would like to suggest, that nascent "nationalistic" feelings at Alalah led a certain Šarruwa to sponsor the making of a statue and to inscribe it with his own version of the deeds of Idrimi, founder of the last independent dynasty to rule the city-state. ...the result was a historiographic masterpiece which promoted an awareness of Alalah's glorious past even as it offered solace in detailing the manner in which that past was itself built upon inauspicious beginnings. It spoke of days when Alalah's leaders were able to muster control of territories, Amae and Niya, which ... never fell under the domination of Mukiš/Alalah. But more understandable in view of the strong anti-Hittite sentiments which must have festered during the long centuries of subjugation, Idrimi was made to gloat over successful forays into Hittite territory. (1981, 323)

Sasson's reconstruction has now been rendered impossible by Fink's (2010) reanalysis of the statue's find-spot, which placed it in the Level III, not Level I, temple; see §2.1. However, in suggesting that the inscriptions need not be automatically assumed to have been commissioned by the historical Idrimi, his reconstruction has made a lasting impact on the scholarship. In particular, Sasson's connection of the Idrimi narrative to the category of Mesopotamian literature called *narû* literature, or pseudo-autobiography, provided a historically attested means by which to detach text from historical figure; this possibility is developed in §4.2.

With Fink's (2010) reanalysis of the statue's find-spot comes a new perspective on the relationship of the statue and its inscriptions to the historical Idrimi. If the find-spot of the statue is to be located in the Level III temple, not the Level I temple, then there is no need to choose between a date for the statue and the inscriptions that is either contemporary with the historical Idrimi or centuries removed from his life. In particular, the latter option is now replaced with a scenario that sees the statue and its inscriptions as created sometime after the destruction of the Level IV palace and before Šuppiluliuma I's conquest of Alalah, which marks the end of Level IV. The statue and inscriptions should now be placed within the period of time ca. 1400–1330—in other words, some period of time ranging from decades up to a century after the historical Idrimi's death.

Fink (2010, 97) himself offered a reconstruction of what such a scenario might look like for what he termed "the enthronement inscription of Addu-Nīrārī":

> I would like to raise the possibility that Addu-Nīrārī did not succeed his father, but rather his nephew Ilimilimma. Consequently, Šarruwa, the experienced scribe, who served under Niqmepa and Ilimilimma..., was the kingmaker who enthroned Addu-Nīrārī. I believe that the statue was inscribed during a period of turmoil in the history of Alalakh, following the traumatic destruction of Level IVA^{F}, probably by the Hittites. At this moment of havoc and mayhem (Level III^{W} = early IVB^{F}) there was an immediate need to reestablish the Idrimi dynasty. Thus, the Idrimi inscription constitutes, in fact, the enthronement inscription of Addu-Nīrārī, king of Alalakh, and the re-establishment of the Idrimi (Aleppan) dynasty that conceivably ruled over Alalakh, almost uninterruptedly, from the days of Yamhad onward.

In this scenario, an earlier, oral, version of which (Fink 2005) was accepted by von Dassow (2008, 32–33), the creation of the statue and its inscriptions would date to shortly after the destruction of the Level IV palace, ca. 1400 BCE, so that the statue "stayed in its place of honor in the temple for a generation or two, until, once again, the Hittite army arrived and destroyed Alalah IV together with the image and cult of its hero, Idrimi" (von Dassow 2008, 33), ca. 1330 BCE.

In this book, I also situate the composition of the inscriptions within this period of time following the destruction of the Level IV palace and the end of Level IV. However, my reconstruction depends primarily on a close reading of the text; I consider it a compelling piece of supporting evidence that the conclusions that I reach through close reading correlate with Fink's reanalysis of the statue's find-spot. Differing from Fink, however, I do not assume that the statue and the inscriptions were created at the same time. Indeed, I will argue in chapter 3 that the statue is considerably older than the inscriptions. And, differing from both Fink and von Dassow, in chapter 6 I will consider the possibility that the inscriptions should be dated more toward the end of the relevant time span—in other words, closer to Šuppiluliuma I's conquest of Alalah and the end of Level IV, ca. 1330, than to the destruction of the Level IV palace, ca. 1400.

2.4. ART HISTORICAL APPROACHES

Alongside these discussions of the statue's date, a parallel conversation has occurred among art historians who have tried to date the statue on the basis of stylistic similarities with other objects. However, this conversation has been somewhat hampered by value judgments that can be surprisingly pejorative. While Woolley described the statue in neutral terms in a prewar popular publication,[9] after the war he instead highlighted its (negative) aesthetic value, observing that "it is not, technically speaking, a good piece of sculpture … it is almost grotesquely ugly" (Woolley *apud* Smith 1949, 8). In the wake of Woolley's judgment, art historians echoed both his pejorative statement and his description of its style as provincial. So, for instance, in his review of Smith 1949, Anton Moortgat (1949, 176) declared that "der Wert der Idri-mi-Statuette als Bilddenkmal reicht bei weitem nicht an die historische Bedeutung ihrer Inschrift heran. Sie trägt provinziellen Charakter und ist das Werk eines Kleinfürsten, der ohne grosse Hilfsmittel um seine Stellung hat kämpfen müssen." Similarly, in his survey of ancient Near Eastern art, Henri Frankfort (1955 [1996], 252) dismissed the statue as "a most clumsy and primitive piece of carving," continuing, in a somewhat evolutionary strain, that "if it had not been for the text, [the statue] would probably have been ascribed to the third millennium." Indeed, by 1980, the Statue of Idrimi's poor aesthetic quality had become prevailing doctrine to the extent that Gates was able to declare that the "very poorly modeled" statue "has become a standard handbook illustration for the supposedly clumsy provincial style of mid-second millennium Syria" (Gates *apud* Sasson 1981, 319; it is worth stressing that Gates actually distances herself from this judgment by qualifying the sculptural style as "*supposedly* clumsy" [emphasis added]).

Alongside aesthetic pronouncements, the primary approach to the statue by art historians has been focused on identifying a home for it within the taxonomy

[9] He wrote that it had "a curious resemblance to Sumerian work, suggesting that a provincial North Syrian art had preserved some of the characters of its prototype for hundreds of years after Sumer had ceased to exist" (Woolley 1939c). Maloigne (2017, 210) has discussed Woolley's description within the context of the division of finds at the end of the 1939 season, whereby Woolley needed to demonstrate that the statue was unexceptional because, as described in §1.2, although the excavating institution and the host country shared all movable finds from an excavation season equally, the director of antiquities for the host country was allowed to retain any "exceptional items from the excavator's lot."

of ancient Near Eastern artistic style. Again, this taxonomic work began with Woolley's introduction to Smith's (1949) edition, where he backed away from a "Sumerian-influenced" style, as quoted above, and instead pointed to the statues from Iron Age Tell Halaf for stylistic parallels (Woolley *apud* Smith 1949, 8). In his review of Smith 1949, Moortgat (1949, 176) agreed with the choice of Iron Age parallels, remarking that the style of the statue

> ist uns bekannt durch in ihrem Wesensausdruck ganz ähnliche Gestalten auf den frühen orthostaten des Burgtores in Zencirli. Bezeichnend das Profil mit der fliehenden Stirn, der weit vorspringenden Nase und der unterentwickelten Mundpartie.... Wäre demnach nicht die Inschrift auf der Idri-mi Statuette, so wäre man geneigt, sie dieses Stiles wegen und trotz ihrer Gewandung, die an Denkmäler aus der Zeit um 1500 erinnert, möglichst nah an die Kunst der nordsyrischen Kleinfürstentümer aus der Zeit kurz nach 1000.

Were it not for the statue's inscriptions, then, and despite its garments (on which see below), Moortgat would have been inclined to date the statue to the beginning of the first millennium BCE.

However, because of the inscriptions, Moortgat (1969, 111) later dated the statue to the Late Bronze Age and, in his famous survey of ancient Near Eastern art, considered it to be representative of an otherwise largely unattested "Mittanian-Hurrian" (or, alternatively, "Hurrian-Mittanian") artistic style. Moortgat believed that the statue showed "a combination of Syrian and Mitannian-Hurrian features," the Syrian features found primarily in the statue's accoutrement. On the other hand, "the style and character of this statue make an impression of an abstract, divorced from nature." Moortgat found a parallel for "this same geometrical abstract style ... in the two lions which decorate the string-board of the stairs in the same building of Idrimi," concluding that "it is difficult to think of other works of art comparable in style. If some day these are proved to be Hurrian-Mittanian, then they will in some way form part of the small group of decorative objects which, apart from glyptic, we can consider as part of Hurrian-Mitannian art."

This positioning of the statue as representative of Hurrian or Mittanian art has been sharply criticized by subsequent scholars. For instance, Ruth Mayer-Opificius (1981, 285) explicitly objected to Moortgat's attribution, remarking: "doch sind wird bis heute nicht genügend über die Kunstäußerungen der Menschen dieses Ethnikons unterrichtet.... Es ist überdies auch keineswegs gesichert, daß Idrimi oder der Künstler, der das Werk schuf, tatsächlich Churriter waren." And Diana Stein (1993–1997, 296) rejected the very categories of "a distinctive Mittanian art ... along with the concept of Hurrian art.... Both have been countered by surveys of individual iconographic motifs, which are shown to vary regionally within the realm and period of M[ittani]."

However, even after rejecting the chimera of a Hurrian or Mittanian style, art historians continued to locate the statue within a broader taxonomy of ancient Near Eastern artistic style and have come to little agreement. Some have stressed Middle Bronze Age parallels (e.g., Spycket 1981, 327 and Bonatz 2000a, 133, 175 n. 79, 206 n. 79). Others have followed Woolley in emphasizing the statue's similarities to Syro-Hittite art from the Iron Age (e.g., Stein 1993–1997, 296). Still others have looked to Egypt (e.g., Mayer-Opificus 1981, 285).[10] And Gates considered that "the statue does not … bear any stylistic features which characterize it chronologically" (Gates *apud* Sasson 1981, 319).[11]

Within this search for stylistic parallels, one area where there has been some agreement concerns the statue's garments, specifically the conical hat and so-called *Wulstsaummantel*. Some of the earliest statements about these garments are found in Moortgat's review, where he noted that "von der älteren syrischen Welt hat Idri-mi nur noch etwas in seiner Tracht gerettet. Sein Gewand soll der Mantel mit schwerem Wulstsaum sein, den wir von der Mischrife-Bronze, vom Götterkopf aus Djabbul und von vielen guten Rollsiegeln der Zeit unmittelbar nach dem Ende der Hammurabi-Dynastie kennen" (Moortgat 1949, 170; see also Moortgat 1969, 111). Mayer-Opificius, who otherwise objected to Moortgat's description of the statue, agreed with him on this point, noting that "der Fürst trägt die seit altsyrischer Zeit übliche Tracht höher gestellter Persönlichkeiten und Götter: die hohe Kappe … und den syrischen 'Wulstsaummantel" (Mayer-Opificus 1981, 284).

The Middle Bronze Age parallels for the statue's garments were discussed at some length by Dominique Collon (1975, 186–88) in her study of the seal impressions from Alalah. In a section entitled "The Male Figure in a High Oval Head-Dress and Related Figures," she noted that "this figure occurs only on Level VII

---

[10] It is tempting to connect this position, which, to my knowledge, has not been taken up elsewhere, to a similar position advocated some years later by Mayer (1995, 334) that the autobiographical presentation of Idrimi's life derives from Egyptian tomb biographies. For instance, in her article, Mayer-Opificus (1981, 285) remarked "wie bereits oben (s. S. 999) erwähnt, hat man einzelne Motive der Inschrift auf der Statue schon gelegentlich—gewiß zu Recht—mit ägyptischen verglichen." But the reference to a page 999 seems to be a placeholder (possibly meant to be filled with reference to Dietrich and Loretz 1981, 249?) that was not updated before publication and so remains unclear.

[11] Gates did, however, identify parallels for the statue's throne, as reconstructed by Woolley. She noted that "before the Syro-Hittite period…, when lions occur regularly on the statue bases of kings … there exist no parallels for thrones such as Woolley's. Royalty and dignitaries throughout the Bronze Age in Mesopotamia sit on simple stools or chairs. This practice extended to Syria, if one can judge from a few apparently standard illustrations…. Only at the very end of the Late Bronze Age are dignitaries shown on elaborate thrones of the sort envisaged by Woolley…. On the strength of the parallels for Idrimi's throne, therefore, it is more likely that the statue dates to the very end of the Late Bronze Age" (Gates *apud* Sasson 1981, 319).

seals, with the possible exception of a figure on sealing 193 from Level IV," which, in fact, she suggested elsewhere might have been reused and thus might date to Levels VI–V (Collon 1975, 103 n. 2). Collon considered identifying the figure wearing this headdress as "the ruler of Iamhad in many cases, and with high officials and dignitaries in other cases, though the distinction is difficult to draw." This

> distinct, tall oval head-dress ... replace[s] the round cap with a band round the bottom worn on sealings and paintings from Mari. ...The mantle also illustrates a later stage in the history of Syrian dress: whereas at Mari the garment had patterned borders, at Alalakh these have been replaced ... by a mantle which has thickly rolled edges.

On the other hand, "seals from the time of Niqmepuh onwards show another type of garment which was probably made from thinner material, was longer, and was trimmed with narrower borders."

However, even if the conical hat and the *Wulstsaummantel* did not continue into the Late Bronze Age in the glyptic from Alalah, with the possible exception of the Level IV sealing AOAT 27, no. 193, it is clear that these garments are still found in Late Bronze Age statues and statuary at other sites. For instance, Sasson (1981, 320) observed that "this type of clothing ... is known as early as Alalakh VII ... and into Late Bronze Age Ugarit." To the extent, then, that Idrimi's conical hat and robe can be used to date the statue, they ground it more firmly in the Bronze Age, in contrast to the Iron Age parallels pointed out for other features. But it is difficult to be more precise solely on the basis of the garments themselves.

If aesthetic judgments and the search for stylistic parallels comprise a relatively large proportion of art historical approaches to the statue, the consideration of text and image as an integrated whole has received considerably less discussion from art historians. The relative absence of such discussions is surprising because, as Hélène Maloigne (2017, 202–3) emphasized, the Statue of Idrimi is "a prime example" of "the interconnection and interdependence of text and image throughout the history of the ancient Near East." In particular, Maloigne cited Zainab Bahrani's (2003) discussion of the Akkadian word *ṣalmu*, often translated as "image, effigy, representation"; importantly, this word is twice used in the body inscription to refer to the statue on which it is inscribed (ll. 92 and 99; see §3.2). As explained by Bahrani (2003, 123), *ṣalmu* is "part of a pluridimensional system of representation" but one that did not rely on mimesis, "for it was not mimesis that made the image a valid functioning representation of the person. A combination was necessary. Substitution by image required the image, the name, and the utterance of the name, and may have also required further contact with the organic body" (129). According to this line of reasoning, the inscriptions on the statue do not serve simply to identify the king or to provide a complementary body of information about him; rather, the very "writing presence" (133) of the cuneiform signs upon the statue is an integral component in the process of representation and "the immanent nature of the real."

To my knowledge, the only art historian to have approached the Statue of Idrimi from this framework is Cory Crawford (2014), who used it as his primary case study in a chapter devoted to studying the relationship between image and text in the ancient Near East from an emic perspective that sought to move away from a modern, Western approach that reads "images as texts" and so can be characterized as "logocentric" (252). Crawford emphasized that the cheek inscription needed to be understood as "a standalone composition" (256). In an innovation, he argued that it ran "not from the mouth of Idrimi, but from his right eye to the deeds presented in the inscription" (257)—that is, to the body inscription. Furthermore, he pointed out that, even though modern scholars typically take the cheek inscription as requesting an audience to read the inscription on the body, the verb in question, which Crawford followed most previous scholars in taking as *liddagal* for "the probable use of *dagālu* in the Gtn stem," actually does not "enjoin … an act of reading … but an act of iterative *viewing*" (257; emphasis original). The result is an apt illustration of Bahrani's (2003) argument outlined above, "in what amounts to a kind of verbal hypallage, the acts of the ruler cling ontologically to him, visually constituted and open to the viewer's devoted gaze" (258).

To be sure, one can question some of the details of Crawford's (2014) claim. For instance, he did not consider Jean-Marie Durand's (2011) argument, adopted in this study, for reading the crucial precative verb in the cheek inscription as a form of *tukkulu*, "to trust," as opposed to *dagālu*, "to see, look at"; see the commentary to line CI 2 in §A.1. And I find it hard to agree that the cheek inscription points to Idrimi's eye; it is placed below his eye and above his ear and runs from his cap to the end of his beard. Nonetheless, I do not think that either of these points diminishes Crawford's (2014, 257) larger claim that the cuneiform signs of the body inscription function more as "a visible instantiation of Idrimi's deeds" than as a text to be read. Indeed, as discussed in §5.3, the paleographic variation that is found throughout the body inscription, combined with the setting of the statue's deposition, probably would have made it impossible to actually read the body inscription. These observations only emphasize Crawford's argument that viewing, not reading, the body inscription was the point. At the same time, as also argued in §5.3, there is good reason to think that other versions of the Idrimi narrative were in circulation, and that the statue's audience would have been familiar with them, so that when they viewed the "visible instantiation of Idrimi's deeds" on the statue's body, they would recall the narrative.

2.5. PHILOLOGICAL APPROACHES

What follows in this section is avowedly guilty of Crawford's (2014, 255) criticism of the "logocentric" approach to the inscriptions; it focuses on text editions (and reviews), translations of all or much of the text for anthologies, and the text's treatment in the dictionaries. Publications that offer important new readings for selected lines (e.g., Na'aman 1980a, 113–16) are not discussed below, although these publications are, of course, cited in the relevant lines of the commentaries in the appendix.

As mentioned previously, the first edition of the Statue of Idrimi inscriptions was published by the British Museum Assyriologist Sidney Smith in 1949. Smith's pioneering edition provided a transliteration, a translation, sporadic notes, a glossary, photographs of the inscription, a hand copy of the same, a paleographic sign list, and a list of logograms. He offered more discursive sections between the edition and the glossary—a fairly straightforward presentation of the orthography and language of the inscription as he understood it and more idiosyncratic discussions of historical geography, chronology, and personal names related to the inscriptions. The edition was prefaced by Woolley's valuable introduction (already mentioned above), which offered important insight into the archaeologist's thinking at this time about the material form and archaeological context of the statue.

Smith was well aware that his readings were possibly, even probably, wrong in a number of places due to the paleographic variation used in the inscriptions,[12] and a number of important new readings were suggested in the first wave of reviews that followed the publication of his edition (see, in particular, Albright 1950, Goetze 1950, Nougayrol 1951, and Speiser 1951).[13] The reviews of René Dussaud (1950) and Oliver Gurney (1950, 1951) focused more on the questions of chronology and historical geography raised by the statue and its inscriptions, while that of Moortgat (1949) unsurprisingly considered the statue from an art historical perspective ("Der Wert der Idri-mi-Statuette als Bilddenkmal"). Finally, A. Leo Oppenheim's (1955) review appeared quite late, so it was consciously "focused on an evaluation of the text as a literary document" (199) as opposed to offering new

---

[12] See, e.g., Smith 1949, iv: "The first edition of an inscription, particularly in the case of a shallow cutting, where the mason's work has been badly done, and the scribal copy, from which the mason worked employed unusual or otherwise unknown forms of signs, is bound to need many corrections. I apologise for my errors in advance; such errors should be attributed, not to lack of care, but either to mere ignorance or inability to foresee the possibilities that may present themselves to others"; and, in reference to the inscriptions' paleographic variation, Smith 1949, 10: "The effect is chaotic, and I must confess that I have only been able to decipher many signs after copying the original several times and drawing up the table of forms. Even so, many readings have only been possible because the context suggested the sign meant. I have tried to indicate every case where I think doubt legitimate. For my own errors I have no other excuse than the right to guess." Smith marked those readings of his where he considered "doubt legitimate" with an asterisk in the transliteration.

[13] The review of Benito Celada (1951) mostly summarizes the inscription and Smith's monograph.

readings. The result was one of the first sustained statements to stress the body inscription's similarity to narratives from the Hebrew Bible in explicit contrast to those from "the ancient Near East" (199).[14]

While important work on the statue and its inscriptions occurred in the 1950s and 1960s, the first complete re-edition did not appear until the early 1970s. This new edition, by Aharon Kempinski and Nadav Na'aman (1973) in Hebrew, offered a transliteration of the text, a translation into modern Hebrew and a limited commentary. The readings were based on the photographs published in Smith (1949), not the authors' personal collation of the inscription, but Kempinski and Na'aman were able to put forward a number of important and insightful suggestions nonetheless. In addition to the philological comments on specific lines, their edition also provided discussion on different aspects of the inscription that had previously generated and continue to generate discussion—namely, "Origins of the Idrimi Dynasty," "Idrimi's Escape and His Return to the Monarchy's Throne," "Idrimi's Journey to Hatti," "Addu-nerari, the Priest," and "Sharruwa's Self-blessing."

Kempinski and Na'aman's 1973 re-edition of the inscriptions was the first in a wave of publications on the statue and its inscriptions that appeared in the 1970s and early 1980s.[15] The next to appear was by Edward Greenstein and David Marcus (1976), written by these scholars of the Hebrew Bible and Northwest Semitics while they were graduate students at Columbia University. This article, the first full edition of the Idrimi text in the English language since Smith's original publication, comprised a lengthy introduction, a transliteration, a translation, and a commentary. Greenstein and Marcus did not personally collate the inscriptions, although they tried to frame this omission as a virtue (see the comments on method below). The introduction was noteworthy for offering some extended discussion of the language of the inscription. Both the introduction and the commentary were also characterized (not surprisingly, given the academic background of these scholars) by a strong interest in finding parallels for the text in the Hebrew Bible; see, for instance, their comment to lines 26–27 of the body inscription (Greenstein and Marcus 1976, 75–77), where they based their interpretation of the passage on perceived parallels to the stories of Jepthah and David.

The trajectory of the analysis in this particular comment—in which their interpretation of a problematic passage in the Idrimi inscriptions was based on a perceived parallel outside the text—also serves to highlight the defining feature of the edition: its method. As mentioned above, Greenstein and Marcus (1976) did not collate the inscriptions. But, in an explicit discussion of their method in the

[14] Although note that Albright (1950, 20) ended his review by pointing out parallels between the Idrimi narrative and the biblical story of Joseph.

[15] Some of these publications had an enormous impact on the scholarship but did not focus on re-editing the inscription and so are discussed elsewhere; e.g., Sasson 1981 (see §2.3).

introduction to their edition, they attempted to turn this omission into a virtue, writing:

> The inscription was written in cuneiform in an inconsistent and idiosyncratic manner. ...We must therefore contend with a multitude of signs whose reading can only be guessed until the requisite interpretation is determined through philological analysis.... Our philological approach, then, begins with a decipherment of the cuneiform that readily yields meaningful Akkadian and then proceeds to suggest appropriate readings for the more obscure passages. The correct decipherment of the more obscure cuneiform follows from philological determinations and not vice versa. Oppenheim ... has voiced the need for a fresh collation of the inscription. We have not had the opportunity of making such a collation from the original monument. However, to our mind, such a collation can only have value after a careful philological study of the inscription has been done, and we have tried to provide such a study here. ...our approach is characteristically more comparative than that of others. That is, we have found in the inscriptions several passages where the comparative material from Akkadian (particularly Mari, Boghazkoi, Amarna, Ras Shamra, and Assyria) and Northwest Semitic (particularly biblical) sources helps elucidate the inscription of Idrimi significantly. (59–60)

In this discussion of method, Greenstein and Marcus essentially distinguished epigraphy ("decipherment of cuneiform") from philology, contrasted the two, and identified each with inductive and deductive approaches to the text, respectively. They argued that, when epigraphic/inductive readings are not obvious, the best approach is philological/deductive. In emphasizing that their "approach is characteristically more comparative," they meant that they used perceived parallels to the inscriptions in Akkadian and West Semitic texts to establish what a particular passage in the inscriptions *should* be about, which, in turn, led them to suggest particular readings or signs or, especially, emendations.

For instance, in their discussion of the curse in line 95, they followed Mattitiahu Tsevat (1958, 124) in reading the sign following *ma-at-šu* as KU/ŠE$_3$ for the Akkadian word *eblu*, "rope, cord." They understood *ebla* to be the direct object of *madādu* for "an expression semantically and etymologically equivalent ... in 2 Sam. 8:2..., 'He (David) defeated Moab. He measured them with a rope, lying them down on the ground. He measured two rope-lengths to be executed and one full rope-length to be spared'" (Greenstein and Marcus 1976, 94–95). Accordingly, Greenstein and Marcus normalized this apodosis as *ebla limdudūšu* and translated it as "Let them have him executed (lit., measure him by rope)," remarking that "the practice may well be western and the idiom West Semitic." However, from both epigraphic and orthographic perspectives (i.e., inductive ones), the sign in question seems better read not as KU/ŠE but as KI and taken as the determinative following *mātu*—in other words, *ma-at-šu*^{ki}. Numerous parallels for the form of the sign occur in the body inscription, and in line 84 the determinative is written with *mātu* after the possessive pronominal suffix (*ma-ti-ia*^{ki}). In sum, as Gary Oller (1977a, 5–6) remarked, although Greenstein and Marcus "propose many new and interesting readings and interpretations ... many of their solutions while ingenious cannot be reconciled with the signs on the statue" (see also Dietrich and Loretz 1981, 203).

Only one year after Greenstein and Marcus's article, Oller's (1977a) University of Pennsylvania dissertation was the next edition of the Idrimi inscriptions to appear, written under the direction of archaeologist James Muhly, with the thesis committee also including the Penn Assyriologists at the time: Barry Eichler, Erle Leichty, and Åke Sjöberg.[16] The dissertation was the first book-length treatment of the statue and its inscriptions since Smith's 1949 edition and is, to my knowledge, the only other to have appeared prior to this book. The dissertation consists of two parts: a text edition and a historical and literary analysis. The edition was based on Oller's own personal autopsy of the inscriptions and consisted of a normalization and translation of the text followed by a "detailed treatment of the text"—namely, a transliteration, short line-by-line notes on alternate readings that had been put forward in previous literature, and a very detailed commentary. Oller's collations of the texts resulted in one extraordinary discovery: while Smith (1949, 22) had indicated that the ends of lines CI 2–3 (ll. 103–104 in Smith's numbering) were no longer preserved on the statue, Oller (1977b) discovered that, in fact, they were! Otherwise, Oller's (1977a) edition is characterized by a conservative approach; if he was not sure of the identification of one or more signs, he left them untransliterated or in transliteration but without a normalization and translation.

In the dissertation's second part, "Related Historical and Literary Studies," Oller focused on the historical Idrimi, historical geography, and historical method and offered a reconstruction and assessment of Idrimi's career in a final concluding chapter. If the conclusion offered mostly a paraphrase of the body inscription, the chapter on historical method, which discusses the fictive ("literary") nature of the text and its use a historical source, remains one of the best things that has been written on the statue and its inscriptions and is discussed more fully below in §2.8. Finally, the edition was supported by a sign list and a hand copy of the inscriptions in two appendices.

Four years later, Manfried Dietrich and Oswald Loretz (1981) published the next edition of the inscriptions in a lengthy article in *Ugarit-Forschungen* (*UF*), the journal that they founded and edited. This article was one of a trio in that volume

---

[16] My guess is that the position of Muhly as the primary advisor to the thesis instead of an Assyriologist derives from the fact that Oller did his PhD in the Program (now Graduate Group) in Ancient History, and not the Department of Near Eastern Languages and Civilizations, at Penn. Accordingly, his primary advisor needed to have an appointment in the Program in Ancient History, but then the rest of the committee was populated by the Assyriology faculty from the Department of Near Eastern Languages and Civilizations.

of *UF*, appearing together with a historical commentary on the historical Idrimi, the statue, and the inscriptions by Horst Klengel (1981) and an archaeological commentary on the statue and its find-spot by Mayer-Opificius (1981). Like Oller's (1977a) before them, the edition by Dietrich and Loretz was based on their own personal autopsy of the inscriptions. Furthermore, they were provided with a plaster cast of the inscriptions by Cyril Bateman, keeper of conservation at the British Museum at the time,[17] which must have afforded them, quite literally, a valuable new perspective on the signs.

The edition by Dietrich and Loretz (1981) consisted of a transliteration, translation, and commentary supported by three different sign lists (paleography, syllabic values, and logographic values) and photographs of the inscriptions. It put forward many new and important identifications of signs, possibly the most important of which was to identify a sign in the cheek inscription (l. CI 2) as DUB, for *ṭuppu*, "tablet," in place of Smith's ALAM, for *ṣalmu*, "statue" (but see the comment to the line in §A.1 for a different identification of the sign altogether). Sandwiched in between the sign lists and the photographs is a study of the text that considered it within the genre "Autobiography" (quotation marks original), recapitulating the text and exploring parallels to it in the Hebrew Bible and Hittite literature. This literary-critical approach to the inscriptions also included a source-critical approach to the text that was heavily dependent on identifying Smith's ALAM in line CI 2 as DUB, as mentioned above, which is discussed more fully in §2.7.

The latest major edition of the text to have appeared is by Durand (2011), who published it as part of the proceedings of a colloquium on "le jeune héros" held at the Collège de France in 2009. Durand presented a transliteration and translation of the text and offered a number of new readings and explanatory notes. He did not collate the inscriptions himself, and the transliteration depends heavily on the copy and transliteration in Dietrich and Loretz (1981), with only sporadic citation of previous literature, as he more or less acknowledged in an opening footnote.[18] Some of the new readings proposed by Durand were very insightful and are fundamental to understanding the social context of the statue

---

[17] Dietrich and Loretz 1981, 203: "Wir sind deshalb nicht nur den Autoritäten des British Museum für die Erlaubnis des Studiums des Originals dankbar, sondern auch Herrn C.A. Bateman, der uns einen naturgetreuen Gipsabguß der Inschrift angefertigt hat."

[18] Durand 2011, 94 n. 1: "il faut souligner que leur [= Dietrich and Loretz's 1981] édition est un véritable chef d'œuvre au niveau de la compréhension graphique des signes et des lectures qui sont dès lors proposées; les progrès qu'ils ont obtenus dans ces deux domaines ont profondément transformé le texte d'Idrimi et il en est sorti beaucoup plus accessible. Leurs propositions rendent dès lors caduque une bonne partie de la littérature antérieure, accessible néanmoins grâce leur abondant commentaire critique auquel il faut se reporter. Je n'ai pas cru bon, chaque fois que je suivais leur édition, de refaire le point bibliographique qu'ils avaient si bien établi."

and its inscriptions. For instance, in place of the reading of the final verb in line CI 2 *li-i[d-da]g-gal-šu-nu*, as established by Oller (1977a, 1977b, 129), for a Gtn precative of *dagālu* formed off of the Gtn base ("let one constant[ly lo]ok upon them," in Oller's (1977a, 18) translation), Durand (2011, 150) suggested reading the same signs as *li-t[a]k*$_3$*-kal-šu-nu*, for a D precative of *takālu* ("afin qu'elle les [= mes descendants] rendent confiants" in his translation).

Durand's (2011) text edition was preceded by a lengthy discussion of the text in which he attempted to contextualize it within the social world of the Amorites as known from the Mari letters and other Old Babylonian sources.[19] For instance, he found a parallel to Idrimi's position as a younger son in the histories of many Amorite kingdoms, including such famous examples as Samsi-Addu I and Zimri-Lim (Durand 2011, 96–98). Similarly, he found the ceremony or ritual that accompanies Idrimi's acknowledgment of Parattarna I's hegemony—and Parattarna I's acceptance of Idrimi's fealty—to be analogous to ceremonies "qui se passait à Der de l'Euphrate pour le *kispum* des rois amorrites de Mari et où tous les vassaux et apparentes étaient fermement invités" (Durand 2011, 109). This approach was heavily criticized by von Dassow (2020b, 198–99) on two grounds. First, even if parallels for practices described in the text can be found in letters from Mari, those same practices "can be found across world cultures" (198) and so cannot be assumed to be Mariote, let alone Amorite. Second, it is unlikely that the category "Amorite" had any emic value to its audience, since

> neither the statue inscription nor any other source identifies Idrimi by a gentilic. The same is true of his descendants; in fact, the same is true of almost all of the thousands of individuals attested in the Alalakh tablets.… This indicates that our ethno-linguistic categories do not apply to our subjects—that is, these categories are not valid for the region of Alalakh and its populations. (199)

In addition to and alongside these full editions of the inscriptions, the modern perception of the Idrimi text as a work of ancient Near Eastern literature—in particular, one thought to belong to a West Semitic literary tradition—means that translations have frequently appeared without full editions, either in anthologies or as part of larger, thematic studies. Even if they lack a full scholarly apparatus, sometimes these translations have functioned as responses to previous editions. This tendency is especially true with regard to translations that had to rely primarily on Smith's (1949) edition. In particular, the translations by Rykle Borger (1968; in *Textbuch zur Geschichte Israels*), Oppenheim (1969; in *Ancient Near Eastern*

[19] Durand 2011, 94–95: "Pour le présent réexamen du texte d'Idrimi, c'est à la documentation de l'époque amorite et aux gains que l'on peut estimer avoir faits à partir de la documentation de Mari pour mieux apprécier sa société que je prendrai mes exemples.… Plusieurs thèmes de l'*Inscription* d'Idrimi peuvent ainsi être mis en relation avec la documentation amorrite ancienne."

Texts Relating the Old Testament), and Marie-Joseph Seux (1977; in *Textes du Proche-Orient ancien et histoire d'Israël*) were conspicuous on occasion in not following Smith in some of his readings. For instance, with respect to Smith's suspect ^{giš}GIGIR *ṣa-^{li}lil-te-a*, "my covered chariot" (l. 17), all three scholars pointedly refrained from offering a translation of the signs after ^{giš}GIGIR in their respective translations.

However, other translations have been more derivative and reproduced previous editions in a more or less one-to-one manner. Of course, in some cases the translation was produced by the same individual(s) who authored or coauthored the edition in question. For example, Dietrich and Loretz's (1985; in *Texte aus der Umwelt des Alten Testaments*) translation reproduced their 1981 edition; Tremper Longman's (1997; in *Context of Scripture*) translation reproduced his earlier 1991 translation; and Greenstein's (1995; in *Civilizations of the Ancient Near East*) translation reproduced his own edition coauthored with Marcus (Greenstein and Marcus 1976). In other cases, though, the source of a translation seems to be less the Akkadian inscriptions and more an earlier translation in a different, modern language. For instance, Daniel Snell (2001) offers mostly a translation of Dietrich and Loretz 1981 into English; Cemil Bülbül (2010) translates Greenstein and Marcus 1976 into Turkish;[20] and Marco Bonechi's (2019) work consists largely of a translation of Durand 2011 into Italian.

Finally, it is worth noting briefly the attention that the inscriptions have received in the two major Assyriological dictionaries, *Akkadisches Handwörterbuch* (*AHw*) and the *Chicago Assyrian Dictionary* (*CAD*). According to an electronic search, *CAD* cites "Smith Idrimi" about 180 times across all its volumes, while *AHw* cites "Idr." About 80 times. A little over three decades after the inscriptions' publication, Dietrich and Loretz (1981, 202) were not overly enthusiastic about the dictionaries' citations, which they considered "nur sporadisch auf die Inschrift verweisen, ohne über die Vorarbeiten wesentliche hinauszugelangen, die in der Sekundärliteratur zur Verfügung stehen." While it is true that the earlier volumes are, out of necessity, heavily reliant on Smith's edition, my opinion of the dictionaries' synthesis of secondary literature is somewhat more charitable. For instance, in the discussion section of *CAD* 17, s.v. "šakkanakku," where Smith (1949) has taken two signs as GIR_3.$NITA_2$ (= *šakkanakku*), the editors explicitly preferred the identification of them by Sasson (1981) and Dietrich and Loretz (1981) as LU_2.IR_3 or DUMU IR_3, respectively.[21] Indeed, for volumes published after Dietrich and Loretz's (1981) edition, the editors of *CAD* tended to adopt the readings of the

20 In fact, Bülbül (2010) offers a transliteration and a translation of the text, and the transliteration also reproduces Greenstein and Marcus 1976. See, e.g., lines 103–104 [= CI ll. 2–3] of the transliteration, where Greenstein and Marcus's suggestions for the missing signs at the end of the lines are reproduced, overlooking the fact that Oller (1977b) identified that Smith had inadvertently omitted these signs, which Oller duly made available.

21 For the identification of the first sign as LU_2, see already Oller 1977a, 132.

scholars from Münster; see, for instance, *CAD* 20, s.v. "ullû A" adj., 1a for an example from the last volume of *CAD* to be published.

One also has the impression that Wolfram von Soden was more willing to offer comments, emendations, and new readings in the pages of *AHw* than Dietrich and Loretz's comment, quoted above, suggests, although these comments may be easier to miss due to the understated nature of the editorial apparatus. For instance, in *AHw* 821b, the citation "*ana pa-ni-ia* brachten sie$^{!}$" seems to signal von Soden's discomfort with a plural verb form *ub-lu-u*$_2$*-nim* in line 36 that takes the singular noun *mātiya* in the previous line as its subject. And, in the same fascicle (*AHw* 793a, 5c), he offered the emendation "$^{\mathrm{udu!}}$*n.*$^{!\mathrm{há}}$" for line 89—in other words, von Soden emended the sign U$_3$, to UDU and understood the form of SISKUR$_2$ to be defective; see the commentaries to lines 36 and 89 in §A.2 for more discussion. In addition, von Soden did occasionally incorporate readings that had been proposed in the reviews of Smith 1949; see, for example, *AHw* 429a (citing Albright 1950), or *AHw* 939b (citing Goetze 1950). (Note that most of the work on *AHw* was done before the wave of re-editions of the text appeared in the 1970s and early 1980s.)

2.6. LINGUISTIC APPROACHES

The Idrimi text is written in a variety of western hybrid Akkadian that has been a repeated object of interest for scholars over the years owing to the manner in which it departs from the expectations of standard Old or Middle Babylonian. In part, this interest has been motivated simply by a desire to better understand the text as a basis for further historical or literary study. But the interest has also been motivated by a desire to situate the text's code within the larger phenomenon of western hybrid Akkadian and, in particular, to explain departures from expected forms of Old or Middle Babylonian as the influence of other dialects or languages. In particular, the West Semitic languages have been seen to be very influential, but, as discussed in more detail below, Hurrian and even Old Assyrian influence has been identified in the Idrimi text's particular variety of Akkadian as well.

Smith (1949, 35–39) included an overview of the language of the inscriptions in his pioneering edition, covering orthography, nominal and verbal morphology, and syntax. Because his overview depended on his own first edition and so was not able to incorporate the improved readings suggested by subsequent generations of scholars, a number of errors or misconceptions appear in it, such as two attestations of *wa* as a contrastive conjunction.[22] In other cases, Smith's

[22] Smith 1949, 34, where it is derived from his misreading of ^{m}*šar-ru-wa* ($^{\mathrm{lu_2}}$)DUB.SAR in lines 98–99 as DIŠ(*šumma*) *šar-ru wa* ($^{\mathrm{lu_2}}$)DUB.SAR, "whether king or scribe" and corrected already in the Corrigenda.

observations hold, even if his explanation is no longer generally accepted.[23] Still other conclusions reached by Smith continue to this day to be the dominant explanation for aspects of the inscriptions' nonstandard variety of Akkadian. Chief among these is the occasional use of stative verbs as perfectives, which Smith explained as the influence of West Semitic.[24]

Jussi Aro's (1954) short article on "the language of the Alalah texts" was the first linguistic study of these texts to appear after the publication of Donald J. Wiseman's (1953) edition of the Level VII and Level IV Alalah texts, although Wiseman's own edition did include a brief presentation of grammar (18–22). Aro marked Level VII texts with an asterisk, following Wiseman's practice, but otherwise, and significantly, he treated the texts from Level VII and Level IV together "because no great differences of usage can be observed between them" (Aro 1954, 361 n. 1), and he included the language of the Idrimi inscriptions in this holistic overview as well. Altogether, he cited the inscriptions over forty times in reference to orthography, morphology, and syntax. Even though a number of reviews of Smith's edition had already appeared, Aro (1954) was heavily reliant on it, so that he incorporated Smith's readings into his grammatical description.[25]

Aro (1954, 364) accepted Smith's explanation for the occasional nonstandard use of the stative in the inscriptions as "presumably reflecting the West Semitic perfect"; interestingly, he did not identify any attestations of this use of the stative outside of the inscriptions. Also like Smith (1949, 36), Aro (1954, 364) remarked on the relatively high frequency of indicative verb forms in the Idrimi inscriptions that are marked with a /u/ suffix. He considered the /u/ suffix to be the "subjunctive" (i.e., subordination) marker, seeing a contrast between the variety of Akkadian used in the inscriptions, where "subjunctives often appear instead of indicative," and that used in the cuneiform tablets from Alalah, where "the use of subjunctive is often neglected" (citing one Level VII text and one Level IV text). Unlike Smith (1949, 36), who offered a variety of explanations for the presence of these /u/ vowels, all of which were explicitly taken to be parallel to Franz Böhl's (1909) explanations of verbal forms with nonstandard /u/ suffix in the Amarna

---

[23] See, e.g., "the use of *inūma* after *idu*, *lamadu*, *šemū*, *amaru*, *malaku*, in Am[arna letters]" (Smith 1949, 35), which is still generally accepted, although not as Smith explained it. Now the phenomenon is understood as an Akkadian calque of West Semitic *k*, which, in addition to meaning "that," can mean, like Akkadian *inūma*, "when." For Smith, *inūma* was an exclamation *inu* + enclitic *-ma* that was etymologically related to Classical Hebrew *hinnēh*.

[24] Smith 1949, 37: "in cases where the permansive [i.e., stative - JL] and the narrative imperfect are linked by *u*, the syntax seems to affect the sense of the permansive. There also seems to be some distinction according to the order. Where the imperfect is followed by the permansive, the latter appears to refer to a single event, as the perfect might do in West Semitic languages."

[25] See, e.g., Aro 1954, 364 for the contrastive conjunctive *wa* and *inūma* as an exclamation, as discussed above.

letters, Aro (1954, 364) doubted "whether any law can be derived from these occurrences. In barbaric Akkadian they may be simple mistakes."

Several years later, Tsevat (1958) published a study in two parts titled simply "Alalakhiana." The first part comprised notes on the published texts from Alalah, including a note on line 5 of the statue's body inscription (see the commentary to the line in §A.2 and Lauinger 2022a, 220). The second part focused on "some Syro-Palestinianisms of the Akkadian of Alalah" (Tsevat 1958, 129). In addition to noting two attestations in the Level IV texts of the stative being used as the West Semitic perfect, in parallel to the attestations identified by Smith (1949), Tsevat (1958, 131–33) also focused on the verb *(w)ašābu* in texts from Alalah, because, as he stated, a "good test for the presence of elements of a Canaanite dialect in a Semitic language is the observation of the prepositional constructions of the verb 'to sit on (a chair or throne), to dwell in (a place).'" For instance, in Mesopotamian varieties of Akkadian, the prepositional complement to *(w)ašābu* is *ina*, but in the Canaano-Akkadian of the Amarna letters the preposition *ana*, "to," also occurs frequently. Tsevat observed that *ana* also occurs as a prepositional complement to *(w)ašābu* in Akkadian texts from Alalah. Furthermore, while *(w)ašābu* + *ina* is found only in texts from Level VII, attestations of *(w)ašābu* + *ana* are found in texts from Level VII and Level IV, and in the Statue of Idrimi's body inscription. Accordingly, Tsevat concluded, "by the time of the second group of texts, the fifteenth century, the Canaanism has asserted itself throughout." This conclusion is interesting, because the Akkadian of the Level IV texts is often described as having been impacted more directly by Hurrian, so that one might have supposed that *(w)ašābu* + *ana* would be less, not more, common in the Level IV texts.

George Giacumakis's (1970) revised dissertation remains, as of this writing, the only published book-length study of the orthography and language of the Alalah texts. Unfortunately, it is a flawed work that received extremely negative reviews because of its errors and misunderstandings, for example, collapsing the Level VII texts, the Level IV texts, and the Idrimi inscriptions into a single language and including texts found but not written at Alalah.[26] Altogether,

---

[26] The reviews are Tsevat 1971; Hawkins 1972; von Soden 1972; Draffkorn 1973; and Reiner 1973. Giacumakis's treatment of a single text demonstrates some of the grammatical and lexicographical difficulties found in the book. He claims that "a few of the middle weak verbs double the final radical in the present and in the preterite," citing *i-ši-im-ma* (AlT 6: 6) as the only example of such a purported preterite form (Giacumakis 1970, 56), when, in fact, the verb is simply the form of the G preterite in the standard Akkadian dialects + enclitic *-ma* (*išīm-ma*), and the lexical entry "dawidu *s.*" translates the word as "commander, chief"" (Giacumakis 1970, 71), citing *da-aw-de-*⌜*e*⌝ in the same text as above (AlT 6: 37) as the only attestation of this putative word, even though the word *dabdû*, "defeat," with a spelling *du*-WI-*du-um* documented at Mari and Level VII Alalah, had already entered the dictionaries by the time (*AHw* 148a; *CAD* 3, s.v. "dabdû"); cf. Hawkins 1972, 136: "In the glossary too the author has frequently chosen to ignore the views of the

Giacumakis (1970) cites the Idrimi inscriptions more than 340 times, including in the glossary entries. Accordingly, the volume cannot be ignored in the present work; rather, I follow the injunction with which Tsevat (1971, 352) concludes his review and "use [it] with caution."

Greenstein and Marcus (1976, 60–63) devoted a substantial portion of the introduction to their edition to the language of the Idrimi inscriptions. Comprising three sections ("Orthography," "The Akkadian of Idrimi," and "West Semitic Influence"), theirs was the first linguistic study of the Idrimi text since Smith's (1949) edition that did not collapse the code into a larger dialect of Alalah Akkadian. Greenstein and Marcus documented the influence of both West Semitic and Hurrian in the Akkadian of the Idrimi text. In particular, they observed that "West Semitic influence, linguistic and idiomatic, has always been assumed for the Idrimi inscription, but few legitimate examples have been proffered in the literature" (Greenstein and Marcus 1976, 62). To that end, the scholars carefully isolated "eight instances in Idrimi where WS influence is more than likely" (62–63), noting that some had already been identified. Furthermore, they put forward the provocative suggestion that "most of the West Semitisms occur in the first part of the inscription, in which the scribe relates a narrative unlike the literature of Mesopotamia.... Here the scribe had little dependence on classic Akkadian style and language and would be more apt to lapse into his own idiosyncratic style" (63). Finally, one of the more peculiar features of their linguistic overview is their persistent identification of Assyrian, and particularly Old Assyrian, influence on the Akkadian of the Idrimi text. However, the putative instances of such influence raised by them can and should be explained differently.

Daniel Arnaud's (1988) study was interested in exploring, first, whether features of "le dialecte parlé dans l'Amq au II millénaire" could be isolated in the Alalah texts beneath the Akkadian, Hurrian, and even Sumerian superstrata, and, second, whether this dialect, once isolated, could be situated within the larger context of the West Semitic languages (Arnaud 1998, 144). The approach was synchronic, treating the Level VII texts, the Level IV texts, and the Idrimi text as a single corpus. The Idrimi text was used as potential evidence for the dialect without any real historical contextualization. Arnaud organized his study by linguistic topic (e.g., phonemes, noun patterns, verbal morphology), and much of his evidence derived from the personal names found in the cuneiform texts. However, Arnaud did cite the Idrimi text about twenty-five times in diverse contexts, such as the syllabary, verb-initial word order, the "confusion formelle" (183) between statives and West Semitic perfect verbs, and the demonstrative pronoun *anamû*. Ultimately, Arnaud (1998, 183–84) concluded that the limited available data suggests that the language spoken at Alalah was Semitic, despite writing in Akkadian

Chicago Assyrian dictionary and the *Akkadisches Handwörterbuch*, a thing which Assyriologists do only at their peril, and certainly not without special argument."

with a heavy overlay of Hurrian. Furthermore, although there are differences between the two, he considered that the dialect of Alalah showed a closer connection to the dialect of West Semitic that has been reconstructed at Emar and along the Middle Euphrates than to Ugaritic and Canaanite.

In contrast to most of the preceding studies, Ignacio Márquez Rowe's (1998) examination of the Akkadian of Late Bronze Age Alalah focused on trying to explain nonstandard aspects as reflecting Hurrian, not West Semitic, influence. Márquez Rowe (1998, 64) was very conscientious in defining his corpus. Although the corpus consisted primarily of the Level IV texts, he excluded some of these texts from it because, although they were found at Alalah, they were not composed there; for example, AlT 3, "the treaty between Pilliya and Idrimi concerning runaways, was probably written by a scribe of Pilliya, i.e., from Kizzuwatna." Conversely, he included texts that were not found at Alalah but originated from there, such as SMEA 37:49–50 (RS 4.449), a letter probably sent by Niqmepa of Alalah to Ibiranu, the ruler of Ugarit. Curiously, despite this careful approach to defining a corpus, Márquez Rowe included the Idrimi text within it with no remark besides "in all likelihood, one must also include the Idrimi inscription which was found in level Ib of Tell Atchana."

Márquez Rowe's article is at its most interesting when it attempts to explain features that had been taken as hallmarks of West Semitic influence on the varieties of Akkadian written at Alalah as, instead, examples of Hurrian influence. For instance, he directly addressed Greenstein and Marcus's (1976, 63) claim, mentioned above, that the verb-initial word order found in several places in the Idrimi text derives from West Semitic influence. While admitting that Hurrian tends toward verb-final word order, Márquez Rowe (1998, 71–72) noted that verbs can occur at the beginning of a clause "as a means of topicalization and, more importantly, it can also mark the subordinate clause whenever it ends in the connective = *an* and follows immediately another verbal form.... This Hurrian normal construction thus provides a resultative force to the second, subordinate clause." For Márquez Rowe, this feature of Hurrian syntax was quite important because the majority of verb-initial clauses identified by Greenstein and Marcus (1976) are connected by the conjunction *u* to a verb-final clause. Therefore, it could be argued that the word order in these attestations mirrors Hurrian, not West Semitic, syntax. Similarly, Márquez Rowe (1998, 75) observed that "it can reasonably be argued, in terms of morphology, that a Hurrian scribe would generally choose the Akkadian permansive—as a nominal base bound with pronominal suffixes—as his predilect form.... Indeed the prevalent use of the permansive as a result of Hurrian influence was already pointed out by Wilhelm." Further, he pointed to two attestations of statives in Level IV texts and one in the Idrimi text (l. 61) "where one would have rather expected a finite form with active meaning, and which possibly reflect the scribe's troubles to bring his Hurrian syntax into an Akkadian construction" (Márquez Rowe 1998, 76).

The great value of this article is methodological. As Márquez Rowe (1998, 76) stated in his conclusion, "linguistic affinities, especially as far as a written *lingua franca* is concerned, are no doubt easy to suggest, but difficult to prove." It is not enough to identify West Semitic parallels, the article insists. One also must demonstrate that parallels in other languages and dialects do not exist, otherwise the influence of West Semitic remains only possible, not proven.[27]

Kathryn Medill (2019, 245–46) explicitly addressed Márquez Rowe's methodological concern in an article published twenty years later. Agreeing with Márquez that linguistic features found in both Hurrian and West Semitic should not be used to classify the nonstandard aspects of the Idrimi text's Akkadian, Medill focused on the use of statives as perfective conjugation verbs. She pointed out that, in fact, statives are not used with "punctual and fientive" meanings in the Level IV texts, so that "it would be problematic to use these verbs to argue that the inscription is written in Hurro-Akkadian" (Medill 2019, 246). Conversely, features that have been taken as characteristic of a Hurro-Akkadian code in the Level IV texts, "such as Hurrian glosses, object-subject-verb or subject-verb-object word order, syntactic objects marked as nominative, problems with gender agreement, and use of the conjunction *u* to introduce apodoses" are mostly absent from the Idrimi inscriptions (Medill 2019, 245). Accordingly, Medill attempted to meet Márquez Rowe's challenge by falsifying putative parallels to Hurrian, the code other than West Semitic said to have influenced the Idrimi text's Akkadian, before marshaling an argument in favor of West Semitic influence.

That argument took the form of finding parallels for three different types of nonstandard verbal forms that occur in the body inscription in the Canaano-Akkadian of the Levantine Amarna letters. After discussing the use of statives with perfective meaning, Medill (2019, 43) turned to the so-called hybrid statives in the body inscription, which have not only the Akkadian verbal prefix appropriate for a tense conjugation verb but also the suffix appropriate for a stative (e.g., *urtabbiʾāku* instead of the Dt preterite *urtabbi* or Dt stative *rutabbâku* expected in standard Akkadian). Various explanations had been put forward for these verbal forms in the scholarly literature; building on a comment by Dietrich and Loretz (1981, 213), Medill (2019, 248–49) demonstrated that the hybrid statives in Idrimi's body inscription have parallels in Amarna letters from the Levant, which "were built from prefixed Akkadian bases plus unexpected suffixes." Similarly, Medill (2019, 249–51) found parallels in the Levantine Amarna letters for the nonstandard use of a /*un*V/ suffix on indicative finite verbs in Idrimi's body

27 At the same time, some weaknesses of method must be acknowledged as well. The inclusion of the Idrimi text in the corpus without any justification is questionable. And, despite pointing to features of Hurrian and Hurro-Akkadian, the article never actually cites any of the texts from which these principles have been formulated; the references are primarily to Speiser's (1941) Hurrian grammar and Wilhelm's (1970) study of the language of the Nuzi texts, the former being out-of-date already in 1989.

inscription about which scholars have long disagreed (see the literature cited in Lauinger 2021, 43 and the commentary to line 26 in §A.2 [*iphurūnima*]). Specifically, Medill (2019, 50) noted that "an imperfect interpretation is possible for each" of the relevant forms in Idrimi's body inscription, making it possible that the forms represent a 3mp West Semitic imperfect conjugation suffix (*yaqtulūna*) on an Akkadian base.

Medill's (2019) argument that the Idrimi inscriptions are written in a variety of Northwest Semitic-Akkadian parallel to the Canaano-Akkadian of the Levantine Amarna letters represents an important contribution in the study of the inscriptions' language as much for its method as for its conclusions.[28] Methodologically, the two significant contributions respond to Márquez Rowe's critique not just by finding possible parallels for nonstandard forms in a particular linguistic code but also by falsifying parallels in another possible code. They also identify parallels as elements of a single system and not by reference to a hodgepodge of *ad hoc* explanations.

However, perhaps the most significant methodological advance in studying the variety of Akkadian found in the Idrimi text appeared in a different article that was published in the same year by Mark Weeden (2019). His aim in this article was to advocate for the concept of "personal syllabaries." He adopted this position in contrast to the typical approach to syllabaries found in the scholarship, in which "the syllabary" refers "to the composite totality of syllabic values in use in the writing at a site or period" (Weeden 2019, 134). With the term "personal syllabaries," Weeden shifted the focus onto "the syllabaries that would have been available to individual scribes when writing" (Weeden 2019, 134). There are a number of different benefits to studying the personal syllabaries of scribes. For instance, we become open to the possibility of scribes as agents able to invoke additional associations through their choice of signs: learned, contemporary, and foreign, to name just a few possibilities. We may be able to infer something of the life histories, or at least education, of scribes on the basis of the signs that they employ or do not employ. And we mitigate the risk that we are "treating text corpora as homogenous blocks written as if everyone responsible for their creation had been to the same school" (Weeden 2019, 149), thereby avoiding the danger of assessing historical evidence against a Frankenstein's monster that never actually existed.

The Idrimi text plays an important role in Weeden's primary case study, which is the personal syllabary of Šarruwa (rendered by Weeden as Šarruwe), the Level IV scribe responsible for a number of legal texts who had already been the subject of investigation by Na'aman (1980b). Šarruwa is, of course, also the name of the scribe who claims to have inscribed the body inscription, and, as discussed

[28] On the Idrimi text's code as Northwest Semitic-Akkadian, as distinct from Canaano-Akkadian, see Medill 2019, 255.

in more detail in §6.1, a majority view in the scholarship has considered these two scribes to be one and the same. As Weeden (2019, 134–35) noted, Na'aman (1980b) had previously established that both of these scribes "use a variety of peculiar and rare sign-values and learned writings," and Weeden built on this analysis by working through the syllabaries of the Level IV legal texts and the Idrimi inscriptions more systematically. His first observation is that, when one considers the totality of Level IV scribes, "the only scribe among these who uses signs from the Š-series for /s/, whatever the phonetic reality of the Š-series, is Šarruwe" (Weeden 2019, 137). Moreover, this same characteristic also appears in the body inscription attributed to Šarruwa. Indeed, one particular word, *masiktu*, is written with IGI(*ši*) in both the body inscription (l. 4) and one of the Level IV scribe's legal texts (AlT 17 [31.3]: 8). In the use of Š-series signs for /s/, we may therefore have a "fingerprint" of Šarruwa's personal syllabary. Furthermore, the fact that this same feature appears in AlT 3 [1.2], the anonymously written treaty between Idrimi and Pilliya of Kizzuwatna, lets Weeden (2019, 139) suggest that Šarruwa may have been responsible for this text as well. Yet Weeden (2019, 142) also found notable differences between the signs used to represent stops in Šarruwa's legal texts and the Idrimi text. In particular, where the Level IV scribe uses only TA for the syllable /ta/, we find both TA and DA(*ta*2) used to write /ta/ in the Idrimi text.

After working through the evidence, Weeden stepped back to make two points that are very important, methodologically speaking, for how we study western hybrid Akkadian (although he did not use this term). The first point concerned the interpretation of variants. Considering the different treatment of stops in the Level IV legal texts and the Idrimi text, Weeden (2019, 142) remarked that "it then becomes very difficult to decide how to explain these differences. They may have to do with the nature of the inscription itself, possibly demanding an archaizing spelling style.... Or they may simply be due to the fact that this scribe Šarruwe is not the same as the other Šarruwe who wrote the documents." In other words, how consistent (or not) should we expect ancient scribes to have been in their choice of particular signs for particular syllables?

For his part, Weeden (2019, 142) considered "genre-expectations" to be decisive in the repertory of available signs for syllables, so that, for him, variation across texts in the signs chosen for a single syllable does not preclude these texts' having been written by a single scribe. He also considered genre expectations to be one component of "stylistic variation" more generally, which opens the door to other reasons why a scribe might have varied the signs he used for a particular syllable. For instance, employing obscure sign values can signal learning, which, in turn, "becomes a means of establishing pedigree and signalling superiority" (Weeden 2019, 142–43; see §4.1 for more discussion).

Weeden's second important methodological point considered the possibility that the differences in the way that stops are written in Šarruwa's legal texts and the Idrimi text could reflect the fact that the Level IV scribe and the scribe named in the body inscription were two different people. This possibility, Weeden (2019, 142) noted, "would also explain the alleged West Semitic substrate behind the inscription compared to the clear Hurrian interference in the Akkadian of the documents." Indeed, earlier in his article, Weeden had noted the various explanations put forward to account for the presence of these different substrate influences in texts supposedly written by the same scribe. For instance, Na'aman (1980b, 110) considered genre expectations to have played the decisive role; thus "the textual tradition of the ruler's fictionalised autobiography that Šarruwe was using would have been West Semitic, so he tended to use a West Semitic influenced Akkadian for that purpose, and allowed Hurrian to interfere with his Akkadian in more everyday documents" (Weeden 2019, 140). On the other hand, von Dassow (2008, 32 n. 74) suggested that "the old scribe Šarruwe, whose primary language was Hurrian, collaborated with a younger colleague, whose primary language was West Semitic," explicitly noting that this suggestion and others that can be imagined are "all impossible to substantiate."

Von Dassow's caveat aside, both she and Na'aman are trying to resolve a perceived "problem" (Weeden 2019, 141) that derives from a shared assumption that texts produced by a single author should show the influence of primarily one substrate language. However, if we accept the idea, which I think has particular resonance for western hybrid Akkadian, "that writing forms a system largely autonomous from the spoken word," then it necessarily follows that we must

> conceive of the written text as having more than one genealogy for the elements of its code. We may have West Semitic elements sitting alongside Hurrian ones, in the same text. This is a reflection of the contributions of the multiple actors who have participated in the formation of the script as far as the point of time at which the relevant document is being written down, of the form of writing that is in use at a particular site in a particular time by an individual with his or her own history. This perspective allows us to have a West Semitic *quttil* form (*wušširšu*, *pullilšu* with an *Interpretatio Hurritica* that mixes up the transitive and intransitive uses of the root) in a single line in one text next to a Hurrian Essive pleonastically reproducing the function of an Akkadian preposition (*ana maryanna*). (Weeden 2019, 141)

In other words, the co-occurrence in a single text of features from more than one linguistic code is not a "problem"; rather, it is reflective of both diachronic and synchronic processes and exigencies.

2.7. SOURCE-CRITICAL APPROACHES

If a text is the output of a single scribe and so reflects both the direct and indirect influences on the scribe's training as well as the scribe's own constraints and choices during the process of textual production, we must also consider that a text may have a long and complicated history, and that the version to which we have access may have been shaped by multiple scribes. Indeed, several scholars have adopted what are essentially source-critical approaches to the Idrimi text, whereby they have employed close reading in order to infer the sources on which the text depends and reconstruct the different stages that may have preceded the version of the text that is inscribed on the statue. Accordingly, this section looks at the source-critical arguments that have been advanced by three different (groups of) scholars—Dietrich and Loretz (1981), Durand (2011), and Vidal (2012)—before considering how approaching the text from a material perspective emphasizes, instead, that it be considered as an integrated whole.

A natural place to start any examination of putative sources for the inscriptions is with the relationship of the cheek inscription to the body inscription. This relationship has provoked discussion since Smith's (1949) decision to place the text of the former at the end of the latter and give it the sequential line numbers 102–104. As discussed in §1.4, Jean Nougayrol (1950, 154 n. 1) objected to this positioning already in an early review, stating that the cheek inscription was better understood as a prologue to the body inscription, while Sasson (1981, 312–13) considered it to be better described as a caption or legend to the statue than as part of the body inscription. But it is Dietrich and Loretz (1981, 244–47) who first developed in a sustained manner the idea of the cheek inscription as distinct from, yet related to, the body inscription. Crucially, their argument depended on a new reading for line CI 2 (= l. 103, according to the traditional line numbering), where they identified a sign that Smith (1949) had read as ALAM (= *ṣalmu*), "statue" instead of as DUB (= *ṭuppu*), "tablet." Accordingly, Dietrich and Loretz translated the final two lines of the cheek inscription as "Mein Taten habe ich auf meine Tafel geschrieben. Man möge sie betrachten / und meiner ständig segnend gedenken!"

Because of the reference to a tablet in these lines, Dietrich and Loretz (1981, 245) understood the cheek inscription to be neither a prologue nor an epilogue to the body inscription but a stand-alone text. Furthermore, the contents of this stand-alone text implied that the Idrimi narrative, at a minimum, was originally written on a tablet that had been installed or deposited together with the statue, perhaps as a votive offering, because "am Ende der Mitteilung wird dann eine Verbindung zwischen Statue und Tafel hergestellt; denn es wird gefordert, die Tafel zu lesen und den König segnend in Erinnerung zu behalten" (Dietrich and Loretz 1981, 245). Therefore, according to Dietrich and Loretz, the statue, the three-line inscription on the statue, and the tablet with the narrative of Idrimi's life originally formed "eine Einheit aus drei Teilen, die in sich geschlossen und voll verständlich ist" (Dietrich and Loretz 1981, 245).

Accordingly, the cheek inscription was the first, and originally only, text inscribed on the statue. At some time later the text on the tablet was also inscribed on the body of the statue, but it is unclear whether that inscription represents "den vollen Wortlaut jener 'Tafel' oder einen Auszug aus ihr" (Dietrich and Loretz 1981, 245). Meanwhile, the body inscription's colophon, and especially Šarruwa's statement in line 99 "daß er für die Beschriftung der Statue verantwortlich sei" (Dietrich and Loretz 1981, 246), signifies that this individual was responsible for transferring the text written on the putative tablet onto the statue, either supervising the work of the stone masons or, Dietrich and Loretz (1981, 246) suggest, perhaps even carving the inscription himself. Indeed, it was only at this time that the colophon would have been composed and carved onto the statue's body together with the narrative.

For Dietrich and Loretz, this reconstruction, especially the temporal separation of the composition of the narrative originally on a tablet and its transfer onto the statue, carries with it three significant implications. First, it means that Šarruwa is excluded from being the author of the narrative (Dietrich and Loretz 1981, 246). Second, it explains how the body inscription can end with a request for blessings for Šarruwa, not Idrimi, as the latter was presumably already dead at the time the body inscription was carved.[29] Finally, it renders invalid any hypothesis that is based on the idea of "ein einheitlicher Text" (Dietrich and Loretz 1981, 247).

Ultimately, Dietrich and Loretz reconstruct a scenario in which a votive statue of a ruler was transformed into a statue intended for veneration by virtue of its close association with a tablet narrating that ruler's accomplishments. As they conclude:

> Den Anfang konnte eine Statue des Königs ohne jede Beschriftung darstellen, die vom Herrscher im Tempel einer Gottheit geweiht wurde. Gleichzeitig oder zu einem anderen Zeitpunkt wurde im Tempel oder an einem anderen Ort, der der Öffentlichkeit zuganglich war, eine Tafel mit dem Bericht über die Großtaten des Königs aufgestellt. Nach dem Tod Idrimis wurden auf den Backenbart der Statue Z. 102–104 geschrieben. Es ist jedoch auch möglich, daß die Statue erst nach dem Tod des Herrschers zusammen mit der Inschrift Z. 102–104 angefertigt wurde. Mit der Beschriftung der Z. 102–104 war der Zweck der Statue jedenfalls neu festgelegt: Sie wurde entweder jetzt erst in den Ahnenkult einbezogen oder, falls sie bereits vorher für den Ahnenkult bestimmt war, durch den schriftlichen Vermerk für diesen Zweck besonders hervorgehoben. (Dietrich and Loretz 1981, 249–50)

It is important to stress how innovative this reconstruction is within the history of scholarship on the Idrimi inscriptions. For the first time, scholars departed from the interpretive framework that Smith had created by placing the cheek inscription at the end of the body inscription and took the two inscriptions seriously on their own terms. At the same time, the question of *why* and *when* the narrative of Idrimi's life was transferred from a tablet onto the statue is left unexplained;

[29] Although Dietrich and Loretz (1981, 247) did remark that "solch ein Akt sei nur innerhalb einer Gesellschaft möglich gewesen, in der Lesen und Schreiben einer kleinen Gruppe vorbehalten war und die Schreiber gegenseitig damit einverstanden gewesen seien."

Dietrich and Loretz (1981, 250) write: "Den Abschluß der Beschriftung führt dann der Schreiber Sarruwa mit der Übertragung des biographischen Berichtes von der bis dahin gesondert aufgestellten Tafel auf die Statue durch." But this statement is more descriptive than explanatory. And, again, absolutely fundamental to the reconstruction is the attestation of a tablet (DUB) in line CI 2 (= l. 103). However, as discussed in the commentary to the line in §A.2, after personal collation, I consider this sign to be better identified as UGU. With the absence of the putative tablet, Dietrich and Loretz's innovative reconstruction is hard to maintain.

This same putative tablet also plays a crucial role in Durand's (2011, 130–34) source-critical discussion, in which he accepted the tablet's existence, remarking, "il faut remarquer cependant qu'Idrimi mentionne à la fois une statue (l. 92, l. 99) et une tablette (l. 103). Tout traitement du passage qui ne tient pas compte de cette ambiguïté risque de ne pas rendre compte de l'histoire du texte" (Durand 2011, 132; referring to the putative DUB sign, he stated in footnote 111 that "la lecture matérielle semble assure"). Despite accepting Dietrich and Loretz's identification of the sign, Durand reconstructed the Idrimi text's source history differently. He envisioned that the narrative was originally written on a tablet that "devait représenter le texte authentique composé par Idrimi et qui a dû servir de modèle, selon un schéma désormais bien connu pour Mari et pour Émar, pour la rédaction d'une statue" (Durand 2011, 132). This tablet represents the first redaction of the text. The narrative on the tablet together with the curse formulae and the first mention of the scribe Šarruwa in line 98 were then inscribed on a statue in what represents a second redaction of the text. That inscribed statue, however, is now lost, and the Statue of Idrimi as we have it represents a second statue on which is written a third redaction of the text, added by either the same scribe Šarruwa, now much older, or by another scribe of the same name. This third redaction of the text differs from the second in that lines 99–101, comprising the second attestation of Šarruwa's name together with his request for blessings, were added at this time.

In addition to the identification of the sign DUB in line CI 2 (= l. 103) as DUB, Durand's source critical approach to the Idrimi text depends on a few key readings in lines 92–101, the text of the body inscription that follows the narrative. The first of these occurs with the initial attestation of Šarruwa in line 98, where I tentatively read ^{m}*šar-ru-wa* DUB.SAR $^{⌜\text{lu}_2?⌝}$ARAD, "Šarruwa is the scribe, the servant (of DNs)." As discussed in more detail in the commentary to the line in §A.2, the sign taken here as LU$_2$ has been identified differently, and Dietrich and Loretz (1981, 207), in particular, proposed identifying it as DUMU: "Šarruwa is the scribe, the son of the servant (of DNs)." Durand (2011, 131, 149) adopted this identification but read the sign with the value TUR (= *ṣehru*), taking it with the preceding DUB.SAR for "apprentice scribe." He contrasted this qualification of this Šarruwa as an apprentice scribe with the attestation of Šarruwa's name and title in the following line 99, where the putative TUR is absent. This alternation is one clue, according to Durand, that we are dealing with two redactions by the hand(s) of Šarruwa(s) (133).

A second moment in the colophon that suggested to Durand that we are encountering a text with multiple prior redactions is "une anticipation inattendue" of the predicate *piriḫšu lilqut* in line 93 before the same predicate in line 94. According to Durand (2011, 133), this repetition represents a seam in the text, "un indice qu'un rédaction se terminait 1. 93 après une très courte malédiction et que, par la suite, les l. 93b–98 ont été sur-ajoutées, lors d'une nouvelle rédaction." In other words, the first attestation of Šarruwa's name in line 98, in which, as discussed above, Durand understood the name to be qualified as apprentice scribe, was actually added during the subsequent redaction of the text by Šarruwa in order to make clear that the earlier redaction belonged to his juvenilia or to attribute that redaction to a junior scribe of the same name. The majority of the curse formulae would then also have been added by the older or second Šarruwa as part of the final redaction.

Finally, Durand's (2011, 133–34) third point in favor of multiple redactions of the text on two different statues is the alternation of the DINGIR determinative before ALAM (*ṣalmu*), where the sign is omitted before the first attestation in line 92 but present before the second attestation in line 98. For Durand, this variation signifies that the statues possessed different functions. Like the original, putative tablet, the first statue—which, again, is no longer preserved and on which the attestation of ALAM lacked a DINGIR determinative—had the function of conferring royal legitimacy.[30] On the other hand, the second statue—namely, the Statue of Idrimi that Woolley discovered—in which the attestation of ALAM is preceded by the DINGIR determinative, served the purpose of ancestor veneration because, on the basis of textual parallels going back to Ebla, the determinative's presence "devrait signifier que la statue représente quelqu'un qui est désormais divinisé, donc déjà mort et intégré à un culte" (Durand 2011, 134).

Chronologically, the final redaction must have occurred a number of years after the historical Idrimi's death, because Šarruwa, the fully-fledged scribe, is to be identified with Šarruwa, the Level IV scribe active during the reign of Idrimi's successor, Niqmepa. Moreover, "tout indique ... que cette seconde statue représente une initiative personnelle du scribe puisqu'il semble prendre une part si grande dans sa réalisation que c'est sur lui, mort ou vif, que sont désormais appelés les bénédictions divines" (Durand 2011, 134). Thus, Durand attempts in his reconstruction to account for the unexpected blessings on behalf of Šarruwa that have caused consternation in the scholarship.

Durand's source-critical approach to the text is attentive to details, and his comments about an ancestor cult being the social context for the (second) statue

---

30 Durand 2011, 134: "Si donc il est légitime de penser que la tablette dont parle Idrimi (et corollairement la première statue qui devait comporter le text) a été faite sur son ordre et fondait ainsi la lignée dynastique d'Alalah."

are particularly appreciated; see chapter 3, where I develop this social context still further. Ultimately, however, the reconstruction is weakened by a few factors, such as the identification of some signs, an overemphasis on variation, and some contradictions in internal logic. With regard to the first factor, Durand accepted Dietrich and Loretz's identification of the sign DUB in line CI 2. This tablet represents his first redaction of the text, but, as discussed above and in the commentary to the line, the identification does not seem to hold up after collation. However, Durand's reconstruction relies on the existence of a tablet in a different way than Dietrich and Loretz's reconstruction, and removing it from Durand's reconstruction may actually strengthen it; see the discussion later in this section. More serious is his identification of the sign following DUB.SAR in line 98 as TUR, such that this Šarruwa is qualified as an "apprentice scribe." As discussed in the commentary, this identification is not certain, and it is dangerous to ask it to support a larger argument.

Indeed, in the commentary to line 98 in §A.2, I note that one reason to prefer a different identification of the sign that has been proposed, LU$_2$, is that it results in an orthographic variation with the attestation of DUB.SAR in line 99 that is part of a larger rhetorical strategy employed in the body inscription. In other words, from the perspective of method, Durand's reconstruction depends heavily on taking variant writings as indices of different redactions. For instance, the fact that the two attestations of the logogram ALAM appear with and without the divine determinative (ll. 92, 99) signifies that we are dealing with two redactions of the text. So, too, is the putative reference to Šarruwa as DUB.SAR TUR in line 98 as opposed to just DUB.SAR in line 99. However, as argued in §4.1, variation in both orthography and paleography is deliberately used in the body inscription for rhetorical purposes. Therefore, the presence of variant writings cannot be taken as a "fingerprint" of different redactions.

Finally, Durand's reconstruction of the sources behind the Idrimi text is marred in places by difficulties in logic. In some places, a difficulty can perhaps be explained away. For instance, according to Durand, the second redaction of the Idrimi text was inscribed on the first, no-longer-preserved statue by Šarruwa, "the apprentice scribe." Is it likely that a document central to a dynasty's royal legitimacy would have been entrusted to an apprentice scribe? We can explain this difficulty by remembering that, according to Durand's reconstruction, it is actually the second/later putative Šarruwa who qualified the first/earlier putative Šarruwa as an apprentice, and he may have had his own reasons for doing so (perhaps a desire to distance himself from his predecessor's or his own earlier efforts).

However, other difficulties in the logic are harder to explain. For example, if the text on the putative tablet was only ever a draft copy to be used as an aid in inscribing the first putative statue, why does line CI 2 mention the tablet at all? In contrast to Dietrich and Loretz's (1981) reconstruction, where the tablet played an important role in its own right, having been deposited together with the statue, for Durand the tablet served only as a model. It was simply a step in a process of scribal production that should have had little value, save perhaps for archival purposes, after the first putative statue was inscribed. For that matter, why was the cheek inscription carved at all? Again, for Dietrich and Loretz (1981), the cheek inscription directed viewers to the associated tablet, but if the tablet was only a draft, this interpretation is impossible. Finally, it is hard to accept from a scholar who has contributed so much to our understanding of the *kispum* ritual and the veneration of royal ancestors in the second millennium BCE (see, e.g., Durand and Guichard 1997, 63–70) that the second putative statue could play a role in an ancestor cult, but that it should be a private devotional act on the part of a scribe instead of being intrinsically connected to the political context of the time.

A third source-critical approach to the Idrimi text was taken by Vidal (2012), who, in contrast to Durand, was more interested in the narrative, and especially its first part, than the colophon and the cheek inscription. Vidal's analysis depended in a large part on the widely accepted literary reading of the narrative, discussed in detail in §2.8, that sees the narrative as comprising two main parts, one in which Idrimi is presented as a folk hero and another in which he is presented as a good king. With regard to the second part of the narrative, Vidal considered that "it is reasonable to assume that Sharruwa could use official documentation preserved in the archives of Alalakh in order to write the section devoted to the adult Idrimi" (Vidal 2012, 81). In particular, he observed that lines 45–51, in which Idrimi narrates how he wrote to Parattarna I, the king of the Hurrians, about the good relations that existed between their respective ancestors, function "as a historical prologue…, the same kind of information registered in the Hittite treaties. So it is reasonable to consider lines 45–51 as a summary of a section of non preserved treaty between Idrimi and his overlord Barrattarna, king of Mittani" (Vidal 2012, 81).[31]

With regard to the first part of the narrative, however, Vidal considered that "it is unlikely that the official documentation preserved in the archives of Alalakh held any information on Idrimi before his installation as the king of the city. In fact, as we have seen, the story of the young Idrimi is based on folk tales and not archival documents" (Vidal 2012, 81). In this case, Vidal inferred two possibilities: Either the scribe Šarruwa composed a completely original story about Idrimi using "motifs and themes" from folklore, or there were preexisting "oral and/or written traditions on the young Idrimi" that Šarruwa "compile[d] and edit[ed]" (Vidal 2012, 81).

Vidal's (2012) claim was that a careful reading of the narrative argues in favor of the second scenario. His basic point was that, when one looks at three episodes of the first part of the narrative that are among the most folkloric (the "bad thing"

---

[31] Vidal cited Greenstein and Marcus 1976, 83 on this point: "We may surmise that the account Idrimi inscribed on his statue is but a synopsis of sections of a written treaty between himself and Barattarna"; see also Márquez Rowe 1997, 181.

that forced Idrimi and his family to flee Halab, Idrimi's departure from Emar and journey into the desert, and his seven-year sojourn with the *habiru*), one finds that they provide "scarce and difficult to interpret information," especially in contrast to other ancient Near Eastern narratives that feature the same literary topos (Vidal 2012, 82–83). For Vidal, the "existence of excessively short passages which provide obscure and laconic information" implied that these passages must be "summaries of pre-existing longer reports ... folk tales well-known by the population of the country" (Vidal 2012, 86). Because this population possessed the necessary background, the mention of Idrimi's name together with an appropriate keyword (e.g., *masiktu* or *habiru*) essentially acted as a prompt to this audience, which, "unlike us, allow[ed] them to fully understand and reconstruct the information registered in the statue. Thus Sharruwa actually would have acted not as the author of the story but as the compiler and editor of earlier material on the young Idrimi" (Vidal 2012, 86).

Vidal's attempt to illuminate the existence of source material for the Idrimi narrative is insightful and provocative. To be sure, it depends on certain assumptions about the audience of the inscriptions, but these assumptions are not necessarily incorrect and can be productively explored; see §5.3 for more discussion. At the same time, Vidal's approach also depends on a binary between preexisting oral or written traditions, on the one hand, and a completely original story, on the other hand, that is not necessarily warranted. For instance, to put forward a (relatively) recent analogy, it is well established that Shakespeare incorporated numerous sources when he wrote *King Lear*, such as Raphael Holinshed's *Chronicles of England*, John Higgins's *Mirror for Magistrates*, and the anonymous play *The True Chronicle History of King Leir and His Three Daughters, Gonorill, Ragan, and Cordella* (Fitzpatrick 2011, 35). No one, however, would describe Shakespeare as having simply "compile[d] and edit[ed]" preexisting texts. Rather than approaching a study of the Idrimi texts and its sources as a binary, then, it seems more productive to locate the text on a continuum with the use of source material excerpted but otherwise unchanged occupying one pole and composition without reference to any external sources occupying the other; see §2.9 for such an attempt.

2.8. LITERARY-CRITICAL APPROACHES

Scholars have also approached the Idrimi text with the tools and methods of literary criticism. In contrast to source-critical approaches, the literary-critical approaches have reinforced the position that the inscriptions are a unified text by showing how different topoi, motifs, or structural units work together and anticipate each other. Questions about the relevance of the modern categories of "literature" and "history" to the ancient text have also been central to literary-critical approaches, particularly with an eye to how the Idrimi inscriptions can be used as sources for writing a modern history.

One of the earliest and still best articulations of these issues is found in Dietrich and Loretz's (1966) review of the first volume of Horst Klengel's (1965) magisterial history of Syria. Klengel (1965, 227) opened his discussion of the reign of Idrimi in his chapter on Alalah under Mittanian hegemony with the statement "Idrimi ist der uns am besten bekannte König von Alalah," with the remainder of the discussion of Idrimi's reign (227–31) simply comprising a retelling of the inscriptions. Indeed, this same tendency to take the Idrimi text at face value as a historical source for Idrimi's reign is found throughout the scholarship. To mention only a few, more recent examples, Wilfred van Soldt (2000, 110) described the inscriptions as "our most important source for the history and chronology of Syria after the fall of Halab." He considered that "the Idrimi inscription provides us with the following data," naming six moments from the narrative, including Idrimi's sojourn with "king Zakkar of the Suteans," a seven-year stay in Canaan, and a thirty-year reign. Similarly, in his own discussion of the chronology of the Late Bronze Age, Frank Zeeb (2004, 87–89) took Idrimi's thirty-year reign at face value ("As Idrimi mentions himself that he ruled at Alalah 30 years after his victorious return, we can … give the following framework") and spent several pages considering what historical events could be identified with the *masiktu* mentioned in line 4 of the body inscription. Even Mario Liverani, whose literary-critical approach to the Idrimi text is discussed later in this section, took the body inscription at face value in his textbook on ancient Near Eastern history when he discussed the politically fragmented nature of Syria and the Levant in the Late Bronze Age. He noted that some of the small states "were involved in coalitions. This was the case of Aleppo, which at the time of the plot against Idrimi's father controlled a large portion of northern Syria (from Aleppo to Mukiš, Niya, and Ama'u)" (Liverani 2011, 337).

Returning to Dietrich and Loretz's (1966) review of the earliest of these examples, Klengel 1965, these scholars objected that Klengel's substitution of a paraphrase of the body inscription for the events of Idrimi's reign "geben zu erkennen, daß der Verf. der literarischen Analyse zu wenig Rechnung getragen hat" (559). Particular concerns of theirs included the use of a literary topos such as "der 'sozialen Neuordnung'" (556) as evidence that Idrimi settled nomadic persons, or numbers such as seven or thirty used for chronological as opposed to symbolic value (558). Because of the presence of literary motifs or symbolic numbers known from other ancient Near Eastern texts in the Idrimi text, Dietrich and Loretz (1966, 559) considered that "brauchen wir dringlichst weiteres kontemporäres Quellenmaterial" in order to use the text as a source for history writing. In the absence of such sources, they noted that it may simply be impossible to apprehend "eine[n] klareren Bild der geschichtlichen Ereignisse…, von denen her die Gestalt Idrimis zu deuten ist." However, to Dietrich and Loretz (1966, 559), this impossibility would not mean that the Idrimi text was without historical value; rather, it would still be a valuable source for the understanding of "altorientalischen Geschichtsschreibung.… Damit stellt die Idrimi-Inschrift ein treffendes Beispiel für die Art der Geschichtsbetrachtung der vorindustriellen Gesellschaft dar, in der die Geschichte plastisch also Epos oder Drama von handelnden Einzelpersonen verstanden wird."

In the years that have followed, one can find examples in the scholarship of both approaches to the Idrimi text—assembling contemporary evidence that corroborates or contradicts details of the text or approaching the text as an example of ancient, not modern, history writing—although the first approach has been pursued in a sustained way only by von Dassow (2008, 33–45). In this discussion, von Dassow stated that her goal was "to know why the inscription tells us what it does, both fact and fancy, and which bits of the tale really happened" (33), although she acknowledged that achieving this goal would be "severely constrain[ed]" by "the impossibility of defining the historical context within which the statue and inscription were produced." In the face of this obstacle, her approach began (35–39) by trying to establish whether there are any "point[s] of contact" (35) between what we know about the historical Idrimi exclusively from evidence outside of the inscriptions and the narrative of his life as presented in the body inscription. She identified three such points of contact. Two of these occur in one Level IV text: both Idrimi's allegiance to Parattarna I, king of Mittani (ll. 42–60) and his campaign against "the land of Hatti" (ll. 64–77) find points of contact with AlT 3 [1.2], the treaty between the historical Idrimi and Pilliya, the ruler of Kizzuwatna (e.g., "Hatti"),[32] in which Idrimi explicitly acknowledged the hegemony of Parattarna I (ll. 40–42). The third point of contact relied on von Dassow's attribution of the construction of the Level IV palace to Idrimi (on which, see the discussion in §2.3), which she identified with "the act of housebuilding described in the inscription" (36; see l. 80).

Having established that points of contact do exist between the narrative of Idrimi's life and what we know about the historical Idrimi from evidence outside of the inscriptions, von Dassow (2008, 43) acknowledged that the only means of evaluating other details of the narrative is indirect; one would have to identify corroborating "circumstantial evidence … in the Alalah IV archives" or "details that cannot be explained by reference to a likely fifteenth- or fourteenth-century agenda." As an example of corroborating circumstantial evidence, she pointed out that administrative texts from Level IV Alalah "record *habirū* troops, enlisted in the time of [the historical Idrimi's] son Niqmepa," and observed that, "under Niqmepa, *habirū* appear to have made up over half of Alalah's army, which stands to reason if Idrimi conquered Alalah with an army of *habirū* to begin with" (43; see ll. 27–30). As an example of a narrative detail that cannot be explained by a political agenda, she contrasted Idrimi's claim that Halab was his paternal estate with his exile to Emar (ll. 3–5), noting that "Idrimi's Halabite origin could be a

[32] Von Dassow 2008, 37–38: "Kizzuwatna had again become subject to Hatti, and it was annexed as a Hittite province in the early fourteenth century … an invasion of Kizzuwatna could reasonably be represented as a campaign 'against Hatti.'"

specious claim, intended to link him to the long-vanished glory of Yamhad. But exile in Emar would not appear to serve any later agenda; there does not seem to have been any reason to claim that a king of Alalah had family in Emar, unless it were in fact true" (43).

Von Dassow's final step in evaluating the historicity of the narrative was to extrapolate from these details to the larger narrative "framework." Although she was careful to note that an "assumption of historicity should not be extended to every detail of the narrative," such as the "folkloristic elements" (43), her basic position was that

> if two elements of the tale, the part about Emar and the part about the *habirū*, hold up to scrutiny by the admittedly limited means available, then the framework of which these elements are parts is thereby upheld, to some correspondingly limited degree. Thus, if we take it as fact that Idrimi's family fled to Emar from Halab, we then assume the validity of the claim that Halab was Idrimi's paternal home; similarly if we decide that Idrimi did in fact conquer the realm of Alalah with an army composed of *habirū*, we then assume that his sojourn in Canaan, preparatory to his advance upon Alalah, actually took place, too. (43)

While von Dassow is to be credited for making her assumptions and reasoning explicit here, I am not sure that they hold up. For instance, there is no reason why admitting that Idrimi's family fled from Halab to Emar means that we must also assume "the claim that Halab was Idrimi's paternal home" to be valid. Indeed, as quoted above and earlier on the same page, von Dassow acknowledged that Idrimi's claim to be from Halab could be "specious … intended to link him to the long-vanished glory of Yamhad." Even if we were to accept Idrimi's flight to Emar as historical because "exile in Emar would not appear to serve any later agenda," this detail would tell us only that Idrimi spent time in Emar; it says nothing about where he came *from*. But, more importantly, I am very hesitant to identify a detail of the narrative as historical simply because I myself, removed over three millennia from the narrative's composition, cannot identify an agenda behind it. Indeed, it feels presumptuous to think that our grasp of social and political life is finely tuned enough to be confident in such assessments.

The use of the Level IV administrative texts as circumstantial, corroborating evidence for the historicity of details found in the Idrimi text is also problematic. For instance, von Dassow used administrative texts recording *habirū* in Niqmepa's army to corroborate the Idrimi text's claim that he conquered (better: invaded) Alalah with an army of *habirū*, from which corroboration she felt comfortable assuming that the description of him assembling this army during a sojourn in Canaan was historical as well. But, to begin, it seems possible that, if Idrimi had assembled the army of *habirū* from somewhere else but wished to obscure their origin, then the body inscription might attribute a different origin—say,

Canaan—to them. On the basis of our present knowledge, I do not think we can rule out the possibility, and, therefore, we need to be careful to treat the other claim also as just one possibility.

More importantly, though, the difficulty in the chain of reasoning actually begins a step earlier, as already recognized by Vidal (2012). He noted that "there are other equally valid possibilities regarding this issue. Thus, for example, Sharruwa (if he was responsible for the creation of this tale) bearing in mind the relevance reached by the *habiru* in Alalakh's army years after the death of Idrimi, could try to link them with the military rise of the founder king" (Vidal 2012, 80–81). In other words, if the inscriptions were composed during the reign of Niqmepa or even later, which von Dassow (2008, 33) has explicitly acknowledged as a possibility,[33] then the detail about Idrimi's army being comprised of *habirū* might function as a just-so story to explain and justify the presence of *habirū* in Alalah's military at that time. Accordingly, only the first step in von Dassow's chain of reasoning—the three points of contact between the historical Idrimi and the narrative—withstands scrutiny, and even the identification of the Level IV palace as the historical "house" (l. 80) that Idrimi ordered to be built is not certain. And these two or three points of contact do not provide much of a basis for evaluating the historicity of the rest of the narrative.

Therefore, Dietrich and Loretz's (1966) second proposed approach as outlined above—namely, to take the narrative as an example of ancient historiography—is, to my mind, more productive, and this approach is also the one that has received more attention in the scholarship. The scholarship operating with this approach is characterized by two sorts of analysis. The first of these has focused on the structure of the text, especially the narrative, which has been recognized to consist of two major units. To my knowledge, the earliest statement to this effect was made by Nougayrol (1951, 151), who considered the narrative of Idrimi's life to consist of "le récit des faits qui ont précédé et déterminé son avènement" and "celui des événements marquants de son règne."[34] The second sort of analysis has focused on the identification of literary tropes or folklore motifs within the narrative, following the approach made famous by Vladimir Propp. So, for instance, Liverani (2004b), in an influential article first published in 1972 and discussed in more detail in §5.2, identified a literary motif of a solitary hero leaving for the desert in a chariot in lines 13–15 of the narrative as well as in other ancient Near Eastern texts. Other motifs have been identified in the narrative, such as the younger brother who is cleverer than his older brothers, a sojourn with

[33] Von Dassow 2008, 33: "In short, it cannot be determined whether the statue and its inscription were produced soon after the reign of Idrimi or almost a century later."

[34] It is possible that these narrative units are also marked linguistically, with the first unit showing a more pronounced departure from standard Akkadian than the second unit; see Greenstein and Marcus 1976, 63 and Medill 2019, 254–55.

an "irregular" population, and the repeated mention of the number seven, already discussed above.[35]

These two types of analysis are quite complementary. In particular, all of the literary motifs just mentioned occur in the first half of the narrative. They combine to cast Idrimi's "departure and ... eventual journey" into "a kind of 'trial,' permitting the protagonist to qualify as a 'hero'" (Liverani 2004b, 94). Or, as Oller (1977a, 192–93) described it, the motifs used in the first half of the narrative work to depict Idrimi "both as the unfortunate slighted refugee heir ... and as the questing hero who against impossible odds gains his rightful position in life." In the second narrative unit, the action shifts. The narrative now depicts Idrimi on a victorious military campaign, focusing on building projects at home and other domestic concerns, and, finally, Idrimi's attention to the veneration of ancestors. In other words, as Oller (1977a, 193) has explained, the narrative "is designed to show Idrimi as a good ruler, and hence presents further justification for his legitimacy." Indeed, Oller stressed that the two units of the narrative work in tandem towards this legitimizing end, in that "the purpose of the Idrimi text seems to be to first tell the story of the ruler's life in a way which positively asserts his legitimacy as king of Alalah and then prove it by an enumeration of his good deeds as king" (199).

I agree wholeheartedly with these observations, although I would offer one modification—namely, that the narrative comprises three, not two, units. The tripartite structure becomes clear when we look at where Oller sees the demarcation between his two putative sections. For Oller (1977a, 191–92), the "fairy tale" ends in line 63 and the recitation of the good king's deeds begins in line 64. However, there is nothing in the context of lines 42–60, what I call the Parattarna episode, that is consistent with presenting Idrimi as a fairy tale or folklore hero other than an appearance of another period of seven years. But the number seven appears in the "good king" narrative unit as well, in the form of the seven Hittite cities that Idrimi plundered; the number seven seems more to characterize the narrative as a whole than to be characteristic of any one unit within it.

The sense that these lines stand apart from what comes before and after in the narrative has been remarked upon before. As discussed above (§2.7) and in more detail below (§2.9), several scholars have suggested that this passage paraphrases or quotes a no longer preserved treaty between Idrimi and Parattarna I. I will argue below that, if the passage has an actual, no longer extant treaty as its source material, it has considerably reworked that source. But this argument is not at odds with the observation that the vocabulary of the passage is immersed in the language of Late Bronze Age diplomatic texts; see, for instance, the repeated mentions of *māmītu* (ll. 50, 52, 53, 54), *mānahtu* (ll. 47, 51, 54; see the

---

[35] For "L'histoire du 'jeune héros' selon la codification de Propp" applied to the Idrimi narrative, see Liverani 2011, 13 Table 1.

extensive discussion of this word in chapter 4), and *šulmu* (l. 54). Even the very first word of this proposed unit, *appūna*, "moreover, in addition" (l. 42), signals to a reader that the narrative is transitioning into something new not just by its meaning but also by its prevalence in Late Bronze Age treaties and diplomatic correspondence.[36] And, indeed, if we consider the end of the first narrative unit, we find that lines 41–42 present a scene that is very fitting for the conclusion of the fairy tale, in which Idrimi, the younger brother who achieved what his older brothers could not, takes his brothers in and becomes their lord and protector; see also the commentaries to lines 8 and 39 in §A.2 and especially the twofold appearance of *ittiyama* with emphatic *-ma* in lines 8 and 41.

From the perspective of the narrative, the Parattarna episode encompasses a limbo period in Idrimi's life, one in which he is effectively the ruler of Alalah but not yet formally acknowledged as its king. It ends with that formal acknowledgment by Parattarna I: "In my status as a retainer, in my loyalty, I seized *this abandoned hem* for him, and so I was king. Kings from all around *came up to me* at Alalah, and I was their equal" (ll. 57–60). Only after this moment does the narrative shift into its third unit, enumerating Idrimi's proper royal actions.[37] Accordingly, the narrative is best understood as having a tripartite structure, with the Parattarna episode serving as a crucial linchpin. In line with this important structural function, the episode was also the location of an argument addressed to the inscriptions' contemporary audience, as I discuss in more detail in chapter 4.

As an aside, it is worth noting that the narrative's literary structure outlined here does not reflect the arrangement of the inscription on the statue's body. As described in §1.4, the body inscription is arranged in four divisions on the statue's body that move, seen from a viewer's perspective, from the left chest (ll. 1–23), down to the left leg (ll. 24–51), over to the right leg (ll. 52–74) and, finally, up to the right chest (ll. 75–100). This arrangement means that, while the fairy tale literary unit begins, necessarily, at the beginning of the body inscription, the Parattarna episode begins about two thirds through the second division, and the

---

36 For instance, the second section of one manuscript of Šuppiluliuma I's treaty with Niqmaddu II of Ugarit begins "Moreover, all of the land of Ugarit, together with its borders, together with its mountains, together with its fields (and) meadows, together with […]," *ap-pu-nu-ma* KUR ^{uru}*u*$_2$*-ga-ri-it gab-*⸢*bu*⸣ *a-du* ZAG-HI.A-*šu a-du* HUR.SAG.MEŠ-[*šu*] *a-*⸢*du* A⸣.ŠA$_3$.HI.A A.GAR$_3$.MEŠ-*šu* ⸢*a-du*⸣ […] (PRU 4 52 [RS 17.639A]: 21′–23′). Huehnergard (2011, 195) described *appūna* as "rare in the Ugaritic text"; cf. van Soldt 1991, 464: "*appūna*(*ma*), 'moreover,' occurs in two older legal texts (Niqmaddu II and Niqmepa)." The word is now attested at least seven times in the Akkadian letters from the House of Urtenu (RSOu 23). Altogether, I am aware of at least sixteen attestations in the Akkadian legal and epistolary texts from Ugarit.

37 Differently than Oller, I understand this third and final narrative unit to begin three lines earlier in line 60, where the difficult lines 60–63 seem to describe Idrimi rebuilding defensive fortifications prior to a military campaign.

Figure 2.2. The vertical ruling between divisions 2 and 3.

good king literary unit begins almost ten lines into the third division. Indeed, the absence of any concern in this regard can be seen in the transition from the second division on statue's left leg to the third division on its right leg—that is, from line 51 to 52—which occurs in the middle of a periphrastic genitive construction: *ma-na-ha-te*.HI.A / *ša pa-nu-ti-ni*, "the tribute / of our ancestors." And the transition from the third division on the right leg to the fourth division on the left chest—that is, from line 74 to line 75—occurs in the middle of the list of persons to whom Idrimi distributed plunder from Hatti after his military campaign there.

One reason why the text's physical arrangement does not correlate with its content may be that the process by which the signs were incised on the statue was not worked out in advance by, for example, being inked on the stone before being carved, as is known to have been done with cuneiform inscriptions from other times and places. We can best appreciate the ad hoc nature of the process if we look at the two divisions of text inscribed on the statue's left and right legs (see fig. 2.2).

These two units are separated from each other by a vertical ruling. This ruling was probably thought to be necessary because the statue's legs are sculpted in the form of an undifferentiated rectangular block and lack any plastic feature that could also serve as a divider between the text. (In contrast, no ruling separates the text on Idrimi's left and right chest because the plasticity of his arms and beard already helps to keep the two divisions of text separate.) As is clear in figure 2.2, one significant feature of the vertical ruling is that it does not extend all the way to the end of the text on Idrimi's left leg but stops about three quarters of the way down. The reason the vertical ruling terminates early is that line 45, a line from the second division on the left leg, has run over into the space on the right leg. From the fact that the vertical ruling stops before the run-over text of line 45, we can infer that the vertical ruling was incised only after the left leg was already inscribed with text.[38]

The conclusion that the narrative of Idrimi's life comprises three, not two, literary units that work together to communicate a larger image of Idrimi serves only to emphasize the central claim of previous scholars who have argued that the narrative is not a straightforward account of the events of Idrimi's life to be taken at face value and referred to as a "history" of his reign. How, then, should we approach it? For Dietrich and Loretz (1966) and Liverani (2004b), the answer to this question was to take the narrative as an example of ancient historiography—what, as quoted above, Dietrich and Loretz (1966, 559) described as "ein treffendes Beispiel für die Art der Geschichtsbetrachtung der vorindustriellen Gesellschaft." One aspect of this answer is unproblematic, in that the text is undeniably premodern. However, the answer is more problematic if it positions the text as representative of a premodern approach to the past ("*die* Art" as opposed to "*eine* Art"). In the current state of our knowledge, many aspects of the Statue of Idrimi and its inscriptions are *sui generis*; see, for instance, the discussion in §3.3 of the fact that statues of royal ancestors are *anepigraphic* in the Bronze Age. Taking the statue and its inscriptions as representative, then, risks distorting our conception of ancient historiography when we need to begin by exploring their historical situatedness.

Liverani (2004b) moved in this direction toward the end of his contribution, mentioned already above, on the motif of the hero who leaves for the desert in a chariot. In a similar vein to Dietrich and Loretz (1966), he compared the narrative of Idrimi's life to modern history, observing that, "although the storyteller wants to provide us with a 'true' story, he has a concept of 'historical truth' that is in general slightly different from ours" (Liverani 2004b, 95). Liverani used the motif of seven years to illustrate what he meant by this statement, noting that, from the perspective of the ancient author and audience,

> the line between historical exactness and literary motif is not clear cut. What does it matter if a period of time was seven years, or six, or nine? Such a piece of accuracy has no relevance whatsoever in a society—like the Syrian society of the Late Bronze period—that does not keep records of the lengths of reigns, that has no dating formulae or any other system to distinguish the single years of the past, and that "dates" its juridical documents only insofar as it says that they are valid "from now on" and "forever." The storyteller cannot know, and is not interested

38 For a discussion of why this line from the second division on the left leg runs over into the right leg, see §2.9.

> in knowing, how long a period was. He just states that it lasted "seven years," in order to emphasise that "in the seventh year" the situation was reversed. And his audience knows that "seven" has no numerical significance, but has a specific narrative function related to the reversal of a given situation or the end of a given phase. (95)

For Liverani, then, the modern historian's task "is not to understand whether a detail is exact or not, but to understand why such a detail was used" (96).

It is in this statement that Liverani moved past holding the text up as a representative example of ancient historiography to focus instead on the text's historical situatedness:

> Idrimi tells the story of his life along the lines of a fairy tale, because he has a definite interest in doing so: he has to face the opinion of a public that was troubled by the irregular way he ascended to the throne.... Idrimi needed to demonstrate to public opinion that his accession to the throne was the result of his heroic capabilities and supernatural assistance. (Liverani 2004b, 96)

Oller (1977a, 199–200), too, emerged from his discussion of the structure of the narrative in a very similar place. Although, as quoted above, he emphasized that "the purpose of the Idrimi text seems to be to first tell the story of the ruler's life in a way which positively asserts his legitimacy as king of Alalah and then prove it by an enumeration of his good deeds as king," he went on to connect this function to the inscriptions' historical situatedness, "the creation of [a] specific document ... the work of a scribe ... who selected motifs and themes ... and recast them to present the life and career of his monarch to the best possible effect" (Oller 1977a, 199–200).

Yet if Liverani (2004b) and Oller (1977a) both emphasized the inscriptions' historical situatedness, neither took the next step of trying to identify or describe that moment, other than to infer that it related to the historical Idrimi's irregular accession (which, in fact, is not known to have been regular or irregular outside of the evidence of the Idrimi text). On the other hand, as discussed in §2.3, both Sasson (1981) and Fink (2010) have taken this step. Sasson's (1981) attempt to situate the inscriptions in a context of incipient nationalism and resistance to Hittite hegemony at Alalah toward the end of the thirteenth century was provocative and trailblazing, but the historical reconstruction depended on Woolley's Level I find-spot for the statue and needs to be abandoned now in light of Fink's (2010) reanalysis of the archaeological record. Fink (2010, 97–98) offered his own contextualization of the text as "the enthronement inscription of Addu-Nīrārī," which was "inscribed during a period of turmoil in the history of Alalakh, following the traumatic destruction" of the Level IV palace by the Hittites. However, to support this scenario, he offered only a few parallels between details of the narrative and what he imagined would have been the situation for Addu-nerari at that time, stating that these parallels "would have served the political agenda" of the king.

Leaving aside the question of whether the enumerated details of Idrimi's life would have been the same faced by Addu-nerari, Fink (2010) leaves unarticulated the more pressing question of how and why parallels would serve a political agenda in the first place.

2.9. APPROACH OF THE BOOK

Indeed, if we step back from the question of why Idrimi's life was cast in the several molds of fairy tale hero, Mittanian client, and archetypical good king, we can see that even those scholars who have done the most sensitive work on these aspects of the narrative have assumed answers to some basic questions or not asked them at all. Chief among these questions are: Why was the story of Idrimi's life inscribed on a statue at this particular time and place and in this particular way? Who would have read it? The aim of this book is to try to answer these questions and explore how those answers inform our understanding of the social and historical context of the statue and the inscriptions. Doing so represents a next step in the line of inquiry that Liverani (2004b) and Oller (1977a) stopped short of fleshing out in their attention to the historical situatedness of the statue and the inscriptions.

In trying to define a social and historical context for the statue and its inscriptions, I combine a close reading of the text with close attention to the materiality of the statue. The close reading treats the body inscription and the cheek inscription as individual texts and explores them in light of legal, epistolary, and administrative cuneiform corpora from Late Bronze Age Anatolia, the Levant, and Egypt (i.e., other western hybrid Akkadian texts), on the one hand, and the Akkadian scholarly and so-called literary texts with which cuneiform scribes, using the term in its broadest sense, of Late Bronze Age Anatolia, the Levant, and Egypt would have been familiar, on the other. This close reading of the text emerges from and is developed by an engagement with the materiality of both the inscriptions and the statue on which they have been inscribed. It is important to emphasize that I would never have been able to reach the conclusions arrived at in this book by studying the Idrimi inscriptions in the form in which they are most often encountered—namely, as a disembodied, anthologized text.

Having dedicated this chapter to scholarly approaches to the Statue of Idrimi over the past seven decades, it seems only fair to the reader to end this chapter with a sample of my own method, a concrete illustration of what combining a careful close reading of the text with an analytic framework emphasizing the materiality of the inscription looks like in action. My subject is one that has already come up twice in this chapter: lines 45–51 of the body inscription. As discussed above (see §2.7), this passage from the Parattarna episode has been identified by Greenstein and Marcus, Márquez Rowe, and Vidal as a summary or synopsis of the historical prologue of an actual treaty between the historical rulers Idrimi and Parattarna I. And I had occasion to discuss it again in my comparison of the literary structure of the narrative with the physical arrangement of the body inscription on the statue, especially the line (l. 45) that runs over from the second division of text on the statue's left leg into the space on the statue's right leg (see §2.8). Now I want to consider what combining a close reading of lines 45–51 with a look at these lines not as a disembodied text but as signs actually carved onto a statue can show us about the extent to which this passage has the historical prologue of an actual treaty as its source material. The passage in question reads:

> 43 [M]U 7.KAM.HI.A ^{m}*pa*$_2$*-ra-at-tar-na* LUGAL *dan-nu* 44 LUGAL ERIN$_2$.⸢MEŠ⸣ *hur-ri*^{ki} *u*$_2$*-na-kir-an-ni* 45 ⸢*i*⸣*-na š*[*e*]*-eb-*⸢*i*⸣ *ša-na-ti a-na* ^{m}*pa*$_2$*-ra-at-ar-na* LUGAL^{ri} 46 LUGAL ⸢ERIN$_2$⸣.MEŠ^{an}*-wa-an-da aš-ta*$_2$*-par*$_2$...
>
> over seven [ye]ars, Parattarna (I), the mighty king, king of the armies of Hurri, turned hostile towards me. In the seventh of (those) years, to Parattarna (I), the king, king of the Umman-manda, I sent a message...

I begin by looking at line 45, the line that extends from the text on the left leg into the space of the right leg (see fig. 2.3). As discussed previously, the extension of line 45 has the effect of terminating the text of the third division at line 74, well before the text of the second division, which continues for another six lines. But why does line 45—and none of the previous twenty-two lines in the same division—run over onto the right leg in the first place?

Figure 2.3. The ends of lines 44–46, showing the extension of line 45 onto the right leg.

One answer could be that line 45 ends in the name and title of the Hurrian king Parattarna I, and the scribe did not want to divide the signs for this important name across two lines or to separate the royal name from its title. Yet this answer immediately provokes another question: Why is this line longer than all of its companion lines? Or, to generalize the question: Is there any rationale to the line breaks in the inscription other than simply the dictates of spacing? In the case of line 45, there does seem to be a rationale, for if we step back and look at the line's larger context, we see that lines 43–46 are actually a carefully structured unit. In contrast to the presentation of these lines immediately above, here is a normalization and translation of the lines that reflects this structure:

43. *sebe* [*šan*]*āti Parattarna šarru dannu*
44. *šar ummānāt Hurri unakkiranni*
45. *ina š*[*e*]*bī šanāti ana Parattarna šarri*
46. *šar Umman-wanda aštapar*…

over seven years, Parattarna (I), the mighty king,
king of the armies of Hurri, turned hostile towards me.
In the seventh of (those) years, to Parattarna (I), the king,
king of the Umman-manda, I sent a message…

This unit can be described as an example of verse because parallelism gives it a clear ABAB structure.[39] Lines 43 and 45 open with a statement about seven years and end with the mention of Parattarna I, the king; lines 44 and 46 open by restating "king of the ERIN$_2$-MEŠ(*ummānu*)" and ending with the main verb of the clause.

However, within the fundamental balance of this parallelism, we encounter, as so often in the body inscription, deliberate variation. For instance, apart from the necessarily different verbs, LUGAL *dan-nu* in line 43 is replaced with the visually similar string LUGAL^{ri} in line 45; the sign sequence ERIN$_2$.MEŠ that appears in the traditional royal title *šar ummānāt Hurri* in line 44 is transformed into the first half of the ethnonym Umman-manda for the royal title *šar Umman-wanda* in line 46;[40] in Parattarna I's name, a doubled consonantal writing in line 43 alternates with a broken writing in line 45. But the variant most relevant to the extension of line 45 onto the statue's right leg is found in the alternation of the logographic writing of the cardinal numerical phrase MU 7.KAM.HI.A with the syllabic writing of the ordinal numerical phrase *i-na še-eb-i ša-na-ti*. Significantly, the syllabic spelling takes up approximately half of line 45, and it is in the intersection of this deliberate orthographic variation with the need to maintain the poetic line for parallelism that we can find an explanation for why line 45 runs over onto the right leg.

In sum, studying the material manifestation of the text on the statue can lead to a new understanding of the text. In the case of line 45, it led to an understanding that lines 43–46 were formally structured as a quatrain so that each line was balanced against the others and line breaks, consequentially, could not be haphazard. This new understanding has important ramifications. For instance, it opens to

[39] It is worth noting that, to the extent the topic has been raised, the Idrimi text has not generally been characterized in this way; see, e.g., Sasson 1981, 312: "Unless one stretches to the breaking point the definition of 'poetry' or even that of 'semipoetry,' it is difficult to regard Idrimi's inscription as poetic in style."

[40] See the commentary to line 44 in §A.2 on the normalization of ERIN$_2$.MEŠ as a plural form of *ummānu* and not *ṣābu*. See also the commentary to line 46 in §A.2 for the reading "Umman-wanda" instead of a different reading that involves an emendation followed by a personal name; i.e., LUGAL ⸢ERIN$_2$⸣.MEŠ <*hur-ri*^{ki}> ^{m}*an-wa-an-da*.

door for a larger study of the poetics of the Idrimi narrative, which is not an approach that has been applied to this text. It also gives us a new perspective on the larger passage to which lines 43–46 belongs, and which has been identified as having a no longer extant treaty between Idrimi and Parattarna I as its source. To my knowledge, scholars have not typically considered contemporary Late Bronze Age treaties to display such a formal structure at the level of the line, and, while it can be difficult to identify sufficiently preserved passages for comparison, it does seem like line breaks can vary across the historical prologues of duplicate manuscripts of the same text.[41] Of course, recognizing this difference between the Idrimi text and Late Bronze Age treaties does not mean that this passage in the Idrimi text could not have an actual, no longer extant treaty between Parattarna I and Idrimi as its ultimate source. However, it implies that such a source, if it existed, was considerably reworked by an author, and this implication means that we are justified in exploring historical contexts for the Idrimi inscriptions that assume "a unified text."

This example, then, is intended to illustrate this book's approach in the chapters that follow, why and how I believe that close reading and an engagement with the materiality of the statue and its inscriptions can work together to offer new insight into an often-studied text. I begin my study of the Statue of Idrimi in earnest in chapter 3, "Ancestors," by exploring one particular context for it: ancestor veneration. The conclusions reached in that chapter—namely, that the Statue of Idrimi represents the transformation of a collective ancestor into an individual one and a site of religious action into a political one—provide the entry point into defining a historical context for the statue and its inscriptions. This entry point is developed in chapter 4, "Arguments," in which I look at the interaction of the cheek inscription and the body inscription and locate this interaction within both Mesopotamian literary traditions and Syro-Anatolian political discourse. In chapter 5, "Audience," I step back to consider who would have been able to access the Idrimi text and how this potential audience informs our reading of that text and contributes further to our reconstruction of a historical context for the statue and its inscriptions. In chapter 6, "Šarruwa and IM-nerari," I consider some possible identifications of persons named in the body inscription with persons attested in other cuneiform corpora from Late Bronze Age Anatolia, the Levant, and Egypt. These identifications are explicitly speculative and intended to emphasize the numerous possibilities about the past that we must acknowledge coexist. In a short concluding chapter, chapter 7, I summarize the arguments made in the previous chapters. Finally, I offer extended philological commentaries on the inscriptions in the appendix because the inscriptions can be quite difficult to comprehend on paleographic and linguistic grounds, and because attempts to resolve the various

[41] Compare, for example, the line breaks of the historical prologue of the Akkadian and Hittite manuscripts of Šuppiluliuma I's treaty with Aziru of Amurru (*CTH* 49; see del Monte 1986, 116, 128).

difficulties of comprehension have generated a large quantity of secondary literature. The commentary aims to make clear how I am reading the text in various places, why I am reading the text that way, and what other possible readings have been proposed, which could change the interpretation but which I am not following.

In the course of producing the commentary, I produced two other resources that I have decided to disseminate both in the spirit of transparency (i.e., to clarify what I was seeing or thinking) and also in the hope that they may be useful to others. Specifically, as anyone who has worked with the Idrimi inscriptions in the cuneiform will not be surprised to learn, I found it necessary to engage with the paleography of the inscriptions in a sustained manner. Sometimes I was interested in pursuing a particular paleographic question across a given line. However, because the inscription is written along the curves of the statue's body and garment, it is impossible to photograph a single line in its entirety, so the photographs published by Smith (1949) and Dietrich and Loretz (1981) present most lines in piecemeal fashion, with a given line often spread out over three different photographs. In order to be able to explore the paleography of a single line and its neighbors more easily, I created composite photographs of each individual line in its entirety; the plates at the end of this book provide these images. Other times, I wanted to be able to compare each attestation of a single sign wherever it appeared in the inscriptions. While both Smith (1949) and Dietrich and Loretz (1981) have published sign lists, the signs were presented in copy, not as photographs, and neither sign list illustrates every attestation. Therefore, I created a sign list that includes a photograph of every single sign arranged by *MZL* number and by line number therein. Due to production costs, it was not possible to include the sign list as part of this book. However, it is available as a free download at https://www.sbl-site.org/assets/pdfs/pubs/SBL2835S.pdf.

Finally, it is worth mentioning an electronic resource that accompanies this book. When I first began this project, I released the Electronic Idrimi, an annotated edition of the inscriptions, on the Oracc workspace.[42] I found that the dynamic nature of this online edition allowed me to engage with the inscriptions in new and unexpected ways. I also appreciated the ability to update the edition in light both of colleagues' suggestions, whether published or privately communicated, and of changes in my own thinking as I wrote this book. Although the transliteration, translation, and commentary in this book, once published, is frozen at a particular moment in time, I look forward to updating the Electronic Idrimi as our understanding of the inscriptions continues to develop in the future.

---

42 The Electronic Idrimi, Oracc, http://oracc.museum.upenn.edu/aemw/alalakh/idrimi/.

3
Ancestors

A natural place to begin the work of trying to define a historical context for the Statue of Idrimi and its inscriptions is by considering the ostensible raison d'être of the statue: its role as a locus of religious action and, in particular, as the focus of veneration in an ancestor cult. Although this second role for the statue is frequently invoked in the scholarly literature, there are dissenting voices, and it cannot be assumed. Accordingly, I begin this chapter by approaching the Statue of Idrimi and its inscriptions from both textual and material perspectives to argue in support of the position that the statue was used in an ancestor cult in antiquity. However, there is an important point of contrast between the Statue of Idrimi and other Bronze Age statues used in ancestor cults. The latter are anepigraphic because they represented collective ancestors, while the Statue of Idrimi is famously inscribed with the life story of an individual. In fact, a close examination of the statue reveals that it, too, was originally anepigraphic, and the inscriptions were added at a later date. This act transformed the representation of a nameless, collective ancestor into a specific, historical ancestor and a locus of religious action into a locus of political action. The final line of the narrative that identifies IM-nerari as the individual responsible for providing offerings to the deceased Idrimi's ghost thereby also identifies him as the new, legitimate ruler of Alalah.

3.1. ANCESTOR VENERATION OR VOTIVE INSTALLATION?

A number of different scholars have understood the *Sitz im Leben* of the Statue of Idrimi to be an ancestor cult, often justifying this position on account of the statue's find-spot. For instance, in his introduction to ancient Near Eastern art, Anton Moortgat (1969, 11) remarked: "the seated figure in stone of this king [Idrimi] stood in a sort of temple at Alalakh, probably a tomb building, where it had been erected as an ancestral image and received the worship due to it." While vigorously disagreeing with Moortgat's suggestion that Idrimi was actually interred in the annex to the temple (Mayer-Opificius 1981, 287), Ruth Mayer-

Opificius nonetheless affirmed his general position about the statue's role in an ancestor cult:

> Es muß nun an dieser Stelle jedoch betont werden, daß wir nur in Alalah mit Sicherheit von der Ausübung eines *echten* Ahnenkultes sprechen dürften.... Daß in den letzten dreihundert Jahren der Geschichte von Alalah das Bild des Fürsten Idrimi ständig Verehrung genoß—von anderen Herrschern in dieser Stadt läßt sich das nicht nachweisen—dürfte daran liegen, daß der König eine neue Ära der Macht für die Stadt und ihre Umgebung heraufführte.... Diesem wichtigen Ahnherrn des königlichen Hauses errichtet man daher durch all Zeiten eine neu 'Ahnenkapelle,' die dem eigentlichen Tempel immer wieder hinzugefügt." (289, emphasis original)

Jack Sasson, too, inferred a role for the statue in an ancestor cult on the basis of its find-spot:

> The presence of an altar in the vicinity of the seated statue may indicate that Idrimi was venerated, if not worshipped. That this occurred in the annex rather than the temple proper may further suggest that the veneration may have been private in nature, perhaps on the part of Šarruwa and the city's leaders, rather than priestly and cultically official. There is evidence, however, that the statue and its throne were to be transported outside the temple, probably during important ceremonies. (Sasson 1981, 323–24)

This list of scholars who connected the statue to an ancestor cult could be continued.[1] Interestingly, however, the statue's own excavator, Sir Leonard Woolley, did not share the opinion that Idrimi's statue was related to the deceased king's presence in an ancestor cult. Considering the historical Idrimi not to have been worthy of such veneration, he instead preferred to see the statue as an ancient art object, valued in its own time as "a 'primitive,' the oldest surviving

[1] Durand (2011, 134), e.g., stated that "la statue représente quelqu'un qui est désormais divinisé, donc déjà mort et intégré à un culte," while Greenstein (1995, 2424) proposed "the hypothesis that … Sharruwa had provided the statue and composed the inscription as an object of veneration, perhaps in an ancestral cult" and continued: "The theme of respect for the 'fathers' sits well with the notion that Idrimi should be enshrined for ancestor worship." Note that neither these scholars nor others who share this opinion have engaged with the difficult question of whether the putative veneration of Idrimi as an ancestor and any offerings such veneration implied "indicate a type of propitiation, based on the belief that the dead were powerful and dangerous" or "suggest a type of commensality that involved the sustenance of the dead" (Suriano 2018, 156; see n. 76 there for bibliography on the question, which is methodologically relevant even if its subject is Iron Age Judah). For a discussion of a possible reciprocal relationship between the dead Idrimi and the living, see §3.2.

monument of the local school of art" that was put on display in the temple (Woolley 1953, 118).[2]

An alternative scenario that is perhaps more convincing was put forward by Nadav Na'aman (1980a, 212), who saw in Idrimi's statue an example of the well-known ancient Near Eastern practice of a "king setting up his statue before the god" as a votive. In Na'aman's reconstruction, Idrimi's statue would not have received veneration itself but would have continually communicated the king's own veneration to a deity.[3] Manfried Dietrich and Oswald Loretz (1981, 250–51) suggested that Idrimi's statue may have originally been installed in the temple of a divinity as a votive and taken on a role in an ancestor cult only after his death (see §2.7). This suggestion was echoed by Dominik Bonatz (2000a, 133), who traced a path of ancient Near Eastern statuary, "der vom frühdynastischen Weihbild über die Statue des Idrimi zum syro-hethitischen Grabdenkmal führt."

Since the possibility that Idrimi's statue was a votive would account for its find-spot in a temple as much as its role in an ancestor cult would, we cannot use the find-spot in the temple alone as evidence for its role in an ancestor cult. Accordingly, I open this consideration of the historical context of the statue and its inscriptions by exploring this possible role more fully from both textual and material perspectives. I begin by discussing several passages in the inscription that are indicative of its role in an ancestor cult, a discussion that culminates in a reinterpretation of Idrimi's statement in lines 87–91 that he reestablished prayers and sacrifices at Alalah. Having confirmed the statue's role in an ancestor cult, I compare and contrast Idrimi's statue to other Syro-Anatolian ancestor statues dating to the Bronze Age. Doing this work highlights an important difference between the Statue of Idrimi and the other Bronze Age ancestor statues: They are all anepigraphic, in contrast to Idrimi's statue, which is famously inscribed. This observation allows us to return to lines 87–91 in order to take up the question of why Idrimi's statue is inscribed at all. These lines permit me to offer one possible answer to this question and, in turn, point the way forward to defining a historical context for the statue and its inscriptions.

---

[2] So also Woolley *apud* Smith 1949, 8: "It may be that an independent school of North Syrian sculpture began in Idri-mi's reign and was fostered by him, his own statue being the first major work of that school; if that were so, and if the fact were recognized, a high value might well be set by local patriotism on an outstanding 'primitive' of the local art tradition."

[3] Similarly, as discussed in §2.2, Goedegebuure (2012, 424) observed that "without being present the king was still present through the statue. So when the troops of Suppiluliuma entered the temple of Alalakh and discovered the Statue of Idrimi, they toppled and destroyed the statue (without damage to the inscription), not out of vandalism but in order to break the nexus between a ruler from the dynasty of deposed kings of Alalakh and its gods."

3.2. TEXTUAL PERSPECTIVES

From a textual perspective, there are indeed several indications in the inscriptions that seem to contextualize the statue in an ancestor cult. Perhaps the most important indication is that the body inscription twice refers to the object on which it is inscribed with the Akkadian word *ṣalmu* (ll. 92, 99). As discussed in §2.4, this difficult-to-translate word, for which the translation adopted herein, "statue," is inadequate, refers more accurately to a concept of visual (re)substantiation of a person rather than to a mimetic representation of him or her. In ancient Near Eastern contexts, the word had wide currency in both expressions of royal ideology (Bahrani 2003, 121–48) and ancestor veneration. With regard to the latter, the West Semitic cognate word *ṣlm* is used in Iron Age funerary inscriptions to refer to the image of the deceased that is engraved on the stelae. For instance, the funerary stele of Si'gabbar from Neirab (*KAI* 2.226) opens with the statement *śgbr kmr šhr bnrb znh ṣlmh*, "Si'gabbar, priest of Sahar in Neirab. This is his *ṣlm*" (*KAI* 2.226: 1–2; translation following McCarter 2000). Significantly, in these two lines the combination of text (the name of the deceased) and reference to his image (*ṣlm*) succinctly announces how the lengthier inscription that follows and the visual representation of Si'gabbar on the stele combine to encapsulate the deceased's identity (see also Suriano 2018, 152).

In discussing attestations of *ṣlm* in funerary contexts, Bonatz (2000a, 146) specifically highlighted the attestation of *ṣalmu* in the Idrimi inscription to emphasize how this word "wird in Syrien im 2. Jahrtausend noch ausschließlich auf Statuen angewandt" (146), in contrast to the first millennium, when it began to refer to images in relief as well. For him, this terminological development parallels a conceptual one as well: "Es wird nicht mehr allein das bezeichnet, was ein Monument ist, wie im Fall der Kultstele, sondern das, was es darstellt" (147). But Bonatz also freely admitted that "die Entwicklung hierzu verläuft unweigerlich graduell, wobei sich die Statuarik wiederum als konservatives, das Flachbild hingegen als innovatives Medium präsentiert" (147). Since, as discussed in more detail below (see §3.3), some of the first-millennium examples of funerary monuments more conservatively formed as statues display the same form as the Idrimi statue—not just the seated position but also the placement of the arms—it is possible to see a continuity in the sense in which *ṣalmu* is used in the body inscription with the sense of *ṣlm* in the first-millennium Iron Age funerary stelae.

Furthermore, in its second reference to the statue, the body inscription prefaces the word with the divine determinative: ^{d}ALAM(*ṣalma*) *an-ni-na-ti*$_{3}$, "this (divine) statue" (l. 99). Jean-Marie Durand (2011, 133–34 with n. 114) remarked about this writing that "dans les listes d'Ancêtres d'Ébla et d'Ougarit les noms humains sont précédés de l'idéogramme divin ou de la mention 'dieu'," and so he considered "d'après des parallèles syriens…, cela devrait signifier que la statue représente quelqu'un qui est désormais divinisé, donc déjà mort et intégré à un culte."[4] In this regard, it is worth noting that attestations of *ṣalmu* in two different texts from Middle Bronze Age (Level VII) Alalah, AlT 366 [40.05]: 12 and 22 and AlT 63 [22.11]: 21, refer to the funerary statue of a king and to the votive statue of a king brought into a temple, respectively. Significantly, in the instance of the funerary statue mentioned in AlT 366 [40.05], the word *ṣalmu* appears twice and is written both times with the divine determinative: *an-na* KU$_3$.BABBAR *ša* ^{d}ALAM, "*This is* the silver for the (divine) statue" (l. 12) and ŠU.NIGIN$_2$ 1 *me-at* 30 KU$_3$.BABBAR *ša* ^{d}ALAM, "Total: 130 (shekels) of silver for the (divine) statue" (ll. 21–22).[5] However, in the instance of the votive statue, which occurs in AlT 63 [22.11], the divine determinative is omitted: ALAM-*šu a-na* E$_2$ ^{d}IM *ú-še-lu-u*$_2$, "(The year in which) he (i.e., the king of Yamhad) brought his statue into the temple of Addu" (ll. 21–22). Therefore, the body inscription's twofold use of the word *ṣalmu* to refer to the object on which it is inscribed and, in particular, the presence of the divine determinative with the second attestation of the word suggests that the statue was understood to be a divinized ancestor.[6]

Another moment in the body inscription that is suggestive of a larger context of ancestor veneration occurs in the epithet of the Sun God in line 100, where this deity is called *bēl elûti u šaplīti bēlu eṭemmī*, "the lord of the Upper World and the Lower World, the lord of ghosts" (see the commentary to line 100 in §A.2 on the construct state form *bēlu*). These epithets are significant because they appeal to the Sun God in this deity's capacity to have power over the netherworld, as opposed to, for instance, associations with justice or favorable omens.[7] The choice of these

[4] Durand's statement should not be taken to mean that the presence of a divine determinative before ALAM occurred only in reference to statues of divinized ancestors. See, e.g., Emar 282: 2, 8, an inventory that lists "precious metals and stones that were used to adorn cultic statues and other sacred objects" (Rutz 2013, 132). In this text, however, the writing of ALAM with the divine determinative refers to specific statues of deities that were mentioned earlier in the text by name.

[5] For commentary on these lines and the argument that the text's reverse records the disbursal of silver as a raw material for the manufacture of a statue of a deceased king and not the melting down of a divine statue for burial goods, as argued elsewhere, see Lauinger 2022b, with discussion of previous literature (to which add Charpin 2008, 80–81).

[6] The absence of the divine determinative from the first attestation probably reflects an interest in orthographic variation more than a difference in the ontological status of the statue. Cf. the presence and absence of the determinative LU$_2$ before DUB.SAR in lines 98–99; see the commentary to line 98 in §A.2.

[7] See already Nougayrol 1951, 153–54 n. 13 ("Šamaš est bien connu dans sa double puissance, d'où découle son pouvoir, non moins attesté, de faire 'monter' les spectres"); Greenstein and Marcus 1976, 96 ("we are no doubt dealing here with the epithet of Šamaš as *bēl eṭemmī* 'lord of the spirits,'" citing the Cuthean Legend of Naram-Sin from Sultan Tepe [MC 7 337: 26]); Oller 1977a, 142–43 ("the epithet *bēl eṭemmi* is often found with Šamaš"); Dietrich and Loretz 1981, 229 ("Zur Beziehung zwischen der Sonne und den Toten in Ugarit, [citing Healey 1980]"); and all of the references cited in *CAD* 17, s.v.

epithets, in turn, implies that the afterlife is a primary concern of the inscription.[8] Second, once we recognize that the cheek inscription is distinct from the inscription on Idrimi's body (see §1.4), we also recognize that this invocation of the Sun God is actually the final note on which the body inscription concludes. In both its content and placement, then, the invocation of the Sun God establishes concern for the afterlife as the proper context for viewing the statue and reading the inscription.

Turning from the body inscription to the cheek inscription, we can see that it reflects a context of ancestor veneration as well. For instance, the cheek inscription's opening statement, "I was king for thirty years," implies that Idrimi's reign is over and that he is dead, yet he continues to speak to us through the inscription and so endures in the afterlife. More tellingly, the following statement that Idrimi inscribed his "labors" (*mānahtu*, l. CI 2) on the statue so that these labors might "encourage" (*tukkulu*, l. CI 2; see the commentary to the line in §A.2 on reading the signs as this verb rather than *dagālu*) his descendants, and in return they continually or regularly "pray" (*karābu*, l. CI 3) to him captures the reciprocal relationship between the dead and the living—the belief that the dead have agency in the world of the living and so require veneration and propitiation—that so often underlies the worship of ancestors.

At this point, a careful reader might note that the three textual moments raised so far as reflecting the statue's role in antiquity in an ancestor cult—its self-designation as a divine statue (^{d}ALAM = *ṣalmu*), the invocation of the Sun God as "the lord of above and below, the lord of ghosts," and the cheek inscription's positioning of the deceased Idrimi as standing in a reciprocal relationship with a living viewer—all occur outside the body inscription's narrative. Indeed, as discussed in §2.7, Dietrich and Loretz (1981, 245–46) argued that both the colophon and the cheek inscription are later additions to text that originally consisted of just the narrative (ll. 1–91). A distribution of textual reflections of an ancestor cult in parts of the Idrimi text that are exclusively external to the narrative could be taken as support for this argument. Accordingly, it is important to look at a passage from the body inscription's narrative that also reflects a context of ancestor veneration.

In the final passage of the narrative, Idrimi describes how he established regular offerings in accordance with divine signs (ll. 87–91); these offerings are typically read as being for Idrimi's ancestors, in the plural. For instance, here is Durand's (2011, 147–48) translation of the text:

> tout comme lorsque nos Pères fixèrent les rites réguliers des dieux de la ville d'Alalah et, lors, les offrandes de sacrifices pour nos Ancêtres, celles qui étaient

"šaplâtu," 2. For the netherworld aspect of the Sun God in Mesopotamia, see Krebernik 2009–2011, 605; for the same aspect in the Levant, see T. Lewis 1989, 38.

[8] It also finds an echo in the Mesopotamian literary text the Cuthean Legend of Naram-Sin; see §4.2 and the commentary to line 45 in §A.2.

accomplies pour eux, moi-même, je (les) ai faites point par point pour eux; celles-là-mêmes, les ayant faites pour eux, les ayant commises au soin d'Addu-nêrârî, mon fils.

This passage can be understood to have a double significance. Idrimi's statement that he provided offerings for his ancestors and then entrusted those offerings to the next generation would both highlight his own piety and instruct an ancient reader to provide offerings for *their* ancestor, Idrimi, now manifest in the statue standing before them.

If this interpretation seems relatively straightforward, things unfortunately get a little less so if when we look more closely at the crucial line, 89, in which Idrimi supposedly provides offerings to his ancestors. Durand transliterated the first half of the line as SISKUR$_2$.HI.A *ni-iq-qi* [*sic*].HI.A *ša a-bi-i-ni* and translated "les offrandes de sacrifices pour nos Ancêtres." However, if one looks at the signs being read in this edition as *a-bi-i-ni* for *abbīni*, "our ancestors, lit., our fathers," the reading of the third sign in the word as *-i-* seems very doubtful (see fig. 3.1), even allowing for the great degree of paleographic variation one routinely encounters in the Idrimi inscription. The presence of a large *Winkelhaken* in the middle of the sign simply does not fit.

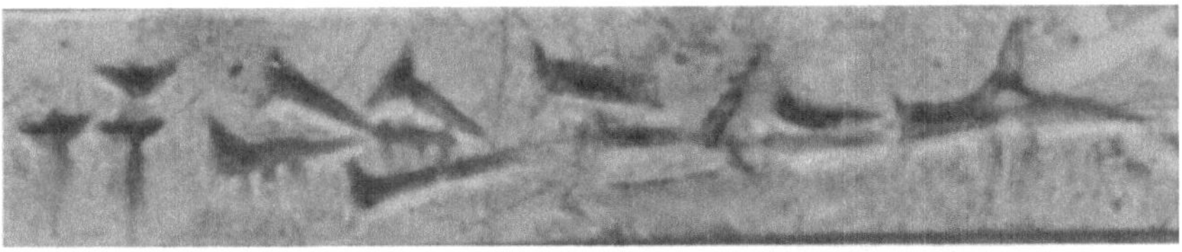

Figure 3.1. Signs read as *a-bi-i-ni* by Durand (2011, 147) in line 89.

Indeed, if we work backwards through the scholarship, we see that this reading was first put forward more tentatively by Dietrich and Loretz (1981, 206) as *a-bi-i*$^?$*-ni*. Some earlier editors of the text, however, had read the sign not as I but as BI. So Edward Greenstein and David Marcus (1976, 66) read the sign string as *a-bi-bi-ni* and understood it to be a crasis of *abi abini*, literally "our father's father" but translated by them as "our forefathers" (92). On the other hand Aharon Kempinski and Nadav Na'aman (1973, 214), followed in turn by Gary Oller (1977a, 113), chose to see the second putative BI as an example of dittography and deleted it: *a-bi-*<<*bi*>>*-ni.* [9] Yet a quick glance at the sign lists for the Idrimi

[9] Note that Kempinski and Na'aman (1973, 214) saw the emended form as plural (אבותי), while Oller (1977b, 16) took it as singular (*abī*{*bi*}*ni*, "our father"). The significance of a singular as opposed to plural form is taken up again later in this chapter (see §3.5); cf. Dietrich and Loretz (1981, 217), who objected to a form in the singular on contextual grounds!

inscription assembled by Dietrich and Loretz (1981, 232, 234), by Oller (1977a, 219, 221), and by me as an accompanying online resource to this book (see §2.9) shows that—again, even admitting the great degree of acceptable paleographic variation found in the inscription—reading the sign in question as either I or BI is not really satisfactory.

However, if we go back in the scholarship to Sidney Smith's original edition, we can find a solution to the problem. Smith's reading of the sign as NINDA$_2$ has been almost entirely ignored by later scholars, even though it is quite satisfactory from an epigraphic perspective. Figure 3.2 shows the sign in question juxtaposed with NINDA$_2$ as it appears in a manuscript of a paleographic list from Emar (Emar 538: 199 [Msk 74175a]; see Emar 6/2 444 and Gantzert 2011, 40 x 3]; see also Roche-Hawley 2012). Contextually, this reading fits the sense of the passage well. While NINDA$_2$ is most often used as a logogram for the Akkadian word *ittû*, "funnel (for a seeder-plow)," the sign does occur with the Akkadian equivalent *abu*, "father," in the lexical list Lu, albeit as preserved only in a first millennium manuscript of that lexical list (K.2051+: rev. ii 16; see MSL 12 127: 69; the equivalence is cited in *CAD* 1, s.v. "abu A," lexical section and discussed in 6).[10]

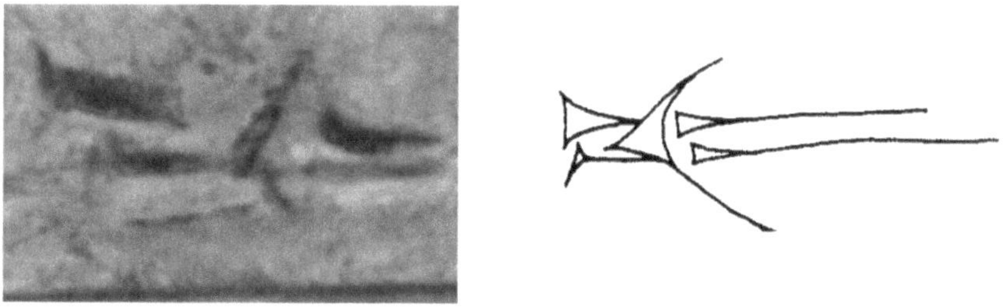

Figure 3.2. Juxtaposition of the sign read as I or BI in line 89 (left) with NINDA$_2$ from Emar 538 (right).

In fact, it was for this precise reason that Oller (1977a, 117), the only scholar known to me to have engaged with Smith's reading, dismissed it for being "rather obscure." But this dismissal may be too hasty. Implicit in Oller's objection to Smith's reading is the assumption that the body inscription's scribe could not have been familiar with the lexical list Lu. We may question if this assumption is reasonable, however. Lu had a fairly wide circulation in Syria and Anatolia during the Late Bronze Age,[11] and at those sites where it has been found, the text played

[10] The equivalence of *abu* for NINDA$_2$ is restored, but the restoration is certain from the attestations of *abu* that come before and after the entry; see below for a transliteration of the larger context.

[11] See Rutz 2013, 206 for references to manuscripts of Lu from Ekalte, Emar, Hattuša, and Ugarit as well as Nuzi farther to the east. The identification of the text from Ekalte, WVDOG 102: 81A, as a manuscript of Lu is tentative owing to the fact that only six lines

a role in cuneiform education (see, e.g., van Soldt 1995, 173–74; Veldhuis 2014, 282). Moreover, that curricular role and, indeed, the shape of the scribal curriculum in general seem to have been more or less the same across these sites.[12] Since other lexical lists that formed part of the scribal curriculum are attested at Late Bronze Age Alalah (S^{a}, Ura, and Diri; see §5.1 for the references and more discussion), the absence of Lu may be due to accidents of preservation and excavation, and we should actually *expect* Lu to have been known at the site as well. And, since the Idrimi inscription's scribe was clearly deeply trained in Akkadian cuneiform (see the discussion of orthographic and paleographic variation in §4.1), we should again *expect* him to have written out the text at some point as part of that training. To put things another way, the burden of proof should be on those who wish to argue that the body inscription's author *could not* have been familiar with Lu.

Alongside these deductive guiding principles, the larger context of the passage supports reading the sign in question as NINDA$_2$ = *abu* as well. If we look back at the larger context of the sign in question, we see that, two lines earlier, the scribe has used another logogram, A.A, to write the same word *abu*, "father." This logogram is also usually attested in lexical texts,[13] and, significantly, the two logograms A.A and NINDA$_2$ appear in sequence in the manuscript of Lu, mentioned above, that establishes a reading *abu* for NINDA$_2$ in the first place:

AD.DA : *a-bu* | NINDA$_2$ ⸢:⸣ [*a-bu*]
A.A : *a-bu* | PA$_4$: ⸢*a*⸣-[*bu*]
AB.BA : *a-bu* | ^{giš}GIBIL : ⸢*a-bi a-bi*⸣
A.A.A : *a-bi a-bi* | AB.BA : *še-e-bu*

AD.DA : "father" | NINDA$_2$: "[father]"
A.A : "father" | PA$_4$: "fat[her]"
AB.BA : "father" | ^{giš}GIBIL : "grandfather"
A.A.A : "grandfather" | AB.BA : "old man" (K.2051+: rev. ii 16–19)

Accordingly, Smith's reading *a-bi* NINDA$_2$-*ni*, instead of *a-bi-i-ni* or *a-bi-bi-ni* fits well both epigraphically and contextually, and Idrimi's claim to have sacrificed to his ancestor can continue to have instructed the ancient reader to do likewise.

---

of text are preserved; see, e.g., CDLI's classification of its subgenre as "Lu?" (https://cdli.ucla.edu/P347326).

12 For instance, according to Veldhuis (2014, 294), "The advanced (or rather advanced-elementary) curriculum [to which Lu belongs] in Ugarit, according to van Soldt's reconstruction, followed a sequence that is much like the Old Babylonian one" and "this group, in essence, defines the Emar lexical corpus."

13 Although see EA 300 [Gezer] for an attestation in western hybrid Akkadian that is in an epistolary, not lexical, context: *lu*-⸢*u*$_2$⸣ *i-ru-da-am* LUGAL EN-*ia ki-ma ša* A.A-*ia*, "I want to serve the king, my lord, just like my father" (ll. 20–22).

A reader might protest at this point that we have spent several pages only to end up more or less where we started out in our discussion of lines 87–91. Such is not actually the case. In addition to having put the reading of the sign in line 89 on firmer ground (not a bad thing), we now must read the first half of that line as SISKUR$_2$.HI.A$^{ni\text{-}iq\text{-}qi_2\text{.HI.A}}$ *ša a-bi* NINDA$_2$-*ni* and translate "the offerings (Akk. gloss: the offerings) for our grandfather" in the singular in place of, for example, Durand's "les offrandes de sacrifices pour nos Ancêtres" in the plural.[14] This shift from a chronologically floating plurality of ancestors to a historically situated single ancestor is extremely significant, and I take it up again at the end of the chapter. However, in order to appreciate its significance, we must move from textual perspectives on the role of the statue in an ancestor cult back to material perspectives.

3.3. MATERIAL PERSPECTIVES

At the beginning of this chapter, I noted that the primary reason the statue has been connected to ancestor veneration is its find-spot in a temple or temple annex. However, as discussed there, this find-spot could equally derive from an ancient function for the statue as a votive object. I return to the statue's find-spot and associated material culture below, but for now I observe simply that one primary reason why Idrimi's statue can be considered to have had a place in an ancestor cult is its visual similarity to other statues from the Syro-Anatolian cultural horizon that are generally understood to have had this function. Although such statues date from the Middle Bronze Age into the early Iron Age, in order to minimize the variables at play I restrict the discussion here to the corpus of stone statues dating to the Bronze Age that has been gathered by Katharina Teinz (2014). This corpus consists of fourteen statues; the relevant details are summarized in table 3.1.

The similarity between these statues and Idrimi is clearly shown by a juxtaposition of the Idrimi statue with the two statues that stood in front of the Royal Hypogeum at Qaṭna (see fig. 3.3 on p. 96). Like Idrimi, these statues show seated males who stare straight ahead and whose laps take the shape of square projections. Yet table 3.1 also makes clear that there are significant differences between the Statue of Idrimi and the ancestor statues from Qaṭna and elsewhere, which it lists.[15] For instance, almost all of those statues clasp a vessel in their right hand

[14] For a discussion of whether the signs *ni-iq-qi*$_2$.HI.A should be taken a gloss to SISKUR$_2$.HI.A or as a second noun, see the commentary to line 89 in §A.2.

[15] The table does not communicate another significant difference between the Statue of Idrimi and the other statues—namely, its relatively large size. Even when not seated on its throne, the Statue of Idrimi is about 20 percent taller than the tallest statues in table 3.1, the pair from the Royal Hypogeum at Qaṭna (85 cm in height); it is about 1000 percent taller than the statue from Area C of the Southern Palace at the same site (11 cm in height).

Site (find-spot)	MBA/LBA	Sex	Seated?	Holds bowl?	Inscription?
Ebla (Temple P2)	MBA	Male	Yes	Yes	No
Ebla (Temple P2)	MBA	Male	Yes	Yes	No
Ebla (near the South-West Gate)	Uncertain	Male	Yes	Yes	No
Hazor (Area H temple)	Uncertain	Male	Yes	Yes	No
Hazor (Area H temple)	Uncertain	Male	Yes	Yes	No
Hazor (Area F, surface)	Uncertain	Male	Yes	Yes	No
Hazor (Shrine of the Stelae)	LBA	Male	Yes	Yes	No
Nagar (Mittani palace, room 11)	LBA	Male	Yes	Yes	No
Qaṭna (Royal Hypogeum)	MBA (although LBA find-spot)	Male	Yes	Yes	No
Qaṭna (Royal Hypogeum)	MBA (although LBA find-spot)	Male	Yes	Yes	No
Qaṭna (secondary context in refuse pit)	LBA	Male	Yes	Damaged	No
Qaṭna (*Coupole de Loth*)	LBA	Male	Yes	Damaged	No
Qaṭnab\ (Area C of Southern Palace)	LBA	Male	Yes	No	No
Ugarit (near the *Sanctuaire aux rhytons*)	LBA	Male	Yes	Damaged	No

Table 3.1. Statues of ancestors from Bronze Age Syro-Anatolia.

Figure 3.3. Juxtaposition of the Statue of Idrimi (left) with statues from the Royal Hypogeum at Qaṭna (right). Source: Adapted by Author from Pfälzner 2006, 17. Copyright: Qaṭna Project of the University of Tübingen. Photo: K. Wita.

(the one exception is the small statue from the Southern Palace at Qaṭna), while Idrimi's right hand is empty and raised to cross his chest. And, of course, all of the other statues are anepigraphic, while Idrimi's statue bears the lengthy inscription across his body and another smaller inscription on his cheek.

The absence of a cup or bowl is no minor omission, for this object would have held libations, the liquid aspect of the deceased's mortuary repast. Bonatz has eloquently articulated the central place of the mortuary repast in the Syro-Anatolian belief system. Referring to the statue's later cousins, funerary stelae like the famous Katamuwa stele from Zincirli, Bonatz (2016, 184) explained that "the table laid with food and drink forms the focus of interaction between the living and dead … where the here and the hereafter are merged in a single visual space." With figures in the round, reference to the mortuary repast is made by the cup held ready for libations and also, perhaps, by the "cubic shape" of many statues' lower half which may have functioned as a table.[16] The absence of a cup in

[16] Bonatz 2016, 177: "One could also imagine a table set in front of figures in order to accommodate food and drink offerings, but in fact the table is already incorporated into the tectonic model of the statues. Especially in the case of the two female figures from Tell

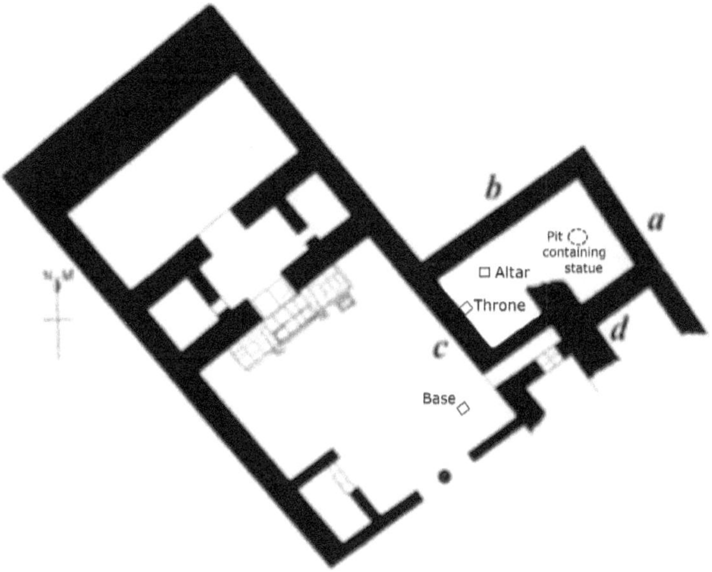

Figure 3.4. Reconstructed plan of Level IB temple and annex showing the find-spots of the pit containing the Statue of Idrimi, the statue's throne and base, and the altar. Adapted by author from Fink 2010, 24, plan 6.

Idrimi's hand, then, would seem to remove from the statue the central iconographic element that enabled it to collapse the realms of living and dead into a single mutually habitable space—that is, the element that would have allowed the statue to function meaningfully in an ancestor cult in the first place.

However, reference to a mortuary repast is absent only if we consider the statue in isolation, and not if we widen our gaze and consider Idrimi's statue as one part of a larger assemblage that comprised the statue's throne and, more importantly for this discussion, an altar. (See fig. 3.4 and §2.1 for more detailed discussion of the archaeological context of the statue, throne, and altar.) While thrones are well attested in rituals involving deceased kings (see Suriano 2009, 8, discussing previous literature), it is the altar that provides a visual representation of the statue's mortuary repast. In his discussion of the Idrimi statue and, in

Halaf, the lower part of the body is sculptured in a cubic shape turning the knees and thighs into a horizontal flat surface that in theory would easily have allowed use of this part of the sculpture as a table for offerings placed next to the cup in the right hand." While the Statue of Idrimi shares this cubic shape at a superficial level, the statue's lap is too sloped and narrow for offerings to have been placed there. (I thank my colleague Theodore Lewis for this observation.)

particular, the troubling absence of a vessel from its right hand, Bonatz (2000a, 132) already moved in this direction by noting that "zwar fehlt es der Statue … an dem Trinkgefäß in der Hand, doch weist ein davor aufgestellter Altar mit dem Reliefbild eines Tisches darauf hin, daß dem Bildnis Opfer dargebracht wurden." As can be seen in figure 3.5, the relief decoration on the altar actually depicts the heads and necks of waterfowl, perhaps ducks or geese. These waterfowl must be what Bonatz is referring to when he describes the altar as decorated "with the relief image of a table," for in their arrangement, they transform the altar into the characteristic "folding table" depicted laden with offerings in numerous first millennium Syro-Anatolian funerary reliefs. But not mentioned by Bonatz—yet possibly even more significant—is the decision to depict these "table legs" as waterfowl in the first place, since waterfowl are a common food offering in images of mortuary repasts (Bonatz 2000a, 94–95; Struble and Rimmer Hermann 2009, 31; Sanders 2013, 45). They are also well attested textually as offerings in funerary rites (e.g., the Ugaritic funerary text *KTU* 1.161 [RS 34.126]: 30; see T. Lewis 1989, 27) or to gods of the Underworld (e.g., the Hittite ritual *CTH* 446; see Collins 1997, 170). As an assemblage, then, statue and altar do refer to the mortuary repast, thereby creating a space where living and dead could mingle, even if Idrimi's statue does not grasp the traditional cup or bowl.[1]

Figure 3.5. The altar, showing relief decoration. Adapted by author from Wooley 1955. Plate LII.

In this visual reference to a mortuary repast, as well as in its seated position and cube-like lower half, Idrimi's statue fits well with the fourteen other Bronze

[1] It should also be emphasized that the position of Idrimi's arms is not without parallel; Schachner, Schachner, and Karablut (2002) published two Iron Age statues (Girbel 2 and Girbel 3) that have their arms in a similar position (see esp. 120 for their comparison of the statues to the Statue of Idrimi). The Statue of Idrimi and Girbel 2 and 3 may therefore belong to a tradition of seated male ancestor statues that is less attested than the tradition in which the seated male holds a bowl.

Age Syro-Anatolian statues of ancestors. These similarities make the statue's remaining difference all the more remarkable: As is clear from table 3.1, the fourteen other statues are all anepigraphic while the Statue of Idrimi is inscribed with a lengthy inscription. Indeed, the anepigraphic nature of these statues may have been as important to their ancient role in an ancestor cult as the visual references to the mortuary repast. To return to the Royal Hypogeum at Qaṭna and the pair of statues that stood outside its entrance, Peter Pfälzner (2012, 218) has argued with respect to the accumulated bones that made up the tertiary and quaternary burials therein:

> no inscriptions are present, in the form of stone engravings, written tablets or inscribed seals, which would identify the buried persons or support their individual re-identification among the anonymous assemblage of collective burials within the tomb after a certain period of time. Ultimately, this also explains why the two completely identical ancestor statues, placed next to the entrance to the grave chambers in the ante-chamber of the Royal Hypogeum of Qatna and which were definitely venerated here as dynastic royal ancestors through ritual activities, lack any inscription or any individual rendering.

In other words, the absence of any inscriptions on the pair of statues from Qaṭna is not happenstance but a purposeful omission, one that was meant to deny the statues any individual identities and instead enable them to embody the ghosts of the royal family's collective—and therefore nameless—ancestors.

The fact that the other Bronze Age examples of these seated ancestor statues are also anepigraphic suggests that they, too, played a similar role in facilitating the veneration of collective ancestors. This suggestion seems probable in light of Teinz's (2014, 15) observation, made in connection with the statues from Ebla, that the existence of the roughly contemporaneous statue of Ibbit-Lim at the site demonstrates "that royal statues at that time could be inscribed" in contexts that did not involve the veneration of ancestors. Indeed, this understanding of why Bronze Age ancestor statues are anepigraphic is very much in keeping with the conclusions reached by Bonatz (2000a, 159–65; 2000b, 210) in his studies of Syro-Anatolian funerary monuments, in which the appearance in the early Iron Age of funerary monuments that are inscribed with the names of specific deceased persons is contextualized as a response of social patterns to new historical conditions.

3.4. A MIDDLE BRONZE AGE DATE FOR THE STATUE?

So why was Idrimi's statue inscribed? In fact, as discussed in more detail below, there is evidence to suggest that originally it was not; rather, the statue was anepigraphic and existed in this state probably for a substantial period of time before the inscription was added to it. As discussed in §2.7, a similar suggestion has been made before, but for different reasons, by Dietrich and Loretz (1981, 245–50). According to them, Idrimi's statue was originally an anepigraphic votive statue,

Figure 3.6. The beginning of lines 10–12.

and the narrative of his life (ll. 1–91 in the inscription) was originally written on a tablet. At some point in antiquity, statue and tablet were brought together, and lines 102–104 (= CI 1–3) were carved onto the statue's cheek to emphasize that the two objects functioned as an assemblage. Only at a later date still were lines 1–91 copied from the tablet onto the statue, at which time the curse formulae and colophon (ll. 92–101) were added as well. However, the claim that a tablet containing the narrative of Idrimi's deeds had a stand-alone existence depends on identifying the eighth sign of line CI 2 as DUB(*tuppu*). As discussed in the commentary to the line, collation does not support this identification, and, with the disappearance of the putative tablet from line CI 2, the scenario reconstructed by Dietrich and Loretz cannot be sustained.

However, other evidence does support seeing the Statue of Idrimi as originally anepigraphic: In at least three places on the statue, the cuneiform signs carved on the statue have clearly been inscribed around damage, which therefore must have occurred to the statue before it was inscribed. One example of such damage occurs near the beginning of the text, in lines 11–12, lines that are among the more cryptic in the entire inscription. They come at the time when Idrimi has the realization that spurs him to leave the safety of Emar and begin his adventures in an active as opposed to reactive capacity. As discussed in the commentary to line 12 in §A.2, there have been many different interpretations of what exactly Idrimi's realization is, in part because the lines do not seem to display the parallel structure we expect, and in part because some damage at the beginning of line 12 has conveniently allowed scholars to offer restorations and work around that problem.

In his study of the scribe Šarruwa, however, Na'aman (1980b, 113) observed that "nothing was written at the beginning of line 12. That there was a break in the stone from the very beginning can be seen also in line 11, where the first sign was shifted beyond that break." Dietrich and Loretz (1981, 212) subsequently confirmed Na'aman's position ("Der Anfang der Zeile ist unbeschriftet"), as has my own personal collation of the line (see fig. 3.6). As can be seen in the figure, the damage to the surface of the statue at the beginning of line 12 continues up into line 11. But the surface of the top half of line 11 has not been damaged, and it is clear that nothing was inscribed in that space; the first sign of line 11 is LU, which has been indented to begin after the damage. In this regard, the first sign of line 12, A, is even more striking. It is indented even further into the line and occupies a raised position in the line, as if it had been fitted into the small amount of space remaining above the damage to the surface of that line. It is worth noting that lines 1–23 of the inscription (i.e., the lines inscribed on the right half of Idrimi's chest) are not typically indented. Besides lines 11–12, only line 4 is indented. (The reason for that line's indentation is unclear.)

To be sure, determining whether damage to the surface of the statue occurred before the statue was inscribed can be very difficult. For instance, line 14 is atypical because, as can be seen in figure 3.7, the line continues well past the end of the other lines above and below it, continuing to just above Idrimi's thumb. The line is also noteworthy because there is a large space between the signs NA and MA in the phrase *ina māt*. Why would so much space be left between these two signs if there were still so many more signs to be written in the line? Is it significant that there is damage to the surface of the statue in the very space that has been left between *ina* and *māt*? Could it be that this damage already existed when the signs were inscribed so that the scribe was forced to leave the space between the signs even if it meant that the end of the line would run over? Such a conclusion is tempting but ultimately speculative. The scribe could have left the space between *ina* and *māt* for some other reason and only subsequently decided not to divide the construct chain *māt huribte* over two lines; the damage between *ina* and *māt* could then have occurred after the statue was inscribed.

Figure 3.7. Composite image showing the extent of line 14 and space between NA and MA signs.

Nonetheless, line 73 does provides another instance where the surface of the statue had clearly suffered damage before the statue was inscribed, as can be seen in figure 3.8 on the next page. This line, which occurs near the bottom of Idrimi's left leg, describes the inanimate plunder that Idrimi seized from the Hittites during

Figure 3.8. The end of lines 72–74.

his raid into their land: *nam-ku-ri-šu-⸢nu bu⸣-še-šu-nu ba-ši-tu-<šu>-nu*, "(I took) their valuables, their luxury goods, <the>ir precious items." Significantly, there is damage to the surface of the statue at the end of the line; the final two signs of the line, TU and NU, have been inscribed off the statue's body and at a 90-degree angle on the throne so as to avoid this damage.[18]

The position of the signs *a-na-ku*, at the beginning of line 90, next to Idrimi's index finger, provides a third example in which it seems indisputable that the signs were carved around preexisting damage to the statue. But this example also illustrates how complicated the relative sequences of surface damage and inscription were. As can be seen in figure 3.9, there is a crack in the surface of the statue in line 90 that runs from Idrimi's fingertip through the A and NA signs before curving downward into line 91. This crack runs into a large abrasion that occupies the bottom of line 90 and the top of line 91. Significantly, the third sign in line 90, KU, is squeezed into the small space above the damage to the bottom of this line. Consequently, the abrasion, but not the crack, was present on the surface of the statue before *a-na-ku* was inscribed. Next, the signs *a-na-ku* were inscribed in the space in front of and above the abrasion. Subsequently, a crack spread out from the abrasion, moving through the A and NA signs to the left and down into the abrasion, either because the abrasion had already created a weak point on the surface of the statue or because the statue sustained additional damage. Accordingly, while the surface of the statue was clearly damaged in some place *after* it was inscribed, the placement of the KU sign into the top half of line 90 demonstrates that the statue's surface was also damaged in places *before* it was inscribed.

[18] See the commentary to line 73 §A.2 for discussion of the emendation. Smith's (1949, 20) unfortunate transliteration of the line's final word as *ba-ši-tu-[šu]-nu* in his edition (i.e., as a restoration and not an emendation) subsequently created confusion in the scholarship.

Figure 3.9. The beginning of lines 90–91.

What do we make of these three examples of the preexisting damage to the surface of the statue, to which some others, albeit less conclusive, could still be added? Smith seems to have considered the raw material from which the statue was carved to have been of poor quality.[19] Similarly, with regard to the damage at the beginning of lines 11–12, Na'aman (1980b, 113) considered that "there was a break in the stone from the very beginning." Neither scholar offered any additional discussion, but their comments assume one possible explanation for the preexisting damage: The particular block of stone that was chosen for the statue possessed flaws, perhaps from the process of quarrying or transporting the stone or from carving the statue. This scenario is difficult to confirm or deny. On the one hand, the statue is made of magnesite, which is a soft and brittle stone that is easily damaged, so it is possible that the raw material could be damaged during the various stages of the *châine opératoire*;[20] on the other hand, should we imagine that the artisan(s) and patron(s) responsible for the statue knowingly and willingly went ahead with a piece of stone the surface of which was marred in multiple places?

However, there is another possible explanation for the damage—namely, that the statue had some period of use before it was inscribed and that it was damaged during this time. According to this scenario, the statue possessed an intrinsic significance such that this surface damage was not enough to disqualify it from being the inscription. Again, the scenario is difficult to confirm or deny completely, but its explanatory power is greater than the scenario above because it accounts for another characteristic of the statue that has been much remarked upon. As discussed in §2.4, the statue's dress, specifically the conical hat and the

---

[19] See, e.g., his comment in the introduction to the original edition: "Faults in the basic stone, and in some cases superficial damage, have everywhere been avoided in the cutting of the inscription" (Smith 1949, 10). See also his note to line 73, where he remarked, "after *ši* there is a long piece of bad surface avoided by the scribe" (Smith 1949, 21).

[20] For a discussion of the statue's material, see Lauinger 2019, 26 n. 17 and 27–28. In that article, I suggested that the unusual choice of magnesite may have been motivated in part by the knowledge that the statue was to be inscribed. The stone's relative softness would have made it easier to carve, and, if the signs were subsequently painted, the white color would have helped them stand out. In light of the argument presented here that the statue was originally anepigraphic, this suggestion needs to be abandoned.

Figure 3.10. Niqmepa of Yamhad wearing a conical hat and robe with fringed hem. Source: Adapted by author from Collon 1975, no. 6.

robe with fringed hem (the so-called *Wulstsaum*), is characteristic of the Middle Bronze Age and is well attested in images of kings in the glyptic found at Level VII Alalah itself, as can be seen in the example in figure 3.10. However, the conical hat and fringed robe seem to have disappeared, with one exception from the glyptic of Late Bronze Age (Level IV) Alalah, although parallels can be found in statuary dating to the Late Bronze Age at other sites.

The explanations found over the decades in the scholarship for why a statue dated to the Late Bronze Age (whether early or late) wears such distinctive Middle Bronze Age dress has varied. For instance, Moortgat (1949, 176) saw in this dress simply the survival of a Middle Bronze Age stylistic feature. More recently, Tallay Ornan (2012, 9–10) suggested, with regard to a similarly attired statue from Late Bronze Age Hazor, that the sculptor could have deliberately "imitated an older outfit." But, of course, the need to explain why the statue is adorned in dress more characteristic of the Middle Bronze Age vanishes if we understand the statue to have actually been created during the Middle Bronze Age and thus to have had a substantial period of use—centuries, perhaps—before the historical Idrimi ruled Alalah, let alone before the statue was inscribed. This period of use would have provided ample opportunities for damage to occur to the surface of the statue before it was inscribed.[1]

[1] For a similar situation with a statue bearing an inscription of Samsu-iluna, see Weeden and Lambert 2020, 18. Mark Weeden (personal communication) also points to the Hieroglyphic Luwian ANDAVAL inscription; see Hawkins 2000, 514–15, where it is described as "part of stele cut down to circular fragments for reuse (column base?)."

3.5. FROM COLLECTIVE ANCESTOR TO HISTORICAL ANCESTOR

It must be stressed that this scenario—an anepigraphic statue existed for a period of time before being inscribed—cannot be conclusively proven. Nor can the other scenario that has been raised—the statue was carved from a flawed piece of stone—be conclusively falsified. However, the first scenario seems preferable because it does not require us to posit that the artisan(s) and patron(s) responsible for the statue knowingly and willingly went ahead with a flawed piece of stone, and it accounts for the style of the statue's dress, which is more characteristic of the Middle than the Late Bronze Age. Positing an original Middle Bronze Age date for the Statue of Idrimi also means that the situation for this statue—created in the Middle Bronze Age but used into the Late Bronze Age—is actually quite similar to the situation for the pair of statues from Qaṭna from outside Royal Hypogeum, which were created in the Middle Bronze but found *in situ* outside a structure whose final period of use was in the Late Bronze Age (Novak 2004). And if we remember Pfälzner's (2012, 281) remarks quoted above (§3.3), also in relation to Qaṭna statues, that the ancient rationale for those ancestor statues' being anepigraphic was to deny them individual identities and allow them to embody the royal family's collective ancestors, we can truly appreciate the significance of inscribing an originally anepigraphic statue at Alalah. The act would have transformed a nameless, collective ancestor into a very specific one—namely, Idrimi.

In fact, this action has a textual echo in the inscription itself, specifically in lines 87b–91, the passage at the end of the narrative where Idrimi claims to have made the proper cult offerings. This passage was discussed above (see §3.2) to argue for the identification of the sign NINDA₂ in line 89, and I give here the larger context:

> Just as our father, himself, attended to the signs of the "gods" (i.e., divinized ancestors) of Alalah, so I, myself, was regularly performing the offerings (Akk. gloss: the offerings) for our grandfather that he had regularly caused to be performed. I regularly performed these things, and then I entrusted them to the authority of IM-nerari, my son. (ll. 87b–91)

In addition to following Durand (2011) in seeing the "gods of Alalah" as a reference to divinized ancestors at the city (as argued in the commentary to l. 88 in §A.2), a primary way in which this translation differs from many, although not all, previous translations is in taking A.A in line 87 and *a-bi* NINDA₂-*ni* in line 89 as singular forms.[22] Accordingly, in the passage at the end of the narrative of his life in which Idrimi speaks of the cult, he specifically mentions the prayers and offerings "our" father made for "our" grandfather. In other words, just as the act of

22 Oller (1977a, 16, 113, 115, 117) also understood both A.A (l. 87) and *a-bi* NINDA₂-*ni* (read by him as *a-bi-*<<*bi*>>*-ni*) as singular forms, although to different effect.

carving the inscription into the statue transformed it from a collective ancestor into a specific, historically situated one, so, too, does the passage at the end of the inscription speak of an ancestor cult in terms of specific, historically defined generations.[23]

Furthermore, as Oller (1977a, 117) observed, the historically situated nature of this important passage "allows for a neat [progression]—my father did, I do, my son will do." It looks not just to the past but also to the future. In particular, in line 91, the final line of the narrative of Idrimi's life, Idrimi states that he "entrusted" (*iptaqid*) the ancestral offerings to the care of his son, the mysterious IM-nerari, an individual who is not otherwise attested in the Late Bronze Age documentation from Alalah, and who has been described alternately as a successor king to Idrimi and simply as an official with religious duties (see §6.2 for some discussion of the secondary literature). Significantly, what has not been noted in the many discussions about IM-nerari is that the root **pqd*, "to entrust," has a special resonance in the context of ancestor cults.

In particular, the root appears in Akkadian as an active participle, *pāqidu*, to designate an individual who was responsible for providing offerings to the ghosts of the dead (Bayliss 1973, 116; Suriano 2018, 180–83). One of the most famous attestations of *pāqidu* in this context comes, of course, from Tablet XII of the Standard Babylonian recension of Epic of Gilgamesh, when Gilgamesh asks the ghost of Enkidu, *ša eṭemmašu pāqida lā īšû tāmur*, "Did you see the one whose ghost does not have a *pāqidu*?," and Enkidu's ghost answers, *ātamar šukkulāt diqāri kusīpāt akali ša ina sūqi nadâ ikkal*, "I have seen (him). He eats the scrapings from a pot (and) crumbs of bread that are dropped in the street" (SB Gilg. XII 152–153).[24] But, when used in this sense, the root was productive, and finite verbal forms occur just as in line 91. For instance, in the Great Hymn to Šamaš, the Sun God is invoked in his capacity as a god who cares for (*paqādu*) the gods of the Underworld, the Anunnaki: *šaplāti m[a]lkī Kusu Anunnaki tapaqqid*, "In the Underworld, you care for the counselors of Kusu, the Anunnaki" (*BWL* 126:31).

In the temporal realm, the individual who served as a *pāqidu* of ghosts was typically a familial relation; such is implied, for instance, by the placement of this passage in the Epic of Gilgamesh, which follows a series of questions in which Gilgamesh asks Enkidu's ghost whether he saw men with an increasing number of sons, who are reported to be in increasingly happier situations in the Underworld. But an individual could also act as the *pāqidu* for ghosts to whom he was not genetically related. This possibility is made clear most poignantly in the famous Genealogy of Hammurabi, which opens with a list of the deceased kings of

---

[23] The use of the plural pronominal possessive suffix "our" rather than "my" may make it more likely that Idrimi refers to the two generations of Alalah's rulers who preceded him than to his own biological father and grandfather, unless he presumed that his audience would be his siblings.

[24] One manuscript has *pāqidu* as a substantivized plural (*pa-qi₂-di*; ms N: vi 9).

Babylon to whose ghosts Ammi-ṣaduqa provides offerings but then concludes: *awīlūtum kališin ištu ṣītim adu erbim ša pāqidam u sāhiram lā išû alkānimma anniam aklā anniam šitiā ana Ammi-ṣaduqa mār Ammi-ditana šar Bābili kurbā*, "As for all humanity from east to west that lacks a *pāqidu* and *someone to invoke their name*, come here, eat this, drink this, (and) bless Ammi-ṣaduqa, son of Ammi-ditana, king of Babylon" (*JCS* 20 96–97: 36–43). As Matthew Suriano (2018, 183) has described it:

> The effect is extraordinary. Not only does Ammi-saduqa claim royal ancestors as his own, but he also portrays himself as the great *pāqidu* for his people, rendering care for both the living and dead. The *kispu*, the ritual feeding of the dead, would never be denied to any subject of Ammi-saduqa. The Babylonian king's actions appealed to genealogy. Although his concept of genealogy was narrowly defined and quite exclusive, he was still able to cast this appeal broadly across the Amorite cultural landscape of the Middle Bronze Age through his reference to an important social obligation: care for the dead.

Suriano went on to note that "the same strategy is at work in the Ugaritic tablet *KTU* 1.161," the funerary text for deceased royal ancestors already mentioned in §3.3 (2018, 183 n. 16).

Indeed, in an earlier study of this text from Ugarit, Suriano (2009) explored how providing offerings to both the dynasty's long-dead collective ancestors and the ghost of the recently deceased king played a crucial role in "the process in which a dead king joined the royal ancestors and his son became the new king" (17; for Niqmaddu III of Ugarit as recently deceased, see T. Lewis 1989, 34–35 with n. 149). Within the context of an ancestor cult, then, the body inscription's use of the root **pqd* (tellingly, in the form *aptaqidšunu*; i.e., in Idrimi's own voice) identified IM-nerari as the new *pāqidu* responsible for providing offerings to the ghosts of Idrimi and his immediate predecessor on the throne of Alalah. In doing so, it also identified IM-nerari as the new, legitimate holder of that dynasty's throne. Just as the inscription transformed a nameless, collective ancestor into a specific, historical, and dynastic one, it transformed the statue from a locus of religious action into one for political action as well.

But what are the historical circumstances that provoked this transformation? Relatedly, how is the identity of IM-nerari entangled with them? In the next chapter, I will try to show that the inscriptions are not simply describing events but making an argument that had contemporary relevance. Understanding that the inscriptions are advancing an argument implies that the succession of IM-nerari was anticipated to meet with resistance. Both the specifics of this argument and the recognition that the succession was contested will allow us to begin to define a historical context for the inscriptions more closely.

4
Arguments

Although it may be an unexpected way to try and establish a historical context for the statue, this chapter begins by looking at the inscriptions' paleography and orthography. The reason for beginning with paleography and orthography is that these features of the inscriptions are characterized by a great degree of variation, and I argue in this chapter this variation is in fact a paralinguistic strategy that reflects—and so evidences—a larger textual program. I locate the larger textual program in attestations of the word *mānahtu* in the cheek and body inscriptions. In the cheek inscription, the word evokes *narû* literature, a modern term for Mesopotamian pseudo-autobiographical texts in which kings left first-person accounts of their misfortunes so that future kings might learn from them. In the body inscription, the word is used with a meaning, "tribute," that derives from the political discourse of Late Bronze Age Syro-Anatolia. The use of the word in the cheek inscription transforms Idrimi into a royal figure whose actions should serve as an example; the uses in the body inscription show how this is so. In their interaction, the inscriptions are making an argument, and their paleography and orthography support this argument by signaling learning and pedigree.

4.1. PALEOGRAPHY AND ORTHOGRAPHY: MAKING SENSE OF VARIATION

The paleography of the inscriptions, like the statue itself, has been the object of value judgments to a surprising degree.[1] (See §2.4 for a review of literature on the statue's aesthetic value.) These value judgments began already in Sidney Smith's (1949) original edition, where he described the carving as "a shallow cutting, where the mason's work has been badly done" (iv). A similar sentiment is found in the reviews of Smith's edition, where, for instance, A. Leo Oppenheim (1955,

[1] This section incorporates, revises, and expands upon material published in Lauinger 2019.

199) characterized the paleography as "abominable." Moving forward through time, Gary Oller (1977a, 3) catalogued "for example 22 different variations on the KI sign, 13 on the NA, and 5 on the URU," concluding that "an explanation for this hodge-podge is difficult to obtain, ... [but] much of the fault must lie with the stone mason who carved the statue." A few years later, Jack Sasson (1981, 316) echoed this statement, noting that the body inscription's narrative succeeds "despite the irritating ignorance displayed by the carver of the inscription," while Edward Greenstein (1995, 2424) remarked with somewhat more restraint that "the inscription was written inconsistently and copied onto the stone with less than complete professionalism."

The leap to value judgments of the sort that describes the variation in the paleography of the Idrimi inscriptions as "abominable"—a descriptor not commonly met in academic discourse—suggests that something other than putatively objective scholarly analysis is at work behind the scenes. Perhaps it is simply frustration with sign forms that anyone who has spent time seriously working with the text knows are quite difficult. But is it also possible that this scholarly opinion has been influenced by a modern, typographical perspective that prizes consistency and condemns variation, one that associates uniformity with more serious or more formal documents and variation with an informal or even childish register? What if the paleographic variation we encounter in the inscriptions was actually deliberate?

Indeed, despite his opinion that the carving had been poorly done, such was actually Smith's (1949, 11) opinion, for he wrote in his introduction that "the present inscription is peculiar not so much in the types of error, as in the apparently intentional variation in the form of signs; incompatible forms of one and the same sign occur within a few lines, sometimes in the same line, occasionally next to one another." However, Smith chose not to develop this observation,[2] and the idea that the inscriptions' paleographic variation was deliberate has received relatively little attention in the scholarship over the subsequent three quarters of a century. Two exceptions are Benno Landsberger and Carole Roche-Hawley, both of whom suggested that paleographic variation could be deliberately employed in the inscriptions as a marker of learning and erudition. For instance, Landsberger (1954, 58 n. 117) remarked that "Šarruwa zeigt seine Gelehrsamkeit, indem er alle im Paläographie-Unterricht ... gelernten Zeichenformen alternierend verwendet..., auch die Schreibweisen ständig variiert (z.B. *ah-hé*.HI.A und LÚ.MEŠ.ŠEŠ.MEŠ)." Similarly, while Roche-Hawley (2024, 38) qualified the overall result made by the inscriptions as "fairly poor" from a modern perspective, she remarked that "while many scholars have insisted on the eccentric aspects of

---

2 "But why ... different forms should be employed side by side remains, to me, a mystery" (Smith 1949, 12); cf. Oller (1977a, 3), who, in the continuation of the quote cited above, admitted that blaming the stone mason "does not explain the larger variations from one type of sign form to another."

this syllabary, it does not seem any more bizarre to us than that which appears in school texts in more or less contemporary corpora such as the paleographic list RS 14.128+ from Ugarit." She concluded that "the result for the 'reader' in ancient Alalah is evident: a statue in the likeness of Idrimi bears a text inscribed in a highly valued and prestige imbibed form of cuneiform—prestigious in its own right—after the fashion of the great Mesopotamian monarchs of the past" (Roche-Hawley 2024, 38). In a note, she specified further the means by which the statue made its impression on its ancient reader, describing him as "[a] 'reader' who would have been more likely to 'view' rather than 'read.'" (n. 13; for more discussion of this important point, see §5.3).

Landsberger's and Roche-Hawley's suggestions that the paleographic variation that has so infuriated modern editors of the text is a deliberate feature, intended to display the scribe's erudition by showing his broad knowledge of sign forms, archaic and contemporary, monumental and cursive, is worth engaging seriously because the material expression of a text has, of course, great potential to influence its contemporary reception. However, paleography can be difficult to discuss; what seems like a meaningful difference in sign forms to one observer may be considered by another observer to be lacking in significance, understood as a scribal error by yet another, or as the basis for identifying a different sign altogether.[3] For instance, in line 61 of the body inscription, a string of signs seems to employ two different forms of the QA sign in order to spell the word *qaqqari* as *qa-qa-ri* (see fig. 4.1). Indeed, in his comment to this line, Smith (1949, 19) noted "the careful distinction between two forms of *qa*, the first being the form common in B.K. [= "Texts found at Boğaz Köi"], the second an irregular variant of the Babylonian form." But Nadav Na'aman (1980b, 115) subsequently objected to this reading on precisely these grounds, considering it "doubtful since the repetition of two different signs in both lines can hardly be accidental" (where "the repetition of two different signs" means the repetition of two different forms of the same sign), so he wanted to identify the signs differently (although he did not, in fact, offer a new reading).[4]

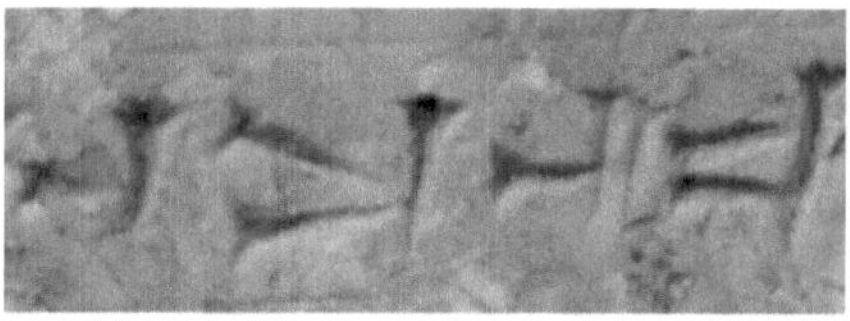

Figure 4.1. The word *qa-qa-ri* (l. 61), showing paleographic variation of the QA sign.

[3] For a more theoretical discussion and a methodology for overcoming this interpretive difficulty, see Homan 2020, esp. 10–34. Unfortunately, the method described there requires a larger sample of sign forms than the Idrimi inscriptions provide.

[4] It is of some methodological value to make explicit the assumptions underlying Na'aman's objection. The first assumption is that we should expect attestations of a single sign to be identical in form. The second assumption is that, if the forms of a single sign are different,

Therefore Landsberger's observation, quoted above, that paleographic variation and orthographic variation should be seen as two facets of a larger program, points a way forward. Establishing orthographic variation is more straightforward (once there is a consensus as to the identification of signs), so one can move more quickly from arguing about data to interpreting that data. And if it can be shown that orthographic variation not only exists in the text but seems to have been intentionally deployed, then there is good reason to suppose that the paleographic variation that occurs alongside it was also, as Landsberger suggested, intentional.[5]

And there is a good deal of orthographic variation in the text. Just as the inscriptions seem to steadfastly resist using a single form for any sign, so, too, do they resist writing words in any sort of consistent manner. For instance, the body inscription employs nine different ways of pluralizing forms in cuneiform: the plural markers MEŠ and HI.A, which appear alone and accompanying syllabic spellings of the plural, the plural marker DIDLI, the reduplication of a logogram, pluralized determinatives, and pluralized determinatives used with the plural marker HI.A, in addition to straightforward syllabic spellings of plural forms. Of course, to some extent, writing plural forms in a multiplicity of ways can be seen as a feature of cuneiform in general and, even more so, of the way in which cuneiform was used to write western hybrid Akkadian during the Late Bronze Age. By way of comparison, plural forms are written four different ways in EA 55, a well-preserved letter of sixty-six lines sent by Akizzi, king of Qaṭna, to the Egyptian pharaoh: the plural markers MEŠ and HI.A after logograms, straightforward syllabic spellings of plural forms, and pluralized determinatives used with the plural marker MEŠ.

This comparison is not meant to suggest that the Idrimi inscriptions indicate the plural in ways that are otherwise unattested in western hybrid Akkadian texts. For instance, two ways of indicating a plural form found in the Idrimi inscriptions but not in EA 55—the reduplication of logograms and DIDLI—are both attested elsewhere in the Canaanite Amarna correspondence (e.g., KUR.KUR in EA 74: 2 [Byblos] and URU.DIDLI.MEŠ in EA 65: 9 [Amurru]; see Rainey 1996, 1:27–28 for a general discussion of the orthography of plural forms in the Amarna letters). In fact, all of the strategies for marking plurality found in the Idrimi

---

the difference is the result of an accident. Of course, these two assumptions are not necessarily valid.

[5] The inscriptions' orthographic variation has received a bit more attention in the scholarship than the paleography. For instance, Borger (1968, 22) remarked on the difficulty of reading the text "wegen ihres barbarischen Akkadisch und ihrer 'gelehrten' Orthographie." Similarly, Moran (1975, 161 n. 37) invoked the Idrimi inscriptions in his explanation of the Jerusalem scribe's use of a rare sign value in EA 286: 22: "We suspect the answer to be that we are dealing with a 'learned' provincial scribe (see Šarruwa of the Idrimi inscription) who is displaying his learning, probably in the hope of impressing his colleague in Egypt."

inscriptions were also used by other scribes writing western hybrid Akkadian. Rather, the hypothesis being explored here is whether the Idrimi text brings together a multiplicity of ways of indicating plural nominal and adjectival forms in cuneiform as a deliberate strategy to display the scribe's erudition, as suggested by Landsberger, Rykle Borger, and William Moran.

Against this hypothesis, one could argue that the multiplicity of plural forms simply reflects the scribe's education, in which students conventionally learned to write some words in the plural one way and other words in another way. The fact that individual words are written in multiple orthographies in the inscriptions argues against this scenario, though. For instance, the polysemic word *mānahtu*, which is freighted with great significance in the inscriptions, as discussed in detail later in this chapter in §4.2 and §4.3, is pluralized three different ways in the space of less than ten lines. In all three instances, the plural form is spelled syllabically, but one time it is marked further with the plural determinative MEŠ (*ma-na-ha-te*.MEŠ; l. 54), one time with the plural determinative HI.A (*ma-na-ha-te*.HI.A; l. 51), and, in its first appearance, with what seems to be an unusual variant for HI.A, HE$_2$ (*ma-na-ha-*[*te*].HE$_2$; l. 47).

However, the best evidence to support the view that the widespread orthographic variation in the Idrimi inscriptions is deliberate comes from two syllabic spellings of the word *ahhēya*, "my brothers." One of these attestations was actually highlighted by Landsberger (1954, 58 n. 117), in the quotation discussed above, as his example of orthographic variation. But whereas Landsberger compared the syllabic spelling with a logographic spelling of the same word later in the text, it is in fact more profitable to compare the syllabic spelling with another syllabic spelling that appears in the body inscription's very next line. Lines 41–42 of the inscription read: [*a*]*h-he*.HI.A-*ia it-ti-ia-ma in-na-hu-u*$_2$ / [*a*]*h-he*$_2$.HI.A-*ia*! *aṣ-ṣur-šu-nu*, "My [br]others were laboring for me, myself; / I protected my brothers." (see also fig. 4.2). As is clear from figure 4.2, not only do the two attestations of *ahhēya* appear in consecutive lines, but each attestation of the word also occupies the exact same position at the very beginning of each line so that the first attestation is quite literally on top of the second. Yet in the first line the syllable /he/ in *ahhēya* is written with HI (= *he*), while in the second it is written with GAN (= *he*$_2$). This juxtaposition can only be deliberate.

Figure 4.2. The beginning of lines 41–42.

In sum, orthographic variation is widespread in the inscriptions. But this variation, as the pluralization of *mānahtu* in three different ways shows, is not the passive reproduction of previously learned spellings. Rather, orthographic variation actively signals an interest in juxtaposing variants, as the striking juxtaposition of [*a*]*h-he*.HI.A-*ia* and [*a*]*h- he*$_2$.HI.A-*ia* makes clear. Given that these statements are valid for orthographic variation, it is reasonable to consider whether the "22 different variations on the KI sign, 13 on the NA, and 5 on the URU," among the other variants cataloged by Oller (1977a, 3), were not the responsibility of an illiterate and poorly trained stonemason but were produced by a scribe with an active interest in paleographic variation.

As with the juxtaposition of the orthographic variants [*a*]*h-he*.HI.A-*ia* and [*a*]*h-he*$_2$.HI.A-*ia*, the frequent juxtaposition of paleographic forms suggests that the paleographic variation was likewise intentional. Sometimes these juxtapositions are horizontal; in other words, they occur within a single line. For instance, line 38 of the body inscription contains four attestations of the sign KI, each of which is underlined in the transliteration: [*m*]*a-at mu-ki-iš-he*$_2$^{ki} *u*$_3$ ^{uru}*a-la-la-ah*^{ki} URU.KI-*ia*, "the land of Mukiš, and Alalah, my city." And, as can be seen in figure 4.3, each of these KI signs has a different form.

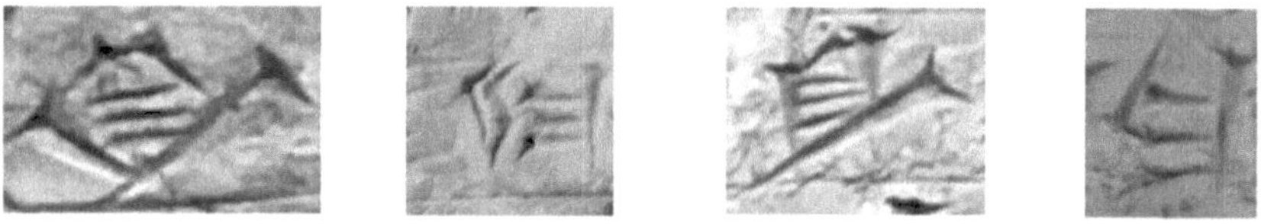

Figure 4.3. Forms of KI in line 38.

Paleographic variants are also found juxtaposed vertically; in other words, they occur in successive lines, as with the orthographic variation in the spellings of *ahhēya* in lines 41–42 discussed above. For instance, the sign U$_3$ is attested four times in lines 53–56, once in each line, and in each attestation the internal feature of the sign's LU component is different. As can be seen in figure 4.4, in line 53 the internal feature of the sign's LU component is PA, in line 54 it is U$_2$ (i.e., adding a vertical wedge to PA), in line 55 it is AŠ (i.e., a single horizontal wedge), and in line 56 it is DIŠ (i.e., a single vertical wedge). Approached from this perspective, the paleographic variation looks less like a "hodge-podge" whose "explanation … is difficult to obtain" (Oller 1977a, 3) and more like a progression of forms obtained by adding or alternating features in a systematic fashion, whether or not the resulting form is expected. In this regard, the vertical juxtaposition of paleographic variants of U$_3$ in lines 53–56 has something of the same spirit found in the famous example of Mesopotamian lexical or scholarly lists that proceed through

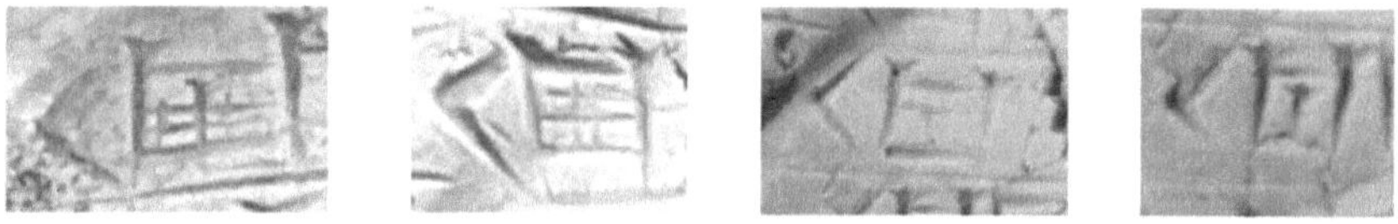

Figure 4.4. Forms of U$_3$ in lines 53–56.

Figure 4.5. The word *qa-qa-ri* in lines 61–62.

a standard sequence of colored animals (white, black, red, speckled, yellow), even if the resulting animal is never found in nature.

Indeed, the example of *qa-qa-ri* in line 61, already mentioned above, displays paleographic variation both horizontally and vertically if we step back to look at the line together with line 62 (fig. 4.5). As can be seen in the figure, within the two attestations of the word *qaqqari* there is horizontal variation because the successive QA signs are formed quite differently, with the former being more cursive than the later. There is also a vertical dimension to the variation because the final RI signs are formed differently, with either two oblique wedges or a *Winkelhaken* before the sign's final vertical wedge.

As the examples discussed in this section demonstrate, it is very difficult to see the widespread orthographic and paleographic variation in the inscriptions as anything other than intentional, and the suggestion put forward originally by Landsberger, supported by Borger, Moran, and Roche-Hawley that the variation was intended to display the scribe's "Gelehrsamkeit" seems the most logical explanation. Such a use of orthographic and paleographic variation would by no means be unique in the cuneiform writings of Late Bronze Age Anatolia and the Levant. For instance, Theo van den Hout (2020, 325–31) has discussed Hittite scribes' use of archaic or archaizing signs in the colophons of texts from Hattuša, a practice that he noted "is also known in Syro-Mesopotamia from the Middle Babylonian period onwards" (326, with n. 175, citing previous literature). He suggested that, "as the scribal counterpart of the classical Roman *poeta doctus* ideal, these scholar-scribes probably reveled in such small displays of learning to be appreciated by the circle of their immediate colleagues only" (326).

A related perspective on this issue, although with a somewhat different emphasis, is given in Mark Weeden's discussion of the rare or unconventional sign-values found in legal documents from Level IV Alalah that are written by the scribe Šarruwa. (See §6.1 for discussions of the relationship between this Šarruwa and the Šarruwa named in the body inscription.)

> Using rare and possibly learned, perhaps even pretentious, sign-values on a statue is one thing, but did one really need to do this on legal documents? The act of writing itself becomes a signifier in that learning can be demonstrated besides the communication of content. The syllabary available to the scribe thus becomes a means of establishing pedigree and signalling superiority. In this sense not only does every scribe have a personal syllabary of sign-usage available to them, but every document becomes a performance of that syllabary modulated according to generic function. (Weeden 2019, 142–43)

Although Weeden is interested only in orthographic variation in this quotation, his remarks are equally relevant to paleographic variation. For him, employing orthographic (and paleographic) variation can have the effect of creating an additional paralinguistic signifier for a written utterance that communicates the pedigree and superiority of the author alongside the utterance's content.

Applied to the Idrimi inscriptions, this observation provokes another question: Why would the creator of these inscriptions wish to communicate his pedigree and superiority? If the answer to this question lies in the situatedness of an utterance—a particular content that is addressed to one or more particular audiences at a particular moment in time—we can ask: What is the particular content of the Idrimi inscriptions, and who is (are) the particular audience(s) of those inscriptions, such that the scribe desired to communicate his pedigree and superiority when producing the inscriptions—that is, in performing the written utterance?

4.2. THE IDRIMI INSCRIPTIONS AND *NARÛ* LITERATURE

A good place to begin answering this question is in the cheek inscription, the three-line text that descends down Idrimi's face and beard:[6] "I was king for thirty years. I inscribed my labors on my[s]elf. May it (i.e., the inscription) encourage them (the descendants) so that they (the descendants) pray to me regularly." Because these lines stand apart from and comment on the body inscription, it is quite significant that the scribe has chosen the word *mānahtu*, "labors," a *maprast*-noun derived from *anāhu,* "to be(come) weary," to encapsulate the narration of Idrimi's life. As far back as 1962, scholars recognized that this choice of word immediately evokes another scribe's use of *mānahtu* in a different literary context—namely, the prologue to the Standard Babylonian Epic of Gilgamesh:[7] *[u]r-ha ru-uq-ta il-li-kam-ma a-ni-ih u šup-šu-uh* / *[ša*$_2$*-k]in i-na* ^{na_4}NA.RU$_2$.A *ka-lu ma-na-ah-ti*, "He came a distant road and was weary but granted rest, / he [set d]own on a *narû* all (his) labors (*mānahtu*)" (SB Gilg. I 9–10). In fact, this attestation of *mānahtu* in the cheek inscription is not the only textual moment in the Idrimi inscriptions where we may see allusions to the Epic of Gilgamesh. For instance, Jean-Marie Durand (2011, 146 n. 175) has drawn attention to the use of *ibru* and *tappû* as synonyms in lines 76 and 83 of the body inscription ("on remarque l'alternance de l'*ibru* occidental

---

6 This section incorporates, revises, and expands upon material published in Lauinger 2019.

7 The intertextuality was suggested, if not developed, by Gadd *apud* Wiseman 1962, 187 with n. 3 and later by Greenstein and Marcus 1976, 81–82. These passages from the Epic of Gilgamesh and the Idrimi inscription were placed next to each other in both dictionaries (*AHw* 601b and *CAD* 10.1, s.v. "manahtu," 1) without further comment and discussed together by Tigay (1982, 144), who did not, however, suggest an explicit connection between the two texts.

avec le *tappu* akkadien, laquelle a son écho dans l'épopée de Gilgamesh!"); see the commentary to line 76 in §A.2. Idrimi's claim to have settled the kingdom's inhabitants in a secure dwelling (*šubtu nēhtu*) may echo not just royal inscriptions but also Tablet VII of the Epic of Gilgamesh, where Šamaš states that a *šubtu nēhtu* is one of the honors that Gilgamesh will award to Enkidu after the latter's death; see the commentary to line 85 in §A.2. Perhaps most striking, Idrimi's twofold declaration in both the cheek inscription and the body inscription, "I was king" (*šarrāku*, ll. CI 1, 58), seems intended to answer—not just in its content but also, perhaps, in its morphology—the Standard Babylonian Epic of Gilgamesh's rhetorical question in its prologue, *man-nu* … *ki-i* ⸢d⸣GIŠ-*gim-maš i-qab-bu-u*$_2$ *a-na-ku-ma* LUGAL, "Who … can say like Gilgamesh, 'I was king'" (SB Gilg. I 45–46).

In this regard, it is important to emphasize that, while the Standard Babylonian prologue is conventionally associated with the first-millennium recension of the text, a manuscript of the epic with this prologue from the House of Urtenu at Ugarit demonstrates that a version of the prologue was already in circulation in the Levant during the Late Bronze Age.[8] To be clear, the Epic of Gilgamesh itself is not attested at Late Bronze Age Alalah, but other scholarly materials, comprising lexical lists, incantations, omina, and hymns are known from the site at this time (von Dassow 2005, 27; Lauinger 2005, 54; von Dassow 2017; see §5.1, and see the discussion of the lexical list Lu in §3.2). Given this larger context for cuneiform scholarship at Alalah as well as the popularity of the Epic of Gilgamesh in the Late Bronze Age Syro-Anatolian world, it is not too great a leap to suggest that both the scribe of the Idrimi inscriptions and his audience would have been familiar with the text. Indeed, as with the lexical list Lu, the burden of proof perhaps should be on those who want to argue that the Epic of Gilgamesh would not have been known in the scribal community of Late Bronze Age Alalah. The question of literacy at Late Bronze Age Alalah is taken up at more length in the following chapter.

In the Standard Babylonian recension, part of the prologue's significance is that it frames Gilgamesh's subsequent wanderings as *narû* literature, a modern scholarly designation for Mesopotamian pseudo-autobiographical literary texts in which kings left accounts of their misfortunes in stone for a didactic purpose: so that future kings might learn from their example.[9] For example, the Cuthean

[8] Arnaud 2007, no. 42; see also George 2007, 238–48; Sasson 2013, 265–77; and Milstein 2016, 124–36. According to George (2007, 238), the text is a "pedagogical exercise" that shows some discrepancies with the parallel lines in the first-millennium version as well several errors and omissions; the relevant lines (ll. 9–10) read: *har-ra-na ru-uq-ta* GIN-*ma a-ni-ih u*$_3$ *šup-šu-uq* / GAR-*nu-šu-ma na-ru-*<*u*$_2$> *ka-lu ma-*<*na*>*-ah-*<<erasure>>*-ti*. See especially George's (2007, 246–47) discussion of the variant *šupšuq* for the first-millennium recension's *šupšuh*.

[9] The term "*narû* literature" was coined by Güterbock (1934, 19; see 62–86 for discussion) in his Leipzig dissertation. The Akkadian word *narû* literally means "stele"; since not all

Legend of Naram-Sin purports to be an autobiographical account of the Old Akkadian king Naram-Sin, who narrates his military defeats after going into battle despite unfavorable omens. The text utilizes Naram-Sin's account to communicate a more general didactic message—"that kings who carry out projects in the face of unfavorable omens are doomed to catastrophe" (Foster 2005, 348)—and, further, makes explicit that this message is intended for future rulers in the opening lines of the Standard Babylonian recension:

1 [*tup-šin-na pi-te-ma* ^{na_4}]NA.RU$_2$.A *ši-ta-si*
2 [*ša a-na-ku* ^{m}*na-ram-*^{d}30] DUMU ^{m}LUGAL-GI.NA
3 [*iš-ṭu-ru-ma e-zi-bu-šu ana*] *u$_4$-me ṣa-a-ti*

[Open the tablet box] and read out the *narû*
[that I, Naram-Sin], son of Sargon
[inscribed and left for] future days.[10]

---

relevant examples report having been inscribed onto stelae, and since other texts, such as "historical" royal inscriptions, can refer to themselves as *narû*, some scholars prefer the terms "pseudo-autobiography" or "fictional autobiography." However, *narû* can signify an inscribed memorial monument more generally (see Walker 1981, 192 and Tigay 1982, 144 n. 11, citing Ellis 1968, 144–47; see also the references gathered in *CAD* 11.1, s.v. "narû A," 1a–b). I retain the term *narû* literature in order to stress the central (fictional) conceit of the genre—that an original version of the text was inscribed by a king. On the existence or not of *narû* literature as an emic genre and debates as to its utility as a modern heuristic category, see, among others, Reiner 1978, 179–80; B. Lewis 1980, 87–90; Longman 1991; Westenholz 1997, 16–20; Pongratz-Leisten 1999, 74–90; Gilan 2015, 2–3; and Pongratz-Leisten 2020, 31. For an earlier discussion of the Idrimi inscriptions within the context of *narû* literature, see Sasson 1981, 312–13. Sasson's point of departure is the pseudo-autobiographical nature of the inscriptions; he does not discuss the attestation of the word *mānahtu* in the cheek inscription. In turn, Longman's (1991, 60–66) analysis of the inscriptions as fictional autobiography depends on Sasson's conclusions.

[10] The translation adapts MC 7 300–301. Although the opening of the text is damaged, the restorations are assured by the text's epilogue, which likewise admonishes future rulers to read the stele. The text quoted here is from first-millennium copies, but it is much older. Two manuscripts are known from Old Babylonian Mesopotamia, while a third manuscript is from Middle Babylonian Hattuša (and so is roughly contemporaneous with the Idrimi inscriptions). Neither the beginning nor ending of the text is preserved in the older manuscripts, however. Other textual connections between the Cuthean Legend and the Idrimi inscriptions have been suggested. For instance, in the final note to her edition, Westenholz (1997, 331) remarked that the Cuthean Legend's "conclusion reminds one of the Idrimi inscription"; cf. lines CI 2–3 with the final lines of the Standard Babylonian Cuthean Legend: "You who have read my inscription / and thus have gotten yourself out (of trouble) / you who have blessed me, may a future (ruler) bless you!" (*šu-ut* ^{na_4}NA.RU$_2$.A-*e-a ta-mu-ru-ma / pu-ut-ka tu-še-ṣu-u / šu-ut ya-ši* ⸢*tak-tar-ba*⸣ *ar-ku-u / lik-ta-rab-ka ka-a-ša$_2$*, ll. 177–180;

The Standard Babylonian Epic of Gilgamesh gives similar instructions to its reader at the end of its prologue (SB Gilg. I 24–28):

I 24 [*a-mur?*] ^{giš}*tup-šen-na ša*2 ^{giš}ERIN
I 25 [*pu-uṭ-ṭe*]*r? har-gal-li-šu ša*2 ZABAR
I 26 [*pi-te-m*]*a?* KA2 *ša*2 *ni-ṣir-ti-šu*
I 27 [*i-š*]*i?-ma ṭup-pi* ^{na4}ZA.GIN *ši-tas-si*
I 28 [*mim-m*]*u-u*2 ^{d}GIŠ-*gim-maš* DU.DU^{ku} *ka-lu mar-ṣa-a-ti*

[*Find*] the tablet box of cedar,
[*release*] its clasps of bronze!
[*Open*] the lid of its secret,
[*lift*] *up* the tablet of lapis lazuli and read out
[all tha]t Gilgamesh went through, all the misfortunes!

In these lines, the phrase "all the misfortunes" (*kalu marṣāti*) corresponds to the phrase "all the labors" (*kalu mānahti*) appearing fourteen lines earlier, which the text uses to describe the subject matter Gilgamesh inscribed on a memorial monument. As Walker (1981, 194) has explained, the *narû* is thus the same as the lapis lazuli tablet that the reader is instructed to read out.

In the version of the prologue from Ugarit, we find some recensional differences from the first-millennium version. Instead of Gilgamesh setting up a single stele inscribed with his labors, multiple steles relating them are set up for him (GAR-*nu-šu-ma na-ru ka-lu ma*-<*na*>-*ah*-<<erasure>>-*ti*, l. 10). More significantly, the contents of the tablet of lapis lazuli are no longer "all the misfortunes" that Gilgamesh experienced but the famous description of the city of Uruk that immediately precedes this passage in the first-millennium version (SB Gilg. I 20–23) and then recurs as Gilgamesh's instructions to Ur-šanabi at the epic's end (SB Gilg. XI 324–328):

22 *pi-te-ma tu-up-ni-in-na ša* ^{giš}EREN
23 *pu-uṭ-ṭe-er har-gal-li-šu*2 *ša* ZABAR
24 *i-šam-ma ṭup-pi* $^{na4!}$ZA.GIN3.NA *ti-ša-*⌜*as*⌝*-si*
25 *um-ma* SIG4-*ša la a-gur-rat*
26 *uš-ši-šu*2 *la id-du-u*2 7 *mu-un-tal-ku*
27 ŠAR2^{ar2} URU ŠAR2^{ar2} KIRI6.MEŠ ŠAR2^{ar2} *es-su*2*-u pi-tir* ⌜E2 *iš*8*-tar*2⌝[11]

translation following Westenholz 1997, 331). Greenstein and Marcus (1976, 96) drew attention to Šamaš's epithet as "lord of above and below" in line 26 of the Cuthean Legend and line 100 of the body inscription. Parattarna I's epithet "king of the Umman-manda" in line 46 of the body inscription may also be meant to evoke the enemy that defeats Naram-Sin in the Cuthean Legend.

[11] The transliteration of the line follows George 2007, 241.

28 *ša-la-aš*$_2$! *ša-ri u*$_3$ *pi-tir u*$_2$*-ru-uk*…[12]

Open the tablet box of cedar,
release its clasps of bronze,
lift up the tablet of lapis lazuli, (and) read out
thus: "Is not its brickwork made of kiln-baked brick.
did not the seven sages lay its foundations?
One šar is the city, one šar are the orchards, one šar are the clay pits, (and) one-half (šar is the temple of Ištar:
Three šar and one half is Uruk.…

That lines 25–28 are intended to be understood as a quotation is made clear by *umma* in line 25. The version from Ugarit, then, also instructs the reader to read out the preexisting Epic of Gilgamesh. A primary difference between the two versions would seem to be an emphasis in the first-millennium version on Gilgamesh's suffering (i.e., "all the misfortunes"), whereas the emphasis in the version from Ugarit is on the didactic message (i.e., built works and other products of civilization as a king's avenue for immortality). In this regard, the version from Ugarit can be seen as one more change in focus at another moment in the epic's history.[13] In both the versions, however, the addition of the prologue thereby frames the preexisting Epic of Gilgamesh as *narû* literature while still preserving its original form.[14]

To return to the Statue of Idrimi, the dynamic between the cheek inscription and the longer inscription on the statue's body is similar to the dynamic between the prologue of the Epic of Gilgamesh and the narrative that follows. By choosing to describe and summarize the body inscription as Idrimi's *mānahtu*, the scribe was

---

[12] The transliteration of the line follows George 2007, 241. As George (2007, 243) noted in his comment to the line, one expects *tamšīhu*, "area" for the copy's *li-ih*!?-⌜*šiš*⌝ at the end of the line. Perhaps emend the text to *li-ih*!?-<*ha*>-⌜*šiš*⌝, for an N precative of *hasāsu*, showing š for s, "let it be recalled!"? Cf. the forms of this verb in line 9 of the body inscription (*ah-šu-šu, ih-šu-uš*).

[13] See, e.g., Abusch (2001, 621–22), who argued that "in the Old Babylonian version, Gilgamesh finds a meaningful context within the bosom of the family, creating children who will represent him in the future, and accepts the role of builder-king. In the eleven-tablet version, he becomes a responsible ruler who rules his community with wisdom and creates human cultural achievements that outlast his own reign and are passed down to future generations. In the twelve-tablet version, he readies himself to become a normal god who judges dead human beings for eternity."

[14] See also George 2003, 1:32 ("The new prologue converted the epic into autobiography in the third person, a genre of Mesopotamian belles-lettres known today as *narû* literature") and Suriano 2017, 296 ("As a literary device, the *narû* transforms the epic into a type of 'third-person autobiography'"). Note that the epic only presents itself as *narû* literature. As Tigay (1982, 144) pointed out, "the epic itself, a third-person narrative, is not a piece of *narû* literature, which typically is a first-person narrative."

consciously connecting the cheek inscription to the Gilgamesh prologue and, likewise, using the cheek inscription to frame the body inscription as an example of *narû* literature. The repetition of the nominal predicate *šarrāku*, "I was king," which occurs in both the cheek inscription (l. CI 1) and a culminating moment of the body inscription (l. 58), echoes another moment early in the Epic of Gilgamesh and underscores that the body and cheek inscriptions are meant to be read alongside both each other and the epic. Indeed, the occurrence of this particular allusion in the cheek inscription reinforces an understanding of the Idrimi narrative as a work of *narû* literature because, as Matthew Suriano (2017, 296–97) has noted in reference to the Epic of Gilgamesh's rhetorical question, "the allusive language of lines 45–46 … is an allusion to the opening words of a *narû* inscription. Not only does this line refer to an individual who speaks, it also quotes the initial word encountered in a *narû* inscription (the first person pronoun *anāku*…) and associates this speech with royal status (*šarru*)." Furthermore, the placement of the short framing inscription on the statue's cheek can be seen as a rhetorical move. Sasson (1981, 313) observed that the very fact that this important summary passage is inscribed on Idrimi's cheek makes the words seem "to issue from Idrimi's own mouth" and emphasizes their autobiographical origin, thereby reinforcing their status as *narû* literature.[15]

But if the cheek inscription presents the body inscription to the reader as *narû* literature by calling it Idrimi's *mānahtu*, what is the body inscription's didactic message? As discussed above, the central conceit of *narû* literature is that the pseudo-author kings recorded their stories in stone in order to communicate a didactic message to future kings. So, for example, the didactic message of the Cuthean Legend of Naram-Sin is, as mentioned above, that kings disregard omens at their peril. And, although it is a text with more layers than the Cuthean Legend, the Standard Babylonian version of the Epic of Gilgamesh famously conveys the message, among others, that a king's energies are best directed toward "communal responsibility" (Absuch 2001, 620). But what about the inscription on Idrimi's body?

4.3. *MĀNAHTU* IN THE POLITICAL DISCOURSE OF ANATOLIA AND THE LEVANT DURING THE LATE BRONZE AGE

To my knowledge, a didactic message for the Idrimi inscriptions has not been hitherto suggested in the scholarly literature,[16] but it is not too difficult to find. In

---

[15] Cf. Crawford's (2014, 257–58) different understanding of the position of the cheek inscription; see the discussion in §2.4.

[16] Sasson (1981, 312) acknowledged that the text should have a "'didactic' dimension," which he declared "not easily identified." Longman (1991, 66) simply omitted any discussion of a possible didactic function, seemingly because he classified the text among the pseudo-autobiographies "with a blessing and/or curse ending," which he distinguished

fact, the inscription quite helpfully signals its message by marking it with three more attestations of the word *mānahtu*. These attestations were discussed in §4.1 in reference to variations in their orthography, specifically the different ways in which plurality is marked. This point is significant. In contrast to the attestation of *mānahtu* in the cheek inscription, which is singular, the attestations of *mānahtu* in the body inscription are plural, and I discuss the difference in number in more detail immediately below.

The attestations of *mānahtu* in the body inscription are also significant in their placement in the narrative because all occur in the passage in which Idrimi swears an oath of loyalty to the king of Mittani, a pivotal episode in the narrative that transforms Idrimi from "questing hero" into "good king" (see §2.8). I quote here the larger context in which the three attestations of *mānahtu* appear, leaving that word and another instance of what I will argue is the same root untranslated this time:

> Moreover, over seven years, Parattarna (I), the mighty king, king of the armies of Hurri, turned hostile toward me. In the seventh year, I sent a message to Parattarna (I), the king, king of the Umman-manda, and I spoke of the *mānahtus* of my forefathers, (namely) that my forefathers *ṅh-ed for them and our ancestors belonged to the kings of the Hurrian armies. Because this was pleasing (to the kings of Hurri), they established a powerful oath between them. The mighty king heard about the *mānahtus* of our ancestors and the oath that was between them, and he respected the oath. Because of the words of the oath, and because of our (former) *mānahtus*, he received my peace offering. So I made a brazier already heavy for sacrifice even greater, and so I returned a household that was lost to him. In my status as a retainer, in my loyalty, I seized this abandoned hem for him, and so I was king. Kings from all around came up to me at Alalah, and I was their equal.

From this passage, it is clear that the word *mānahtu* has a different sense here than in the cheek inscription and the prologue to the Standard Babylonian Epic of Gilgamesh. The editors of *CAD* 10.1 shared this opinion, because they gave these three attestations of *mānahtu* their own meaning, which they translated as "vassal service" (*CAD* 10.1, s.v. "mānahtu," 5).[17] Setting aside the obvious and much-discussed difficulties presented by retrojecting vassalage into the ancient Near East, differentiating these attestations from that of *mānahtu* in the cheek inscription is absolutely correct. However, in isolating the attestations in their own meaning, the editors missed a larger point, which is that the plural form of the

---

from pseudo-autobiographies with a didactic *ending* (97–129), so he understood only the latter subgenre to have possessed a didactic function.

[17] In *AHw* 601b, the three attestations are cited under the same meaning as the attestation in CI 2 but kept apart as a distinct, plural usage.

word *mānahtu* had broader valence in the political discourse of Anatolia and the Levant during the Late Bronze Age.

Prior to 2016, the word *mānahtu* in the plural was known from only one attestation in the Akkadian of Ugarit, which occurred in a fragmentary, if suggestive, context:

> ^{0} (traces) ^{1} (traces) ^{2} ⸢*ma-na*⸣*-ha-ti*.MEŠ ^{3} ⸢*a*⸣-[*n*]*a* LUGAL KUR *kar-ga-miš* ^{4} *it-ta-din* ⸢*u*$_3$⸣ LUGAL KUR *kar-ga-miš* ^{5} *ma-na-ha-ti*.MEŠ *ša-a-šu-nu* ^{6} *a-na* LUGAL KUR *u*$_2$*-ga-ri-it*
>
> ^{7} *it-ta-din-*⸢*ma*?⸣ KU$_3$.BABBAR.MEŠ ŠAM$_3$.MEŠ-*šu-nu* ^{8} *il-te-qe*$_3$
>
> (single ruling)
>
> (seal impression of Ini-Teššub, king of Carchemish)
>
> "[…] gave *mānahtus* to the king of the land of Carchemish, and the king of the land of Carchemish gave those *mānahtus* to the king of the land of Ugarit, and he (i.e., the king of the land of Carchemish) took silver as their purchase price." (PRU 4 293b [RS 19.55]; the line numbering and new readings follows Huehnergard 1986)

In part because the first two lines of text are illegible, different interpretations of the meaning of *mānahtu* in this text can be found in the literature. For instance, both Wolfram von Soden and the editors of *CAD* 10.1 cited these attestations under a well-attested meaning for the word in agricultural contexts, "Pl. Arbeitsertrag, erworbene Güter" (*AHw* 602b), "installations, equipment (mostly in the plural)" (*CAD* 10.1, s.v. "mānahtu," 3d). This sense for the word was explicitly accepted by both John Huehnergard (1986, 453) and Sylvie Lackenbacher (2002, 175 n. 576). Ignacio Márquez Rowe (2006, 247 n. 130), on the other hand, suggested that the word should be understood in the context of "the mutual loyalty of the kings of Ugarit and Carchemish," making an explicit connection to "the use of the derived substantive *mānahtu* in the inscription of the Statue of Idrimi."

However, the 2016 publication of 130 more letters in syllabic cuneiform from the House of Urtenu (RSOu 23) has now provided us with fifteen attestations of *mānahtu* in the plural across six different letters. Three of these letters were sent by members of the Hittite administration, and three no longer have the name of the sender preserved.[18] Altogether, the attestations make clear that the word designated some sort of a delivery of grain, as this passage from RSOu 23 21 [RS

---

[18] Sender is a member of the Hittite administration: RSOu 23 21 [RS 94.2571]: 9, 19, 23, 27, 28, and 30; RSOu 23 22 [RS 94.2185]: 19; RSOu 23 27 [RS 94.2585]: 9, 23, 25, 33. Name of sender not preserved: RSOu 23 81 [RS 94.2524]: 32; RSOu 23 104 [RS 94.2481+]: 10; RSOu 23 107 [RS 94.2540]: 15′, 19′.

94.2571], a letter sent by the Hittite prince Tasi to the *sākinu*-prefect of Ugarit, illustrates:

> [6] *ša a-kan$_2$-na taš$_3$-pu-⸢ra⸣-an-ni* [7] *um-ma-a šum-ma* ^{giš}MA$_2$.MEŠ [8] *iš-tu* ^{uru}*ki-na-a-ni* [9] *ma-na-ha-ta u$_2$-še-re-du-mi* [10] *u$_3$ u$_2$-še-bal-ku-mi* [11] *i-ia-nu-me-e mi-ri-il-ta$_2$* [12] *ša te-er-ri-ša-an-ni* [13] *u$_2$-še-bi-la-ku-mi* [14] *⸢u$_3$⸣ mi-⸢ri-il-ta$_2$⸣* [15] *⸢ša⸣ tu-⸢še-bi-la⸣* [16] *mi-na-a e-er-ri-iš* [17] *šum-ma i-na lib$_3$-bi-ka* [18] DUG$_3$.GA-*ut-tu ša-ak-nat* [19] *u$_3$ ma-na-ha-tu$_4$* [20] *⸢ša⸣ e-te-er-ša-ak-ku* [21] *re-eh-ta$_2$ šu-bi-la* [22] *⸢u$_3$⸣ bul$_2$-li-ṭa-an-ni* [23] *pa-na-nu* KUR *u$_2$-ga-ri-it aš-šum ma-na-ha-ti* [24] *u$_2$-ul ul-⸢tu⸣* ^{uru}*ši-an-ni-i bal-ṭu* [25] *i-na-an-na i-na* MU.KAM$_2$^{ti} *an-ni-⸢ti⸣* [26] NUMUN *i-za-⸢ar⸣-ru u$_3$ i-na* MU.KAM$_2$^{ti} [27] *ša il-la-ka ma-na-ha-tu$_4$ i-ma-ʾa-⸢da⸣* [28] *u$_3$ ša ⸢i-na⸣-an-na at-ta ma-na-ha-⸢ta$_2$⸣* [29] *tu-še-ba$_2$-la a-na-ku* 3^{šu} *u$_2$-ra-da-ku* [30] *u$_3$ aš-šum ma-⸢na-ha⸣-ti* [31] *ša e-ri-⸢iš-ka⸣* [32] *i-ia-nu lu-u$_2$ la-a ta-qab$_2$-bi.*
>
> About that which thus you sent as a message to me, saying: "If the boats bring *mānahtus*[19] down from (the city of) Kinanu,[20] then I will deliver (them) to you. If not, I will deliver (another) request that you make of me,"—as for (the other) request that you would deliver, what request would I make? If friendship is placed in your heart, then, as for the *mānahtu*s that I requested from you, deliver the remainder and keep me alive! Previously was the land of Ugarit not alive because of *mānahtu*s from (the city of) Siyannu?[21] Now, in this year, seed is being sown, and in the year that is coming, *mānahtu*s will be many. So, *for now*, you, yourself, can deliver the *mānahtu*s. (Then) I, myself, will add threefold for you. Regarding the *mānahtu*s that I requested from you, you must not say, "There are none"!

As discussed by Lackenbacher and Florence Malbran-Labat (2016, 48) in their commentary to the text, the attestations of *mānahtu*, all of which are in the plural, "souligne le lien de ces *mānahatu* avec la production du grain: le prince Tâsi y demande au préfet de lui en faire parvenir par bateaux, en rappelant que l'Ugarit avait pu survivre grâce à un envoi de ce genre et il promet de rembourser au triple l'année suivante, quand les semailles auront porté le fruit escompté." They go on to demonstrate that the other attestations of *mānahtu* in the letters from the House of Uretenu that are similarly in the plural also signify grain intended for subsistence (48). The clearest example comes from RSOu 23 81 [RS 94.2524], where the *mānahtu*s are explicitly described as wheat.[22] Another important attestation is

---

[19] The word *mānahtu* is construed as a triptotic plural throughout the letter.

[20] Cf. the city (URU) *Kinani* known from Level IV texts from Alalah, which are taken by RGTC 12.2, s.v. "*Kinʿanu/Kinahnu/Kinahhu" as instances of the toponym Canaan, also attested in the Level IV texts but otherwise marked there, as elsewhere, with KUR. Alternatively, see Cohen 2021, n. 7 ("That Canaan is intended here … is without doubt").

[21] Note the placement of the negative particle before the prepositional phrase *ultu Siyannu*.

[22] *[a-nu]-ma ma-na-ʾa-ti ša-a a-kan$_2$-na [taš$_3$?]-⸢pu⸣-ra ma-a a-nu-um-ma* 10 GUR GIG.MEŠ *[ul?]-te-bil$_2$ u$_3$* GIG.MEŠ *ša-a tul$_2$-te-bi-la-an-ni* 9 GUR GIG.MEŠ, "[N]ow, as for the

RSOu 23 22 [RS 94.2185], where the sender requests *mānahtu*s for his servants and then exclaims: *i-na bu-bu-ti lu-u2 la-a i-ma-at-tu2*, "They must not die from hunger!" (ll. 21–22).

According to Lackenbacher and Malbran-Labat (2016, 49), the choice to refer to these shipments of subsistence grain by the word *mānahtu*, as opposed to simply calling them "grain," is significant:

> On voit que, dans ce corpus, *mānah(ā)tu* désigne des denrées alimentaires en se référant non pas à leur nature (grain, cultures vivrières) mais au système dont elles relèvent. Le fait que ce soit le pouvoir impérial qui impose leur livraison au roi d'Ugarit—et pourrait seul l'en exempter—et que les personnages qui demandent d'en bénéficier soient des princes hittites incite à penser à une contribution en nature, occasionnelle ou non, destinée à constituer des réserves stockées sur place et envoyées là où le besoin s'en faisait sentir dans l'empire.

This understanding of these plural forms of *mānahtu* has largely been accepted by scholars who have subsequently worked on the texts. So, for instance, Elena Devecchi (2022, 295) considered the term to designate "a contribution of food supplies occasionally requested from the kingdom of Ugarit," going on to add the nuance that "these texts convey the impression that the *mānaḫ(ā)tu*-supplies did not have to be delivered on a regular basis or meet a particular deadline but could be requested in case of need on the basis of the current good relations between the parties and even paid back in the future" (296).

Yoram Cohen and Eduardo Torrecilla (2023) proposed, further, understanding this sense for the attestation of *mānahtu* in the plural in PRU 4 293b [RS 19.55]: 2, cited above. Indeed, on the basis of the letter sent by the Hittite prince Tasi RSOu 23 21 [RS 94.2571], also cited above, they made a compelling case that the opening lines of PRU 4 293b [RS 19.55] refer to the king or city of Siyannu, so that the text reads, with restorations: "[*The king/city of Siyannu*] gave *mānahtu*s to the king of the land of Carchemish, and the king of the land of Carchemish gave those *mānahtu*s to the king of the land of Ugarit, and he (i.e., the king of the land of Carchemish) took silver as their purchase price." According to this interpretation, which, again, goes back to Tasi's reference to the fact that Ugarit had been kept alive because of *mānahtu*s from Siyannu, the text would record the sale of something described as *mānahtu*s to Ugarit with the viceroy of Carchemish functioning as a middleman. The crucial takeaway is that the no-longer-preserved subject in the opening lines could not sell the *mānahtu*s to Ugarit directly, seemingly because *mānahtu*s were deliveries of staples that occurred within the framework of Hittite hegemony.

---

*mānahtu*s that [you se]nt thus sent, saying: 'Now, [I ha]ve sent 10 *kurru* of wheat,' the what that you sent to was (only) 9 *kurru* of wheat" (RSOu 23 81 [RS 94.2524]: 32–35).

One place where the foregoing analysis of the attestations of *mānahtu* may require some nuance is in the letter RSOu 23 107 [RS 94.2540], which was clearly sent by a lower-ranking individual to his superior, as is evident from the fact that the former addresses the latter as "my lord." Cohen and Torrecilla (2023, 68) translate the relevant passage as:

> $^{14'}$*ša-ni-tam* EN-*ia*$^{!}$ *a-nu-ma* $^{15'}$*ma-na-ah-ta a-na muh-hi-ka* $^{16'}$*ia-a-nu u*$_3$ *i-na* $^{17'}$*bu-bu-ti* E$_2$^{ti} IR$_3$-*ka* $^{18'}$*i-mu-tu*$_4$ *u*$_3$ EN-*ia* $^{19'}$*ma-na-ah-ta a-na* IR$_3$-*ka* $^{20'}$*i-din* 1^{en} *u*$_4$-*mi* EN-*ia* $^{21'}$⸢*la*$^{?}$⸣ *i-ša-ga-ar*
>
> Another thing, my lord: grain staples (*ma-na-aḫ-ta*) from you are not to be had! (The people of) the household of your servant will die of hunger (*ina bubūti*)! My lord—give grain staples (*ma-na-aḫ-ta*) to your servant! My lord should not delay for even one single day.[23]

This translation follows the editors of RSOu 23 in taking the form of *mâtu* in line 18′ as present-future. The parallel that both the editors of RSOu 23 and Cohen and Torrecilla seem to have in mind is RSOu 23 22 [RS 94.2185], mentioned above, where the sender requests *mānahtus* so that his servants will not die from hunger (*ina bubūti lū lā imâttū*). However, the verb in RSOu 23 107 [RS 94.2540] is not a prohibitive. As written, the form of *mâtu* is ambiguous; it could be present-future (*imuttū*) or preterite (*imūtū*).

There are at least two other noteworthy features of this passage. The first feature is that the two attestations of the word *mānahtu* appear in the singular in this letter, not the plural, as in all of the other attestations of the word when it refers to an obligatory delivery of staples. The second feature is that the first attestation of *mānahtu* is described by the letter's sender as *ana muhhika*. Cohen and Torrecilla translated the compound prepositional phrase as "(*m.*) from you," but this translation requires some justification because it reverses the expected direction of motion; in other words, *ana muhhi* is "to," not "from." Lackenbacher and Malbran-Labat translated it as "(les subsistances) *qui t'incombent*," with italic indicating the translation's tentative nature. This qualification seems appropriate because, even if *ana muhhi* frequently means "incumbent upon," it is questionable whether the author of the letter would describe the grain that he was requesting from his superior in terms of a legal obligation.

I suggest that this triad of features—the indicative form of *mâtu*, the singular form of *mānahtu*, and the compound prepositional phrase *ana muhhi*—can be

---

[23] The final verb is difficult. Cohen and Torrecilla (2023, 68 n. 22) tentatively suggest taking it as a by-form of *šahāru*, "to delay (> *ahāru*?), while the Lackenbacher and Malbran-Labat translate, "que *pas* un seul jour, mon seigneur, il n'ait (encore) faim!" Seemingly, they have understood a denominative *šagāru*, which is itself a Sumerian loanword, from ša$_3$-gar, "hunger," which is used as a logogram from Akkadian *bubūtu* (Cohen and Torrecilla reached the same inference).

explained if we understand *mānahtu* to designate another facet of the obligation of a subordinate to the Hittite hegemon. If the plural form of *mānahtu* designated the grain staples that the subordinate was required to deliver, the singular form of the noun might designate the dependent labor force that was responsible for cultivation or even simply their labor. If we combine this understanding of *mānahtu* with an analysis of *i-mu-tu*$_4$ as a 3mp preterite form and a straightforward translation of *ana muhhika* as "to/for you,"[24] we may translate the letter as: "Something else: My lord, now there is no *mānahtu for* you. They died from a famine in (lit. of) your servant's house.[25] So, my lord, give a *mānahtu* to your servant. My lord should not *be hungry/delay* for one day."[26]

In this interpretation, the labor force is "for" the superior (*ana muhhika*) because the grain produced by this labor force is intended for him. However, since the economic unit of production under the responsibility of the letter's sender (*bīti ardika*) died previously, grain cannot be cultivated to be sent on to the superior. Therefore, "my lord" is urged to send a replacement labor force so that he, the superior, can continue to receive shipments of grain. This reinterpretation of RSOu 23 107 [RS 94.2540] does not contradict the conclusions of Lackenbacher and Malbran-Labat or those of Cohen and Torricelli, discussed above, that, when used in the plural, the word signifies shipments of grain that the ruler of Ugarit was obliged to deliver. In using the singular form of the same noun to signify a different aspect of a system of obligatory service, RSOu 23 107 [RS 94.2540] emphasizes that it is precisely the obligatory service that is at stake in all of these letters; that is, the base semantic meaning of *mānahtu* is obligatory service or labor, and the word can express different nuances of that meaning in different forms.

This conclusion, in turn, provides context for one further attestation of *mānahtu*, which occurs in a land grant from Emar (LN-104; previously published as Gs-Kutscher 6). This attestation is quite important, as it illustrates that the use of *mānahtu* to designate aspects of obligatory service had a wider currency in the Akkadian of Anatolia and the Levant. In this land grant, which has been re-edited with important new readings by Cohen and Maurizio Viano (2016), *mānahtu* is used twice to describe a service that the recipient of the grant, a certain Irib-Baʿlu, did for the ruler of Emar, for which he and his sons received an appointment as

24 In the interpretation presented here, *muhhu* does not add any semantic nuance to *ana* but is a collocation with the pronominal suffix, which, of course, cannot attach directly to *ana*; see Huehnergard 2011, 190–91 ("Often clauses with *ana* plus a noun are paralleled by others with *ana muhhi* plus a pronoun").

25 Taking *bubūti* as a construct form; for the unexpected /i/ vowel, cf. the very next word, where the same phenomenon occurs (*bīti* for expected *bīt*). Alternatively, one can follow Lackenbacher and Malbran-Labat, as well as Cohen and Torrecilla, and translate "(The people) of the household of your servant died from hunger" without complicating the interpretation of *mānahtu* presented here.

26 See above on the difficult form *i-ša-ga-ar*.

šangû-priest and temple administrator of the temple of Nergal-of-the-Marketplace. According to the text, the ruler of Emar was required to deliver four of his daughters together with precious stones, four thousand shekels of silver, and four hundred shekels of gold to the king of Mittani, presumably as tribute, but Irib-Baʿlu made a payment to the king of Mittani and thereby redeemed the ruler of Emar's daughters:

> [16] … *u*$_3$ *ma-na-ah-ta* GAL [17] <*ša*> *liṭ-ṭi* URU^{lis}-*šu* *u*$_3$ *be-li-šu* [18] *e-te-pu-uš* *u*$_3$ *ki-i-mu-u*$_2$ *ma-na-ah-ti-šu* [19] *ša liṭ-ṭi* URU^{lis}-*šu* *u*$_3$ *be-li-šu* [20] *ša i-pu-šu* LUGAL *u*$_3$ ^{uru}*e-mar* [21] *a-na* ^{lu_2}SANGA *ša* E$_2$ ^{d}NE$_3$-IRI$_{11}$-GAL [22] *ša* KI.LAM *u*$_3$ *a-na ra-be bi-ti* [23] DUMU-*šu* DUMU.DUMU-*šu* NUMUN-*šu* [24] NUMUN.NUMUN-*šu* *iš-ku-un-šu*

> "…He did a great *mānahtu* <for (lit. of)> the hostages of his city and his lord. In return for his *mānahtu* for (lit. of) the hostages of his city and his lord that he did, the king and (the city of) Emar appointed him, his son, his grandson, his offspring, and his offspring's offspring as *šangû*-priest of the temple of Nergal-of-the-Marketplace and as temple administrator."[27]

Significantly, the word *mānahtu* appears here in the singular. In their re-edition of the text, Cohen and Viano (2016, 59) translated it as "service," referring explicitly in their commentary (62) to the attestations of the word in the Idrimi inscriptions.

More recently, Cohen (2023, 61) understood it as "tribute," translating "(he) had paid the heavy tribute of the hostages of his city and his lord." Cohen's reevaluation of the word *mānahtu* in this text derived from his and Torrecilla's (forthcoming) analysis of the attestations of the word in RSOu 23. However, as discussed above, they did not consider the idea that uses of the word in the singular might designate a different aspect of a subordinate's obligatory duties to a hegemon. Indeed, the land grant from Emar supports the idea that *mānahtu* designates labor when used in the singular and the products of that labor when used in the plural. Cohen translated *mānahta* … *ētepuš* as "(he) had paid … the tribute," but we would expect the verb to be a form of *nadānu* in the context of delivering tribute (see, e.g., RSOu 23 107 [RS 94.2540]: 20′, cited above). The verb *epēšu* signifies the performance of an activity.

Again, the importance of the attestation of *mānahtu* with this sense in a land grant from Emar is that it demonstrates that the sense had a broader use in Late Bronze Age Anatolia and the Levant than it did at Ugarit. The Emar land grant also expands the chronological horizon of this sense of the word. Cohen and Viano (2016, 64) have argued that the land grant is to be dated to the period of time before Šuppiluliuma's conquest, when Emar acknowledged the hegemony of Mittani. Therefore, the text is closer in time to the Idrimi inscriptions than to

[27] I am grateful to Martin Worthington for suggesting the emendation in line 17; cf. line 19.

the letters from the House of Urtenu, and it also reflects a similar set of political relationships and vocabulary; note in particular that the king of Mittani is named throughout the text as "the king of Hurri-land" just as Parattarna I is in the body inscription on Idrimi's statue.

To return to Ugarit, Juan-Pablo Vita (2021b, 120) has suggested that the word *mānahtu* appearing in the Akkadian syllabic texts is the vocalized version of the term *mnḥt* that appears in alphabetic cuneiform texts from the site; see also Cohen and Torrecilla 2023, 71. The alphabetic term encompasses a variety of different objects, both finished products and raw materials (Vita 2021b, 119) and has been understood to designate either a gift or tax (McGeough 2020, 409–10). The suggestion that Akkadian *manahtu* and Ugaritic *mnḥ* are related goes back to William Foxwell Albright (1957, 35) in his notice of the then recently published volume PRU 4, where he commented on the text PRU 4 293b [RS 19.55], quoted above:

> the word *manahātu* is scarcely the plural of Accadian *mānahtu*, "toil," but is rather the plural of the noun which appears as *minḥah*, "gift, offering," in Hebrew, *m(a)nḥītu* as a loanword in New Egyptian with the same meaning, and *mnḥ*, probably with the same sense, in Ugaritic (from the secondary derivative *mnḥ*, "to give, bestow," found also in Arabic). With this meaning the text acquires new importance for the practices governing relations between reigning princes in Syria during the thirteenth century B.C.

In addition to this etymology of the noun *mnḥ* from **mnḥ*, "to deliver," Cohen (2023, 62) seems to suggest a *mem*-preformative noun from **nwḥ*, "to rest," as a possibility, to the extent that in Classical Hebrew the root "in the Hiphil stem … can mean 'to cause to rest' … and 'to place, set down.'"

To return, finally, to the Statue of Idrimi, the possible connection of Akkadian *manahtu* and Ugaritic *mnḥ*, as well as the root of the latter word, are important for understanding the Parattarna episode in the body inscription because, in addition to referring to the *mānahātu* of Idrimi's ancestors, the inscription qualifies the *mānahātu* in line 48 as something that those ancestors did for the Hurrian kings with a verb written as *in-na-hu-u₂* (see line 41 for another attestation of the verb). Among the various suggestions for this verb found in the scholarship are *anāhu*, "to toil," and *nâhu*, "to be at rest"; see the commentary to line 41 in §A.2. Apart from the fact that we might expect the 3mp N-stem durative of *nâhu* to be *innuhhū* and not **inahhū*, the best reason to see the verb in the body inscription as a form of *anāhu* is that the clearest attestations of this verb with the same sense exist in texts found at, but not always written at, Ugarit (so already Kühne 1982, 246).

The texts of four royal deeds in which individuals are granted property or exemptions by the king of Ugarit use a form of *anāhu* to state explicitly that the grant has been made because the individual "labored" for the king; note, in particular, that it is impossible to derive *anih* or *ētanah* from *nâhu*.[28] As Márquez Rowe (2006, 246–47) has explained, the verb *anāhu* is employed in these texts to indicate that "the royal grants, promotions or immunities in question are in fact a reward for faithful service."[29] Furthermore, a similar use of *anāhu* occurs in a manuscript of the famous treaty between Šuppiluliuma I and Niqmaddu II of Ugarit.[30] Since the treaty was written at the Hittite chancellery and subsequently sent to Ugarit, this attestation demonstrates that the use of *anāhu* to indicate "sustained, continuous, and lasting effort or service" is found outside of Ugarit and also that it could describe interpolity relations, not just intrapolity ones.

At this point, I have already mentioned Cohen 2023 twice without addressing the article's major claim—namely, that the attestations of *mānahtu* in the Parattarna episode in the Statue of Idrimi's body inscription should be understood in light of the attestations of the same word in the plural in RSOu 23 as referring to obligatory payments made by Idrimi's ancestors to Parattarna I's ancestors, for which "tribute" is an approximate translation. I am in complete agreement with the claim, even if I might disagree with a couple of the details, such as how to understand the singular form of the noun in Emar land grant LN-104 or the verb *in-na-hu-u*$_2$ that appears in line 48 of the body inscription. I also wholeheartedly agree with what Cohen (2023, 64) sees as one of the larger implications of his

---

[28] ^{m}IR$_3^{du}$ *a-na* LUGAL *a-ni-*⸢*ih*⸣ *u*$_3$ *ša uš-bal-*⸢*ki*⸣*-it ni-id-na an-na-a* ^{d}IM EN HUR.SAG *ha-zi li-iš-al-šu*, "(PN$_1$ will deliver 10 shekels yearly. He is exempt (of obligations) to the overseer of chariot(s) and the *hazannu*-official).... PN$_2$ [= PN$_1$'s father] labored for the king, so, with regard to whoever undoes this gift, let Baʿlu, the lord of Mount Hazzi, call him to a reckoning!" (PRU 3 83–84 [RS 16.157]: 24–28); *a-na* UGU LUGAL⸢*ri*⸣ [EN-*šu* ^{m}*si*$_2$]*-na-ra-*[*nu*] *e-ta-na-*⸢*ah*⸣ [*šu-u*$_2$] ⸢*u*$_3$ E$_2$⸣*-šu a-na* ⸢DUMU⸣.MEŠ *ša* ⸢*re*⸣*-ši*, "(As of today, PN is exempt.)... PN has labored on behalf of the king, [his lord. (Now) he] and his household *belong to* the sons of the *ša rēši*-official" (PRU 3 107–108 [RS 16.238+]: 15–17); [*a*]*-na* LUGAL *e*$^{!}$(A)*-ta-na-ah* LUGAL *ip-*⸢*ṭu*$_2$⸣*-ur-*⸢*šu*⸣ [*u*$_3$] ⸢*u*$_2$⸣*-za-ak-ki-šu ki-i-ma* ^{d}UTU^{ši}, "(From this day on, RN has exempted PN, the female servant.)... She labored [f]or the king, (so) the king released her (text: him) [and] exempted her (text: him) like the sun" (PRU 3 110 [RS 16.267]: 7–8); *a-na* LUGAL EN-⸢*šu*⸣ *a-ni-ih dan-niš*$_2$ *dan-niš*$_2$*-ma*, "(The king has transferred houses ... to PN and his sons forever.) He labored greatly for the king, his lord" (PRU 3 140–41 [RS 16.132]: 29–30).

[29] Márquez Rowe (2006, 246 n. 128) also put to rest an earlier interpretation of these verbs by Kestemont (1974, 557), who wished to derive them from a root **hnh*, which he understood on the basis of a Classical Hebrew parallel to have the base meaning "to diminish, weaken" and an extended, juridical, sense "to assume a legal obligation, to be(come) obliged to a person."

[30] *an-nu-ma-ma* ^{m}*ni-iq-ma-an-du* ⸢*it*⸣*-ti* ^{lu2}KUR*-ia na-ki-ir u*$_3$ *it-ti ša-la-mi*$_3$*-ia ša-lim u*$_3$ *a-na* ^{d}UTU^{ši} LUGAL GAL *be-li-šu i-ta-na-ah dan-niš*$_2$ *u*$_3$ *ri-kil*$_2$*-ta ša-la-ma ša* KUR *ha-at-ti na-ṣi-ir*, "Now Niqmaddu (II) is at war with my enemy and at peace with my ally. He has labored greatly for the Sun, the Great King, his lord. He has observed the peace treaty with (lit. of) the land of Hatti" (PRU 4 48–52, 67–70 [RS 17.340+]: rev. 11′–14′).

analysis, that it allows us "to ... gain one more step in the reconstruction of the history of imperial Mitanni about which so little is known." Indeed, I would extrapolate still further and say that the attestations of *ʾnḫ in both the Hurrian and Hittite spheres of influence—in documents produced by both hegemons and their subordinates, as verbs and as nouns, and, possibly, in both Akkadian and Ugaritic—demonstrate that the words *anāhu* and *mānahtu* held a vibrant and productive place in the political discourse of Anatolia and the Levant during the Late Bronze Age, which they did not in contemporary Mesopotamia.

4.4. ARGUMENTS FOR ACKNOWLEDGING THE HEGEMONY OF MITTANI

We see, then, that the meaning of *mānahtu* in the body inscription is very different than the meaning of the same word in the cheek inscription, but this difference in meaning is actually the point! Using the word *mānahtu* in the cheek inscription to frame the narrative in the body inscription as *narû* literature transformed Idrimi into the royal figure whose actions *should* serve as an example for future kings. The attestations of the same word in the Parattarna episode served as signposts, guiding the ancient reader toward an understanding of precisely *how* Idrimi could function as a positive example. The plural forms of the word in the Parattarna episode, however, distinguish the meaning of the word from its meaning in the cheek inscription. These attestations were drawn from the vocabulary of political discourse in Anatolia and the Levant during the Late Bronze Age in order to portray Idrimi as a ruler who seeks to become a political subordinate of the kings of Mittani. The didactic message is clear: acknowledging the hegemony of Mittani is not just desirable but necessary.

Indeed, according to the inscriptions' perspective, such political subordination is the only true path to legitimate rule. To continue the passage quoted above, it is only when Idrimi swears a loyalty oath to the Mittani king that he really becomes king of Alalah: "In my status as a retainer, in my loyalty, I seized *this abandoned hem* for him, and so I was king. Kings from all around *came up to me* at Alalah, and I was their equal" (ll. 57–59). In particular, the nominal predicate *šarrāku*, which appears in the cheek inscription (l. CI 1) as well as in this passage (l. 58), has already been discussed above (see §4.2) as an answer to the Epic of Gilgamesh's question, "Who ... can say like Gilgamesh, 'I was king'?" The use of *šarrāku* at the end of the Parattarna episode and in the cheek inscription thus not only emphasizes the close connection between the cheek inscription and this pivotal passage concerning the desirability of acknowledging the king of Mittani's hegemony but also ties the cheek inscription still more tightly to the Epic of Gilgamesh and the framing device employed in the prologue of the Standard Babylonian recension.

I want to conclude this chapter by returning to the question of orthographic and paleographic variation in the inscriptions with which the chapter opened. We left off discussion of these features by citing Weeden's (2019, 142–43) observation, made more in reference to legal texts from Level IV Alalah than the Idrimi inscriptions but still germane, that the employment of orthographic (or, equally, paleographic) variation adds another level of signification to a written utterance, "establishing pedigree and signalling superiority" over and above the utterance's content. We asked what the particular content of the Idrimi inscriptions was that impelled its scribe to establish his pedigree and superiority, and we began discussing the cheek inscription and the Parattarna episode in order to answer this question. We are now in a position to provide that answer. As described above, the inscriptions are making an argument about the need for the ruler of Alalah to acknowledge the hegemony of the king of Mittani. By signaling pedigree and superiority, the orthographic and paleographic variation that runs through the inscriptions makes a second, paralinguistic, argument portraying them as wise and erudite texts, steeped in cuneiform learning, whose primary-level argument should therefore be accepted.

Recognition that the inscriptions on the Statue of Idrimi were making arguments to one or more contemporary audiences is welcome not just because it helps us to make sense of key features of the texts, such as the interconnection between the words written on Idrimi's body and those on his cheek or the rampant paleographic and orthographic variation that has so frustrated modern scholars, but also because those arguments themselves become valuable evidence in reenvisioning the statue, its inscriptions, and, perhaps most crucially, the statue's own transformation from the representation of a nameless, collective ancestor to a particular, historically situated one. However, recognizing that the inscriptions are making arguments provokes another question: Who was (were) the audience(s) for these arguments? The next chapter attempts to answer this question.

5
Audiences

The previous chapter ended by recognizing that the inscriptions on the Statue of Idrimi were making an argument to one or more contemporary audiences and asking, consequently, who the audience(s) may have been. In this chapter, I identify Alalah's nobility, the *maryannu*, as one audience that was targeted for the argument. I open the chapter by demonstrating that the *maryannu* of Late Bronze Age Alalah probably possessed an advanced education in cuneiform Akkadian and so represent a potential audience for the Idrimi text. I then explore the portrayal of Idrimi himelf as a *maryannu* in the narrative and contend that this portrayal implies that the city's *maryannu* were not just a potential audience but a targeted one. After a short excursus as to how the *maryannu* might have accessed the Idrimi text, I end the chapter by considering why the text's argument in favor of acknowledging Mittanian hegemony might have been addressed to the city's *maryannu*: these men could influence the city's political direction, and their willingness to accept the ruler of Alalah's decisions could not be taken for granted.

5.1. LITERACY AND THE *MARYANNU* AT LATE BRONZE AGE ALALAH

Who was or were the audience(s) for the Idrimi inscriptions? A partial answer to this question is readily available. Whoever the contemporary audience(s), they must have had a relatively high degree of scribal training in order to be able to recognize the allusions to texts like the Cuthean Legend of Naram-Sin or the Epic of Gilgamesh and to appreciate the diversity of sign forms, archaic and contemporary, inscribed on the statue. Other intertextual allusions in the text, such as a probable reference to the lexical list Lu in the sequential use of the logograms A.A and NINDA₂ for *abu*, "father," in lines 87 and 89 (see §3.2), also indicate that at least one intended contemporary audience had scribal training. This partial answer then points one way forward. If we can identify who would have had a relatively high degree of scribal training at Alalah a time contemporary with the statue, then we can identify one *potential* audience for the inscriptions' argument.

One immediate difficulty with this approach is the relative lack of Late Bronze Age texts that, like the Idrimi inscriptions, postdate the destruction of the Level IV palace. However, I believe that there is some justification for trying to answer the question by exploring who had a relatively high degree of scribal training during the somewhat earlier time period documented by the Level IV corpus and then considering that answers we find in this corpus are also valid for Alalahian society during the period of time after the destruction of the Level IV palace but before Hittite conquest of the city—namely, Sir Leonard Woolley's Level III(/II), Amir Fink's (2010) Level IVB^{F}, or the current excavation's Period 3 (Yener, Akar, and Horowitz 2019a). Doing so seems warranted because "the end of Level IV" is essentially a statement about architecture and not one about social and political (dis)continuities (see §2.1). These discontinuities would be expected later, after the Hittite conquest.

When we talk about scribes and scribal training in the Level IV corpus, we need to acknowledge that we are dealing with a continuum. As Theo van den Hout (2020, 293–94) has explained, "the ancients themselves are at least partly to blame for this confusing situation: they use the same term (DUB.SAR) for what might be best described as both scribe and scholar." At the one end, we must imagine scribes who operated in institutional or noninstitutional contexts and produced administrative texts in the course of tracking the receipt and disbursement of commodities. Speaking of the Hittite world, van den Hout (2020, 293) described these scribes as "a work force of average tablet writers and clerks, simple scribal craftsmen working in chancelleries, temples, and all kinds of offices doing the bookkeeping and drawing up of standard documents." These activities would have required a relatively low level of literacy and numeracy and not necessitated any exposure to literary texts during scribal training. Looking at the Level IV corpus, we find one example of a scribe who seems to have belonged on this end of the continuum: a certain PN, the son of Ewri-Kiaše, who was a member of the *ehelle* social class and who is listed and identified by his profession among leatherworkers, a cartwright, and other professional specialists in the census list AlT 153 [413.17 = *SSAU* 2 33]: 30.

At the opposite end of the continuum, we can imagine individuals who were highly educated in cuneiform and who would have been familiar with the Mesopotamian literary tradition as a result of this education. One such group conceivably functioned as "palace scribes," and so were attached, for example, to a chancellery, acted as the supervisors of the clerks such as PN, the son of Ewri-Kiaše, described above, and were the ones who actually composed treaties, royal inscriptions, and other prestige documents for the king. A second group of individuals at this end of the continuum would have played a role as magico-religious specialists, whose day-to-day activities necessitated their familiarity with incantations, hymns, omina, and other specialized scholarly literature. Finally, we might also find at this end of the continuum wealthy, high status individuals, *les hommes d'affaires* who were not employed as scribes by anyone at all but whose literacy and numeracy enabled them to pursue their own business affairs (writing letters and contracts) and, just as importantly, afforded them cultural capital. Furthermore, it is important to note that none of these three descriptions are mutually exclusive; a single individual could conceivably have been a wealthy religious functionary who combined duties at a temple with managing his own business affairs and was asked on occasion to help draft important state documents.

A group of tablets from Level IV Alalah that has been described by Eva von Dassow (2005, 47) as a "scholar's library" seems to have belonged to just such an individual. The excavations of Woolley, as well as Aslıhan Yener and Murat Akar discovered scholarly texts at Alalah, which have already been mentioned several times because their presence at the site demonstrates that advanced scholarly activity was occurring at the site. Specifically, these scholarly texts comprise lexical lists, incantations, omina, and hymns. While most of the lexical lists lack any firm archaeological context,[1] at least seven other scholarly texts were found together in the central courtyard (room 1) of the Level IV palace.[2] In her analysis of the archaeological context of the Level IV tablets, von Dassow (2005, 48) concluded that the find-spot of these tablets implies that they fell from the upper story of a suite of two rooms (C1-D1) that ran along the courtyard's northeastern side and adjoined the Level IV palace.

This conclusion is important because three tablets, seemingly the remnants of an archive belonging to a certain Kabiya, were found on the ground floor inside of suite C1-D1.[3] One of these texts, AlT 15 [36.1] records Kabiya and his sons' "promotion to *maryanni*-status and appointment as priest" of ^{d}EN.LIL$_{2}$. Both the archaeological association of AlT 448–453a to suite C1-D1 and the fact that "scribal training and possession of incantation tablets, omen tablets, and hymns

1 One lexical list found by Woolley's excavations, AlT 447 [5.3], was found below the floor of the Level III/II fortress and so may date to Level IV. The other two lexical lists found by his excavations (AlT 445 [5.1] and 446 [5.2]) and the three lexical fragments found by Yener's excavations (*JNES* 64: 55–56 and *NABU* 2017/53 [AT 13062], 2017/53 [AT 22997]) were all discovered near the surface or otherwise in an unspecified secondary context; see the discussion of von Dassow (2017).

2 Incantations: AlT 448 [6.1], 449 [6.2], and 450 [6.3]. Omen collections: AlT 451 [6.4] and AlT 452 [6.5]. Hymns: AlT 453 [6.6] and 453a [6.7]. These tablets were recorded on a single field card with the excavation numbers ATT/38/34–42. As the count of tablets with excavation numbers (nine) exceeds the count of published tablets (seven), two tablets from this group may be missing; see von Dassow 2005, 40.

3 AlT 15 [36.1] (grant of *maryannu* status and appointment as *šangû*-priest); AlT 87 [32.1] (testament); AlT 88 [32.2] (transfer of property). The principal actors in AlT 88 [32.2] do not have any explicit relationship to Kabiya and his family, so an explanation for the presence of this document in suite C1-D1 is not readily apparent; see von Dassow 2008, 272 for discussion.

would be consonant with their [= Kabiya and his sons'] role as priests" have led von Dassow (2005, 48) to infer that the "scholar's library" originally belonged to Kabiya. On the basis of scholarly tablets actually discovered at Alalah, then, we know that one individual who had advanced scribal training at Level IV Alalah was both a member of the *maryannu* class and also a *šangû*-priest, whose connection to Alalah's ruling family was strong enough for him to have apparently inhabited a residence literally attached to the palace.[4] In the figure of Kabiya, then, we seem to meet an individual with advanced scribal training who acted as a magico-religious specialist. We might speculate further that Kabiya functioned on occasion as a "palace scribe" on account of his close physical association with the palace.

From the list of witnesses who appear together in Kabiya's testament, AlT 87 [32.1], it seems clear that Kabiya was also at home among the wealthy, high-status residents of Level IV Alalah. In the Level IV witness lists to legal texts, the practice (as in cuneiform legal texts from other times and places) was for the scribe who drew up the text to list himself last. The witness lists themselves generally comprise a small recurring group of individuals of high status, such as *šukkallu*-ministers, *šangû*-priests, and *hazannu*-mayors, and one concurs with Christian Niedorf's (2008, 144) impression "daß dieselben Männer der führenden Gesellschaftsschicht sich vor dem König gegenseitig ihre Geschäfte bezeugen." For our purposes, the key observation when looking at the witness lists is that a single individual sometimes functioned as the scribe to a legal text and other times simply acted as a witness within this circle of friends.[5] We can illustrate this point with three examples, beginning with the witness list to Kabiya's testament, AlT 87 [32.1], mentioned above.

Eleven individuals appear in this witness list, which begins (ll. 23–34) with a certain Taguhli, the son of Uštaya, who can be securely identified as a *maryannu* (von Dassow 2002, 844), and Ilimi-ilima, the son of Tuttu, both father and son being very prominent men (see below and §5.4). The witness list also includes, among others, a Taguwa, who is identified as "the son of the *šukkallu*-minister" (l.

[4] Von Dassow (2005, 48) noted that "if Kabiya did indeed dwell here, next door to the king, Suite C1-D1 was probably not his only residence, for AlT 87 indicates that his household was sizable." Subsequently, von Dassow (2008, 272) raised the intriguing possibility that Suite C1-D1 could have been Kabiya's workplace, not his residence.

[5] For a similar situation in the Hittite world in ca. 1250–1200, see van den Hout (2020, 306–7), who discusses scribes who appear as witnesses in three Hittite treaties together with "the highest military, diplomatic, administrative-economic, and judicial competencies of the state, those otherwise closest to the king (the *tuhkanti* or second-in-command, princes, some in-laws), and probably the most important vassal kings … as well as some local governors…. Serving as witnesses alongside others belonging to the highest echelons of Hittite society, this is indisputable evidence of elevated status of the seven scribes listed. For most of them we do not have tablets that they themselves wrote but all of them have connections to the scribal profession."

27), an individual named Tehiya (*ti-hi-ia*), and the tablet's scribe, a certain Kušah-ewri (^{d}30-EN DUB.SAR, l. 33). This Kušah-ewri is attested a scribe in at least two other legal texts (AlT 48 [353.2]: 22; AlT 103 [37.4]: rev. 7′ [restored]); if we follow von Dassow's (2008, 454) suggestion to identify him with an individual with the hypocoristic name Kušaya, he would be attested as a scribe in three more legal texts as well (AlT 16 [36.2]: 24; AlT 46 [352.1]: 18; AlT 98e [37.1]: rev. 6′). However, this Kušah-ewri seems to have been more than just a scribe, for in AlT 104 [37.5]: rev. 4′, the name appears in the witness list followed by the title "*šuk-kallu*-minister" (^{d}30-EN SUKKAL), and the presence in lines rev. 1′–2′ of this witness list of two of the same individuals who also appear in the witness list to AlT 87 [32.1]—Taguhli and Tehiya—strongly suggests that we are dealing with the same individual, a *šukkallu*-minister who also drew up legal texts for other high status individuals who were, at a minimum, acquaintances. And the fact that all of these individuals appear as witnesses to Kabiya's testament implies that he, too, had a place among them, in addition to his role as religious official.

Most of the attestations of scribes in the Level IV documentation occur in the witness lists to legal texts (von Dassow 2008, 285–86 gathers the references), designating the scribe who drew up the document; when we follow the individuals designated as such through the Level IV corpus, we find them in alternative roles and also possessing high status, similar to the example of Kušah-ewri, the scribe and *šukkallu*-minister. For instance, in the marriage contract AlT 91 [33.1]: 23, Ašraqama is attested as the document's scribe;[6] other witnesses include the Taguhli we met above (l. 21), a certain Agi-^{d}IM (l. 21), and even Šarruwa (l. 22), probably the famous Level IV scribe, although not acting in that capacity in this text. In AlT 67 [341.2]: 11, we also find Ašraqama in the witness list, again with Agi-^{d}IM (now identified as a *šangû*-priest, l. 13) and Taguhli (*ta-gu*$_{5}$*-hu-*<*li*>, l. 12), but now not functioning as the document's scribe, who is instead a certain Tuppiya (l. 14). Indeed, in this text, Ašraqama is listed as the very first witness, suggesting that he had a higher status than the *šangû*-priest Agi-^{d}IM and Taguhli and that his position after them in the witness list of AlT 91 [33.1] was due only to his role as that document's scribe.[7]

---

[6] Because of Ašraqama's position at the end of the witness list, von Dassow's (2008, 278 n. 54) suggestion to read the profession following his name as DUB.SAR seems certain to me; cf. the readings SUKKAL, found in Niedorf 2008, 266 and Dietrich and Mayer 1996, 185, and E$_{2}$.[GAL.LI]M, found in Na'aman 1980b, 111.

[7] These are the only three attestations of the personal name Ašraqama in the Level IV corpus, but the same individual may also be encountered in the solitary attestation of the name Ašriya (AlT 74 [342.3]: 19), possibly a hypocoristic of Ašraqama (von Dassow 2008, 285). Ašriya is the scribe of AlT 74 [342.3] and appears in its witness list in the company of a number of highly ranked individuals, so this identification, if correct, would add further support to the argument about his high status presented here.

But it is the legal text AlT 74 [342.3] that gives us our best example of a high-status individual identifying himself as a scribe on some occasions but not others. This individual is a certain Biriyaššura, who appears as a witness to four legal transactions. In these transactions, the creditor is either a father or his son, once a certain Tuttu (AlT 74 [342.3]) and three times his son Ilimi-ilima (AlT 48 [352.3], 49 [352.4], and 70 [341.5]). Tuttu and Ilimi-ilima, whom we briefly met above in connection with Kabiya's testament (AlT 87 [32.1]) and who are discussed again later in this chapter (see §5.4), were two of the wealthiest and most important men attested in the Level IV corpus, with the son securely identified as a *maryannu* (Bunnens 1978; von Dassow 2008, 170, 294–97). In the earliest of the texts, AlT 74 [342.3], in which Ašriya is the scribe, Biriyaššura appears in the witness list alongside well-attested individuals such as Pallanuwe, the royal administrator (*šatam šarri*; von Dassow 2008, 171); Irkabtu, "a prominent official with responsibilities for the army" (von Dassow 2008, 147); and Iri-Halba, who is known to have been a *maryannu* (von Dassow 2008, 390). In the three later texts, Biriyaššura appears consistently in the witness lists with the *maryannu* Taguhli and twice with Tehiya; see above. In two of these texts (AlT 49 [352.4], 70 [341.5]) Biriyaššura is the scribe, but in one (AlT 48 [352.3]) he is not. Like Ašraqama, we encounter a situation where sometimes Biriyaššura takes his turn as the scribe responsible for a legal text but other times is just a witness.

But the most significant attestation of Biriyaššura has to be AlT 109 [2.6], a letter sent by the man himself to Alalah's ruler, Niqmepa (and so representing one of his earlier attestations, with AlT 74 [342.3] and 353 [44.15]). In this letter, Biriyaššura addresses the king by name, not title, and with a surprisingly familiar greeting formula: *a-na* ^{m}*niq*$_{2}$*-me-pa um-ma* ^{m}*bi-ri-a-šur-ru-ma bu-lu-uṭ* SIG$_{5}$-⸢*qi*$_{2}$⸣-*iš a-na mi-im-mu-ka lu-u*$_{2}$ *šul-mu*, "Thus says Biriyaššura to Niqmepa: Live in good health! May your possessions be well!" (ll. 1–5). This greeting formula contrasts strongly with the note of deference that we expect an inferior would show in writing to his lord; compare, for instance, the opening of AlT 107 [2.4]: *a-na* LUGAL^{ri} *be-li-i*[*a*] *qi*$_{2}$*-bi*$_{2}$*-ma um-ma* ^{m}*ir-te-šu-ba* [(…)] *a-na* GIR$_{3}^{pi_{2}}$ *be-li-i*[*a*], "Speak to the king, my lord! Thus says Ir-Teššub: (I fall) at the feet of my lord!" (ll. 1–4).

Indeed, the contrast is so great and unexpected that von Dassow (2008, 286 n. 69) doubted that the sender of AlT 109 [2.6] could be the same as "the scribe Biriyaššura who was employed in Niqmepa's administration." But this doubt rests on the assumption that the authors of legal documents were "scribes" who were "employed" and so postulates another individual simply in order to fit this assumption. However, the name Biriyaššura is uncommon in the Level IV corpus (AlT 109 [2.6] is the only attestation besides the ones found in the witness lists and legal texts discussed above), so it seems better to follow Niedorf (2008, 40 with n. 47) in accepting that the sender of AlT 109 [2.6] is the same as the Biriyaššura of the legal texts. Indeed, Niedorf suggested that the familiar greeting formula is evidence of "ein großes Vertrauensverhältnis, evtl. sogar eine enge Verwandtschaft" between Biriyaššura and the king.[8]

Indeed, the fact that nothing seems to distinguish those individuals who are sometimes qualified as scribes in legal texts (and sometimes not) from the other high-status individuals who appear as witnesses in the same lists implies that the sometime scribes possessed the same high status and that scribal training was widespread among these individuals during Level IV. The conclusion that the sometime scribes, sometime witnesses who appear in the witness lists of the Level IV legal texts were members of the upper echelons of Alalah's society is reinforced by several administrative texts in which many of these same men mentioned above appear together in groups in connection with some task they all had in common, from the perspective of the royal administration.

For instance, there is AlT 156 [415.5], an administrative text listing individuals associated with a temple of Kubi, in which we find both our sometime-scribes Ašraqama and Biriyaššura, as well as Iri-Halba, Taguhli, a *šangû*-priest, and two sons of a *šukkallu*-minister.[9] AlT 353 [44.15], an administrative text listing individuals with and without sheep, includes our Biriyaššura, as well as the *šatam šarri* Pallanuwe, Iri-Halba, a *šangû*-priest, the *šukkallu*-minister, at least one of the *šukkallu*-minister's sons, and other high-status individuals known from other texts. As von Dassow (2002, 910–11) summarized it, "the men named in AlT 353 … evidently constituted a group of prominent residents of Alalah … who were closely associated with the palace. …It is tempting to suggest that AlT 353 records the distribution or collection of sheep on some particular occasion, involving important Alalahians." Finally, a number of these same men, such as the sons of the *šukkallu*-minister, and others that we have met in the legal texts discussed above, such as Ilimi-ilima and Taguhli, appear in a third tablet, AlT 128 [414.1], listing *maryannu* who "were probably resident in the city of Alalah," some of whom "were also members of what could be called the royal court" (von Dassow 2002, 847).

One last text must be mentioned in connection with this discussion of literacy at Level IV Alalah. AlT 51 [352.6] is a legal text whose caption to the seal impression on the obverse of this text identifies the seal as belonging to an unnamed ^{lu_2}GIR$_3$ DUB.SAR. While the logogram (^{lu_2})GIR$_3$ is often used to designate relatively low-level functionaries responsible for conveying goods from their place of disbursement to their place of final use, it does not seem to indicate such a role in AlT 51 [352.6]. As Niedorf (2008, 384) noted, the seal impression of this ^{lu_2}GIR$_3$ is in the exact place on the tablet where the royal seal was typically impressed,

---

[8] Cf. AlT 403 [47.12], where a certain Biriyaššuwa—a similar, but not identical, name—receives twenty talents of copper from the palace for a business venture (*harrānu*) to the land of Hatti.

[9] Von Dassow (2002, 856) notes that other names listed in the text "are attested elsewhere as names of members of the *maryanni* class," while cautioning that "some of these names, as well as additional ones, are also attested as members of the *hupše* class."

meaning that the individual qualified as ^{lu_2}GIR$_3$ DUB.SAR "als Stellvertreter des Königs die Rechtmäßigkeit des hier festgehaltenen Geschäfts garantierte" and so had "eine hohe administrative Stellung." Accordingly, Niedorf suggested that ^{lu_2}GIR$_3$ is an abbreviation for a longer logogram, such as ^{lu_2}GIR$_3$.NITA$_2$, *šakkanakku*, "governor," or ^{lu_2}GIR$_3$.ŠE$_3$.GA, *sākinnu*, "prefect." Von Dassow (2015a, 188) considered this a "weakly-founded supposition," preferring instead that "this tablet should be understood as a document drawn up independent of royal authority—that is why witnesses and the scribe seal it instead of the king." But von Dassow's interpretation ignores the office that occurs before DUB.SAR in the caption, ^{lu_2}GIR$_3$. Indeed, there is actually no reason why this ^{lu_2}GIR$_3$ DUB.SAR was necessarily the scribe responsible for AlT 51 [352.6];[10] if he was not, his decision to identify himself as a scribe nonetheless would be even more suggestive of how this qualification had meaning as a marker of identity outside of simple legal functionalism. Ultimately, the seal impression of the ^{lu_2}GIR$_3$ DUB.SAR at the site where we normally find royal seal impressions in AlT 51 [352.6] is tantalizing, but, on the basis of our current knowledge, we can only speculate as to its significance.

Nonetheless, the Level IV legal and administrative texts still allow us to draw a picture of who possessed the ability to read and write Akkadian cuneiform during the second half of the fifteenth century BCE: occupational specialists on par with craftsmen such as leatherworkers and cartwrights, to be sure, but also the city's nobility—a wealthy, influential, and relatively closed circle of men. We are not always, or even usually, able to determine their social class, but when we are, these individuals are *maryannu*. And, as discussed above, there is good reason to think that this picture of cuneiform literacy is also applicable to the first half of the fourteenth century—namely, Woolley's Level III(–II), the current excavation's Period 3, and the range of time during which the Statue of Idrimi and its text(s) need to be dated, because there is no reason to understand the transition from Level IV to Level III to have been accompanied by any political or social transformation, since Alalah continued to acknowledge the hegemony of Mittani during Level III until the second half of the fourteenth century. As we stated in chapter 4, recognizing an argument in the Idrimi inscriptions implies the existence of a contemporary audience for that argument. Wealthy and high status individuals such as the kingdom's *maryannu* in the early fourteenth century, who had the time and resources to enjoy a more advanced education in Akkadian cuneiform, represent one such potential audience.

---

[10] Because the scribe responsible for a legal text typically appears as the final name in the witness list, the scribe of AlT 51 [352.6] was probably named Tu-[…]. However, the ^{lu_2}GIR$_3$'s seal inscription identifies its owner as [Y]ana-[…]. Of course, it is possible that Tu-[…] used a seal that he had inherited, in which case he could be identified with the ^{lu_2}GIR$_3$.

5.2. AUDIENCE IDENTIFICATION: IDRIMI AS *MARYANNU*

But can we identify Alalah's *maryannu* not just as a potential audience but as a targeted audience for the inscriptions' arguments?[11] If we look at the portrayal of Idrimi as hero in the body inscription, I believe we can. Significantly, the narrative of Idrimi's life portrays him as a *maryannu*. This portrayal should be understood as a rhetorical strategy, conscious or unconscious on the part of the author, to strengthen audience members' connection to the text and their receptivity to the text's arguments by encouraging them to see a reflection of themselves, or what they aspired to be, in the narrative's hero. The literature on audience identification is vast, spanning disciplines such as literary criticism, media studies, and psychology, and cannot be easily summarized here. (For one theoretical framework coming out of the empirical study of literature, see Oatley 1994 and Oatley 1999.) But, in short, a central finding is that audiences respond favorably to characters in narratives who remind them of themselves; the authors of narratives, aware of this truth, create characters who reflect their target audience in order to provoke this favorable response.

To be sure, studies on audience identification are generally based on contemporary audiences' engagements with contemporary media, and it would be anachronistic to simply assume that Late Bronze Age audiences engaged in the same ways we do with the narratives that they encountered. However, it would also be patronizing to dismiss out of hand the possibility that a Late Bronze Age audience could identify with a narrative's protagonist. For instance, in an extended reading of the mythological composition from Ugarit known as the Baal Cycle, Aaron Tugendhaft (2018) argued that this narrative of deities sending messengers, building houses, banqueting, fighting, and dying served as a Late Bronze Age critique of the "divine foundation" of contemporary politics (127). While Tugendhaft's reading of the text as "subversive criticism" (Pardee 2019, 172) has not received wholesale support, his larger point—that the narrative cannot be automatically read as representative of some timeless Canaanite cosmogony "emerging from the distant past" (Tugendhaft 2018, 28) but needs to be first approached within the immediate historical context of the narrative's manuscripts—seems unimpeachable. And, whether the Baal Cycle is thought to have been composed, adapted, or simply thought relevant enough to recopy at Late Bronze Age Ugarit, what emerges from such an approach is a reading of the text in which gods are represented as human rulers in order to make an appeal to an audience of human rulers.[12] There is good reason, then, to think that the authors of other

---

[11] This section incorporates, revises, and expands upon material published in Lauinger 2021.

[12] That the ruler of Ugarit was one of the audiences that Tugendhaft (2018) has in mind for the Baal Cycle is my own inference. Despite referring to one or more audiences for the text throughout the book (e.g., "the dynamic relationship between audience and text" [5]

Late Bronze Age narratives, especially one like the Idrimi narrative that was composed in the Late Bronze Age, had their audience(s) in mind, consciously or not, in the portrayal of their protagonists.

The point is important because if we can grant some level of audience identification with the Idrimi narrative, we can work backward from the representation of Idrimi in the narrative to the audience for whom that representation was intended; in other words, we can begin to define the inscriptions' targeted audience. However, the claim that Idrimi is portrayed as a *maryannu* in the narrative requires some support, because a half century of scholarship, going back to A. Leo Oppenheim's 1955 review of Sidney Smith's edition (61), has found a home for the narrative of Idrimi's life—a younger son loses his home, sojourns far away, and wins a kingdom—in a Levantine, West Semitic–speaking literary context, which makes it almost a temporal analog to the Baal Cycle, a universal Canaanite tale "emerging from the distant past," to use Tugendhaft's words, quoted above. We should be cautious, though, in attributing this type of story—what Edward Greenstein (2015) termed "the fugitive hero narrative pattern"—too readily to the Levantine world. In a perceptive study that acts as a critique of the universalizing approaches of twentieth century pioneers of narratology such as Lord Raglan, Vladimir Propp, and Joseph Campbell and their inheritors, Greenstein identified the fugitive hero pattern in stories from Egypt, Hatti, and first-millennium Assyria and Babylonia. However, Greenstein was more interested in their differences than their similarities: "Beyond the shared structure, each fugitive hero narrative develops its own individual themes and objectives. In looking at a particular story, the variations on the pattern are especially significant and poignant. One is interested in seeing how each text departs from, adapts, or otherwise transforms the shared story pattern" (2015, 24). With Greenstein and Tugendhaft, we are interested less in the fact that the Idrimi narrative might share features with other ancient Near Eastern texts and more in the narrative's particularity.

As discussed in §2.8, the fugitive hero narrative pattern serves functionally, as it does in so many of the other texts in which it is found, to justify a usurper king's rule. Specifically in its first section, Idrimi's status as a younger brother, his flight from Halab following a political crisis, a seven-year period of exile, and a divine encounter give the narrative the character of "a kind of 'trial,' permitting the protagonist to qualify as a 'hero'" (Liverani 2004b, 94). This character has the effect of deemphasizing Idrimi's illegitimate origins and emphasizing his divine favor. Then, following a divine encounter, Idrimi seizes control of Alalah, and the action of the narrative shifts. In short order, Idrimi engages in diplomatic negotiations, launches a successful military campaign, commences building projects throughout

---

or "the poem's ancient Ugaritic audience" [102]), he does not, to my knowledge, define those audiences or the mode of their access to the text.

his kingdom, and reestablishes the proper performance of religious rites. As Gary Oller described it, "the second section … is designed to show Idrimi as a good ruler, and hence presents further justification for his legitimacy" (1977a, 193). In other words, Idrimi's actions as king provide additional proof of his divine favor and render irrelevant any concerns as to his—or his successors'—legitimacy.

But what about the specific manifestation of the pattern that we find in the Idrimi narrative, the ways in which it "departs from, adapts, or otherwise transforms the shared story pattern," to which Greenstein in the quotation above urges us to be sensitive? In other words, if Idrimi is a fugitive hero, whose hero is he? At this point, we want to look more closely at one sentence in the body inscription, which follows immediately upon the difficult passage in which Idrimi has the epiphany that prompts him to leave Emar and take up his adventure in earnest. Before he leaves Emar and enters the desert, the narrative pauses for Idrimi to note what he brought with him on his journey: [AN]ŠE.KUR.RA-[*i*]*a* ⸢^{giš}GIGIR⸣-*ia u*$_3$ $^{\text{lu}_2}$IŠ-*ia* [*el*]-*te*-⸢*qe*$_2$⸣-*šu-nu*, "I took my horse, my chariot, and my chariot-driver" (ll. 13–14).[13]

The details are striking in part because they are superfluous. As Jean-Marie Durand (2011, 156) remarked, "il est intéressant en tout cas de voir qu'il n'y a plus mention par la suite de ce *kîzum* [*sic*] (qui de toute façon reste pour nous un inconnu)."[14] Neither horse nor chariot reappear in the narrative either,[15] and the plot could continue in exactly the same way it does if all three were never mentioned. Still, though, of the three, the greatest surprise would seem to be the inclusion of the chariot driver, for, in his seminal study already quoted above, Mario Liverani (2004b, 89) traced the appearance and reappearance of a literary motif across the Late Bronze Age in which "the hero is alone, on a chariot, and ventures into the desert." For Liverani, the function of this motif "always is to emphasize the hero's valour by pointing out his loneliness" (87). If a solitary adventure is the point of the topos, why does the text seem to undermine the topos by having Idrimi begin it "mit … nur einem Begleiter" (Klengel 1981, 274) and, especially, one who will play no further role in the narrative?

In fact, as Liverani described, the solitary nature of the hero's adventure is only one of two aspects of the topos "leaving by chariot for the desert." The other aspect is "helpers or tools," which Liverani observed "at first seems to contradict the hero's isolation, an isolation that is crucial to the story" (Liverani 2004b, 91),

---

13 On the logogram $^{\text{lu}_2}$IŠ (= *kizû*) and the possible translations of the word as "chariot-driver" or "archer," see the commentary to line 13 in §A.2.

14 See the commentary to line 16 in §A.2 for the suggestion, not generally accepted in the literature, that the 3ms pronominal suffix -*šu* in line 16 in the clause *iš-ti-šu* … *bi-ta*$_2$*-ku*, refers back to the *kizû* in line 13 ("I spent with night with him").

15 Smith (1949, 15) read the partially preserved sign(s) at the beginning of line 17 as [^{giš}]GIGIR. This reading no longer seems possible after collations by Oller (1977a, 10, 34); Dietrich and Loretz (1981, 204); and myself; see the commentary to line 17 in §A.2.

just as in the Idrimi narrative. Liverani noted that these helpers and tools, which typically take the form of "chariots, horses, and grooms" in the Late Bronze Age expressions of the topos, in fact play two roles in the narrative. On the one hand, they provide the hero with a tangible means of transport. On the other hand, and less tangibly, "the prestige of the horse, a symbol of social status, and its privileged connection to the hero, [has] a psychological and social basis that is very strong and concrete in the Near East of the fifteenth to thirteenth centuries BC" (Liverani 2004b, 92). From the perspective of the narrative, Liverani concluded, "Idrimi might have been able to get from Emar to Ammiya on foot," but if he did not arrive in a chariot drawn by a horse, "he would never have been recognized by the refugees there as 'the son of their lord'" (Liverani 2004b, 92; see also Liverani 2011, 20: "le jeune héros du Bronze récent ne pouvait pas ne pas avoir un char, deux chevaux et un cocher").

The details in line 13 of the horse and chariot, then, work to give Idrimi a social and political identity. But what is the identity, and how does the presence of the chariot driver relate to it? Significantly, administrative documents from Level IV Alalah make clear that a close association existed between chariots and the *maryannu*, a characteristic social class of Late Bronze Age Syro-Anatolia that is particularly well attested at Level IV Alalah, as already seen in the discussion of literacy that opened this chapter. Some caution is required here, because many myths exist about *maryannu* and chariots. Happily, the social class has been the object of extended study by von Dassow (2008, 268–314, who lucidly dismantles the myths; see, esp. 87–90, 290, and 300–304), and her methodical examination of the evidence makes it clear that a close association existed between *maryannu* and chariot. For instance, even if a *maryannu* did not need to possess one in order to belong to the social class, census lists from Late Bronze Age Alalah show a careful concern in documenting whether or not individual *maryannu* possessed them at the moment of the texts' composition (von Dassow 2008, 303–4),[16] other administrative tablets "provide evidence that the palace supplied chariots, as well as horses, to members of the *maryann*[*u*] class" (von Dassow 2008, 309),[17] and the

[16] See, e.g., AlT 131+ [413.3 = *SSAU* 2 1]: 61–65, part of the section on *maryannu* of a census list of the town of Alime, which reads: "Maduwa—one with (lit. of) a chariot; Taguya—he does not have a chariot; Tagiya—he does not have a chariot; Kuša[x-x]-zi—he does not have a chariot; Ewiya—one with (lit. of) a chariot" (61 ^{m}*ma-du-wa ša* ^{giš}GIGIR 62 ^{m}*ta-gu*$_{5}$*-ia* ^{giš}GIGIR NU.TUK 63 ^{m}*ta-gi*$_{5}$*-ia* ^{giš}GIGIR NU.TUK 64 ^{m}*ku-ša*-x[x-x]-*zi* ^{giš}GIGIR NU.TUK 65 ^{m}*e-wi-ia ša* ^{giš}GIGIR).

[17] See, e.g., AlT 329 [44:1], which bears the heading "Tablet of yearling horses" (*tup-pi*$_{2}$ ANŠE.KUR.RA.HI.A MU.DIDLI, l. 1) and ends with a section that records the disbursement of teams of horses to three individuals and concludes, "They took (the horses) for *maryannu*" (*a-na ma-ri-a-na-te* : *il-qe*$_{3}$*-u*$_{2}$, l. 18). The nominal form *ma-ri-a-na-te* is difficult and has been interpreted either as a "Hurrian collective noun *maryannardi* or as an Akkadian

class analogous to Alalah's *maryannu* at Nuzi were termed *rākib narkabti*, "chariot rider," so that the chariot is literally written into the name of the social class.

Significantly, some of the same census lists that document *maryannu* and their chariots also list individuals who are identified as *kizû*, "chariot driver," and, interestingly, these chariot drivers are generally qualified as belonging to someone, usually the king.[18] As von Dassow, who also considered the *kizû* to have been a chariot driver, concluded:

> While a *maryann*[*u*] could employ his own *kizû*, the royal administration, in the person of the king, employed a number of *kizû*s. Therefore, besides providing horses and chariots for *maryann*[*u*] serving in the chariotry, the administration could also have provided them with chariot-drivers if … they had no *kizû* of their own. Each *maryann*[*u*] who went to war would set forth with his horse(s), his chariot, and his *kizû*, like Idrimi in the passage of the statue inscription that describes its hero setting out on his quest for kingship. (von Dassow 2008, 314)

Thus the chariot driver, together with the horse and chariot, represents simply one more piece of Idrimi's professional accoutrements so that, far from starting his adventure with an unexpected companion, Idrimi remains as solitary a figure when he leaves for the desert as the other heroes whom Liverani (2004b) studied. Horse, chariot, and chariot driver work together to present Idrimi both as a *maryannu* and as a heroic ideal.

At this point, we want to return to some of the central claims and implications of the phenomenon of audience identification that were discussed above: the creators of narratives are aware, consciously or not, of their audiences' favorable response to characters who "look" like them; these creators construct protagonists who reflect their targeted audience in order to increase the likelihood of a favorable response; and therefore the representations of these protagonists can serve as evidence for the intended audiences of the narratives. From the portrayal of Idrimi in the body inscription as a *maryannu*, then, the nobility of Late Bronze Age Alalah, ca. 1400–1350 BCE, emerges not just as a potential audience for the inscriptions but as a targeted one. The men who comprised the kingdom's *maryannu* would have found immediate appeal in the story of a *maryannu* who "left by chariot for the desert" to make his fortune. The kingdom's *maryannu* were one audience for the body inscription's argument about the need for the ruler of Alalah to acknowledge the legitimacy of Mittani.

---

feminine plural *maryannāti* … serving as an abstract noun" (von Dassow 2008, 306 with n. 111, citing previous literature).

18 See, e.g., AlT 131+ [413.3 = *SSAU* 2 1], the census list of the town of Alime mentioned above in connection to *maryannu* and chariots. It also lists a certain Huliga, the king's *kizû*, among the members of the *ehelle* social class resident at the town ([m]*hu-li-ga* [lú]IŠ LUGAL, line 47).

5.3. EXCURSUS: AUDIENCE ACCESS TO THE TEXT

At this point it is worth considering how the *maryannu* might have accessed the text of the Idrimi inscriptions. I have framed this section as an excursus in order to emphasize that demonstrating the ability of the *maryannu* to access the text is not fundamental to the claim that the inscriptions are making arguments to them. The claim that the *maryannu* are an intended ancient audience derives from a close reading of the statue and its inscriptions. Accordingly, at least some *maryannu* should have had access to the text, even if the manner of their access is not readily apparent to us. Nonetheless, it is still important to consider the question.

There would seem to be three possible modes by which an ancient audience could have accessed the text: they might have read it in the form of the inscription carved onto the statue, they might have read (versions of) it in the form of other manuscripts in circulation besides the inscription, or they might have heard (versions of) it transmitted orally. I believe that the first possibility can be ruled out, although with some qualification. Given its role in an ancestor cult (see chapter 3), one or more living persons must have interacted with Idrimi's statue during the presentation of the mortuary repast. Yet I do not believe that the inscriptions carved onto the statue were themselves ever meant to be read. Rather, the materiality and "presence" of the inscriptions on the statue would have had a profound effect on a beholder, especially in contrast to other contemporary, typically anepigraphic, ancestor statues with which he or she would have been familiar (again, see chapter 3).[19]

Indeed, the high degree of paleographic variation would have made the version of the text inscribed on the statue very difficult, if not impossible, to read. In fact, the variation implies that the version of the text on the statue was actually not intended to be read.[20] But the paleographic variation carries two additional implications with it. It implies that the inscriptions on the statue did have a contemporary audience who could observe and be impressed by the inscription's paleography. And it implies that at least some constituent part of this audience would have already been familiar with text and its argument in favor of Mittanian hegemony in order for the paralinguistic argument of this other version of the text that they could not read—the inscriptions on the statue—to succeed.

So we return to the question of how this audience would have accessed the text. As outlined above, the remaining possibilities are that the text existed in written form in other manuscripts and/or that it was transmitted orally. With regard to the latter possibility, Jordi Vidal (2012) has made an interesting argument in

[19] I borrow the concept of "presence" from Pongratz-Leisten (2021, 330), for whom it does not just convey the literal presence of writing on an object but is to be understood in "dynamic terms," whereby the presence of writing on an object is "conceived as co-presence with the beholder in an emphatic sense."

[20] So already Roche-Hawley 2024, 38 n. 13; see §4.1 for the quotation.

favor of the existence of "folk tales" about Idrimi that existed before the composition of the text. He observes that key moments in the narrative—the bad event that occurred at Halab, Idrimi's sojourn with the Suteans, and his stay with the *habiru*—are much shorter than the depictions of similar moments in other ancient Near Eastern texts (e.g., the Annals of Muršili II). He argued that the descriptions of these events in the narrative are abridged to such an extent that "the information granted by Sharruwa would be clearly insufficient, putting his contemporary reader in a position very similar to ours, i.e. unable to reconstruct the concrete meaning of his words" (Vidal 2012, 83–84). Essentially, taken on their own, the abridged descriptions of events would be unable to do the narrative heavy lifting required of them. Accordingly, Vidal inferred that "pre-existing longer reports" were "well-known by the population of the country" so that "readers of the inscription should possess a background on the young Idrimi that, unlike us, allow them to fully understand and reconstruct the information registered on the statue" (86).

Although he did not commit to a mode of transmission ("oral and/or written," [86]), Vidal thus opened a door to the possibility that stories about Idrimi were being transmitted earlier than the text inscribed on the statue. But these stories would comprise the source material for the Idrimi narrative and need be to kept distinct from the text inscribed on the statue, for the text on the statue is inextricably tied up with writing. As argued in §4.2, the text deploys the word *mānahtu* in the cheek inscription in order to frame the narrative in the body inscription as *narû* literature and thereby to present Idrimi as a royal figure whose example is to be followed. Significantly, the second line of the cheek inscription has Idrimi say, *ma-na-ah-ti-ia* ⸢*a*⸣-*na* ⸢UGU⸣-*ia aš-ṭu₂-ur*, "I inscribed my labors on my[s]elf" (l. CI 2). In other words, and according to the text itself, the body inscription gains its didactic function only upon being *written*.

At this point, we might feel like we face a conundrum. The text communicates to a reader that the narrative has a didactic function through the cheek inscription's framing of the inscription on the statue's body, yet we have argued above that this manifestation of the text could probably not be read by an ancient audience and required previous knowledge of the texts. But this conundrum comes about only if we take the cheek inscription literally. Readers, both ancient and modern, have easily understood as literary fictions the claims of Gilgamesh and Naram-Sin in the eponymous Epic and the Cuthean Legend, respectively, to have inscribed their experiences on stelae; so, too, Idrimi's statement may originally have been a literary fiction. Indeed, to run the risk of tautology, this literary fiction may have inspired the act of inscribing the Idrimi text on an originally anepigraphic statue in the first place! The fact that the didactic message of the text is intrinsically connected to its existence in a written form while the sole exemplar we have, the inscription on the statue, is (deliberately?) unreadable implies that an audience has preexisting knowledge of the text, so there is good reason to infer that other manuscripts of the Idrimi text existed at some point.

In fact, this suggestion has been made before, if for different reasons. As discussed in more detail in §2.7, Manfried Dietrich and Oswald Loretz (1981, 244–47) argued for a scenario in which only the cheek inscription was originally inscribed on the statue. The cheek inscription implored visitors to the statue to read a tablet, installed nearby, on which the narrative of the body inscription was written. For Durand (2011, 132), the tablet was only ever a template; it "devait représenter le texte authentique composé par Idrimi et qui a dû servir de modèle, selon un schéma désormais bien connu pour Mari et pour Émar, pour la rédaction ultérieure d'une statue." As Durand noted, in most cases these tablets seem to have been produced by scribes who were working to prepare texts to be inscribed on a variety of objects.

While the actual evidence for the scenario proposed by Dietrich and Loretz falls apart with the new identification of the sign taken by them as DUB instead as UGU (see the comment to l. CI 2 in §A.2), it is not necessary to maintain the reading DUB in order to still postulate the existence of such a tablet. Indeed, keeping in mind Durand's comments, quoted above, we might actually consider the existence of a tablet that functioned as a template for the inscriptions to be carved on the statue as an acceptable baseline assumption, shifting the burden of proof onto anyone wishing to argue for the opposite position—namely, that such a tablet never existed. And, indeed, several of the errors in the inscriptions do seem to support a scenario in which a template was used in the process of inscribing the inscriptions onto the statue. Chief among these errors are two examples of dittography (<<NIN>> NIN-*ia* in l. 2 and <<*pi*$_2$*-ri-ih-šu li-il-qu*$_2$*-ut*>> in l. 93) as well the defective UB (text: HI) in line 78; see the commentaries to the lines in §A.2 for more discussion. These instances of dittography, taken together with historical parallels of templates for inscriptions, demonstrate that at least one manuscript of the Idrimi text existed in the past, in addition to the version inscribed on the statue. Circumstantial evidence makes it very plausible that other exemplars of the text were in circulation among Alalah's *maryannu* as well. But, to end this excursus as it began, it is ultimately not necessary to determine definitively how this ancient audience accessed the text. Some sort of audience access is implied by the fact that the text is making an argument, a conclusion that was reached in chapter 4 by a close reading of the inscriptions.

5.4. THE POLITICAL INFLUENCE OF THE *MARYANNU*

If we accept that the Idrimi text is making an argument to Alalah's *maryannu*, who would have accessed the text either orally or via other manuscripts in circulation, we may still ask: Why was this particular argument addressed to them at all? To return to the figure of Kabiya, we saw at the beginning of this chapter that Niqmepa of Alalah promoted him to the *maryannu* class and appointed him *šangû*-priest of ^{d}EN.LIL$_2$, as recorded in AlT 15 [36.1]. Von Dassow (2008, 274) remarked about this text that "it is worth spelling out the obvious: the king had a role in determining who was *maryanni*." This conclusion seems indisputable, but it is also worth considering whether the king was the only one to play a role in securing Kabiya's promotion and appointment, even if the text in question leaves us only the king's fingerprints. Was the decision to promote Kabiya entirely the king's own? What influence might the kingdom's *maryannu*, or Kabiya himself, have had on the ruler of Alalah?

With regard to Kabiya's promotion and appointment, we will almost certainly never know for sure. But it is clear that the *maryannu* of a kingdom could and did have power or influence over a local ruler in Late Bronze Age Syro-Anatolia, as is most famously illustrated by a section in Šuppiluliuma's treaty with Šattiwaza (*CTH* 51: §4) describing resistance that Šuppiluliuma faced in northern Syria during the First Syrian War. For instance, after Šuppiluliuma conquered Aleppo and Mukiš, Taguwa, the ruler of Niya, traveled to Mukiš in order to swear allegiance to the Hittite king but lost his throne to an insurrection at home while he was away:

> ^{30b} ^{m}*ta-gu*$_{5}$*-wa* LUGAL ^{uru}*ni-ya su-lum-me-e* ^{31} *a-na* KUR ^{uru}*mu-ki-iš-he a-na pa-ni-*[*ia it-ta-al-k*]*a* EGIR ^{m}*ta-gu*$_{5}$*-u*$_{2}$*-a* ^{m}*a-gi-it-*^{d}IM *a-hu-šu* KUR ^{uru}*ne-ia u*$_{3}$ ^{uru}*ne-ia* ^{32a} *it-ta-kur-šu-nu-ti u*$_{3}$ ^{m}[*a-gi-it-*^{d}IM ^{lu_2}]$^{.meš}$*mar-ia-an-nu an-nu-u*$_{2}$ *a-na* 1^{en} *ut-te-er-šu-nu-ti*

> Taguwa, the ruler of (the city of) Niya [wen]t to the land of (the city of) Mukiš, before [me] for peace. After Taguwa (departed?), Agi-Teššub, his brother, *made* the land of (the city of) Niya and (the city of) Niya *hostile*, and *this* [Agi-Teššub] united the *maryannu* (lit. transformed into one).[21]

Significantly, in order to seize the throne from his brother, Agi-Teššub needed to bring the kingdom's *maryannu* together into a united coalition, which, interestingly, implies that they possessed diverse viewpoints before Agi-Teššub convinced them to rebel.

---

21 Beckman 1996, no. 6A obv. 30–32; see Devecchi 2018, n. 1 for previous editions. On the transitive sense of *nakāru*, cf. Beckman's translation (Beckman 1996, 39): "his brother Aki-Teshshup brought(!) the land of Niya and the city of Niya to hostility." *CAD* 11.1, s.v. "nakāru," 1a–1′ cites the attestation as an intransitive use, "to become hostile" but provides only an excerpt of the line, omitting the subject, and without translating. The sense of *arki*—and even whether it is a preposition or subordinating conjunction that introduces an abbreviated subordinate clause—is unclear; for discussion, citing various interpretations, see Devecchi 2013, 91 with n. 21. The understanding of the demonstrative pronoun *annû* as modifying the restored PN follows Beckman; although the word order is very difficult, both the singular form and the fact that Agi-Teššub has already been mentioned in the text support it. Alternatively, see, e.g, *CAD* 18, s.v. "târu," 12a–5′, where the editors took *annû* with *mariyannū* ("these chariot drivers"), but this interpretation suffers from the facts that *annû* is singular and that the *maryannū* have not yet been mentioned in the text.

Agi-Teššub was joined in his resistance to the Hittite king by a certain Agiya, king of Arahtu. But the text seems to state that Agiya was compelled to resist only after his city was captured by a coalition of its own influential men:

> ^{32b} ^{m}*hi-iš-mi-ia* ^{m}*a-si-ri* ^{33} ^{m}*zu-ul-ki-ia* ^{m}*ha-ba-a-hi* ^{m}*b*[*ir-ri-i*]a *u*$_{3}$ ^{m}*ni-ru-wa-bi qa-du* ^{giš}GIGIR.MEŠ-*šu-nu a-na* ERIN$_{2}$.MEŠ-*šu-nu it-ti* [^{m}]*a-gi*$_{5}$*-ia* ^{34} LUGAL ^{uru}*a-ra-ah-ti a-na* 1^{en} *ut-t*[*e-er-r*]*u* ^{uru}*a-ra-ah-ti iṣ-ṣa-ab-tu-ma i*[*t*]*-ta-ak-ru um-ma šu-nu-ma it-ti* LUGAL GAL LUGAL KUR ^{uru}*ha-at-ti* ^{35a} *ni-im-ha-aṣ-mi*$_{2}$
>
> Hišmiya, Asiri, Zulkiya, Habahi, B[irriy]a and Niruwabi, together with their chariots and! (text: to) their troops united (lit. transformed into one) *against* Agiya, the ruler of (the city of) Arahtu. They seized (the city of) Arahtu, and they became hostile. They spoke as follows: "Let us fight with the Great King, the king of the land of Hatti!"

Gary Beckman (1996, 39) translated the beginning of the passage as "(PNs$_{1-6}$) made common cause with Akiya, king of Arahtu. They seized the city of Arahtu." Presumably, this translation depends on taking the preposition *itti* with its base meaning "with." But *itti* often has an adversarial meaning (i.e., "against") in contexts of hostility in western hybrid Akkadian. Indeed, it has this sense in line 34 of this very passage (*itti šarri rabî*).[22] And the context of the passage suggests just such an adversarial context—for instance, if the six named men were "making a common cause with" Agiya, why does the text state that they seized his city in the very next clause? Note also the intransitive use of *turru* in this passage in contrast to the transitive use in line 32; it seems as though the six men came together on their own accord, captured the city, and compelled Agiya to rebel. Indeed, it is to them that the text attributes a speech featuring the cohortative verb *nimhaṣ*: "Let us fight with the Great King, the king of the land of Hatti!" Undoubtedly, the exhortation paraphrases or stands in for longer arguments that were made at the time. These six men successfully advanced anti-Hittite policy in Arahtu, coming together as an alliance in order to seize the city and compel its ruler, Agiya, to become hostile to Šuppiluliuma. The cohortative in particular signifies that the six men used rhetoric alongside force to sway Agiya (and others) to their position.

Furthermore, although the text does not specifically describe the six men as *maryannu* in this passage, in the lines that follow immediately after the passage quoted above, the text states that ^{m}*a-gi*$_{5}$*-ia* LUGAL ^{uru}*a-ra-ha-ti* ^{m}*a-gi*$_{5}$-^{d}IM^{ub} ŠEŠ-*šu ša* ^{m}*ta-gu*$_{5}$*-wa u*$_{3}$ $^{lu_2.meš}$*mar-i*[*a-a*]*n-ni-šu-nu … il-te-qe*$_{2}$*-šu-nu*, "he (Šuppiluliuma) took away Agiya, the king of (the city of) Arahtu, Agi-Teššub, the brother of

[22] See also, e.g., EA 45, a letter sent from the ruler of Ugarit to Egypt: "Something else: It should not be that [the king of the land of Hatti] becomes hostile to me!" (*ša-ni-tam as-su*$_{2}$*-ri-im-*[*ma* LUGAL KUR *ha-at-te*] *it-ti-ia i-na-ki-ir*, ll. 30–31). For this sense of the preposition more generally at Ugarit, see Huehnergard 2011, 187 and van Soldt 1991, 453 s.v. "epēšu" and "nakāru."

Taguwa, and their *maryannu*" (ll. 35–36). Because the text specifies "their" *maryannu* but *maryannu* have hitherto only been explicitly mentioned in reference to Agi-Teššub (so that one would expect "his" *maryannu*), the implication seems to be that the six named men were *maryannu* from the city of Arahtu.

The influence—and threat—that *maryannu* could represent to a local ruler is also very clear in two letters, TT3 and TT4, that were found at near-contemporaneous Qaṭna, near the southern end of the Orontes Valley. Both of these letters, written in a thick dialect of Hurro-Akkadian, were sent by Hittite royal interests to Idadda, the ruler of Qaṭna and an ostensible Hittite ally. But Idadda's loyalty seems to have been in doubt from the Hittite perspective, so the letters feature both threats and promises of protection in an attempt to keep Qaṭna's policy aligned with the Hittites.

Significantly, both letters are addressed, either directly or indirectly, not just to Idadda but also to the city's *maryannu*. The direct address occurs in TT3, where the letter's greeting formula reads: *a-na* ^{m}*id-a-an-da u*$_3$ *a-na* $^{\text{lu}_2\text{.meš}}$*mar-ia-ni-na um-ma* ^{m}*ha-an-nu-ut-ti u*$_3$ *um-ma* ^{m}*ta*$_2$*-gu*$_5$*-wa* ŠEŠ-*ka bu-lu-uṭ a-na* UGU-*ku-nu lu-u*$_2$ *šul-mu*, "A message from Hannutti and a message from Taguwa, your (sg.) brother to Idadda and to the *maryannu*. Stay well (sg.)! May you (pl.) be healthy!" (ll. 1–6). After this opening, the letter from Hannutti, a Hittite military officer, and Taguwa, who is generally identified as the same ruler of Niya attested in the Šattiwaza treaty mentioned above, communicates to them an order from the Hittite king that they fortify (?) Qaṭna,[23] and it recalls the unfortunate fate of another city that defected from Hittite loyalty and was destroyed (ll. 7–19). The letter's third and final section is from Taguwa alone: *u*$_3$ *um-ma* ^{m}*ta*$_2$*-gu*$_5$*-wa*, "a message from Taguwa" (l. 20). In this section, the tone of the letter changes as the ruler of Niya promises to send troops to protect Qaṭna. Significantly, this section is also addressed not just to Idadda but to the *maryannu* as well, because Taguwa uses the second person plural pronoun throughout.[24] For good measure, he also ends the

---

[23] Cf. the discussion of Oliva (2018, 276–77), who understands the crucial verb *du-un-ni-in-ku-nu* and its Hurrian gloss ***da-ab-be-eš*** in lines 10–11 to mean "to threaten." Here and in what follows Hurrian words are transliterated in bold italic, following the convention of Richter and Lange (2012) and Oliva (2018).

[24] "You (pl.) should not {Hur. despair}!" (lit. "Your (pl.) {Hur. despair} should not exist," using an anticipatory genitive construction, "of you (pl.), {Hur. despair} should not exist," *u*$_3$ *ša at-tu*$_4$*-nu* : ***za-za-al-ki-mu*** *lu-u*$_2$ *la i-ba*$_2$*-aš-ši* (ll. 23–24); cf. "You (pl.) {Hurr. should not despair!} I will offer protection," *u*$_3$ *at-tu-nu* : ***za-za-lu-uk-ku*** *a-na-ṣa-ru*$^{?}$ (ll. 30–31). The interpretation of the Hurrian words follows Richter's analysis in the notes to the edition in Richter and Lange 2012 and the cross-references provided there; see also Oliva 2018, 280–81.

letter with the instruction *ṭup-pu a-na pa-ni* $^{\text{lu}_2\text{.meš}}$*mar-ia-ni-na* : ***u$_2$-ru-uš-te***, "{Hurr. Show} the tablet to the *maryannu*!" (ll. 32–34).[25]

While TT4, the other letter, is explicitly addressed to Idadda alone and is sent only by Hannutti (*a-na* ^{m}*id-a-an-da um-ma* ^{m}*ha-an-nu-ut-ti a-na lu-u$_2$ šul-mu* UGU-*ka*, "A message from Hannutti to Idadda. May you (sg.) be healthy!," ll. 1–3), the *maryannu* of Qaṭna are also its intended audience, as is abundantly clear from the opening of the letter's first body section, which reads $^{\text{lu}_2\text{.meš}}$*mar-ia-ni-na ša* ^{uru}*qaṭ$_3$-na* : ***pu-uk-lu-uš-te*** *u$_3$ ṭup-pu lu-u$_2$ il$_9$-te-ne$_2$-mu-šu-nu*, "{Hur. Gather} the *maryannu* of Qaṭna so that they may repeatedly hear the tablet!" (ll. 4–6; see Oliva 2019, 297 for some discussion of both verbs). The remainder of the letter communicates a missive from Šuppiluliuma, the king of Hatti, in which the Hittite king seems to recount recent actions on the part of Qaṭna that have angered him and threatens to withhold support when Qaṭna is endangered. Significantly, the letters use second person plural forms throughout, further emphasizing that it is addressed to the *maryannu* and not just Idadda.[26]

In a recent article, Eduardo Torrecilla (2022, 334) has reflected on the significance of the fact that these letters have the *maryannu* of Qaṭna as much as Idadda as their intended audience:

> That TT3 and TT4 advised Idanda to gather the maryannu of Qaṭna to read Šuppiluliuma's message is most likely an indicator that both Idanda and Šuppiluliuma suspected that an uprising could surge from the Qaṭna nobility. Addressing the maryannu no doubt means that they had a say in the talks, that they had already expressed their conditions, and that Idanda could not leave them aside in the negotiations. It was the whole nobility of Qaṭna, and not just Idanda, who had to be convinced to submit to Ḫatti. Otherwise, Idanda was at risk of being deposed by his own people, just like Takuwa was deposed by a coup perpetrated by Aki-Teššup and the maryannu of Niya, as related by *CTH* 51.

To return to Alalah, is there any reason to think that the relationship between that kingdom's ruler and its *maryannu* was different? Could Alalah's ruler always be confident in his nobility's continuing loyalty, or might they have had concerns similar to those of Idadda of Qaṭna? Consider from this perspective the presence in the palace of legal texts documenting the property rights of *maryannu* not known

---

25 For an analysis of the Hurrian form *ur* = *ušt-e*, see Richter's note to line 34 in Richter and Lange 2012, 57.

26 See, e.g., "You (pl.) know that Mittani is destroyed, but you (pl.) are afraid of these three chariot(s). You (pl.) will see (Hur. gloss: you (pl.) will see) that which they will do (Hur. gloss: *the things they* will do)" (*at-tu$_4$-nu-ma ta-am-mar$_6$-ku-nu* : ***wu-ri-da-aš$_2$-šu$_{11}$*** *ša e-pu-uš-šu-nu* : ***da-na-aš$_2$-te-da-še-na***, ll. 37–39). In his note on the Hurrian gloss in line 39, Richter remarked that it was "morphologisch singularisch," but "es sich um eine syntaktische Pluralform handelt" (Richter and Lange 2012, 63); cf. Oliva's (2019, 302) comment on the line, where the verb is explicitly taken as morphologically plural.

to be members of the royal family, and, in particular, the eight or nine legal texts in which a certain Ilimi-ilima, who has the same name as the last attested ruler of ruler of Level IV Alalah, or his father, Tuttu, appears as the principal.[27]

We have already met Ilimi-ilima, the son of Tuttu, a number of times in the witness lists and administrative texts that feature *maryannu* and other high-status individuals (see §5.1). For instance, he appears in the list of thirty-four *maryannu* resident at Alalah (AlT 128 [414.1]: 26). From his identification as a *maryannu*, the scope of his and his father's business affairs, and other indications such as the text AlT 330 [44.2], where he is listed as the recipient of a pair of horses (lines 12–13) two entries after Ilimi-ilima, the prince (DUMU LUGAL, lines 7–8), it is clear that Ilimi-ilima, the son of Tuttu, was one of the more important persons extant in the Level IV documentation. In an earlier study, Guy Bunnens (1978, 6) described how the legal texts in particular "permettent de saisir sur le vif comment un homme que le sort a placé dans une situation privilégiée peut à la fois étendre sa puissance et accroître sa fortune," later characterizing him as "un bourgeois âpres au gain" (9). In a more neutral tone, von Dassow (2008, 294) noted that "both Tuttu and Ilimi-ilima are attested in a fairly wide range of roles and contexts" and that father and son "possessed substantial wealth which they used for its own increase" (297).

Two hypotheses have been advanced to explain the presence in the palace of legal texts documenting the property rights of Tuttu and Ilimi-ilima. According to one, the presence of the tablets in the palace reflects the fact that Ilimi-ilima, at least, lived or worked in the palace. According to the other, the presence of the tablets in the palace reflects the palace's interest in the legal transactions, even if the ruler of Alalah was not a principal in the transaction itself. Niedorf (2008, 129–33) considered the idea of royal interest but preferred the first hypothesis because

27 AlT 16 [36.2], 46 [352.1], 47 [352.2], 48 [352.3], 49 [352.4], 66 [341.1], 70 [341.5], 74 [342.3], and perhaps 93 [33.3], which concerns the daughter of a certain Ilimili(ma); see von Dassow 2008, 295–96 for descriptions of all of the texts. Also germane but not discussed here is a dossier of texts concerning a certain Zaze that was found in room 10 of the palace and consists mostly of administrative texts relating to the production of furniture: AlT 114 [2.11], 417 [46.1], 418 [46.2], and 421 [46.5]; see von Dassow 2005, 24 and von Dassow 2008, 321–23. In those references and elsewhere (2008, 298–99), von Dassow highlights two other texts found in room 10: AlT 419 [46.3], a small list of furniture intended "for the house of Iri-Halba" (*a-na* E₂ ^{m}*i-ri-hal-ba*₂, l. 4), and AlT 92 [33.2], a marriage contract involving this same Iri-Halba. This same Iri-Halba probably appears in witness lists (AlT 17 [31.3]: 22, 69 [341.4]: 21, and 74 [342.3]: 14), as well as both the administrative text documenting the temple of Kubi (AlT 156 [415.5]: rev. a 2) and the disbursement or collection of sheep (AlT 353 [44.15]: 22); he therefore clearly belonged to Alalah's nobility. Since Zaze's dossier and AlT 419 [46.3] are thematically connected on the basis of furniture, and AlT 419 [46.3] and 92 [33.2] are connected by virtue of their association with Iri-Halba, possibly it is the person of Iri-Halba more than Zaze who ties together the entire constellation of texts; see already von Dassow 2008, 299.

four legal texts found in the palace lack a royal seal or the statement that they occurred before the ruler of Alalah, which, to him, should be indicators of royal interest in a legal transaction. While von Dassow also initially accepted the first hypothesis,[28] she subsequently distanced herself from it and adopted the second hypothesis, developing it as part of a larger argument about the ontological status of legal texts at Level IV Alalah; for example, she noted: "the fact that these transactions were concluded before the king can be explained thus: these tablets were sealed by the king for the same reason that they were kept in his palace, and this reason was that they record transactions or agreements in which the king did in fact have an interest, even though his interest is not explicitly stated" (von Dassow 2010, 45).[29]

Von Dassow's hypothesis finds additional support in the presence in the palace of three administrative texts—AlT 128 [414.1], 156 [415.5], and 353 [44.15]—discussed earlier in this chapter (see §5.1), which list "prominent residents of Alalah" together in connection with particular tasks or occasions. While these administrative texts can be taken to indicate the palace's authority over these persons, the opposite interpretation is equally possible; namely, it was precisely the palace's anxiety about its authority vis-à-vis its *maryannu* that drove its interest in monitoring them on clay. For instance, von Dassow (2002, 856) spoke of men "enlisted to do" something "at the temple of Kubi," in reference to AlT 156

[28] See, e.g., von Dassow 2005, 47: "It appears that members of Alalah's local nobility might conduct their affairs and store their records within the palace. This is clearest in the case of Ilimi-ilima, son of Tuttu, whose tablets were found mostly in Room 22." See also: "It is of course possible that individuals such as ᶠZaze, Iri-Halba, Tuttu, and Tuttu's son Ilimi-ilima did have official roles or family relationships to the king," but the presence of the tablets in the palace are "most simply interpreted as evidence for close relationships integrating high-status members of Alalahian society with the ruling family and thus the state. Although other explanations for the presence of individual or family archives within government buildings are conceivable, an explanation predicated on assuming that the people and their activities occupied the same space as their documents accords best with the limited information available from the contents of the archives at issue, the prosopography of those individuals attested outside their own documents (e.g., as witnesses to other documents drawn up before the king), and the fact that each archive was found in a distinct location" (50).

[29] See von Dassow 2008, 297: "The fact that the transactions recorded by these tablets took place in the king's presence and required his seal, together with the tablets' findspot in the palace, implies that they did affect the king's interests, even though the documents do not explicitly state how." See also von Dassow 2015a, 183: "First, the particular transactions of which written records are extant were ones that affected the interests of the royal administration, or in some instances the interests of its members, like Ewrihuda and Irkabtu. In other words, documents of Ilimi-ilima and others were kept in the palace because they touched the king's interests. Second, most transactions did not interest the king or his administration, and were not recorded in writing at all."

[415.5], on the basis of the tablet's fragmentary heading, which she translated as "of the temple of Kubi, *according to* the rites/regulations [...]" ([... *š*]*a* E$_2$ ^{d}*ku-bi ki-ma par*$_2$-⸢*ṣi*$_2$ x ... x]x-*ku*, l. 1). Her translation of *parṣu* as "rites/regulations" clearly derives from the immediately preceding mention of the temple of Kubi. However, it is worth noting that the word was often used with the sense "custom, practice" in western hybrid Akkadian, including in another text from Level IV Alalah.[30] If the word is being used with this sense in AlT 156 [415.5]: 1 ("of the temple of Kubi, *according to* the custom[s]"), then the text would witness the palace's monitoring a group of *maryannu* who had been brought together by a customary source of authority that represented an alternative to the palace.

Similarly, although it is unclear whether AlT 353 [44.15] records the distribution or collection of sheep to or from some of the most prominent men of Alalah, one of the text's most salient features is that roughly one-third of the individuals either had not contributed or not received sheep at the time of the text's composition; either the palace had not been able to compel these men to contribute the sheep, or it was concerned enough that they had not yet received their sheep to make a record of the fact. But the best evidence for the influence that *maryannu* may have had with the rulers of Level IV Alalah is the letter AlT 109 [2.6], which a certain Biriyaššura sent to Niqmepa, the ruler of Alalah. As discussed above (see §5.1), the name is so uncommon that there is good reason to identify this Biriyaššura with the elite individual attested as a scribe and witness in Level IV legal texts. Strikingly, Biriyaššura addresses Niqmepa as an equal, with a brief greeting formula that omits any royal title or indication of obeisance.[31]

Taking this letter together with the find-spots of the legal texts involving *maryannu* and the administrative texts documenting *maryannu*, we can reconstruct a scenario in which the city's *maryannu* represented a potent force that the ruler of Alalah could not simply take for granted during Level IV. To be sure, the reconstruction is speculative, and other scenarios could account for the same constellation of evidence. But the scenario laid out here seems superior to the contrary one—namely, that the city's *maryannu* were *not* a potent force during Level IV and the ruler of Alalah *could* take them for granted—because of the

30 "(PN$_1$ asked to marry the daughter of PN$_2$) and he delivered to him a gift according to the custom of Halab" (*u*$_3$ *ki-ma pa-ra-aṣ* ^{uru}*ha-la-ab*^{ki} *ni-id-na i-za-ab-bil-šu*, AlT 17 [31.3]: 5). See *CAD* 12, s.v. "parṣu," 6 for attestations of the word with this sense more generally.

31 The body of the letter, which, to my knowledge, has not been re-edited since Wiseman's (1953, 59) original publication, and which is obscure in places, maintains a familiar tone. Biriyaššura seems to complain to the ruler of Alalah that, although he sent "them" (the referent is not specified), the palace did not give "them," so he asks that "they be made to cross over here" (*aš-ta-par*$_2$*-šu-nu* E$_2$.GAL *la i-din-šu-nu* ⸢*u*$_3$⸣ *lu(-)ul-te-bi-ru-n*[*im*], ll. 9–11). The tablet is also sealed with what Collon (1975, 115 n. 1) has suggested was Biriyaššura's personal seal; see AOAT 27, no. 210 for a drawing of the anepigraphic impression, which is not attested on any other extant tablets.

relative power of the *maryannu* as documented at near-contemporary Niya and Qaṭna. Indeed, to repeat once more a refrain that has occurred several times already through this study, the burden of proof would seem to be on anyone who wishes to maintain that the *maryannu* were not an influential group of men who needed to be taken into account at Late Bronze Age Alalah.

Ultimately, the most compelling reason to consider *maryannu* as such is that the program of the statue and its inscriptions present arguments addressed to them. Because this conclusion derives from a close reading of the text, not from the evidence presented in this section, we do not run the risk of tautology in making it. Both the examples of influential *maryannu* at Niya and Qaṭna and the rereading of texts and find-spots from Level IV Alalah simply increase the likelihood of the conclusion. Now, however, we want to take stock of this conclusion and the others reached in this study as to the historical context of the Statue of Idrimi and its inscriptions in order to present a final, speculative suggestion about when and why the inscriptions were carved on the statue and, in particular, how the program of statue and inscriptions might relate to the enigmatic IM-nerari who is named in the final line of the narrative of Idrimi's life.

6
Šarruwa and IM-nerari

Because the existence of an argument implies the existence of (at least one) audience, the previous chapter attempted to define the audience implied by the inscriptions' arguments. It identified the *maryannu* of Alalah as a primary audience because some of these individuals were influential players in the local politics of Alalah at the time. Their support would be necessary if IM-nerari was to follow the pro-Mittanian policy that the Idrimi text urged; indeed, the *maryannu*'s support could possibly compel him to adopt such a position in the first place. From this perspective, IM-nerari himself emerges as a second possible audience for the Idrimi text.

Although the body inscription is clearly designed in part to affirm IM-nerari's legitimacy by casting him as a new Idrimi, we should be careful not to automatically equate the text's viewpoint with IM-nerari's own. Indeed, the remarkable attribution of at least the body inscription to a scribe named Šarruwa actually acts to separate the text's point of view from IM-nerari's own. Accordingly, as a kind of coda to this study of the historical context of the Idrimi statue and its inscriptions, this chapter offers some final thoughts about the identities of Šarruwa and IM-nerari. Let me emphasize the speculative nature of this chapter. I am not suggesting that the scenarios proposed here are the most likely reflections of past reality, or even more likely than other scenarios that have previously been put forward; indeed, in some respects, they may be less likely. But I do not think that, on the basis of the evidence currently at our disposal, these scenarios can be falsified. Accordingly, I take the liberty here of working through them as alternatives that must be acknowledged in other reconstructions of the past and as hypotheses that will hopefully be able to be tested in the future as our knowledge of Late Bronze Age Alalah and surrounding regions deepens.

6.1. ŠARRUWA

I begin with a discussion of the inscriptions' ostensible author, Šarruwa. The final lines of the body inscription attribute some sort of creative role in the program of statue and inscriptions to a certain Šarruwa, "the scribe": ^{m}*šar-ru-wa* DUB.SAR $^{⌜lu_2?⌝}$ARAD 10 20 30 *u*$_3$ ^{d}INANNA ^{m}*šar-ru-wa* ^{lu_2}DUB.SAR ⌜*ša*⌝ ^{d}ALAM *an-ni-na-ti*$_3$ *iš-ṭu*$_2$*-ru-šu*, "Šarruwa is the scribe, the servant of the Storm God, the Sun God, the Moon God and IŠTAR. Šarruwa is the scribe who *šaṭāru*-ed this (divine) statue" (ll. 98–99). I have left the verb *šaṭāru* in line 99 untranslated here in recognition of the fact that it can be used in Akkadian with multiple senses, including "to write," "to inscribe," and even "to copy." In light of the verb's direct object in line 99, *ṣalmu*, "statue," the first of these senses does not seem appropriate, although it is found in some translations with the use of parentheticals to make it work.[1] While the third sense, "to copy," is theoretically possible, it also seems inappropriate, given the verb's direct object, *ṣalmu*, "statue," we would expect *ṣalmu* to be an indirect object with this sense ("to copy something *onto* a statue"). On the other hand, the second possible sense, "to inscribe," is works quite well with the direct object *ṣalmu*, "statue," as has long been recognized in the scholarship. The editors of *CAD* 17.2, s.v. "šaṭāru," 1c–1′a′("to inscribe an object—a stele—in general") cited this attestation as the first one of the sub-usage, and it is found in most treatments of the line from Sidney Smith's (1949, 23) original edition ("who inscribes this divine statue") to Jean-Marie Durand's (2011, 149) more recent one ("qui a inscrit cette statue"). This sense of *šaṭāru* also fits well with the similar "scribal signatures" in Luwian inscriptions, where the relevant verb used, when one occurs, is SCALPRUM, "to carve."[2]

However, this sense and the resulting attribution of the inscriptions to the scribe Šarruwa would seem to contradict the cheek inscription, in which the voice of Idrimi claims in line CI 2 that he *šaṭāru*-ed the text "on my[s]elf" (*ana* [*m*]*uhhiya*). While the presence of an indirect object theoretically opens the door for understanding *šaṭāru* to have here the sense "to copy," the cheek inscription's central conceit—that the Idrimi text represents Idrimi's own words—makes it impossible to understand Idrimi as only the copyist of his own autobiography. But reminding ourselves of this conceit also points a way forward. Although the cheek inscription is emphatic that the Idrimi text represents Idrimi's own words—perhaps, to this

---

1 See , e.g., Oppenheim 1969, 558 ("who has written [the text of] this statue") and Greenstein and Marcus 1976, 68 ("who has written [the text of] this statue for him").

2 See van den Hout 2020, 353 for a connection of the lines in the body inscription to the Luwian "scribal signatures," and 361–62 and 365 for more general references and discussion; cf. Payne (2010, 184), who states that the verb for "to inscribe, engrave" is "/*kwaza-*/, written REL-*za*, sometimes determined with the double logogram CAPERE+SCALPRUM." After discussing various and different verbs meaning "to write," she concludes that "a distinction was made between 'writing' and 'engraving'" (185).

end, placing them on the cheek in order to connect them to his mouth; see the comments of Jack Sasson (1981, 313) quoted in §4.2—it is simultaneously also clear that Idrimi's claim to authorship is fictional, in that *narû* literature is pseudo-autobiographical by definition. And, just as Idrimi's claim of authorship is fictional, I suggest that we should consider the possibility that Šarruwa's claim to have inscribed the statue in lines 98–99 is fictional as well.

Smith (1949, 22–23) himself did not recognize the personal name Šarruwa in the original edition of the inscriptions. Instead, he read the signs somewhat tortuously as DIŠ *šar-ru wa* DUB.SAR, with DIŠ to be read as *šumma* and *wa* as a putative West Semitic conjunction, and translated "whether king or ... scribe." This interpretation is found throughout the pages of Smith's edition, including the vocabulary, until the corrigenda, where Smith acknowledged Donald Wiseman's suggestion to read the sign string as a personal name and profession: ᵐ*šar-ru-wa* DUB.SAR. Wiseman's recognition of this personal name, Smith noted, derived from the former's work on the texts from Level IV Alalah, where the name is fairly well attested.

In these texts, Šarruwa is first and foremost the name of a scribe responsible for at least four legal texts.[3] All four texts in which the attestations of Šarruwa the scribe occur date securely to the reign of Niqmepa, as does one of the damaged attestations (AlT 91 [33.1]). The other damaged attestation, in AlT 104 [37.5]: rev. 5′, dates to the reign of Ilimi-ilima. Šarruwa the scribe also appears in at least one Level IV administrative text, AlT 159 [415.7], a "list of palace personnel," according to von Dassow (2008: 330 n. 158; cf. Niedorf 2008, 78–79). According to Christian Niedorf (2008, 78 n. 295), he may also appear in AlT 156 [415.5], the administrative text listing individuals associated with the temple of Kubi (see §5.1 and §5.4); Niedorf reads line i 9 as ᵐ*šar-ru-we* ˡᵘ²DUB, whereas Eva von Dassow (2002, 853) read ᵐ ⸢x-x⸣-*we* ˡᵘ²ŠIM?.[4]

---

[3] AlT 15 [36.1]: 20, 17 [31.3]: 23, 47 [352.2]: 20, and 72 [342.1]: 16—he is identified as a scribe in all. The name may also be present in two other legal texts, AlT 91 [33.1]: 22 and 104 [37.5]: rev. 5, although it is damaged in both. AlT 91 [33.1]: 22 reads IGI [*ša*]*r*?-*ru*-[*wa*?]; the end of the line is damaged, but there does not seem to be space for the PN's occupation. This individual is the penultimate witness, but the final witness is identified as a *šukkallu* and may have had that position as a mark of respect so that the penultimate position is not incompatible with the final position in which the scribe drawing up a document is typically listed. AlT 104 [37.5]: rev. 5′reads [IGI *šar*?-*r*]*u*?-*wa*. Von Dassow (2008, 470) did not include AlT 91 among her attestations of Šarruwa in the Level IV corpus, although it is unclear whether she considered it doubtful or omitted it in error.

[4] Various other individuals named Šarruwa are attested in Level IV texts as well. One of these individuals was a chariot maker (*naggar narkabāti*) active during the reign of Niqmepa (AlT 422 [46.6]: 8 and 425 [46.8]: 12; see Niedorf 2008, 108–9 for a description of the texts). Another Šarruwa was one of a number of men connected to the town of ᵘʳᵘ*za-bu*-[...] who received a standard disbursement of four *parīsu*s of grain in AlT 304 [432.6]: ii 14. Another Šarruwa is listed among men assigned to military duty (?) in the town of

A majority view in the scholarship has identified this scribe named Šarruwa who was active during Level IV with the Šarruwa attested in the body inscription, who claims to have "inscribed" the statue. Indeed, Nadav Na'aman (1980b, 109) has pointed out a "fondness for playing with signs and words" in the legal texts produced by the Level IV Šarruwa that also fits well with the impression one receives of the body inscription's putative scribe. The examples Na'aman gives include spelling the common name "Irkabtu" with the inventive spelling URUDU-DUGUD (i.e., Akkadian *erû* + *kabtu*) in AlT 15 [36.1]: 16 and multiple instances of variant spellings of a single personal name within a single text.[5]

However, the next year, Sasson (1981, 318) presented an alternative identification in the Alalah corpus for the Šarruwa of the Idrimi inscription. In keeping with his argument that the statue and inscription were created in the stratum in which Sir Leonard Woolley reported having found them (see §2.3), he pointed to a fragmentary letter in the Hittite language, AlT 124 [ATH 1], whose addressee is named *šar-r*[*u-*...].[6] Sasson suggested that the name be restored as Šarr[uwa] and that this letter's "correspondent" may have been the same as the body inscription's scribe.

With the statue now placed within a time frame of ca. 1400–1330 BCE because of the revised archaeological context (see §2.1), and not ca. 1250 BCE as Woolley recorded it, Sasson's suggestion must be abandoned. Yet the consensus opinion that identifies the Šarruwa of the body inscription with the Level IV scribe of the same name is still possible, if in a modified form. Since the Level IV Šarruwa was already active and prominent during the reign of Niqmepa, ca. 1425 BC (von Dassow 2022, 475), if he was responsible for the inscriptions, their date of composition needs to be closer to beginning of the new time frame, ca. 1400 BCE.

Akubiya (AlT 147 [415.4]: i 44; see von Dassow 2008, 850–52). Finally, one should mention the name Šarruwanta, listed as the head of a household of the *tuppallenni* class from the town of Zalaki (AlT 192 [412.9]: ii 9); perhaps Šarruwa is a hypocoristic of Šarruwanta?

5 In AlT 47 [352.2], e.g., Aštabi-šar is first spelled as ^{m}*aš-ta-bi*-LUGAL (l. 5) and then in the immediately following line as ^{m}*aš*$_2$-*ta*$_8$-*bi-šar*, using the sign HI with the unusual value *ta*$_8$; in the same text, the name Ilimi-ilima also shows less exotic variation, being spelled as *i-lim*-DINGIR-*ma* (l. 3) and DINGIR-DINGIR-*ma* (l. 7). Two other examples not mentioned by Na'aman are the scribe's writing of his profession after his own name with plene phonetic complements in AlT 72 [342.1]: 17–18 as DUB.SAR$^{ru\text{-}ru_3}$, perhaps to be read syllabically as *ṭup-šar-ru*^{ru_3} (see Niedorf 2008, 332) and the orthography of the word *masiktu* in AlT 17 [31.3]: 8, which is the same as in line 4 of the body inscription (*ma*-IGI(*si*$_{17}$)-*ik-tu*$_2$; see Weeden 2019, 137–38).

6 In the 1953 catalog, Wiseman was inconsistent in representing damage to the second sign of the name in his transliteration. It appears as *šar-r*[*u?*] in his summary of the text (so also Hagenbuchner 1989, no. 330) and as *šar-ru*-[...] in the actual transliteration. In the copy (Wiseman 1954, 10), only traces of the sign identified as RU are visible, although these traces are consistent with that identification. As Sasson noted, other restorations are possible; Klengel (1965, 251) had previously suggested restoring the name as *šar-r*[*u-up-ši*].

The originator of the statue's revised archaeological context, Amir Fink (2010, 98), was of this opinion, suggesting a scenario in which the Level IV Šarruwa played the role of "king maker," reestablishing Idrimi's dynastic line at Alalah following the destruction of the Level IV palace:

> The king maker of somewhat unusual capture of the throne must be an honorable person, preferably old, who represents the Idrimi dynasty, and could be the voice of its legacy. No one could be better as a king maker than the old scribe Šarruwa, who served under Niqmepa and Ilimilimma, and whose written documents for many years stood as the word of the king. Šarruwa must have signified the continuity of the Idrimi dynasty and the livelihood of the city and kingdom, desired by those people of Alalakh who survived the destruction.

This scenario certainly seems possible. However, the line of reasoning that underlies it still applies if the inscriptions were composed toward the end of the possible time frame, ca. 1330.

To paraphrase Fink's words quoted above, the author of a somewhat unusual narrative about capturing the throne of Alalah would ideally be a wise person, preferably old, who had been alive during the Idrimi dynasty. The Level IV scribe Šarruwa, who served under Niqmepa and Ilimi-ilima and whose written documents testified to his deep familiarity and ability with the cuneiform script, would have been a natural choice. Attributing the authorship of, or at least the act of inscribing, the body inscription to Šarruwa would have served as an ideal rhetorical strategy, making the same paralinguistic argument as the variation in paleography and orthography identified in §4.1—namely, that the body inscription's argument came from a place of wisdom and learning. Just as the pseudo-autobiographical nature of the narrative framed it as *narû* literature, the fictitious attribution of authorship engaged with another literary trope of the ancient Near East (and, indeed, the ancient world more widely), that of the wise counselor.

This scenario is as speculative as any of the others, but it may possess a slight advantage in explanatory power in its ability to accommodate the blessings for Šarruwa that are invoked at the very end of the body inscription (ll. 99–100). Scholars have tied themselves into knots in attempting to account for the appearance of Šarruwa here where one might expect Idrimi, suggesting far-fetched explanations such as Šarruwa taking advantage of a largely illiterate society to "stealthily" insert his own name in place of the king's (Kempinski and Na'aman 1973, 217–18; Na'aman 1980b, 107), or Idrimi having been so delighted with the scribe's crafting of the narrative of his life that he allowed Šarruwa to receive blessings in his own place (Oller 1977a, 141).[7] If the historical Šarruwa had, in

---

[7] For a review of these suggestions and others that have been made, see Oller 1989, 412–14 and Fink 2010, 96–97. Fink (2010, 98) himself considered that "the blessing for Šarruwa can be attributed to his special status as king maker, which allows him some liberties in the

fact, been dead for at least half a century before the scribal colophon was composed, it is natural that the subject matter would take the form of a request for blessings, especially in a text deeply invested with the theme of ancestor veneration (see, especially, §3.2).

6.2. IM-NERARI

In the original edition of the text, Smith (1949, 40) proposed that the IM-nerari to whom Idrimi "entrusts" the regular offerings for his grandfather should be identified with a certain Addu-nerari, ruler of Nuhašše, who is the sender of the Amarna letter EA 51 and is also known from various Hittite texts (discussed in more detail in §6.3).[8] However, Smith's suggested identification was promptly rejected by Oliver Gurney (1951, 93) in his review of Smith's edition,[9] and to my knowledge the suggestion has subsequently received no discussion. Instead, the general opinion has been that IM-nerari was an otherwise unattested Alalahian and member of the royal dynasty, either a son or other relation of Idrimi.[10] The major issue that has occupied scholars following this line of interpretation, then, has been the absence of IM-nerari from contemporary Level IV texts. For some scholars, the absence can be explained if IM-nerari died before or just after taking

inscription—as an old man he is praying to the gods to give him good health, protect him, and be his guardians."

8 Smith 1949, 40: "The name of this son is the same as that of a prince who addressed a letter in the Amarna archive, no. 51, to a king of Egypt. This name, famous as that of Assyrian kings in subsequent centuries, cannot have been common in Syria in the fifteenth century.... There is no sound reason for refusing to identify Idri-mi's son with the writer of the letter, if the chronological circumstances allow that course."

9 "Adad-nirari the son of Idri-mi was an elder brother of Niqmepa and his predecessor on the throne of Alalakh. Dr. Smith's identification of this Adad-nirari with the writer of Amarna Letter No. 51 appears in any case to be forced. The latter is most naturally taken to be a king of Nuhassi."

10 For some more statements to this effect, see, e.g., Márquez Rowe 1997, 180–81 ("Now, if we accept that the text is a posthumous 'autobiographical' composition, I understand that the mention of 'by Idrimi' by his own successor can only mean that Addu-nirari was at the time of Šarruwa's composition the living king of Alalah, who may be ascribed in turn to levels VB/IV"); Niedorf 2008, 283 ("der Erstgeborene Idrimis"); von Dassow 2008, 32 ("the dynasty of Idrimi regained power under a descendant named Addu-nirari," although she nuances this statement as follows: "it mattered little whether Addu-nirari was literally Idrimi's 'son' or whether, in reality, Idrimi could possibly have designated him as heir; as always, what mattered was what people wanted to believe in"); and Weeden 2019, 140 ("We do not know what relationship Niqmepa may have had to what must have been his brother [i.e., IM-nerari]").

the throne.[11] For others, IM-nerari is to be identified with Idrimi's son and successor, Niqmepa, who changed his name upon assuming the throne.[12] And for still others, the absence is explained by the fact that IM-nerari was only a religious official and did not rule.[13] Consistent among all of these suggestions is the idea that the inscriptions date to the time of the historical Idrimi or just after, for the absence of any attestation of IM-nerari in the Level IV archives is noteworthy only if the attestation of him in the body inscription is more or less contemporaneous with those archives.[14]

---

[11] See, e.g., Weeden 2019, 140 ("I myself prefer the shorter novella that has Addu-Nerari dying or being killed before taking the throne or being otherwise effaced from the documentary records before Niqmepa takes over").

[12] See, e.g., Collon 1975, 167 n. 3 ("In the statue inscription Idrimi says that he handed on his duties to his son Adad-nirari. There is no other mention of this son: it may be that he died shortly afterwards, without ever coming to the throne, it may be that only religious duties were involved, or it is possible that Adad-nirari changed his name to the old, West Semitic, dynastic name of Niqmepuh/Niqmepa when he ascended the throne.") and Durand 2011, 129–30 ("Mais une autre hypothèse, non envisagée également, pourrait tout aussi bien être avancée. Nous ne savons rien de l'octroi des basilonymes à Alalah dans la lignée d'Idrimi. Or, on est à une époque qui montre de façon tangible que l'on n'est pas toujours roi sous son nom de naissance. Les rois hittites, par exemple, changent de nom en montant sur le trône et la basilonymie assyrienne fait suspecter la même chose, lorsque l'on voit des princes qui n'étaient pas appelés à être rois proclamer par leur nom leur qualité d'aîné, tel un Assurbanipal. Addu-nêrârî a donc pu devenir roi sous le nom de Niqmepa; la dynastie d'Alalah pratique de fait, de façon ostensible une dénomination traditionnaliste, comme celle de plusieurs de ses contemporains, et 'Niqmepa' est un nom royal typique de la Côte occidentale, comme le montre la documentation d'Ougarit").

[13] To my knowledge, this position was first advanced by Goetze (1950, 229): "He [= Idrimi] merely puts the presumptive heir to the throne in charge of the state cult much in the same way as Hittite kings did." See also, among others, Oller 1977a, 154–55 ("The mention of ᵈIM-nirāri, a son of Idrimi, in his inscription, creates a special problem. Scholars have interpreted this passage as indicating the transfer of royal power from Idrimi to his son; ᵈIM-nirāri was Idrimi's successor. This seems unlikely for a number of reasons. We have no evidence for an actual throne tenure for ᵈIM-nirāri. No texts mentioning him were found in the Alalah IV corpus.... The most likely explanation, however, is that ... the Idrimi inscription should be interpreted as indicating only the transfer of religious duties to ᵈIM-nirāri and not the actual royal succession") and Dietrich and Loretz 1981, 253 ("nach Wiederherstellung der Ordnung dieses Aufgabenbereiches hat Idrimi die Durchführung des Kultes seinem Sohn anvertraut").

[14] Interestingly, the first proponent of a low date for, and so pseudo-autobiographical reading of, the inscriptions, Sasson (1981, 314–15) still thought that the statement about IM-nerari should be understood as restricting his purview to religious affairs: "the influx of Halabite/Emarite population allows him [Idrimi] to introduce foreign worship in Alalah's temples and to have his son, Adad-nirāri, supervise the cult"; he remarks in n. 15, "I side with those who do not regard Adad-nirāri as a royal successor to Idrimi."

However, the revised time frame for the statue, 1400–1330 BCE, necessarily changes the questions we ask about the attestation of IM-nerari in the body inscription and the scenarios we reconstruct as a result. The two scholars who have discussed IM-nerari within the revised time frame have dated the inscriptions toward the beginning of the period. So, for instance, building on Fink's (2005) initial reanalysis, von Dassow (2008, 32–33) reconstructed a scenario in which,

> after the Alalah IV palace was destroyed ... the dynasty of Idrimi regained power under a descendant named Addu-nirari ... Šarruwa, a fairly aged scribe now, having served both Niqmepa and Ilimilimma, helped Addu-nirari propagandize his rule and legitimacy by composing an inscription commemorating the dynasty's founder, Idrimi, and portraying Addu-nirari as that founder's designated successor. ... [The statue] stayed in its place of honor in the temple for a generation or two, until, once again, the Hittite army arrived and destroyed Alalah IV together with the image and cult of its hero, Idrimi.

Fink (2010, 98) incorporated von Dassow's scenario in his own subsequent reconstruction:

> Addu-Nīrārī could have been the biological son of Idrimi, a blood relative of the admired king or even just an ordinary person, who claimed that Idrimi designated him as his heir, as suggested by von Dassow (2008, 32). Assuming he was the son of Idrimi, he could have been born shortly before his father's death, and thus he was in his late thirties-early forties by the time the Level IVAF palace was destroyed—ready to take over the kingdom.

But what if the inscriptions date toward the end of the possible time frame of ca. 1400–1330 BCE? This relative date is also possibility, although not to my knowledge one that has been considered. And if the inscriptions do date toward the end of the time frame, then Smith's (1949) original identification of IM-nerari with Addu-nerari of Nuhašše actually becomes possible. Prior to the reevaluation of the statue's find-spot, there were very good chronological reasons for ignoring Smith's identification. If the historical Idrimi ruled ca. 1450 BCE and, according to Woolley, the statue was discovered in Level IB, ca. 1250, while Addu-nerari of Nuhašše is dated to after Šuppiluliuma I's First Syrian War, ca. 1330 BCE, the latter ruled either a century after or before the inscriptions were composed, depending on whether one dates them to the historical Idrimi or the statue's find-spot. But Addu-nerari of Nuhašše's dates of activity fall within the revised time frame of ca. 1400–1330 BCE if the inscriptions were composed toward the end of the period.

So an identification of Addu-nerari of Nuhašše with the IM-nerari of the body inscription is, in fact, possible. Furthermore, contemporaneously with Smith's (1949) publication of the Idrimi text, a second Addu-nerari, this one the ruler of Qaṭna, entered the historical record (Bottéro 1949a and Bottéro 1949b), and this Addu-nerari of Qaṭna is attested again in documents discovered more recently (Richter and Lange 2012). These developments make it worthwhile to explore the possibility of identifying the body inscription's IM-nerari with Addu-nerari, ruler of Nuhašše or Addu-nerari, the ruler of Qaṭna. In doing so, however, I want to emphasize that they are only explored here as just that—possibilities. I am not claiming that an identification of IM-nerari with Addu-nerari, ruler of Nuhašše or Addu-nerari, ruler of Qaṭna, is more likely than the possibility that IM-nerari was a native Alalahian and member of Idrimi's dynastic line. Rather, establishing that these possibilities exist, particularly if they cannot be disproven, serves to remind us that this other historical reconstruction is only one possibility among several. At the same time, to the extent that an identification of IM-nerari with Addu-nerari, ruler of Nuhašše or Addu-nerari, ruler of Qaṭna, can be disproven, then the argument that IM-nerari was a native Alalahian and member of Idrimi's dynastic line is actually strengthened.

6.3. ADDU-NERARI, RULER OF NUHAŠŠE

Addu-nerari of Nuhašše is attested in three sources:

- *CTH* 46, an edict issued by Šuppiluliuma I that describes a coalition of three Syrian kingdoms, including one led by Addu-nerari of Nuhašše against Niqmaddu II of Ugarit;[15] *CTH* 45 and *CTH* 47 form part of the same dossier but do not mention Addu-nerari of Nuhašše by name
- EA 51, a letter sent by Addu-nerari of Nuhašše to the Egyptian pharaoh, in which he recounts having rejected Hittite overtures and requests Egyptian support
- EA 53, a letter sent by Akizzi of Qaṭna to the Egyptian pharaoh, in which he reports, among other things, Addu-nerari of Nuhašše's hostility to Hatti and loyalty to Egypt.

Several other texts, all treaties issued by the Hittite state, are also germane to the topic; they are introduced below when relevant.

CTH 46 would seem to present the primary obstacle to identifying Addu-nerari of Nuhašše with the IM-nerari of the Idrimi statue's body inscription. As mentioned above, this text describes Addu-nerari of Nuhašše as part of a coalition of three Syrian kingdoms. The other two kingdoms are Niya, led by a certain Agi-Teššub, and Mukiš, led by a certain Itur-Addu. Should not the contemporaneity of Addu-nerari as ruler of Nuhašše with Itur-Addu as ruler of Mukiš exclude an identification of Addu-nerari of Nuhašše with IM-nerari of the body inscription? If the kingdom of Mukiš was ruled by Itur-Addu during the reign of Addu-nerari

---

[15] *CTH* 46 is often described as a "treaty." For a reevaluation of its genre and the text's identification as an "edict," see Devecchi 2012.

of Nuhašše, as evidenced by *CTH* 46, then how could that Addu-nerari have ruled Alalah as the IM-nerari of the body inscription?

In fact, the contemporaneity of Addu-nerari as ruler of Nuhašše with Itur-Addu as ruler of Mukiš is not a very good objection to identifying Addu-nerari as ruler of Nuhašše with the IM-nerari of the body inscription, and one can push back against it from at least three sides. First, being identified as the ruler of Mukiš (LUGAL KUR *Mukiš*) in *CTH* 46 cannot necessarily be equated with political control of Alalah. While two terms can be synonymous,[16] two facts suggest that the situation was not always as one-to-one in antiquity as we might assume it to be: "the land of Mukiš" also represented one region within the earlier Level IV kingdom controlled by the rulers of Alalah, and there was a city of Mukiš that may have served on occasion as the center of political power in that larger kingdom.[17] Second, and similarly, we cannot necessarily assume that "the kingdom of Mukiš" only had one ruler (*šarru*) at a time. To my knowledge, there is no evidence for multiple rulers coexisting at Alalah-Mukiš, but such may well have been the situation at contemporary Nuhašše (see below), so the possibility must at least be kept open. Finally, and perhaps most importantly, we must remember that *CTH* 46 captures only a snapshot in time. Points one and two are important and productive avenues for exploration, but, in the interest of brevity, it is this third possibility—whether Addu-nerari of Nuhašše could have ruled Alalah at some point prior to Itur-Addu of Mukiš's reign—that I wish to work through here as a sort of thought experiment.

At this point, we need to be clear about the date of the coalition against Ugarit. While earlier scholarship dated the coalition to during Šuppiluliuma I's First Syrian War,[18] more recent scholarship has coalesced around a date after this war.[19] Accordingly, as von Dassow (2020a, 204) has put it, "The moment when Itūr-Addu, Addu-nirari, and Agi-Teššob were all kings of their respective realms and combined to oppose Ḫatti can be roughly fixed to the years following Šuppiluliuma's initial conquest of Mukiš, thus sometime in the 1330s." This date,

---

[16] See, e.g., AlT 2 [1.1], where Niqmepa bears the title "king of the land of Mukiš" in the preamble (l. 1) but "king of the city of Alalah" in the caption to his seal impression.

[17] On Mukiš as a constituent region of the Level IV kingdom, see von Dassow 2008, 55. For the city of Mukiš as a possible "alternative capital" for the kingdom after the destruction of the Level IV palace, see von Dassow 2008, 61–62. Adding to the sense that the referents "land" and "city" can have particular political resonances, note that in *CTH* 46 Addu-nerari and Itur-Addu are describes as rulers of the lands (*mātu*) of Nuhašše and Mukiš, respectively, but Agi-Teššub is described as the ruler of the of the city of Niya ([uru]*ni-i*, l. obv. 3).

[18] See, e.g., Klengel 1965, 240; Singer 1999, 632–36; and Altman 2001a, 12–13.

[19] See, e.g., Devecchi 2013, 84; Gromova 2013, 111; Stavi 2015, 95–86; Wilhelm 2015, 76–77; and von Dassow 2020a, 204. Note, however, that Richter in Richter and Lange 2012, 156–60 still prefers to date the coalition to the First Syrian War.

sometime in the 1330s, then serves as our *terminus ante quem* for Addu-nerari of Nuhašše's hypothetical rule over Alalah, because, since we are exploring only the third possibility discussed above, control would need to have transferred to Itur-Addu by then. A date sometime around 1400, when the Level IV palace and castle were destroyed and the Level IV textual documentation ends, serves as our *terminus post quem*, because Ilimi-ilima is the last attested ruler of Alalah in those texts.

The textual evidence for Alalah-Mukiš during these seven decades has been reviewed by von Dassow (2020a, 201–4), and it is extremely sparse. The texts are:

- *CTH* 135, a fragmentary treaty between Hatti and Tunip that "narrates a conflict between Alalah and Tunip in which Ilimi-ilima figures as the aggressor" (von Dassow 2020a, 201)
- *CTH* 75, the Aleppo treaty, which describes different Hittite conquests of Aleppo, not Alalah, although these conquests are often taken as proxies for conquests of Alalah (see von Dassow 2020a, 201 on this point)
- KpT 1.11 (Wilhelm 2019), a tablet from Kayalıpınar that "narrates events in the land of Kizzuwatna that involve (an) Alalaḫ(ian), and tells of the missions of two personages named Ehli-Tenu and Ilī-Šarruma" (von Dassow 2020a, 203), who are otherwise unknown
- *CTH* 136, a fragmentary treaty between Hatti and Mukiš itself (Devecchi 2007), in which the name of neither the king of Hatti nor the ruler of Mukiš is preserved[20]
- *CTH* 51, the Šattiwaza treaty, which states only that Šuppiluliuma I "overpowered" (*le'û*) "the land of Aleppo and the land of Mukiš" during the First Syrian War, without mentioning the ruler of either, before moving on to describe military actions in the lands of Niya and Nuhašše

Simply put, none of the extant evidence precludes the possibility of Addu-nerari having controlled Alalah-Mukiš sometime in the years before the 1330s.

Therefore, we need to extend our thought experiment to its next logical step and consider if it is possible to move from a situation in which Addu-nerari ruled Alalah to one in which Addu-nerari ruled Nuhašše, Itur-Addu ruled Alalah-Mukiš, and these two rulers were allies—in other words, the state of affairs documented in *CTH* 46. Again, we are interested in exploring the possibility because if we discover that such a development is impossible, then we can safely exclude identifying Addu-nerari of Nuhašše with IM-nerari of the body inscription.

Two possible scenarios could account for such a development. First, Addu-nerari ruled just Alalah-Mukiš; then, at some point, he gained control of Nuhašše

[20] Devecchi (2007, 211, citing previous literature) attributed it to Šuppiluliuma I; von Dassow (2020a, 204) suggests that the ruler of Mukiš may have been Itur-Addu, so that the treaty would date to the aftermath of the coalition against Ugarit's defeat, although she is quite clear to maintain that such an identification is only a suggestion.

and subsequently gave the rule of Alalah-Mukiš to Itur-Addu. Second, Addu-nerari ruled just Nuhašše; then, at some point, he gained control of Alalah-Mukiš and subsequently gave the rule of Alalah-Mukiš to Itur-Addu. I describe Addu-nerari giving the rule of Alalah-Mukiš to Itur-Addu because the two appear as allies in *CTH* 46. It is also possible that Itur-Addu seized control from Addu-nerari, yet the two rulers were subsequently reconciled. For the purpose of the discussion here, we will play out only the one scenario and ask if it is conceivable that Addu-nerari, putatively the ruler of both Nuhašše and Alalah-Mukiš, might transfer control of Alalah-Mukiš to Itur-Addu. In fact, one can imagine many possible reasons why Addu-nerari might have preferred to have an ally (and family member?) in direct control of Alalah-Mukiš—for instance, in a time of military emergency. Accordingly, the need for Addu-nerari to relinquish control of Alalah-Mukiš is not sufficient grounds for falsifying a scenario in which he ruled Alalah-Mukiš prior to Itur-Addu sometime in the years before the 1330s.

For the purposes of this discussion, let us again choose to follow only one of the various possible scenarios outlined above—specifically, the idea that Addu-nerari first ruled Nuhašše and then conquered Alalah-Mukiš—because this scenario fits more easily with the image of a ruler concerned with his legitimacy. Is there anything about the history of the kingdom of Nuhašše itself that could preclude the idea that Addu-nerari ruled there in the years before the 1330s and later gained control of Alalah-Mukiš as well?

While there are many references to Nuhašše in the Amarna letters and the Idadda archive from Qaṭna during the First Syrian War (and after),[21] some of our best knowledge of Nuhašše at this time derives primarily from two texts, again, both Hittite treaties. The first is *CTH* 51, the Šattiwaza treaty, which is discussed briefly above in connection with the history of Mukiš in the time period ca. 1400–1330, also describes Šuppiluliuma I's conquest of Nuhašše. Specifically, after stating that Šuppiluliuma I "took" (*leqû*) Nuhašše, it narrates that a certain Šarrupše fled and that Šuppiluliuma I installed a certain Tagib-šarri, "a servant of Šarrupše," in kingship over the city of Ukulzat. The second, *CTH* 53, the Tette treaty, presents a different image of Šarrupše in its historical prologue. The prologue narrates how the king of Mittani invaded Nuhašše in order to kill Šarrupše, Šarrupše appealed to the king of Hatti for help, and the king of Hatti's troops subsequently drove the Mittani invading forces out of Nuhašše. While these two texts seem to offer contradictory depictions of Nuhašše's political relations vis-à-vis Hatti, they also seem to agree in documenting that the ruler of Nuhašše during the First Syrian War was a certain Šarrupše.[22] Because it is generally agreed that

---

[21] See the excellent summary of these letters by Abrahami 2016, 130–32.

[22] Cf. Richter 2002, 610: "Was die Verhältnisse in Nuhašše betrifft, so sind derzeit keine sicheren Aussagen möglich, da sich Sattiwaza-Vertrag und Tette-Vertrag in Bezug auf Sarrupse widersprechen: Laut Sattiwaza-Vertrag ging Suppiluliurna gegen diesen vor, laut Tette-Vertrag rettete er ihn vor der Bedrohung durch den König des Landes Mittani. Ich

the First Syrian War occurred before the coalition against Ugarit (see above), this point would seem to falsify the very scenario that we have been exploring—namely, that Addu-nerari ruled Nuhašše, subsequently gained control of Alalah-Mukiš, and then gave control of Alalah-Mukiš to Itur-Addu prior to the coalition against Ugarit.

Significantly, however, neither *CTH* 51 nor *CTH* 53 ever describes Šarrupše as the "ruler" (*šarru*) of Nuhašše, in contrast to other individuals mentioned earlier in *CTH* 51 (e.g., Taguwa, the ruler of Niya, or Agiya, the ruler of Arahtu). Some scholars have understood him to be its ruler, nevertheless.[23] For other scholars, the omission of *šarru* reflects the fact that Šarrupše never actually gained the throne of Nuhašše.[24] But there is another possibility as well. For instance, *CTH* 49 is a treaty between Šuppiluliuma I and a certain Huqqana of the land of Hayasa, in which Huqqana is also never designated as the ruler (*šarru*). In his introduction to the text, Gary Beckman (1996, 22–23) explained this omission in light of the fact that the text assumes in its stipulations that Huqqana "must exert his powers of persuasion on another potentate of Hayasa rather than simply command him" and concluded that Hayasa "stood at a lower stage of political development than Hatti, being ruled in the time of Suppiluliuma I by a number of tribal chiefs, paramount among whom was Huqqana." Putting aside an evolutionary model of the stages of political development, *CTH* 49 suggests that we should at least consider the possibility that the absence of the title *šarru* in association with Šarrupše may reflect the fact that the sociopolitical organization of Nuhašše was different than in Mukiš or Niya at the time. It may have been more decentralized, with multiple individuals wielding power and influence.

In fact, this conception of Nuhašše can be found in the scholarly literature from over half a century ago. On the basis of evidence such as *CTH* 51, where Nuhašše is described as consisting of multiple "lands" ("When I went to the land of Nuhašše [KUR [uru]*nu-haš-ši*], I took all of its lands [KUR.KUR.MEŠ *gab₂-ba-ša*]," l. 38), and letters of Aziru of Amurru from Amarna, where he complains of "rulers of the land of Nuhašše" in the plural (LUGAL.MEŠ KUR *nu-ha-aš-še*, EA

---

gehe davon aus, daß Sarrupse zunächst als Nachfolger des Adad-nīrārī durch Suppiluliuma I. eingesetzt wurde und sich die Angaben des Sattiwaza-Vertrages auf ein späteres Ereignis beziehen."

[23] See, e.g., Beckman's (1996, 39) translation of the relevant passage in *CTH* 51 ("When I went to the land of Nuhashishi…, (its king) Šarrupshi alone escaped") or the statements of Stavi 2015, 86 ("the king of Nuhašše is said to be Šarrupši") and von Dassow 2020a, 204 ("the text relates his invasion of Nuḫašše, which he captured, and whose king Šarrupše he replaced").

[24] See, e.g., Altman 2001b, 37–45, esp. 36 ("the reason for the omission of the title 'king' following the name of Šarrupši is that he was never actually king"); Altman 2004, 261–62 ("a contender for the crown"); and esp. Torrecilla 2022 for discussions that have treated the Qaṭna letters written by or mentioning Šarrupše.

160: 25, 161: 36), Michael Astour (1969, 387) described Nuhašše as "subdivided into several small states with their own kings, of whom one, however, was the senior ruler." Similarly, Horst Klengel (1998–2001, 610) understood these texts to demonstrate "daß N[uhašše] zu dieser Zeit kein einheitlicher Staat war, …wohl unter Einbeziehung verschiedener Herrschaftsgebiete." More recently, Philippe Abrahami (2016, 131) has considered that the reference to a plurality of kings of Nuhašše "fait en effet référence aux différents royaumes de cette zone comprenant notamment Barqa, Yaratu et l'État éponyme du Nuhašše."

Nuhašše at this time should probably be understood as what Brendan Benz (2016, 95–97), in his study of the sociopolitical organization of the Levant in the Late Bronze Age, has termed a "multipolity decentralized land"—that is, "a political coalition of cities and centralized lands that retained their local independence and identities under the authority of their respective kings, *hazannūti*, and/or collective representative bodies," in contrast to a "centralized land," which "consist[ed] of an integrated political unit under the authority of a single leader, who governed his domain from a centralized administrative hub." One of Benz's (2016, 141–79) case studies of this form of sociopolitical organization concerns Amurru, as documented in the Amarna letters. He demonstrates that Amurru was at first a multipolity decentralized land that ʿAbdi-ʾAširte controlled by influencing local sources of authority, but that ʿAbdi-ʾAširte's son Aziru transformed it into a centralized land with a central administrative city. Significantly, the example of Amurru thus demonstrates that forms of sociopolitical organization were not fixed but were fluid and open to change.

Understanding Nuhašše as a multipolity decentralized land opens up space for Addu-nerari to have ruled one constituent part of it at the same time as Šarrupše ruled another.[25] There is also space for him to have consolidated control, perhaps with the aim of organizing Nuhašše as a more centralized polity. Much as Aziru of Amurru effected his transformation of Amurru in part by skillfully navigating tensions between the larger geopolitical powers of Hatti and Egypt, so Addu-nerari may have done with respect to Hatti and Mittani. Conceivably, the king of Mittani's invasion of Nuhašše in an attempt to kill Šarrupše, as described in in *CTH* 53 (see above), might have been instigated by Addu-nerari as part of his attempt to gain control over all the lands of this multipolity decentralized land,

[25] For this reason, I think that Benz's model of a multipolity decentralized land is preferable to Turri's (2020, 292) attempt to account for the references to multiple lands or rulers of Nuhašše described above. Turri suggested that the term "Nuhašše" could function not just as a political referent that signifies only "a well-defined kingdom" but also as a geographical referent that signifies "a wide region that encompasses the entire area east of the middle Orontes" that includes the kingdoms of Qaṭna, Tunip, Niya, and Nuhašše itself, as well as others. However, this suggestion does not accommodate a situation in which there are multiple rulers of Nuhašše, the "well-defined kingdom."

and one could imagine that Addu-nerari seized control of Alalah-Mukiš at this time as well.

The preceding discussion has established, I hope, that we cannot exclude an identification of IM-nerari in the body inscription with Addu-nerari of Nuhašše as a historical possibility on the basis of our current state of knowledge. If we want to connect the program of the Statue of Idrimi and its inscriptions to his having seized control of Alalah, the invasion of Nuhašše by Mittani would be one possible moment, as it would explain both the concern for establishing a conquering ruler's legitimacy and the pro-Mittani argument advanced by the inscriptions, which would also have served to remind the new ruler with which geopolitical power his interests lay.

6.4. ADDU-NERARI, RULER OF QAṬNA

In addition to Addu-nerari of Nuhašše, we also need to consider whether another Addu-nerari who dates to this time frame could possibly be identified with IM-nerari of the body inscription. This Addu-nerari was a ruler of Qaṭna during the Late Bronze Age. He is known from two sources. The first is *RA* 43 139–175, Inventory I, which was discovered during Robert du Mesnil du Buisson's excavations in 1927. The text, which exists in four recensions, is an inventory of donations made to the temple of NIN.GAL, and it mentions Addu-nerari as a king of Qaṭna twice as responsible for donations (l. 249, ll. 323–333) and once in a damaged context in a colophon ([...]-*um* / [MU n.KAM *ša* ^{md}IM]-*ne*$_{2}$-*ra-ri*, ll. 327a–b). In another colophon, Addu-nerari's name has been restored (MU 45.KAM *ša* <$^{\text{m!?}}$>^{d}[IM- *ne*$_{2}$-*ra-ri*(?)] LUGAL; l. 363a); if correct, this restoration is quite important because it would be evidence that he reigned for at least forty-five years. The second source, TT6, is a legal document from the more recently excavated Idadda archive, in which Addu-nerari settles certain men in an area for military service and specifies both their responsibilities (labor, taxes) and to whom those responsibilities are due. Dating to before Idadda's reign, the text is one of the oldest in the archive (Richter and Lange 2012, 76, 163 n. 75).

On several occasions, the editor of the Idadda archive, Thomas Richter, has suggested that Addu-nerari of Qaṭna should be identified with Addu-nerari of Nuhašše.[26] While acknowledging that direct proof for the identification of the two rulers does not exist (and probably never will), Richter raised two pieces of indirect evidence that make the identification compelling to his eyes. The first is the unlikelihood of two neighboring kingdoms being ruled by persons with the same Akkadian name, especially given the relative lack of Akkadian names in Syria at this time. Second, the "geographisch unrichtig" (Helck *apud* Richter and Lange 2012, 158 n. 29) appearance of Qaṭna in *CTH* 51 as one of Šuppiluliuma I's

---

26 See, e.g., Richter 2002, 608–9; Richter 2008, 195–96 with n. 85; and Richter and Lange 2012, 158 with nn. 28–29.

conquests after Niya but before Nuhašše would become explicable because "das gut befestigte Qaṭna eines der Machtzentren des Adad-nīrārī gewesen ist," and so it needed to be subdued before Nuhašše could be conquered.[27]

While Richter's observations are insightful, his proposal has not been generally accepted in the scholarship.[28] Indeed, a primary difficulty with the identification of the two rulers would seem to be that, according to the Amarna letters, Addu-nerari of Nuhašše was a contemporary of Akizzi of Qaṭna, but, according to the texts from Qaṭna itself, Addu-nerari of Qaṭna's reign not only preceded Akizzi's but was separated from it by the reign of Idadda *and* may have lasted at least forty-five years. In other words, Addu-nerari of Qaṭna's reign should be placed before ca. 1350, while Addu-nerari of Nuhašše's reign should be placed after. Nonetheless, we should consider whether Addu-nerari of Qaṭna could conceivably be the IM-nerari of the body inscription, even without being identified with Addu-nerari of Nuhašše.

Unfortunately, on the basis of the limited extant evidence, it is very difficult to falsify or confirm the possibility. On the face of it, the possibility is at first sight quite attractive because of Addu-nerari of Qaṭna's seemingly expansive geographical control; in particular, the toponyms in TT6 suggest that his influence extended southward into the Lebanon mountain range (see Richter and Lange 2012, 76 note to l. 3). Taken together with the possibility of a long reign of at least forty-five years, this extent implies a good deal of political and/or military power, and one is tempted to imagine that he extended his control similarly northward. While at least six different kingdoms were attested in the upper (i.e., southern) and middle Orontes in subsequent decades,[29] what if the Orontes Valley was a territorial political unit at some point during the reign of Addu-nerari of Qaṭna? In the end, we do not know.

Such is a fitting sentiment for this chapter's final words as well. Ultimately, there are a number of different possibilities for the identity of the IM-nerari who is mentioned in the final line of the Idrimi narrative as the legitimate successor of the Idrimi dynasty. Perhaps he was actually a member of the royal family. Perhaps he was an Alalahian, a *maryannu* or someone else, who assumed the throne and was not a member of the dynasty but claimed to have been. Perhaps he was not from Alalah at all. Perhaps he was the same as Addu-nerari of Nuhašše, who took advantage of Mittani military incursions to consolidate control of Nuhašše, Alalah-Mukiš, and maybe even other adjacent regions as well ("in one day, as one man, the land of Niya, the land of Ama'u, the land of Mukiš, and Alalah, my city,

---

[27] But cf. Wilhelm's (2015) discussion of the text's organization, especially the observation that "it is not a linear narrative of a sequence of events but a text which follows the principle of association and thus mixes events … with associated events from a later period" (74).
[28] See, e.g., Wilhelm 2012, 239 n. 49; Devecchi 2013, 92; Stavi 2015, 112; and Torricella 2022, 326.
[29] As attested in the Amarna letters; see Abrahami 2016, 120.

looked favorably at me"). Perhaps sometime around 1370 BCE, the long-lived Addu-nerari of Qaṭna controlled a kingdom that stretched along the entire Orontes Valley. Or perhaps IM-nerari was someone completely different.

7
Conclusion

The preceding six chapters have offered an extended study of the Statue of Idrimi and its inscriptions. The goal of this chapter is to summarize and synthesize those chapters. In the appendix that follows this chapter, readers can find commentaries on philological and material aspects of the inscriptions that are at the heart of this study.

In chapter 1, I introduced the Statue of Idrimi. Among other discussions, I gave background on the ancient city of Alalah, where the statue was found, and reviewed the chief excavator Sir Leonard Woolley's contemporary and near-contemporary reports on its archaeological discovery. I also introduced the inscriptions carved on the statue's body and cheek, explaining why I treat what has customarily been taken as a single inscription as two distinct inscriptions.

In chapter 2, I reviewed some of the different ways scholars have approached the Statue of Idrimi and its inscriptions since its discovery in 1939. I also described my own approach in this book, which combines a close reading of the Idrimi text and an engagement with the materiality of the statue and its inscriptions. Specifically, I have read the Idrimi text within the context of the cuneiform corpora from Late Bronze Age Syro-Anatolia—not only the archival texts but also the Mesopotamian lexical and literary texts with which the scribes would have been familiar. At the same time, these readings originated from and were developed by engagement with the statue and its inscriptions as material objects.

The argument of chapter 3 is a case study in this regard. My argument was derived first of all from textual references to the veneration of ancestors found within the inscriptions. However, it was also grounded in studying the statue together with other objects found in association with it, most notably the altar; in juxtaposing the statue with other statues of ancestors from Bronze Age Syro-Anatolia; and in observing details of how the inscription was placed on the statue's body, which in turn implied that there had been prior damage to the statue's surface. Together, these points and others led to me to claim that the Statue of Idrimi functioned as a locus for offerings in the context of an ancestor cult, but that the statue was originally anepigraphic and represented a nameless, collective ancestor. At some point, both the cheek and the body of the statue were inscribed, and these inscriptions transformed the statue into a specific individual—Idrimi, a former king of Alalah—and identified a certain IM-nerari as Idrimi's *pāqidu*, the individual responsible for providing offerings to the deceased king and his royal line, as well as the new, legitimate ruler of Alalah.

But the lengthy inscription on the statue's body and the shorter inscription on its cheek did much more than that, as I explored in chapter 4. At the heart of this chapter's argument was the observation that the Akkadian word *mānahtu*, which has the basic meaning of "weariness, toil," is used in the cheek inscription and the body inscription in two different ways. The attestation of *mānahtu* in the cheek inscription has the sense of "labors" and is in dialogue with *narû* literature, a genre of Mesopotamian pseudo-autobiography in which kings narrate their lives in order to communicate a didactic message to future kings, as known from texts such as the Cuthean Legend of Naram-Sin or, with an additional narrative layer, the Epic of Gilgamesh. However, the three attestations of *mānahtu* in the body inscription have the sense of "tribute," which is at home in the political discourse of Late Bronze Age Syro-Anatolia, as made clear especially by Akkadian letters found in the House of Urtenu at Ugarit. The central claim of the chapter was that the two inscriptions work together. The attestation of *mānahtu* in the shorter cheek inscription frames the longer narrative of Idrimi's life on the body as *narû* literature and, so, as didactic. In the case of the Idrimi narrative, the didactic message is communicated primarily through the attestations of *mānahtu* in the body inscription, and that message is the desirability and even necessity for a ruler of Alalah to acknowledge the hegemony of Mittani. Essentially, cheek and body inscriptions combine to advance an argument that acknowledging the hegemony of Mittani was the only path to legitimate rule. Tellingly, this ancient argument was accompanied by a second, paralinguistic one that took the form of widespread orthographic and, most notably, paleographic variation in the inscriptions. Rather than being an indicator of "abominable" workmanship, this variation was intended to portray the inscriptions as objects steeped in cuneiform learning and possessed of great erudition and pedigree, and, thereby, to make the text's audience more receptive to its primary-level argument in favor of Mittani's hegemony.

If the conclusions of chapter 4 implied an audience for the inscriptions, I explored the nature of this audience in an explicit manner in chapter 5. I began by exploring what we can say about literacy at Level IV Alalah, after justifying why conclusions about that period of time may cautiously be extended to the time after the destruction of the Level IV palace but before Šuppiluliuma I's conquest of the city. Moving between an archaeologically excavated assemblage of scholarly texts, on the one hand, and a prosopographic study of persons identified as "scribe" in legal texts, on the other, I argued that Alalah's nobility—the *maryannu*, a wealthy, influential, and relatively closed circle of men—were literate and so represented one potential audience for the inscriptions' argument. In fact, the presentation of

Idrimi as himself a *maryannu* in the text's narrative suggested that Alalah's *maryannu* were not just a potential audience but a targeted one. In a manner similar to the inscriptions' virtuosic display of paleography, making Idrimi look like a *maryannu* was a rhetorical choice, conscious or not, to make an audience of *maryannu* more receptive to him as a protagonist, thereby facilitating their acceptance of the inscriptions' argument. And the *maryannu* were a target audience because they were probably people of influence at Late Bronze Age Alalah. Obtaining their endorsement would be crucial for IM-nerari if he were to pursue the course of action advocated in the Idrimi text and seek (or seek to maintain) Mittanian recognition of his rule at Alalah.

However, I began chapter 6 by urging caution in assuming that the perspectives of IM-nerari and the Idrimi text are one and the same. The caution is appropriate because the text distances itself from IM-nerari by attributing the body inscription to a certain Šarruwa, the scribe, and this distance opens up the possibility that IM-nerari was a second audience for the text. Just as the text was making an argument about the desirability of Mittani as a regional hegemon to one audience, Alalah's *maryannu*, it may have simultaneously addressed that argument to IM-nerari. Accordingly, in chapter 6, I explored possible identities of Šarruwa and IM-nerari, emphasizing that the exploration was not to advocate for one or another identity in particular. Rather, I hoped to put forward alternative scenarios about the past to see if one or more of them could be falsified, thereby increasing the likelihood of others that could not be. In particular, I was interested in scenarios that date toward the end of the revised time frame for the inscriptions, ca. 1330 BCE. For instance, the scribe named in the body inscription, Šarruwa, has most often been identified with a scribe of this same name who is attested in legal and administrative texts from Alalah IV. If the inscriptions date toward the beginning of the revised time frame, ca. 1400, this identification is possible. But I also raised the possibility that the attribution of the inscription to Šarruwa could have been fictitious, in which case the memory of this wise and learned scribe was invoked half a century after his death as part of its larger rhetorical strategy.

Prior to the revised time frame for the statue and inscriptions, scholarship on the identity of IM-nerari was preoccupied with the absence of a son of Idrimi and ruler of Alalah with this name from the Level IV texts. The primary explanations were that IM-nerari had a short rule, changed his name, or was only a religious official. Within the revised time frame, it has been suggested that he was member of Idrimi's dynasty who took over the throne shortly after the Level IV palace was destroyed and the documentation ceased. Accordingly, he would date to the beginning of the revised time frame, ca. 1400 BCE. But viable scenarios exist for dates at other moments in the time frame as well. In particular, two individuals named Addu-nerari are attested as rulers of the kingdoms of Nuhašše and Qaṭna, respectively, in this period; Sidney Smith (1949) had already suggested an identification with Addu-nerari of Qaṭna in his pioneering edition of the text. After presenting the extant evidence, I demonstrated that an identification of either of these individuals with the IM-nerari of the body inscription cannot be disproven. Therefore, given the present state of our knowledge, it is possible that IM-nerari was a member of the Idrimi dynasty or another Alalahian who assumed the throne of Alalah after Level IV, but it is also possible that Addu-nerari of Nuhašše or Addu-nerari of Qaṭna ruled the city at some point.

It can be uncomfortable to have to live with multiple, coexisting possibilities about the past. One way forward is to evaluate some possibilities as more or less likely than others. I hope that we will make such evaluations as we continue to think and write about the Statue of Idrimi and its inscriptions. I would only ask that we are cautious—and explicit—about the assumptions we are making if we find ourselves writing some version of "it is more likely that…"

Appendix
Commentaries on the Cheek Inscription and the Body Inscription

See chapter 1 for a translation and transliteration of the inscriptions.

A.1. CHEEK INSCRIPTION

CI 1. MU 30.K[AM.M]EŠ LUGAL-*ku*

The majority of scholars have translated LUGAL-*ku* in one of two ways: "I was king," or "I ruled/reigned." In other words, the stative form LUGAL-*ku*, normalized as *šarrāku*, is understood either to function as a nominal predicate or as a West Semitic suffix conjugation verb. Either interpretation is possible with the temporal construction *šalāšā šanāti*, "for thirty years" (accusative of time). The choice of a nominal predicate derives from the interpretation of the same form in line 58 and what is understood to be an intertextual allusion to a nominal predicate *anākuma šarru* in SB Gilg. I 46; see the commentary to line 58 in §A.2 and §4.2.

CI 2. ma-na-ah-ti-ia ⸢*a*⸣*-na* [U]GU-*ia aš-ṭu*$_2$*-ur li-*⸢*tak*$_2$⸣*-kal*$_2$*-šu-nu*

For a discussion of *mānahtiya*, "my labors," as an intertextual allusion to the prologue of the Epic of Gilgamesh (SB Gilg. I 10), see §4.2.

Smith (1949, 22) transliterated the sign identified here as [U]GU instead as ALAM but made clear in a note that he preferred to identify it as UGU, and that its identification as ALAM was based on context.[1] The sign does not seem to

[1] Smith (1949, 23): "*ṣalmi*: the form might be MUH [= UGU], but the context leads me to think it must be the form of No. 329 [*sic*] common in early times from the Agade dynasty onwards." Perhaps because of this note, Giacumakis (1970) recorded the sign in his glossary as UGU and ALAM, although without discussion; see 66 s.v. "ana" and 89 s.v. "muhhi"

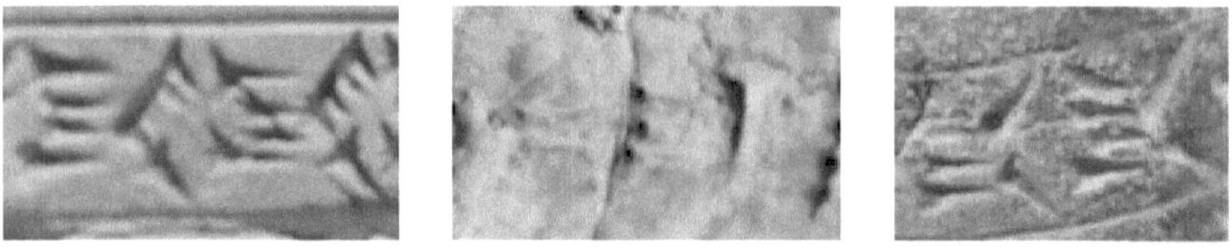

Figure A.1. Comparison of ALAM signs in lines 92 (left) and 99 (right), with putative ALAM in line CI 2 (center).

resemble ALAM. As can be seen in figure A.1, the only *Winkelhaken* is at the beginning of the sign, while other examples of ALAM in the body inscription have *Winkelhaken* in their middle and at their end. Furthermore, the sign in question ends in a vertical wedge.

In 1981, Dietrich and Loretz (1981, 207) proposed a new identification of the sign as DUB, and that identification subsequently played an important role in the source-critical approach to the Idrimi text; see §2.7. A comparison of the sign to the two attestations of DUB in the body inscription shows that, while it is closer in form to these signs, the interior vertical wedges that occur in other examples of DUB in the body inscription are missing from the sign in line CI 2; see figure A.2. See also figure A.3 for examples of the sign in two fragments of Paleographic S^a from Emar, Emar 538: 72 [Msk 74175a] (see Emar 6/2 443 and Gantzert 2011, 38 iii 21), and Msk 74193a (see Emar 6/2 475 and Gantzert 2011, 41 iii 16); see also Roche-Hawley 2012. Instead, the sign in question shows only two horizontal wedges; what appears to be a topmost third horizontal wedge is actually the head of a vertical wedge.

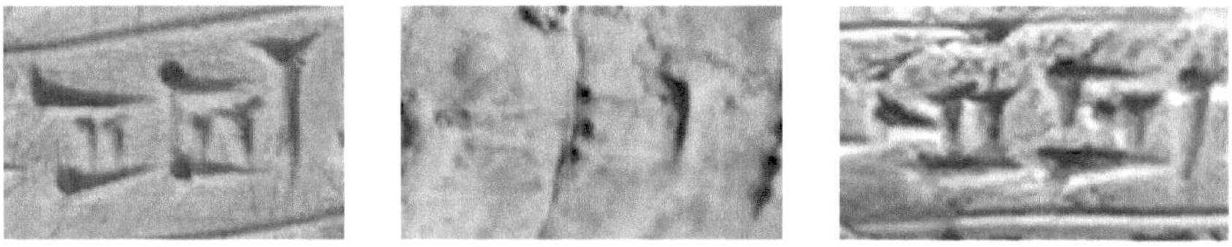

Figure A.2. Comparison of DUB signs in lines 98 (left) and 99 (right), with putative DUB in l. CI 2 (center).

[*sic*]. Smith's identification of the sign as "No. 329" seems to be an error for no. 358, since no. 329 is RA in his sign list, while ALAM is no. 358 (Smith 1949, plate 16; his comment on page 23 continues to state that the putative ALAM in l. CI 2 was not included in the sign list).

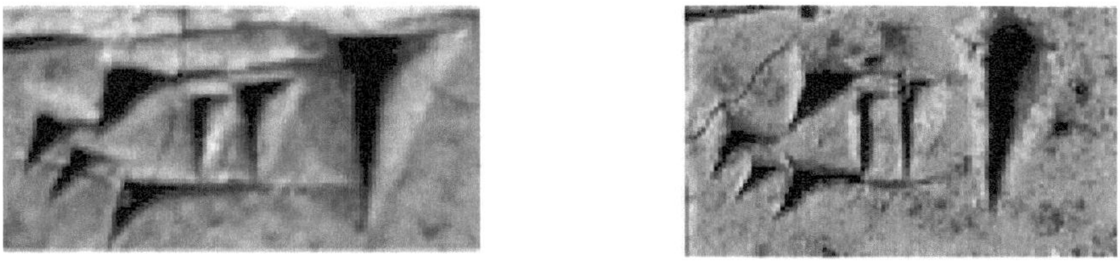

Figure A.3. Two examples of DUB in paleographic lists from Emar (Msk 74145+ on left, Msk 74193a+ on right). Courtesy C. Roche-Hawley.

Collation of the sign suggests that the top half of a *Winkelhaken* was recognizable emerging from the damage at the very beginning of the sign after collation, and is still barely visible in the photograph of the sign. This shape supports Smith's original preference to read the sign as UGU; see the comparison with other attestations of UGU, including one in the very next line, in figure A.4. Note in particular that the attestation in line 48 has only one medial vertical wedge, unlike the example in line CI 3. As mentioned above, this medial vertical wedge is present in the sign in CI 2, but its shape is obscured by a crack running along the length of the wedge that has also has the effect of suggesting that the wedge's head is in fact a horizontal wedge.

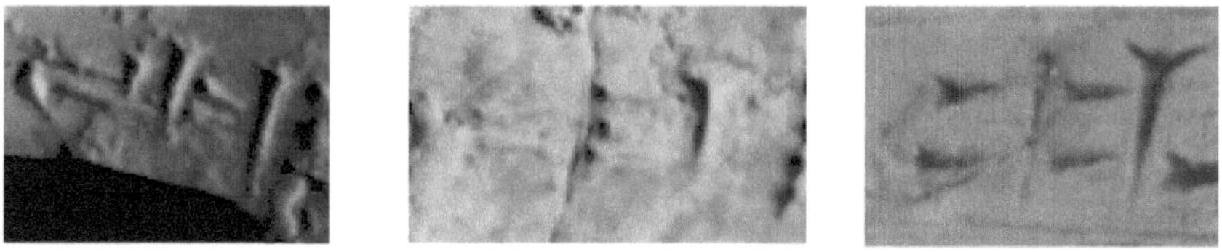

Figure A.4. Comparison of UGU signs in lines CI 3 (left) and 48 (right), with UGU in line CI 2 (center).

The verb at the end of the line was inadvertently omitted by Smith (1949) from his copy and thereby indicated as no longer preserved in his transliteration. After collating the inscription, Oller (1977b) realized that the signs were, in fact, present on the statue. The damaged sign(s) have been restored variously as -I[D-DA]G-, -⸢DAG⸣-, and -⸢DAG$_3$⸣-. The space available suggests that only one sign should be restored. The traces that are preserved suggest that the sign is DAG, not DAG$_3$, especially when one compares them to the form of DAG in a manuscript of Paleographic S^a from Ugarit; see figures A.5 and A.6 on the next page.

Whether the damaged sign was restored as -I[D-DA]G-, -⸢DAG⸣-, and -⸢DAG$_3$⸣-, prior to Durand's (2011) edition, it was taken as a precative formed off of the G present tense of *dagālu*. While the form of the precative is not in accordance with the expectations of the standard dialects of Akkadian, there are good examples of similarly constructed precatives in other western hybrid Akkadian

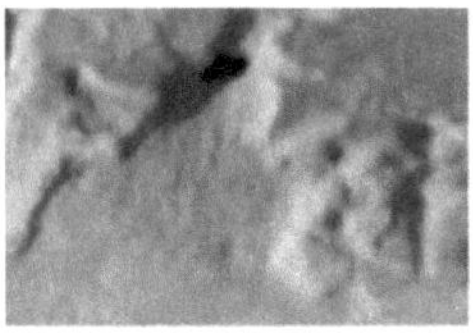

Figure A.5. Damaged DAG in line CI 2.

Figure A.6. Example of DAG in RS 14.128+. Courtesy C. Roche-Hawley.

corpora (see, e.g., Izre'el 1991, 1:165–66). However, there are difficulties with the semantics and syntax of this interpretation of the verb. For instance, in the literature, the verb is translated with the preceding clause as something like, "upon my statue I wrote my accomplishments. Let one constant[ly lo]ok upon them" (Oller 1977a, 18).[2] Semantically, there is a bit of legerdemain involved in this translation because, although *dagālu* is transliterated literally as "to look," the sense intended is actually "to look at in order to read." Yet the verb *dagālu* is not used in Akkadian with the sense of looking at something in order to read it; that verb, as is clear from restorations of the text prior to Oller's (1977b) "discovery" of the signs at end of the line, is *amāru*, "to see."[3] Syntactically, there are also problems with the plural or impersonal subject and with the referent of the 3mp pronominal suffix. In Akkadian, an impersonal use of the verb requires a 3mp form, but the verb is singular. Dietrich and Loretz's attempt to get around this difficulty by read the GAL sign with a CVCV value *-galu-* has no basis; the verb is singular and requires a singular subject. With regard to the verb's 3mp pronominal suffix, all of the translations understand the referent to be the word they translate as "accomplishments," "Taten," achievements," or "deeds" (although note that the pronominal suffix drops out of von Dassow's translation)—in other words, *mānahtiya*. But, although the translations of the word in question may be plural, in the text that word is singular, so it cannot be the referent for *-šunu*, especially since the word *is* used quite intentionally in the plural elsewhere in the inscription; see §4.3.

For these reasons, I am inclined to accept Durand's (2011, 150) suggestion to see the verb as a precative of *tukkulu*, "to make trust," rather than *dagālu*. Understanding a D precative of *takālu* resolves the problems encountered with previous translations, as it allows *mānahtiya* to function as the subject, not the object and so provides a singular subject for the verb; it also allows "them" to refer to Idrimi's

---

[2] Cf. Dietrich and Loretz 1981, 207: "Meine Taten habe ich auf meine Tafel geschrieben. Man möge sie betrachten und meiner ständig segnend gedenken"; Greenstein 1995, 2428: "My achievements I have inscribed on my statue. Let them look upon them, and let them continually bless me"; Liverani 2014, 333: "I wrote my deeds on my statue, (so that everyone) may see them and bless me"; and von Dassow 2015b, 2: "I wrote my deeds on my tablet. Let them look and keep invoking blessing upon me."

[3] *CAD* 1.2, s.v. "amāru A," 3 gathers references from all periods of Akkadian. Only Crawford (2014) has explicitly advanced a discussion of *dagālu* with the sense "to look" that does not involve reading; see §2.4.

descendants, who then function as the plural subject of the verb in the following line (but, admittedly, are not explicit in either line).

CI 3. (erasure) *u*$_3$ *a-na* UGU-⸢*ia*⸣ *li-ik-ta-na-*⸢*ra-bu*⸣

There seems to be an erasure at the beginning of the line, directly below the *ma-* of the preceding line.

As discussed in the comment to line CI 2 (*litakkalšunu*), Smith omitted the final signs from his copy and transliteration, and their existence was "rediscovered" by Oller (1977b). See that comment, as well, for the nonstandard form of the precative *liktanarrabū*, which is built off of the Gtn present. The verb *karābu* can communicate either the petition that is made to a deity or the blessing that results from the deity's having accepted the petition. While previous scholars have been uniform in understanding the compound prepositional phrase *ana muhhiya* to signify that prayers should be made to an unnamed deity for Idrimi's benefit (e.g., von Dassow 2015b, "Let them … keep invoking blessings upon me"), the understanding here is that prayers are to be made to Idrimi in his role as a deified ancestor with the implicit understanding that he will then act in their favor.

Indeed, it is unclear why the inscription (whether it "encourages" or is "looked at") should bring blessings upon Idrimi. Was the idea to remind a viewer of all the good things that Idrimi did in his life for Alalah and thereby convince them to provide offerings to the statue out of a sense of indebtedness? This is possible but not entirely convincing. On the other hand, inscribing Idrimi's accomplishments on his body makes good sense within the framework of a transactional, *do ut des*, concept of prayer. The accomplishments would show his capabilities in life and therefore, implicitly, in the hereafter as well, marking him as an effective ancestor to direct their prayers to for their own benefit—in other words, to encourage (*tukkulu*) them.

A.2. BODY INSCRIPTION

1. ⸢*a-na-ku*⸣ ^{m}*id-ri-mi* DUMU ^{m}DINGIR-*i-li*$_3$*-ma*

The majority of commentators consider *anāku Idrimi* to be a nominal sentence, "I am Idrimi…," in parallel to the well-attested formula found in West Semitic and Luwian inscriptions of the first millennium. This formula has been studied by Hogue (2019), who considered that "the use of the personal deictic 'I' statement actually produce[d] the presence of the implied speaker by conjuring them within the imagination of the audience" (325). He suggested that the formula "likely originated in Akkadian based on the earlier use of I-deixis in Sumerian inscriptions" (326). The success of the Akkadian version of the formula, in particular, came from fronting the "I (am)" statement, which "initiated deictic projection from the beginning of the inscription" (339), in contrast to earlier Sumerian "(am) I" statements, in which the deictic projection is delayed. Evidently, though, it took some time for the formula to achieve the wide popularity it enjoyed in the Iron Age. Hogue noted the existence of only three attestations of the formula from the Bronze Age, including the example on the Statue of Idrimi. The earliest attestation is an inscription of Kaštiliasu III from Babylonia, and Hogue considered it impossible to know if the formula came to Alalah from Babylonia or was independently arrived at (327). He also considered inconclusive the possibility, raised by others, that the third attestation of the formula, in an inscription of Šuppiluliuma II, was transmitted from Alalah to the Hittites (327–28).

On the historical Idrimi, see §2.3. The name "Idrimi" is most often taken to be constructed from the West Semitic root *ʿḏr*, "help," a position put forward by Smith (1949, 69) in his original edition of the text. Indeed, Greenstein and Marcus (1976, 69) pointed out that one such name, Hadad-ʿezer, is written as ᵈIM-*id-ri* in Shalmaneser III's royal inscriptions (e.g., RIMA 3 36: ii 27 et passim), and Golinets (2018, 372) listed a number of other examples of similar spellings in cuneiform sources. Nonetheless, the etymology of Idrimi remains unclear.[4] For instance, Greenstein (1995, 2424) suggested that it means "(The God) is my help." However, his translation emphasized that personal names constructed with this root, as the example of Hadad-ʿezer shows, are typically theophoric (see the discussion immediately below), while Idrimi's name consistently omits any theophoric element, even in the king's own seal inscription (AOAT 27, no. 189). Smith (1949, 69) tried to avoid the problem of an absent theophoric element by understanding *-mi* to be the direct speech marker and translating the name as "'My help!'" because "the natural inference is that the birth of a male heir constituted the 'help,' and that the name derives from an exclamation at the time of birth"; cf. Arnaud (1998, 157), who translated it as "(C'est) mon aide, je le dis." As Oller (1977a, 22) noted with reference to Smith's (1949) interpretation, understanding *-mi* as the direct speech marker on a name seems "a bit far-fetched."

Alongside the consensus view that the name "Idrimi" is constructed from the root *ʿḏr*, we should also consider the possibility of a different root. Golinets (2018, 368–70) observed that the root *ġzr* is also productive in Semitic onomastica and could lie behind a spelling ID-RI in cuneiform. This root is well attested at Ugarit with the meaning "youth" and the extended meaning "hero, warrior."[5] Presumably, then, the suffix *-mi* is the enclitic marking emphasis that is found in other western hybrid Akkadian texts and may derive from West Semitic (see, e.g., Huehnegard 2011, 210; Izre'el 1991, 1:330–33; and Rainey 1996, 3:240–48).

---

[4] A few scholars have objected to a West Semitic etymology for the name and instead tried to understand it as Hurrian; see, e.g., Speiser 1951, 151 and Draffkorn [Kilmer] 1959, 134–35 (included among "names that may be Hurrian"). But, to my knowledge, a suitable root does not exist (*id-* I, "to break, smash?"; see Richter 2012, 109).

[5] Its other attestations include use as a frequent epithet for Aqhat ("Aqhat the Hero," *aqht ġzr*) or his father Dani'ilu ("the hero, the Harnemite man," *ġzr mt hrmny*) in the Tale of Aqhat.

However, we might expect the *pirs*-formation noun to be a noun of action, although cf. Arabic *ṭifl*, "child."

Another possible etymology may be suggested by attestations of a name spelled as *ydrm* in alphabetic texts from Ugarit; see, e.g., *KTU* 2.70 [RS 29.093]: 1 and *KTU* 4.102 [RS 11.857]: 6; and cf. the PN *ydrmt* in *KTU* 5.1 [RS 1.016]: 5. The last of these texts is a scribal exercise listing PNs that begin with *y* and may offer the feminine analog to *ydrm*. In addition to beginning with *y*, these texts also spell the second letter as *d* and not *ḏ*. These points suggest that the first element of the name is not the noun derived from *ʿḏr* bur rather a verb with /d/ as one of its root consonants.

Ilimi-ilima, the father of Idrimi, was probably the ruler of Halab during his lifetime (von Dassow 2008, 19 and 24 n. 57). He is not otherwise attested outside of this inscription, although a certain Ilimi-ilima may be attested in a fragment of the res gestae of Hattušili I.[6] After the historical Idrimi, the name was borne by two individuals known from Level IV Alalah: Idrimi's grandson, the son of Niqmepa and the last known ruler of Alalah attested in the the Level IV palace, and the son of a certain Tuttu who, together with his father, is a principal in a dossier of legal texts discovered in the Level IV palace (on whom, see §5.1 and §5.4). Ilimi-ilima, the ruler of Alalah, is also probably to be identified with the Ilimi-ilima associated with Alalah in *CTH* 135, a treaty between Hatti and Tunip (von Dassow 2008, 60 with n. 146).

Smith (1949) did not offer an etymology of the name written as ^{m}DINGIR-*i-lim-ma*. Following his publication, an initial flurry of discussion tried to understand the name as Hurrian but soon fizzled. A concurrent and more persistent vein of scholarship has sought a Semitic etymology. Most attempts locate the etymology in the Semitic word for god (*ilu*, *ʾil*, etc.), the Amorite divine name "Lim," or some combination of these two nouns. Because the name appears not just in the body inscription but also in the Level IV archives, there are a good number of attestations and variant writings; von Dassow (2008, 444) has gathered the attestations. Some notable examples are: DINGIR-DINGIR-*ma*, *i-lim-i-lim-ma*, DINGIR-*mi-li*, and *i-li-mi-li*. The first and shortest writing confirms that the name comprises two elements. The last two attestations are sandhi writings and confirm that the first LIM sign in the second attestation in the list needs to be read as *lim* and not *li*$_{3}$.[7] The contrast between the first two attestations and the second two reveals an abbreviated form of the name in which the final -*ma* could be omitted.

---

[6] KUB 36 103: 2′; The name is spelled there ^{m}*a-na-an-ma*, but Kühne (1972, 248) suggested that this spelling reflects a misunderstanding of the oral pronunciation of a name written ^{m}DINGIR-DINGIR-*ma*. The same text also mentions the city of Halab (l. 6′ of duplicate KBo 3 56), but, as the two proper nouns are separated by a section ruling, there is no reason to associate one with the other.

[7] This observation presents an obstacle to Durand's (2011, 135 n. 116) analysis of the name as written in the body inscription, in which he suggested reading LIM with the value *lum*$_{2}$.

Given these data, one possible normalization of the name could be *Ilīmi-ilī(ma)*, "Indeed, my god is my god," where the suffix *-mi* on the first element is the emphatic *-mi* possibly found in Idrimi's name; see the discussion above and see already Albright 1964, 41 n. 8. The spelling of the name as DINGIR-DINGIR-*ma* suggests an abbreviated form in which the enclitic *-mi* might be omitted instead of the enclitic *-ma* (i.e., *Ilī-ilīma*). The spelling of the name in line 1 of the body inscription as DINGIR-*i-li*$_{3}$*-ma* might be another example of this abbreviation, or, conceivably, DINGIR is to be normalized as *ilim* for a sandhi writing; in other words, *ilim-i-li*$_{3}$*-ma* = *ilīm(i)-ilīma*).

2. ARAD ⌜^{d}⌝[I]M ^{d}*he*$_{2}$*-bat u*$_{3}$ ^{d}*iš*$_{8}$*-tar*$_{2}$ NIN ^{uru}*a-la-la-ah* <<NIN>> / NIN-*ia*

As discussed in the Note on Transliterations, Normalizations, and Translations in the front matter to this volume, the reading of the divine names written logographically as ^{d}IM and ^{d}*iš*$_{8}$*-tar*$_{2}$/^{d}INANNA are uncertain. However, Durand (2011, 135 n. 118) has suggested that the co-occurrence of ^{d}IM with the goddess Hebat may suggest that ^{d}IM refers to Addu of Aleppo in this line. The suggestion is compelling given Hebat's important role in the religious life of Aleppo in the Middle Bronze Age.[8] Indeed, Archi has proposed a Semitic etymology for the divine name Hebat, which is written as ^{d}*ha-a-ba-du* in texts from Ebla, and which Archi etymologizes as *ha(l)abājtu*, "She of Halab" (Archi 2013, 9).[9]

Figure A.7. End of lines 2–3.

The question of how to interpret the pair of NIN signs at the end of the line has been approached differently in the literature. Smith (1949, 14) emended the text, deleting the first NIN, and his emendation has been accepted by many scholars. However, other scholars have transliterated the signs as a reduplicated logogram (NIN.NIN-*ia*) indicating the plural Akkadian form *bēletiya*, "my ladies," referring to both Hebat and IŠTAR. Finally, some scholars have taken the NIN

[8] See, e.g., FM 7 45, in which the goddess is mentioned together with her divine parents Dagan and Šalaš in connection with the *pagrûm*-offerings for the deceased king of Yamhad, Sumu-epuh: [*i-n*]*u-ma pa-ag-ri-a-im ša* ^{d}*da-gan* [^{d}]*ša-la-aš u*$_{3}$ *he*$_{2}$*-ba-at i-na* E$_{2}$.GAL-*lim* [*a*]*-na i-*[*d*]*-ir-tim ra-bi-tim ša su-mu-e-pu-uh wa-aš-ba-*[*nu*], "At the time of the *pagrûm*-rites of Dagan, Šalaš, and Hebat, we were staying in the palace for the great lamenting of Sumu-epuh" (ll. 3–5; see Durand 2002, 150 for discussion).

[9] See already Archi 1994 for a more detailed discussion of the Ebla texts in which the goddess ^{d}*ha-a-ba-du* appears in association with the god Hadda (= Addu) and the city of Halab.

signs simply as two separate words, normalizing the signs as *bēltu bēltiya* and translating, "the lady, my lady," in reference to IŠTAR.

The form and placement of the first NIN signs, which are written right up against Idrimi's beard, supports Smith's decision to emend the text. As figure A.7 shows, there is no room after the first NIN of the final pair for any additional signs without their having to be written on the beard itself. The diminutive and cramped form of that NIN sign also shows that the scribe was conscious of running out of space at the end of the line. As Dietrich and Loretz (1981, 204) noted, the unusual omission of the KI determinative after ^{uru}*a-la-la-ah* in the line may also indicate the mason's awareness that he did not have much more space available to him in the line. Nonetheless, after carving the subsequent NIN sign, the mason realized the following *-ia* sign would need to be carved on Idrimi's beard if it was to follow immediately upon the NIN; not wishing to do this, he decided to run the sign over onto the next line. The decision to also repeat the NIN sign before IA may derive from the fact that line 3 ends E$_2$-*ia*; including NIN before IA avoided two successive IA signs (which might have been interpreted as a scribal error) and clarified the object of the possessive pronominal pronoun. Note that this scenario implies that the mason carving the inscription had access to it in some form such that he knew already that line 3 ended in *-ia* when he was deciding how to complete the end of line 2; see §5.3 for more discussion.

3. i-⸢na⸣ ^{uru}*ha-la-ab*^{ki} E$_2$ *a-bi-ia*

Halab, modern Aleppo, was an important city of great antiquity. Because the site has been occupied up to and including the current day, archaeological excavations have been limited to the citadel, where excavators have discovered Iron Age levels of the temple of the famous Storm God of Aleppo, on whom see below (on the excavations, see, e.g., Kohlmeyer 2009; Kohlmeyer 2013). Evidence for the history of Halab during the second millennium, therefore, comes from textual references from other sites.

Texts from Mari make it clear that Halab was the capital of the kingdom of Yamhad, which was one of the most powerful states in the ancient Near East during the first half of the second millennium. The end of the kingdom of Yamhad was brought about by Hittite campaigns late in the seventeenth and early in the sixteenth century. While the political entity that was Yamhad did not survive these campaigns, its territory was not incorporated into the Hittite state, and a kingdom of Halab seems to have persisted. Unfortunately, the evidence for this kingdom prior to the documentary record from the Hittite New Kingdom is scanty and, in a great part, comes from Late Bronze Age (Level IV) Alalah itself.[10] For instance, AOAT 27, no. 11, the so-called dynastic seal used by Niqmepa, ruler of Alalah,

---

[10] I elide references to the Idrimi text from the following discussion.

bears an inscription of Abba-el, the son of Šarra-el.[11] Although neither of these kings are otherwise attested in texts from Alalah or elsewhere, as von Dassow notes, because the former king "not only associates himself with the chief deities of Halab but bore the same name as an earlier king of Halab, the inference that Halab was the seat of his kingship is virtually compulsory" (2008, 18). Accordingly, we should understand Šarra-el and Abba-el to have ruled sometime during Levels VI or V of Alalah.

Halab appears in five Level IV texts,[12] of which AlT 101 [38.4] is perhaps the most illuminating as to the history of Halab. This text, following Márquez Rowe's (1997, 186–96) re-edition and discussion, is a receipt recording Niqmepa of Alalah's return of fugitives described as "of" (*ša*) a certain Wantaraššura. The receipt is witnessed by an individual named Arnuwar, who is described as the *halzuhhuli*-official of Halab (ll. 9–10). While this office is often described as that of a "governor," Márquez Rowe demonstrated that one of its duties was to return fugitives. As the *halzuhhuli*-official of Halab, then, Arnuwar seems to have been working on behalf of the Wantaraššura named as the owner of the fugitives in the text's opening lines, ad so Wantaraššura was evidently the ruler of Halab during the reign of Niqmepa of Alalah. Márquez Rowe concluded his discussion by observing that Wantaraššura's name, like those of the kings of Mittani, is "at least partially of Indo-Aryan etymology" (197), so that the former may have been put on the throne by one of the latter. The etymology of Wantaraššura's name is perhaps made more significant, Márquez Rowe went on to note, by its contrast to the kings of Level IV Alalah, who "bore clear Semitic royal names and who clearly belonged to an old royal dynasty, paradoxically that of Halab" (197).

Here, Márquez Rowe was referring in part to AOAT 27, no. 11, the so-called dynastic seal of Abba-el, the son of Šarra-el, used by Niqmepa and mentioned above. The name Abba-el suggests a connection to the Middle Bronze Age rulers of Halab, as at least one and possibly two kings of Yamhad bore that name (Lauinger 2015, 202–3, 212–14), and the name Šarra-el is constructed along the same pattern. The qualification of Abba-el in the seal inscription as a "mighty king" (*šarru dannu*) could further indicate his status, or at least presume it, as one of the great kings of the time. In other words, following Muršili I's campaigns, the kingdom of Halab may have continued to be a regional power and to have been ruled by descendants of the kings of Yamhad—or at least by kings who identified

[11] The inscription on this seal reads: [1] *ab-ba*-AN LUGAL KALAG.GA [2] DUMU *šar-ra*-AN [3] IR$_3$ ^{d}IM [4] *na-ra-am* ^{d}IM [5] *si*$_2$*-ki-il-tum* [6] *ša* ^{d}*he*$_2$*-bat*, "Abba-El, the mighty king, the son of Šarra-EL, the servant of Addu, the beloved of Addu, the treasured possession of Hebat." On the reading of the divine name as Hebat and not Addu (in l. 6 as Collon), see Dietrich and Loretz 1997, 222, confirmed by collation of Collon's photograph by von Dassow 2008, 18 n. 40.

[12] AlT 17 [31.3], 101 [38.4], and 161 [414.3]; HAM 6282 [417.6] and 7331/25 [492.23].

with them—until these were removed from the throne and replaced by a ruler from the Mittani "circle" (Márquez Rowe 1997, 197).

A central crux of this line is whether the phrase Idrimi uses in apposition with Halab, *bīt abiya*, literally "the house of my father," means that his father ruled Halab. Ilimi-ilima's status as ruler of Halab is generally assumed in the scholarship but not discussed. Alternatively, Sasson (1981, 313) pointed out that Ilimi-ilima is not actually called "king" and suggested another scenario, "no less conjectural, …that Ilimilimma may have failed in an attempt to usurp Halab's throne." On the other hand, Mayer (1995, 342–43) argued that Ilimi-ilima actually ruled Alalah itself, and that the reference to Halab as *bīt abiya* was to it as a "Stammhaus, in dessen Schutz man zwangsläufig floh, als Alalah abermals den Hethitern in die Hände fiel." In response, Márquez Rowe (1997, 183) pointed out that "other scattered allusions to [Idrimi's] 'paternal house,' claiming for example his rights of succession (l. 10) against his older brothers, as well as his identification by the population as 'their lord's son' … reveal that Ilimilimma had indeed been the earlier ruler of the kingdom of Halab"; see also von Dassow 2008, 23 n. 57. Similarly, Greenstein (1995, 2426) observed that the reference in this line to "the household of my father" is paralleled by Idrimi's statement that he "returned a household that was lost to him" (l. 56) when he formally acknowledges Parattarna I's hegemony after gaining control of Alalah.

Note, however, Durand's (2011, 110) subsequent remarks that "si rien ne dit quel était le statut précis d'Ilum-ilî-ma à Alep, sans doute était-il de grande importance. On sait peu de choses encore sur la société de l'Alep amorrite mais il existe des indices forts, à en juger par les textes de Mari contemporains du royaume du Yamhad, que la tribalité y était importante." In other words, Durand reminds us that the discussion of Ilimi-ilima's status has been conducted as if this status were a binary: either he was Halab's king, or he was not. Yet the data provided by the Mari texts reminds us that the power dynamics of northern Syria during the eighteenth century were very diffuse (e.g., the *merhûm* Bannum), and this reminder can be extended forward in time even if only to consider as a possibility and, hopefully one day, be able to confirm or deny.

4. ma-si$_{17}$-ik-tu$_{2}$ it-tab-ši u$_{3}$ hal-qa$_{3}$-nu / IGI

Collation confirms Oller's (1977a, 24) observation that the first sign in the line is MA, which is indented considerably. While there is some light surface damage to the beginning of the line, I did not see the traces of any signs. There is no obvious explanation for the indentation. Perhaps the surface damage had occurred to the statue before the inscription was carved; see the discussion in §3.4.

Believing text to be no longer preserved at the beginning of the line, previous scholars had understood *masiktu* to be used attributively (e.g., [*nukurtu*] *masiktu*, "an evil hostility"). After Oller's collations, the word has been understood to be a substantive. Most scholars have translated it as "an evil"; von Dassow's (2008, 19) translation of the word as “a bad thing” improves on this etymologically and captures the euphemism.[13] Significantly, the word *masiktu*—also written with IGI(*si*$_{17}$)—appears in AlT 17 [31.3], a legal text from Level IV Alalah.[14] This text is the record of court proceedings in which the ruler Niqmepa returned property that had been confiscated when a certain Apra “turned into a criminal and was killed because of his crime” (^{m}*ap-ra a-na* EN *ma-si*$_{17}$*-ik-ti it-tu-ur u*$_{3}$ *ki-ma ar-ni-šu* GAZ, ll. 7–9). This text has been discussed in relation to line 4 of the body inscription at least as far back as Landsberger (1954, 60 with n. 129). In particular, it has been suggested that the attestation of *masiktu* in AlT 17 [31.3] should refer to an act of rebellion and so, by extension, should the attestation in this line of the body inscription.[15]

Some scholars have proposed that the *masiktu* was the conquest of the city by various Hittite rulers, as recorded in Hittite documentation. These conclusions depend on a variety of unsupported assumptions, beginning with the assumption that the attestation of *masiktu* signifies that Halab was in fact destroyed; they can also involve questionable chronological reconstructions that require the symbolic spans of time found in the inscription to be counted literally. However, just because the arguments that have been put forward attributing the *masiktu* to Hittites cannot be proven does not mean that it *has* been proven that the Hittites were *not* responsible for the *masiktu*.

Otherwise, the *masiktu* has been increasingly understood to have been instigated by the growing power of Mittani. For instance, von Dassow (2008, 44) cautiously describes what she terms “the incident at Halab” as “most likely an early event in the nascent kingdom of Mittani’s imperial expansion.”[16] The two pieces of evidence raised in support of Mittani involvement are, first, the state of enmity that existed between Barattarna and Idrimi after he captured Alalah and their subsequent rapprochement, as detailed later in the inscription (ll. 42–58),

---

[13] She has translated it as “misfortune” subsequently; see von Dassow 2022, 481.

[14] Note that AlT 17 [31.3] is written by the Level IV scribe Šarruwa; see §6.1. For a possible use of IGI with this value in an Amarna letter, see EA 86: 9 [Byblos] ([*ti*]-⸢*ša*⸣-*si*$_{17}$; see Moran 1992, 159 n. 2 for discussion of some other interpretations of the sign string).

[15] For instance, Marquez Rowe (1997, 183) started from the observation that *masiktu* functions as a synonym to *arnu* in AlT 17. Next he established a meaning for *arnu* by looking to the Amarna letters, citing Moran’s comments concerning EA 139, where “the killing of vassal kings and a royal commissioner, as well as breaching another’s city walls, are declared, simply and without further qualification, as crimes (*arnu*) against the crown” (Moran 1995, 570). Finally, Márquez Rowe extended the meaning of *arnu* in the Amarna letters to conclude that “the ‘evil’” (i.e., *mašiktu*) “must have involved the killing of Idrimi’s father as well as the seizure of the town of Halab” (p. 183).

[16] See also von Dassow 2008, 19: “most likely an event that occurred in the course of Mittani’s conquest of the region.” Subsequently, she has suggested that the *masiktu* “may have been Mittani’s seizure of Halab after the Hittites destroyed the city and withdrew (alternatively, it may have been the Hittite destruction)” (von Dassow 2022, 481–82).

and, second, the use of word *masiktu* as a descriptor itself, which is taken as being deliberately vague.[17] However, this interpretation runs into the comparison with the Level IV text AlT 17 [31.3], where *masiktu* is juxtaposed with *arnu* and seems to refer to a specific action.

In part, the euphemistic impression given by *masiktu* derives from the verb *ittabši*, where the inchoative use of the N stem serves to obfuscate who, exactly, was responsible for the flight of Idrimi and his brothers. Without denying this impression, it is worth noting that the perfect tense of *bašû* in the N stem is also commonly used in the protases of omen texts; sometimes these protases omit *šumma*.[18] The use of the verb *ittabši* may have the effect of suggesting, then, that the criminal act that drove Idrimi and his brothers from Aleppo was a sign, and that the following narrative was predetermined.

The verb *halqānu* is one of several attestations of an Akkadian stative used as West Semitic perfective, as is common in the Canaano-Akkadian of the Amarna letters. This use was recognized already by Smith (1949, 37) and has been maintained by most subsequent scholars; see, most recently, Medill 2019, 245–46, discussing previous literature. The West Semitic influence on *halqānu* (and also the verb of the following clause, *ašbānu*) is also apparent in the larger syntax in which the verbs appear. As Smith also noted, the clause-initial position of the stative/suffix conjugation verbs, immediately following the conjunction *u* and preceded by a clause with a prefix conjugation verb, seems to be a clear example of the sequence of tenses found in West Semitic languages. As Medill (2019, 252) put it, "from the very first sentence of the Early History [= ll. 3–60a of the body inscription] the reader is nudged into a Northwest Semitic linguistic frame as he immediately encounters verbs which are Akkadian in form but Northwest Semitic in meaning."

In support of seeing IGI at the end of line 5 as text that has run over from line 4 and not a suffix -*ši* with *a-ha-te*.HI.A in line 5, see Lauinger 2022a, 220 n. 6. In addition to the observation about the horizontal ruling below line 5 made there, note that none of the objections to understanding IGI as a prepositional use of *pānu* really hold up. In particular, Greenstein and Marcus's (1976, 71) assertion that prepositional uses of *pānu* are "generally confined to later texts in Akkadian"

---

[17] See, e.g., Astour 1969, n. 4 ("The inscription is very evasive about these events"); Oller 1977a, 205 ("the reason for Idrimi's reluctance to be specific in naming the cause of his misfortune is obvious … Idrimi had made peace with Barrattarna … in this new relationship, he could hardly name him as the main cause of his father's demise and his family's exile"); and Zeeb 2004, 90 ("Not naming the *mašiktu* by its real character would then be a rhetorical device motivated by the wish not to put the foregoing actions of the partner into a bad light, once an agreement was finally reached").

[18] See, e.g., "(if) a footprint like the footprint of an ostrich occurs" (*šēpu kīma šēp lurmi ittabši*, CT 20 32: 70). This reference and many others, with and without *šumma*, can be found in *CAD* 2, s.v. "bašû," 4c-2′.

is inaccurate. *CAD* 12, s.v. "panu," 1h gives several examples from the second millennium where *pānu* functions as preposition itself, and Vita (1997) has gathered additional examples attested in western hybrid Akkadian corpora. Furthermore, as Greenstein and Marcus acknowledged, a prepositional use *pānu* occurs later in the body inscription (l. 33).

5–6. ⌜LU$_2$⌝.HI.A ^{uru}*e*$^!$*-mar*^{ki} *a-ha-te*.HI.A

The seeming description of Idrimi's aunts (literally, "sisters ([o]f my mother") as "men of Emar" has generated substantial discussion; see Lauinger 2022a for a review of the literature. As suggested there, the seeming contradiction can be resolved by a well-attested distinction in Late Bronze Age Syrian texts, including from Emar itself, between "sons" of a town or city and "men" of a town or city. The "sons" are the indigenous population, who could own city property and participate in collective decision making, while "men" either refers to the entire population resident at a town or city or, more specifically, to resident aliens who could not own property or participate in decision making. This interpretation is supported by the marginal status of the Idrimi's aunts at Emar, as evidenced by Idrimi's rhetorical questions in lines 10–12, which, alhough obscure, ends by asking "but (who) is, indeed, a servant to the citizens (DUMU.HI.A) of Emar?"; see the commentary to line 12 below.

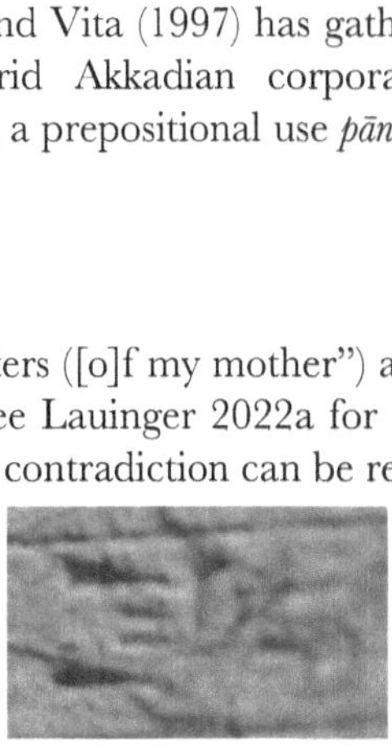
Figure A.8. Defective E$^!$ in line 5?

It is difficult to determine whether the E sign in the toponym *Emar* is defective or just damaged; see figure A.8.

6. [*š*]*a um-mi-ia u*$_3$ *aš-ba-nu a-na* ^{uru}*e-mar*^{ki}

For *ašbānu* as an Akkadian stative used as a West Semitic perfective and for its clause initial position also reflecting West Semitic syntax, see the commentary to line 4 above (*halqānu*). The verb *ašbānu* shows another characteristic of West Semitic in its prepositional complement, which is *ana* instead of *ina*, the preposition used with *ašābu* in the standard Akkadian dialects. The use of *ana* was discussed by Tsevat (1958, 131–33), who pointed out that "a good test for the presence of elements of a Canaanite dialect in a Semitic language is the observation of the prepositional constructions of the verb 'to sit on (a chair or throne), to dwell in (a place),'" in that the former use the preposition *l*- while the latter use *ʿal* or *b*-. Similarly, he observed that one finds a parallel situation when one compares the "Canaanite Akkadian" of the Amarna letters and Alalah with "standard Akkadian," in that the former uses *ašābu ana* as often as it uses *ašābu ina*. In other words, *ašābu ana* is a calque of West Semitic *yṯb l*-

7. ah-he$_2$.⌜HI.A⌝*-ia ša* UGU*-ia* GAL.GAL.HI.A

In *CAD* 14, the attestation of GAL.GAL.HI.A appears s.v. "rabbû," a-2′because GAL.GAL is attested in lexical and bilingual texts as a logogram from *rabbû*, "very big." Otherwise, those scholars who have normalized the logogram have been unanimous in seeing the signs as a logogram for *rabû*, "big." A majority have taken it to be a 3mp G stative, *rabû*; a stative seems logical because it fits the sense of the passage (in that being older is not fientive). However, Durand (2011, 136), who did not himself offer a normalization, objected to the G stem, remarking in a note: "La répétition de l'idéogramme indique sans doute une forme plus complexe qu'un permansif G, *rabû*." That is, a seeming problem with a normalization of GAL.GAL.HA$_2$ as *rabû* is that, while the plural form accounts for the 3mp ending, the G stem does not account for the reduplication of the logogram GAL; if number is indicated by a plural determinative, then the reduplication should indicate a stem other than the G stem. To some extent, however, Dietrich and Loretz (1981, 211) anticipated this objection. They pointed to line 97 of the body inscription, where the phrase *ilānu rabûtu* is written logographically as DINGIR-MEŠ GAL.GAL.E.NE; that is, the plural form of the exact same word, *rabû*, is conveyed both by the plural determinative E.NE as well as by reduplication of the logogram (see the commentary to line 97 below). Indeed, as discussed in §4.1, there are a number of attestations in the body inscription of words spelled with what might be described as pleonastic plurals, such as syllabic spellings + postposition determinatives, multiple postposition determinatives, preposition determinatives + postposition determinatives, and even preposition determinatives + syllabic spellings + postposition plural determinative. Therefore, while *rabbû*, "much older," remains a possible normalization and translation for GAL.GAL.HA$_2$, there is reason to understand the combination of reduplication and plural determinative as pleonastic and to normalize simply *rabû*.

8. it-ti-ia-ma aš-bu-u$_2$ u$_3$ ma-an-nu-um-ma

The nuance in meaning conveyed by the enlitic *-ma* on the preposition *ittiyama* has generally been ignored in by scholars, and those who have attempted to convey its nuance have translated it with the sense "also, as well."[19] However, the sense of the passage that results argues against this interpretation. If "we" fled to Emar, and "we" stayed there, and "my" brothers stayed there "also," who else accompanied Idrimi to comprise "we"? In other words, this "we" is typically understood to be Idrimi and his brothers, but his brothers are actually excluded from the group if we understand *-ma* in line 8 to mean "also, as well," or the like. It seems better to consider whether the enclitic *-ma* may convey a different nuance, thereby

[19] See, e.g., Greenstein and Marcus 1976, 67: "(My older brothers) also stayed with me," so also Buccellati 1962, 96 and Dietrich and Loretz 1981, 204.

maintaining the conventional understanding that the "we" of *halqānu* (l. 4) and *ašbānu* (l. 6) consists of Idrimi and his brothers.

Two scholars have gone this route. In his discussion of the uses of enclitic *-ma* in the inscription, Smith (1949, 34) remarked that, while generally the suffix "is used with a force that can be understood but cannot always be neatly rendered," the attestation in line 8 was an exception that could be understood as "adversative in force." This interpretation was grounded in Smith's understanding of *rabû* in the previous line as meaning that Idrimi's older brother "grew great against me," but still they "abode with me nevertheless," where "nevertheless" translates the enclitic *-ma*. However, *rabû* is better understood to communicate that Idrimi's brothers were older than him, and since the initial condition that Smith's interpretation relied on no longer exists, an interpretation of *-ma* as adversative needs to be abandoned.

Although Durand (2011) did not comment explicitly on the line, we can infer from his translation, "(Mes frères) les voilà qui habitent avec moi-même," that he understood the suffix to emphasize the 1cs pronoun *-ya* that is also suffixed to the preposition *itti*. This interpretation has much to commend it. It fits the context of the line, which one expects to be pejorative (i.e., even though my brothers were older than me and should have been out there doing something about the situation, they stayed with me, the baby of the family). It also preserves the possibility of seeing Idrimi's brothers as the other persons who comprised the subject "we" in lines 4 and 6. And, finally, it sets up a frame with lines 39–42. If lines 3–12 open the episode of Idrimi's wanderings through a description of his status vis-à-vis his brothers, lines 39–42 reintroduce his brothers to close the episode, using the exact same form, *ittiyama*, to emphasize the change to their respective statuses; see the commentary to line 41 below.

9. ⸢*a*⸣*-wa-te.*MEŠ *ša ah-šu-šu u₂-ul ih-šu-uš*

This line contains two forms of the verb *hasāsu* which show a confusion of sibilants that cannot be resolved by recourse to orthography, as ŠU does not have a value for the syllable /su/. A similar confusion of sibilants occurs in forms of this verb found in Amarna letters sent from Qaṭna and Hazor.[20] While the verb *hasāsu* has a base meaning of "designat[ing] the mental functions 'to mind, respect, remember, recall'" (Heimpel 1999), a majority of scholars have translated the verb rather neutrally with the meaning "to think."[21] However, a few scholars have understood *hasāsu* to have a different sense, "to plan"; for example, Oppenheim

[20] EA 56: 14 [Qaṭna] (*i-ha-aš-ša₁₀*(SA)-⸢*ša*⸣-[*an-ni*]) and EA 228: 18 [Hazor] (*li-ih-šu-uš-mi*).

[21] For a representative sample, see, e.g., Albright 1950, 16 ("but none of them thought the things which I thought"); Seux 1977, 43 ("mais aucun ne pensait aux affaires auxquelles je pensais"); and Dietrich and Loretz 1981, 204 ("Aber keiner erwog Dinge, die ich überlegte").

(1969, 557): "but none of them had the plans I had." While this translation gets closer to the meaning of the verb, it nonetheless misses out on another nuance of the verb that needs to be taken into account—namely, that it is followed by *umma anāku* (l. 10).

As is well known, this phrase is commonly used in Akkadian to introduce direct speech, and, indeed, direct speech is occasionally found juxtaposed with the verb *hasāsu*. In these instances, the verb has the sense of externalizing recall—that is, of making others conscious of something by referring to or mentioning it.[22] For instance, in a letter from Mari, we find the statement, "These men were referred to in this report, (which stated): *i-na ṭe$_4$-mi-im an-ni-im* … LU$_2$.MEŠ *šu-nu-ti ih-su$_2$-su-nim um-ma-a-mi it-ti* PN [I]R$_3$ PN$_2$ [*i*]*d-bu-bu*, "'They spoke with PN, the servant of PN$_2$'" (ARM 28 20: 6–12; see LAPO 16 397 [no. 252]). Similarly, in an Old Babylonian letter from Larsa, one finds seven attestations of *hasāsu*, one of which is explicitly used in connection with the phrase *ana pî wardim*, "according to the mouth of a servant":

> *i-nu-ma wa-ar-du-um i-na bi-tim iṣ-ṣa-ab-tu a-lu-um i-ša-al-šu-ma* DUMU PN *ih-su$_2$-us* DUMU A.ZU *u$_2$-ul ih-su$_2$-us* … *u$_2$-uṣ-ṣi$_2$$^!$-ṣu$_2$-šu-ma* DUMU PN-*ma ih-su$_2$-us a-na pi-i wa-ar-di-im ma-ar a-wi-li it-ta-na-ad-di$^?$-nu* … *i-na še-e ša-ra-qu$_2$-tim u$_2$-ul ih-ha-si$_2$-is* … *iš-tu i-na a-li-ni wa-aš-bu i-na sa$_3$-ar-tim ma-ti-ma šu-um-š*[*u*] *u$_2$-ul ha-si$_2$-is a-wi-lum pa-na-nu-um u$_2$-ul ha-si$_2$-is i-na-an-na ma-an-nu-um ih-su$_2$-sa$_3$-ku-uš-šu* (AbB 14 144: 6–9, 11–13, 22–23, 26–30, citing previous literature)
>
> When the servant was seized in the house, the city interrogated him. He mentioned the son of PN, he did not mention the physician's son…. They interrogated him, but he mentioned only the son of PN. Is it *customary to extradite* free citizens on the basis of a servant's testimony?… He was not mentioned concerning the stolen barley…. Since he has been living in our city, his name has never been mentioned concerning a crime. Previously, the man has not been mentioned. Who, now, mentioned him to you?

Outside of Mesopotamia proper, one finds *hasāsu* with *umma* in an Amarna letter sent by the pharaoh to Aziru of Amurru: *gab$_2$-bi a-wa-te*.MEŠ *ša taš$_3$-pur* UGU-*ši-na šar-ru-um-ma* LUGAL *ih-su$_2$-us um-ma-a la-a šal-mu gab$_2$-bu ša ta-aq-bu$_2$*, "As for all of the words that you sent (in messages), the king, himself, made mention of them, saying: 'Everything that you say is insincere'" (EA 162: 20–21 [Egypt]). While *CAD* 6, s.v. "hasāsu" cited this reference under meaning 6 ("to be intelligent, understanding")—the same meaning under which the attestations of the verb in this line of the Idrimi body inscription are found—there are over half a dozen other instances of *umma* in this same letter, and all introduce direct speech, both inside and outside of epistolary contexts, so there is every reason to assume the same for this instance that follows *hasāsu*.

---

22 *AHw* 330a, 2; *CAD* 6, s.v. "hasāsu," 5 ("to refer to [something/somebody], to mention").

Understanding the verb *hasāsu* to have the sense "to refer to, to mention" carries with it a few implications. First, it suggests a literal translation of the direct object *awâte* as "words" rather than the more abstract sense "affair, matter, situation" that occurs in most translations; indeed, the more literal sense fits the plural form of the word better. Second, as both the Mari and Larsa parallels cited above suggest, the fact that the "words" are "mentioned" rather than being simply spoken communicates that they are something that other people already knew, even if they were not currently thinking of them; that is, the "men" were "referred to" in a report previously given, and the servant "mentioned" two persons already known to the city. This implication, in turn, suggests that lines 10–12 may be a proverb or maxim, even if it is one that is adapted by Idrimi to his present circumstance; see the commentary to line 10 below. Finally, it is even possible that the attestations of the verb *hasāsu* are meant to communicate that Idrimi spoke lines 10–12 aloud to his brothers. If this understanding is correct, so that Idrimi's brothers were in possession of the same insight as Idrimi (even if they needed to be reminded of it by him), then the text is emphasizing even more strongly the brothers' inaction in contrast to Idrimi's own action.

10. um-ma a-na-ku-ma ma-an-⌜nu⌝-um E₂ *a-bi-šu*

The MA sign appears three times in the line in three different forms, illustrated in figure A.9. The attestations of the interrogative pronoun *mannum* in this line and in the following line are marked by mimation through a final -V*m* sign. Mimation does not generally occur in the inscriptions except in the case of final CVC signs and interrogative and demonstrative pronouns like this one or *annâm* (l. 57). For a similar situation in the Akkadian of Ugarit, see Huehnergard 2011, 99–100.

Going back to Smith's (1949, 15) edition, *mannum* is often translated as "whoever" in the scholarly literature. Elsewhere in the body inscription, we find the generalizing relative pronouns *mannumma* (l. 8) and *mannummê* (ll. 92, 96), so we might expect *mannum ša* in place of just *mannum* here if the generalizing relative

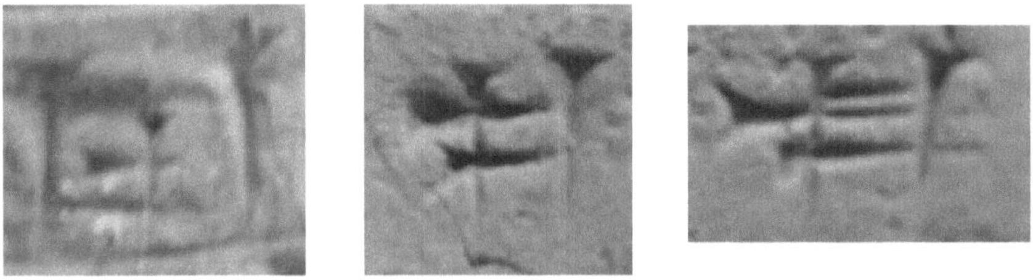

Figure A.9. Three different forms of MA in line 10 (first = left; second = center; third = right).

pronoun and not the interrogative pronoun was intended.[23] However, Wilhelm (1970, 81–82) has shown that at Nuzi both *mannum* and *mannummê* could function as generalizing relative pronouns. For instance, he gave the following example, which clearly shows *mannum* alone in a variant of the common penalty clause that uses *mannum ša*: *ma-an-nu i-na be-ri-šu-nu ib-bal-kat*, "Whoever among them violates the contract (will pay silver and gold)" (HSS 9 22: 27–28, cited p. 81). In a related fashion, one can also find *mannum* functioning almost as a synonym for the indefinite pronoun *mamman*: *šum-ma* A.ŠA$_3$ *ša ma-an-ni-im pi*$_2$*-ir-qa ir-ta-ši*, "If the field of anyone will have acquired a claim…" (*RA* 23 38: 13–15; cited p. 82). Indeed, this same use of *mannu* occurs at Late Bronze Alalah in the treaty between Niqmepa and Ir-^{d}IM of Tunip (and so is more indicative of the usage of Akkadian at Tunip than Alalah): *šum-ma* LU$_2$ *lu* LU$_2$.SAL-*tum* GU$_4$ ANŠE *u*$_3$ *šum-ma* ANŠE.KUR.RA *iš-tu* E$_2$ *ma-an-nim yu-da*$_2$*-šu*…, "If a man or a woman identified an ox, donkey or a horse in the house of someone…" (AlT 2 [1.1]: 32–33; see Dietrich and Loretz 1997, 216). The same use is found in the Amarna letters in a letter from Rib-Addi of Byblos: *ša-ni-tam* ^{giš}MA$_2$-MEŠ *ša ma-ni i-zi-zu* UGU-*ia*, "Something else: Whose boats have taken a stand against me?" (EA 101: 11–12). The use of interrogative *mannum* as a generalizing relative or indefinite pronoun, then, has a wider use in the Late Bronze Age than just the Hurro-Akkadian milieu.

Finally, there is still one more possibility that needs to be considered. In Northwest Semitic, the vocalization of the interrogatives "who?" and "what?" is the opposite of their vocalization in Akkadian; for example, Ugaritic *my*, "who?" and *mh*, "what?"[24] Presumably as a reflection of this situation, in the Amarna correspondence the Akkadian interrogatives *mannu*, "who?" and *mīnu*, "what?" are occasionally used for each other, so that one can find *mannu* with the meaning "what?" and *mīnu* with the meaning "who?" (see already Böhl 1909, 29). For instance, IR$_3$-Heba, the ruler of Jerusalem, begins the body of one letter by asking *ma-an-na ep-ša-ti a-na* LUGAL EN-*ia*, "What did I do to the king, my lord?" (EA 286: 5). These parallels may be behind Durand's (2011, 136) translation of this line of the body inscription as "Quelle est sa famille?"

In sum, there are three valid possibilities for *mannum*. It could be used as an interrogative pronoun "who?," a generalizing relative pronoun "whoever," or an interrogative pronoun "what?." In the commentary to line 9 above, I suggested that the use of *hasāsu* together with the phrase indicating direct speech may communicate that lines 10–12 represent a maxim or proverb that has been refashioned to fit Idrimi's immediate circumstances. The repetition of *mannu*—with any of the three meanings—fits this context very well, especially if the lines

---

[23] Cf. *AHw* 603b, where meaning 3 gathers instances of the phrase *mannum ša* with the meaning "wer auch immer; jeder der," with lines 10–11 of the Idrimi inscription listed under usage c ("nur *mannum*") together with one not-very-similar reference from Hattuša.

[24] For an overview of the interrogative pronouns "who?" and "what?" in the Semitic languages, see Burlingame 2021, 212–14.

are structured as parallelism. This parallelism can be synonymous, as in the case of two lines from the so-called "Assyrian Collection" of proverbs: *man-nu gi-it-ru-nu man-nu ša-ru a-na man-ni ut-li a-na-ṣar*, "Who is accumulating wealth? Who is rich? For whom do I guard my lap?" (*BWL* 227: 19–20). Or it can be antithetical, as the famous quotation from Gilgamesh and Huwawa in the so-called Dialogue of Pessimism that uses the interrogative *ayyû*: *a-a-u*$_2$ *ar-ku ša*$_2$ *a-na* AN^e *e-lu-u*$_2$ *a-a-u*$_2$ *rap-šu*$_2$ *ša*$_2$ KI.TIM *u*$_2$*-gam-me-ru*, "Who is (so) tall that he goes up to the Heavens? Who is (so) wide that he encompasses the Underworld?" (*BWL* 148: 83–84).

The syntactic role of *bīt abīšu* in the clause is difficult. The phrase has been taken as a direct object for scholars who have read the signs following *lu-u*$_2$ in line 11 as a transitive verb, which is also the interpretation followed here; see the commentary to line 11 below. Similarly, Oller (1977a, 28), following a suggestion of Shaffer, considered "*bīt a-bi-šu* as a sandhi for *bīt a-bi-*<*i*>*-šu*," thus supplying him a verb of possession (*īšu*) that can take *bīt abi* as its direct object ("Whoever possesses (his) family seat"). Dietrich and Loretz (1981, 204, 211–12) may have understood *bīt* as an adverbial accusative, because they translated *bīt abīšu* as "im Haus seines Vaters." Durand (2011, 136) interpreted *mannum bīt abišu* as a nominal sentence ("Quelle est sa famille?").

11. lu-u$_2$ *i-⸢dag*$^?$*⸣-gal u*$_3$ *ma-an-nu-um*

The signs following *lū* in this line, shown in figure A.10, have generated substantial literature. In one vein of scholarship, these signs have been taken as one or more verbal forms, and, in the other, as nominal forms. The determining factor is whether the third sign was identified as I and so taken as a verbal prefix, or as DUMU/TUR. For instance, Smith (1949, 14–15) was the first scholar to take the signs as a verbal form, identifying four signs, *i-*šu li-kal*, and translating "(Whoever still) has an inheritance, let him hold (thereto)" (taking *li-kal* as an unexpected precative of *kullu*). Goetze identified Smith's putative ŠU and GAL and single sign, GIŠIMMAR, which he read with the syllabic value *sa*$_6$ for *i-sa*$_6$*-kal* as a form of *sakālu*, "to acquire" (with theme vowel /a/ for expected /i/). And Na'aman (1980b, 113) suggested *i-dàg*$^!$*-gal*, translating "(Who) will own (his patrimony)"; note that *CAD* 3, s.v. "dagālu," 1c records this usage of *dagālu* as restricted to OA, NA, and NB, and, to my knowledge, no new attestations of the word with this

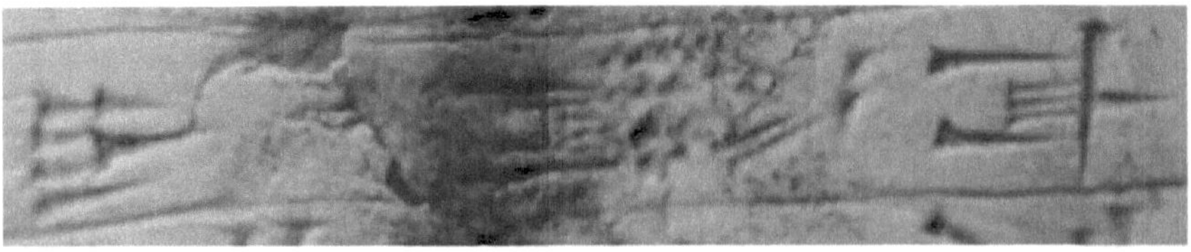

Figure A.10. The third, fourth, and fifth signs of line 11.

usage have since been published that would change this chronological and geographic distribution.

The first scholar to take the signs as a nominal form was Landsberger (1954, 55 n. 99), who identified them as DUMU SU.BIR$_4$, translating "ein Sohn des grossen (Landes) Suburtu." Putting aside the paleographic difficulty of identifying the sign before GAL as EDIN (= BIR$_4$) (so already Goetze 1957, 22 nn. 5–6), Landsberger's translation makes little sense contextually. But his suggestion that the sign identified by as Smith as I should instead be identified as DUMU/TUR has continued to characterize this vein of scholarship. So, for instance, Kempinski and Na'aman (1973, 211) identified the signs as DUMU NISAG (= MURU$_2$) GAL. Paleographically, MURU$_2$ is much better than SU.BIR$_4$,; this reading was followed by Greenstein and Marcus (1976, 64) and arrived at independently by Oller (1977a, 73). In one interpretation, NISAG was taken as a logogram for *ašarēdu*, "foremost (one)," so that the phrase *māru ašarēdu rabû* would be "great foremost son." However, only Oller (1977a, 73) noted the difficulty of NISAG being a logogram for *ašarēdu* because "the equation NISAG = *ašarīdu* is only attested lexically … and while *ašarīdu* does occur in titles for royal heirs … the appellation DUMU.NISAG.GAL is nowhere else attested."[25] Meanwhile, Dietrich and Loretz (1981, 211) suggested that NISAG was a logogram for the Akkadian word *šakkanakku*, "(military) governor," although this word is usually written logographically as ŠAGIN. In support of this reading, they cited *ABZ*. However, *MZL* now reads the attestation in question as SIMUG = *nappāhu*.

Durand (2011, 13) maintained Kempinski and Na'aman's identification of the logogram, but he read it more conventionally as MURU$_2$ with the Akkadian equivalence *qablu*, "middle." He saw the signs TUR MURU$_2$ GAL as a sequence, "small, middle, large," and took them to refer to social rank. He remarked that cuneiform texts from Ekalte (Tall Munbaqa) show that "la société de Munbaqa … était divisée en 'tur' et 'gal' et que les deux corps se réunissaient lorsqu'il fallait prendre une décision politique majeure" (112). While the Ekalte texts do not attest to a "middle class" (*qablu*), as Durand proposed to read in this line of the body inscription, he explained the absence as follows:

> Le murub$_4$ = *qablu* … devait représenter un assez compréhensible 'entre-deux', soit des 'tur' qui ont grandi (sans doute pour des raisons économiques), soit des 'gal' qui sont sur le déclin; il est vraisemblable qu'il s'agissait là d'un 'statut de fait,' mais qui n'avait pas sa place dans une nomenclature officielle, toujours

---

[25] In fact, the equation does not actually exist. It is derived from the composite edition of á A = *nâqu* (MSL 14 332) and was cited by *CAD* 1.2, s.v. "ašarēdu," lex. (ni-sag MURÚ = *a-šá-ri-du*). However, the line is preserved in two tablets; for one the Akkadian is no longer preserved, and in the other (BM 09037), the sign in question is NISAG$_3$ (= MURU$_{13}$). See already Durand 2011, 111 n. 61.

binaire idéalement, et cela explique sans doute que les textes officiels n'en parlent pas (112).

While taking the signs following *lū* as (a) nominal form(s) has the benefit of bringing lines 10–11 into closer parallelism, given the nominal predicate *lū arad* in line 11, the first sign of the string is better identified as I than DUMU, as the comparison with an I sign a few lines later and a DUMU sign in the following line makes clear; see figure A.11. And, in keeping with the vein of scholarship outlined above, once the first sign in the string is identified as I, it is very hard to see the sign string *i*-⸢*x*⸣-GAL as anything other than a verb form. The second, damaged, sign in the string is very conceivably an archaizing form of DAG or DAG$_3$, even if it be somewhat different in form than the poorly preserved attestation of the sign in the cheek inscription; see the commentary to CI 2 in §A.1. For these reasons, Na'aman's suggestion to read *idaggal* for a 3cs G present form of *dagālu*, "to see, look" seems the best interpretation of the signs found in the literature.

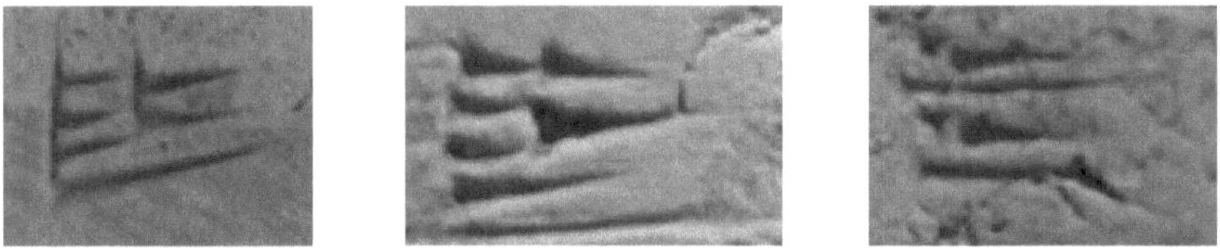

Figure A.11. The third sign of line 11 (center) juxtaposed with attestations of I (l. 14, left) and DUMU (l. 12, right).

However, Na'aman's translation of the verb with the sense "to own, possess" seems questionable given, as discussed above, the chronological distribution of the attestations of the verb with this sense. It seems possible that Na'aman sought to parallel earlier interpretations of the signs that had read there the verb *išû*, "to have, possess." The common sense of the verb *dagālu*, "to see, look" fits the context in that the lines can be understood as a pair of rhetorical questions commenting on Idrimi's poor situation. He is surrounded by the household of his father yet a servant to others. This observation, then, is what spurs him to action, beginning in line 13. In this regard, it is very tempting to read the verb as *i*-⸢*tak*$_2$⸣-*kal*$_2$, for a 3cs G present of *takālu*, "to trust in, rely on" and translate, "Who, indeed, relies on the household of his father, but who is, indeed, a servant to the citizens of Emar?" However, in the G stem, the verb *takālu* consistently takes its object with *ana* or a dative pronominal suffix. Therefore, one would need to emend line 10 to <*a-na*> E$_2$ *a-bi-šu* in order to take the verb as *itakkal*.

12. a-[*n*]*a* DUMU.HI.A ^{uru}*e-mar*^{ki} *lu-u*$_2$ ARAD

Before 1980, signs were thought to be missing from the beginning of the line, and different restorations, mostly [*lā īšu*], were preferred. In 1980, however, Na'aman

Figure A.12. The second half of line 14, showing extent to the right.

(1980b, 113) observed that the beginning of the line, although damaged, had been left blank; see the discussion and figure in §3.4.

13. [AN]ŠE.KUR.RA-[*i*]*a* ⸢^{giš}GIGIR⸣-*ia* *u*$_3$ $^{\text{lu}_2}$IŠ-*ia*

The logogram $^{\text{lu}_2}$IŠ-*ia* is perhaps to be read KUŠ$_7$ or ŠUŠ$_3$, and, while it is clear in texts from Late Bronze Age Anatolia and the Levant that the profession designated by this logogram, *kizû*, accompanied a *maryannu* into combat, there is some disagreement as to whether he was the chariot driver or archer. For more discussion, citing previous literature, see Lauinger 2021, 38 n. 17; see also the discussion of this line in §5.2.

Not discussed there but worth asking: is anything to be made of the fact that the text specifies only a single horse for Idrimi? In the Level IV administrative texts from Late Bronze Age Alalah, horses are typically disbursed in pairs (*tāpalu*) for service pulling chariots; see, for example, AlT 329 [44.1], 330 [44.2], and 338 + 33.9 [44.7], and the discussion in von Dassow 2008, 305–7, especially n. 108. Also, with regard to this line, cf. Albright's (1950, 16) translation, "my horse(s)" and Liverani's (2014, 332) translation "my horses."

14. [*el*]-*te*-⸢*qe*$_2$⸣-*šu-nu* *u*$_3$ *i-na ma-at hu-ri-ib-te*^{ki}

The end of line 14 extends far past the other lines in this division of the statue; the signs -*ri-ib-te*^{ki} are written after the horizontal rulings have ended and above the statue's hand, as shown in figure A.12. The identification of the signs *i-na* for the preposition *ina* has received discussion on the basis of the form of the sign NA and the resulting syntax, in that the verb *etēqu* does not typically take its object with *ina*; see, for example, Oller 1977a, 33–34. Paleographically, the identification of the sign as NA is not problematic; the characteristic feature of the sign is the initial component consisting of crossed wedges. As can be seen in figure A.13, the

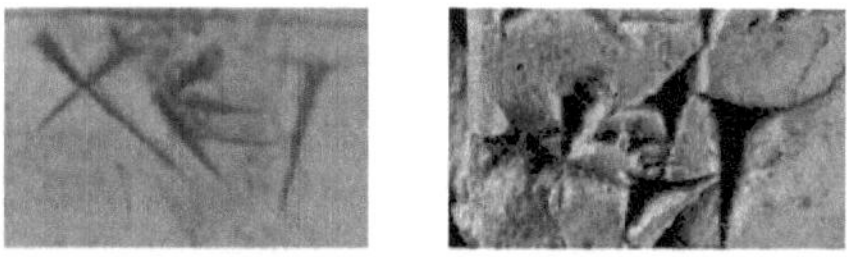

Figure A.13. The sign NA in line 14 (left) and Msk. 74193a+ (right). Courtesy C. Roche-Hawley

initial components of a NA sign are crossed in a somewhat similar, if more perpendicular, fashion in a manuscript of Paleographic S^{a} from Emar (Emar 538: 164′ [Msk 94193a]; see Emar 6/2 475; Gantzert 2011, 42 i 25; and Roche-Hawley 2012).

The use of *ina* as a prepositional complement to *etēqu* may be less unexpected than has been presented. A simple review of the dictionaries reveals several attestations where *etēqu* is used with *ina*, although, admittedly, none are from texts written in western hybrid Akkadian.[26] Perhaps more tellingly, though, in Ugaritic, the cognate verb *ʿtq* seems to take the preposition *b* as its complement; see, for example, a fragment from the alphabetic letter of Puduhepa to Niqmaddu III: *tʿtq . by . ḥwt .* […], "(the caravans) must pass through the land of […]" (*KTU* 2.73 [RS 17.434+]: 4′; see Pardee 1983–1984, 322 and Pardee 2002a, 96). Note especially the similar context: the Ugaritic letter and the Idrimi text share the context of crossing through a land.

Although *huribtu* is typically translated as "desert" in the literature, Durand (2011, 136 n. 126) has argued that the word is better understood as a formerly inhabited place that is now abandoned; see also Durand 2011, 101 n. 24 ("Le 'pays en ruines' s'oppose au monde des villes, le désert réel étant désigné alors par le terme de *madbarum*"). Accordingly, Durand understood that the word "indique qu'Idrimi emprunte les routes qui passent par des régions abandonnées, alors que l'on imagine qu'à l'époque amorrite ces régions étaient encore peuplées" before he reached in the following lines, "l'endroit où, éventuellement, il n'y a plus que des nomades qui passent de temps en temps y laissant la trace de leurs abris précaires."

15. ⸢*e-te-ti-iq*⸣ *u*$_3$ *li-bi* ERIN$_2$.MEŠ *su-tu-u*$_2$^{ki}

This attestation of *libbu* is the only occurrence of the word in the inscriptions where it is used prepositionally and not in a compound prepositional phrase.

The Suteans are well attested throughout the second millennium BCE in cuneiform corpora from a number of different sites as a tribally organized population that pursued seminomadic pastoralism.[27] The narrative function of Idrimi's sojourn among them is open to debate. Some scholars have emphasized the nomadic character of the Suteans; in particular, Greenstein (1995, 2426) has evoked the role of the "makeshift housing" of the Suteans within a larger reading of the text that focuses on the theme of house and home in the narrative. However,

---

[26] See, e.g., in the Middle Assyrian Laws: *šum-ma* DAM^{at} LU$_2$ *i-na ri-be-e-te te-te-ti-iq*, "If the wife of a man passed through a city square" (KAV 1: ii 14–15; cited *CAD* 4, s.v. "etēqu," 1).

[27] The bibliography on the Suteans, beginning with the famous but now out-of-date study by Heltzer and Arbeli-Raveh 1981, is vast; see, in particular, Streck 2002 and Ziegler and Reculeau 2014.

it is also possible that it is the desert, not the Suteans, that has narrative significance. As demonstrated by Liverani (2004b) and discussed in more detail in §5.2, the topos of a journey into the desert plays an important role in framing Idrimi as a fairy tale hero, and it may be that the Suteans are mentioned in the text because they reinforce the desert setting of Idrimi's sojourn.

16. ⸢e⸣-te-ru-ub ⸢iš⸣ -ti-šu-<nu> a-na li-bi

The preposition taken here as *ištišu<nu>* presents several difficulties and is often omitted in translations of the text. The identification of the first sign as IŠ seems correct. Even though it is damaged, the sign in question clearly comprises three horizontal wedges followed by a large *Winkelhaken* and ending in two vertical wedges, the first of which is smaller than the second. It is very similar to the attestation of IŠ in line 21, shown in figure A.14. Reading the first sign of the preposition as IŠ means that the preposition is, with Oller, *išti* and not *itti*. This difference does not change the meaning of the text, as both prepositions mean "with," but it is interesting from the perspective of dialect because, broadly speaking, *išti* is at home in the Assyrian dialects, while the Babylonian dialects employ the preposition *itti*.

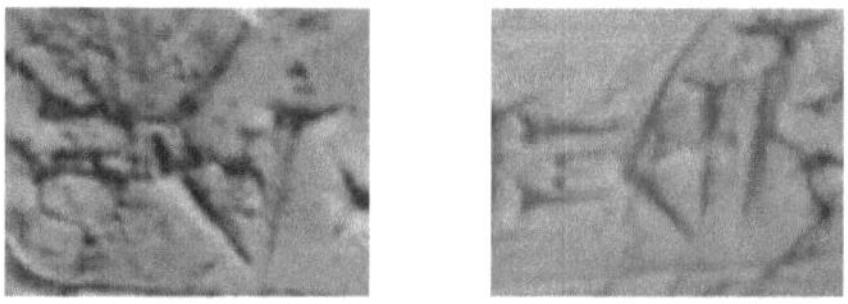

Figure A.14. IŠ (l. 16, left) juxtaposed to IŠ (l. 21, right).

According to de Ridder's (2018, 304–5) data, one typically finds the form *ilte* before pronominal suffixes, with /št/ instead of /lt/, not the historical form **ište*. However, this latter form, followed by the expected vowel before the pronominal suffix, is what is found in this line of the body inscription. Therefore, since *ištu*, *išti-* is attested already in Old Akkadian texts, it may be better to understand the employment of *išti* before the pronominal suffix as a deliberate archaizing form than a sign of Assyrian influence.

While some scholars have considered that the ostensibly singular pronominal suffix on the preposition refers to the *kizû*-chariot driver mentioned in line 13, such a referent does not seem likely, given that, as argued in §5.2, the *kizû*-chariot driver is the functional equivalent of Idrimi's horse and chariot—that is, only an accoutrement indicative of his social status. Accordingly, most scholars considered that the possessive pronoun must refer back to the Suteans in the immediately preceding line; to my knowledge, Greenstein and Marcus (1976, 73) were the first scholars to explicitly comment on this difficulty and suggest emending the text.

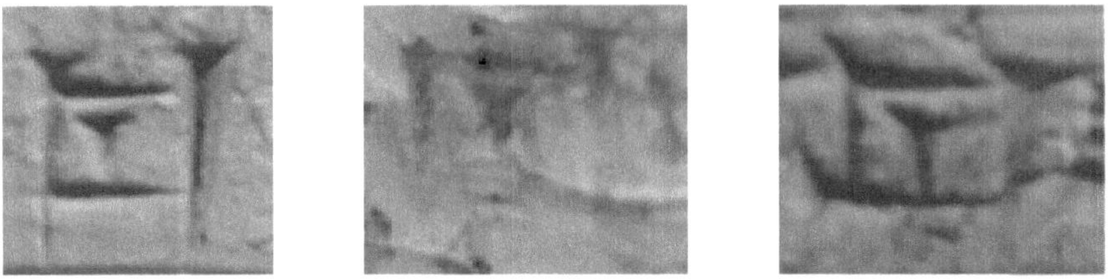

Figure A.15. The damaged sign at the beginning of line 17 (center) juxtaposed with KU signs in line 10 (left) and later in line 17 (right).

17. ⌜KU$^{?}$⌝-[*x*(-)*x*]*x-zak*$^{?}$*-kar bi-ta*$_{2}$*-ku i-na ša-ni u*$_{4}$-⌜*mi*⌝

The condition of the beginning of line 17 has deteriorated since excavation, as is clear from comparing Smith's (1949) copy with Oller's (1977a). While Smith's copy shows damage only at the very beginning of the line so that every sign is preserved, Oller's copy shows only a few wedges remaining from Smith's putative third and fourth signs (ZA and LI). At the time I studied the statue, the line's condition had deteriorated even further; the top of first sign is still preserved, but the second and third signs are almost entirely missing. A number of different interpretations, none of them satisfactory, have been put forward in the literature for reading the beginning of line 17. After collation, I agree with Oller (1977a, 10) and Dietrich and Loretz (1981, 204) that the first sign should be identified as KU against other identifications of the sign as GIGIR(LAGAB×BAD) because there is not a BAD sign inside the putative LAGAB component. Rather, there is a small interior vertical wedge; the forms of KU in lines 10 and later in the same line provide good parallels (see figure A.15). Nothing now remains of the next one, or possibly two, remaining signs. For the following sign, Dietrich and Loretz's (1981, 204) ZAG is also a good fit epigraphically. A possible difficulty could be the sign's first large *Winkelhaken*, where we expect a horizontal wedge. But see figure A.16 for an example of ZAG in a manuscript of Paleographic S^{a} from Ugarit that has a *Winklehaken* in place of the horizontal wedge (Roche-Hawley 2024). Because the sign ZAG can be read as *zak*, Dietrich and Loretz (1981, 204) took the wedges that Smith (1949, 15) read, with difficulty, as *-te-a* to be a single sign, KAR. Epigraphically, this reading works well, and the resulting syllabic string *zak-kar* is reasonable.

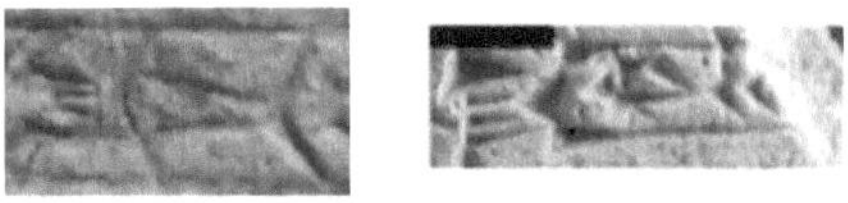

Figure A.16. The second preserved sign in line 17 juxtaposed with an example of ZAG in RS 86.2222+. Image on right courtesy of C. Roche-Hawley

Nonetheless, despite being in agreement with Dietrich and Loretz epigraphically, I find it more difficult to accept their interpretation of the signs *zak-kar* as a personal name Zakkar, most famously borne by the first millennium ruler of Hamath (Dietrich and Loretz 1981, 213). Personal names are not mentioned in the Idrimi text unless they serve some larger narrative purpose. It is possible that some significance or association was attached to a putative Zakkar that is now lost to us. But, on the other hand, if the Suteans are primarily window dressing, mentioned mainly in order to flesh out the desert through which Idrimi passes, and which does serve an important narrative purpose, then we would scarcely expect to find a personal name mentioned here.[28]

I do not have an interpretation of the sign string to offer, owing in part to the fact that some of the signs are no longer preserved. But I do think that one can make a few inferences within the parameters of the sign identifications as discussed above. First, the signs at the beginning of line 17 should be a nominal form that is the object of the preposition *ana libbi*. Second, the word [x]-*zak-kar* would seem to be clause final; the morphology and position in the clause suggest that it may be a verb. Indeed, this idea fits with the occurrence at the end of line 16 of the prepositional phrase *ana libbi*, since this prepositional phrase does not work very well with the verb *biātu*. While verbs in the preterite and perfect tenses dominate the narrative, there are five attestations of verbs in the present tense; in four of these attestations, the present tense is used aspectually, to describe an ongoing action in past.[29] Fourth and finally, following this logic, we expect the damaged sign at the head of the string [x]x-*zak-kar* to be a verbal prefix. However, while the reading of that sign by Smith and others as LI fits the morphological context, in that it could mark the precative and the precative is formed elsewhere in the Idrimi text with a present tense base, a precative does not fit the sense of the passage. Because the putative verb seems to be singular, Idrimi and not the Suteans would seem to be the subject. One would expect the sign to be A, although AZ or AŠ$_2$, with assimilation of an infixed /t/, could be possible. However, after comparing the preserved traces and the copies of Smith and Oller to the potential roots, especially **zkr*, I have not been able to come up with a satisfactory reading, and it is possible that this chain of reasoning is incorrect.

18. [*an*]*-mu-uš-ma u*$_3$ ⸢*a*⸣-[*n*]*a ma-at ki-in-a-ni*$_7^{ki}$

The first sign of the verb [*an*]*mušma* was no longer preserved on the statue when I studied it, but it is clear in Smith's copy and photograph and in Oller's copy. Evidently, the loss of this sign is another instance of the continued deterioration of the statue's surface.

---

[28] See, already, Durand 2011, 102: "je ne crois pas que ce soit une bonne idée de trouver en ces lieux un dénommé Zakkar, totalement inconnu par ailleurs."

[29] See *u*$_2$*-ra-ak* (l. 27; verbal hendiadys?); *in-na-ḫu-u*$_2$ (ll. 41, 48; aspectual); *u*$_2$*-uš-ša-bu* (l. 85; aspectual); and *e-te-ne-pu-uš*$_{10}$*-šu-nu* (l. 90; aspectual). Note also the nonstandard precatives forms *li-*⸢*tak*$_2$⸣*-kal*$_2$*-šu-nu* and *li-ik-ta-na-ra-bu* in lines CI 2–3.

The attestation of "the land of Canaan" in this line and the following have been much discussed, primarily as fodder for arguments about whether the phrase signified "a definite territorial entity or a 'diffuse and vague' designation for a region whose size, location, and inhabitants were largely unknown even to the individuals who populated the southern Levant during the L[ate] B[ronze Age]" (Benz 2016, 100, citing Lemche 1991, 39). "The land of Canaan" is attested at Late Bronze Age Alalah, but its significance is not entirely clear. The toponym is attested in several texts from Level IV; one in particular, AlT 188 [412.5], qualifies three lower-class individuals as from "the land of Alašiya," "the land of Nuhašše," and "the land of Canaan" (ll. 5–6, 8), suggesting that these three toponyms were understood to be equivalent from the scribe's perspective. Two other texts seem to conceive of "Canaan" as a settlement, because they use the URU determinative.[30] From the perspective of the narrative, the references to "the land of Canaan" in the Idrimi text seem primarily intended to localize the city of Ammiya; for a discussion of the narrative significance of this second toponym, see the commentary to line 20 below.

20. ^{uru}⌜*am*⌝*-mi-ia*^{ki} *aš-bu i-na* ^{uru}*am-mi-ia*^{ki}

With regard to the morphology of the verb *aš-bu*, most of the scholars who have commented have understood the suffix to be another example of what they considered to be the misapplication of the Akkadian subordination marker; see, for example, Greenstein and Marcus 1976, 74 ("the final *u* is a peculiar feature of this text [cf. *ittūru* in line 30, etc.] in which a reckless suffixation of subjunctive u abounds") and Oller 1977a, 35 ("subjunctives occurring where indicatives are expected"). Keeping in mind that ancient Near Eastern settlements were conceived of as people as much as places, perhaps a simpler solution is to take *aš-bu* as a 3mp stative with Ammiya as its subject. This interpretation allows the verb to have the same meaning, "to reside," as the attestation of the same verb in line 23, in contrast to the meaning "to be situated," as it would otherwise need to be translated. Furthermore, there are several other occasions in the text where an ostensibly singular place seems to take a plural verb. For instance, in lines 35–36, the singular noun *mātu* is the subject of two plural verbs: *ma-ti-ia iš-mu-un-ni-ma* GU_4.HI.A u_3 UDU.HI. … *ub-lu-*u_2*-*ni_7, "my land heard (about this), so they brought oxen and sheep." And in lines 70–71, the subject *māt Hatte* stands as the subject of both the

---

30 AlT 48 [352.3]: 5 (see Niedorf 2008, 370, discussing previous literature) and BM 131938 [493.29]: 3, an unpublished text that is cited by Niedorf 1998, 530 and RGTC 12.2, s.v. "*Kinʿanu/Kinahnu/Kinahhu." Note that the British Museum online collections database (https://www.britishmuseum.org/collection/object/W_1954-0712-178) indicates that this museum number belongs to a different object, a pottery ostracon with three lines of an inscription in Pahlavi that was found in Nizamabad, Iran and dates to the sixth-eighth centuries CE.

singular verb *iphur* and the plural verb *illikū*: *ma-at* ⸢*ha*⸣*-at-te*^{ki} *u_2-ul ip-hur u_3 a-na* ⸢UGU⸣*-ia u_2-ul il-li-ku*, "The land of Hatti did not gather and march because of me" (see the commentary to l. 71 below).

The city that is at the center of these lines, Ammiya, is quite significant. In addition to the attestations in the Idrimi text, Ammiya is attested in the Level IV documentation from Alalah and in a number of different Amarna letters, mostly written by Rib-Addi and Ili-rapi of Byblos, but once in a letter sent by the pharaoh to its ruler. In the Level IV texts, the toponym is used to qualify different individuals appearing in lists. The best preserved of these is AlT 181 [414.7], a list of twenty armed *habiru* who were resident in the town of Anaše; one individual named Aziru is qualified as "of Ammiya."[31] The other two attestations, AlT 166 [415.11]: 19 and *SSAU* 4 11 [412.20]: 11 are quite fragmentary, so that the overall purpose of the lists is not explicit, but the toponym is used to qualify individuals in those texts as well. If nothing else, these attestations demonstrate that the city of Ammiya was known to the administrators of earlier Level IV Alalah.

In the Amarna letters, Ammiya is presented by Rib-Addi of Byblos as a cautionary tale for what will happen to him should the pharaoh not intervene. Early letters report that ʿAbdi-ʾAširte of Amurru sent messages to "the men of Ammiya" encouraging them to kill their lord (*bēlu*, *eṭlu*) and join the *habiru* (EA 73: 25–29 and 74: 24–27). Subsequently, they did just that (EA 75: 32–34 and 81: 11–14). As Benz has stressed, when the men of Ammiya followed ʿAbdi-ʾAširte's encouragement to assassinate their ruler, "this decision *did not* involve the Ammiyites replacing their leader with ʿAbdi-Aširta" but rather joining the *habiru* (Benz 2016, 161; emphasis original).[32]

The city of Ammiya has been identified with the modern town of Amioun, about 20 km due south of the Lebanese Tripoli and about 10 km inland (RGTC 12.2, s.v. "Ammiya"; see now Turri 2021). Accordingly, Ammiya was located approximately 300 km to the south of Alalah. Why was this very specific, fairly distant location chosen to serve as the place of Idrimi's arrival after his journey through the desert? On the one hand, it may be because the historical Idrimi did spend time in that city. But, given the literary nature of the text, it seems important to consider also whether having the city of Ammiya serve as a setting for Idrimi's encounter with the displaced citizens of his father's kingdom could be fictive and serve a narrative function. Durand (2011, 104) has suggested that the name of the city actually derives from West Semitic *ʿammu*, "people," and that "il est donc possible qu'Ammiya n'ait été à l'origine qu'une concentration humaine formée par l'établissement de ces réfugiés de tous bords." Alternatively, if we keep in mind one possible date for the Idrimi inscriptions in the late fourteenth century (see §2.1

---

[31] They are from all over, including Emar (l. 4) and Canaan (l. 9). Another individual is identified as a Sutean (DUMU *su-ti*; l. 17).

[32] Still later, it seems that Ammiya once more had a ruler, this time called a king (*šarru*), whom ʿAbdi-ʾAširte's son, Aziru, killed (EA 139: 13–14 and 140: 10–11).

and chapter 6), the Idrimi text could actually have been composed at about the same time as the events described in the letters of Rib-Addi of Byblos, when the men of Ammiya killed their lord and joined the *habiru*. In a text that has, among its various interests, the goal of justifying the once and future incorporation of outsiders into a community, the city could have been seen as an apt location for a gathering of displaced persons; see, variously, §2.7, the commentary to line 86 below, and Lauinger in press.

21. [D]UMU.MEŠ ^{uru}*ha-la-ab*^{ki} DUMU.MEŠ *ma-at mu-ki-iš-he*^{ki}

On Halab, see the commentary to line 3 above. On Mukiš, see §1.1.

22. DUMU.MEŠ *ma-at ni-hi*^{ki} *u*$_{3}$ D[UMU.M]EŠ *ma-at*

The well-preserved DUMU sign at the beginning of line 22 is quite different from the two DUMU signs in line 21, shown in figure A.17 (the second DUMU sign in line 22 is too damaged for comment). Indeed, the variation is so sharp that Dietrich and Loretz (1981, 204) read the sign as HE$_{2}$ and remarked that the form "ist es epigraphisch höchst problematisch. Es weicht nämlich von den sonst üblichen DUMU-Zeichen wesentlich ab und ist am ehesten an die Normalform des HÉ (siehe Zeichenliste) anzuschleifen. Dies erklärt sich aufgrund der Annäherung der Zeichen TUR (DUMU) und HÉ in der mB Schreibweise, in deren Tradition auch sonstige DUMU-Zeichen stehen" (208).

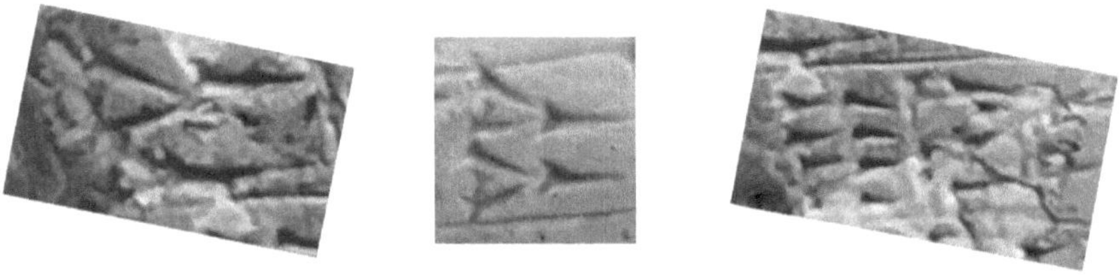

Figure A.17. Attestations of DUMU in lines 21–22.

The toponym Niya is well attested in Late Bronze Age texts, in which it is written, variously, as *ni-e, ni-i, ni*-HI, and *ni-he*$_{2}$. Because it is attested with both the KUR and URU determinatives, it seems to have designated both a city and the surrounding land. The city seems to have been located on the eastern side of the Orontes and just north of Tunip, so in the al-Ghab plain; see Röllig 1998–2001, 313–14.

The second DUMU sign in this line has been restored as [ERIN$_{2}$] or [LU$_{2}$] in previous editions. For instance, Oller (1977a, 30) read [LU$_{2}$].MEŠ with the following epigraphic remarks:

Although one would expect the restoration DUMU.MEŠ *māt Amae* so as to parallel the preceding groups cited, the available space in the copy precludes this choice. The traces of the sign remaining on the statue can be reconciled with both an ERIN$_2$ or a LU$_2$. Even though ERIN$_2$ fits the amount of room better, a LU$_2$ such as those found in lines 5, 75, or 76 cannot be entirely precluded, and I have opted for the latter since it makes a bit better sense in context.

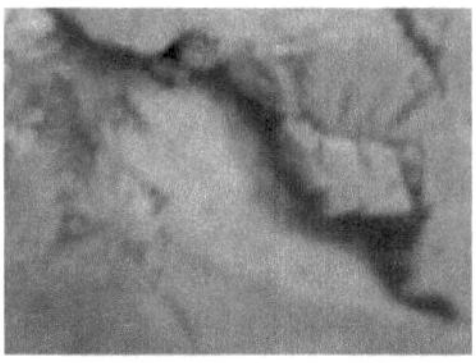

Figure A.18. D[UMU.M]EŠ, line 22.

However, as can be seen in figure A.18, Oller's opinion that there is too little room for a DUMU sign (note his puzzling remark about "available space in the *copy*" [emphasis added]) does not seem warranted. Both the traces and the space could accommodate DUMU, and, since, as Oller noted, this sign is also what context demands, it seems prudent to read the sign as D[UMU].

23. a-ma-e^ki^ aš-bu

This line, which contains only six signs, is one of the shortest in the body inscription in terms of number of signs because it is written at the very bottom of the right arm. There is no horizontal ruling below it.

The toponym "Ama'u" is not as well attested as "Mukiš" and "Niya." Because of this fact and because otherwise Mukiš, Niya, and Nuhašše appear as allies in a coalition of three Syrian kingdoms in *CTH* 46 (see §6.3), Astour (1969, 385) wished to see Ama'u as an alternate designation for Nuhašše. Later, he also suggested identifying it with the toponym 'Ama, which is attested in texts from Ebla (Astour 1988, 141 n. 23). Astour's earlier claim can no longer be maintained because the toponym Ama'u is now attested in a few contexts in texts from Level IV Alalah, which establish that it cannot be the same as Nuhašše (see RGTC 12.2, s.v. "Ama'u"). Rather, the toponym refers to a settlement and its surrounding land that form part of the Level IV kingdom of Alalah-Mukiš. It may also have been the name of one of the kingdom's administrative districts; see von Dassow 2008, 55. However, Astour's later identification of the toponym with Eblaite 'Ama has, to my knowledge, been neither proven nor disproven.

24. i-mu-ru-un-ni-ma

This line, comprising only six signs, is also one of the shortest in the body inscription; it corkscrews over the surface of the statue as it moves from the left side of Idrimi's leg, over the hem of his robe, and finally onto the flat surface of his lap.

The form of *amāru* written as *i-mu-ru-un-ni-ma* has generated substantial discussion in the literature; see Medill 2019, 250, table 3 for a summary of some different interpretations. Medill herself (in personal communication with the author and see her n. 41) parsed the form as *īmur-ūn(a)-ni-ma*, where *-ūna* is the 3mp suffix of the West Semitic imperfective (*yaqtulu*) conjugation, with elision of the final vowel before the 1cs suffix. However, I now take the suffix written as *-unni* as a by-form of *-ūni*, with a long open syllable becoming a short, closed syllable, and interpret it as the alternate form of the 3mp suffix attested in other western hybrid Akkadian corpora; see the commentary to line 26 below (*iphurūnima*). An advantage of this interpretation in the immediate context is that there is no longer a 1cs accusative pronominal suffix on the verb, eliminating otherwise awkward syntax ("They saw me, that I was…").

25. i-nu-ma DUMU *be-li-šu-nu a-na-ku u*₃ *a-na* UGU*-ia*

The use of *inūma* with the meaning "that" is well attested in other western hybrid Akkadian corpora and may represent a calque of West Semitic *k*, which can mean both "when" and "that"; cf. Izreʾel (1991, 1:306), who noted that the attestations "occur in the Amarna letters from Canaan, but also in [peripheral Akkadian] dialects which seem to be outside the area of direct influence by WS dialects, such as Boghazköy."

*26. ip-hu-ru-ni*₇*-ma a-ka-a-na-ka ur-tab-bi-a-ku*

See Medill 2019, 249 for some discussion of previous literature on the verb written as *ip-hu-ru-ni*₇*-ma* and in particular its suffix(es). In line with her interpretation of the verb *i-mu-ru-un-ni-ma*, she understood the suffix to be *-ūna*, the 3mp suffix of the West Semitic imperfective (*yaqtulu*) conjugation, with elision of the final vowel before the 1cs suffix; see the commentary to line 24 above (*īmurunnima*). This interpretation requires understanding the /n/ to be reduplicated (see her normalization *iphurūnnima* on 250).

A different explanation for the verbal morphology that has not, to my knowledge, been put forward may be that *-ūni* is an alternative 3mp suffix attested in other texts written in western hybrid Akkadian. For instance, Huehnergard (2011, 168) observed *-ni(m)* occurring at Ugarit in verb forms in legal texts where it did not "have its normal force." Furthermore, these verbs would "occur frequently in the sg., invariably without the ventive ending," but "have *-ni*(7) the one or two times they are pl." From this distribution, he concluded: "it seems likely, therefore, that the scribes simply considered *-ū* and *-ūni* to be variant markers of plurality." Izreʾel (1991, 1:137–41) had already independently come to the same conclusion regarding the ending *-ni(m)* on verb forms in the earlier subcorpus of letters from Amurru. He noted that this ending "adds no semantic or morphosyntactic denotation" and that, furthermore, "when a pronominal suffix is attached to the verb, the additional syllable *-ni* is omitted," so that "the endings *-ū* and *ūni*" are in "complementary distribution" (137). From these data, he concluded that "the ventive allomorph *-ni(m)* had joined the suffix *-ū* of the 2nd and 3rd person of the plural to form a new plural suffix; that is, *-ūni*" (137; see also Izreʾel 2012, 204 for a summary). Thus the suffix *-ūni* that is found on the verb *iphurūnima* in this line and on other verbs elsewhere in the body inscription can be identified as additional examples of this alternative 3mp suffix found in western hybrid Akkadian texts from Ugarit and Amurru.

Following Dietrich and Loretz (1981, 213), the form *akannaka* is tentatively understood to be the adverb *akanna* + enclitic *-k(a)*, which is attested in Ugaritic as having deictic force.

The verb *urtabbiāku* is an example of a so-called hybrid perfect that is well attested in the Canaano-Akkadian of the Amarna letters sent by Levantine rulers, although it is not one of the relatively restricted set of verbs for which the hybrid perfect is attested in that corpus. For more discussion, see Medill 2019, 247–49; note especially 248 for her objections to Durand's (2011, 138–39) suggestion that *a-ku* is not the 1cs stative suffix but "une forme enclitique de *anâku*" intended to disambiguate verbal forms with regard to person.

27. u_2-ra-ak u_3 a-na li-bi ERIN$_2$.MEŠ ^{lu_2}SA.GAZ

The verb spelled *u_2-ra-*AG has been variously taken as a form of *riāqu*, *wâru*, or *arāku*, and even as a West Semitic loanword.[33] The suggestion to see a form of *arāku*, which is tentatively adopted here, is first found, to my knowledge, in Oppenheim's (1969, 557) translation: "(There I grew up) and stayed for a long time." From this translation, one infers that Oppenheim understood *arāku* to be used in a hendiadys construction with the following stative *ašbāku*; Oller (1977a, 38) subsequently objected that "semantically *arāku* in the D really does not bear the meaning 'to stay for a long time.'" But a similar collocation of *arāku* with *wašābu* is found in a Mari letter, even if the syntax is quite different: *u_4-mi-šu-nu i-na wa-ša-bi-im u_2-ur-ri-ku*, "(Because the sheikhs and Bedouin have not met their brothers who dwell in town for a long time), they have extended their stay" (LAPO 17 488 [no. 733]: 35; see Sasson 2015, 300).

28. a-na MU 7.KAM.MEŠ *aš-ba-ku* MUŠEN.HI.A *u_2-za-ki*

The statement that Idrimi "released" (*zukkû*) birds should mean that he released them in order to observe their flight pattern, as opposed to sacrificing them in order to inspect their carcasses. The opposition is emphasized by the subsequent clause in line 29, which states that Idrimi also inspected (*barû*) the entrails of sacrificial lambs. This practice of ornithomancy is different than the Mesopotamian divinatory practices involving birds, in which either captured birds were sacrificed and their external and internal organs inspected for ominous features, as with sheep and lambs (see Anor and Cohen 2021, discussing previous literature) or the calls of wild birds were interpreted as signs (see Miglio 2022, 176–77, discussing

33 Landsberger *apud* Mazar 1963, 311 n. 3 read *sa-ra-ak* and translated "I was *captain* over the *awêlûtu Hapirû*," noting that "the author thus uses a word borrowed from West Semitic (*śār*) to express the concept of 'captain of a band.'"

previous literature). On the other hand, the practice of observing not just the physical features of birds but also their flight is well attested in texts from Hattuša (see Minunno 2013, 125, citing previous literature).[34] Thus, in lines 28–29, Idrimi states that he took omens according to two different practices.

For some scholars, the juxtaposition has been understood to mean that Idrimi took omens according to both "western" and Mesopotamian traditions; for example, Oppenheim 1969, 557 n. 2.[35] Alternatively, Durand (2011, 108 n. 47) was troubled by the lack of a coordinating conjunction between the two verbs and so rejected the idea that Idrimi took omens via two different techniques at the same time, suggesting instead that for seven years Idrimi relied on ornithomancy as an inexpensive type of divination, and then, in the seventh year, he switched to the more prestigious and expensive practice of divination via extispicy. A third possibility is that the mention of two different divinatory practices was intended to function as a merism for all possible types of divination.

29. SILA$_4$.HI.A *ab-ri-ma u*$_3$ *še-eb-i ša-na-ti* ⸢d⸣[I]M

Most previous scholars have taken *šeb ī* as an ordinal number followed by a singular form of the noun *šattu* ("in the seventh year") instead of what appears to be the plural oblique form. There have been a number of different attempts to resolve the discrepancy between expected singular form and what the text says. For example, Dietrich and Loretz (1981, 214) suggested that the form refers to "eine westsem. Tradition ... in der das wurzelhafte -n- auch im Sg. nicht in Kontaktstellung zur F.-Endung -t- steht."[36] Durand's (2011, 138) translation, "et, lors—

---

[34] Note that birds are well attested in various contexts in texts from both Level VII and Level IV Alalah. For example, a number of Level VII ration lists record disbursements to individuals identified as *usandû*. While this profession is often translated as "bird-catcher, fowler," it is better understood to be a ritual and/or divinatory specialist; see Zeeb 2001, 280–82 and Minunno 2013, 90. Similarly, the Level IV text AIT 355 [44.17] records a disbursement of eight birds and details of their deaths in connection with the king's movements in what is probably a ritual or divinatory context; see Minunno 2013, 90.

[35] Compare George's (2013, 109–10) discussion of late Old Babylonian omen texts from Tigunanum, in which he identified "two different written traditions of divinatory lore. In the majority are the many omen texts whose spelling, language and content speak for their origin in the north and northwest, particularly at Aleppo.... Alongside them are tablets that display the same ductus but whose content, style, vocabulary and spelling show them to be copies of good southern texts." In the discussion, George (2013, 109) noted that "an explicit mark of northern—specifically north Syrian—origin is the rubric on three tablets that attributes the preceding texts to Adad *bēl Halab* "lord of Aleppo" himself"; cf. the text of the body inscription that follows immediately (ll. 29b–30a).

[36] See already Liverani 1967, 51 with n. 5. Martin Worthington (personal communication) has reminded me that a singular form could also be at home in the Hymno-Epic dialect of

les années étant sept—(le dieu de l'Orage s'étant mis de mon côte)" takes the opposite approach, seeing *šebî* as a cardinal number with the plural noun *šanāti*. However, with a cardinal number expression, as opposed to an ordinal number expression, we expect a durative, not a punctual, verb, which is what we have with the verb *ittūru*; see the commentary to line 30 below. I understand *šebî* as a substantivized cardinal and adverbial accusative in construct with the plural *šanāti*; cf. line 45 where a similar expression uses the preposition *ina*.

30. ⌜*a*⌝*-na* SAG.DU*-ia it-tu-ru u*$_3$ *e-te-pu-uš* ^{giš}MA$_2$.⌜HI⌝.A

The final sign of the verb *ittūru* was identified as RU by Smith (1949, 16), and this identification was accepted by all scholars, even though it resulted in a verb form unexpected in the standard Akkadian dialects, until Dietrich and Loretz (1981, 204) identified the sign as UR, which resulted in the expected verb form. However, collation of the inscription suggests that Smith's original identification of the sign as RU is better. As can be seen in figure A.19, the sign in line 30 has two initial *Winkelhaken*, the tails of which cross three vertical wedges, which are positioned above a horizontal wedge. The example of RU in line 99, although much more clearly formed, shows an identical position of the third vertical wedge raised above the previous two. In contrast, the two closest parallels among the attestations of UR are notably different, as can be seen in figure A.20. In particular, while the attestation in line 77 has an initial *Winkelhaken*, there is only one, not two; more importantly, the sign lacks the bottom horizontal wedge. On the other hand, while the attestation of UR in line 98 has the bottom horizontal ruling, it does not have any initial *Winkelhaken*.

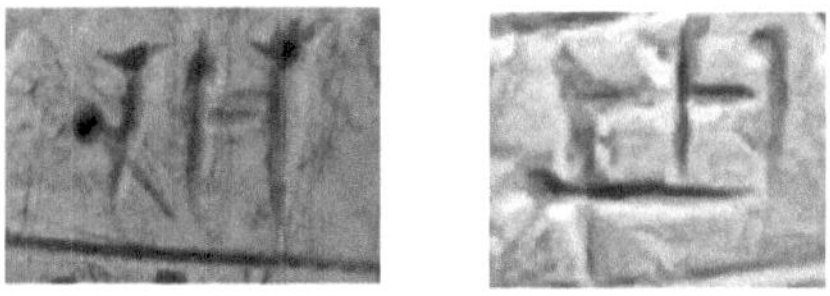

Figure A.19. RU in line 30 (left) juxtaposed with RU in line 99 (right).

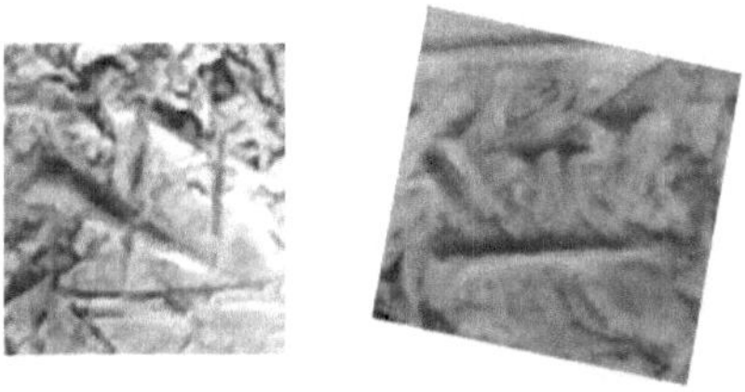

Figure A.20. Two attestations of UR in line 77 (left) and line 98 (right).

Of course, maintaining Smith's original identification of the sign as RU and not UR means that one must grapple with the form of *ittūru*, which is G perfect and marked with an unexpected final /u/. In light of the remark in the commentary to line 29 above that this verb form is durative, discussion must begin with the use of the G perfect tense. It is suggested here that the use of the G perfect tense derives from lexical

Akkadian, where an epenthetic /a/ often appears before the feminine marker /t/; see Hess 2010, 109.

considerations—namely, that certain verbs have the perfect tense as their expected or fixed form of the G stem, similar to how certain verbs seem to have been learned with or without an infixed -t- in the Canaano-Akkadian letters from Amarna (Baranowski 2016, 111–14).

To greatly simplify matters, if the perfect tense is typically used to specify the action of a verb in relation to another verb in the standard Akkadian dialect of the second millennium BCE, in the Idrimi text, certain verbs seem have the perfect tense as their expected or fixed form in the G stem. For instance, all four attestations of *leqû* appear in the G perfect (ll. 14, 64, 74, 77), even though that use of this tense makes little sense from the perspective of standard Akkadian; for example, line 14, where [*el*]*teqešunu*, "[I] took ([m]y [h]orse, my chariot, and my chariot-driver)," is the first verb in a sequence of three, all of which are G perfect. In addition to the four attestations of *leqû*, the verb under discussion in this line, *târu*, is attested four times (ll. 30, 39, 56, 77), and the only attestation that is not G perfect is in the D stem (l. 56). The two attestations of *epēšu* in the G stem are in the perfect tense (ll. 30, 72); the other four are in the Gtn (l. 90 [2×]) or Š stems (ll. 80, 89).

Otherwise, some verbs may appear in the G perfect because they occur in a sequence with another G perfect verb and so are primed to appear in this form. For example, two verbs, *erēbu* and *elû*, are attested in both the G perfect and in other tenses in the G stem; the attestations in the G perfect (*ēterub* in l. 17 and *ēteli* in l. 65) occur in narrative sequences initiated by *leqû*, which, as noted above, is attested only in the G perfect tense. However, because the majority of the verbs attested in the G perfect occur only one time in the inscription, it is difficult to tell whether the use of the G perfect tense relates to verb base, priming, standard Akkadian syntax, or something else.

The /u/ suffix on the verb *ittūru* has been taken as one of the examples of "indicative *u*" or a misapplied subordination marker thought to occur throughout the text. In most instances, the /u/ suffix can be interpreted as either the 3mp suffix or the subordination marker, as discussed where relevant in the commentary; see, already, Medill 2019, 249 n. 41. However, this particular form is one where I believe that the /u/ suffix is, in fact, best interpreted as an instance of "indicative *u*," or, better put, as marking the imperfective (*yaqtulu*) prefix conjugation, as regularly occurs in the Canaano-Akkadian texts from Amarna and Taanach. Medill (2019) has argued that a number of verb forms ending in *-uni* in the body inscription should be interpreted as the imperfective (*yaqtulu*) prefix conjugation 3mp suffix *-ūna* + the 1cs accusative pronominal suffix *-ni* with an elision of the /a/ vowel. While I now consider that these suffixes are better interpreted as examples of *-ūni*, an alternative 3mp marker found in Akkadian cuneiform texts from Amurru and Ugarit (see the commentary to l. 26), understanding *ittūru* as a 3ms imperfective (*yaqtulu*) prefix conjugation has explanatory power. Medill (2019, 249 n. 41) herself raised this possibility before preferring Dietrich and Loretz's identification of the final sign as UR, which, of course, made interpreting the form as the imperfective (*yaqtulu*) prefix conjugation both impossible and unnecessary. However, with Smith's original identification of the final sign as RU supported through collation, the /u/ suffix returns, and the imperfective (*yaqtulu*) prefix conjugation fits the context established by the clause's cardinal number expression very well.

The phrase ^{d}IM *ana qaqqadiya ittūru* literally translates as "the Storm God was turning to my head," and most scholars have understood this expression to mean that the Storm God was favorably inclined to Idrimi. In particular, Greenstein and Marcus (1976, 79) pointed to the parallel expression *ana yâšim ittūrūni* in line 39 as support for both the general meaning of the expression and also for understanding *qaqqadu* as a reflexive pronoun. However, other translations of *târu* are possible. For instance, *CAD* 18, s.v. "târu," 2d translated "Adad returned to me," which, if correct, would carry with it the implication that the Storm God had previously abandoned Idrimi. The verb *târu* also has the meaning "to transform, to change state, to turn into," and one could conceivably argue for a third meaning of the verb, "the Storm God transformed for me" that perhaps signals a change in Idrimi's devotions from Addu of Aleppo (see the commentary to l. 2 above) to Teššub or Baʿlu; note lines 33–34, where Idrimi's first act upon arriving at the shores of Mukiš is to climb to the top of Mount Hazzi (= Mount Ṣapunu), the traditional home of Teššub and Baʿlu (see the commentary to l. 34 below). Note that this last translation and the traditional translation are not mutually exclusive.

31. ERIN$_2$.MEŠ *nu-ul-la a-*⸢*na*⸣ ^{giš}⸢MA$_2$.HI⸣.A *u$_2$-šar-ki-ib-šu-nu*

To my knowledge, the substantive *nullû* is not found in either *AHw* or *CAD* 11.2 but is recognized in the literature as a loanword into Akkadian from Hurrian *nuli*, which designates a type of weapon or soldier (Richter 2012, 281–82). Durand (2003) has argued that *nuli*-soldiers in Hurrian were the equivalent of *rēdû*-solders in Akkadian. The syntactic relationship between ERIN$_2$.MEŠ and *nullâ* is unclear. The normalization *nullâ* provided here is meant to reflect a base *nul(l)i* + *-a* (accusative case marker). The accusative case marker means that the word cannot be in a genitive construction with ERIN$_2$.MEŠ. The two words could be in apposition ("troops, that is, *nullû*-soldier[s]"), or they could be coordinated without an explicit coordinating conjunction ("troops (and) *nullû*-soldier[s]"). In either case, *nullâ* is evidently construed as a collective unless we understand the troops to have been accompanied by a single *nullû*-soldier. Finally, *nullâ* could be an adjective being used attributively instead of a noun. In this case ERIN$_2$.MEŠ would also need to be normalized in the singular and taken as collective, as in line 64. The

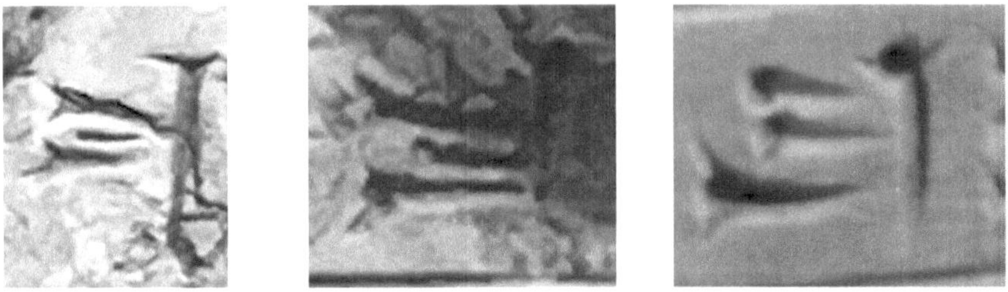

Figure A.21. Juxtaposition of ŠU in line 31(left) with attestations of ŠU in line 34 (center) and line 96 (right).

first two options seem preferable because they allow ERIN$_2$.MEŠ to be normalized in the plural and resumed by the plural pronominal suffix on the verb. However, much about this statement remains opaque, most obviously the significance of the *nullû*-soldiers' presence. Perhaps it is related to the fact that the expedition to Mukiš proceeded via the sea, since no *nullû*-soldiers are mentioned in the context of Idrimi's campaign against Hatti (l. 64), which proceeded over land.

The form of ŠU in the pronominal suffix at the end of the verb *ušarkibšunu* is oddly formed, consisting of only three horizontal wedges, and resembles a cursive MA. However, context requires that it be identified as ŠU, and there are two other occurrences of the sign that are similarly shaped with three horizontal wedges, as shown in figure A.21.

33. eṭ-he$_2$*-e*$^{!?}$*-ku u*$_3$ *pa-*⸢*an*⸣ HUR.SAG *ha-zi*

The identification of the third sign as E$^{!?}$ and the reading of the signs as a single word *eṭ-he*$_2$*-e*$^{!?}$*-ku* was first proposed by Nougayrol (1951, 152), although he took the signs to be a form of *nêʾu*, "to turn back." As is clear from the juxtaposition of this sign with an attestation of E in the following line in figure A.22, the sign is very defective if it was intended to be E. Conceivably, the error might have occurred if the mason omitted the interior horizontal wedges at the beginning of the sign and interpreted the head of the bottom of the two superimposed vertical wedges as a horizontal wedge. If the identification of the sign as a defective E is correct, then *eṭhêku* is easily interpreted as a hybrid perfect from *ṭehû*, which often takes its object with *ana*; see, for example, *ṣa-bu-um a-na ṣu*$_2$*-up-ri-im*^{ki} *i-ṭe*$_4$*-eh-he-em*, "the troops will approach Ṣuprum" (ARM 2 44: 20).

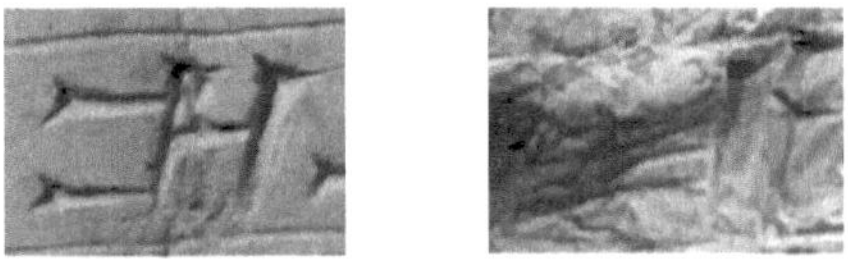

Figure A.22. Juxtaposition of E$^{!?}$ in line 33 (left) with E in line 34 (right).

Mount Hazzi, known in the modern day as "Bald Mountain" (Jebel Aqra in Arabic and Kel Dağı in Turkish), is located on the Mediterranean near where the north-flowing Orontes empties into the Mediterranean Sea having turned southward after its great bend. The mountain was famous in antiquity as the home of various Storm Gods because of the impressive thunderstorms that routinely gather around its summit. In Hurrian and Hittite texts, it was the home of Teššub; at Ugarit, where the mountain was known as *Ṣapunu*, it was the home of Baʿal Zaphon. This latter identification persisted into the first millennium (e.g., Esarhaddon's treaty with Baal of Tyre, SAA 2 5) and is reflected in the Hebrew Bible. In Greek sources, the mountain was known as *Kasios* (Greek) or *Casius* (Latin) and was the home of Zeus Kasios and Jupiter Casius, respectively (Healey 2007).

34. ⸢*a*⸣*-na ta*$_2$*-ba*$_2$*-li*$_3$ *ak-šu-ud e-li-ia-ku*

On the form of ŠU, see the commentary to line 31 above.

Because the context requires that the action is fientive, the verb written as *e-li-ia-ku* should be interpreted as either a "hybrid perfect" (i.e., *ēliyāku*) or as a stative functioning as a West Semitic perfective conjugation (i.e., *eliyāku*). Coming directly after a description of Idrimi reaching dry ground in front of a mountain, the verb must refer to going up that mountain. However, only Smith (1949, 98) and Dietrich and Loretz (1981, 205) have translated the verb with this meaning, while other scholars understand it to refer either to going ashore or to moving inland (see, esp., Durand 2011, 139 with n. 138). The verb should signify that Idrimi ascended the home of Teššub and Baʿal to perform a sacrifice or other ritual. Possibly the oxen and sheep brought to Idrimi in lines 35–36 represent offerings in this regard as well.

35. u$_3$ *ma-ti-ia iš-mu-un-ni-ma* GU$_4$.HI.A *u*$_3$ UDU.HI.A

As the subject of *išmûnnima* (l. 35) and *ublūni* (l. 36), the noun *mātiya* seems to be construed as plural, as are other attestations of this noun or toponyms in the body inscription; see, for example, *Ammiya ašbū* (l. 20) and *māt Hatte … ul illikū* (ll. 70–71), and the commentary to line 20.

For *-unni* on the verb *išmûnnima* as an allomorph of the 3mp suffix, see the commentary to line 24 (*īmurunnima*) and line 26 (*iphurūnima*).

36. a-na pa-ni-ia ub-lu-u$_2$*-ni*$_7$ ⸢*u*$_3$⸣ *i-na* UD 1.KAM

For *-ūni* on the verb *ublūni* as an allomorph of the 3mp suffix, see the commentary to line 26 (*iphurūnima*). As mentioned in the comment to *išmûnnima* in line 35, the subject of *ublūni* is understood to be *mātiya*, construed as plural in number. It is also possible that it is an impersonal use of the 3mp verb ("oxen and sheep were brought").

37. ki-ma 1^{en} LU$_2$ *ma-at ni-he*^{ki} *ma-at a-ma-e*^{ki}

There are three attestations of KI in the line, and all three are strikingly different in form, as shown in figure A.23; cf. the forms of KI in line 38 as well as the discussion in §4.1.

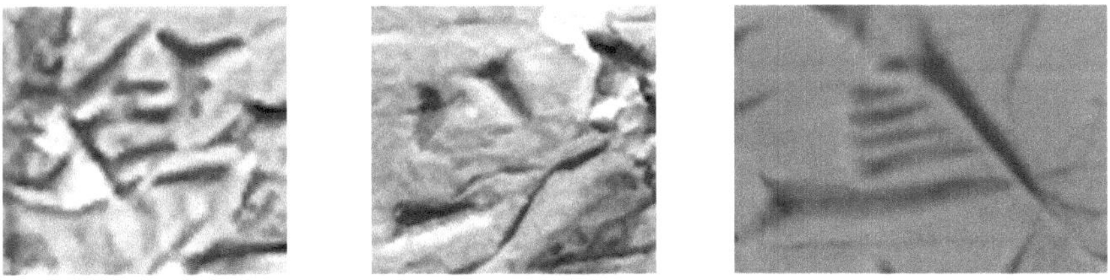

Figure A.23. The first, second, and third attestations of KI in line 37.

Greenstein and Marcus (1976, 80–81) claimed that "to [their] knowledge there is no parallel in Akkadian" to the phrase *kīma ištēn amīli*, because "to express 'in unison,'" Akkadian texts employ *ištēniš* (from OAkk on)," citing the article in *CAD* 7. On the other hand, they considered the phrase to have "an exact equivalent in Hebrew" (citing several examples) and "are therefore compelled to regard Idrimi's expression as a calque from West Semitic." The phrase is well attested in texts from Mari, where, of course, it could still reflect West Semitic influence; see, for example, *ma-a-tum ši-i [k]a-lu-ša ki-ma* 1 LU$_2$ *a-na ṣe-ri-ia ib-ba-la-ka-[a]t*, "That entire land defected to me in unison (lit. like one man)" (ARM 1 29: 21–24). For the possible attestation of the phrase in a fragmentary context in a letter from Tell Leilan, see PIHANS 117 92: 19.

On the toponyms Niya and Ama'u, see the commentary to lines 22 and 23, respectively.

38. [m]a-at mu-ki-iš-he$_2$^{ki} *u*$_3$ ^{uru}*a-la-la-ah*^{ki} URU.KI-*ia*

There are four attestations of KI in this line, and all four are strikingly different in form; see §4.1 with figure 4.3 for discussion, and cf. the commentary to line 37.

On the toponym Mukiš, see §1.1.

39. ⸢*a*⸣*-na ia-ši*$_2$*-im it-tu-ru-ni*$_7$ ⸢ŠEŠ.MEŠ⸣*-ia*

The suffix *-ūni* on the verb *ittūrūni* may be interpreted as the 3mp marker + 1cs dative pronominal suffix, resuming the prepositional phrase *ana yâšim*, or as the alternative form of the 3mp marker found elsewhere in the body inscription; see the commentary to line 26 (*iphurūnima*).

For *târu* with the meaning "to turn (favorably)," see the commentary to line 30 (*ittūru*), but cf. the translation in *CAD* 18, s.v. "târu," 2b ("returned to me"), which implies that Idrimi formerly controlled the lands. Conversely, Durand

(2011, 97 n. 7) has argued that the phrase does not mean that Idrimi controlled the lands, only that they are not hostile to him. Elsewhere, he stated that these lines describe

> les lieux d'où converge vers lui une population qui va devenir celle de la ville refondée. Il faut comprendre que la nouvelle Alalah a eu comme population tous ces gens que l'on doit considérer comme autant de 'paysans-colon'. Les autres régions continuent à exister car ce sont leurs rois qui vont, par la suite, reconnaître la nouvelle fondation et dont Idrimi se prétendra l'égal (ll. 59–60). (Durand 2011, 118)

The reference to Idrimi's "brothers" (*ahhēya*) has been taken to refer either to his biological brothers, who are mentioned in line 7, or to his peer rulers in the area. I understand the former sense because of the narrative function of lines 39–42. These lines conclude the narrative of Idrimi's wandering; his brothers act as a frame to this narrative, which opens with his departure from them at Emar and closes with his settling in Alalah. His brothers' acknowledgment of his hegemony marks his changed status;[37] see the commentary to line 8.

40. [i]š-mu-u$_2$*-ma u*$_3$ *a-na mah-ri-ia il-li-ku-u*$_2$

Is the compound prepositional phrase *ana mahriya* meant to convey a different nuance than the compound prepositional phrase *ana pāniya* in line 36?

*41. [a]h-he.*HI.A*-ia it-ti-ia-ma in-na-hu-u*$_2$

See §4.1 with figure 4.2 on the orthography of *ahhēya* in this line and line 42.

The verb written as *in-na-hu-u*$_2$ has been variously understood to be a form of *ahû* II, "to fraternize"; *anāhu*, "to toil"; *nâhu*, "to be at rest" (with extended meanings "to be reconciled, to be in friendly alliance"); and *nêʾu*, "to turn back." The verb *anāhu*, "to toil" is probably what is intended, because this verb is used in royal grants and decrees from Ugarit to indicate that an individual has performed service to his or her lord faithfully; see the discussion in §4.3, citing attestations. As discussed there, the verb is used in the same sense in the famous treaty between

---

37 On the narrative function of these lines, see already Liverani 1970, 863 ("Da questa differenza di atteggiamento tra Idrimi che decide di partire alla riconquista del regno paterno perduto, e i suoi fratelli che non osano e si accontentano del misero stato di esuli, deriva la fortuna di Idrimi; e quando questa si è realizzata e l'eroe è diventato re, ecco ricomparire i fratelli") and Dietrich and Loretz 1981, 252 ("Aus dem in Z. 39–42a vorliegenden Topos, daß der jüngere Bruder die Führung und den Schutz der älteren übernimmt, dürfte nur schwer zu entnehmen sein, welche Vorgänge sich tatsächliche abgespielt haben. Konnte sich Idrimi nur einen Teil des väterlichen Erbes sichern und sich nicht gegen seine Brüder durchsetzen? War er gezwungen, sich am Rande des Herrschaftsgebietes von Halab anzusiedeln?").

Šuppiluliuma I and Niqmaddu II of Ugarit. See also the discussion in §4.2 and §4.3 of the derived noun *mānahtu*, which also occurs four times in total in the cheek and body inscriptions.

However, if the form in which the verb appears is not problematic, the preposition complement *itti* is. In the attestations of the verb used in this sense from Ugarit, it appears with either the preposition *ana* or the compound prepositional phrase *ana muhhi* to indicate that someone labored "for" someone else. The other attestation of this verb in line 48 of the body inscription similarly uses the compound prepositional phrase *ana muhhi*. On the face of it, then, the preposition *itti* should indicate that Idrimi's brothers joined him in acknowledging the hegemony of some unnamed third party. However, it seems difficult to believe that the text would leave the third party unnamed, especially when Idrimi's acknowledgment of the hegemony of Parattarna I comprises a lengthy and central episode in the narrative. Furthermore, as discussed in the commentary to line 8 above, lines 39–42 constitute the concluding half of a frame to Idrimi's wandering, and, according to the frame's narrative logic, the brothers should be subordinate members of Idrimi's household, not the household of someone else. So much is implied by the emphatic *-ma* on the preposition + 1cs suffix *ittiya*, which is identical to the identical preposition *ittiyama* in line 8. It is also implied by Idrimi's claim in the following line that he protected his brothers. At the risk of tautology, it is possible that *itti* is used in this line precisely because this preposition is the one that is used in the pejorative description of the brothers in line 8; see the commentary to line 53 for discussion of the use of *itti* as an unexpected complement to *palāhu*.

42. [a]h-he$_2$.HI.A-*ia aṣ-ṣur-šu-nu ap-pu-na*

Collation supports Dietrich and Loretz's (1981, 205) identification of the first sign of the verb as AZ. A key point of their identification of the sign was their recognition that all five of the AZ signs in the body inscription have the ZA component of the sign placed at the very beginning of the sign form, as shown in figure A.24. Once this characteristic of AZ signs is understood, the ZA component of the sign in line 42 can be recognized, damaged and faint, but visible immediately after the preceding *-ia*. While the remainder of the sign in line 42 is more complicated than some other attestations of AZ, such as the example in line 58, it is similar in form to the attestation in line 69.

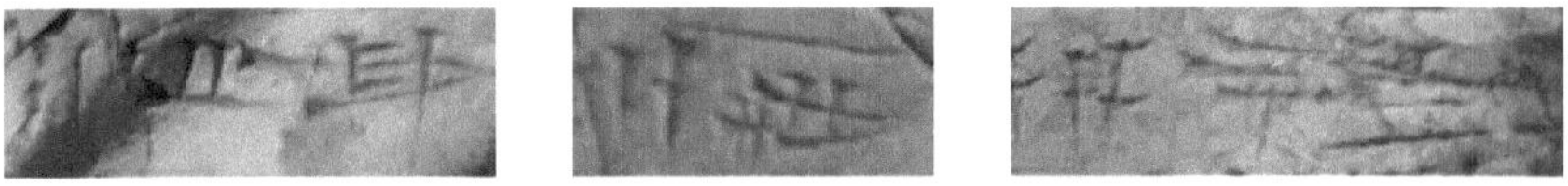

Figure A.24. Juxtaposition of AZ in line 42 (left) with attestations of AZ in line 58 (center) and 69 (right).

43. [M]U 7.KAM.HI.A ^{m}*pa*$_{2}$*-ra-at-tar-na* LUGAL *dan-nu*

For this line (which technically begins with *appūna* at the end of the previous line) as introducing the so-called Parattarna episode, the second pivotal episode of the narrative, see §2.8; for line 43 as the first line of a quatrain, see §2.9.

Parattarna I, the first historically attested king of Mittani, ruled in the middle of the fifteenth century (Wilhelm 1993–1997, 293; von Dassow 2022, 474); the name is also attested in line 45 in an alternate spelling. Outside of the Idrimi inscription, Parattarna I is attested only at Level IV Alalah and Terqa (see Rouault 1992, 254; the Parattarna whose death is mentioned in an administrative list at Nuzi is likely to be distinguished as Parattarna II, for which see von Dassow 2022, 473). At Alalah, Parattarna I is known from AlT 3 [1.2], the treaty between the historical king Idrimi of Alalah and Pilliya of Kizzuwatna, Alalah's neighbor to the north, where the treaty's concluding stipulation implies Parattarna's I hegemony over Idrimi. None of the attestations of Parattarna I explicitly qualify him as "king of Mittani," and he is qualified only as "king of the Hurrian people" in the following line of the body inscription. Nonetheless, as Wilhelm (2003–2005, 339) observed, it seems likely the polity ruled by Parattarna I was already known as the kingdom of Mittani, since the earliest attestation of "Mittani" seems to predate him by a short time; see also von Dassow 2022, 475.

Parattarna I is qualified as *šarru dannu*, "mighty king," and Bunnens (1973) has suggested that this qualification was not simply a descriptive epithet (e.g., *CAD* 3, s.v. "dannu," 4a, "a ferocious king") but also had a political valence. He considered the reference to a plurality of kings in line 49 (LUGAL.HI.A *ša* ⌜ERIN$_{2}$⌝.MEŠ *hur-*⌜*ri*⌝^{ki}) to indicate that "les Hurrites sont gouvernés par une série de roitelets…, qui discutent entre eux des affaires qui concernent leur communauté"; a king in this group who held command or influence over his peers, then, bore the title *šarru dannu*, "mighty king." While Bunnens's claim seems to have been accepted by some scholars,[38] Oller (1977a, 54–59) raised a number of objections, including that the meaning and significance of the title *šarru dannu*, as Bunnens interpreted it, derived from his understanding of Hurrian political organization as a sort of federation of "kinglets," but this interpretation derived from Bunnens's own misunderstanding of line 49, which refers to a plurality of single kings over time, not a multiplicity of kinglets at one time.[39]

---

[38] See, e.g., Klengel 1978, 92 n. 9 and Klengel 1981, 276 with n. 49; cf. Astour 1978, 9 n. 81 (*šarru dannu* as the equivalent of *šarru rabû*); Freu 2003, 31 ("le titre significatif," without specifying what it signified); and Durand 2011, 140 ("un roi de premier rang," without further discussion).

[39] Subsequently, the possible significance of the phrase was considered by Guichard (2003, 205). On the basis of his reading of the "royal letters" found at Mari (ARM 28), he considered whether *šarru dannu* might have been reserved as a title only for kings with subordinate kings in the Middle Bronze Age. Ultimately, however, he rejected the idea that the phrase had some deeper "distinction de entre les deux catégories de rois."

44. LUGAL ERIN$_2$.⸢MEŠ⸣ *hur-ri*^{ki} *u*$_2$*-na-kir-an-ni*

With one exception, previous scholars have unanimously normalized ERIN$_2$.MEŠ in the phrase LUGAL ERIN$_2$.⸢MEŠ⸣ *hur-ri*^{ki} as a form of *ṣābu* without comment. The same scholars are fairly evenly divided in translating *ṣābī Hurri* as "Hurrian people, Hurrians" or as "Hurrian warriors, troops," although, again, without any comment as to why they think the phrase should signify either the general population or soldiers specifically. The one exception is Durand (2011, 140), who translated ERIN$_2$.MEŠ *Hurri* as "des bandes hourrites," remarking in a note (n. 144): "Lire sans doute *ummân Hurri*. C'est de la même façon que sont désignés les Hourrites dans les textes d'Emar. Ces derniers datent cependant apparemment de la fin de la puissance hourrite au Proche-Orient; il est intéressant de voir qu'ils retrouvent alors ce qui était vérité avant la création du Mittani." Durand's suggestion seems correct. Besides the parallels from Emar (on which texts, see Vita 2002, 116–21, citing previous literature), lines 43–46 are marked by a high degree of parallelism, as discussed in §2.9; reading *ummānāt Hurri* in line 44 and *ummānwanda* in line 46 heightens this parallelism. And, of course, if the reading of ERIN$_2$ in line 44 is established to be *ummānu* and not *ṣābu*, one does not need to debate whether a translation "people" or "troops" is preferable, since *ummānu* has only the latter meaning.

The verb *unakkiranni* is written in a rare morphographemic spelling (*u*$_2$*-na-kir-an-ni*). Beginning with Smith's (1949, 17) edition, scholarship has been unanimous in translating the verb as some variation of "(Parattarna) became hostile to me," without comment. But the morphosyntax and semantics of this form are not so straightforward. The sense "to be(come) hostile" is much better attested in the G stem of this verb. While the dictionaries do attest to a few uses of *nukkuru* with this sense,[40] the verb is generally used in this stem in the sense "to move something

[40] In addition to the attestation in the Idrimi text, *CAD* 11.1, s.v. "nakāru," 7a ("*nukkuru* turn hostile") lists one attestation from a Hittite treaty (*CTH* 41.I), a Neo-Assyrian treaty (SAA 2 6), and a royal inscription of Darius I. The attestation in *CTH* 41.I should be deleted. The verbal prefix is not preserved, and restoring a D-stem form results in a preterite tense verb ([*u*]*nakkir*) where one expects the present tense. On the other hand, restoring a G-stem form [*i*]*nakkir* results in the expected present tense, not to mention the more common G-stem form; see, e.g., Kitchen and Lawrence 2012, 326. *AHw* 720a, 11 ("verfeinden") lists only the Neo-Assyrian attestation for *nukkuru* with this sense. To my knowledge, the attestation of *nukkuru* in the Idrimi text is not cited in *AHw*. Note also two attestations of *nukkuru* with the factitive meaning "to make enemies, incite others to enmity" in the Amarna letters, both of which seem to need to be understood as suffix conjugation forms: EA 132: 41 (*a-bu-šu nu-ki-ir* URU.⸢MEŠ⸣, "His father made the cities hostile" [Byblos]), cited by *AHw* 720a, 12 as "kan. Pf. Pass." and by *CAD* 11.1, s.v. "nakāru," 12 in its own meaning; and EA 179: 19′ ([*nu*]*-kur*$_3$ KUR.MEŠ ⸢*a*⸣*-mu-ri*, "[*He made*] the lands of Amurru *hostile*" [possibly Ṭubihu], not cited by the dictionaries). For EA 335: 10, the other attestation cited under *CAD* 11.1 s.v. "nakāru," 12, correct the line number to 11 and read

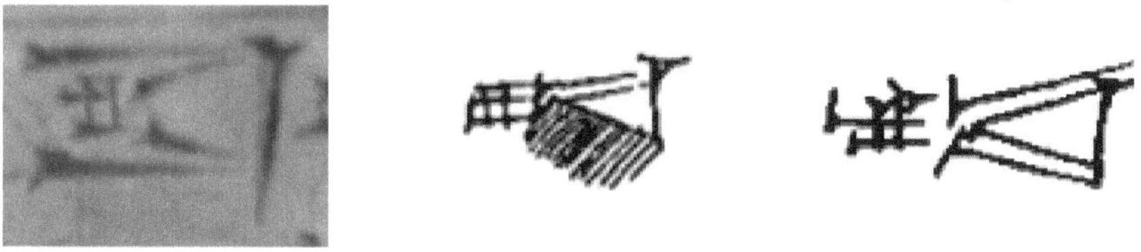

Figure A.25. Juxtaposition of AD in line 45 (left) with attestations of AD in RS 20.121 line 153 (center) and line 168 (right).

away, to change something," while the sense "to make enemies, incite others to enmity" uses the Š stem in the standard Akkadian dialects. We can also ask why the verb takes a direct object. In the second millennium, the G-stem attestations with the meaning "to be(come) hostile" cited by *CAD* 11.1, s.v. "nakāru," 1 take the object with a preposition, usually *itti*. On the other hand, the use of *nukkuru* in the D stem with the standard sense "to move something away, to change something" does take its object in the accusative case. If the scholarship is correct in understanding *unakkiranni* to mean something like "he turned hostile toward me," as is tentatively followed here, we should note a disconnect between the morphosyntax and the semantics of the verb relative to the verb's use in the standard dialects of Akkadian.

45. ⸢i⸣-na š[e]-eb-⸢i⸣ ša-na-ti a-na ^{m}pa$_2$-ra-at-ar-na LUGAL^{ri}

This line extends from the second division of text on the left half of Idrimi's legs into the third division of text on the right
half of his legs; see §2.8 and §2.9 for discussion.

One interesting epigraphic feature of these lines is the AD sign used to spell Parattarna I's name. It is written with an initial interior component that does not occur elsewhere in the inscription. Accordingly, Oller (1977a, 53–54) understood it to be defective and emended to *-at*$^{!}$-. However, near parallels for the form can be found in a manuscript of the god list An from Ugarit, *Ugaritica* 5 220 [RS 20.121]: 153 and 168, as shown in figure A.25. Furthermore, there is an AD sign almost directly below this one that lacks the initial interior component, as shown in figure A.26. Therefore, the otherwise unattested form of AD in line 45 may be better understood as an example of paleographic variation on a vertical dimension that is discussed in §4.1.

Figure A.26. The signs *-ra-at-*, line 45 above *ad-bu-*, line 46.

The desire for variation, which is a hallmark of lines 43–46 in particular, may also explain the different

NU.⸢KUR$_2$⸣ for the noun *nukurtu*, "hostility." (This reading does not fit the context of EA 179: 19′, which is why the signs there are read syllabically.)

writing of the name Parattarna, which, in contrast with line 43, omits the *-ta-* sign. Accordingly, there does not seem to be a need to emend the text to ^{m}*pa*$_{2}$*-ra-at-*<*ta*>*-ar-na*, as does Oller (1977a, 50).

46. LUGAL ⌜ERIN$_{2}$⌝.MEŠ^{an}*-wa-an-da aš-ta*$_{2}$*-par*$_{2}$ *u*$_{3}$ *ad-bu-ub*$^{!}$(TE)

The central crux of these lines is what to do with the epithet of Parattarna I that opens line 46, specifically the sign string AN-WA-AN-DA that follows LUGAL ERIN$_{2}$.MEŠ. The two basic options were laid out already by Smith (1949, 18) in the original edition: either to read the signs together as a form of *Umman-manda*, the "enemy horde" of Mesopotamian literature and scholarship, or to understand a textual error, emending the text so that ERIN$_{2}$.MEŠ <*hur-ri*^{ki}> in this line is parallel to ERIN$_{2}$.MEŠ *hur-ri*^{ki} in line 44 and then taking the signs AN-WA-AN-DA as a personal name. Smith preferred the latter option, stating that "the decisive argument against [the former] is grammatical. The copula before *atbute* demands an object for *ašdapar* immediately before the verb." He also saw a possible DIŠ between ERIN$_{2}$.MEŠ and AN ("only a scratched line is clearly visible"), which he interpreted as the *Personenkeil*.

Both of these objections can be laid to rest. The putative DIŠ has been the object of repeated collation (Gadd *apud* Cornelius 1963, 168; Oller 1977a, 60; Adalı 2011, 9), and my own collation of the inscription agrees with all of them that there is not a vertical wedge between ERIN$_{2}$.MEŠ and AN (contra, e.g., Klengel 1981, 276, who states that "der Personenkeil weist jedoch auf einen Personennamen"), as can be seen in figure A.27. Furthermore, the verb *šapāru* is amply attested without an explicit direct object. In this use, the verb has the meaning "to send a message," which fits the context of line 46 very well (so already Oller 1977a, 62). The question was discussed in a detailed manner by Oller (1977a, 59–67), who concluded, "I have opted for the reading Ummān-wanda on the basis of my collation (no DIŠ sign), the extremely tenuous nature of the hypothetical An-wanda, and the possibilities for a link between the Hurrians and Ummān-manda" (67). Nonetheless, scholarship on the line has continued to be more or less evenly split between reading ERIN$_{2}$.MEŠ^{an}*-wa-an-da* and emending

Figure A.27. The beginning of line 46.

the text to ERIN$_2$.MEŠ <*hur-ri*^{ki}> ^{m}*an-wa-an-da*, with the emended reading found as recently as Durand 2011, 140 and Bonechi 2019, 80.

In my opinion, Oller's reasons for preferring not to emend the text and to read ERIN$_2$.MEŠ^{an}-*wa-an-da* are as valid now as they were then, and they can be further supported by the close link between the narrative and *narû* literature, as argued in §4.2. In particular, the Umman-manda are explicitly named in the Hittite version of the Cuthean Legend of Naram-Sin as the enemy horde that devastates the king of Agade (*CTH* 311.2.A; see Otten and Rüster 1973, 86).[41] Since *narû* literature is of great importance to the Idrimi text's primary argument, and the Parattarna episode itself is central to that argument, it is actually not too surprising to meet an allusion to a prime example of *narû* literature in the episode's opening lines. Indeed, other allusions to the same text may occur in the Sun God's epithet as "lord of the Upper World and the Lower World, lord of ghosts" in line 100, the body inscription's final line, which is, of course, another emphatic moment in the text (see the commentary to l. 100 and §3.2) as well as the nominal predicate *šarrāku* that is attested in the cheek inscription and the Parattarna episode (see the commentary to l. 58 and §4.2).

In considering that the string ERIN$_2$.MEŠ AN WA AN DA could be an allusion to the Umman-manda, two questions naturally arise. First, why should the ethnonym be written with /w/ insteand of /m/? And, second, why call Parattarna I "the king of Umman-manda," at all? Adalı (2011, 10) has reviewed some attempts in the literature to answer the first question. For instance, Nougayrol (1951, 152 n. 8) cited his earlier study of omen texts (Nougayrol 1950, 20) in which the Umman-manda appear in apodoses written with /b/ in place of /m/, while Cornelius considered a change of /m/ > /w/ to be a characteristic of Hittite toponyms,[42] although it is unclear how this change, if accurately identified, is relevant. Adalı (2011, 11–12) himself raised the possibility of Hurrian influence, where the initial consonant of *manda* was understood to be a Hurrian labial fricative /f/, which is occasionally represented with either m-series signs or WA; the main point of Adalı's suggestion that should be emphasized is that *Ummān-wanda* would not be "the original form of writing the term" but "a local Alalah form" (12). In keeping with the line of Adalı's thinking, we might also consider the change of /m/ > /w/ to be a hypercorrection on the author's part, an attempt to archaize the ethnonym that is in line with the paleographic and orthographic displays of erudition found throughout the inscriptions (see already Oller 1977a, 62 on the possibility of "the reverse, a m > w interchange," although without suggesting a reason).

---

[41] Glassner (2024) now suggests that a very fragmentary attestation of the Umman-manda appear in one of the Akkadian language manuscripts of the Cuthean Legend from Hattuša.

[42] "Der Lautwandel von m zu w, der für das erste Jahrtausend ja allbekannt ist, ist in Nordsyrien an hethitischen Ortsnamen schon für das 2. Jahrtausend zu belegen" (Cornelius 1963, 168 n. 7, citing "Am deutlichsten ist Ijaruwata für Jarimuta").

As for why Parattarna I might be referred to as a king of the Umman-manda, after reviewing various attestations of the ethnonym in second millennium contexts, Oller (1977a, 65–66) highlighted one in particular, a passage in the res gestae of Hattušili I, which is already famous in Alalahian studies for mentioning a certain Zukraši of Halab who may provide a synchronism with the Level VII texts; see Lauinger 2015, 205–6. The same passage, KBo 7 14: 14, also mentions a certain Zaludi with the title GAL ERIN$_2$.MEŠ *Manda*. As Oller (1977a, 67) discusses, the context of the passage "suggests a confrontation between the Hittites on the one hand and the ruler of Halab and his Hurrian allies on the other." Since Zukraši is a Halabean general, Zaludi *rab ummān manda* could well be his Hurrian ally, "thus providing a link between the term Umman-manda and Hurri" (Oller 1977a, 67; see also Adalı 2011, 4). In this regard, it is worth noting references to *mandu* soldiers in a text from Chogha Gaveneh in western Iran (Abdi and Beckman 2007, 54 no. 18; see Adalı 2011, 3–4 and de Boer 2014, 167, 187). In referring to Parattarna I as "the king of Umman-wanda," we may have a complicated situation where the text is taking a traditional term for a Hurrian military leader, "chief of the *mandu* troops," which it is then identifying with the Umman-manda of the Cuthean Legend for programmatic reasons and, further, archaizing by writing /m/ and /w/ for literary effect.

The reading of the final sign in line 46 as UB was first proposed by Albright (1950, 18 n. 29) "instead of the enigmatic *at-bu-te* of the *editio princeps*." Contextually, this reading seems correct, but the sign in question does seem to be TE, which would then need to be understood as written in error. For instance, compare the sign in question with an attestation of UB, on the left, and TE, on the right in figure A.28.

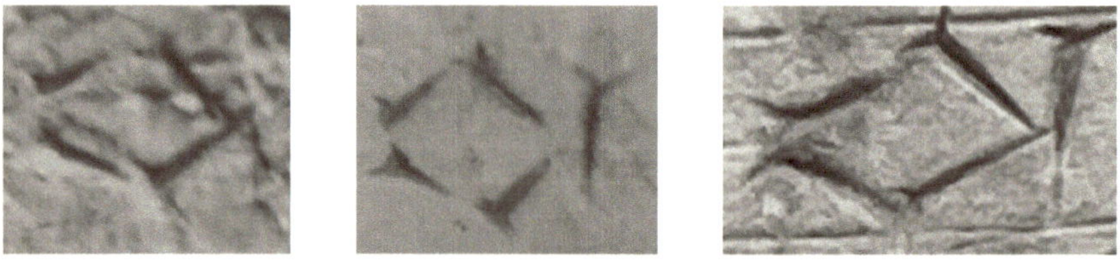

Figure A.28. Juxtaposition of *ub*!(TE) in line 46 (center) with attestations of UB in line 16 (left) and TE in line 47 (right).

47. ma-⌜na-ha⌝-[te].HE$_2$ *ša a-bu-te*.HI.A-*⌜ia i⌝-nu-ma*

The first word of the line, *mānahā[te]*, also provides us with the first attestation in the body inscription of a word that is central to the Idrimi text's argument to its ancient contemporaries, as discussed in chapter 4. Given the importance of *mānahtu* to this argument, the use of the sign HE$_2$ in what seems to be a variant of the plural determinative HI.A in this first attestation of the word in the body inscription is noteworthy. Oller (1977a, 68) objected to the interpretation, remarking, "since HI.A is used in the very next word in line 47…, it seems difficult to assume the use of HÉ as a plural indicator here and never again in the entire text. However, I am at a loss to explain its presence." But in a text that has variation as a hallmark, Oller's objection does not carry as much weight as it might with other texts. Indeed, variation is often used for emphasis in the Idrimi text, and it is precisely in this context that we might expect to find some form of variation intended to communicate the scribe's erudition given the importance of this particular word to the text; see, already, Márquez Rowe 1997, 201 n. 22 ("This unique writing may also be understood within the framework of Šarruwa's scribal skill"). In this regard, one might speculate that the HE$_2$ is an artificial variant of HI.A in which the /i/ and /a/ are contracted to /e/, as in Mari Akkadian, despite, of course, the plural determinative not being Akkadian.

48. ⸢a-bu⸣-te.⸢HI⸣.A-*ia a-na* UGU-*šu-nu in-na-hu-u*$_2$

On the interpretation of the verb *in-na-hu-u*$_2$ as a form of *anāhu*, "to be(come) tired," see the commentary to line 41 (*innahū*).

49. ⸢u$_3$ *pa-nu-ti⸣-ni a-na* LUGAL.HI.A *ša* ⸢ERIN$_2$⸣.MEŠ *hur-⸢ri⸣*^{ki} *da-mi-iq*

The reading of the first noun in line 49 as *⸢pa-nu⸣-ti-ni* goes back to Dietrich and Loretz (1981, 205)—note that they do not indicate any damage to the surface!—and is tentatively confirmed by collation. In particular, the first sign of the word seems to be comprised of a vertical wedge crossed by horizontal wedges, as shown in figure A.29. This form seems decisive for a reading of the sign as PA over WA.

The reference to a plurality of Hurrian kings is almost uniformly understood in the literature to refer to multiple kings over a period of time, only one of whom was ruling at any given moment. The exception to this understanding is found in Bunnens (1973, 149), where, in the course of his arguments about the royal epithet *šarru dannu*, this line is cited as evidence that "les Hourrites sont gouvernés par une série de roitelets"; again, see the commentary to line 43. Note the periphrastic genitive construction with determinative *ša* in this line (LUGAL.HI.A *ša* ERIN$_2$.MEŠ), whereas in the close parallel in line 44 that has the word "king" in the singular, the *ša* is omitted, and the genitive construction uses the construct state (LUGAL ERIN$_2$.MEŠ). For the normalization of ERIN$_2$.MEŠ as *ummānu* and not *ṣābu*, see the commentary to line 44.

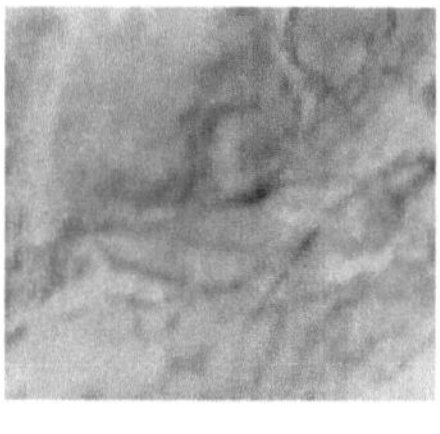

Figure A.29. The sign *⸢pa⸣*, line 49.

The interpretation of *⸢u*$_3$ *pa-nu⸣-ti-ni a-na* LUGAL.HI.A *ša* ⸢ERIN$_2$⸣.MEŠ *hur-⸢ri⸣*^{ki} as a nominal clause that stands apart from *damiq* was first proposed by Durand (2011, 141). This interpretation resolves the perceived lack of agreement in number without needing to posit a "Kollektivkonstruktion" (Dietrich and Loretz

1981, 218). It also has another advantage that Durand did not remark upon. If *damiq* belongs with the clause in line 49 that is coordinated with the clause in line 48 by the conjunction *u* at the beginning of line 49, then this second clause would be dependent on the subordinating conjunction *inūma* at the end of line 47, and we would expect it to be marked with the subordinate marker. In contrast to other corpora of western hybrid Akkadian, where the subordination marker is not typically employed,[43] the morphology of the verb following the relative *ša* or a subordinating conjunction in the narrative portion of the body inscription meets the expectations of the standard Babylonian dialects exactly. Therefore, not only does Durand's interpretation resolve any difficulties with number and gender agreement, it also removes what would otherwise be an anomalous instance of a verbal predicate in a subordinate clause which lacks the subordination marker.

However, Durand's understanding of the sense of *damiq* requires some nuance, in my opinion. According to him:

> *Damâqum* ne signifie pas 'être bon,' ce qui est le propre de *ṭiâbum*, mais 'prouver sa qualité intrinsèque'; la racine est ainsi utilisée pour toutes manifestations d'amitié ou de services rendus. Dans les textes de Mari le *mudammiqum* est, de la sorte, 'celui qui rend un service,' voire le héros militaire, tout particulièrement 'l'ancien combattant.' *Damiq* indique ici l'amitié qui existait entre les deux groupes humains." (Durand 2011, 151)

While he is undoubtedly correct that the word has a political valence here, we should not assume that valence to be the same as it is centuries earlier at Mari. Indeed, if it were, we might expect to find it in the plural here; for example, "They (the forefathers) were allies," or similar.

A different social-political valence of *damqu* may be found in a text from Level IV Alalah—namely, in AlT 3 [1.2], the treaty of the historical Idrimi with Pilliya of Kizzuwatna. Márquez Rowe (2001) argued that the group of men identified in that text as $^{lu_2.meš}$SIG$_5$ (l. 39) signify "members of the political elite and the wealthy class" (459). But that context, with $^{lu_2.meš}$SIG$_5$ seemingly needing to be read as *damqūtu* for a substantivized verbal adjective, is different from the 3ms predicate we find in the Idrimi text.

---

43 For Amurru Akkadian, see, e.g., Izre'el 1991, 1:166: "The Akkadian subjunctive morpheme is not used in Amurru Akkadian, a structural reduction frequently attested in PA dialects." For the Canaano-Akkadian of the Amarna letters sent from the Levant, see Rainey 1996, 2.197: "It can be stated categorically that the scribes writing Akkadian in Canaan do not use the subjunctive marker, either the Babylonian or the Assyrian"; see also Tropper and Vita 2010, 87: "Das KA verwendet den Subjunktiv definitiv nicht, und zwar offenbar deshalb nicht, weil die Subjunktivendung *-u* (*iprusu*) mit der Endung der kan. PK^L (*yaqtulu*) identisch wäre. Verben in abhängigen Sätzen weisen im KA also die gleiche Form auf wie Verben in Hauptsätzen."

A better parallel may be found at Amarna in attestations of *damāqu* or *damqu* where the following clause is introduced by the conjunction *u*, with the sense of something being pleasing or acceptable (*damāqu*) before the king, to the effect that (*u*) royal action is subsequently taken. These attestations occur in the stative,[44] as in this line in the Idrimi text, or in the precative or jussive.[45] (Although the editors of *CAD* 3 captured this sense for the attestations of *damāqu* in the precative, which are kept apart as meaning 1b from other, more general, uses of the verb, the attestations of stative are unfortunately mingled with other attestations that are quite dissimilar—for example, concerning a good harvest—simply on the basis of morphology.) Because of this construction, the coordinating conjunction *u* that introduces the following clause has the sense "so, so that," as is found for this conjunction in Canaano-Akkadian.[46]

50. [*u*$_3$] ⸢*a-na*⸣ *bi-ri-šu-nu* NAM.ERIM$_2$ *dan-na*

The logogram NAM.ERIM$_2$, is common for the word *māmītu*, "curse, oath," in all periods of Akkadian. The logogram appears here and in line 52, while the word *māmītu* is spelled syllabically in lines 53 and 54. The difficulty arises because the word *māmītu* is feminine, yet the adjective modifying NAM.ERIM$_2$ in this line, *danna*, is masculine. Accordingly, one approach in the scholarship has been to consider NAM.ERIM$_2$ to be a different, masculine, word with the same meaning as *māmītu*. Another approach has been to understand NAM.ERIM$_2$ as *māmītu* but with a (perceived) lack of gender agreement.[47] A third approach has been to emend the text to *dan-na-*<*ta*>. This last suggestion cannot be discounted. As can be seen in figure A.30 on the next page, there is plenty of space at the end of the

---

44 Generally when the writer is querying, often for rhetorical effect, whether some action has received royal approval; e.g., "is it pleasing before the king … that the sons of ʿAbdi-ʾAširte do what they want?" (*da-*⸢*mi*⸣*-iq i-na pa-ni* LUGAL^{ri} … ⸢*u*$_3$⸣ *ti-pu-šu-na* DUMU.MEŠ ^{m}IR$_3$*-a-ši-ir-ta ki-*⸢*ma lib*$_3$⸣*-bi-šu-*⸢*nu*⸣, EA 84: 8–13 [Byblos]).

45 When a request for royal approval or action is actually being made; e.g., "(the hostility against me is severe,) so may it be pleasing before the king, my lord that he dispatch a senior official in order to guard me (*u*$_3$ *yi-da-mi-iq i-na pa-ni* LUGAL^{ri} EN*-ia u*$_3$ *yu-wa-ši-ra* 1 ^{lu2}GAL *a-na na-sa-ri-ia* > *na-ṣa-ri-ia*, EA 64: 9–13 [Gath]).

46 The sign U$_3$ is no longer preserved on the surface of the statue. Smith (1949, 16) transliterated the sign as fully preserved, and Oller (1977a, 13) transliterated it as fully restored ([ù]), but then Dietrich and Loretz (1981, 205) transliterated it as fully preserved once more, so it is unclear when during the statue's post-excavation history this part of its surface deteriorated and the sign was lost.

47 Durand (2011, 141 n. 152) argued that *danna* was, in fact, an older form of a feminine noun in which gender was marked with /a/, not /at/, and which is indeclinable. According to him, then, there is no gender incongruence.

Figure A.30. The end of lines 49–51.

line for another sign (the lines both before and after are longer). The presence of this space may reflect the fact that a sign has been inadvertently omitted; cf. the discussion of the suggested emendation *i-ip-pa-aš*$_2$*-ši-*<*iṭ*> in the commentary to line 96. Otherwise, it may be slightly more probable that a different, masculine, word underlies the logographic writing than that there is a lack of gender agreement between noun and adjective because, with the exception of cardinal numbers and demonstrative pronouns, the three other attestations of syllabically spelled adjectives in attributive use in the body inscription are in the expected gender. Furthermore, two of these attestations are examples of the same adjective as in this line.

51. ⌜*iš-ku*⌝*-nu-ni*$_7$*-na* LUGAL *dan-nu ma-na-ha-te.*HI.A

The suffixes on the verb form written ⌜*iš-ku*⌝*-nu-ni*$_7$*-na* have created some difficulties in the literature. Smith (1949, 106) recognized that the final *-na* was the West Semitic energic suffix. However, this identification has not been accepted by some subsequent scholars, who have emended the text to *-ma* for the expected Akkadian enclitic suffix. The preceding suffix, written with the sign NIM, generated little attention until Oller's (1977a, 68–69) discussion of the verb form. Oller noted that taking *-ni(m)* as the ventive is quite difficult because parallel forms of *šakānu* in similar idiomatic expressions from Alalah or Ugarit lack this suffix, while taking it as the 1cs dative suffix is also difficult because it "doesn't really make sense in the context." I take the suffix as the alternate form of the 3mp suffix attested in other corpora of western hybrid Akkadian; see the commentary to line 26 (*iphurūnima*).

52. ša pa-nu-ti-ni u$_3$ NAM.ERIM$_2$ *ša bi-ri-šu-nu*! *iš-me-ma*

The signs at the end of this line curve above and around Idrimi's lap, which may account for some epigraphic oddities. For instance, the NU in *bi-ri-šu-nu*! consists of only a horizontal wedge (i.e., AŠ), as shown in figure A.31. Note also what appears to be a small *Winkelhaken* just above the head of the wedge that resembles an oblique check mark. Possibly this wedge comprises part of the sign, so that this form of NU is similar to a form of the sign found elsewhere in the body inscription; for example, lines 25, 42, 48, 51, 65, *et passim* (see figure A.32). But a similar "check mark" wedge is found directly to the right of the head of the vertical wedge in the sign ME that occurs two signs later in line 52, as shown in figure A.33 on the next page. The function of these check marks, if the wedges are not meant to be part of the signs or simply scribal errors, is unclear; for an overview of check marks and a study of the phenomenon at Mari, see Arkhipov 2019b.

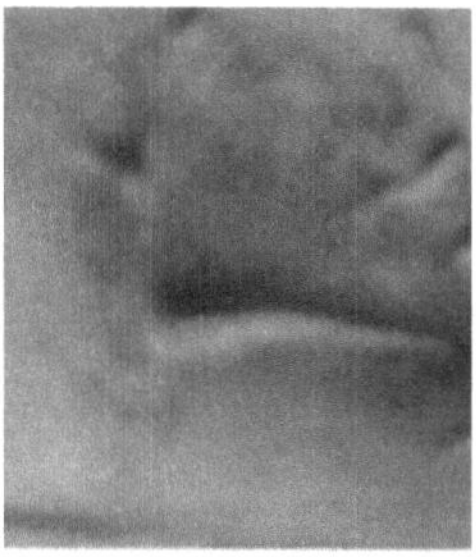

Figure A.31. Second occurrence of NU, line 52.

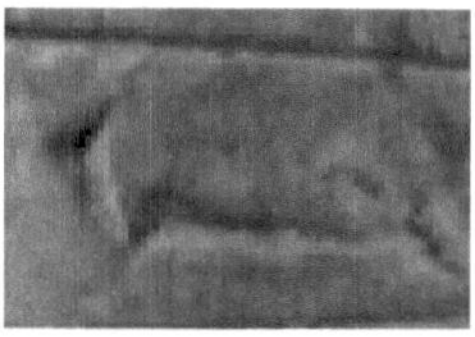

Figure A.32. Form of NU in line 65.

53. u$_3$ it-ti ma-mi-ti ip-ta-la-ah aš-šum a-wa-at

Oller (1977a, 75–76) recognized that what had been read by Smith (1949, 16) and Landsberger (1954, 55 n. 100) as two signs (ZU and ŠU) was, in fact, one sign (LA),[48] and that what had been read as one sign (AH) was, in fact, two signs (AŠ and ŠUM, for *aššum*, in parallel to l. 54). Recognition of the latter string removed a putative sequence AH-AH that Smith wanted to take together (on account of his perceived repetition of the sign) and allowed Oller to read the remaining AH with the previous three signs for *ip-ta-la-ah*. The most questionable reading is the first sign, as shown in figure A.34 on the next page. Despite the form of IB,[49] *ip-ta-la-ah* seems the strongest reading of the sign string; it has been followed by all subsequent scholars and is accepted here, too.

However, identifying the sign string as *ip-ta-la-ah* has created a philological difficulty with the reading of the preceding signs ID and TI. In the original edition, this sequence of signs possessing the syllabic values *it-ti* that is followed by a noun in the genitive was naturally interpreted as the preposition *itti* by Smith (1949, 16, 99), and this interpretation was followed by all subsequent scholars prior to Dietrich and Loretz (1981). The difficulty with this interpretation lies in *itti* then having to function as a complement to the following verb, *iptalah*, if one accepts the reading after collation of Oller (1977a, 75–76).

---

48 Oller considered the form to be defective, since he transliterated *-la*!-.

49 Oller (1977a, 76) remarked: "Despite the lack of inner verticals, the basic shape of the IB/P sign conforms to the others in this text…, and the rather odd inverted v lines between the two verticals cannot really be related to anything in cuneiform." Ultimately, Oller considered this form to be defective, since he transliterated *ip*!-.

This issue was already anticipated by Oller (1977a: 13, 76), who translated *itti* as "with regard to" and acknowledged the difficulty in his commentary: "A problem is presented by *itti* which should not really be translated 'with regard to' … one would expect *palāhu* to either take a direct object or employ *ana* with the meaning 'to have fear, honor concerning."[50] In the subsequent four decades, most scholars have simply ignored this difficulty and followed Oller in reading the verb as *iptalah* and then taking the prepositional phrase *itti māmīti* to introduce the verb's direct object.

Figure A.33. ME with check mark in line 52.

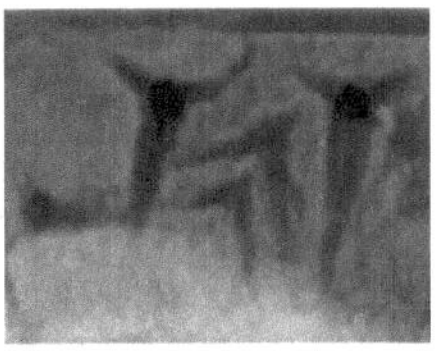

Figure A.34. IB, line 53.

The primary exception has been Dietrich and Loretz (1981, 205), who accepted Oller's reading of the verb as a form of *palāhu* and then took a logical step toward resolving this difficulty by reading the sign string *it-ti* not as the preposition *itti* but as the noun *ittu*, "sign" (*AHw* 406a s.v. "ittu II," *CAD* 7, s.v. "ittu A"), pointing to a later attestation of this same word later in the text (l. 88). They normalized the form as *ittī* (218), for a masculine plural oblique in construct with the following genitive, translating "(und fürchtete sich vor) dem Inhalt des Eides" (205). In this way, *palāhu* took a direct object, mitigating Oller's concern about *palāhu* used with the prepositional complement *itti*. However, there are two difficulties with the interpretation. First, while *itti* is valid as a singular construct form of the noun *ittu*, "sign, characteristic" in the nominative or accusative case, we expect the plural oblique construct form to be *ittāt* because the noun is feminine, although not marked as such in the singular. Second, "Inhalt" (Dietrich and Loretz 1981, 205) is not really a good translation of *ittu* in the plural, while "Zeichnen," the more accurate translation found in their comment to the line (Dietrich and Loretz 1981, 218), does not seem to fit the context of this passage.

These difficulties were understood by Durand (2011, 142 with n. 155: "le sens n'en apparaît pas"), who attempted to nuance Dietrich and Loretz's interpretation of the sign string as a form of the noun *ittu* by reading the first sign logographically as A_2 and the second sign as a phonetic complement. This reading allowed him to normalize the noun as *idāti* or *ittāti*; that is, with an explicit feminine plural. However, as Durand himself noted, this form is still not entirely satisfactory because the expected form in construct is actually *idāt* or *ittāt*.

[50] In their study of *palāhu* and other verbs of fearing in Akkadian, Svärd et al. (2021) focused only on the semantics of these verbs, not how they take their objects; see esp. 486–89.

Durand's own translation "les clauses [du serment]" also seems difficult to accept given that no support for it is offered.

Although the attempts of Dietrich and Loretz, as well as Durand, to avoid the difficulty of *palāhu* taking its object with the preposition *itti* by interpreting the string instead as the noun *ittu*, "sign" are creative, they ultimately bring as many, if not more, difficulties. Note also that a third potential noun has come to light subsequent to their work; Arkhipov (2019a) has convincingly argued for a word *ittu*, "moment," from the root **wʿd*, and this reading is now recognized in the famous phrase *ana ittišu* that refers to the repayment of debts, which is to be distinguished from *ittu*, "sign." However, this word is also feminine, except in the Assyrian dialects, where it seems to have a masculine plural, so we would expect to find *idat* or *idāt* if it occurred in this line of the body inscription.

To return to considering the string as a preposition, one possibility is that the use of *itti* with *palāhu* is calquing a preposition that would be used with a verb of fearing in a different, probably West Semitic, language. For example, there are a number of instances of *palhu* taking its object with *ištu pāni* in Amarna letters sent from Amurru and Tyre, where the use of this prepositional phrase seems to be a calque of the West Semitic use of *yrʾ* with the compound preposition *mn* + *pn*; see Rainey 1996, 3:52 for discussion. Could something similar be occurring with this use of *palāhu* with *itti*?

The preposition *itti* does seem to be used differently on occasion in western hybrid Akkadian texts than in the standard Akkadian dialects. For instance, while van Soldt (1991, 452–53) confirmed that *itti* is used in the Akkadian of Ugarit as a "comitative" that generally "corresponds to Mesopotamian practice," he also noted an exception in which *itti* is used with *leqû* with the meaning "to receive from DN" in a literary context. Indeed, Cohen (2023, 62) seems to have had this passage in mind when he argued in favor of interpreting the string in this line as the preposition and not the noun when he remarked, "reading here *it-ti* seems to be the simplest solution," with the explanation to take it "in a separative sense, 'to be respectful, fearful of, from', as the use of *itti* with *leqû*, 'to take from.'" But if a separative sense lies behind the use of *itti* with *leqû* in the example from Ugarit, then it does not seem to fit the context of this attestation of the preposition in the body inscription, since a separative sense of *ina* should require motion.

Meanwhile, in his survey of prepositions in the Akkadian of Ugarit, Huehnergard (2011, 188) noted "a curious example" in which "*itti* denotes 'to.'" The example in question comes from EA 47, in which the preposition seems to occur with the verb *šapāru*, "to send": [^{lu_2}]DUMU KIN-*ri-ka it-ti-šu-nu* [*ta-ša*]-⸢*par*$_2$⸣, "You send your messenger to them" (EA 47: 16–17). In fact, this sense of *itti* occurs elsewhere in the Amarna letters as well, such as in a letter sent from Byblos where it is used with the verb *wuššuru* in a passage that is, amusingly, put in the mouth of the Egyptian official Amon-appa: *ta-aš-ta-na a-wa-ta*$_5$ *a*-⸢*na*⸣ *ia-ši uš-ši-ra-mi* LU$_2$-*ka it-ti-ia*, "You repeated a command to me, 'Dispatch your man to me!'" (EA 82:

14–15). In these and a handful of other occurrences, it seems that *itti* is used with these verbs because it has assumed the directional meaning of West Semitic *ʿm*.

However, while these examples demonstrate the potential of prepositions to be used as verbal complements in ways that are different from the standard Akkadian dialects, I do not have a clear explanation for why, specifically, *itti* should be used with *palāhu*. As a tepid argument in favor of interpreting the sign string as the preposition *itti*, we can note that this preposition seems to be used unexpectedly with *anāhu* elsewhere in the body inscription as well; see the commentary to line 41. But we should also keep in mind that perhaps some ambiguity in whether the string *it-ti* should be interpreted as *itti*, "with"; *ittu*, "sign"; or even *ittu*, "moment" was precisely the point. Indeed, a similar ambiguity between *itti*, "with" and *ittu*, "sign" may occur in the Standard Babylonian Epic of Gilgamesh, specifically in the opening of the flood tablet, when the gods decide to cause the flood. There the list of five gods who swear an oath ends with Ea: ^{d}*nin-ši-ku*$_{3}$ ^{d}*e*$_{2}$*-a it-ti-šu-nu ta-mi-ma*, "Ninšiku, Ea, was also under oath with them" (SB Gilg. XI 19). Noegel (1995) has argued that the polysemous *ittišunu* offers competing readings as *ittišunu*, "with them" and "their sign." He suggested that the word was a phenomenon of Janus parallelism in this polysemy because "when read as 'with them' [it] parallels the list of gods present in the assembly, and as 'omen, sign,' it parallels 'their words' (*amassunu*) in the following line." These and other examples of Janus parallelism "result [in] a text that challenges the reader and gives cause for contemplation of its interpretation."

54. ma-mi-ti u$_{3}$ *aš-šum ma-na-ha-te.*MEŠ*-ni šu-ul-mi-ia*

Smith (1949) recognized that *šulmu*, "health," was being used in an extended sense, translating it as "peace" in the text edition (17) and as "greeting" in the glossary (106). Subsequently, however, many scholars have understood *šulmu* to mean here "greeting-gift"—that is, the gift that accompanied written or oral greetings and that is well attested in Late Bronze Age letters in the cognate noun *šulmānu*.[51] While this understanding seems to derive from the fact the *šulmu* is the direct object of *mahāru*, "to receive," neither of the dictionaries recognizes any attestations of *šulmu* with the meaning of a concrete greeting gift,[52] so proponents of this sense have offered various arguments in its favor. In particular, Dietrich

[51] Goetze (1950, 228 n. 20) moved in this direction in taking the 1cs pronominal suffix *-ni* as I$_{3}$ (= *šamnu*, "oil") and then seeing *šaman šulmiya* as a gift ("the acceptance of a present on the part of the other party … underlines the equality of the two parties who conclude the treaty"). Landsberger (1954, 55) was the first to understand the word *šulmu* itself with the meaning of a concrete gift concrete gifts ("meine Gaben").

[52] *CAD* 17.3, s.v. "šulmu," 1f-1′ ("referring to written messages—in gen.") read *aššum mānahāteni šu-ul-mi-ia imdahar* and translated "because of our efforts he accepted my greetings." *AHw* 1268b–1269a, to my knowledge, does not cite this attestation s.v. "šulmu."

and Loretz (1981, 219) looked to Ugarit, where "der hiesige Gebrauch von *šulmu* im Sinne von *šulmānu* 'Begrüßung, (Amts-)Geschenk' (siehe *AHw.*, S. 1268) erinnert an ug. *šlm*, das sowohl 'Wohlbefinden, Frieden' also auch 'Gruß, (Begrüßungs-)Geschenk' ... bedeuten kann," citing an attestation from the first tablet of the Legend of Kirta (*KTU* 1.14 [RS 2.[003]+]: III 26–27).

This parallel is worth developing, if in a somewhat different direction. In the passage, *šlm* occurs in the context of a dream that El sends to Kirta, promising him military victory over a certain King Pabuli; in particular, the word appears in a message sent by Pabuli to Kirta that is delivered by two messengers, where it encompasses the various items that Pabuli offers to give Kirta in an attempt to convince Kirta to withdraw his army: *qh . krt . šlmm šlmm . wng mlk . lbty*, "Take, O Kirta, offerings—offerings of peace! But fly, O king, from my palace" (translation following Greenstein 1997, 17). In other words, the context is a diplomatic message in which one ruler attempts to convince another, stronger ruler to cease hostilities, a context that is strikingly similar to the context of *šulmiya* in the Idrimi text, where Idrimi has sent a message (*aštapar*, l. 46) to Parattarna I, the mighty king (*šarru dannu*, ll. 43, 50, 51) in order to convince him to cease being hostile (*unakkiranni*, l. 44).

Note that, while Dietrich and Loretz recognized only one word *šlm* in Ugaritic that has both the meanings "wellbeing, greeting, greeting-gift" and "peace," *DULAT* disambiguated two distinct words, *šlm* (I), "peace, health, well-being, prosperity" and *šlm* (II), "communion victim / sacrifice, peace-offering," with the attestation cited by Dietrich and Loretz filed under *šlm* (II). Whether or not the words should be disambiguated, it is clear that *šlm* could designate a tangible offering for peace or well-being. Furthermore, other uses of *šlm* in alphabetic texts from Ugarit make clear that the word could function not just as a general term for p eace offerings but more specifically as a sacrifice. For instance, numerous texts document sacrificial sheep that are qualified as *šlmm*, "a peace-offering."[53] While *šlm* typically occurs in the plural when it is used in this sense, it may occur in the singular in the funerary text concerning the internment of Niqmaddu III, where Pardee (2002b, 115 n. 130) has remaked that "it is uncertain whether *šlm* represents here a rare use of the singular for the sacrifical term ... or whether the expression is non-technical."[54]

Not only does the sense of Ugaritic *šlm* fit the context of *šulmu* in this line of the body inscription, but the larger sacrificial context in which the words occurs

---

[53] See, e.g., *KTU* 1.109 [RS 24.253]: 10–11: "A ewe for Ṣapunu as a burnt-offering. And as a peace-offering: the same," *dqt l ṣpn . šrp . w šlmm kmm* (translation following Pardee 2002b, 31; cf. Pardee 2000, 603, where *šlmm* is translated as "sacrifice de bien-être").

[54] *KTU* 1.161 [RS 34.126]: 30–31: "You shall present bird(s) of well-being," *tq⌜d⌝m ʿṣr šlm* (translation following Pardee 2002b, 88; cf. Pardee 2000, 818, where the clause is translated, "Tu présenteras [un/deux] oiseau[x] en sacrifice salutaire"). See also lines 31–34 for additional attestations of *šlm* in the text.

at Ugarit accords well with the the following line, which, if obscure, clearly mentions "a sacrifice" (*nīqu*) and perhaps a brazier (*kinūnu*); see the commentary to l. 55.

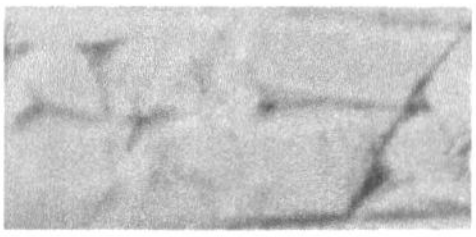

Figure A.35. NU NU in line 55.

55. im-ta$_2$-har u$_3$ ki-nu-[n]u$^?$ ša kab$^?$-tu$_3$-u$_2$ ša SISKUR$_2$

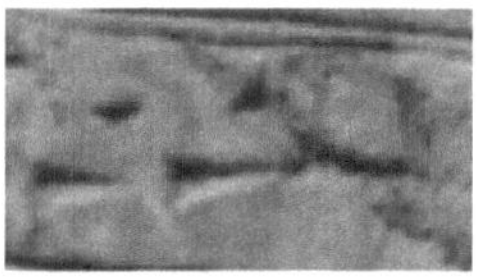

Figure A.36. BU in line 62.

Figure A.37. NU in line 69.

Figure A.38. NU in line 51.

The sign string read here as *ki-nu-nu$^?$ ša kab$^?$-tu$_3$-u$_2$* is difficult, and a number of interpretations can be found in the literature. Table A.1 gathers the primary interpretations of lines 55b–56a. Epigraphically, the first sign in this difficult string, KI, is clear. The problems begin with the wedges that Smith and many other scholars read as NU NU, Landsberger as NU TI$^!$, and Oller as a single sign, BU, as shown in figure A.35. Oller's reading BU depends on seeing a *Winkelhaken*, now poorly preserved, as having been originally inscribed in the damage to the surface of the statue directly before the final horizontal so that the sign would have originally resembled an attestation of BU, as is found in line 62, shown in figure A.36. After personal collation, I agree with both Smith and Oller that the traces of a *Winkelhaken* are indeed present. Yet the second wedge of the sign, which is more a vertical than a *Winkelhaken*, seems difficult to reconcile with BU. Furthermore, the first three wedges, taken together, do find parallels in forms of NU elsewhere in the inscription. For instance, as can be seen in figure A.37, the NU in line 69 shows the same sequence of horizontal-vertical-horizontal as the first three wedges above. And the wedge sequence of an initial *Winkelhaken* followed by a horizontal wedge is also used to form other examples of NU elsewhere in the inscription; see, for example, line 51, shown in figure A.38. Furthermore, there are good parallels in the body inscription for signs written in proximity showing paleographic variation; see the discussion in §4.1. Therefore, both paleograpically and contextually, there are reasons to read the signs in question as two different forms of NU; that is, NU NU.

The second sign in this string that is difficult from as epigraphic perspective is the putative KAB or RI, shown in figure A.39 on page 238. There are two issues here. First, while all other examples of RI begin with a horizontal wedge crossed

Author	Transliteration	Translation
Smith 1949, 16–18	*u ki-nu-nu ša emidū(du-u)-ša GAZ*	" And (I made a great) brazier whereon I put a sacrifice"
Landsberger 1954, 55 n. 100	*u_3 ki-nu-ti! ša kab-du u_2-ša*-AMAR×ŠE	" " und meine Treue (ki-nu-ti!), die stark war (kab-du), machte ich … (ú-ša-
CAD 8, s.v. " kinūnu," 2a	uncert.: *ki-nu-nu ša* UŠ(or *ri-*)*du-ú ša* SIZKUR.SIZKUR	[no translation offered]
Greenstein and Marcus 1976, 65, 67	ù ki-nu-ti ša kab-tu ú-ša <*mhir*(?)> SISKUR$_x$(*niqê*)	" Then I *pr<esented>* the (*gestures of*) loyalty, which were considerable, (I made great)
Oller 1977a, 113, 77–79	u KI.BU ša RI.DU.Ú ša SIZKUR	" And .... sacrifices (I increased)."
Na'aman 1980b, 114	*ù gi_5-nu $a^?$-ša-ri-du-ú ša* SIZKUR$_x$ (*niqê*)	" and (I have added) selected(?) offerings of sacrificial animals."
Dietrich and Loretz 1981, 205	*ù ki-nu-nu ša ri-du-ú ša niqê* (SÍSKUR)	" Im folgenden Kinūnu-Monat (habe ich) Gußopfer (reichlich gespendet)."
Durand 2011, 142	*ù ki-nu-nu ša re-du-ú ša* $siskur_2$	" lors, le *kinûnu* qui suivait (était le moment) des offrandes sacrées; (je [les] offris plus grandement

Table A.1. Various interpretations of line 55b.

by two vertical wedges, in no other examples are the vertical wedges spaced apart from each other to this degree; compare, for example, the attestation from line 79 shown in figure A.40. The attestation from line 79 reveals another epigraphic difficulty with reading the sign in question as RI. The form of the sign in line 79 shows the same archaizing rendering of the sign's final *Winkelhaken* with two oblique wedges instead. However, it lacks the two small horizontal wedges before these oblique wedges that occur in the putative RI from line 55. Indeed, such wedges are not found in any of the seventeen examples of RI among the many that occur on the statue.

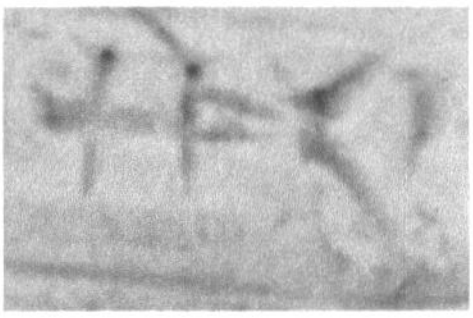

Figure A.39. KAB in line 55.

Figure A.40. RI in line 79.

Landsberger's suggestion to read the sign as KAB is more difficult to assess because there is only one attestation of the sign, where it is to be read as *gub*$_3$, on the statue, as shown in figure A.41. The form of the sign actually matches the sign in question in line 55 quite well. It has two initial horizontal wedges that cross a vertical wedge and that are somewhat spaced apart, and there is a small horizontal wedge superimposed above the tail of the initial horizontal wedge, which has been extended, before the oblique wedges at the end of the sign. From an epigraphic perspective, then, KAB seems to be preferrable to RI.

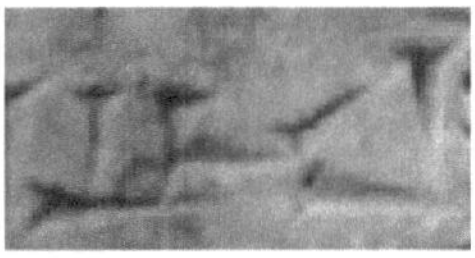

Figure A.41. The sign *gub*$_3$ (KAB) in line 59.

Having reviewed these epigraphic issues, the best identification of the signs in the string seems to me to be *u* KI NU NU ŠA KAB DU U$_2$ ŠA SISKUR$_2$—essentially Landsberger's reading of the line without his emendation. In what is essentially a conflation of Smith's and Landsberger's interpretations, this sign string could be read as *ki-nu-nu ša kab-tu*$_3$*-u*$_2$ *ša* SISKUR$_2$ and normalized as *kinūnu ša kabtu ša nīqi*, "(I/he made great) a brazier that was heavy, the one for (lit. of) the sacrifice," understanding the brazier to be heavy with the peace offerings mentioned in the previous line.

However, this reading presents two grammatical difficulties. First, *kinūnu* is marked with /u/, the ending expected for the nominative case, instead of /a/, the ending expected for the accusative case, as the direct object of *ušarbi*, and there are no other examples of the direct object of a transitive verb being marked with a vowel other than /a/ for the accusative.[55] Second, the sign DU is not used

[55] For suggestions in the literature that E$_2$ *hal-qu*$_2$ (l. 56) is a direct object marked in the nominative case, see the discussion immediately below.

elsewhere with the value *tu*3. More generally, it might be objected that, while some otherwise unattested grammatical features do occur in isolation in the inscription, a reading that requires the co-occurrence of multiple otherwise unattested grammatical features is suspect.

As a response to this latter objection, one can point to line 70 and specifically the verb form *eh-te-pi*3*-šu-nu-ti*. This verb form provides the only attestation of the Babylonian form of the 3mp accusative suffix *-šunūti*, as opposed to the short form *-šunu*, in both inscriptions.[56] It also contains only one attestation of the syllable /pi/ written with the sign BAD (*pi*3), as opposed to BI (*pi*2), in both inscriptions. Therefore, there is a parallel for the co-occurrence of multiple isolated grammatical features, and one might even suggest that it is precisely the co-occurrence that makes the interpretation more probable. Accordingly, I suggest reading the line as *kinūnu ša kabtu ša nīqi*, "(I made great) a brazier which was heavy, the one for (lit. of) the sacrifice," taking *kinūnu* literally as "brazier," with Smith, and not as the month Kinunu, with Dietrich and Loretz and Durand, on account of its qualification as "heavy" (*kabdu*).

*56. u*2*-šar-bi u*3 E2 *hal-qu*2 *u*2*-te-er-šu*

The sense of the "house that was lost" is not immediately clear because of the polysemy of both *bītu* and *halqu*. I follow Klengel's (1981, 276) interpretation of *bītu* as referring to the royal household. Na'aman's (1980b, 114–15) idea to see a reference to fugitive families is attractive because of the importance of extraditing fugitives as part of political alliances at this time and place, as he noted, and also because the administration at Level IV Alalah did use the word *bītu* in some of its internal accounting of its population (the so-called "group B census lists"; see von Dassow 2008, 154–56). However, the fact that *bītu* stands in the singular, as opposed to plural, as in the group B census lists, makes Klengel's interpretation more probable, so that we should envision a subordinate household "returning" to the authority of its previous hegemon. However, this statement need not imply that Parattarna I or one of his predecessors was involved in the events that forced Idrimi and his family to flee Halab. Rather, the verb *turru*, "to return (someone or something)" is simply in keeping with the assertion earlier in the passage that Idrimi's forefathers and ancestors had acknowledged the hegemony of the Hurrian kings, even if this assertation has no basis in fact.

In addition to the possible senses for *bītu*, scholars have had to wrestle with the case vowel on *halqu*, especially since *bītu* seems to be the direct object of transitive *turru*. If *halqu* modifies *bītu*, the attributive adjective *halqu* is marked with the

[56] The form *-šunu* for the 3mp accusative suffix is used widely in western hybrid Akkadian. Although this form is also found in the Assyrian dialects, its appearance in western hybrid Akkadian is better understood as an example of "systemic simplification" (Izre'el 1991, 1:101) than as an Assyrianism.

wrong case vowel. (The case of *bītu* is obscured by the word's logographic writing.)[57] Two other interpretations of the line can be found in the literature that step around this difficulty. Kempinski and Na'aman (1973, 213) transliterated and normalized E$_2$(*bīt*) *hal-qu* [*sic*]. From their translation, it is clear that they understand an asyndetic relative construction in which *bītu* stands in the construct state and *halqu* is taken not as an attributive verbal adjective marked for the nominative case but as a 3ms stative with the subjunctive marker.[58] A different interpretation of the grammar was put forward by Durand (2011, 142 n. 158), who suggested "lisant *utter-šu(m)*, au D/2 (passif) pour expliquer le nominatif *bîtu halqu*." None of these three interpretations can be excluded, and E$_2$ *hal-qu*$_2$ is tentatively understood here as an asyndetic relative construction because it allows the words to be read in accordance with the standard Akkadian dialects without positing that accusative *halqu* is marked with an *u* vowel (although cf. *kinūnu* in the previous line) or the unexpected orthography *u*$_2$*-te-* for *utt-*.[59]

57. i-na LU$_2$*-ti-ia i-na ki-nu-ti-ia* SI$^?$ ŠUB *an-na-am*

The end of line 57 has occasioned much discussion, especially the sign(s) before AN NA AM, which are written around the corner of Idrimi's lap. One widely adopted interpretation goes back to Nougayrol (1951, 153), who took the wedges together as PAD$_3$ (= IGI + RU) and understood the logogram to function as the object of the verb in the following line, with the phrase having the meaning "to swear an oath."[60] However, other interpretations can be found in the literature as well, and Oller (1977a, 80) cautioned that

> while PÀD is semantically appropriate…, no Akkadian reading for PÀD by itself as a noun meaning "oath" seems to exist. Further confusion arises from the fact that everywhere else in the text the scribe uses either *māmītu* … or NAM.ERÍM … for oath. If the word "oath" is meant by the PÀD, one wonders why the scribe chose it rather than the standard term he has employed elsewhere.

57 This lack of agreement has received very little discussion in the literature cited above. To my knowledge, only Greenstein and Marcus (1976, 89) raised the issue when they cited the form of *halqu* as one of the other examples of "erroneous case endings" found in the inscription in their comment on line 79.

58 This interpretation was also independently suggested to me by Baruch Halpern (personal communication).

59 Although see AIT 3 [1.2]: 45 for the writing *i-ti-iq* for a form that is in the protasis of a curse formula and so universally taken as G present and normalized as *ittiq*.

60 Interestingly, Nougayrol seems to have understood PAD$_3$ to be a logogram for the verb *tamû*, "to swear" and not a noun that is the direct object of *ṣabātu*. From his translation of lines 57b–58 ("je prêtai serment. Je le (= Baratarna) saisis de la chose et je fus roi"), it is clear that he understood the words to belong to two different clauses.

From an epigraphic perspective, there is one clear horizontal wedge and traces of others before a RU sign, shown in figure A.42. Therefore, either there is another sign before RU, or RU is the second component of a larger sign. According to their copies, both Smith and Oller saw two vertical wedges crossing the clear horizontal wedge, and my personal collation confirms the presence of these wedges. Smith and Oller's primary disagreement was whether or not there is a *Winkelhaken* before the horizontal wedge. Smith copied a *Winkelhaken*, while Oller did not, remarking, "the RU is definitely present, ...the initial winkelhocken of the IGI, copied by Smith, is not entirely confirmed by collation" (1977a, 80 n. 1). Nonetheless, he considered Nougayrol's reading of the wedges as a single sign, PAD$_3$, to be "best." However, Oller's doubts about the presence of a *Winkelhaken* seem correct; what Smith evidently took as the wedge's bottom half instead seems to be a crack in the surface of the statue that curves downward and extends into the top of the following line.

Figure A.42. SI$^{!?}$ ŠUB, line 57.

Considering that the visible elements of the sign before the putative RU consist of a horizontal wedge and two vertical wedges, I tentatively suggest reading it as a damaged or defective SI$^{!?}$. This reading is attractive because SI is a logogram for *qannu*, "hem," the main verb is *ṣabātu*, and the phrase *qanna ṣabātu*, literally "to seize the hem," is a common idiom for acknowledging the hegemony of another ruler. The sign RU can be read as ŠUB, a logogram for the adjective *nadû*, which is well attested with the meaning "abandoned." The signs AN NA AM following ŠUB are clear, and the only debate has been whether to take them with the preceding sign as part of a larger word or to read them independently as either the substantive *annu*, "consent, approval," or the demonstrative pronoun *annû*, "this." The presence of mimation should indicate taking it as the demonstrative pronoun, because mimation does not generally occur in the inscriptions except in the case of final CVC signs and interrogative and demonstrative pronouns; see the commentary to line 10.[61]

58. aṣ-bat-šu u$_3$ LUGAL-*ku a-*⸢*na* ^{uru}⸣*a-la-la-ah*^{ki}

Similar to the attestation of LUGAL-*ku* in line CI 1, the majority of scholars have translated the end of the line in one of three ways: "I became king," "I became

[61] Durand (2011, 142 n. 161), who accepted Nougayrol's identification of the sign(s) before the demonstrative pronoun as PAD$_3$, "oath," has remarked that *annû* can have a sense of "renvoyant à quelque chose de déjà connu et qui n'a pas de sens prospectif, attesté dans la langue de l'Ouest depuis Mari jusqu'à Emar." For him, the text qualified the oath (PAD$_3$) as "antérieur" in order to clarify that it is only a reference to the earlier oath (*māmītu*) in lines 53–54. However, this sense of *annû* no longer works if the preceding signs are identified as a word that does not mean "oath."

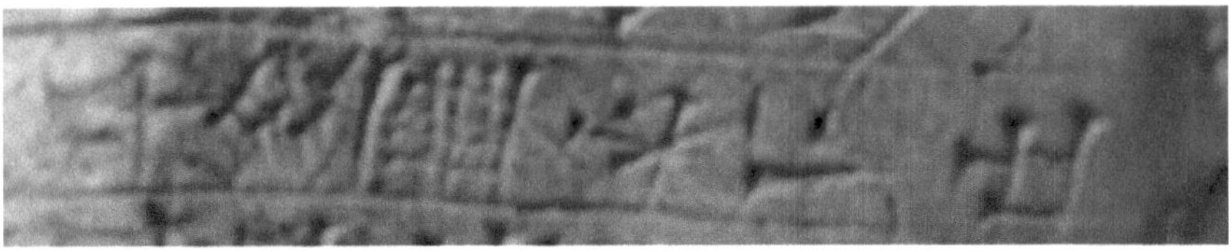

Figure A.43. The second half of line 59.

king of Alalah," or "I ruled over Alalah"; see the commentary to line 57. In other words, as with line CI 1, the question is whether the stative form LUGAL-*ku*, normalized as *šarrāku*, functions as a nominal predicate or a West Semitic suffix conjugation verb. However, unlike the attestation of the same form in line CI 1, there is also the question in this line as to whether the following words *ana Alalah* belong to part of the same clause as *šarrāku* or to the following clause.

If *šarrāku* is being used as a West Semitic suffix conjugation verb, the resulting verb-initial word order is exactly what we would expect from other attestations of statives used in this manner in the body inscription. For instance, in the coordinated clauses *hal-qa*$_3$*-nu* … *u*$_3$ *aš-ba-nu a-na* ^{uru}*e-mar*^{ki}, "we fled … and stayed at Emar" (ll. 4–6), not only does *ašbānu* show the influence of West Semitic in its initial placement in the clause, but, as discussed in the comment to line 6, the use of *ana* as its complement seems to be a West Semitic calque, as West Semitic *yṯb* takes the preposition *l*-, whereas in the standard dialects of Akkadian *wašābu* takes the preposition *ina*. However, the fact that *ana* is used in line 58 may actually be an argument *against* taking the prepositional phrase *ana Alalah* with *šarrāku* as an example of West Semitic influence, because the corresponding verb in West Semitic, *mlk*, takes the prepositions *ʿal* or *b*- and not *l*-, as would be expected for *ana*.[62]

59. LUGAL.MEŠ *ša* ZAG-*ia u*$_3$ GUB$_3$-*ia il*$^?$*-lu-an-ni-ma*

The second half of the line presents epigraphic difficulties. While the final three signs are AN NI MA, it is unclear whether there are two or three signs before these, and, furthermore, which wedges belong with which signs, as shown in figure A.43. Smith's (1949, 18–19) reading **il-lu-an-ni-ma* for a form of *elû*, "to go up," has been widely adopted. However, the first sign does not seem like a good fit for IL because there are multiple interior *Winkelhaken* before

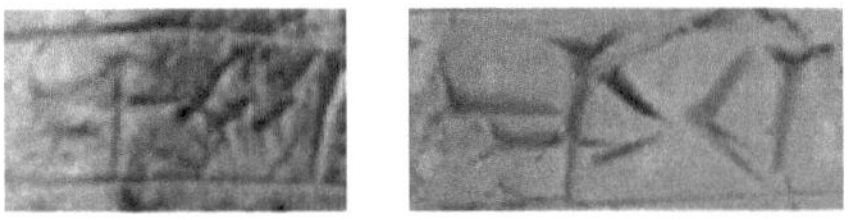

Figure A.44. Juxtaposition of putative IL in line 59 (left) with IL in line 40 (right).

[62] Cf. van Soldt's (1991, 443–47) discussion of verbs + *ana* in the Akkadian of Ugarit, where he concluded: "if we compare the combinations of verbs and *ana* with their Ugaritic counterparts … in all but one of these examples *ana* corresponds to an attested *l*; only with *ʿrb* does *ana* equal *b*" (446–47).

expect only a single *Winkelhaken*, as in the attestation of IL in line 40 in figure A.44 and the two other attestations of the sign in the inscription (ll. 71 and 81). For this reason, Dietrich and Loretz (1981, 220) suggested that it could be "eine Sonderform für IL (Mischform von IL und ID) mit Hinweis auf ähnliche Formen im a/mA und mB Bereich."

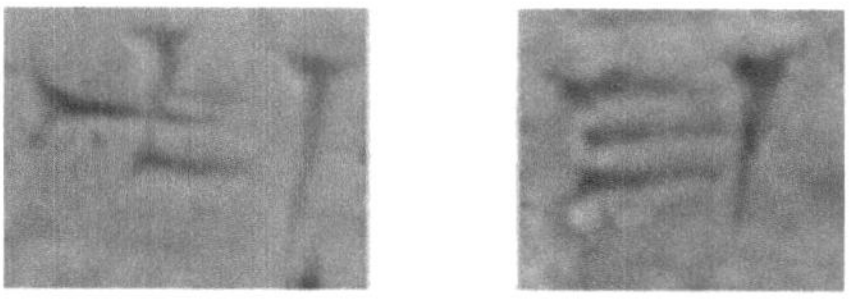

Figure A.45. The first and second attestations of MA in line 60.

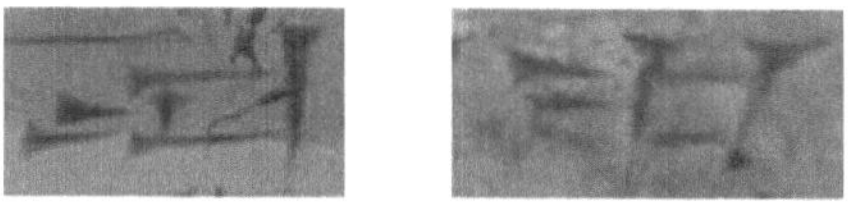

Figure A.46. Juxtaposition of UM in line 11 (left) with UM in line 60 (right).

Alternatively, Durand (2011, 143) suggested a different identification, taking the wedges instead as two different signs, ⌜E⌝ and LI. But this suggestion does not stand up epigraphically. Durand's putative ⌜E⌝ is not damaged, it is missing the first vertical wedge of the A component, and what he seems to be taking as the head of the lower of the two superimposed final verticals is actually a horizontal wedge. However, his larger point—that the wedges should be taken as two signs instead of a single sign—may be correct, although I do not have an identification to offer.

The following sign can be identified as LU; see, for example, the clear paleographic parallels in lines 36, 84, 100. This identification brings its own difficulties, however, because it seems to result in an uncontracted sequence of vowels that is not otherwise attested in the body inscription or, indeed, expected (Goetze 1950, 228–29). Furthermore, if the /u/ is the 3mp marker, we would expect the form of the ventive before the 1cs accusative suffix to be *-ninni*, not *-anni*. And, of course, if the verb really is a form of *elû*, we expect a dative suffix, not an accusative suffix.

60. u$_3$ *ki-ma šu-nu-ti-ma um-ta*$_2$*-ši-la-ku ki* BAD$_3$-*šu-nu*

Epigraphically, the second occurrence of MA in the line is remarkable for being the only occurrence of a cursive form of the sign that is otherwise always written in archaizing form, including earlier in the same line (although see the comment to -*šu*! in l. 96); see figure A.45. The sign identified as UM, following both Smith (1949, 18) and Dietrich and Loretz (1981, 206), was read as AL by some scholars in the intervening decades. The sign differs from six other forms of UM that are attested in the inscriptions in that its initial vertical wedge is much larger. Compare, for instance, the form of the sign in this line with a representative form found earlier in the body inscription, in line 11, shown in figure A.46. To be sure, still another form of UM is found in the body inscription, shown in figure A.47 on the next page, but the two variations of this form are quite different, and both occur in the curse formulae. Unfortunately, the only attestation of AL in the

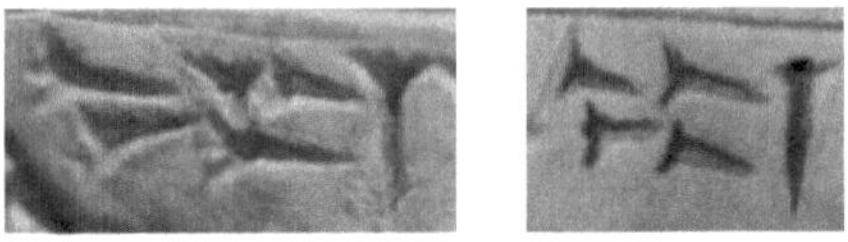

Figure A.47. Attestations of UM in line 92 (left) with UM in line 96 (right).

markedly different than the sign in line 60, in that it has an interior horizontal wedge in its second component (see figure A.48) that is entirely absent from the sign in line 60.

If the sign is identified as UM, the resulting form, *umtaššilāku*, can be understood as a D stem "hybrid perfect" verb; see the commentary to l. 26 (*urtabbiāku*). This interpretation largely follows the analysis first put forward by Dietrich and Loretz (1981, 221) and followed by subsequent scholarship, except that these scholars interpreted the stem and tense as Dt preterite, not D perfect (e.g., "I was made king"). However, the semantics of *muššulu* + *kīma* make a passive unnecessary, as discussed in the commentary to line 84.

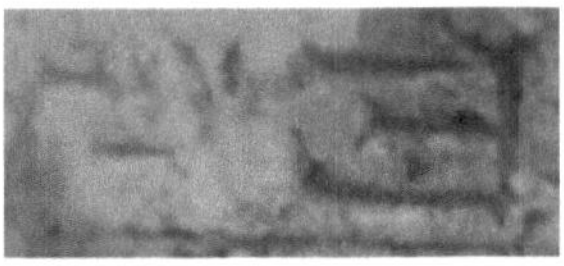

Figure A.48. Attestation of AL in line 19.

*61. ša a-bu-te.*HI.A *i-na qa-qa-ri tab-ku-*⸢*u*₂⸣

See §4.1 with figure 4.1 on the paleography of *qa-qa-ri* in this line and the next.

For the use of the preposition *ina* + *qaqqari* with the meaning "on the ground," where one might expect a different preposition, such as *eli*, in the standard Akkadian dialects, see *CAD* 13, s.v. "qaqqaru," 1a–1′, where this passage is cited together with a parallel from the Disputation between Tamarisk and Palm: *tabkū erūya ina qaqqarima*, "my branches are scattered on the ground" (*BWL* 160: 3). The line is also preserved in the manuscript of the text that was discovered at Emar subsequent to the publication of *BWL* (Emar 783: 34′) ; on this tablet, see Jiménez 2017, 28, 30–33, citing previous bibliography.

The verb form *tabku* is interpreted as a true stative and not a stative used as a suffix conjugation verb. In this use, the sense of *tabāku*, "to pour out, lay flat" is unproblematic, as opposed to the sense of the verb for those scholars who take it as active and perfective, where it must be translated "to heap up, pile up"; see already Durand's (2011, 143) comment (n. 165): "Mais *tabâkum* n'est pas *šapâkum*!"[63] Durand (2011, 116–17) considered this line to indicate that Alalah was an abandoned city at the time of Idrimi's enthronement.

[63] Although note that *CAD* 18, s.v. "tabāku," 1b cited this attestation of the verb under the usage "to make stacks, layers of bricks."

62. u$_3$ a-na-ku i-na qa-qa-ri u$_2$-ša-at-bu-u$_2$

Although the signs of the verb at the end of the line are clear, the final U$_2$ was emended by Smith (1949, 18) to KU (*u-ša-at-bu-*ku*) in order to provide a form of the verb, *tabāku*, that he expected. Smith's emended reading has continued as one primary line of interpretation of the verb in the secondary literature, although the fact that it requires emendation has dropped out of the literature; see, for example, Greenstein and Marcus 1976, 65; Na'aman 1980b, 115. However, a Š form of *tebû* fits the context well; see, for example, already Goetze 1950, 229: "In our passage there is a contrast between 'they' (60) and 'I' (62) and between *tab-ku-ú*, 'they have spread out' and *ú-ša-at-bu-ú*, 'I caused to rise,'" although note that Goetze takes *abbūte* in as the subject of *tabkū/u* in line 61.

Following Medill (2019, 249 n. 41), I understand the verb to be part of the subordinate clause introduced by *kī* in line 60 so that the final /u/ is the subordination marker. Although we might expect the /a/-vowel in the *ša*-prefix to become /e/ in this *e*-class final weak verb, because the inscriptions tend to display Babylonian vowel harmony, the forms *ušatba* and *ušatbi* are well attested in a number of different dialects and genres of Babylonian. In the Š stem, *šutbû* needs to be transitive, although no direct object is specified. That object is tentatively understood to be *dūru* (l. 60). While the most common senses of *šutbû*, "to make someone get up, to remove a person from an office or an illness from a person, to mobilize a workforce, to make winds rise up," are not really appropriate to this context, *CAD* 18, s.v. "tebû" does note a sense of *tebû* in the Š stem "to erect a building" (meaning 16). The two references cited there are both from a single Neo-Assyrian letter, SAA 10 14, written by the chief scribe of the Assyrian king, and Parpola (1983, 12) has suggested that this sense of *šatbû* is an Aramaism. Perhaps the use of *šutbû* with the same sense in line 62 can be understood either as a calque or as otherwise deriving from West Semitic influence.

63. u$_3$ a-na AN.TA$_2$ *u$_2$-šaq-qu$_2$-u$_2$-šu-nu*

The sign string A NA AN DA has received much scholarly attention. One school of thought, following a suggestion of Albright (1950, 18 with n. 32), has taken it as a form of the word *anantu*, "battle, strife," although *CAD* 1.2, s.v. "anantu" declined to accept this reading. Oller (1977a, 88) put forward a different suggestion to read AN.DA as AN.TA$_2$ and equate it with AN.TA = *eliš*, "up above, upwards." As he remarked, understanding AN.TA$_2$ as a form of *eliš*, or even *šamû*, fits the context of constructing a city wall perfectly. The reading AN.TA$_2$ for expected AN.TA is not problematic because the Sumerian ablative-instrumental case *-ta* is sometimes written *-da*, and this orthography occurs in references cited in the bilingual section of *CAD* 4, s.v. "eliš." Therefore AN.TA$_2$ can be understood as a learned writing designed to show scribal competency, which occurs throughout the inscriptions; see §4.1 on other such displays of learning in the inscription. The preposition *ana* before *eliš* is more problematic, though, because the sense of direction is communicated by the locative-terminative ending *-iš* on *eliš*, and this difficulty seems to have been behind Oller's (1977a, 88) suggestion to emend the text to *a-na-*<*ku*>. However, it is possible that the pleonasm *ana eliš* is a hypercorrect locution on the scribe's part. Or perhaps it is not as unexpected as we assume.[64]

Albright (1950, 18 with n. 32) read the verb as *u-šak-lu-ú-šu-nu*, which he analyzed as "the causative of *kalû*, 'to stop,'" translating, "I made them stop fighting," taking the preceding sign string A NA AN DA as a form *anantu*, "battle, strife," as mentioned above. This interpretation of the verb dominated the literature for decades. However, it requires identifying the third sign in the verb form as LU despite the fact that it is a clear KU; so already Goetze 1950, 229 and Oller 1977a, 87. The unambiguous form becomes evident in juxtaposing the sign with typical examples of KU and LU in the body inscription, as shown in figure A.49, because these sign forms are not very similar.

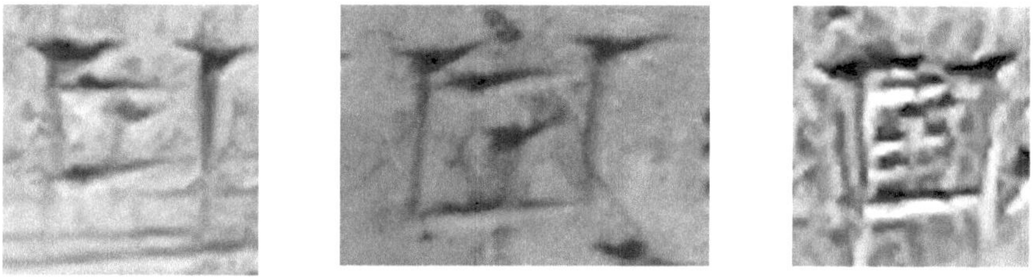

Figure A.49. Juxtaposition of KU in line 62 (left) with KU(*qu*$_2$) in line 63 (center) and LU in line 69 (right).

Oller (1977a, 14, 83, 87) was the first to understand the verb as a form of *šaqû*, and this reading has been adopted by most subsequent scholars. However, the verb's object, seemingly indicated by the 3mp accusative pronominal suffix, remains difficult. Durand's (2011, 143 n. 164) confident statement, "bàd = *dûrî* (acc. plur.)," seems intended to address this problem, but it cannot be accepted without support. Tentatively, I understand *-šunu* as dative, not accusative; see the commentary to line 84 on *-šunu* as a form of the dative pronominal suffix, in addition to the accusative pronominal suffix. If this interpretation of the pronoun is correct, then the referent should be either the populace of the city, in which case the referent is implicit, or, if explicit, perhaps the "forefathers" mentioned in line 61 or the "troops" mentioned in line 64, athough see the commentary to line 64 on ERIN$_2$.MEŠ^{ba_2} as a singular, collective noun.

---

64 See, e.g., the restored phrase in a letter from Mari: "When a man from the Yaminites comes here (going) from <do>wnstream to upstream, (they will seize him)," [*i-nu-m*]*a* 1 LU$_2$ *i-na* DUMU.MEŠ *ia-mi-na* [*an-ni-i*]*š iš-t*[*u*] <*ša*>*-ap-la-nu-um* [*a-na e-li*]*-iš i-la-ku* (ARM 2 102: 19–21; see LAPO 17 423–24 [no. 680] and ll. 10, 12 for other attestions of *eliš* in the letter).

64. ERIN$_2$.MEŠ^{ba_2} *el-te-qe$_2$ u$_3$ a-na ma-at ha-at-te*^{ki}

The scholarship is divided as to whether the PA sign that follows ERIN$_2$.MEŠ is a logogram that qualifies ERIN$_2$.MEŠ (either an adjective or a noun in a construct chain) but whose reading is unknown or is to be read *ba$_2$* and taken as a phonetic complement with ERIN$_2$.MEŠ for a normalization *ṣāba*. Oller (1977a, 92) explicitly argued against the latter interpretation, pointing out that the "phonetic complement is grammatically incorrect—one should expect *ṣābē* or *ṣābāte*." However, Greenstein and Marcus (1976, 87) cited several passages from the Amarna letters (all Byblian) where ERIN$_2$.MEŠ is construed with a singular predicate (Albright and Moran 1948, 245) so that there are parallels in western hybrid Akkadian for the logogram being written with the plural determinative yet still construed as singular in number.

There may also be a good reason why ERIN$_2$.MEŠ is written with a phonetic complement in this line and not elsewhere in the text. The logogram ERIN$_2$ can also be read as *ummānu*, "troops," and both readings occur in the body inscription. For instance, the literary context of the passage implies a reading of the sign as *ummānu* in lines 44 and 49; see the commentary to line 44. But from the immediate context of the attestation ERIN$_2$.MEŠ *Sutu* in line 15, which does not involve war or corvée, *ṣābu* is the more appropriate reading there. Given the martial context, both *ṣābu* and *ummānu* are possible readings of the sign in this line, so the phonetic complement may serve the purpose of disambiguation.

The precise meaning of "the land of Hatti" in the inscription is not immediately clear, so already Oller 1989, 197. It seems to designate both a geographically defined area and a political entity. The toponym appears first to designate a geographic area, since Idrimi takes troops and goes up to the land of Hatti, using the verb *elû*. The third and final attestation of *māt Hatte* also designates a geographic entity, because when Idrimi leaves it, he brings plunder down from it, using the verb *šūrudu* (l. 80). Within this frame, however, Hatti appears not as a geographical area but as a political entity, an agent that can act (or, more accurately, that chooses not to do so).

As for the location of the geographical area described twice by *māt Hatti*, von Dassow (2008, 37–38) suggested that the phrase describes Kizzuwatna, the region immediately to the north of the kingdom of Alalah-Mukiš. As she observed, Kizzuwatna

> had been subject to Hatti in the time of Hattušili I, recovered its independence once the Hittite Old Kingdom began its decline (late sixteenth century), then became subject to Mittani in the time of Idrimi (as indicated by AlT 3, discussed above); by the end of the fifteenth century Kizzuwatna had again become subject to Hatti, and it was annexed as a Hittite province in the early fourteenth century. Therefore, an invasion of Kizzuwatna could reasonably be represented as a campaign "against Hatti," especially from the standpoint of the fourteenth century.

In other words, Kizzuwatna is a suitable candidate for the descriptor *māt Hatti* because it was a Hittite province and because we know that the historical Idrimi had a conflict with Kizzuwatna. The location of Kizzuwatna also fits with the use of the verbs *elû* and *arādu* to describe Idrimi's movement to and from *māt Hatti*, and the toponyms in *māt Hatti* that Idrimi seized and that can be localized do seem to be in the area of southern Kizzuwatna/northern Mukiš; see the commentary to lines 66–68.

65. e-te-[l]i u$_3$ 7 URU.DIDLI.HI.⸢A *aṣ*⸣*-bat-šu-nu*

The verb *ēteli*, from *elû*, "to go up, go upstream, go north" has frequently been translated as "to attack, march against" in previous literature. This translation is not entirely inaccurate from a freer perspective, inasmuch as Idrimi does in fact attack Hittite settlements, but it misses the parallelism with line 80, where Idrimi refers to the prisoners and booty that he "brought down" (*ušēridu*) from the land of Hatti. In communicating movement northward, the verb *elû* not only places the action in a landscape but also reveals the author's own mental map.

The DIDLI sign is, in fact, an archaizing form of HAL. While the HAL sign can consist of only two successive horizontal wedges, so that it is identical to DIDLI (AŠ-AŠ) in the Late Bronze Age, older forms of these two signs were not similar; DIDLI was still composed of two successive horizontal wedges, but HAL was written with a horizontal wedge crossed by two oblique wedges—that is, it looked like AN without the vertical wedge. This sign is what we find in line 65 and in the two other attestations of the sign in lines 69 and 87, as shown in figure A.50. Despite the widespread acceptance that the three attestations of this sign are to be identified as DIDLI and not HAL, there has been little discussion of the phenomenon in the scholarly literature other than descriptive statements by Giacumakis (1970, 27) and Oller (1977a, 92–93). Possibly, the scribe was familiar with both the contemporary form of HAL written with only two successive horizontals, as well as the more archaic form with oblique wedges. Accordingly, he used the latter as an archaic form of DIDLI on the basis of the analogy of the identical, contemporary forms of the two signs. The unexpected form of DIDLI, then, may give us some insight into the creative process of composing and inscribing the sign forms.

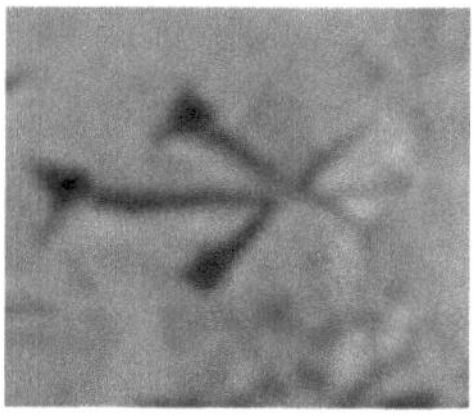

Figure A.50. DIDLI in line 65.

66–68. ^{uru}*pa-aš-ša-he*$_2$^{ki} ^{uru}*ta*$_2$*-ma-ru-ut-la*^{ki} ^{uru}*hu-luh-ha-an*^{ki} ^{uru}*zi-la*<$^{\text{ki uru}}$>*i-e*^{ki} ^{uru}*u*$_2$*-lu-zi-la*^{ki} *u*$_3$ ^{uru}⸢*za*⸣*-ru-na*^{ki}

Despite the fact that the URU determinative occurs only six times in lines 66–68, recognition that these lines contain seven toponyms goes back to Smith's (1949, 18) edition. He read the final two toponyms in line 67 as ^{al}*zi-***si**^{KI} *i-e*^{KI}, noting (21) that "the form interpreted as KI does not exactly resemble any other form; if it had a short oblique before the horizontal it would be a fairly common form." In this regard, he also remarked on the absence of an URU determinative before *I'e* and stated that he had originally considered taking "all the signs from *zi* to *e* inclusive as one name, thus securing *al* and KI the usual positions," but he observed that "there were two objections to this: the signs do not produce a credible geographical name, and the number of city names given is then six, not seven, as stated in 65." Kempinski and Na'aman (1973, 213) were the first to suggest emending the text to <uru>*i-e*; in my opinion, the likelihood of a scribal error increases with the identification of Smith's putative SI KI as a single sign, LA, so that the KI determinative after the toponym Zila has also been omitted; see the discussion below.

While many identifications and localizations have been offered for all seven toponyms, usually on the basis of perceived phonetic similarities to other ancient or modern toponyms, only I'e and Zaruna are clearly attested elsewhere and localizable in a general way. The first three toponyms, Paššahe, Tamarutla, and Huluhhan, as well as the sixth, Uluzila, are not attested outside of the body inscription.[65]

The fourth toponym, Zila, is also not attested elsewhere, but it requires a bit of clarification. The signs were identified as *zi-si*^ki by Smith, who was followed by many subsequent scholars, and this putative Zisi or Zise was identified with a toponym known as Sis in the Old Assyrian correspondence at Kanesh (Smith 1949, 78; Kühne 1982, 212) and Sissu in Neo-Assyrian royal inscriptions, which, in turn, has been equated with classical Sision and modern day Kozan in Cilicia;[66] with Zizziya, a settlement in Kizzuwatna attested in the Hittite treaty with Išmirikka;[67] or with classical Issos in the Gulf of Iskendrun;[68] see von Dassow 2008, 37 n. 89.

However, the identification of the signs as *zi-si*^ki cannot be maintained. As mentioned above, Smith already considered the form of the KI determinative to be unusual in the original edition, and Oller (1977a, 96) developed this observation. He remarked that "the KI sign after URU *Zi-si*, while not impossible, is extremely poor—especially when compared to the nicely made KI signs which follow all the other city names in the list—and the same observation might be made about the SI sign which precedes it"; see figure A.51 on the next page. Oller

---

65 Tamarutla is normalized with initial /t/ here because *tam(a)* seems to be a productive element in Anatolian/Hittite place names; see RGTC 6.1, 391–93 and RGTC 6.2, 157–58.

66 Smith 1949, 78–79; Astour 1965, 41; RGTC 7.1, s.v. "Sissû"; and RGTC 12.2, s.v. "Zisi."

67 Goetze 1950, 230 and Na'aman 1980b, 116; see RGTC 6.1, s.v. "Zijazija" (which does not mention the Idrimi text).

68 Gates 2000, 79.

made about the SI sign which precedes it"; see figure A.51 on the next page. Oller went on to suggest that Smith's two signs might be better taken as together as LA, pointing to the first LA sign in the toponym *Alalah* in line 58 as a parallel. Subsequently, Dietrich and Loretz (1981, 206) combined Kempinski and Na'aman's emendation, described above, with Oller's new identification of the sign as LA and took the next logical step, considering the determinative KI as well as the following URU to have been omitted from the text—that is, they emended to the text to ^{uru}*Zi-la*<^{ki} ^{uru}>*I-e*^{ki}.

Figure A.51. Smith's putative SI KI in line 67, better identified as LA.

Both the identification of Smith's SI KI as LA and these emendations have much to commend them. The putative SI is so small that it seems necessary to take it as one component of a larger sign and not as an independent sign; the height of signs is one aspect of the body inscription that is fairly consistent. And, as noted by Oller, the LA in line 58 does offer a close parallel, as do the LA signs in lines 31 and 78 (second LA). Dietrich and Loretz's emendations, furthermore, result in the expected number of seven, not six, toponyms in the list, and attestations of a settlement named I'e in texts other than the body inscription (see below) allow us to feel comfortable that we are not engaging in an exercise in tautology.

The toponym I'e is one of the two in the list of seven toponyms that is attested outside of the body inscription. It appears in the Level IV text *SSAU* 2 4 [492.31], a census list from Level IV Alalah that enumerates residents who are classified as *ṣābū namê* (i.e., a group comprising both *hupše* and *haniahhe*); see also Na'aman 1980b, 116. Although Klengel (1981, 278 with n. 62) first drew attention to the attestation of the toponym in the census list, that attestation has received almost no attention since, which may be because, as von Dassow (2008, 37 n. 89) pointed out, it is for some reason missing from both of the standard collections of toponyms in the Alalah texts; see Niedorf 1998 and RGTC 12.2. Since the fragment, which I have collated from a photograph, can be classified as a "Group A" census list, according to von Dassow's terminology, it dates to late in Niqmepa's reign (von Dassow 2008, 222), and we can conclude that the settlement formed part of the kingdom of Alalah-Mukiš at this time.

The final toponym, Zaruna, is the best attested of the seven because it appears in the Annals of Hattušili I, where it is destroyed by the Hittite king (KBo 10.1: obv. 31 and 10.2: ii 11–12). The campaign against Zaruna was immediately followed by a campaign against Haššuwa; see Oller 1977a, 87 for a detailed description of the campaigns. Haššuwa is identified with the toponym Haššum that occurs in Old Assyrian texts (sometimes written as Haššuwa) and texts from Mari (e.g., ARM 32: 252, recording the delivery of gifts from Anum-Hirbi, king of Haššum), and it seems to have been located in southwestern Anatolia (Barjamovic 2011, 201–2 with n. 756, also 207ff. on Anum-Hirbi). Accordingly, the town of Zaruna may have been in southwestern Anatolia as well. Possibly, Zaruna is to be identified with the toponym Saruna (Goetze 1950, 230), which is attested in an inscription of Tiglath-pileser III as one of the cities of the land of Bit-Agusi (RINAP 1 43: ii 5) and has been identified with Tall Ṣūrān, located about 22 km northwest of Aleppo; see the discussion in RGTC 7.1, s.v. "Saruna." This localization of Saruna is in harmony with the localizations of Zaruna that have been put forward on the basis of the Annals of Hattušili I and the location of Haššuwa.

In sum, only two of the toponyms in lines 66–68, I'e and Zaruna, are attested outside of the body inscription, and only Zaruna can be roughly localized. Its location does not contradict the suggestion that the geographic area designated by the "land of Hatti" should be identified with ancient Kizzuwatna (see the commentary to l. 64). And if the toponym I'e was located to the north of the kingdom of Alalah-Mukiš's northern border prior to its incorporation into the kingdom of Alalah-Mukiš during the reign of Niqmepa, its location would fall within Kizzuwatna as well. Therefore, von Dassow's suggestion, cited above, that the *māt Hatte* that Idrimi attacked refers to Kizzuwatna is supported to the extent possible and, just as importantly, not contradicted by the toponyms listed in lines 66–68.

69. an-mu-u$_2$ URU.DIDLI.HI.A *aṣ-bat-šu-nu u*$_3$ *ul-lu-u*$_2$

While *ullû*, "that," is a common deictic pronoun of distance in the standard Babylonian dialects, the deictic pronoun of proximity also occurring in this line, *anmû*, "this," is much rarer; the more common deictic pronoun of proximity is *annû*. The pronoun *anmû* also appears in line 90 of the body inscription, and both attestations are unusual for seeming to be singular in number where one expects a plural form; see, for example, the treaty between Tudhaliya II and Sunaššura of Kizzuwatna: URU.DIDLI.HI.A *an-mu-ut-tim*, "these cities" (KBo 1 5: i 14).

Despite the fact that *anmû* is a pronoun of proximity and *ullû* a pronoun of distance in almost all of the scholarship on this line, the two pronouns have often been taken in apposition and seen as referring to the same object—that is, the preceding seven cities. For instance, Oller (1977a, 14) translated "These (*anmû*) cities (under) their protection / I destroyed them (*ullû*)." Part of the issue is the signs following URU.DIDLI.HI.A, which, following Goetze (1950, 229) and prior to Dietrich and Loretz (1981, 206), most scholars identified as *ṣa-lul-šu-nu* and took as a by-form of *ṣalūlu*, "roof, protection." As discussed in the commentary to line 42, Dietrich and Loretz established that what had been taken as an independent ZA sign was in fact the initial component of AZ as it is formed consistently in the body inscription. Accordingly, they identified the signs as *aṣ-bat-šu-nu*.

Recognizing the verb *ṣabātu*, "to seize" in line 69 is important because the subsequent verb in line 70 is a form of *hepû*, "to break, destroy," and the contrast between seizing and destroying implies a contrast between *anmû* and *ullû* as well. However, it is only in the edition of Durand (2011, 144) that we see the possibility that the words could actually be in juxtaposition, not apposition. Durand translated "ces diverses villes-là j'annexai; lors, d'autres / ayant forcées," remarking in his note to the line (n. 169): "La différence de traitement est que certaines de celles qui ont été emportées de vive force (*hepûm*) sont gardées (*ṣabâtum*, donc annexées), les autres étant apparemment simplement pillés." In other words, understanding that the pronouns contrast makes clear that the inscription is emphasizing that the seven named settlements were actually annexed; the fact that at least one settlement, I'e (see note to l. 67), formed part of the kingdom of Alalah-Mukiš during the reign of Niqmepa makes this statement even more meaningful.

If Durand's interpretation of *anmû* as the deictic pronoun of proximity and *ullû* as the deictic pronoun of distance is insightful, his decision to translate *anmû* as attributive is open to question. He is not alone in this decision. There is a distinct tendency in later scholarship, beginning with Oller's (1977a, 14) edition, to translate *anmû* as modifying URU.DIDLI.HI.A; to my knowledge, the only exception after Oller's edition is Liverani's (2014, 333) translation: "these were their cities and these I destroyed." The tendency is noteworthy because, prior to Oller's edition, the word was typically taken in the scholarship as a substantive.[69] While an adjective being used attributively can precede the noun it modifies in elevated or poetic registers of Akkadian,[70] the other examples of attributive adjectives in the body inscription all follow the nouns they modify. Furthermore, substantival use in a nominal sentence results in the expected case (although not number). Therefore, the earlier scholars seem to be correct; because *anmû* precedes URU.DIDLI.HI.A, it should be used substantively. In an attributive use, it should follow the noun it modifies and be marked for a different case; cf. URU.DIDLI.HI.A *an-mu-ut-tim* in the Sunaššura treaty cited above. Note also that *anmû* is used substantively in its other attestation in the inscription (l. 90). However, unless one takes *ullû* as an example of *casus pendens*, this word is marked with an unexpected ending for its case as well as its number.

70. eh-te-pi$_3$*-šu-nu-ti ma-at* ⸢*ha*⸣*-at-te*^{ki}

The verb *ehtepišunūti*, written as *eh-te-pi*$_3$*-šu-nu-ti*, is unique in the inscriptions for two reasons. First, the spelling represents the only time in the inscriptions that the syllable /pi/ is written with BAD. The four other occurrences are written with BI, including one that occurs in an instance of dittography; see the commentary to l. 93 below). Second, the accusative pronominal suffix *-šunūti* is the only example of this standard Babylonian form in the inscription, which otherwise uses the short form *-šunu* exclusively.

---

[69] See, e.g., Greenstein and Marcus 1976, 88: "These are the towns under their (the Hittites') protection," following earlier scholarship in reading the signs taken here as *aṣbatšunu* instead of *ṣalūlšunu*, "their protection," as described above.

[70] See, e.g., *li-kun-ma an-nu-u*$_2$ *zi-kir-šu*, "may this name of his be permanent," MC 16 126: 54 (reference courtesy Martin Worthington).

71. u$_2$-ul ip-hur u$_3$ a-na ⸢UGU-*ia*⸣ *u$_2$-ul il-li-ku*

Because the preceding verb *iphur* is singular with *māt Hatte*, some scholars have interpreted the /u/ suffix on *illikū* as one of the examples of an indicative verb with "an inappropriately applied subjunctive suffix" (Greenstein and Marcus 1976, 79). I follow Dietrich and Loretz (1981, 223) in understanding the text as shifting its representation of "the land of Hatti" from a collective to a multiplicity; see the commentary to line 20 (*ašbū*). Note also that in the following line (line 72) we meet a plural referent again in the pronominal possessive suffix found on the recitation of the booty that Idrimi takes: he captured "their prisoners" (*šallātešunu*), not "its (the land of Hatti's) prisoners."

72. ša ŠA$_3^{bi}$*-ia e-te-pu-*⸢*uš šal*⸣*-la-te.*HI.A*-šu-nu*

The secondary literature is split as to whether *šallātu* is a general term for booty or refers to human captives. In the end, the answer seems to revolve around the relationship between *šallātešunu* and the three other types of goods that Idrimi pillages, which are identified in the following line as *namkūrīšunu*, *būšēšunu*, and *bāšītušunu*. Supporters of the interpretation of *šallātu* as a general term for booty see this subsequent list of three words as specifying what makes up the more general designation *šallātu*, while supporters of *šallātu* as a term for human captives see "the division of booty by the scribe into two distinct groups—human (*šallatu*—prisoners-of-war) and inanimate objects (*namkūru*, *būšu*, and *bāšītu*)" (Oller 1977a, 102). The key to understanding that *šallātu* refers here to human captives lies, in my opinion, in the repetition of all four words in lines 78–79. In those lines, however, *šallātu* is now coordinated with a new noun, *maršītu*, which should mean "livestock" in that context (see the commentary to l. 79), while the following three nouns are coordinated together. This arrangement makes clear that we are dealing with a contrast between animate and inanimate plunder in lines 78–79, and by extension in lines 72–73 as well.

73. aš$^!$-lu-ul-ma nam-ku-ri-šu-⸢*nu bu*⸣*-še-šu-nu ba-ši-tu-*<*šu*>*-nu*

There are two epigraphic oddities in the line. At the beginning of the line, even if the uppermost horizontal wedge is damaged, it is clear that the sign AŠ consists of two superimposed horizonal wedges, instead of a single horizontal wedge, as shown in figure A.52. At the end of the line, the final inscribed two signs, TU and NU, are written on the other side of a large break so that there is a significant gap between ŠI and TU; see §3.4 with figure 3.8. As discussed there, the placement of these signs is some of the best evidence for preexisting damage to the statue, before it was inscribed. The emendation at the end of the line may

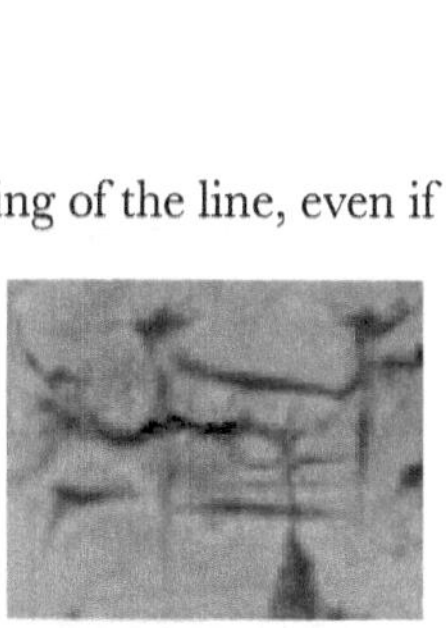

Figure A.52. AŠ$^!$ Followed by LU in line 73.

perhaps be explained as haplography with the second part of TU having been read as ŠU so that the mason inscribed NU immediately after TU instead of inscribing ŠU. Possibly the odd placement of the line contributed in some way to this error.

With regard to the sequence of nouns *namkūrīšunu būšēšunu bašītu<šu>nu*, the question is whether these three words are being used as synonyms in order to convey a sense of totality through repetition,[71] or whether there is a meaningful distinction between the three words that the text is trying to communicate. Many scholars have simply translated these three words with three different words in the target language without much thought about this question.[72] To my knowledge, the only scholar to have taken seriously the idea that the text is specifying three different types of property is Smith in the original edition. Smith (1949, 21) translated the words as "trade goods, household goods, and personal possessions," and he discussed the meanings of all three words in a lengthy note to the glossary entries for *būšu* and *bašītu*.

In my opinion, a survey of attestations of these nouns in other second-millennium corpora suggests that the three nouns refer to valuable inanimate property more than staple goods such as grain, but they otherwise overlap semantically and are synonymous. Their nature as valuable items can be seen in a letter from Mari where a lying merchant claims that his *bašītu* consisted of 30 minas of bronze, 20 minas of *šakattum*-garments, 3 bronze spears, 60 pieces of linen, and 10 donkeys.[73] Meanwhile, the overlap of *bāšītu* and *būšu* is evident in another Mari letter, where the writer states: *i-na-an-na* KU$_3$.BABBAR-*šu* KU$_3$.GI-*su*$_2$ *u*$_3$ *ba-ši-is-su*$_2$ *la-ma a-ṣa-ab-ba-tu-šu-ma šu-*[*s*]*u*$_2$ *i-na bu-še-e qa-ti-šu ša u*$_2$*-še-ṣu*$_2$*-u*$_2$, "Now, as for his silver, his gold, and his *bāšītum*, even before I seized him, they were (already) confiscated from the *būšu* available to him that I was going to confiscate" (ARM 28 105: rev. 27′–28′).

In a marriage contract from Level IV Alalah, AlT 94 [33.4]: 21–23, *būšu* is also used as an umbrella term for valuable items. The stipulation determines who gets to keep the silver of the bride price (designated by the Hurrian word *waturanni* as opposed to the Akkadian word *terhatu*) and other items designated by the

71 See, e.g., *CAD* 21, s.v. "zâzu," 5a: "whatever goods (and) personal possessions they (had)."

72 A good example is found in *CAD* 2, s.v. "bāšītu," 1d, where the editors translated "their goods, their possessions, and their valuables," while in the same volume s.v. "būšu" usage b-2, they translated "their property, valuables, goods," so that the word used to translate *namkūru* s.v. "bāšītu," 1d is used to translate *bašītu* s.v. "būšu," b-2′, and the word used to translate *bašītu* s.v. "bašītu" mng. 1d is used to translate *būšu* s.v. "būšu," b-2′.

73 A.2500+: obv. 3–13; see Durand 1990, 75–77 and LAPO 18 61 [no. 926]. Note that, while this enumeration of a *bāšītu* includes donkeys, these donkeys seem to be connected to the transport of the merchandise. Although cf. FM 3 136: 14, where the *bašītu* of a Sim'alite Hana who is absent without leave is said to consist of two hundred sheep and five donkeys.

Akkadian word *unūtu* in the event of divorce. These objects are then described as a collective by the word *būšu*; see Niedorf 2008, 294–95, citing previous literature. Meanwhile, an overlap of *unūtu* with the last of the three words, *namkūru*, is evident in the treaty of the citizens of Ugarit with the merchants of Carchemish, where *namkūru* is repeatedly used together with *unūtu* to describe what needs to be reimbursed by Ugarit if merchants of Carchemish bearing the "tribute" (*mandatti*) of Ugarit are killed.[74]

Of course, this brief survey may well gloss over local differences or nuances in the meaning of the words *namkūru*, *būšu*, and *bāšītu* that could have existed even at a single time and place. But the impression that one gets is that the list is intended to comprise three general synonyms for valuable inanimate objects, and that the emphasis may be on three synonyms because these items are distributed to three different groups in lines 74–76.

74. el-te-qe$_2$ *u*$_3$ *u*$_2$*-za-iz a-n*[*a*] ⸢ERIN$_2$⸣.MEŠ *til-la-ti-ia*

While the form *zâzu* in the D stem, *uza'iz*, in which the middle radical is an *aleph*, is found in the standard Akkadian dialects, Aro (1954, 363) noted that this form is characteristic of Middle Babylonian but not Old Babylonian, where the D stem is inflected as a weak verb. Aro cited only *GAG* (§104r) in support of this claim, where we find the statement that in "aB [Old Babylonian] war die Flexion anscheinend noch schwach."[75] The inflection of *zâzu* as a strong verb in the D stem is noteworthy in the context of Greenstein and Marcus's (1976, 62) statement that "the inscription of Idrimi shows no particular acquaintance with Middle Babylonian," pointing to the absence of the sound changes /w/ > /m/ and /št/ > /lt/.

The reading ⸢ERIN$_2$⸣.MEŠ *til-la-ti-ia* goes back to Smith's corrigenda to the 1949 edition and has been accepted by all scholars. There is also remarkable consistency, with two exceptions (discussed below), in translating the phrase as "auxiliary troops." But this translation provokes questions. What is the main body of troops to which these are auxiliaries? Why does Idrimi not share the plunder with the main body of troops as well? Why should auxiliary troops mentioned before the "brothers" and "comrades" in the list of recipients?

Some scholars have noted that the phrase *ṣābū tillati* occurs in texts from Mari and in Amarna letters sent by Levantine rulers to the pharaoh. In the Amarna correspondence, the attestations of *ṣābū tillatu* designate local, Levantine troops that can be called on for support or mobilized by Egyptian commissioners, as distinct from the *ṣābū piṭṭāti*, the regular Egyptian army that periodically campaigned (or did not) in the Levant. This meaning is difficult to apply to the situation in line 74 of the body inscription. In the Mari texts, *ṣābū tillati* means

---

[74] PRU 4 154–57 [RS 17.146]: 9, 15, 17, 24, 31, 41.

[75] Citing "das Pf. *uzzīz* VAB VI 234, 13." But that form, when republished in AbB 2 159, was reread as *us-zi-iz* by its editor (Frankena) and interpreted as a Š preterite (i.e., *ušzīz*).

troops provided by an ally. Thus, when Hammurabi of Babylon attacked Larsa not just with his own army but also troops from Yamhad and Mari, those latter two contingents were his *ṣābū tillati*. This meaning seems to be adopted for the phrase in line 74 by Durand (2011, 144) and Bonechi (2019, 80), who translated "aux troupes de mes alliés" and "le truppe dei miei alleati," respectively. This interpretation is tentatively adopted here, too, because it solves the problem of why the *ṣābū tillati* appear first in the list of the recipients of plunder, in that it would be appropriate to honor the troops of one's allies first. However, the further question arises of who exactly these allies were who provided Idrimi with the troops. The text makes no mention of any allies in its earlier descriptions of the campaign.

75. $^{\text{lu}_2\text{.meš}}$*ah-he*$_2$.HI.A-*ia*

This line is one of the shortest in the inscription, consisting of only seven signs, because the lines below it (both the signs and the rulings) curve up and into what would be its space in order to compensate for having less surface to inscribe on the statue's shoulder. This observation suggests that the mason already knew that he would have less space for line 75 and thus ended this line after only seven signs.

In contrast to the references to brothers in the episode of Idrimi's wandering (see the commentaries to ll. 8 and 39), it is unclear whether the "brothers" in this line should be understood biologically or in an extended or metaphorical sense (e.g., to indicate a peer ruler). In either case, the position of the "brothers" after the *ṣābū tillati* is noteworthy because we might expect Idrimi's brothers, whether biological or his peers, to appear first, as discussed in the commentary to line 74.[76]

76. u$_3$ $^{\text{lu}_2\text{.meš}}$*ib-ru-te*.HI.A-*ia ka-ka*$_4$*-šu-nu-ma*

The interpretation of the sign string IB-*ru-te* as a plural form of *ibru*, "friend, colleague," was first suggested by Albright (1950, 18) and has been followed by all subsequent scholars. There has been almost no discussion, however, of who these "friends" were, why they appear at the end of the listing of "allies' troops" and "brothers," and whether the term designates some sort of formal or informal social-political group or, rather, individuals with whom Idrimi had a close personal relationship. To my knowledge, the only exception is Oller's (1977a, 110) remark in his comment to the word *tappūte* in line 83 that this word is "a good synonym to *ibru*" and that "if the reading of ŠEŠ is correct in line 82, a parallelism exists with lines 75–76—LÚ.MEŠ *ahhē* and LÚ.MEŠ *ibrūte* parallel LÚ.MEŠ.ŠEŠ.MEŠ and LÚ.MEŠ *tappūte*.HI.A."

---

[76] In one vein of scholarship on these lines, only the *ṣābū tillati* is taken as the direct object of *uzaʾʾiz*; *ahhēya* and *ibrūteya* (l. 76) are taken as the direct objects of *elteqe*. However, this interpretation depends on reading the signs at the end of line 76 as *qa*$_3$*-du-šu-nu-ma* instead of *ka-ka*$_4$*-šu-nu-ma*; see the commentary to line 76 in §A.2.

This comment is astute. The words *ahu* and *ibru* occur together in Mesopotamian texts,[77] and the lexical heading to *CAD* 7, s.v. "ibru" shows that *ibru* and *tappû* were regularly equated in Mesopotamian lexical and synonym lists. Indeed, the discussion section of this article specifies that "the term occurs after the OB period … mostly in the hendiadys *ibru u tappû*." The terms are used as synonyms in a number of Mesopotamian literary texts, including the Epic of Gilgamesh; for example, ^{d}*en-ki-du*$_3$ *ib-ri li-iṣ-ṣur tap-pa-a li-šal-lim*, "Enkidu should protect (his) comrade, he should keep (his) companion safe!" (SB Gilg. III 9; see also the discussion in §4.2).

Interestingly, this awareness of the interchangeability of *ibru* and *tappû* is found in other western hybrid Akkadian texts from the Levant. For instance, in EA 126: 16 [Byblos], Rib-Addi uses the word *ibru* in apposition to *hazannu*, the typical term for the Levantine rulers, while he uses the word *tappû* in this same sense in another letter (EA 113: 30). In sum, one has the sense that *ibru* in line 76 reflects less some sociopolitical reality and more a literary association, in which the word was placed in apposition with *ahu*, on the one hand, and substituted for *tappû*, on the other.

The identification of the sign following KA as QA and not DU follows Dietrich and Loretz (1981, 206), as does the reading of the sign string as *ka-ka*$_4$*-šu-nu-ma* against the readings *qa*$_3$*-du-šu-nu-ma* or *qa*$_3$*-tu*$_3$*-šu-nu-ma* that are found in earlier literature. Collation of the sign, depicted in figure A.53, shows it to clearly be QA and not DU. This reading has also been adopted by Durand (2011, 145) and Bonechi (2019, 80). Interestingly, however, Dietrich and Loretz, Durand, and Bonechi all translate *kakkašunuma* as plural despite the fact that the word is clearly marked as singular. And Idrimi's reason for taking the weapons is different in each of the three editions. For Dietrich and Loretz (1981, 223), the weapons were intended for the royal army; for Durand (2011, 145 n. 170), as votive offerings; and for Bonechi (2019, 80), as trophies. If the reading *ka-ka*$_4$*-šu-nu-ma* is correct, the singular form should not simply refer to the weapons of the various members of the land of Hatti, because the other objects that Idrimi took from them in lines 72–73 are explicitly plural (putting aside the difficult form *ba-ši-tu-*<*šu*>*-nu* and noting that the objects are in the singular when they appear again in ll. 78–79). Therefore, one imagines that the singular number of *kakku* is significant and related to Idrimi's reason for taking it, especially in connection with the 3mp possessive pronominal suffix ("their weapon"), but the significance is obscure.

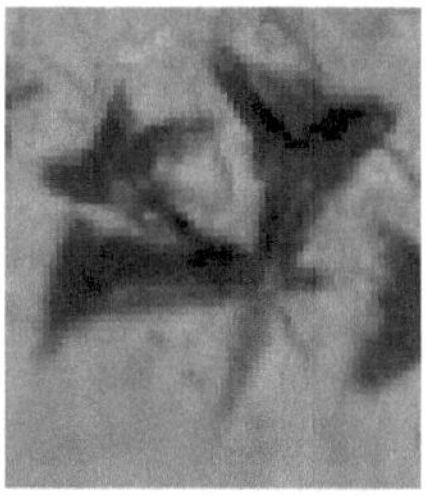

Figure A.53. QA (*ka*$_4$) in line 76.

[77] See, e.g., the Old Babylonian Hymn to Ištar (PBS 1/1 2: ii 29), cited in *CAD* 7, s.v. "ibru," usage c-1′.

78. u$_3$ *e-ru-ub a-na* ^{uru}*a-la-la-ah*^{ki} URU.KI-*ia i-na šal-la-ti*$_3$

The UB sign lacks an interior vertical wedge, similar to the form of the sign in line 36 and in contrast to the form of the sign in line 16, which has the expected interior wedge (see figure A.54). Smith (1949) explained the defective form in the corrigenda as follows: "The sign read *ub* in line 78 was intended for HI, a mason's error in reading HI.A." Because the signs UB and HI are so similar, the mason misinterpreted the uncommon sequence of signs UB A as the common plural determinative HI.A, so he carved HI in place of UB. (I am grateful to Martin Worthington for explaining Smith's explanation to me.) This error may offer an important insight into the process by which the inscription was carved onto the statue.

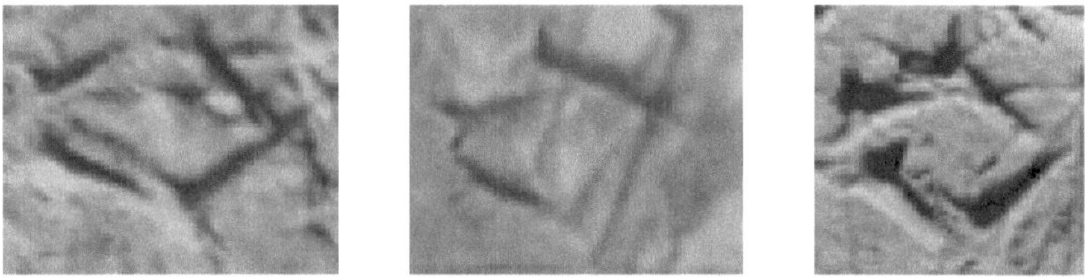

Figure A.54. Juxtaposition of attestations of UB in lines 16 (left), 36 (center), and 78 (right).

If the previous attestation of *šallatu* in line 72 was clearly marked as plural by the plural determinative HI.A, the attestation of *šallatu* in this line seems to be clearly marked as singular, as much by the use of the final CVC sign -*tim* to mark the case ending as by the absence of the plural determinative. A singular form seems necessary also because the word is coordinated with *maršīti* (l. 79), which is unambiguously singular; see the commentary to line 79.

79. u$_3$ *i-na mar-ši-ti*$_3$ *i-na nam-ku-ri i-na bu-ši*$_2$ *u*$_3$ *i*$^{!}$*-na ba-ši-tu*$_2$$^{!?}$

The noun *maršītu* is the only one of the four types of plunder listed in lines 78–79 that does not also appear in the list of plunder in lines 72–73. Etymologically, the word is a *maprast*-formation noun from **ršʾ*, "to acquire," hence the translations of the word one can find in some editions as "property, possessions" more generally. However, the word *maršītu* can also have the specific sense of "flocks, wealth in cattle" (*CAD* 10.1, s.v. "maršītu," 2). Although *CAD* 10.1 did *not* include the line under discussion under this meaning, to my knowledge the dictionary was the first to suggest that the word had this sense in the earlier volume *CAD* 1.2, s.v. "arādu" A, 3a-2′("flocks"), and it is found in a number of other translations as well.

In my opinion, the best reason to see *maršītu* having the sense "flocks" in this line comes from the syntax and especially the use of conjunctions. Paradoxically, Oller (1977a) used this same reasoning to argue that the word must have the sense "property." In a note to his comment on the line (105 n. 1), he argued that the *u* at the beginning of line 79 did not mark a separation between clauses; rather, "the actual purpose of this *u* seems to be to divide the booty between animate (prisoners) and inanimate (goods etc)"—that is, between animate *šallatu* and four inanimate types of plunder that follow (*animate* vs. [*u*] *inanimate-inanimate-inanimate-*and [*u*]-*inanimate*). In fact, the conjunctions in line 79 seem to be used to coordinate between like types of plunder (*animate*-and (*u*)-*animate* vs. *inanimate-inanimate*-and (*u*)-*inanimate*). This interpretation feels more natural because we then find the conjunction, as expected, before the final item, whether the list consists of two items or three items. Accordingly, *maršītu* should be an animate noun: "flocks."

Like the noun *šal-la-ti*$_3$ in the previous line, the nouns written as *nam-ku-ri* and *bu-ši*$_2$ can be singular or plural. They are taken as singular here because *maršīti* is clearly singular. The final noun in the line, *ba-ši-tu*$_2^{!?}$, is also clearly singular, but it is also singular in the list of plunder in lines 72–73, where it is written as *ba-ši-tu-*<*šu*>*-nu*, the difficult form that is both not in accordance with the standard Akkadian dialects and requires emendation; see the commentary to line 73. The form of the word in this line and in particular the identification of the final sign are also difficult and have generated much literature; see figure A.55. Smith (1949, 20) identified it as UD with the value *tu*$_2$, remarking (30) that the phrase normalized by him as *ina bašitu* was one of the only examples of the incorrect use of a case in the text. From this comment one can infer that there seems never to have been any doubt in Smith's mind as to the sign's identification as UD. However, a number of scholars have read the sign as TI instead of UD, which has the benefit of resulting in the correct case for the noun after the preposition *ina*. Oller's (1977a, 104–5) discussion is of the sign is measured. His collation of the sign was inconclusive, and he noted:

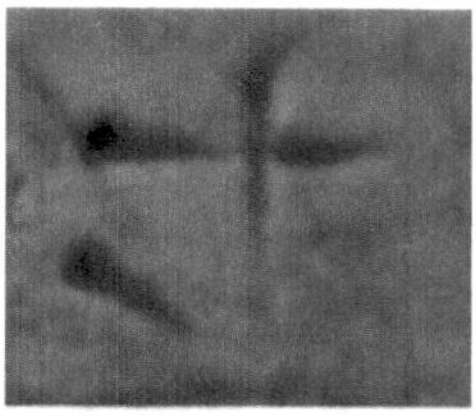

Figure A.55. UD$^{!?}$(*tu*$_2$) in line 79.

> grammatically *bāšītu* should be in the genitive case, and the scribe did put the other nouns in the sequence in the correct case. Unfortunately, this cannot be too strongly emphasized because in line 73, we have *namkūrišunu* and *bušēšunu*, but clearly *bašitu*<*š*>*unu* [*sic*]. Epigraphically the sign is not a good TI because it is missing the winkelhocken at the end. Also, the TÚ in this text is normally drawn like the ERÍN sign…, but note that here the broken vertical is lacking.

After considering these issues, Oller chose to identify the sign as TI$^{!}$.

However, one approach to understanding the form that has not hitherto been mentioned is by comparison with the immediately preceding sign, IGI(*ši*). This sign is not written with superimposed vertical wedges, and it may have influenced the form of the subsequent sign in what may be described as an example of visual dittography. For that reason, I tentatively prefer to identify the sign as a defective UD rather than a defective TI even if this identification results in an unexpected case vowel, especially since the same unexpected case vowel occurs on the same word in line 73.

The defective UD sign is not the only epigraphic issue in this line. Just four signs earlier, an additional vertical wedge has been added to the I sign that forms part of the preposition *ina*, shown in figure A.56. It looks like the mason had begun to carve IA and stopped when he realized the error; see already Smith 1949, 20 ("an unnecessary perpendicular: mason's error").

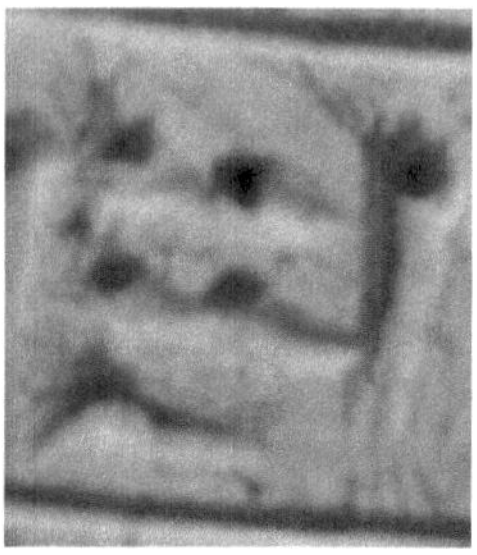

Figure A.56. Defective I in line 79.

80. ša iš-tu ma-at ha-at-te^{ki} *u*$_2$*-še-ri-du* E$_2$ *uš*$_{10}$*-te-pi*$_2$*-iš*

As discussed in the commentary to line 65 above, the verb *šūrudu* is used as a complement to *elû* earlier in the inscription. Whereas Idrimi and his army first "went up" (i.e., ascended to higher ground or went northward) in order to attack "the land of Hatti," so on the return he brought his captives and booty "down" (i.e., descended to lower ground or went southward).[78]

This line contains the first attestation of the sign UZ with the value *uš*$_{10}$ in a form of *epēšu*; two other attestations occur in line 90. Smith (1949, 27) identified the sign as UH$_2$ and remarked, "ÚH is presumably to be read *uš*," looking to Old Assyrian texts for parallels. Smith's identification was uniformly adopted over the next few decades, with the sign UH$_2$ given the value *uš*$_x$. However, several scholars pointed out that the three attestations of the sign are actually a mix of UH$_2$ and

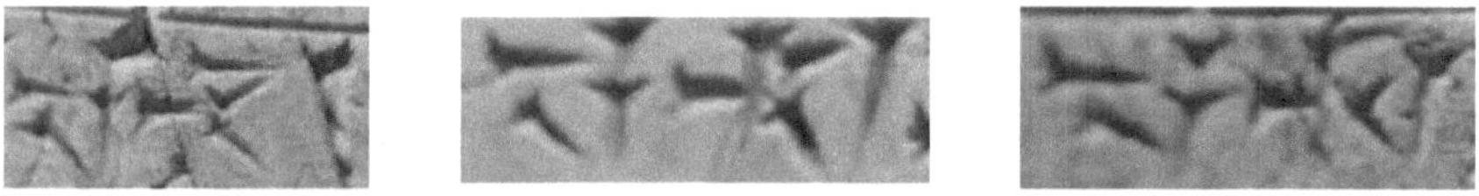

Figure A.57. UZ Formed as UD + HU in lines 80 (left), 90 (first attestation in center, second attestation on right).

[78] See, similarly, Smith 1949, 21: "I brought down" (but cf. the sense of the verb in glossary [97]: "to send southwards"); *CAD* 1.2, s.v "arādu A," 3a, "to bring or send down to lower ground"-2′, "merchandise, booty, object" (cf. mng. 3e. "to take downstream"); and the translation and remarks of Durand (2011, 145): "que l'on avait ramenés du pays de Hatti vers la plaine," with n. 172: "En m. à m.: 'qu'ils avaient fait descendre.'" Le pays hittite est compris comme la région des montagnes qui dominent la plaine syrienne."

UZ because UH$_2$ = UD + KUŠU$_2$ and UZ = ŠE + HU, while the signs inscribed on the statue are UD + HU (see figure A.57). Yet a manuscript of Paleographic S^a from Ugarit has this same form and demonstrates that UD could be the first component of an archaizing form of UZ, as shown in figure A.58 (see Roche-Hawley 2024).[79] Therefore the signs in question in the body inscription can be identified as UZ(*uš*$_{10}$) and not UH$_2$(*uš*$_x$).

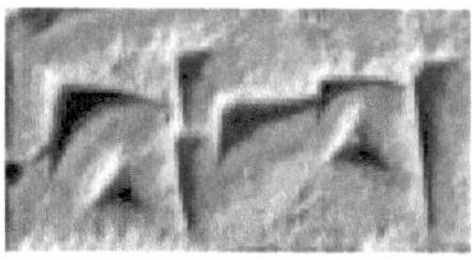

Figure A.58. UZ in RS 14.128+. Courtesy C. Roche-Hawley.

81. ^{giš}GU.ZA-*ia ki-ma* GU.ZA.MEŠ *ša* LUGAL.MEŠ *u*$_2$*-ma-ši-il*

The determinative GIŠ is present before the first occurrence of *kussû* in the line but absent before the second attestation. Note the presence and absence of the determinative in the two writings of *kussû* (^{giš}GU.ZA-*ia* … GU.ZA.MEŠ). Some scholars have emended the text to provide the second attestation with the determinative—that is, <^{giš}>GU.ZA.MEŠ. But the emendation is unnecessary and obscures the fact that the text consistently provides alternate spellings of the same word with and without a determinative; see, for example, both $^{lu_2.meš}$ŠEŠ.MEŠ-*ia* and ŠEŠ.MEŠ and also $^{lu_2.meš}$*tap-pu-te*.HI.A-*ia*-and *tap-pu-te*.HI.A-*šu-nu* in the very next two lines, as well as ALAM-*ia* and ^{d}ALAM (ll. 92, 99) and DUB.SAR and ^{lu_2}DUB.SAR (ll. 98–99) later in the body inscription; see the discussion of orthographic variation in §4.1.

Almost all scholars have taken the verb *umaššil* as 1cs, except for Durand (2011, 145), who translated “Mon trône fut l’égal des trônes des (autres) rois”; see the commentary to line 84 for discussion of the syntax of *muššulu*.

82. $^{lu_2.meš}$ŠEŠ.MEŠ-*ia ki-ma* ŠEŠ.MEŠ *ša* ⸢LUGAL⸣.MEŠ DUMU.MEŠ-*ia*

On the writing of *ahu*, “brother,” with and without a determinative, see the commentary to line 81 (*kussû*).

83. ki-ma DUMU.MEŠ-*šu-nu u*$_3$ $^{lu_2.meš}$*tap-pu-te*.HI.A-*ia ki*$^!$(U$_3$)-<*ma*> *tap-pu-te*.HI.A-*šu*-⸢*nu*⸣

On the writing of *tappû*, “companion,” with and without a determinative, see the commentary to line 81 (*kussû*). For *tappû* as a synonym to *ibru* in line 75, see the commentary to that line.

Somewhat unexpectedly, the inscription has a clear U$_3$ sign where we expect *ki-ma* in light of the previous prepositional statements (see figure A.59 on the next page). This form of U$_3$, in which the initial component is a *Winkelhaken* instead of IGI, is common in the body inscription. Has there been a scribal error, or does

[79] See *Ugaritica* 5 205: iii 84, although note that the tablet is published there as RS 20.135.

IGI, is common in the body inscription. Has there been a scribal error, or does the conjunction *u* have an unusual sense here? While Smith (1949, 99 s.v. "u") preferred the latter option ("between two accusatives governed by *mašalu* II with the same sense as *kima*"), the other scholars who have taken the time to comment on the form have considered the possibility of a scribal error for *ki-ma*. In particular, Durand (2011, 146) suggested, "il vaut mieux le comprendre comme un *ki-ma* incomplet, le *-ma* n'ayant pas été noté par le scribe." This suggestion seems plausible and can be developed a bit further. The signs KI and U$_3$ are not dissimilar, and U$_3$ also appears (correctly) earlier in this same line. Therefore, from a mechanical perspective, the error is explainable as an instance whereby the preceding U$_3$ was miscopied in place of KI. Cf. line 86, where the reverse is true, and it seems that KI has been copied in place of an intended U$_3$.

Figure A.59. U$_3$ in error for KI in line 83.

84. u$_2$-ma-ši-lu-u$_2$-šu-nu TUŠ.MEŠ *ša a-na* ŠA$_3^{bi}$ *ma-ti-ia*^{ki}

The attestation of *muššulu* in this line differs from the other two attestations of the verb in lines 81 and 87 in two ways: it has an /u/ suffix, and there is a 3mp pronominal suffix. Most of the scholars who have discussed the /u/ suffix have taken it to be an example of the suffix that is interpreted as "indicative" /u/ or a misuse of the subordinate marker. Medill (2019, 249 n. 41) suggested that, if the attestations of *kīma* in lines 82–83 were subordinating conjunctions instead of prepositions, perhaps the /u/ could be understood as an expected use of the subordination marker. However, she did not offer a translation, and it is difficult to make the syntax work.

Durand (2011, 145–46) offered the major departure from the consensus view. He took as a series of three nominal clauses ("mes 'frères' [furent] comme les 'frères' des rois; mes administrateurs [furent] comme leurs administrateurs et messieurs mes 'compagnons' [furent] comme leurs 'compagnons'") that is followed in line 84 by a clause consisting of only *muššulu*, "Ils s'égalèrent eux." (Similarly, he understood the form *umaššil* in line 81 to be 3cs, not 1cs, translating "Mon trône fut l'égal des trônes des (autres) rois.") In other words, he interpreted the verb in line 84 as 3mp, thus explaining the /u/ suffix as well as the appearance of the 3mp pronominal suffix. As a crucial component of this interpretation, he argued that, when *muššulu* takes a direct object or is followed by *ana*, it must have the meaning "to be equal to X," as opposed to when the object takes *kīma*, when it can mean "to make like X."

Durand's analysis is insightful and can be developed still further. The verb *muššulu* certainly can have meaning "to be equal to X"; see *CAD* 10.1, s.v. "mašālu," 5, where the one parallel that Durand cited ("*ûl umaššilû-ka* = 'ils ne peuvent pas rivaliser avec toi!'") is listed. But, in fact, an example, taken from Old

Babylonian Agušaya, of *muššulu* construed with *kīma* is also included there among the other attestations of the verb with this meaning. In other words, the use of *kīma* as opposed to *ana* (in the case of a verb with two arguments) or an object in the accusative (in the case of a single argument) does not need to be as determinative of whether *muššulu* is transitive or intransitive as Durand would have it.

One is left with the impression that Durand was actually most concerned with the pronominal suffix on the verb in line 84, which he took as accusative. Accordingly, he focused on the other attestation of the verb with a pronominal suffix that he cited in his note. Because this attestation of *muššulu* + accusative suffix is used with a single argument, he tried to understand *umaššilūšunu* as a verb with a single argument as well. However, in western hybrid Akkadian texts, the short form of the 3mp suffix -*šunu* can serve as a dative pronominal suffix as well as an accusative one; for example, *la-a ia-di-nu-šu-nu* $^{\ulcorner m \urcorner}$*ia-pa*-^{d}ISKUR *a-la-ka*$_{13}$, "Yapa'-Baʿlu /Haddu does not allow them to go (lit. does not grant going to them)" (EA 114: 58–59 [Byblos]). Therefore, the pronominal suffix on *muššulu* can resume the indirect objects introduced by *kīma*, and there is no need to understand *umaššilūšunu* as its own clause with a single argument. Indeed, the abbreviation of the phrase *ša* ⌜LUGAL⌝.MEŠ after the first indirect object to just -*šunu* after the second and third direct objects may have primed the verb for the resumptive pronoun.

The sign in line 84 identified here as TUŠ was read by Smith (1949, 20) as SU. Dietrich and Loretz (1966, 556) were the first to offer a new identification, which has been accepted by most subsequent scholars with little discussion other than Oller's (1977a, 110–11) comment that "epigraphically SÚ or KU are both possible readings for the sign and a determination must be made on the basis of other criteria." After collation, two observations can be made about the sign read as TUŠ (= KU) in this line and twice in the following line (see fig. A.60). First, all three signs have a different form. Second, only the second occurrence of the sign in line 85 looks like KU as it is typically written in the inscription. The form of the other two attestations of the sign is quite noteworthy because KU is otherwise one of the most consistently formed signs in the inscription.

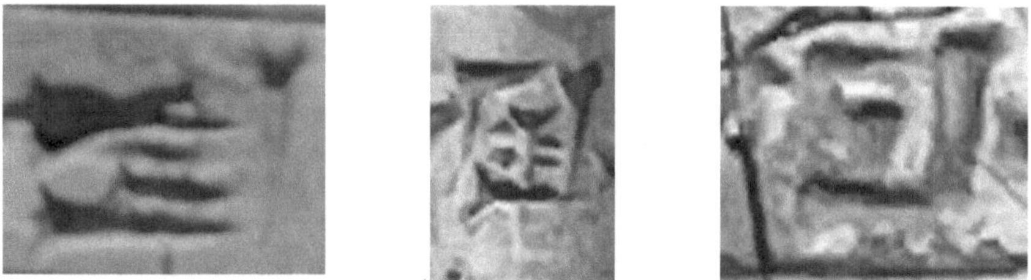

Figure A.60. TUŠ (= KU) in lines 84 (left) and 85 (first attestation in center, second attestation on right).

85. KI.TUŠ-*šu*-⸢*nu*? *ne*$_2$?⸣-*eh*?-*ta*$_5$ *u*$_2$-*še*-*ši*-*ib*-*šu*-*nu* *ša* KI.TUŠ *la u*$_2$-*uš*-*ša*-*bu*

Smith (1949, 20, 101 s.v. "ṭābu") identified the signs following the first occurrence of KI.TUŠ as -*šu*-⸢*nu*⸣ DUG$_3^{tam}$ for *šubatšunu ṭābtam*. In the corrigenda to the edition, he added a further epigraphic note that "the illegible heads have left ends not compatible with *ne*. DUG, not *ih*." This comment was undoubtedly in response to Goetze's remark, either published already (1950, 229) or in private, that "the standard phrase is *šubtam nīhtam* (*w*)*ašābu*(*m*)/*šūšubu*(*m*); ...no doubt to be read here too."

Goetze, however, offered no epigraphic observations in support of the reading. This was left to Greenstein and Marcus (1976, 91), who stated that "what appears as ŠU in our ŠU-*eh-tam* is obviously the first part of a partly broken NE"—that is, reading KI.TUŠ ⸢*ne*⸣-*eh-tam*, so that Smith's -*šu-nu* is taken as a single sign. Subsequently, Oller (1977a, 112) collated the signs and reported:

> epigraphically DU$_{10}$ is better than IH. For an IH in this text, one would expect two horizontals inside the sign.... The sign before the DU$_{10}$ is impossible to see accurately from the photo. Collation reveals that the traces remaining on the statue are compatible with NU although NI cannot entirely be ruled out. Since collation cannot settle the question entirely, context offers a basis for interpretation.[80]

Figure A.61 shows the signs in question. The sign following TUŠ consists of four horizontals followed by an oblique vertical wedge. This form is attested many times for ŠU. However, could it be the first part of NE? There are fewer attestations of NE, but those forms begin with a ŠA component, often minus the final vertical. The oblique vertical following the horizontals in the sign in question therefore does not seem to fit other attestations on NE, although, of course, one cannot exclude that the wedges could be part of a variant form of NE not otherwise attested. Still, ŠU seems the better identification.

---

80 One additional epigraphic interpretation that can be briefly mentioned is that found in *CAD* 1.2, s.v "ašābu," 4c-3′: KI.TUŠ *šu-ub-tam*. In this reading, which was subsequently abandoned in *CAD* 11.2, s.v. "nēhu," usage a-2′-a′ (whose own reading *šub-tu ni-ih-tu* is a mystery to me; RU(*šub*)-TU are not possible) and then revisited in *CAD* 17.3, s.v. "šubtu A," 3e, the ŠU after KI.TUŠ is read as the first sign of a new word and the sign taken as DUG$_3$ or AH read as UB, the traces between these two signs are ignored, and the entire resulting word *šubtam* is understood to be an unmarked gloss of KI.TUŠ.

Figure A.61. The beginning of line 85.

Going into the break are the traces of a damaged oblique wedge, and there is the head of a damaged horizontal wedge in the break. These traces are consistent with NU, but it is difficult to see how they could be part of a NE sign.

Coming out of the break, there are two damaged wedges, one above the other. Both could be horizontal wedges or *Winkelhaken*. Oller's (1977a) assessment that NI cannot be excluded seems accurate.

After the damaged wedges coming out of the break, the first undamaged sign fits HI (= DUG$_3$) better than AH because the body inscription is generally consistent in forming AH with two interior vertical wedges.

In sum, the wedges following KI.TUŠ and going into the break are, with Smith, better read as -*šu*-⸢*nu*⸣ than as ⸢*ne*⸣-. However, Smith's suggestion to read KI.TUŠ-*šu*-⸢*nu*⸣ DUG$_3^{tam}$ does not account for the traces of wedges that are visible coming out of the break—that is, that are present after -⸢*nu*⸣ and before a putative DUG$_3$. In agreement with Oller, these traces seem consistent with NI. Allowing for the following sign to be identified as AH, as opposed to HI (= DUG$_3$) results in a reading of the line that harmonizes the two primary interpretations that have been put forward, in which KI.TUŠ is followed by a possessive pronominal suffix but also modified by the adjective *nēhtam* and not *ṭābtam*.

Epigraphically, the primary objection to this reading is the form of AH without interior wedges. However, unique paleographic variants are attested in the inscription, and this type of a variant would have a parallel in the forms of UB without the expected interior vertical wedge discussed in the commentary to line 78 above. The identification has other epigraphic and contextual advantages. Epigraphically, it allows one to account for the traces of NI coming out of the break. Contextually, it avoids an unexpected collocation of *ṭābtu* with *šubtu* or the need to take *ṭābtu* as an adverbial accusative.[81] It also results, as described above, in a

[81] Smith and most others who have read *ṭābtam* have taken the word as an adverbial accusative. In this interpretation, we need to explain why the adverbial accusative should be marked as feminine, especially since the agreement of the adjective not just in number but also in gender with *šubatšunu* might be seen as one of the strongest arguments in favor of understanding it to be used with an attributive function. A possible explanation is that we have an example of the feminine singular of an adjective used substantively to indicate an

contextually appropriate standard Akkadian idiom, *šubtam nēhtam šūšubu*, "to cause to dwell in security."[82]

86. a-na-ku u$_2$*-še-ši-bu-šu-nu u*$_3$[!](KI) *ma-ti*[ki]*-ia u*$_2$*-ki-in-nu*

The verb *ušēšibušunu* is frequently taken as one of the forms with a nonstandard /u/ suffix that has occasioned much discussion in the literature. Alternatively, Adler (1976, 109) took the form as an example of Hurrian interference, translating the phrase literally as "(die keinen Wohnsitz hatten), bekamen einen von mir verschafft," with a note that "das Subjekt des Satzes ist nicht '*anāku*', sondern '*šunu*.'" According to this interpretation, the /u/ vowel is the 3mp suffix, and the object suffix at the end of the word also marks the subject, a feature that is also attested in the Hurro-Akkadian texts from Qaṭna (Richter and Lange 2012, 40–41; Vita 2020, 364). However, in the parallel constructions gathered by Richter that have an independent pronoun before the verb in addition to a pronominal suffix on the verb, the two pronouns agree.[83] More probably, in line 85, the independent pronoun *anāku* serves either to emphasize the 1cs subject or to disambiguate the verb from 3cs or 3mp forms.[84]

The interpretation of the form adopted here follows Medill (2019, 249 n. 41), who suggested that the verb can be a standard Akkadian use of the subordination marker "if the *ša* clause beginning in line 85 extends through line 86." In other words, the relative *ša* in line 85 governs three successive subordinate clauses, of which the third and final is introduced by the conjunctive *u*. This *ša* lacks an antecedent and is understood to stand in the accusative case for an accusative of means. The conjunction *u* at the beginning of line 87 then serves to coordinate the three subordinate clauses with the main clause. Not only does this interpretation of *ušēšībušunu* and *ukinnu* allow for a minimalist interpretation of the verbal

---

abstract sense (*GAG* §60a); see, e.g., the lemma booked in the dictionaries as *ṭābtu(m)* (*AHw*) or *ṭābtu* B, although note that the majority of the attestations of the lemma are Assyrian and, furthermore, primarily Neo-Assyrian. Alternatively, Durand (2011, 146) attempts to take *ṭābtam* as an attributive adjective, translating "bonnes habitations" and expands on this innocuous translation in a note (n. 177): "On dirait 'meilleures'; 'bonnes' a ici le sens de 'qui méritent vraiment de noms d'habitations,' c'est-à-dire 'bien équipées.'"

82 Note also the collocation of *šubtu* and *nēhtu* in Tablet VII of the Epic of Gilgamesh, when Šamaš responds to Enkidu after the latter has cursed the harlot Šamhat. The Sun God lists the honors that Gilgamesh will pay to Enkidu's body after his death, including that "[he will] set you on a restful seat, the seat to (his) left," [*u*$_2$*-še*]*š-šeb-ka šub-ta ne*$_2$*-eh-ta šu-bat šu-me-li* (SB Gilg. VII 142; see also VIII 86).

83 See, e.g., *at-tu*$_3$*-nu-ma lu-u*$_2$ *i-mar*$_6$*-ku-nu*, "indeed, you all will see" (TT2: 54–55).

84 Although if one is open to seeing a scribal error, one could conceivably read KU as TUŠ and emend the beginning of line 86 to *a-na* <KI>.TUŠ, for *ana šubti ušēšibušunu*, "whom I caused to reside in a dwelling."

morphology because it does not posit a nonstandard morpheme, it also fits well with the larger context of the passage.

Early interpretations of *ušēšibušunu* understood the verb to describe the forced settling of nomads.[85] Subsequently, it was taken as an expression of "a standard literary theme—care for the general well-being of the inhabitants of his land by the king."[86] However, Durand (2011, 120) compared this passage to the phenomenon depicted or alluded to in the Middle Bronze Age texts from Mari about Alalah-Alahtum (*l'Affaire d'Alahtum* [FM 7]) and "le repeuplement d'Alalah" described therein. I have developed this position in Lauinger in press and argued that this passage serves as a post hoc explanation for the settlement of displaced persons (*habiru*) in the Level IV kingdom of Alalah-Mukiš, where administrative texts show the population's having been organized into two different sectors for the purposes of military conscription.

The conjunction following *ušēšibušunu* in line 86 seems to have been written as KI in an error for *u*$_3$. Smith (1949, plate 12) copied the sign with relative accuracy. (What Smith has taken as a second, upper, *Winkelhaken*, I see as the head of the topmost horizontal wedge.) However, Oller's (1977a, 236) copy is misleading. What Oller has taken as interior vertical wedges actually constitutes superficial damage to the surface of the statue; see figure A.62 on the next page. Despite his copy, Smith (1949, 20) read the sign as "*u*" without comment, and there has been little discussion in the literature.[87] Cf. the commentary to line 83, where it is suggested that U$_3$ has been inscribed in place of an intended *ki-*<*ma*>.

[85] This interpretation is found in Smith's (1949, 21) edition, where he translated "those who had no settled abode, I made to abide in one," as well as in *CAD* 1.2, s.v "ašābu," 2a-5′: "those who did not want to live in settlements I made do so," so also 4c-3′; Oppenheim 1969, 558; and *CAD* 17.3, s.v. "šubtu A," 3e.

[86] Oller 1977a, 111, following the analysis of Dietrich and Loretz 1966, 556.

[87] Arnaud (1998) is the only person to have tried to make sense of the passage with a reading of the sign KI as a logogram; in particular, he seems to have also read the second occurrence of KI in the line, taken by everyone else as a determinative with *mātu* (although in l. 84 after the possessive pronominal suffix) also as a logogram: *a-na-ku ú-še-ši-bu-šu-nu* ki *ma-ti* ki-*ia*. But his translation, "Moi, je les sédentarisai dans mon pays," is difficult to map onto this transliteration. It seems that he translated the first KI as "dans" (reading KI as *itti* but meaning "in"?) and took the second KI as a determinative before the *-ia*, despite his transliteration. Note also that he has cited the line in the context of a discussion of the clause-medial position of verbs; with a reading U$_3$!(KI), the verb *ušēšibušunu* is actually clause final.

Figure A.62. Photo of *u*$_3$! (KI) (center) juxtaposed with Smith's (1949, plate 12) copy (left) and Oller's (1977a, 236) copy (right).

Like *ušēšibušunu* earlier in the line, *ukinnu* has generally been taken in the scholarly literature to be one of the verb forms in the inscription that is marked with nonstandard *-u* suffix.[88] A different interpretation has been put forward by Durand (2011, 146), who took the form as 3mp (n. 178: "Ce n'est plus ici une 1re personne à la forme subjonctive, mais une 3e plurielle").[89] Translating "ils affermirent mon pays," Durand took the subject of the verb to be the "inhabitants" of the land in the immediately preceding lines. See the commentary to line 85 above (*ušēšibušunu*) for an understanding of the verb as a 1cs form and the suffix *u* as a standard use of the Akkadian subordination marker.

Durand (2011, 146 n. 178) is also one of the only scholars to have offered an explicit comment as to what Idrimi's statement that he *kunnu*-ed the land actually means. He remarked,

> le verbe *kunnum* signifie 'donner sa stabilité' à un ensemble. L'expression complète est à chercher dans le *išdî mâtim kunnum*, 'assurer la stabilité des fondements du royaume', qui servit de programme de règne à nouveau roi comme Yasmah-Addu de Mari. On trouve ici l'idée intéressante que la stabilité du royaume vient de la sécurité financière et de l'aisance des différentes unités (*bîtum*) dont se compose la pays.

I agree with Durand that we have an echo of Mesopotamian royal inscriptions in the use of this verb, as with the phrase *šubatšunu nēhtam ušēšibšunu* in line 85. At the same time, as mentioned above, I understand the phrase as referring to the historical situation in which the earlier Level IV kingdom of Alalah-Mukiš was organized into two different sectors for the purposes of military conscription.

---

[88] See, e.g., Smith 1949, 101 s.v. "kānu" ("II 1 … impf. 1st s. with indic. *-u* end"); Giacumakis 1970, 81 s.v. "kānu" ("D.pret."); Greenstein and Marcus 1976, 91 ("the 'subjunctive' suffix" that is "inappropriately applied" [79] throughout the inscription); and Dietrich and Loretz 1981, 225 ("D Prt. 1.Sg. *ukīn* mit nicht erklärbarem Subj.").

[89] Some doubt about the verb as a 1cs form is already found in Borger's (1968, 23) translation "So festige ich (?)."

87. u$_3$ u$_2$-ma-ši-il URU.DIDLI.HI.A-*ia ki-me-e pa-nu-ti-ni-ma ki-ma* A.A-*ni-ma*

This is the only attestation of *kīmê* in the Idrimi inscriptions, while *kīma* is attested seven times, including later in this line. The scholarly literature is split as to whether *kīmê* functions as a preposition or subordinating conjunction. However, it must be understood to be a preposition because it serves to mark the direct object of *muššulu* in the same way that *kīma* marked this verb's direct object in lines 81–83 (although the verb is used transitively here). This understanding, in turn, allows us to recognize that *pānûtinima* means simply "earlier ones, previous ones," referring to cities, and not "ancestors," as the word has been translated by many scholars. If *pānûtinima* were to have the meaning "ancestors" in this line, then *umaššil … kīmê pānûtinima* would mean "I made (my cities) equal to our ancestors," which does not make sense. Nor should the oblique plural *pānûtinima* be taken adverbially, an understanding found in the translations both of scholars who take *kīmê* as a preposition and of those who take it as a subordinating conjunction.[90] These translations may get at the sense of the passage from the perspective of a free translation, but they obscure the syntax and are difficult morphologically. If the adjective *pānû* was being used here as an adverbial accusative, we would expect it to be in the singular, *pānâ*, and we certainly would not expect it to have a possessive pronominal suffix.

A central interpretive question has been whether the words *ki-ma* A.A-*ni-ma* stand parallel to the preceding phrase *kīmê pānûtinima* or introduce a new thought. The desire to read the two phrases or clauses as parallel goes back to a perceived overlap not just in syntax (*kīmê* X *kīma* Y) but also in morphology (the twofold presence of the 1cp possessive pronominal suffix) and semantics (because, as discussed above, *pānûtinima* is frequently translated as "ancestors" and A.A is frequently taken as a plural logogram, "fathers"). However, *pānûtinima* refers to earlier cities, and A.A is singular; see §3.2. The perceived overlap in semantics between *pānûtinima* and A.A-*ni-ma* is not actually present, and taking the two phrases/clauses in parallel—"I made my cities equal to our earlier ones (and) equal to our father"—is nonsensical. Accordingly, it seems best to take *kīma abunima* with what follows, where, as we will see, it fits very well with the larger thematic concerns of the passage. It is important to note that the interpretation put forward here is not weakened by the perceived similarity between *kīmê pānûtinima* and *kīma abunima*. This similarity is precisely the point. The tension between the perception of similarity and the actual morphosyntactic dissimilarity is precisely where we can locate an aesthetic appreciation of the text.

[90] See, e.g., Oppenheim 1969, 558 ("like they were previously"), so also Longman 1991, 218; Longman 1997, 480; and Liverani 2004a, 139 ("as before").

88. A₂ₜₑ.MEŠ ša DINGIR.MEŠ ša ᵘʳᵘa-la-lah₃ᵏⁱ u₂-ki-in-nu-u₂-ma

Because the sign A₂ has the syllabic value *it* and is followed by the sign TE, Smith (1949, 20) read the string syllabically as *it-te*.MEŠ. Prior to Durand's (2011) edition, all subsequent scholars followed Smith in this reading, although with differences in opinion as to what the lemma was. Not until Oller's (1977a, 16) dissertation do we find the suggestion that the signs *it-te* are to be connected to the lemma *ittu*, "sign, characteristic mark" (*AHw* 406a, s.v. "ittu II," "sign"; *CAD* 7, s.v. "ittu A," s.). Oller argued:

> the basic connotation for *ittu* in Akkadian is "sign," "indication," or "omen" and so that is what should be expected here. The context of this passage is the correct performance of the religious obligations assigned to the ruler of Alalah which Idrimi tells us he carried out accordingly and eventually turned over to his ᵈIM-nirari. The "signs" which the gods established should then refer to that which indicates the correct times for cult or ritual—i.e, the proper times to perform the sacrifices. (Oller 1977a, 115–16)

The lemma *ittu* fits the context well, as Oller explained, but a central objection to reading the string as *it-te*.MEŠ and interpreting it as a plural oblique form of *ittu*, "sign, characteristic" is that this word is feminine, so one expects a plural *idāte*, or possibly *ittāte*. Durand's (2011, 147) decision, followed here, to read the first sign logographically as A₂ and take the next sign as a phonetic complement allows one to normalize the expected feminine plural oblique form.

Syntactically, recognizing the construction as a periphrastic genitive construction is not problematic (as opposed to the interpretation of the other instances of *ša* in the passage; see the discussion below). However, the phrase has simply been translated as "the gods of Alalah" and taken at face value by almost all scholars from Smith on without any real consideration of what it means or who exactly these gods are. To the extent that there is a deity associated with Alalah—that is, to the extent that the toponym appears as part of the divine name or, at least, as an epithet—that deity is the goddess whose name is written as IŠTAR or INANNA. The goddess appears with the epithet "lady of Alalah" in line 2 of the body inscription, a temple dedicated to the goddess existed at the city for almost a millennium, and attestations of "Ištar of Alalah" are found outside of Alalah proper in Hittite documentation. Significantly, however, there is only one of her, and, given her identity, it is unlikely she had a consort or children. So what does the plural form "gods" of Alalah signify?

To my knowledge, the only scholar to address this point is Durand (2011). Although he translated the phrase as "des dieux de la ville d'Alalah" (147), he noted elsewhere the absence of any report on building or restoring temples in the recitation of Idrimi's good deeds and speculated:

> On peut ainsi se demander si ces “dieux” sont bien les puissances transcendantes que l’on entend généralement par ce terme, ou s’il ne faut pas plutôt y voir les Ancêtres divinisés dont Idrimi relève le culte. Il n’y a pas de mention de temples parce que les Ancêtres reçoivent leur culte dans une structure familiale, fût-elle celle du roi dans son palais. (Durand 2011, 128)

Understanding “the gods of Alalah” to signify the divinized ancestors of the city’s inhabitants not only accounts for the otherwise unexpected plural form of *ilāni* but also finds good parallels in the contemporary Levantine world.[91] It also fits well with the central thematic concern of the passage; see §3.2 and §3.5.

In light of the recognition that A.A-*ni-ma* is singular and not plural (see §3.5 and the comment on l. 87 above), the final -*u* on the verb is understood to be the subordination marker. This interpretation represents a departure from previous scholarship, in which the morpheme is understood to be the 3mp marker, with either “the gods” or “forefathers” (taking A.A as plural) as the subject. As for the sense of the verb, such is the semantic purview of *kunnu*, “to establish” that it easily encompasses all the possible interpretations of *it-te*.MEŠ/A$_2$^{te}.MEŠ that have been proposed. Depending on the choice of subject, one can establish a time, establish a border, establish cultic regulations, or establish ominous signs. The sense of the verb understood here, “to honor, attend to the dead,” is not found in the previous literature and seems also not to be recognized in *CAD* 8, s.v. “kânu.” But that the verb *kunnu* was used in this sense is clear, for example, in *JCS* 34 242–43, a text from the Middle Euphrates region: “PN$_1$ and PN$_2$ shall properly attend to (*ukannū*) the gods and the dead (DINGIR.MEŠ *u*$_3$ *mi-ti*) of PN$_3$ their father” (ll. 25–27; see Pitard 1996, 125).[92]

89. u$_3$ SISKUR$_2$.HI.A$^{ni\text{-}iq\text{-}qi_2.\mathrm{HI.A}}$ *ša a-bi* NINDA$_2$-*ni ša uš-te-pi*$_2$-*šu-u*$_2$$^!$-*šu-nu*

The SISKUR$_2$ logogram, which has the common reading *nīqu*, “libation, sacrifice” and is in fact used for this word in line 55, is followed by a syllabic spelling as *niqqu*. Accordingly, there is disagreement in the scholarship as to whether the syllabic spelling should be understood as an unmarked gloss to the logogram, so that there is one direct object (“the offerings”), or whether SISKUR$_2$ should be read differently here so that there are two direct objects. Scholars in support of the second position have understood the two objects to indicate burnt offerings and libations (see, for example, Goetze 1950, 229: “sacrifices and libations). But it is unclear how SISKUR$_2$ is to be read in this interpretation because the probable reading of the logogram is *ikribu*, “prayer,” if it is not to be read as *niqqu*. On

---

91 For an attestation of *ilu* with the meaning “divinized ancestor” at Late Bronze Age (Level IV) Alalah, see AlT 92 [33.2]: 20 and Niedorf’s (2008, 282) discussion of the passage.

92 See also Durand 1989: “Le verbe proprement akkadien *kunnum* a cependant le sens (courant) d’‘honorer une divinité ou esprits des morts.’ C’est ainsi qu’on trouve normalement dans *Tod und Leben* 84, 26 pour signifier ‘s’occuper des esprits des morts.’”

the other hand, proponents of seeing a logogram followed by a syllabic gloss have noted the parallel phenomenon for AN$^{ša-mu}$ and KI$^{er-ṣe-ti}$ that occurs later in the body inscription (ll. 93, 97). They have also observed the absence of the coordinating conjunction between SISKUR$_2$.HI.A and *ni-iq-qi*$_2$.HI.A, "which the scribe normally inserts between two objects" (Oller 1977a, 117).

For the identification of the sign NINDA$_2$ and the resulting construct chain *a-bi* NINDA$_2$*-ni*, "our grandfather," in the singular, see §3.3.

The U$_2$ in the verb *uš-te-pi*$_2$*-šu-u*$_2^!$*-šu-nu* is defective, being written with an initial *Winkelhaken*; see figure A.63 (the wedge is present in Oller's copy but has been omitted from Smith's copy). Could this error derive from the mason having incorrectly inscribed U or even started to inscribe U$_3$, so that it could be evidence of (auto)dictation? Or could it derive from the mason having started to inscribe NU after the preceding ŠU (note that the following two signs are *-šu-nu*), so that it could be evidence of visual copying?

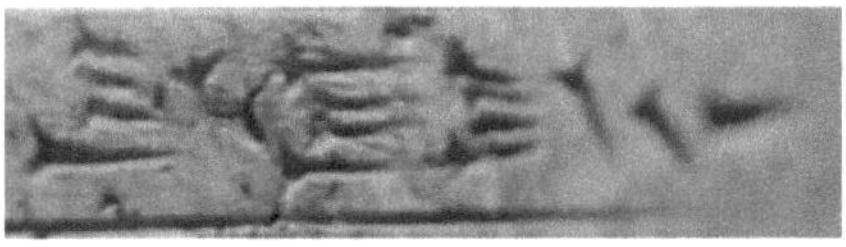

Figure A.63. The signs *-šu-u*$_2^!$*-šu-* in line 89.

90. a-⌜na⌝-ku e-te-ne-pu-uš$_{10}$*-šu-nu an-mu-u*$_2$ *e-te-pu-uš*$_{10}$*-šu-nu*

While much of the discussion of the orthography of the verb *ēteneppuššunu* has focused on the use of the sign UZ with the value *uš*$_{10}$ (on which, see the comment to l. 80), also noteworthy is the use of the sign NE to write the syllable /ne/. The only other occurrences of the syllable /ne/ in the inscriptions are found in lines 85 and 91, where it is spelled with NI (= *ne*$_2$).

The following verb, written as *e-te-pu-uš*$_{10}$*-šu-nu*, seems to have been interpreted as G perfect by most scholars because they translate the form as a simple past tense verb without the addition of "regularly," *vel sim.*, that characterizes their translations of the Gtn form *ēteneppuššunu* earlier in the line. However, understanding the verb to be a Gtn preterite picks up on the Gtn present tense form earlier in the line. The shift from a present to preterite tense captures a shift from the description of an ongoing action in the past to the statement of completed actions with which the body inscription concludes (*ēteppuššunu* … *aptaqid*).

91. u$_3$ *a-na qa-ti* ^{md}IM*-ne*$_2$*-ra-ri* DUMU*-ia ap-ta-qi*$_2$*-id-šu-nu*

On the sense of *paqādu*, see the discussion in §3.5. On possible identities of IM-*nerari*, see the discussions in chapter 6.

92. ma-an-nu-um-me-e ALAM*-ia an-ni-na-ti i-na-as-sah*$_2$*-š*[*u*]

This line is the first line of the curse formula and so the first line of the body inscription after the narrative has ended. However, it is also the last line written on the statue's right lower lap. There was no apparent interest on the part of the scribe and/or mason in having the inscription's placement on the statue map onto the larger structural units of the text because it would have been relatively easy to start this line at the top of right chest; see §2.8 for more discussion of the body inscription's literary structure in comparison to its physical arrangement on the statue's body.

The word *ṣalmu* appears here and in line 99 to refer to the statue on which the inscriptions are carved. For more discussion of this term, its use in cognate Semitic languages, and the spelling with the divine determinative in line 99, see the discussions in §2.4 and §3.2. The noun *ṣalmu* is typically masculine in Akkadian, but it is modified by a demonstrative pronoun, *annīnāti*, that appears to be feminine plural.

93. u$_{3}$ <<*pi*$_{2}$*-ri-ih-šu li-il-qu*$_{2}$*-ut*>> AN$^{ša\text{-}mu}$ *li-iz-zu-ur-šu*

Greenstein and Marcus (1976, 66) were the first to suggest an editorial deletion of <<*pirihšu lilqut*>>. They remarked that "this phrase cannot stand here, as it has no grammatical subject," and so considered it to be "an anticipatory dittograph of *pirihšu lilqut* in the following line." This interpretation seems preferable to others that have taken *šamû*, "Heaven" as the subject of both this clause and also the following *lizzuršu* (e.g., Smith 1949, 23), which have translated *lilqut* as passive (e.g., Kempinski and Na'aman 1973, 215), or which have understood AN and *ša-mu* as two distinct words that serve, respectively, as the subjects to *lilqut* and *lizzuršu*—that is, transliterate AN *ša-mu* instead of AN$^{ša\text{-}mu}$ or ^{d}*Ša-mu* (Durand 2011, 148).[93] Note, though, that Greenstein and Marcus included the first sign of the line, U$_{3}$, as part of the dittograph and so deleted it as well. However, the use of the conjunction *u* to coordinate subordinate and main clauses introduced by a generalizing relative pronoun is common in texts written in western hybrid Akkadian in the Late Bronze Age.[94] (The conjunction does not appear to coordinate

[93] See also Durand 2011, 133 and §2.7 for discussion of the source-critical implications of this interpretation for Durand.

[94] At Level IV Alalah, this use of *u* is found in Idrimi's treaty with Pilliya: *ma-an-nu-um-me-e mu-un-na-ab-ta iṣ-ṣa-bat u*$_{3}$ *a-na be-li*$_{2}$*-šu u*$_{2}$*-ta-ar-šu*, "whoever will have seized a fugitive will return (the fugitive) to his lord" (AIT 3 [1.2]: 15–16). It occurs in the Idadda archive from Late Bronze Age Qaṭna; see, e.g., TT2: 44–47. For Nuzi, see the attestations gathered by Wilhelm (1970, 53). It is worth noting that the coordination of subordinate and main clauses with *u* occurs in most western hybrid Akkadian corpora. For instance, see the discussion of Seminara (1998, 544-545) for Emar. Both Huehnergard (2011, 242) and Rainey (1996, 3:102–6) have connected the phenomenon in texts from Ugarit and the Syro-Levantine Amarna letters, respectively, to the so-called "*waw* of apodosis" found in WS languages. Rainey further pointed to Middle Bronze Age attestation from Mari and suggested "that the Hurrians who founded the Mitanni kingdom inherited this syntactical feature from the Amurrite cultural centers of N. Syria" (102).

the *mannummê* clause and the main clause in lines 96–97, although difficulties with the end of line 96 make it difficult to be certain; see the commentary to l. 96.)

Interestingly, while the verb *nazāru* can be translated "to curse," it is not, in fact, typically used in the sense of a god delivering a curse on a person. Instead, *nazāru* means "to curse" in the sense "to abuse, to insult," as is clear from the passages gathered in *CAD* 11.2, s.v. "nazāru," which almost entirely involve humans cursing or hurling insults at either the gods (meaning 1) or other humans (meaning 2). Indeed, the editors of *CAD* 11.2 seem to have been aware that the usage in the Idrimi text was unusual because they positioned it at the very end of meaning 2a, where it is prefaced by "note in curses" and joined by one other text, a *kudurru* of Marduk-šapik-zeri.[95]

94. ša-ap-la-tu$_2^{er\text{-}ṣe\text{-}tu_2}$ *pi*$_2$*-ri-ih-šu li-il-qu*$_2$*-ut*

The signs read here as *ša-ap-la-tu*$_2^{er\text{-}ṣe\text{-}tu_2}$ were interpreted very differently by Smith (1949, 22), as *ša ab-du-ut-sa *kap-tu*, "(May the gods of Heaven and earth carry away the shoot) of him who plans doing away with it (i.e., the statue)." In this interpretation, Smith (1949, 96 s.v. "abaṭu") understood *ab-du-ut-sa* to be an otherwise unattested noun *abtūtu*, "destruction," derived from *abātu*, "to destroy," with the 3fs possessive pronominal suffix -*ša*, which showed the assimilation of /š/ > /s/ after a dental (although that dental did not assimilate to /s/ as well). He took *kap-tu* as a G stative 3cs + subjunctive of *kapādu*, although he was careful to note that "the reading is a guess from the context, the form written not being recognizable" (102 s.v. "*kapadu"; the written form in question is the sign read by him as *kap*-).

Although Smith's interpretation was taken up by *AHw*, objections from other quarters were swift.[96] Still, the first real substantial improvements did not appear until Greenstein and Marcus's (1976, 66, 68) edition, where they read the signs as *ša-ap-la-nu*$^!$ *er-ṣe-tu*, translating "the Earth below." Epigraphically, this reading is a great improvement. Identifying Smith's putative SA as IR, and his DU as LA are straightforward. The most questionable sign is the one read as ZI$_2$ (*ṣe*); it is difficult to find a parallel form where what is usually a final vertical wedge is instead two oblique wedges; cf. the form of the same sign in the same word in line 97 (see fig. A.64).

---

95 "Šamaš, the great judge of Heaven and earth, should curse him with his pure, irreversible command," ^{d}UTU DI.KU$_5$ GAL *ša* AN *u*$_3$ KI *i-na pi-šu el-li la muš-pe-li li-iz-zu-ur-šu-ma* (*ZA* 65 56: 57–59; see Paulus 2014, 577). In FM 7 39: 33, the one attestation of *nazāru* published since *CAD* 11.2 known to me that has a deity as its subject (who speaks through a prophet), the verb seems to mean "to make an unwarranted claim on territory"; see Durand 2002, 140 note d, citing previous literature.

96 See especially Goetze (1950, 229 with n. 22) and *CAD* 1.1, s.v. "abtu," discussion. The reading was eventually corrected in *AHw* 1541b.

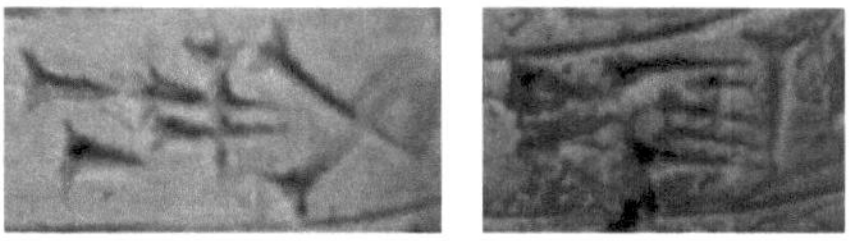

Figure A.64. The sign *-ṣe-* in lines 94 (left) and 97 (right).

In keeping with their deductive approach to the text, Greenstein and Marcus stated that they expected an adverb in the apodosis, and they accordingly emended a clear UD(*tu*$_2$) sign to NU without any further discussion. Subsequently, Dietrich and Loretz (1981, 207) maintained the reading of the sign as UD, with the value *tu*$_2$, so that they read the signs as *ša-ap-la-tu*$_2$ *er-ṣe-tu*$_2$. They considered that that the sign string *ša-ap-la-tu*$_2$ could be *šaplatu*, a by-form of *šapiltu* and so feminine singular adjective modifying *erṣetu*, but placed, unusually, before the word. But they also suggested that it could be a feminine plural substantive that was glossed by *erṣetu*. An unmarked gloss works well with the occurrence of an unmarked gloss in immediately preceding and parallel apodosis. (Although note some circularity here, because part of the reason for seeing a gloss in that line was the presence of an unmarked gloss here.) And further support for taking *erṣetu* as an unmarked gloss is found in line 97, where it glosses the logogram KI.

95. DINGIR.MEŠ *ša* AN *u* KI LUGAL-*ut-šu u*$_3$ *ma-at-šu*^{ki} *lim-du-du-šu*

This writing of the conjunction *u* with U instead of U$_3$ seems to be one of three such writings that occur in the inscriptions. All three occur outside the narrative portion of the body inscription (i.e., in the curse formulae or the colophon, ll. 95, 97, 99), and all three occur only in the phrase AN (*šamê*) *u* KI (*erṣeti*). That being said, it is not entirely certain that the *Winkelhaken* is to be taken as the sign U and not as part of the following KI. Figure A.65 shows the attestations. Of these three attestations, the example in line 99 is the least ambiguous, because the two *Winkelhaken* at the beginning of KI establish that the preceding *Winkelhaken* is an independent sign than needs to be identified as U. On the basis of this phrase, I tentatively understand the first *Winkelhaken* after AN in lines 95 and 97 to be U as well. However, because of the form of KI in those lines, it is possible that the *Winkelhaken* is part of that sign so that one should read AN KI, "the Heavens (and) the Underworld."

Figure A.65. The signs AN *u* KI in lines 95 (left), 97 (center), and 99 (right).

Unlike the curses in lines 94 and 98, which are common in second-millennium Mesopotamian sources, it has been argued that the curse in line 95 requesting the deities "measure out" (*madādu*) someone's kingship and land has parallels in the Hebrew Bible, such as Amos 7:17 ("your land shall be divided by rope"; Tsevat 1958, 124) or 2 Samuel 8:2 ("he measured them off with a rope"; Greenstein and Marcus 1976, 94–95). However, these parallels depend on accepting Smith's (1949, 22) identification of the sign following *ma-at-šu* as KU (= ŠE$_3$) and his understanding of it as a logogram for the Akkadian word *eblu*, "rope, cord," which is cognate to the Classical Hebrew word *ḥebel*, "rope," that occurs in the biblical attestations.

Indeed, figure A.66 clearly shows why Smith read it as KU. However, KU is one of the few signs that is attested many times in a consistent paleography as LAGAB × DIŠ (although cf. the attestations of the sign in ll. 84–85). Accordingly, Goetze (1950, 229) suggested reading Smith's putative KU instead as KI, because this sign that shows a great deal of variation in the inscription, and because the determinative in a similar orthography with *mātu* elsewhere in the body inscription (*ma-ti-ia*^{ki}, l. 84). In particular, in one form of the sign KI that appears in the inscription, the *Winkelhaken* has been flattened into a horizontal wedge that gives the sign the box-like shape that resembles KU, as shown in figure A.67. In light of this variant, the tendency toward homogeneity of KU signs, and the orthographical parallel, it seems better to read the sign as KI.

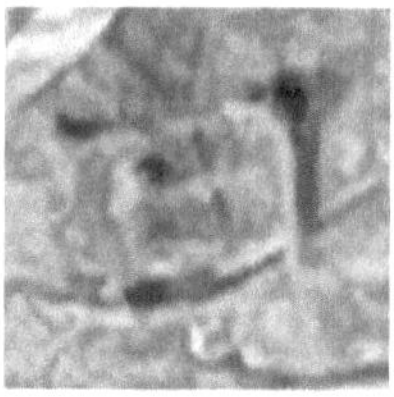

Figure A.66. Determinative KI in line 95 (Smith's putative KU).

Figure A.67. KI in line 57.

If taking the sign as the determinative KI instead of KU removes one half of the proposed parallels to "measuring out by rope" found in the Hebrew Bible, a reanalysis of the verb by Wasserman (2006; reference courtesy Martin Worthington) seems to remove the other half. As is clear from the discussion above, the verb, written *lim*-DU-DU has been read as a 3mp precative of *madādu*, "to measure out," since Smith's edition. However, its use in a curse formula is unusual, since this well-attested verb generally occurs in prosaic contexts having to do with the calculation of capacity, length, or time. For this reason, the editors of *CAD* 10.1, s.v. "madādu A" kept it apart from meaning 1, "to measure (using a measure of capacity of length)," and instead filed it under a separate "uncert. Mng.," together with two attestations of the verb in Old Akkadian curse formulae. They also cross-referenced to this meaning another use of the verb in the D stem, also with an uncertain meaning, in *Ludlul bēl nēmeqi* (*CAD* 10.1, s.v. "madādu A," 4e).

In his reanalysis, Wasserman added a third attestation in an Old Akkadian curse formula and noted that the Old Akkadian attestations and the attestation in *Ludlul* all "involv[e] the verb *madādum*, a divinity, and a geographical designation (mostly river and silt…)." He suggested that the verb is "not *madādum*, but the verb *maṭāṭum*, which to the best of my knowledge is not recorded hitherto in Akkadian, with the meaning … 'to collapse (trans.), to sway, be shaken, to demolish.'" Wasserman derived the meaning of the verb "by comparison to Biblical Hebrew, where the root √mwṭ (closely related to the later √mṭṭ) exists, with the meanings 'to sway, be shaken' (*qal*); 'to be made to stagger, to be made to totter' (*nif.*); 'to reel' (*hitpol*)." Accordingly, he read the verb in this line of the Idrimi inscription as *lim-ṭù-ṭù-šu*, transla-ting the entire curse as "may the gods of Heaven and earth collapse his kingship and land *on* him," commenting on "the slightly dif-ferent idiom and the double accusative construction" compared with the other attestations.

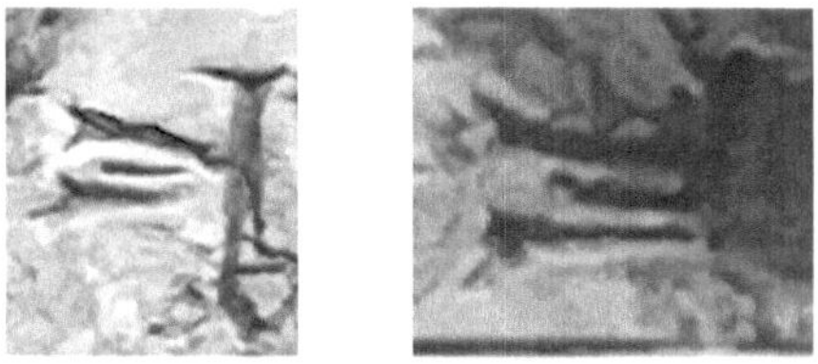

Figure A.68. Attestation of ŠU in line 96 (left) juxtaposed with the second attestation of ŠU in line 95 (right).

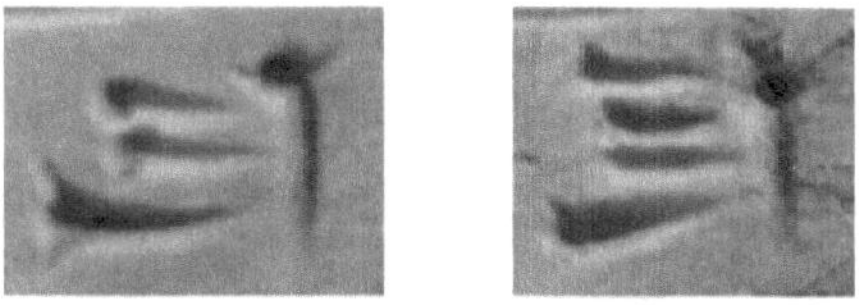

Figure A.69. Attestations of ŠU in lines 31 (left) and 34 (right).

Wasserman's suggestion is very intriguing. Morphologically, the reanalysis of a hollow root as a geminate root, or vice versa, does not seem too problematic. And if the pronominal suffix on the verb is taken as dative and not accusative, there is no double accusative and so no syntactic difficulty. The choice of DU to write /ṭu/ is perhaps a little unusual, since the three other attestations of the syllable use TU = *ṭu*$_2$; note, in particular, that two of the three occur in the immediately following section of blessings (*iš-ṭu*$_2$*-ru-šu*, l. 99 and *li-bal-li-ṭu*$_2$*-u*$_2$*-šu*, l. 100). However, a number of possible explanations, ranging from text-critical to sociolinguistic, could explain the use of DU instead of TU here. The biggest obstacle is the difference in object, for all three other attestations of the verb involve a canal collapsing and being blocked up with silt. A putative attestation in the Idrimi inscription would involve a different object. But, of course, the same is true if the verb is *madādu*.

96. ma-an-nu-um-me-e u$_2$*-na-ak-kar*$_3$*-šu i-ip-pa-aš*$_2$*-ši-*<*iṭ?*>

Although *-šu*, the sign following GAR$_3$, has been identified as such by all scholars going back to Smith's original edition, it is noteworthy because it has only three horizontal wedges, which is especially clear when it is compared to an attestation of the same sign in the previous line (see fig. A.68). However, two attestations of ŠU earlier in the body inscription show a similar form, being comprised of only three wedges (see fig. A.69). Possibly one could consider reading the sign in line 96 as MA and taking it as the enclitic *-ma*. However, it should probably not be identified as MA because MA is almost always written in an archaizing form in the inscriptions, for which the attestation of the sign at the beginning of the same line, shown in figure A.70, can stand as a good example. The only exception to this archaizing form is the second attestation of the sign in line 60, shown in figure A.45 on page 243. Note also that with the sign in question in line 96, the bottom horizontal wedge is longer than the upper two. Since a longer bottom horizontal wedge is a typical feature of ŠU, it seems preferable to read the sign as *-šu* and not *-ma*.

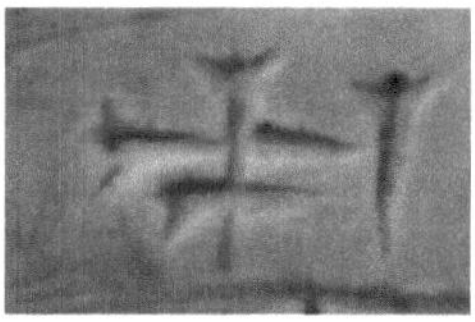

Figure A.70. The first attestation of MA in line 96.

The verb *nukkuru* is translated here with the sense "to alter" in light of the following verb, which seems to be a form of *pašāṭu*, "to erase, efface." However, as discussed immediately below, the form is difficult, and the verb in question may not be *pašāṭu*. In that case, *nukkuru* may have the sense here "to remove," as in the first-millennium grave inscription of Mullissu-mukannišat-Ninua: ˹*mam*$_2$˺*-ma ar-ku-u*$_2$ [*ša*$_2$] ^{giš}GU.ZA-˹*ia*˺ [T]A* *pa-an* GIDIM.MEŠ ˹*u*$_2$˺*-na-kar-*˹*u*$_2$˺*-ni*, "As for any future person who removes my chair from before the ghosts" (*BaghM* 21 474: 18–21; reference courtesy Adam Miglio).

The final word in the line, written as *i-ip-pa-aš*$_2$*-ši*, is epigraphically clear but morphologically difficult and has generated a variety of interpretations. The interpretation tentatively adopted here takes the verb as a form of *pašāṭu*, "to erase, efface" and goes back to Oppenheim's (1969, 558) translation of the line as "whoever changes or erases it(s inscription)"; see also Greenstein and Marcus's (1976, 66, 68) restoration *i-ip-pa-aš-ši-*[*issu*]. Other suggestions found in the literature include *napāṣu*, "to push away, smash" (Smith 1949, 22–23, 104 s.v. "napasu"); *bašû*, "to be, exist" in the N stem (Goetze 1950, 229); *pa'āṣu*, "to break up, crush" (Kempinski and Na'aman 1973, 215, 216); and *epēšu*, "to do, make" (Dietrich and Loretz 1981, 207).

Figure A.71. The ends of lines 93–98.

Taking the verb as a form of *pašāṭu* has the advantage of fitting the context well. However, it does not account for the plene spelling of the verbal prefix, which leads us to expect a I-ʾ verb, and it also requires the emendation of the text. While I cannot explain the plene spelling, the need to emend might find some explanation in the fact that line 96 is noteworthy for ending earlier than any of the lines above or below it; see figure A.71. The empty space suggests that some signs may have been inadvertently omitted, and there is easily enough room to accommodate a form of *pašāṭu*, so that one might consider emending, as opposed to restoring, the text as *i-ip-pa-aš*$_2$*-ši-*<*iṭ*>.

97. ^{d}IM EN AN *u* KI$^{er\text{-}ṣe\text{-}ti}$ *u*$_3$ DINGIR.MEŠ GAL.GAL.E.NE ⸢*šu*⸣*-ma-šu*

The paleography and orthography of DINGIR.MEŠ GAL.GAL.E.NE is striking. For instance, there are no parallels for the form of MEŠ in the inscriptions. As can be seen in figure A.72, MEŠ is typically written as ME followed by three or four *Winkelhaken*, but the form in this line has two rows of superimposed *Winkelhaken* after a vertical wedge. The orthography of the entire phrase DINGIR.MEŠ GAL.GAL.E.NE is also remarkable for employing three different means of marking the plural in cuneiform: The MEŠ determinative, reduplication, and the Sumerian plural morpheme E.NE. Smith (1949, 22) considered the unusual orthography to be "a tag from liturgy," commenting elsewhere (24) that "the phrase in Sumerian … is a tag rather than a series of ideograms. It may imply the use of Sumerian in the scribal schools." The phrase **dingir-gal-(gal)-e-ne** is very common in royal inscriptions from the Old Babylonian period that are written in Sumerian, and Smith's suggestion that the orthography in this line reflects a familiarity with these texts seems reasonable.

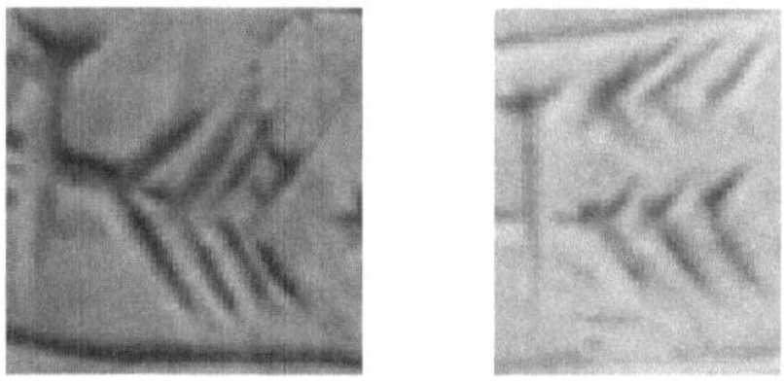

Figure A.72. Juxtaposition of a typical form of MEŠ in line 82 (left) with the form in line 97 (right).

In the standard Akkadian dialects, the expected form of *šumu* in the accusative singular with a pronominal suffix would be *šumšu* and not *šumašu*. When the form has been discussed, the /a/-vowel has typically been taken to be the vowel of the accusative case preserved before the pronominal suffix. For instance, Smith (1949, 30) stated in his discussion of the morphology of the singular construct, "there is only one case of the vowel ending of the acc.," citing this form. Similarly, Aro (1954, 362) remarked that "the rules about case-ending in status constructus and substantives with possessive suffixes are not clear to the scribes," citing this form; see also Greenstein and Marcus 1976, 62. A different interpretation could be to see the /a/ as an epenthetic vowel inserted between the consonant of the noun base and the consonant of the pronominal suffix, similar to the /a/ vowel of *lib-bašu*. Although the phonological context does not require the insertion of a vowel to resolve a consonant cluster, perhaps the form *šumašu* derives from analogy. Note also that an epenthetic /a/ can appear before a possessive pronominal suffix in the Hymno-Epic dialect of Akkadian; see Hess 2010, 108.

98. u$_{3}$ NUMUN.MEŠ-*šu li-hal-liq* ⌈*i-na ma*⌉-*ti-šu* ^{m}*šar-ru-wa* DUB.SAR ⌈$^{lu_2?}$⌉ARAD 10 20 30 *u*$_{3}$ ^{d}INANNA

The reading *li-hal-liq* is significant because it is morphologically singular and so seems to require a singular subject. Accordingly some scholars have taken only ^{d}IM as its subject, normalizing DINGIR.MEŠ GAL.GAL.E.NE in the plural oblique and taking it in construct with *bēl*—that is, "the Storm God, the lord of the Heavens and of the Underworld and of the great gods."[97] However, a parallel for this curse occurs in a treaty from Late Bronze Age (Level IV) Alalah:

> *ma-an-nu-um-me-e a-*[*wa-t*]*e*.MEŠ *an-nu-ut-ti uš-bal-kat-šu-nu* ^{d}IM E[N *x-x*]*x* ^{d}UTU EN-*el di-ni* ^{d}30 *u*$_{3}$ DINGIR.MEŠ GAL.GA[L *lu*$^{?}$-*u*$_{2}$$^{?}$] *u*$_{2}$-*hal-liq-šu* MU-*šu u*$_{3}$ NU-MUN-*š*[*u li*$^{?}$-*ha*]*l-liq i-na* KUR.KI.MEŠ ^{giš}GU.ZA-*šu u*$_{3}$ ^{giš}P[A]-*šu li-iš-bal-kat-šu*
>
> (As for) whoever causes these words to be broken, the Storm God, the lo[rd of…], the Sun God, the lord of judgment, the Moon God, and the great gods *should* make him disappear. [May] *they* make his name and h[is] seed disappear from the lands. May they overturn his throne and his scep[ter]." (AlT 2 [1.1]: 75–77)

While there are a number of difficulties with this passage, the key parallels to the Idrimi text are found in line 76, where there are two attestations of the verb *hulluqu*. Both attestations are damaged, but both are clearly singular in form. Yet the first attestation, tentatively restored here as [*lū*] *uhalliqšu*,[98] has multiple gods as its subject, and the second attestation, which does not have an explicit subject, presumably takes them as its subject as well. Furthermore, the second attestation of *hulluqu* in AlT 2 [1.1]: 76 is not clause final but is followed by the prepositional phrase *ina mātāti*, just as in line 98 of the Idrimi text where *lihalliq* is followed by

---

[97] The reading of the verb in the line as singular came relatively late in the scholarship, as discussed in more detail immediately below. Originally, Smith (1949, 22) read *li-hal-li-***qu*, although this reading requires more than a little disentangling.

[98] Previous editors have restored the marker of plurality E.NE in the damage before the verb; i.e., DINGIR.MEŠ GAL.GA[L.E.NE] *u*$_{2}$-*hal-liq-šu*. This restoration derives, of course, from the curse in the Idrimi text under discussion here. But it is not necessary and results in an unexpected preterite form *uhalliqšu* where one expects a precative. Accordingly, Schwemer (2005, 186 n. 27) considered the text to be corrupt. I restore the modal particle *lū* for an alternative form of the precative [*lū*] *uhalliqšu* that is attested elsewhere in western hybrid Akkadian.

the prepositional phrase *ina mātišu*. Therefore, to return to that line, there is some reason not to take DINGIR.MEŠ GAL.GAL.E.NE in construct with *bēl* but instead as another subject of the verb and to see both the resulting lack of agreement between subject and verb and also the nonstandard word order as a local manifestation of a traditional Mesopotamian curse.

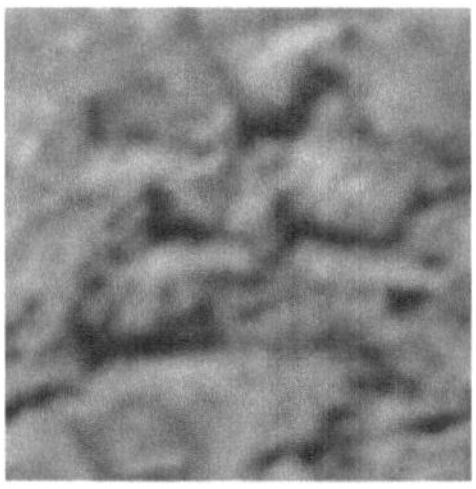

Figure A.73. The sign ⸢LU$_2^?$⸣.

On the scribe Šarruwa, his possible identification with a Level IV scribe of the same name, and the request for blessings for him and not Idrimi, see the discussion in §6.1.

The sign following DUB.SAR has been identified as GIR$_3$, DUMU/TUR, and LU$_2$. As can be seen in figure A.73, it consists of a bottom horizontal wedge with four small *Winkelhaken* or horizontal wedges above it. Accordingly, its identification as GIR$_3$ seems as though it can be safely discarded, because if the sign were GIR$_3$ in an archaizing form, we would expect to see the characteristic "animal head" shape component at its beginning; if the sign were GIR$_3$ in a cursive form, we would still expect to see one or more *Winkelhaken* at the beginning. The sign could conceivably be identified as TUR if the wedges above the bottom horizontal are also interpreted as horizontal wedges written on a slight angle. However, the form would be very cursive, and the TUR signs in the body inscription tend to be archaizing. Even those that are structured as stacked horizontal wedges have at least four of them (see fig. A.74).

The sign LU$_2$ also tends to be written in an archaizing form, but, as Oller noted, there are exceptions. In fact, a striking exception occurs in the immediately following line, and the form of the sign in line 75 is particularly noteworthy as well (see fig. A.75).

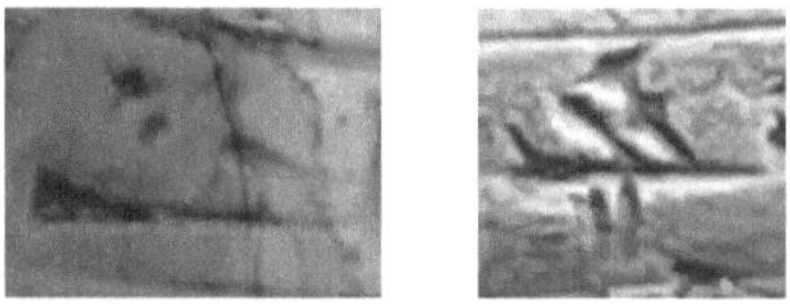

Figure A.74. Two attestations of TUR/DUMU in lines 25 (left).

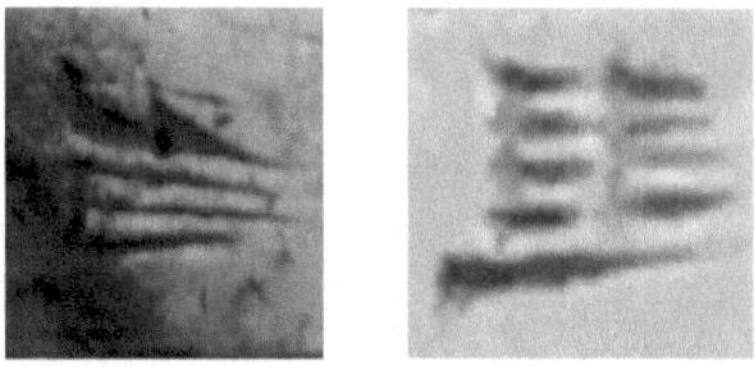

Figure A.75. Two cursive forms of LU$_2$ in lines 75 (left) and 99 (right).

The essential question, then, in identifying the sign in line 98 is whether we interpret the wedges above the bottom horizontal wedge as fewer than expected horizontal wedges or as more than expected *Winkelhaken*. In sum, it is very difficult to decide between LU$_2$ and TUR, and, ultimately, the identification of the sign here as LU$_2$ is based on contextual grounds. Reading the sign as LU$_2$ in line 98 provides an alternation between lines 98–99 that seems in keeping with the inscription's interest in variation, whereby DUB.SAR is written without a determinative, while ARAD is written with one in line 98, and in line 99, DUB.SAR is written with the determinative, while ARAD does not appear at all. The presence and absence of the divine determinative before ALAM in lines 92 and 99 may be another example of this interest in variation in the colophon. However, an identification of the sign as LU$_2$ must remain tentative. Methodologically, a more important point is that, whether one considers an identification LU$_2$ or TUR to be more likely, the identification is not secure and should not be used as a basis for further text critical arguments; see §2.7.

Epigraphically, only the final sign in the sequence of signs 10 20 30 *u*$_3$ ^{d}INANNA has created difficulty; see figure A.76. Scholars have identified this as either MUŠ$_3$ after the divine determinative for ^{d}INANNA or ŠUR for AN.ŠUR, the divine name Aššur. Epigraphically, the difference between SUR and MUŠ$_3$ is only the presence of an additional vertical wedge at the end of MUŠ$_3$ that is not present with SUR. On the face of it, this point would seem to rule in favor of reading the sign as SUR, because such a wedge is absent. However, as Oller (1977a, 135–36) explained, there are good contextual grounds for preferring the form to be a graphic variant of MUŠ$_3$ nonetheless. AN.ŠUR would be a very unusual orthography for the divine name Aššur, which "is never written ^{d}ŠUR." Rather, when it is written with SUR, the divine name is spelled ^{d}*aš-šur*. Furthermore, it would be very unexpected to see the patron deity of Assyria appear in this context. On the other hand, a theophoric element written ^{d}INANNA does in fact occur multiple times in the onomasticon of Alalah IV.[99] Furthermore, Dietrich and Loretz (1981, 229) pointed out that we find the same orthography used to write the patron goddess of Alalah in copies of Šuppiluliuma's treaty with Niqmaddu II of Ugarit.[100] Therefore, whether the logogram is to be read as Ištar, Išhara, or Šaušga (see the Note on Transliterations, Normalizations, and Translations), it seems that we meet the patron goddess of Alalah in this line as well.

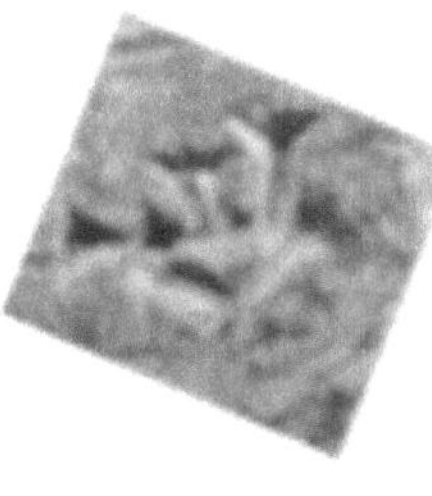

Figure A.76. INANNA in line 98.

The reading of the preceding signs 10 20 30 as divine logograms is first found in Gurney's (1951, 557) review, to my knowledge, although its source is unclear: "It has been suggested to me that the scribe Sharruwa is describing himself in this line as 'servant of (the gods) Adad (= 10), Šamaš (= 20), Sin (= 30) and the goddess Ishtar.'" In connection with this orthography for the Storm God, Schwemer

---

99 Relatedly, in the catalogue of the Alalah texts, Wiseman read this element in the Level IV texts as AN.ŠUR (see, e.g., Wiseman 1953, 129 s.v. "A-ri-AN.ŠUR"), and already the next year Landsberger (1954, 57 n. 111) suggested identifying the sign in question as MIM$_3$ (= INANNA) instead.

100 PRU 4 48–52, 67–70 [RS 17.340+]: rev. 20′: ^{d}INANNA ^{uru}*a-la-la-ah*; see also PRU 4 63–67 [RS 17.237]: 15′.

(2001, 77) has observed that "den frühesten Beleg für die Schreibung des Wettergottes mit dem Zeichen U bietet die Idrimi-Inschrift, die in die erste Hälfte des 15. Jh. datiert." However, on the basis of the redating of the statue to the fourteenth century (see §2.1), this attestation of the orthography can no longer claim such priority.

99. ^{m}*šar-ru-wa* ^{lu_2}DUB.SAR ⸢*ša*⸣ ^{d}ALAM *an-ni-na-ti*$_3$ *iš-ṭu*$_2$*-ru-šu* DINGIR.⸢MEŠ⸣ *ša* AN *u* KI

For discussions of *ṣalmu*, the presence of the divine determinative, and the feminine form of the demonstrative pronoun *annīnāti* that modifies the noun, see §2.4, §3.2, and the commentary to line 92.

100. li-bal-li-ṭu$_2$*-u*$_2$*-šu li-na-ṣa-ru-šu lu-u*$_2$ SIG$_5$^{u_2}-*šu* ^{d}UTU EN *e-lu-ti* / : *u*$_3$ *šap-li-ti* EN$^{lu\text{-}u_2}$ *e-tim-mi* ⸢*lu-u*$_2$⸣ TI.LA-*šu*

On the indentation and *Glossenkeil* at the beginning of the line, conventionally numbered in previous literature as 101, indicating instead that this line is to be understood as part of the previous line, see §1.4.

For the form of *linaṣṣarūšu*, in which the precative is built off the present tense and not the preterite tense, as in the standard Akkadian dialects, see the commentaries to lines CI 2 and CI 3 in §A.1.

The verb form written as *lu-u*$_2$ SIG$_5$^{u_2}-*šu* has been normalized several different ways in the scholarly literature, and it is impossible to determine for certain how the form should be read. Does one interpret the form within the rules of the standard Akkadian dialects as a stative or verbal adjective in a predicative construction because such an interpretation is possible? Or does one consider that the orthographic variation in the choice to write the form logographically opens the door for, or even signals, that we should interpret the sign string as one of the variant precative forms such as are found in other dialects of western hybrid Akkadian? In light of the immediately preceding nonstandard form of *linaṣṣarūšu*, I tentatively prefer the latter option, as it allows the sequence of three precatives to act almost as a *tricolon crescens* of variant precatives. In keeping with such an interpretation, a normalization suggested by Dietrich and Loretz (1981, 207; see also 229), which sees *lū* as uncontracted (*lū udammiqūšu*), seems to heighten the variation and so works well. (Accordingly, I understand the sign U$_2$ that follows SIG$_5$ as a phonetic complement indicating that the logogram should be read as plural in number.)

As discussed in §3.2, the appearance of the Sun God in the final, emphatic position with these particular epithets is no coincidence, because in both Akkadian and West Semitic texts, the Sun God has a particular role with regard to the spirits of the dead, owing to his/her daily movement traversing the world of the living during the day and then the Underworld at night; indeed, it is precisely to this aspect of the Sun God that the epithets "lord of the Upper World and the Lower World, lord of ghosts" refer.

From an epigraphic and philological perspective, however, the epithet "lord of ghosts" is not straightforward because of the signs LU U$_2$ that appear in between EN and *eṭemmu*. Beginning with Smith (1949), many scholars took them as a phonetic complement with the preceding EN since the signs spell the final syllable of the Akkadian word designated by that logogram, *bēlu*. But doing so results in a form of the noun in the construct state, *bēlu*, that is different than the form *bēl*, which is expected in the standard Akkadian dialects.[101] For this reason, other scholars have considered the signs to be a scribal error and deleted them from the text. Dietrich and Loretz (1981, 207) and Durand (2011, 150 with n. 197) have offered still other, more radical, interpretations of the syntax.

The interpretation suggested here is that *bēlu* is a nonstandard form of the noun in the construct state in which the case marker is present. There are good parallels for such forms in western hybrid Akkadian. For instance, in the Akkadian of Ugarit, "a significant majority of the examples" of singular nouns in the construct state "have a case-ending that would not appear in normative Akk[adian]. In all but a few instances, the case-vowel is the one required by context" (Huehnergard 2011, 150).[102] While the preservation of case vowels other than /i/ on nouns in the construct state is not as common in Akkadian texts written at Amurru, the phenomenon does occur.[103] Indeed, the very presence of the signs LU U$_2$ following EN may indicate that the form of the noun in the construct state reflects West Semitic nominal morphology, not the standard Akkadian dialects.

Figure A.77. Juxtaposition of LA in line 100 (center) with attestations of third LA in line 78 (left) and LA in 94 (right).

[101] Anticipating this difficulty, Smith (1949, 22–23) considered "EN-*lu-u*" to be "a 'pausal' form, to indicate unusual emphasis," which the explicit writing of the final syllable would make clear to a reader. Note that a construct state noun ending in -*u* is a feature of so-called Hymno-Epic Akkadian; see Hess 2010, 108–9.

[102] See, e.g., *ši-it be-el-tu*$_4$ E$_2$, "she is the mistress of the estate" (PRU 3 85–86 [RS 16.250]: 23).

[103] See, e.g., another form of *bēltu* in a text found at Ugarit but written at and sent from Amurru: DUMU.MUNUS ^{f}⌜*ra-bi*⌝-*ti be-el*$_2$-*tu*$_4$ *hi-ṭi-ka*, "the daughter of the Great Lady, your criminal (lit. the owner of your crime)" (PRU 4 144–46 [RS 17.318A+]: 15′).

Given that the preceding sequence of precatives shows increasingly nonstandard Akkadian forms (*liballiṭūšu* > *linaṣṣarūšu* > *lū udammiqūšu*), such an interpretation fits well within the immediate literary context of the line.

The identification of the penultimate sign in the body inscription as LA was first proposed by (Oller 1977a, 129) and is excellent from an epigraphic perspective. Oller (1977a, 144) suggested "for [a] comparable LA—cf. l. 78 in *šal-la-tim*)." And Oller could have pointed to more parallels than line 78, for there are a number of similarly formed LA signs in the inscription. For instance, another excellent parallel, if written more distinctly, is found in line 94 in the spelling of *šaplâtu*, the same word that appears in this line, although in a different form. All three attestations of LA can be seen in figure A.77. Oller's identification of the sign as LA means that it can be read with the preceding TI as the logogram TI.LA, which is used to write forms of *balāṭu*, "to live" and so fits the context quite well. My interpretation of the sign string *lu-u*$_2$ TI.LA-*šu* follows the interpretation of the similar sign string of *lu-u*$_2$ SIG$_5^{u_2}$-*šu* earlier in the line. I understand this form also as an uncontracted precative *lū uballiṭšu* as can be found in other dialects of western hybrid Akkadian; note in particular how the only difference between the two orthographies is that SIG$_5^{u_2}$-*šu* has the phonetic complement U$_2$ to indicate that it is plural in number with the plural subject (DINGIR.MEŠ *ša* AN *u* KI, l. 99), while the phonetic complement is omitted with TI.LA-*šu*, which is singular in number with its singular subject (^{d}UTU, l. 100).

References

Abdi, Kaymar, and Gary Beckman. 2007. "A Cuneiform Archive from Chogha Gavaneh, Western Iran." *JCS* 59:39–91.

Abusch, Tzvi. 2001. "The Development and Meaning of the Epic of Gilgamesh: An Interpretive Essay." *JAOS* 121:614–22.

Abrahami, Philippe. 2016. "Les lettres de la correspondance d'El-Amarna expédiées depuis l'Oronte." Pages 119–35 in *Le fleuve rebelle: Géographie historique du moyen Oronte d'Ebla à l'époque médiévale; Actes du colloque international tenu les 13 et 14 décembre 2012 à Nanterre (MAE) et à Paris (INHA)*. Edited by Dominique Parayre. SyriaSup 4. Beyrouth: Presses de l'Ifpo.

Adalı, Selim. 2011. *The Scourge of God: The Umman-manda and Its Significance in the First Millennium BC.* Helsinki: Neo-Assyrian Text Corpus Project.

Adler, Hans-Peter. 1976. *Das Akkadische des Königs Tušratta von Mittani.* AOAT 281. Kevelaer and Neukirchen-Vluyn: Butzon & Bercker and Neukirchener Verlag.

Akar, Murat. 2012. "The Late Bronze Age II City of Alalakh and Its Social Context in the Northern Levant: A Re-Examination of the Post-Level IV Stratigraphic Sequence (I–III) Based on New Excavation Results." PhD diss., Universita' degli Studi di Firenze.

———. 2019. "Excavation Results." Pages 11–75 in *The Late Bronze II City. 2006–2010 Excavation Season.* Vol. 2A (Text) of *Tell Atchana, Alalakh.* Edited by K. Aslıhan Yener et al.. Istanbul: Koç University Press.

Albright, William F. 1950. "Some Important Recent Discoveries: Alphabetic Origins and the Idrimi Statue." *BASOR* 118:11–20.

———. 1957. "Recent Books on Assyriology and Related Subjects." *BASOR* 146:34–35.

———. 1964. "The Eighteenth-Century Princes of Byblos and the Chronology of the Middle Bronze Age." *BASOR* 176:38–46.

Albright, William F., and William Moran. 1948. A Re-Interpretation of an Amarna Letter from Byblos (EA 82)." *JCS* 2:239–48.

Algaze, Guillermo. 2005. *The Uruk World System: The Dynamics of Expansion of Early Mesopotamian Civilization.* Chicago: University of Chicago Press.

Altman, Amnon. 2001a. "EA 59 and the Efforts of Mukiš, Nuhašše, and Niya to Establish a Common Front against Šuppiluliuma I." *UF* 33:1–25.

———. 2001b. "The Submission of Šarrupši of Nuhašše to Šuppiluliuma (CTH 53: a, obv. i, 2–11)." *UF* 33:27–47.

———. 2004. *The Historical Prologue of the Hittite Vassal Treaties: An Inquiry into the Concepts of Hittite Interstate Law*. Bar-Ilan Studies in Near Eastern Languages and Culture. Ramat-Gan: Bar-Ilan University Press.

Anor, Netanel, and Yoram Cohen. 2021. "Bird in the Sky: Babylonian Bird Omen Collections, Astral Observations and the *manzāzu*." *RA* 115:51–80.

Archi, Alfonso. 1994. "Studies in the Pantheon of Ebla." *Or* 63:249–56.

———. 2006. "Alalah al Tempo del Regni di Ebla." Pages 3–5 in *Tra Oriente e Occidente: Studi in Onore di Elena Di Filippo Balestrazzi*. Edited by Daniele Morandi Bonacossi. Padova: S.A.R.G.O.N.

———. 2013. "The West Hurrian Pantheon and Its Background." Pages 1–22 in *Beyond Hatti: A Tribute to Gary Beckman*. Edited by Billie Jean Collins and Piotr Michalowski. Atlanta: Lockwood.

———. 2020. "Linguistic and Political Borders in the Period of the Ebla Archives." Pages 31–40 in *Alalakh and Its Neighbors: Proceedings of the 15th Anniversary Symposium at the New Hatay Archaeology Museum, 10–12 June 2015*. Edited by K. Aslıhan Yener and Tara Ingman. Leuven: Peeters.

Arkhipov, Ilya. 2019a. "*Ittum* 'sign' et *ittum* 'moment' en paléobabylonien." Pages 47–78 in *De l'argile au numérique: Mélanges assyriologiques en l'honneur de Dominique Charpin*. Edited by Grégory Chambon et al. Leuven: Peeters.

———. 2019b. "On the Use of 'Check Marks' in Cuneiform Writing." Pages 10–20 in *The Earliest States of Eastern Europe, 2017–2018: Early Forms and Functions of Writing*. Edited by Timofey Guimon. Moscow: Dmitry Pozharsky University.

Arnaud, Daniel. 1996. "Études sur Alalah et Ougarit à l'Âge du Bronze Récent." *SMEA* 37:47–65.

———. 1998. "Le dialecte d'Alalah: Un examen préliminaire." *AuOr* 16:143–86.

———. 2007. *Corpus des textes de bibliothèque de Ras Shamra-Ougarit (1936–2000) en sumérien, babylonien et assyrien*. AuOrSup 23. Sabadell: Editorial Ausa.

Aro, Jussi. 1954. "Remarks on the Language of the Alalakh Texts." *AfO* 17:361–65.

Astour, Michael. 1965. *Hellenosemitica: An Ethnic and Cultural Study in West Semitic Impact on Mycenaean Greece*. Leiden: Brill.

———. 1969. "The Partition of the Confederacy of Mukiš-Nuhašše-Nii by Šuppiluliuma: A Study in Political Geography of the Amarna Age." *Or* 38:381–414.

———. 1978. "Les Hourites en Syrie du nord: Rapport sommaire." *RHA* 36:1–22.

———. 1988. "The Geographical and Political Structure of the Ebla Empire." Pages 139–58 in *Wirtschaft und Gesellschaft von Ebla: Akten der Internationalen Tagung Heidelberg, 4.–7. November 1986*. Edited by Hartmut Waetzoldt and Harald Hauptmann. Heidelberg: Heidelberg Orientverlag.

Bahrani, Zainab. 2003. *The Graven Image: Representation in Babylonia and Assyria*. Philadelphia: University of Pennsylvania Press.

Baranowski, Krzysztof. 2016. *The Verb in the Amarna Letters from Canaan*. Languages of the Ancient Near East 6. Winona Lake, IN: Eisenbrauns.

Barjamovic, Gojko. 2011. *A Historical Geography of Anatolia in the Old Assyrian Colony Period*. Copenhagen: Museum Tusculanum Press, Carsten Niebuhr Institute of Near Eastern Studies, University of Copenhagen.

Batiuk, Stephen, and Aaron Burke. 2005. "The Tell Atchana Mapping and GIS Project." Pages 145–52 in *Surveys in the Plain of Antioch and Orontes Delta, Turkey, 1995–2002*. Vol.

1 of *The Amuq Valley Regional Projects*. Edited by K. Aslıhan Yener. OIP 131. Chicago: Oriental Institute of the University of Chicago.

Batiuk, Stephen, and Mara Horowitz. 2010. "Temple Deep Sounding Investigations 2001–2006." Pages 161–68 in *The 2003-2004 Excavation Seasons*. Vol. 1 of *Tell Atchana, Ancient Alalakh*. Edited by K. Aslıhan Yener. Istanbul: Koç University Press.

Bayliss, Miranda. 1973. "The Cult of Dead Kin in Assyria and Babylonia." *Iraq* 35:115–25.

Beckman, Gary. 1996. *Hittite Diplomatic Texts*. WAW 7. Atlanta: Scholars Press.

Benz, Brendan. 2016. *The Land before the Kingdom of Israel: A History of the Southern Levant and the People who Populated It*. HACL 7. Winona Lake, IN: Eisenbrauns.

Bergoffen, Celia. 2005. *The Cypriot Bronze Age Pottery from Sir Leonard Woolley's Excavations at Alalakh (Tell Atchana)*. Contributions to the Chronology of the Eastern Mediterranean 5; Denkschriften der Gesamtakademie 31. Vienna: Österreichischen Akademie der Wissenschaften.

Bhabha, Homi. 1994. *The Location of Culture*. London: Routledge.

Boer, Rients de. 2014. "Amorites in the Early Old Babylonian Period." PhD diss., Leiden University.

Böhl, Franz. 1909. *Die Sprache der Amarnabriefe mit besonderer Berücksichtigung der Kanaanismen*. Leipzig: J. C. Hinrichs.

Bonatz, Dominik. 2000a. *Das Syro-hethitische Grabdenkmal: Untersuchung zur Entstehung einer neuen Bildgattung in der Eisenzeit im nordsyrisch-sudöstanatolischen Raum*. Mainz: P. von Zaber.

———. 2000b. "Syro-Hittite Funerary Monuments: A Phenomenon of Tradition or Innovation?" ANESSup 7:189–210.

———. 2016. "Syro-Hittite Funerary Monuments Revisited." Pages 173–94 in *Dining and Death: Interdisciplinary Perspectives on the 'Funerary Banquet' in Ancient Art, Burial and Belief*. Edited by Catherine Draycott and Maria Stamatopoulou. Colloquia Antiqua 16. Leuven: Peeters.

Bonechi, Marco. 2019. "Popoli della bibbia/5—gli Amorrei: Nella Levante delle origini." *Archeo* 411:68–81.

Borger, Rykle. 1968. "Die Statueinschrift des Idrimi von Alalach (um 1400 v. Chr.)." Pages 21–24 in *Textbuch zur Geschichte Israels*. Edited by Kurt Galling. Tübingen: Mohr.

Bottéro, Jean. 1949a. "Les inventaires de Qatna." *RA* 43:1–40.

———. 1949b. "Les inventaires de Qatna (Suite)." *RA* 43:137–215.

Boyes, Philip. 2020. *Script and Society: The Social Context of Writing Practices in Late Bronze Age Ugarit*. Contexts of and Relations between Early Writing Systems 3. Oxford: Oxbow.

Buccellati, Giorgio. 1962. "La 'carriera' di Davide e quella di Idrimi, re di Alalac." *BeO* 4:95–99.

Bülbül, Cemil. 2010. "İdrimi Zamanında Alalah Krallığı." *History Studies: International Journal of History* 2.2:15–27.

Bunnens, Guy. 1973. "À propos de l'épithète royale 'šarru dannu.'" *AIPHOS* 20:145–54.

———. 1978. "Ilim-ilimma, fils de Tuttu 'bourgeois-gentilhomme' d'Alalakh au XVe s. av. n.e." *Akkadica* 10:2–15.

Burlingame, Andrew. 2021. "Ugaritic Indefinite Pronouns: Linguistic, Social, and Textual Perspectives." PhD diss., University of Chicago.

Celada, Benito. 1951. Review of *The Statue of Idri-mi*, by Sidney Smith. *Sef* 11:434–35.

Charpin, Dominique. 2008. "'Le roi est mort, vive le roi!' Les funérailles des souverains amorrites et l'avènement de leur successeur." Pages 69–96 in *Studies in Ancient Near Eastern World View and Society: Presented to Marten Stol on the Occasion of his 65th Birthday, 10 November 2005, and His Retirement from the Vrije Universiteit Amsterdam*. Edited by Robertus J. van der Spek. Bethesda, MD: CDL.

Cohen, Yoram. 2009. *The Scribes and Scholars of the City of Emar in the Late Bronze Age*. HSS 59. Winona Lake, IN: Eisenbrauns.

———. 2021. "The 'Hunger Years' and the 'Sea Peoples': Preliminary Observations on the Recently Published Letters from the 'House of Urtenu' Archive at Ugarit." Pages 47–61 in *Ve-'Ed Ya'aleh (Gen 2:6): Essays in Biblical and Ancient Near Eastern Studies Presented to Edward L. Greenstein*. Edited by Peter Machinist et al. WAW Sup 5. Atlanta: SBL Press.

———. 2023. "The Statue of Idrimi and the Term *mānahtu/mānahātu*." *IOS* 23:56–65.

Cohen, Yoram, and Euardo Torrecilla. 2023. "Grain Tribute in Hittite Syria and the Fall of Ugarit." *BASOR* 389:65–73.

Cohen, Yoram, and Maurizio Viano. 2016. "A Land-Grant Document from Emar: A (Re)-Edition and Discussion of LN-104 (AKA Gs-Kutscher 6)." *Kaskal* 13:57–71.

Collins, Billie Jean. 1997. "Purifying a House: A Ritual for the Infernal Deities." Pages 168–71 in vol. 1 of *Context of Scripture*. Edited by William Hallo and K. Lawson Younger. Leiden: Brill.

Collon, Dominique. 1975. *The Seal Impressions from Tell Atchana/Alalakh*. AOAT 27. Kevelaer and Neukirchen-Vluyn: Butzon & Bercker and Neukirchener Verlag.

Cornelius, Friedrich. 1963. "ERIN-Manda." *Iraq* 25:167–70.

Crawford Crawford. 2014. "Relating Image and Word in Ancient Mesopotamia." Pages 241–64 in *Critical Approaches to Ancient Near Eastern Art*. Edited by Marian Feldman and Brian Brown. Berlin: de Gruyter.

Démare-Lafont, Sophie, and Daniel Fleming. 2015. "Emar Chronology and Scribal Streams: Cosmopolitanism and Legal Diversity." *RA* 109:45–77.

Devecchi, Elena. 2007. "A Fragment of a Treaty with Mukiš." *SMEA* 49:207–16.

———. 2012. "Treaties and Edicts in the Hittite World." Pages 637–45 in *Organization, Representation, and Symbols of Power in the Ancient Near East: Proceedings of the 54th Rencontre Assyriologique Internationale at Würzburg, 20–25 July 2008*. Edited by Gernot Wilhelm. Winona Lake, IN: Eisenbrauns.

———. 2013. "Suppiluliuma's Syrian Campaigns in Light of the Documents from Ugarit." Pages 81–97 in *New Results and New Questions on the Reign of Suppiluliuma I*. Edited by Stefano de Martino and Jared Miller. Firenze: LoGisma.

———. 2018. "Details that Make the Difference: The Akkadian Manuscripts of the 'Šattiwaza Treaties.'" *WO* 48:72–95.

———. 2022. "The Governance of the Subordinated Countries." Pages 271–312 in *Handbook Hittite Empire: Power Structures*. Edited by Stefano de Martino. Empires through the Ages in Global Perspectives 1. Berlin: de Gruyter.

Dietrich, Manfried, and Oswald Loretz. 1966. Review of *Nordsyrien*, by Horst Klengel. *OLZ* 61:554–60.

———. 1981. "Die Inschrift des Königs Idrimi von Alalah." *UF* 13:201–78.

———. 1985. “Historisch-Chronologische Texte aus Alalah, Ugarit, Kamid el-Loz/Kumidi und den Amarna Briefe.” Pages 496–520 in *Historisch-Chronologische Texte*. Edited by Otto Kaiser. Vol. 2. *TUAT* 1/5. Gütersloh: Gütersloher Verlagshaus.

———. 1997. “Der Vertrag zwischen Ir-Addu von Tunip und Niqmepa von Mukiš.” Pages 211–42 in *Crossing Boundaries and Linking Horizons: Studies in Honor of Michael C. Astour on His Eightieth Birthday*. Edited by Gordon Young et al. Bethesda, MD: CDL.

Dietrich, Manfried, and Walther Mayer. 1996. “Hurritica Alalahiana (I).” *UF* 28:177–88.

Draffkorn, Anne. See Kilmer, Anne.

Durand, Jean-Marie. 1989. “Tombes familiales et culte de Ancêtres à Emâr.” *NABU* 1989/112.

———. 1990. “La Cite-État d’Imâr à l’époque des rois de Mari.” *MARI* 6:39–92.

———. 2002. *Le Culte d’Addu d’Alep et l’affaire d’Alahtum*. FM 7. Paris: SÉPOA.

———. 2003. “*nuldânum* = ‘Führer ou Duce.’” *NABU* 2003/76.

———. 2011. “La fondation d’une lignée royale syrienne: Le geste d’Idrimi d’Alalah.” Pages 94–150 in *Le jeune héros: Recherches sur la formation et la diffusion d’un thème littéraire au Proche-Orient ancien*. Edited by Jean-Marie Durand et al. OBO 250. Fribourg and Göttingen: Academic Press and Vandenhoeck & Ruprecht.

Durand, Jean-Marie, and Michel Guichard. 1997. “Les rituels de Mari.” Pages 17–78 in *Recueil d’études à la mémoire de Marie-Thérèse Barrelet*. FM 3. Paris: Société pour l’étude du Proche-Orient ancien.

Dussaud, Réne. 1950. Review of *The Statue of Idri-mi*, by S. Smith. *Syria* 27:157–60.

Ellis, Richard. 1968. *Foundation Deposits in Ancient Mesopotamia*. New Haven: Yale University Press.

Fink, Amir. 2005. “The Enthronement Inscription of Addu-nirari, King of Alalakh.” Paper presented at the Annual Meeting of the American Schools of Oriental Research. Philadelphia, PA, November 18.

———. 2010. *Late Bronze Age Tell Atchana (Alalakh): Stratigraphy, Chronology, History*. BAR International Series 2120. Oxford: Archaeopress.

Fitzpatrick, Joan. 2011. “The Critical Backstory.” Pages 35–59 in *King Lear: A Critical Guide*. Edited by Andrew Hiscock and Lisa Hopkins. Continuum Renaissance Drama Guides. London: Continuum.

Fleming, Daniel, and Sophie Démare-Lafont. 2009. “Tablet Terminology at Emar: ‘Conventional’ and ‘Free Format.’” *AuOr* 27:19–26.

Foster, Benjamin. 2005. *Before the Muses: An Anthology of Akkadian Literature*. Bethesda, MD: CDL.

Frankfort, Henri. 1996. *The Art and Architecture of the Ancient Orient*. Baltimore: Penguin, 1955. Repr. New Haven: Yale University Press.

Freu, Jaques. 2003. *Histoire du Mitanni*. Collection Kubaba, Série Antiquité 3. Paris: L’Harmattan.

Gantzert, Merijn. 2011. “The Emar Lexical Texts.” PhD diss., Leiden University.

Gates, Marie-Henriette. 2000. “Kinet Höyük (Hatay, Turkey) and MB Levantine Chronology.” *Akkadica* 119–20:77–101.

Genz, Hermann. 2006. “Hethitische Präsenz im spätbronzezeitlichen Syrien: Die archäologische Evidenz.” *BaghM* 37:499–509.

George, Andrew. 2003. *The Babylonian Gilgamesh Epic: Introduction, Critical Edition and Cuneiform Texts*. 2 vols. Oxford: Oxford University Press.

———. 2007. "The Gilgameš Epic at Ugarit." *AuOr* 25:238–48.

———. 2013. *Babylonian Divinatory Texts Chiefly in the Schøyen Collection: With an Appendix of Material From the Papers of W. G. Lambert*. CUSAS 18. Bethesda, MD: CDL.

Giacumakis, George. 1970. *The Akkadian of Alalah*. The Hague: Mouton.

Gilan, Amir. 2015. *Formen und Inhalte althethitischer historische Literatur*. THeth 29. Heidelberg: Universitätsverlag Winter.

Glassner, Jean-Jacques. 2024. "L'*ummān-manda* dans la stèle de Cutha." *NABU* 2024/21.

Goedegebuure, Petra. 2012. "Hittite Iconoclasm: Disconnecting the Icon, Disempowering the Referent." Pages 407–52 in *Iconoclasm and Text Destruction in the Ancient Near East and Beyond*. Edited by Natalie Naomi May. OIS 8. Chicago: Oriental Institute of the University of Chicago.

Goetze, Albrecht. 1950. Review of *The Statue of Idri-mi*, by S. Smith. *JCS* 4:226–31.

———. 1957. "The Syrian Town of Emar." *BASOR* 147:22–27.

Golinets, Viktor. 2018. *Verbalmorphologie des Amurritischen und Glossar der Verbalwurzeln*. Vol. 2 of *Das amurritische Onomastikon der altbabylonischen Zeit*. AOAT 271.2. Münster: Ugarit-Verlag.

Greenstein, Edward. 1995. "Autobiographies in Ancient Western Asia." Pages 2421–31 in vol. 4 of *Civilizations of the Ancient Near East*. Edited by Jack Sasson. New York: Scribner's.

———. 1997. "Kirta." Pages 9–48 in *Ugaritic Narrative Poetry*. Edited by Simon Parker. WAW 9. Atlanta: Scholars Press.

———. 2015. "The Fugitive Hero Narrative Pattern in Mesopotamia." Pages 17–35 in *Women, Worship, and War: Essays in Honor of Susan Niditch*. Edited by Saul Olyan. BJS 357. Providence, RI: Brown Judaic Studies.

Greenstein, Edward, and David Marcus. 1976. "The Akkadian Inscription of Idrimi." *JANESCU* 8:59–96.

Gromova, Daria. 2013. "Syria in the Period before, during and after the First Syrian War of Suppiluliuma I." Pages 99–114 in *New Results and New Questions on the Reign of Suppiluliuma I*. Edited by Stefano de Martino and Jared Miller. Firenze: LoGisma.

Guichard, Michaël. 2003. "Lecture des 'Archives royal de Mari,' Tome XXVIII: Lettres royales du temps de Zimrî-Lîm." *Syria* 80:199–216.

Gurney, Oliver. 1950. Review of *The Statue of Idri-mi*, by Sidney Smith. *JRAS* 82:76–77.

———. 1951. Review of *The Statue of Idri-mi*, by Sidney Smith. *PEQ* 83:90–93.

Güterbock, Hans. 1934. "Die historische Tradition und ihre literarische Gestaltung bei Babyloniern und Hethitern bis 1200, Erster Teil: Babylonier." *ZA* 42:1–91.

Hagenbuchner, Albertine. 1989. *Die Brief mit Transkription, Übersetzung und Kommentar*. Vol. 2 of *Die Korrespondenz der Hethiter*. Heidelberg: C. Winter.

Hale, William. 2021. "Turkey and Britain in World War II: Origins and Results of the Tripartite Alliance, 1935–40." *Journal of Balkan and Near Eastern Studies* 23:824–44.

Hawkins, John David. 1972. Review of *The Akkadian of Alalah*, by G. Giacumakis. *BSOAS* 35:135–36.

———. 2000. *Inscriptions of the Iron Age*. Vol. 1 of *Corpus of Hieroglyphic Luwian Inscriptions*. Untersuchungen zur indogermanischen Sprach- und Kulturwissenschaft NF 8. Berlin: de Gruyter.

Healey, John. 1980. "The Sun Deity and the Underworld: Mesopotamia and Ugarit." Pages 239–42 in *Death in Mesopotamia: Papers read at the XXVIe Rencontre assyriologiques internationale*. Edited by Bendt Alster. Mesopotamia: Copenhagen Studies in Assyriology 8. Copenhagen: Akademisk Forlag.

———. 2007. "From Ṣapānu/Ṣapunu to Kasion: The Sacred History of a Mountain." Pages 141–51 in *"He Unfurrowed His Brow and Laughed": Essays in Honour of Professor Nicolas Wyatt*. Edited by Wilfred G. E. Watson. AOAT 229. Münster: Ugarit-Verlag.

Heimpel, Wolfgang. 1999. "Minding an Oath." *NABU* 1999/42.

Heinz, Marlies. 1992. *Tell Atchana/Alalakh: Die Schichten VII–XVII*. AOAT 41. Kevelaer and Neukirchen-Vluyn: Butzon & Bercker and Neukirchener Verlag.

Heltzer, Michael, and Shoshana Arbeli-Raveh. 1981. *The Suteans*. Series minor, Seminario di studi asiatico 13. Naples: Istituto Universitario Orientale.

Hess, Christian. 2010. "Towards the Origins of the Hymnic Epic Dialect." *Kaskal* 7:101–22.

Hogue, Timothy. 2019. "'I Am': The Function, History, and Diffusion of the Fronted First-Person Pronoun in Syro-Anatolian Monumental Discourse." *JNES* 78:323–39.

Homan, Zenobia. 2020. *Mittani Palaeography*. CunMon 48. Leiden: Brill.

Huehnergard, John. 1986. "RS 19.55 (PRU 4, 293b)." *UF* 18:453.

———. 2011. *The Akkadian of Ugarit*. HSS 34. Repr. Winona Lake, IN: Eisenbrauns.

Izre'el, Shlomo. 1991. *Amurru Akkadian: A Linguistic Study*. 2 vols. HSS 40–41. Atlanta: Scholars Press.

———. 2012. "Canaano-Akkadian: Linguistics and Sociolinguistics." Pages 171–218 in *Language and Nature: Papers Presented to John Huehnergard on the Occasion of His Sixtieth Birthday*. Edited by Rebecca Hasselbach and Na'ama Pat-El. SAOC 67. Chicago: Oriental Institute of the University of Chicago.

Jiménez, Enrique. 2017. *The Babylonian Disputation Poems: With Editions of the Series of the Poplar, Palm and Vine, the Series of the Spider, and the Story of the Poor, Forlorn Wren*. CHANE 87. Leiden: Brill.

Kempinski, Aaron, and Nadav Na'aman. 1973. "The Idrimi Inscription Reconsidered" (Hebrew). Pages 211–20 in *Ḥafirot umeḥkarim*. Edited by Yohanan Aharoni. Tel Aviv: Hotsa'at haMakhon learkhe'ologyah ʿal yedei Karṭa.

Kestemont, Guy. 1974. *Diplomatique et droit international en Asie occidentale (1600–1200 Av. J.C.)*. Publications d'Institut orientaliste de Louvain 9. Louvain: Université Catholique de Louvain, Institut Orientaliste.

Khadduri, Majid. 1945. "The Alexandretta Dispute." *American Journal of International Law* 39:406–25.

Kilmer, Anne D. (née Draffkorn). 1959. "Hurrians and Hurrian at Alalah: An Ethno-linguistic Analysis." PhD diss., University of Pennsylvania.

———. 1973. Review of *The Akkadian of Alalah*, by G. Giacumakis. *JAOS* 93:400–401.

Kitchen, Kenneth, and Paul Lawrence. 2012. *The Texts*. Part 1 of *Treaty, Law, and Covenant in the Ancient Near East*. Wiesbaden: Harrassowitz.

Klengel, Horst. 1965. *Nordsyrien*. Part 1 of *Geschichte Syriens im 2. Jahrtausend v. u. Z*. Berlin: Akadamie.

———. 1978. "Mittani: Probleme seiner Expansion und politischen Struktur." *RHA* 36:91–115.

———. 1981. "Historisch Kommentar zur Inschrift des Idrimi von Alalah." *UF* 13:269–78.

———. 1998–2001. "Nuhašše." Pages 610–11 in vol. 9 of *Reallexikon der Assyriologie*. Edited by Dietz-Otto Edzard. Berlin: de Gruyter.

Kohlmeyer, Kay. 2009. "The Temple of the Storm God in Aleppo during the Late Bronze and Early Iron Ages." *NEA* 72:190–202.

———. 2013. "Der Tempel des Wettergottes des Aleppo." Pages 179–218 in *Tempel im alten Orient, 7. Internationales Colloquium der Deutschen Orient-Gesellschaft, 11.–13. Oktober 2009, München*. Edited by Kai Kaniuth et al. Wiesbaden: Harrassowitz.

Krebernik, Manfred. 2009–2011. "Sonnengott. A. I." Pages 599–611 in vol. 12 of *Reallexikon der Assyriologie*. Edited by Michael Streck. Berlin: de Gruyter.

Kühne, Cord. 1972. "Bemerkungen zu kürzlich edierten hethitischen Texten." *ZA* 62:236–61.

———. 1982. "Politische Szenerie und Internationale Beziehungen Voderasiens um die Mitte des 2. Jahrtausends vor Chr." Pages 203–64 in *Mesopotamien und seine Nachbarn: Politische und kulturelle Wechselbeziehungen im Alten Vorderasien vom 4. bis 1. Jahrtausend v. Chr. XXV; Rencontre assyriologiques internationale Berlin, 3. bis 7. Juli 1978*. Edited by Hans-Jörg Nissinen and Johannes Renger. Berlin: D. Reimer.

Lackenbacher, Sylvie. 2002. *Textes akkadiens d'Ugarit: Textes provenant des vingt-cinq premières campagnes*. LAPO 20. Paris: Cerf.

Lackenbacher, Sylvie, and Florence. Malbran-Labat. 2016. *Lettres en Akkadien de la "Maison d'Urtēnu": Fouilles de 1994*. RSOu 23. Leuven: Peeters.

Landsberger, Benno. 1954. "Assyrische Königsliste und 'Dunkles Zeitalter.'" *JCS* 8:31–45, 47–73, 106–33.

Lauinger, Jacob. 2005. "Epigraphic Finds from the Oriental Institute's 2003 Excavations at Alalakh." *JNES* 64:53–58.

———. 2011. "An Excavated Dossier of Cuneiform Tablets from Level VII Alalah?" *BASOR* 362:1–44.

———. 2015. *Following the Man of Yamhad: Settlement and Territory at Old Babylonian Alalah*. CHANE 75. Leiden: Brill.

———. 2019. "Discourse and Meta-discourse in the Statue of Idrimi and Its Inscription." *Maarav* 23:19–38.

———. 2021. "Imperial and Local: Audience and Identity in the Idrimi Inscriptions." *Studia Orientalia Electronica* 9:28–46.

———. 2022a. "Idrimi's Aunts at Emar: On Line 5 of the Idrimi Inscription." Pages 219–25 in *One Who Loves Knowledge: Studies in Honor of Richard Jasnow*. Edited by Betsy Bryan et al. Material and Visual Culture of Ancient Egypt 6. Columbus, GA: Lockwood.

———. 2022b. "The Supposed Recyling of a Silver Statue of a God from Middle Bronze Age/Old Babylonian Alalah (AlT 366 [40.05])." Pages 313–32 in *"Now These Records Are Ancient": Studies in Ancient Near Eastern and Biblical History, Language and Culture in Honor of K. Lawson Younger, Jr*. Edited by James Hoffmeier et al. ÄAT 114. Münster: Zaphon.

———. In press. "Movements of Persons and Populations at Middle and Late Bronze Age Alalah." In *Crossroads IV: Migration and Mobility in the Ancient Near East*. Edited by Jana Mynářová et al. Columbus, GA: Lockwood.

Lemche, Niels Peter. 1991. *The Canaanites and Their Land: The Tradition of the Canaanites*. JSOTSup 110. Sheffield: JSOT Press.

Lewis, Brian. 1980. *The Sargon Legend: A Study of the Akkadian Text and the Tale of the Hero Who Was Exposed at Birth.* Dissertation Series of the American Schools of Oriental Research 4. Cambridge: American Schools of Oriental Research.

Lewis, Theodore. 1989. *Cults of the Dead in Ancient Israel and Ugarit.* HSM 39. Leiden: Brill.

Liverani, Mario. 1967. "Ma nel settimo anno…." Pages 49–53 in *Studi sull'Oriente e la Bibbia: offerti al P. Giovanni Rinaldi nel 60 compleanno da allievi, colleghi, amici.* Genoa: Studio e Vita.

———. 1970. "L'epica ugaritica." Pages 859–69 in *Atti del Convegno Internazionale sul Tema: La Poesia Epica e La Sua Formazione (Roma, 28 Marzo–3 Aprile 1969).* Rome: Accademia Nazionale Dei Lincei.

———. 2004a. "Aziru, Servant of Two Masters." Pages 125–44 in *Myth and Politics in Ancient Near Eastern Historiography.* Translated by Zainab Bahrani and Marc Van De Mieroop. Ithaca, NY: Cornell University Press.

———. 2004b. "Leaving by Chariot for the Desert." Pages 85–96 in *Myth and Politics in Ancient Near Eastern Historiography.* Trans. Zainab Bahrani and Marc Van De Mieroop. Ithaca, NY: Cornell University Press.

———. 2011. "Portrait du héros comme un jeune chien." Pages 11–26 in *Le jeune héros: Recherches sur la formation et la diffusion d'un thème littéraire au Proche-Orient ancien.* Edited by Jean-Marie Durand et al. OBO 250. Fribourg and Göttingen: Academic Press and Vandenhoeck & Ruprecht.

———. 2014. *The Ancient Near East: History, Society, and Economy.* Translated by S. Tabatabai. London: Routledge.

Longman, Tremper. 1991. *Fictional Akkadian Autobiography: A Generic and Comparative Study.* Winona Lake, IN: Eisenbrauns.

———. 1997. "The Autobiography of Idrimi (I.148)." Pages 479–80 in vol. 1 of *Context of Scripture.* Edited by William Hallo and K. Lawson Younger. Leiden: Brill.

Mabie, Frederick. 2004. "Ancient Near Eastern Scribes and the Mark(s) They Left: A Catalog and Analysis of Scribal Auxiliary Marks in the Amarna Corpus and in the Cuneiform Alphabetic Texts of Ugarit and Ras Ibn Hani." PhD diss., University of California, Los Angeles.

Maloigne, Hélène. 2017. "How Idrimi Came to London." *Museum History Journal* 10 (2017): 200–16.

Márquez Rowe, Ignacio. 1997. "Halab in the XVIth and XVth Centuries B.C.: A New Look at the Alalah Material." *WZKM* 87:177–205.

———. 1998. "Notes on the Hurro-Akkadian of Alalah in the Mid-Second Millennium B.C.E." *IOS* 18:63–78.

———. 2001. "The Akkadian Word for *Aristoi*?" *Monografies Eridu* 1:457–60.

———. 2006. *The Royal Deeds of Ugarit: A Study of Ancient Near Eastern Diplomatics.* AOAT 335. Münster: Ugarit-Verlag.

Mayer, Walter. 1995. "Die historische Einordnung der 'Autobiographie' des Idrimi von Alalah." *UF* 27:335–50.

Mayer-Opificius, Ruth. 1981. "Archäologischer Kommentar zur Statue des Idrimi von Alalah." *UF* 13:279–90.

Mazar, Benjamin. 1963. "The Military Élite of King David." *VT* 13:310–20.

McCarter, Kyle. 2000. "The Tomb Inscription of Si'gabbar, Priest of Sahar." Pages 184–85 in vol. 2 of *Context of Scripture.* Edited by William Hallo and K. Lawson Younger. Leiden: Brill.

McGeough, Kevin. 2020. "Taxation and Management of Resources at Ugarit." Pages 399–418 in *Economic Complexity in the Ancient Near East: Management of Resources and Taxation (Third–Second Millennium BC)*. Edited by Jana Mynářová and Sergio Alvernini. Prague: Charles University.

Medill, Kathryn. 2019. "The *Idrimi Statue Inscription* in its Late Bronze Scribal Context." *BASOR* 382:243–59.

Mellink, Machteld. 1957. Review of *Alalakh: An Account of the Excavations at Tell Atchana in the Hatay, 1937–1949*, by Leonard Wooley. *AJA* 61:395–400.

Miglio, Adam. 2022. "Soundscapes, Portentous Calls, and Bird Symbolism in the *Gilgameš Epic*." *JNES* 81:165–85.

Milstein, Sara. 2016. *Tracking the Master Scribe: Revision through Introduction in Biblical and Mesopotamian Literature*. New York: Oxford University Press.

Minunno, Giuseppe. 2013. *Ritual Employs of Birds in Ancient Syria-Palestine*. AOAT 402. Münster: Ugarit-Verlag.

Monte, Giuseppe. del. 1986. *Il tratto fra Muršili II di Hattuša e Niqmepaʿ di Ugarit*. OAC 18. Rome: Istituto per l'Oriente C.A. Nallino: Centro per le antichità e la storia dell'arte del Vicino Oriente.

Moortgat, Anton. 1949. Review of *The Statue of Idri-mi* by Sidney Smith. *BO* 7:175–76.

———. 1969. *The Art of Ancient Mesopotamia: The Classical Art of the Ancient Near East*. Translated by Judith Filson. London: Phaidon.

Moran, William. 1950. "A Syntactical Study of the Dialect of Byblos as Reflected in the Amarna Tablets." PhD diss., Johns Hopkins University.

———. 1975. "The Syrian Scribe of the Jerusalem Amarna Letters." Pages 146–66 in *Unity and Diversity: Essays in the History, Literature, and Religion of the Ancient Near East*. Edited by Hans Goedicke and Jimmy Jack McBee Roberts. Baltimore: Johns Hopkins University Press.

———. 1992. *The Amarna Letters*. Baltimore: Johns Hopkins University Press.

———. 1995. "Some Reflections on Amarna Politics." Pages 559–72 in *Solving Riddles and Untying Knots: Biblical, Epigraphic, and Semitic Studies in Honor of Jonas C. Greenfield*. Edited by Ziony Zevit et al. Winona Lake, IN: Eisenbrauns.

Na'aman, Nadav. 1980a. "The Ishtar Temple at Alalakh." *JNES* 39:209–14.

———. 1980b. "A Royal Scribe and His Scribal Products in the Alalakh IV Court." *OrAnt* 19:107–16.

Niedorf, Christian. 1998. "Die Toponyme der Texte aus Alalah IV." *UF* 30:516–68.

———. 2008. *Die mittelbabylonischen Rechtsurkunden aus Alalah (Schicht IV)*. AOAT 352. Münster: Ugarit-Verlag.

Noegel, Scott. 1995. "Janus Parallelism Clusters in Akkadian Literature." *NABU* 1995/39.

Nougayrol, Jean. 1950. "Textes hépatoscopiques d'époque ancienne conserves au Musée du Louvre (III)." *RA* 44:1–44.

———. 1951. Review of *The Statue of Idri-mi*, by S. Smith. *RA* 45:151–54.

Novak, Mirko. 2004. "The Chronology of the Royal Palace of Qaṭna." *AeL* 14:299–317.

Oatley, Keith. 1994. "A Taxonomy of the Emotions of Literary Response and a Theory of Identification in Fictional Narrative." *Poetics* 23:53–74.

———. 1999. "Meeting in Minds: Dialogue, Sympathy, and Identification in Reading Fiction." *Poetics* 26:439–54.

Oliva, Juan. 2018. "Der hurro-akkadische Brief TT3 aus Qaṭna unter neuem Blick." *UF* 49:275–83.

———. 2019. "Anmerkungen zum hurro-akkadischen Brief TT4 aus Qaṭna und neue geschichtliche Aussichten." *UF* 50:295–312.

Oller, Gary. 1977a. "The Autobiography of Idrimi: A New Text Edition with Philological and Historical Commentary." PhD diss., University of Pennsylvania.

———. 1977b. "A Note on Lines 102–104 of the Idrimi Inscription." *JCS* 29:167–68.

———. 1989. "The Inscription of Idrimi: A Pseudo-Autobiography?" Pages 411–17 in *DUMU-E$_2$-DUB-BA-A: Studies in Honor of Åke Sjoberg*. Edited by Hermann Behrens et al. Occasional Publications of the S. N. Kramer Fund 11. Philadelphia: Babylonian Section, University Museum.

Oppenheim, A. Leo. 1955. Review of *The Statue of Idri-mi*, by S. Smith. *JNES* 14:199–200.

———. 1969. "The Story of Idrimi, King of Alalakh." Pages 557–58 in *The Ancient Near East in Texts and Pictures Relating to the Old Testament*. 3rd edition. Edited by James Pritchard. Princeton: Princeton University Press.

Ornan, Tallay. 2012. "The Long Life of a Dead King: A Bronze Statue from Hazor in its Ancient Near Eastern Context." *BASOR* 366:1–24.

Otten, Heinrich, and Christel Rüster. 1973. "Textanschlüsse von Boğazköy-Tafeln (21–30)." *ZA* 63:83–91.

Pardee, Dennis. 1983–1984. "Ugaritic." *AfO* 29–30:321–29.

———. 2000. *Les textes rituels*. RSOu 12. Paris: Éditions Recherche sur les Civilisations.

———. 2002a. "Puduhepa, Queen of Hatti, to the King of Ugarit (RS 17.434+)." Pages 96–97 in vol. 3 of *Context of Scripture*. Edited by William Hallo and K. Lawson Younger. Leiden: Brill.

———. 2002b. *Ritual and Cult at Ugarit*. WAW 10. Atlanta: Scholars Press.

———. 2019. Review of *Baal and the Politics of Poetry*, by Aaron Tugendhaft. *JNES* 78:166–72.

Parpola, Simo. 1983. *Commentary and Appendices*. Part 2 of *Letters from Assyrian Scholars to the Kings Esarhaddon and Assurbanipal*. AOAT 5.2: Kevelaer and Neukirchen-Vluyn: Butzon & Bercker and Neukirchener Verlag.

Paulus, Susanne. 2014. *Die babylonische* Kudurru-*Inschriften von der kassitischen bis zur frühneubabylonischen Zeit: Untersucht unter besonderer Berücksichtigung gesellschafts- und rechtshistorischer Fragestellungen*. AOAT 51. Münster: Ugarit-Verlag.

Pfälzner, Peter. 2006. "Syria's Royal Tombs Uncovered." *Current World Archaeology* 15:12–22.

———. 2012. "How Did They Bury the Kings of Qaṭna?" Pages 205–22 in *(Re-)Constructing Funerary Rituals in the Ancient Near East: Proceedings of the First International Symposium of the Tübingen Post-Graduate School "Symbols of the Dead" in May 2009*. Edited by Peter Pfälzner et al. Qaṭna Studien: Supplementa 1. Wiesbaden: Harrassowitz.

Pitard, Wayne. 1996. "Care of the Dead at Emar." Pages 123–40 in *Emar: The History, Religion, and Culture of a Syrian Town in the Late Bronze Age*. ed. Mark Chavalas. Bethesda, MD: CDL.

Pongratz-Leisten, Beate. 1999. "'Öffne den Tafelbehälter und lies…': Neue Ansätze zum Verständnis des Literaturkonzeptes in Mesopotamien." *WO* 30:74–90.

———. 2020. "Approaches to the Concept of Literature in Assyriology." Pages 21–40 in *The Ancient Near East and the Foundations of Europe: Proceedings of the Melammu Workshop held in Jena 19th September 2017*. Edited by M. Krebernik and S. Ponchia. Melammu Workshops and Monographs 3. Münster: Zaphon.

———. 2021. "The Aura of the Illegible: A Multimodal Approach to Writing in Mesopotamia." Pages 327–34 in *Klänge der Archäologie: Festschrift für Ricardo Eichmann*. Edited by Claudia Bührig et al. Wiesbaden: Harrassowitz.

Porter, Anne. 2012. *Mobile Pastoralism and the Formation of Near Eastern Civilizations: Weaving Together Society*. Cambridge: Cambridge University Press.

Rainey, Anson. 1996. *Canaanite in the Amarna Tablets: A Linguistic Analysis of the Mixed Dialect Used by the Scribes from Canaan*. 4 vols. HdO 25. Leiden: Brill.

———. 2010. "The Hybrid Language Written by Canaanite Scribes in the Fourteenth Century BCE." Pages 851–61 in *Proceedings of the 53e Rencontre Assyriologique Internationale*. Vol. 2. Edited by Leonid Kogan et al. Winona Lake, IN: Eisenbrauns.

Reiner, Erica. 1973. Review of *The Akkadian of Alalah*, by G. Giacumakis. *Language* 49:500–504.

———. 1978. "Die akkadische Literatur." Pages 151–210 in *Altorientalische Literaturen*. Edited by Wolfgang Röllig. Neues Handbuch der Literaturwissenschaft 1. Wiesbaden: Akademische Verlagsgesellschaft Athenaion.

Richter, Thomas. 2002. "Der 'Einjährige Feldzug' Suppiluliumas I. von Hatti in Syrien nach Textfunde des Jahres 2002 in Mišrife/Qaṭna." *UF* 34:603–18.

———. 2008. "Šuppiluliuma I. in Syrien: Der 'Einjährige Feldzug' und Seine Folgen." Pages 173–203 in *Hattuša-Boğazköy: Das Hethiterreich im Spannungsfeld des Alten Orients. 6. Internationales Colloquium der Deutschen Orient-Gesellschaft, 22.–24. März 2006 in Würzburg*. Edited by Gernot Wilhelm. Colloquien der Deutschen Orient-Gesellschaft 6. Wiesbaden: Harrassowitz.

———. 2012. *Bibliographisches Glossar des Hurritischen*. Wiesbaden: Harrassowitz.

Richter, Thomas, and Sarah Lange. 2012. *Das Archiv des Idadda: Die Keilschrifttexten aus den deutsch-syrischen Ausgrabungen 2001–2003 im Königspalast von Qaṭna*. Qaṭna Studien 3. Wiesbaden: Harrassowitz.

Ridder, Jacob Jan de. 2018. *A Descriptive Grammar of Middle Assyrian*. Leipziger Altorientalistische Studien 6. Wiesbaden: Harrassowitz.

Roche-Hawley, Carole. 2012. "On the Palaeographic 'Syllabary A' in the Late Bronze Age." Pages 127–44 in *Palaeography and Scribal Practices in Syro-Palestine and Anatolia in the Late Bronze Age: Papers Read at a Symposium in Leiden, 17–18 December 2009*. Edited by Elena Devecchi. PIHANS 119. Leiden: Nederlands Instituut voor het Nabije Oosten.

———. 2024. *Babylonian Ceremonial Script in Its Scholarly Context*. Critical Editions of Ancient Texts 1. Columbus, GA: Lockwood.

Röllig, Wolfgang. 1998–2001. "Nihi, Niʾi, Nija." Pages 313–14 in vol. 9 of *Reallexikon der Assyriologie*. Edited by Dietz-Otto Edzard. Berlin: de Gruyter.

Rouault, Olivier. 1992. "Cultures locales et influences extérieures: le cas de Terqa." *SMEA* 30:247–56.

Rutz, Matthew. 2013. *Bodies of Knowledge in Ancient Mesopotamia: The Diviners of Late Bronze Age Emar and Their Tablet Collection*. Ancient Magic and Divination 9. Leiden: Brill.

Sanders, Seth. 2013. "The Appetites of the Dead: West Semitic Linguistic and Ritual Aspects of the Katumuwa Stele." *BASOR* 269:35–55.

Sasson, Jack. 1981. "On Idrimi and Šarruwa, the Scribe." Pages 309–24 in *Studies on the Civilization and Culture of Nuzi and the Hurrians in Honor of Ernest R. Lacheman*. Edited by Martha Morrison and David Owen. SCCNH 1. Winona Lake, IN: Eisenbrauns.

———. 2013. "Prologues and Poets: On the Opening Lines of the Gilgamesh Epic." Pages 265–77 in *Beyond Hatti: A Tribute to Gary Beckman*. Edited by Billie Jean Collins and Piotr Michalowski. Atlanta: Lockwood.

———. 2015. *From the Mari Archives: An Anthology of Old Babylonian Letters*. Winona Lake, IN: Eisenbrauns.

Schachner, Andreas, Şenay Schachner, and Hasan Karablut. 2002. "Vier Sitzbilder aus Bīt-Bahiani." *ZA* 92:106–23.

Schwemer, Daniel. 2001. *Die Wettergottgestalten Mesopotamiens und Nordsyriens im Zeitalter der Keilschriftkulturen: Materialen und Studien nach den schriftlichen Quellen.*. Wiesbaden: Harrasowtiz.

———. 2005. "Texte aus Alalah." Pages 182–86 in *Staatsvertrage, Herrscherinschriften und andere Dokumente zur politischen Geschichte*. Edited by Bernd Jankowski and Gernot Wilhelm. *TUAT* NF 2. Gütersloh: Gütersloher Verlagshaus.

Seminara, Stefano. 1998. *L'Accadico di Emar*. Materiali per il Vocabolario Sumerico 6. Rome: Università degli Studi di Roma "La Sapienza," Dipartimento di Studi Orientali.

Seux, Marie-Joseph. 1977. "L'inscription d'Idrimi (vers 1550–1500 av. J.-C.)." Pages 42–43 in *Textes du Proche-Orient ancien et histoire d'Israël*. Paris: Cerf.

Singer, Itmar. 1999. "A Political History of Ugarit." Pages 603–733 in *Handbook of Ugaritic Studies*. Edited by Wilfred G. E. Watson and Nicholas Wyatt. HdO 1/39. Leiden: Brill.

Smith, Sydney. 1949. *The Statue of Idri-mi*. Occasional Publications of the British Institute of Archaeology in Ankara 1. London: British Institute of Archaeology in Ankara.

Snell, Daniel. 2001. *Flight and Freedom in the Ancient Near East*. CHANE 8. Leiden: Brill.

Soldt, Wilfred van. 1991. *Studies in the Akkadian of Ugarit: Dating and Grammar*. AOAT 40. Kevelaer and Neukirchen-Vluyn: Butzon & Bercker and Neukirchener Verlag.

———. 1995. "Babylonian Lexical, Religious and Literary Texts and Scribal Education at Ugarit and its Implications for the Alphabetic Literary Texts." Pages 171–212 in *Ugarit: Ein ostmediterranes Kulturzentrum im Alten Orient; Ergebnisse und Perspektiven der Forschung*. Edited by Manfried Dietrich and Oswald Loretz. Abhandlungen zur Literatur Alt-Syrien-Palästinas 7. Ugarit und seine altorientalische Umwelt 1. Münster. Ugarit-Verlag.

———. 2000. "Syrian Chronology in the Old and Early Middle Babylonian Periods." *Akkadica* 119–20:103–16.

Soden, Wolfram von. 1972. Review of *The Akkadian of Alalah*, by G. Giacumakis. *ZA* 62:126–28.

Speiser, Ephraim Avigdor. 1941. *Introduction to Hurrian*. AASOR 20. Eugene, OR: Wipf & Stock.

———. 1951. Review of *The Statue of Idri-mi*, by S. Smith. *JAOS* 71:151–52.

Spycket, Agnès. 1981. *La statuaire du Proche-Orient ancien*. Leiden: Brill.

Stavi, Boaz. 2015. *The Reign of Tudhaliya II and Šuppiluliuma I: The Contribution of the Hittite Documentation to a Reconstruction of the Amarna Age*. THeth 31. Heidelberg: Universitätsverlag Winter.

Stein, Diana. 1993–1997. "Mittan(n)i B. Bildkunst und Architektur." Pages 296–99 in vol. 8 of *Reallexikon der Assyriologie*. Edited by Dietz-Otto Edzard. Berlin: de Gruyter.

Stein, Gil. 2014. "Economic Dominance, Conquest, or Interaction among Equals? Theoretical Models for Understanding Culture Contact in Early Near Eastern Complex Societies." Pages 55–67 in *Proceedings of the International Conference of Young Archaeologists*. Edited by M. Hossein Azizi Kharanaghi et al. Tehran: Tehran University.

Streck, Michael. 2002. "Zwischen Weide, Dorf und Stadt: Sozio-ökonomische Strukturen des amurritischen Nomadismus am Mittleren Euphrat." *BaM* 33:155–209.

Struble, Eudora, and Virgina Rimmer Herrmann. 2009. "An Eternal Feast at Samʾal: The New Iron Age Mortuary Stele from Zincirli in Context." *BASOR* 356:15–49.

Suriano, Matthew. 2009. "Dynasty Building at Ugarit: The Ritual and Political Context of KTU 1.161." *AuOr* 27:5–22.

———. 2017. "Kingship and Carpe Diem, Between Gilgamesh and Qoheleth." *VT* 67:285–306.

———. 2018. *A History of Death in the Hebrew Bible*. New York: Oxford University Press.

Svärd, Saana, Tero Alstola, Hedi Jauhianen, Aleksi Sahala, and Krister Linden. 2021. "Fear in Akkadian Texts: New Digital Perspectives on Lexical Semantics." Pages 470–502 in *The Expression of Emotions in Ancient Egypt and Mesopotamia*. Edited by Shih-Wei Hsu and Jaume Llop Radùa. CHANE 116. Leiden: Brill.

Teinz, Katharina. 2014. "Imagery of Ancestors? Bowl-Holding Seated Stone Effigies." Pages 11–28 in *Contextualising Grave Inventories in the Ancient Near East: Proceedings of a Workshop at the London 7th ICAANE in April 2010 and an International Symposium in Tübingen in November 2010, Both Organised by the Tübingen Post-Graduate School "Symbols of the Dead"*. Edited by Peter Pfälzner et al. Qaṭna Studien Supplementa 3. Wiesbaden: Harrassowitz.

Tigay, Jeffrey H. 1982. *The Evolution of the Gilgamesh Epic*. Philadelphia: University of Philadelphia Press.

Torrecilla, Eduardo. 2021. "The Toponym uru*A-la-at-ha* in the Letters RSO 23 28–35 and Elsewhere." *Antiguo Oriente* 19:113–28.

———. 2022. "Reflections on the Qaṭna Letters TT1-5 (I): Hittite Expansionism and the Syrian Kingdoms." *Antigua Orientalis* 40:321–43.

Tropper, Josef, and Juan-Pablo Vita. 2010. *Das Kanaano-Akkadische der Amarnazeit*. Lehrbücher orientalischer Sprachen I/1. Münster: Ugarit-Verlag.

Tsevat, Matitiahu 1958. "Alalakhiana." *HUCA* 29:109–34.

———. 1971. Review of *The Akkadian of Alalah*, by G. Giacumakis. *JBL* 90:350–52.

Tugendhaft, Aaron. 2018. *Baal and the Politics of Poetry*. Ancient Word. New York: Routledge.

Turri, Luigi. 2020. "Geopolitics of the Orontes Valley in the Late Bronze Age." Pages 281–301 in *From the Prehistory of Upper Mesopotamia to the Bronze and Iron Age Societies of the Levant*. Vol 1 in *Proceedings of the 5th "Broadening Horizons" Conference (Udine 5–8 June 2017)*. Edited by Marco Iamoni. Trieste: EUT Edizioni Università di Trieste.

———. 2021. "The Rediscovery of Amioun or the Ancient Ammiya: Geography and Politics in Northern Lebanon during the Second Millennium." *Rivista di Studi Fenici* 49:33–52.

Ussishkin, David. 1970. "The Syro-Hittite Ritual Burial of Monuments." *JNES* 29:124–28.

Van De Mieroop, Marc. 2016. "A Babylonian Cosmopolis." Pages 259–70 in *Problems of Canonicity and Identity Formation in Ancient Egypt and Mesopotamia*. Edited by Gojko Barjamovic and Kim Ryholt. CNIP 43. Copenhagen: Museum Tusculanum.

———. 2023. *Before and After Babel: Writing as Resistance in Ancient Near Eastern Empires*. Oxford: Oxford University Press.

van den Hout, Theo. 2020. *A History of Hittite Literacy: Writing and Reading in Late Bronze Age Anatolia (1650–1200 BC)*. Cambridge: Cambridge University Press.

Veldhuis, Niek. 2014. *History of the Cuneiform Lexical Tradition*. GMTR 6. Münster: Ugarit-Verlag.

Vidal, Jordi. 2012. "Summaries on the Young Idrimi." *SJOT* 26:77–87.

Vita, Juan-Pablo. 1997. "*PĀNI* comme préposition dans l'accadien périphérique du Bronze Récent." *NABU* 1997/124.

———. 2002. "Warfare and the Army at Emar." *AoF* 29:113–27.

———. 2020. "Akkadian as Lingua Franca." Pages 357–72 in *A Companion to Ancient Near Eastern Languages*. Edited by Rebecca Hasselbach-Andee. Blackwell Companions to the Ancient World. Hoboken, NJ: Wiley Blackwell.

———. 2021a. "Akkadian in Syria and Canaan." Pages 1213–65 in *History of the Akkadian Language*. 2 vols. Edited by Juan-Pablo Vita. HdO 1/152.1–2. Leiden: Brill.

———. 2021b. "The Hittites in the Administrative Texts of Ugarit." *Kaskal* 18:111–26.

von Dassow, Eva. 1997. "Social Stratification of Alalah under the Mittani Empire." PhD diss., New York University.

———. 2002. "Lists of People from the Alalah IV Administrative Archives." *UF* 34:835–911.

———. 2005. "Archives of Alalakh IV in Archaeological Context." *BASOR* 338:1–69.

———. 2008. *State and Society in the Late Bronze Age: Alalah under the Mittani Empire*. SCCNH 17. Bethesda, MD: CDL.

———. 2010. "What Did Archives Mean in Mittani? The Case of 15th Century BCE Alalah." *JCSMS* 5:37–53.

———. 2015a. "Genres of Texts and Archives of Tablets." *OLZ* 110:177–90.

———. 2015b. "Idrimi." In *The Encyclopedia of Ancient History*. Edited by Robert Bagnall et al. https://doi.org/10.1002/9781444338386.wbeah26123.

———. 2017. "Diri and S[a] at Alalah." *NABU* 2017/53.

———. 2020a. "Alalah between Mittani and Hatti." *Anteriore Antica. Journal of Ancient Near Eastern Cultures* 2:193–226.

———. 2020b. "Nation Building in the Plain of Antioch from Hatti to Hatay." Pages 190–208 in *Perspectives on the History of Ancient Near Eastern Studies*. Edited by Agnès Garcia-Ventura and Lorenzo Verderame. University Park, PA: Eisenbrauns.

———. 2022. "Mittani and Its Empire." Pages 455–528 in *From the Hyksos to the Late Second Millennium BC*. Vol. 3 of *The Oxford History of the Ancient Near East*. Edited by Karen Radner et al. New York: Oxford University Press.

Walker, Christopher. 1981. "The Second Tablet of *ṭupšenna pitema*, an Old Babylonian Naram-Sin Legend?" *JCS* 33:191–95.

Wasserman, Nathan. 2006. "*maṭāṭum*, 'To Collapse.'" *NABU* 2006/45.

Weeden, Mark. 2019. "Remarks on Syllabaries at Alalah VII and IV: Arguments for an Archival Approach to the Study of Cuneiform Writing." Pages 129–53 in *Keilschriftliche*

Syllabare: Zur Methodik ihrer Erstellung. Edited by Jörg Klinger and Sebestian Fischer. BBVO 28. Berlin: PeWe.

Weeden, Mark, and Wilfred Lambert. 2020. "A Statue Inscription of Samsuiluna from the Papers of W. G. Lambert." *RA* 114:15–62.

Westenholz, Joan. 1997. *Legends of the Kings of Akkade.* MC 7. Winona Lake, IN: Eisenbrauns.

Wilhelm, Gernot. 1970. *Untersuchungen zum Hurro-Akkadischen von Nuzi.* AOAT 9. Kevelaer and Neukirchen-Vluyn: Butzon & Bercker and Neukirchener Verlag.

———. 1993–1997. "Mittan(n)i, Mitanni, Maitani. A. Historisch." Pages 296–99 in vol. 8 of *Reallexikon der Assyriologie.* Edited by Dietz-Otto. Edzard. Berlin: de Gruyter.

———. 2003–2005. "Parattarna I. und II." Pages 339–40 in vol. 1 of *Reallexikon der Assyriologie.* Edited by Dietz-Otto Edzard and Michael Streck. Berlin: de Gruyter

———. 2012. "Šuppiluliuma I. und die Chronologie der Amarna-Zeit." Pages 225–57 in *Kāmid el-Lōz 20. Die Keilschriftbriefe und der Horizont von El-Amarna.* Edited by Rolf Hachmann. SBA 87. Bonn: Dr. Rudolf Habelt.

———. 2015. "Suppiluliuma and the Decline of the Mittanian Kingdom." Pages 69–79 in *Qaṭna and the Networks of Bronze Age Globalism: Proceedings of an International Conference in Stuttgart and Tübingen in October 2009.* Edited by Peter Pfälzner and Michel Al-Maqdissi. Qaṭna Studien Supplementa 2. Wiesbaden: Harrassowitz,

———. 2019. "Die hurritischen Texte aus Šamuha." Pages 197–209 in *Keilschrifttafeln aus Kayalıpınar 1: Textfunde aus den Jahren 1999–2017.* Edited by Elisabeth Riekne. Wiesbaden: Harrassowitz.

Winstone, Harry. 1990. *Woolley of Ur: The Life of Sir Leonard Woolley.* London: Secker & Warburg.

Wiseman, Donald. 1953. *The Alalakh Tablets.* Occasional Publications of the British Institute of Archaeology in Ankara 2. London: British Institute of Archaeology in Ankara.

———. 1954. "Supplementary Copies of Alalakh Tablets." *JCS* 8:1–30.

———. 1962. "Some Aspects of Babylonian Influence at Alalah." *Syria* 39:180–87.

Woolley, C. Leonard. 1936. "Tal Atchana." *JHS* 56:125–32.

———. 1937. "Excavations near Antioch in 1936." *AJ* 17:1–15.

———. 1938. "Excavations at Tal Atchana." *AJ* 18:1–28.

———. 1939a. "Alalakh: The City and Its Sculpture." *Times* (London), August 3, 13–14, 16.

———. 1939b. "Excavations at Atchana-Alalakh." *AJ* 19:1–37.

———. 1939c. "A New Chapter of Hittite Sculpture Opens." *Illustrated London News*, December 9, 867–69.

———. 1947. "Atchana 1946. Summary of a Lecture by Lt.-Col. Sir Leonard Woolley, to the British School of Archaeology in Iraq, 7 October 1946." *Man* 58:60–61.

———. 1948. "Excavations at Atchana-Alalakh, 1939." *AJ* 28:1–19.

———. 1950. "Excavations at Atchana-Alalakh, 1946." *AJ* 30:1–21.

———. 1953. *A Forgotten Kingdom: Being a Record of the Results Obtained from the Excavation of Two Mounds, Atchana and Al Mina, in the Turkish Hatay.* London: Penguin.

———. 1955. *Alalakh: An Account of the Excavations at Tell Atchana in the Hatay, 1937–1949.* Reports of the Research Committee of the Society of Antiquaries of London 18. London: Society of Antiquaries.

Yener, K. Aslıhan, ed. 2005. *Surveys in the Plain of Antioch and Orontes Delta, Turkey, 1995–2002*. Vol. 1 of The *Amuq Valley Regional Projects*. OIP 131. Chicago: Oriental Institute of the University of Chicago

———. 2010. *The 2003–2004 Excavation Seasons*. Vol. 1 of *Tell Atchana, Ancient Alalakh*. Istanbul: Koç University Press.

Yener, K. Alıhan, Murat Akar, and Mara Horowitz, eds. 2019a. "Interpretation and Discussion." Pages 311–41 in *The Late Bronze II City. 2006–2010 Excavations*, vol. 2 of *Tell Atchana, Alalakh*. Edited by K. A. Yener et al. Istanbul: Koç University Press.

———. 2019b. *The Late Bronze II City. 2006–2010 Excavations*. Vol. 2 of *Tell Atchana, Alalakh*. Istanbul: Koç University Press.

Zeeb, Frank. 2001. *Die Palastwirtschaft in Altsyrien nach den spätbabylonischen Getreidelieferlisten aus Alalah (Schicht VII)*. AOAT 282. Münster: Ugarit-Verlag.

———. 2004. "The History of Alalah as a Testcase for an Ultrashort Chronology of the Mid-Second Millennium B.C.E." Pages 81–95 in *Mesopotamian Dark Age Revisited: Proceedings of an International Conference of SCIEM 2000 (Vienna 8th–9th November 2002)*. Edited by Hermann Hunger and Regine Pruzsinszky. Contributions to the Chronology of the Eastern Mediterranean 6. Denkschriften der Gesamtakademie 32. Vienna: Verlag der Österreichischen Akademie der Wissenschaften.

Ziegler, Nele, and Hervé Reculeau. 2014. "The Sutean Nomads in the Mari Period." Pages 209–26 in *Settlement Dynamics and Human-Landscape Interaction in the Dry Steppes of Syria*. Edited by Daniele Morandi Bonacossi. StCh 4. Wiesbaden: Harrassowitz.

Plates

The following plates contain composite photographs of the cheek and body inscriptions that were created using the GNU Image Manipulation Program from photos taken by the author with an SLR camera in January 2019. As discussed in §2.9, my goal in creating these composite photographs was to be able to explore paleography within a single line without having to flip between different pages, as is the case with the plates in Smith 1949 and Dietrich and Loretz 1981. Since a single line of the inscription can curve around the surface of the statue, creating the composite photographs involved varying degrees of image manipulation, with the result that the photographs cannot be used reliably to judge the scale of individual signs relative to each other. In some places on the statue, the curvature of the inscription is so significant that it was impossible for me to avoid negative space between lines when creating a composite photograph. On these occasions, I have filled in the negative space with a color close to that of the surrounding surface of the statue without attempting to obscure its existence.

Plate 1. The cheek inscription.

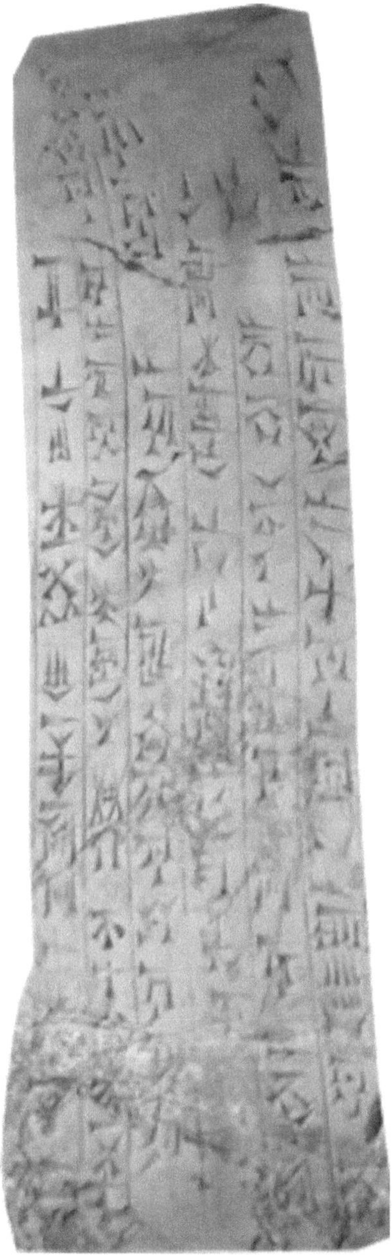

Plate 2. The body inscription, lines 1–6.

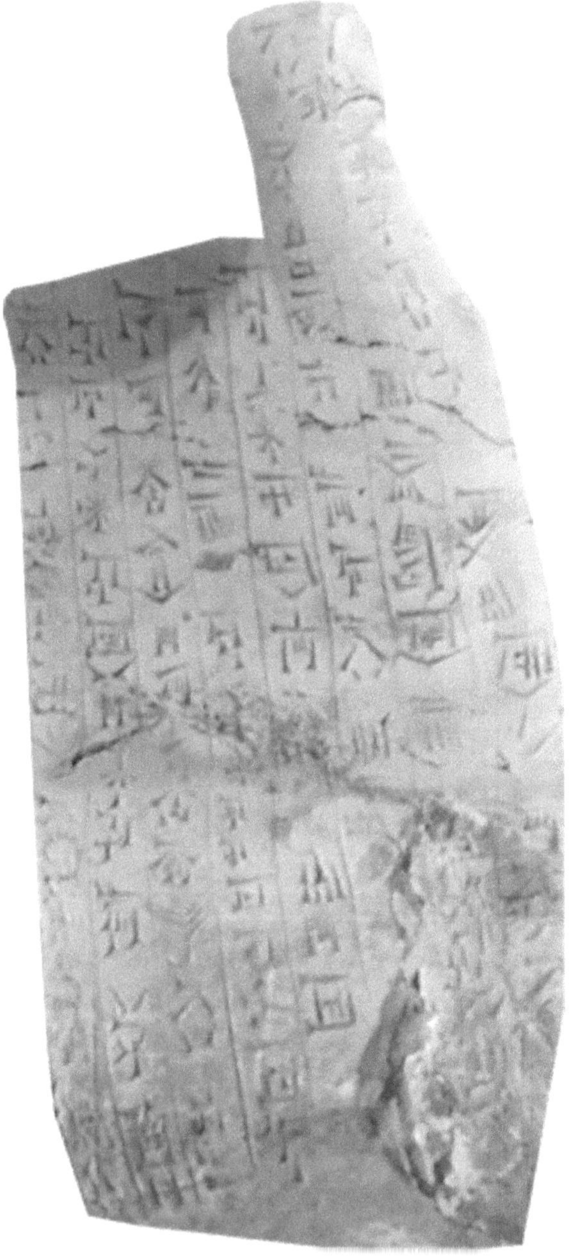

Plate 3. The body inscription, lines 7–14.

Plate 4. The body inscription, lines 15–23.

Plate 5. The body inscription, lines 24–29.

Plate 6. The body inscription, lines 30–36.

Plate 7. The body inscription, lines 37–42.

Plate 8. The body inscription, lines 43–51.

Plate 9. The body inscription, lines 52–58.

Plate 10. The body inscription, lines 59–64.

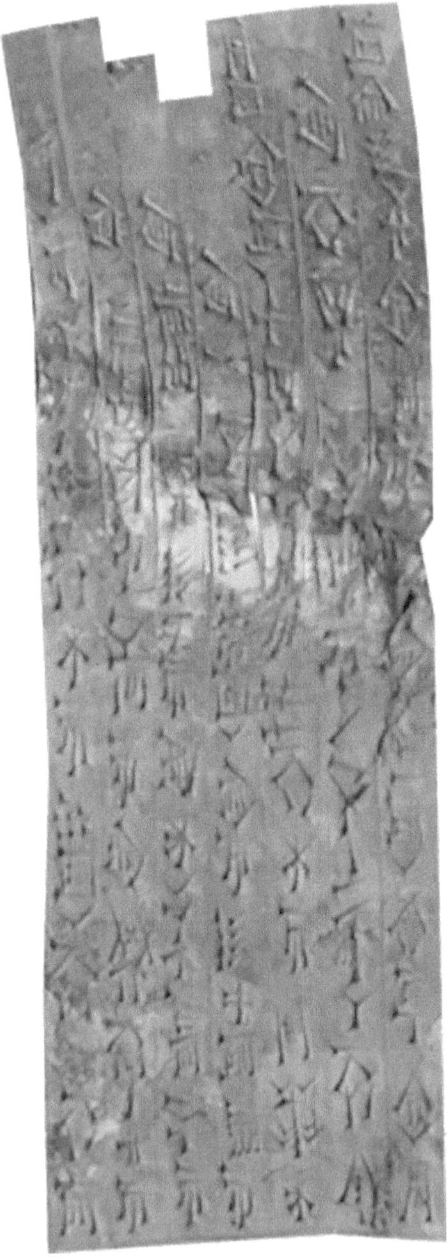

Plate 11. The body inscription, lines 65–71.

Plate 12. The body inscription, lines 72–74.

Plate 13. The body inscription, lines 75–78.

Plate 14. The body inscription, lines 79–86.

Plate 15. The body inscription, lines 87–92.

Plate 16. The body inscription, lines 93–100.

Indices

PRIMARY TEXTS

AbB
2 159 255
9 1:9 22
14 144: 6–9 195
14 144: 11–13 195
14 144: 22–23 195
14 144: 26–30 195
AlT
2 [1.1]: 1 166
2 [1.1]: 32–33 197
2 [1.1]: 75–77 280
2 [1.1]: 76 280
3 [1.2] 37–38, 58, 61, 71, 221, 228, 247
3 [1.2]: 15–16 273
3 [1.2]: 39 228
3 [1.2]: 45 240
6: 6 56
6: 37 56
15 [36.1] 135, 148
15 [36.1]: 16 160
15 [36.1]: 20 159
16 [36.2] 153
16 [36.2]: 24 137
17 [31.3] 37, 188, 190–91
17 [31.3] 5 155
17 [31.3]: 7–9 190
17 [31.3]: 8 61, 160
17 [31.3]: 22 153
17 [31.3]: 23 159
17 [31.3]: 5 155
46 [352.1] 153
46 [352.1]:18 137
47 [352.2] 153
47 [352.2]: 3 160
47 [352.2]: 5 160
47 [352.2]: 7 160
47 [352.2]: 20 159
48 [352.3] 138, 153
48 [352.3]: 5 206
48 [353.2]: 22 137
49 [352.4] 138, 153
51 [352.6] 139–40
63 [22.11]: 21–22 89
66 [341.1] 153
67 [341.2]: 11 137
67 [341.2]: 12 137
67 [341.2]: 13 137
67 [341.2]: 14 137
69 [341.4] 37
69 [341.4]: 21 153
70 [341.5] 138, 153
71 [341.6] 37
72 [342.1]: 16 159
72 [342.1]: 17–18 160
74 [342.3] 137–38, 153
74 [342.3]: 14 153
74 [342.3]: 19 137
87 [32.1] 135–38
87 [32.1]: 23–34 136
87 [32.1]: 27 136–37
88 [32.2] 135
91 [33.1] 137, 159
91 [33.1]: 21 137
91 [33.1]: 22 137, 159
91 [33.1]: 23 137
92 [33.2] 153
92 [33.2]: 20 271
93 [33.3] 153
94 [33.4]: 21–23 254
98e [37.1]: rev. 6′137
99 [37.2] 37

100 [38.3] 37
101 [38.4] 188
101 [38.4]: 9–10 188
103 [37.4]: rev. 7′137
104 [37.5]: rev. 1′–2′137
104 [37.5]: rev. 4′137
104 [37.5]: rev. 5′159
107 [2.4]: 1–4 138
109 [2.6] 155
109 [2.6]: 1–5 138
114 [2.11] 153
124 [ATH 1] 40, 160
128 [414.1] 139, 154
128 [414.1]: 26 153
131+ [413.3 = *SSAU* 2 1]: 47 145
131+ [413.3 = *SSAU* 2 1]: 61–65 144
147 [415.4]: i 44 160
153 [413.17 = *SSAU* 2 33]: 30 134
156 [415.5] 139, 154–55, 159
156 [415.5]: 1 154–55
156 [415.5]: rev. a 2′153
159 [415.7] 159
161 [414.3] 188
166 [415.11]: 19 207
181 [414.7] 207
186 [412.3] 37
187 [412.4] 37
188 [412.5]: 5–6 206
188 [412.5]: 8 206
192 [412.9]: ii 9 160
227 [412.19] 37
304 [432.6]: ii 14 159
329 [44:1]: 1 144
329 [44:1]: 18 144
329 [44.1] 201
330 [44.2] 201
330 [44.2]: 7–8 153
330 [44.2]: 12–13 153
338 + 33.9 [44.7] 201
353 [44:15] 138–39, 154–55
353 [44.15]: 22 153
355 [44.17] 212
366 [40.05]: 12 89
366 [40.05]: 21–22 89
366 [40.05]: 22 89
395 [47.4] 37
401 [47.10] 37
403 [47.12] 139
417 [46.1] 153
418 [46.2] 153
419 [46.3] 153
419 [46.3]: 4 153
421 [46.5] 153
422 [46.6]: 8 159
425 [46.8]: 12 159
445 [5.1] 135
446 [5.2] 135
447 [5.3] 135
448 [6.1] 135
449 [6.2] 135
450 [6.3] 135
451 [6.4] 135
452 [6.5] 135
453 [6.6] 135
453a [6.7] 135
AOAT
27, no. 11 187–88
27, no. 189 37, 184
27, no. 193 45
27, no. 210 155
ARM
1 29: 21–24 218
2 44: 20 216
2 102: 19–21 246
28 20: 6–12 195
28 105: rev. 27′–28′ 254
32: 252 250
BaghM
21 474: 18–21 278
BM
09037 199
131938 [493.29]: 3 206
BWL
126:31 106
148: 83–84 198
160: 3 244
227: 19–20 198
CT
20 32: 70 191
CTH
41.I 222
45 165
46 165–68, 209
47 165
49 82, 169
51 152, 167–69, 171

51: §4 149
51: 38 169
53 168–70
75 167
135 167, 185
136 167
311.2.A 225
446 98
EA
45: 30–31 150
47: 16–17 233
51 162, 165
53 165
55 112
56: 14 194
64: 9–13 229
65: 9 112
73: 25–29 207
74: 2 112
74: 24–27 207
75: 32–34 207
81: 11–14 207
82: 14–15 233–34
84: 8–13 229
86: 9 190
101: 11–12 197
113: 30 257
114: 58–59 263
126: 16 257
132: 41 222
139 190
139: 13–14 207
140: 10–11 207
160: 25 169–70
161: 36 170
162: 20–21 195
179: 19′222–23
196: 13 25
228: 18 194
286: 5 197
286: 22 112
300: 20–22 93
335: 10 222
Emar
282: 2 89
282: 8 89
538: 72 [Msk 74175a] 180
538: 164′[Msk 94193a] 202
538: 199 [Msk 74175a] 92
783: 34′244
FM
3 136: 14 254
7 39: 33 274
7 45 186
Gilg.
I 9–10 116
I 10 179
I 20–23 119
I 24–28 119
I 45–46 117
I 46 179
III 9 257
VII 142 266
VIII 86 266
XI 19 234
XI 324–328 119
XII 152–153 106
Gs-Kutscher 6 *See* LN-104
HAM
6282 [417.6] 188
7331/25 [492.23] 188
HSS
9 22: 27–28 197
Idrimi Statue
CI 1 3, 21, 100, 117, 121, 131, 179, 241–42
CI 2 3, 21, 46, 50–53, 63, 65, 67, 90, 100, 118, 122, 147–48, 158, 179–83, 200, 205, 283
CI 3 3, 21, 50, 53, 90, 100, 118, 181, 183, 205, 283
1–23 75, 101
1–91 90, 100
2 148, 186–87, 215, 270
3 187–89
3–5 71
3–60 191
4 60, 70, 101, 160, 189–92, 194
4–6 242
5 56, 191–92
6 192, 194, 242
7 193, 219

8 193–94, 196, 219–20, 256
9 120, 194–97
10 190, 195–98, 200, 204, 241
11 100–101, 190, 198–200, 243
12 100–101, 192, 200–201
13 143–44, 200–201, 203
13–14 143
14 101, 200–202, 214
15 202–3, 247
16 143, 203, 205, 226, 258
17 53, 143, 204–5, 207, 214
18 205–6
19 244
20 206–8, 217, 253
21 203, 208
22 208–9
23 206, 209
24 209–10, 217
24–51 75
25 210
26 60, 210–11, 214, 217–18, 230, 244
27 205, 211
27–30 71
28 211–12
29 211–13
29–30 212
30 206, 213–15, 218
31 215–17
33 192, 216–217
34 215–17
35 217
36 54, 217, 219, 258
37 218
38 114, 218
39 214–15, 218–19
40 219, 242–43
40–42 71
41 129, 194, 205, 219–20, 227, 234
42 75, 219–20, 251
42–58 190
42–60 71
43 81, 221, 224, 227, 235
43–46 222
44 81, 222–24, 227, 235, 247
45 77, 80–81, 90, 213, 221, 223
46 81, 119, 222, 224–26, 235
47 74, 113, 226–28
48 129–30, 181, 205, 220, 227–28
49 221, 227–29
50 74, 229–30, 235
51 15, 74, 76, 113, 230, 235–36
52 74, 229–32
52–74 75
53 74, 114, 220, 231–34
54 74–75, 113–14, 231, 234–36
55 114, 236–39, 271
56 114, 189, 214, 238–40
57 196, 240–42, 276
57–59 131
57–60 75
58 121, 131, 179, 220, 225, 241–42, 250
59 238, 242–43
59–60 219
60 75, 243–45, 278
61 58, 111, 115, 244–46
62 115, 236, 245–46
63 74, 245–46
64 74, 214–16, 246–48, 251
64–77 71
65 214, 231, 248, 260
66 248–51
67 248–52
68 248–51
69 220, 236, 246, 251–52
70 239, 251–52
70–71 217
70–72 39
71 207, 239, 243, 251, 253
72 214, 253, 258
72–73 253
73 101–3, 253–55, 259–60
74 76, 80, 214, 255–56
75 76, 256, 261, 281
75–100 75
76 117, 256–57, 280
77 213–14
78 148, 258, 265, 284–85
78–79 257
79 238, 240, 253, 258–60
80 71, 73, 214, 247–48, 260–61, 272
81 243, 261–62
82 256, 261, 279
83 256, 261–62, 267
84 49, 244, 246, 261–63, 267, 276
84–85 276
85 117, 205, 263–66, 268
86 208, 262, 266–68

87 105, 266, 269, 271
87–91 90, 105
88 105, 232, 270–71
89 54, 91–92, 94, 105, 214, 271–72
90 102, 205, 214, 251–52, 260, 272
91 102, 106, 272
92 66, 244, 272–73, 283
93 66, 148, 252, 272–74
93–98 66
94 66, 274–75, 285
95 49, 275–77
96 216, 230, 243–44, 274, 277–79
97 193, 272, 274–75, 279–80
98 65–67, 89, 213, 280–83
98–99 158, 261
98–100 21
99 64–65, 67, 88, 158, 213, 273, 275, 277, 282–83, 285
99–100 162
100 21, 89, 119, 225, 277, 283–85
JCS
20 96–97: 36–43 107
34 242–43: 25–27 271
K.
2051+: rev. ii 16 92–93
KAI
2.226: 1–2 88
KAV
1: ii 14–15 202
KBo
1 5: i 14 251
3 56: 6′185
7 14: 14 226
10.1: obv. 31 250
10.2: ii 11–12 250
KpT
1.11 167
KTU
1.14 [RS 2.[003]+]: III 26–27 235
1.109 [RS 24.253]: 10–11 235
1.161 [RS 34.126] 107
1.161 [RS 34.126]: 30 98
1.161 [RS 34.126]: 30–31 235
2.70 [RS 29.093]: 1 185
2.73 [RS 17.434+]: 4′202
4.102 [RS 11.857]: 6 185
5.1 [RS 1.016]: 5 185
KUB
36 103: 2′185
LAPO 17
488 [no. 733] 211
LN
104 127, 130
104: 16–24 128
MC
7 300–301 118
7 337: 26 89
16 126: 54 252
Msk
74145+ 181
74193a 180
74193a+ 181, 201
MSL
12 127: 69 92
14 332 199
PBS
1/1 2: ii 29 257
PIHANS
117 92: 19 218
PRU
3 65 [RS 16.247]: 14 22, 23
3 83–84 [RS 16.157]: 24–28 130
3 85–86 [RS 16.250]: 23 284
3 107–108 [RS 16.238+]: 15–17 130
3 110 [RS 16.267]: 7–8 130
3 140–41 [RS 16.132]: 29–30 130
4 48–52, 67–70 [RS 17.340+]: rev. 11′–14′130
4 48–52, 67–70 [RS 17.340+]: rev. 20′282
4 52 [RS 17.639A]: 21′–23′75
4 63–67 [RS 17.237]: 15′282
4 144–46 [RS 17.318A+]: 15′ 284
4 154–57 [RS 17.146]: 9 255
4 154–57 [RS 17.146]: 15 255
4 154–57 [RS 17.146]: 17 255
4 154–57 [RS 17.146]: 24 255
4 154–57 [RS 17.146]: 31 255
4 154–57 [RS 17.146]: 41 255
4 293b [RS 19.55] 123, 129
4 293b [RS 19.55]: 2 125

RA
23 38: 13–15 197
43 139–175: Inventory I, 249 171
43 139–175: Inventory I, 327 171
43 139–175: Inventory I, 363 171
43 139–175: Inventory I, 323–333 171
RIMA
3 36: ii 27 184
RINAP
1 43: ii 5 251
RS
14.128+ 111, 182, 261
RSOu
23 21 [RS 94.2571]: 6–32 123–25
23 21 [RS 94.2571]: 9 123
23 21 [RS 94.2571]: 19 123
23 21 [RS 94.2571]: 23 123
23 21 [RS 94.2571]: 27 123
23 21 [RS 94.2571]: 28 123
23 21 [RS 94.2571]: 30 123
23 22 [RS 94.2185]: 19 123
23 22 [RS 94.2185]: 21–22 125–26
23 27 [RS 94.2585]: 9 123
23 27 [RS 94.2585]: 23 123
23 27 [RS 94.2585]: 25 123
23 27 [RS 94.2585]: 33 123
23 81 [RS 94.2524]: 32 123
23 81 [RS 94.2524]: 32–35 124–25
23 104 [RS 94.2481+]: 10 123
23 107 [RS 94.2540]: 14′–21′ 126–27
23 107 [RS 94.2540]: 15′123
23 107 [RS 94.2540]: 19′123
23 107 [RS 94.2540]: 20′128
SAA
2 5 217
2 6 222
10 14 245
SSAU
2 4 [492.31] 250
4 11 [412.20]: 11 207
TT
2: 44–47 273
2: 54–55 266
3 151–52
3: 1–6 151
3: 7–19 151
3: 20 151
3: 23–24 151
3: 30–31 151
3: 32–34 152
4 151–52
4: 1–3 152
4: 4–6 152
4: 37–39 152
6 171–72
Ugaritica
5 205 [RS 20.135]: iii 84 261
5 220 [RS 20.121]: 153 223
5 220 [RS 20.121]: 168 223
WVDOG
102 81A 92
ZA
65 56: 57–59 274

ANCIENT PROPER NOUNS

I. Divine Names

Adad 212, 215, 282. *See also* Addu of Aleppo *and* Storm God
Addu of Aleppo 14, 89, 186, 188, 212, 215. *See also* Storm God
AN *See* Šamû
Aššur 282
Baʿal of Tyre 217. *See also* Storm God
Baʿal Zaphon 130, 215, 217. *See also* Storm God
Dagan 186
El 235
Hadda *See* Addu of Aleppo
Hebat 3, 186, 188
INANNA *See* IŠTAR
Išhara 282

Ištar *See* IŠTAR
IŠTAR 3, 9, 120, 158, 186–87, 257, 270, 282
Jupiter Casius 217. *See also* Storm God
Kubi 139, 153–55, 159
Moon God 9, 158, 280
Nergal-of-the-Marketplace 128
Storm God 5, 9, 37, 158, 187, 215, 217, 280, 282
Sun God 9–10, 89–90, 106, 158, 225, 266, 280, 283
Šalaš 186
Šamaš 89, 106, 117, 119, 266, 274, 282. *See also* Sun God
Šamû 273
Šaušga 282
Sin 282. *See also* Moon God
Teššub 215, 217. *See also* Storm God
Zeus Kasios 217. *See also* Storm God

II. Ethnonyms

Hana 254
Sim'al 254
Sutean 4, 70, 147, 202–3, 205, 207
Umman-manda 6, 80–81, 119, 122, 224–26

III. Personal Names

Abba-el 188
'Abdi-'Aširte 170, 207, 229
Addu-nerari 41, 48, 78–79, 91, 162–73, 177–78. *See also* IM-nerari
Agi-dIM 137
Agi-Teššub 149–52, 165–66
Agiya 150, 169
Akizzi 112, 165, 172
Akubiya 160
Ammi-ditana 107
Ammi-ṣaduqa 107
Amon-appa 233
Anum-Hirbi 250
Apra 190
Aqhat 184
Arnuwar 188
Asiri 150
Ašraqama 137–39
Ašriya 137–38
Aštabi-šar 160
Aziru 82, 169–70, 195, 207
Biriyaššura 138–39, 155
Biriyaššuwa 139
Birriya 150
Dani'ilu 184
Darius I 222
David 48–49
Ehli-Tenu 167
Enkidu 106, 117, 257, 266
Esarhaddon 217
Ewiya 144
Ewri-Kiaše 134
Ewrihuda 154
Zaze 153–54
Gašera 13
Gilgamesh 106, 117, 119–20, 131, 147, 266
Habahi 150
Hadad-'ezer 184
Hammurabi (of Babylon) 256
Hammurabi (of Yamhad) 13
Hannutti 151–52
Hattušili I 13, 185, 226, 247, 250–51
Hišmiya 150
Huliga 145
Huqqana 169
Ibbit-Lim 99
Ibiranu 58
Idadda 151–52, 168, 171–72, 273
Ili-rapi 207
Ili-Šarruma 167
Ilimi-ilima 3, 13–14, 33,41, 136, 138–39, 153–54, 159–61, 164, 167, 185–86, 189
IM-nerari 8–10, 21, 82, 85, 105–7, 156–57, 162–67, 171–73, 176–78, 272. *See also* Addu-nerari
Ini-Teššub 123
Ir-dIM 197
IR3-Heba 197
Iri-Halba 138–39, 153–54
Irib-Ba'lu 127–28

Irkabtu 138, 154, 160
Itur-Addu 14, 34, 165–69
Jepthah 48
Joseph 48
Kabiya 135–38, 148–49
Kaštiliasu III 184
Kirta 235
Kušah-ewri 137
Kušaya 137
Maduwa 144
Marduk-šapik-zeri 274
Muršili I 188
Naram-Sin 118–19, 147
Niqmaddu II 75, 130, 165, 220, 282
Niqmaddu III 107, 202, 235
Niqmepa (of Alalah) 10, 13–14, 33, 37–39, 41, 45, 58, 66, 71, 73, 138, 148, 155, 159, 160–64, 166, 185, 187–88, 190, 197, 250–52
Niqmepa (of Ugarit) 75
Niqmepa (of Yamhad) 104
Niruwabi 150
Pabuli 235
Pallanuwe 138–39
Parattarna I 6–7, 38, 52, 68, 71, 74–75, 79–82, 119, 122, 129–32, 189, 191, 220–26, 235, 239
Parattarna II 38, 221
Pilliya37–38, 58, 61, 71, 221, 228, 273
Puduhepa 202
Rib-Addi 197, 207–8, 257
Šamhat 266
Samsi-Addu I 52
Samsu-iluna 104
Sargon 118
Shalmaneser III 184
Si'gabbar 88
Sumu-epuh 186
Sunaššura 251–52
Šarra-el 188
Šarrupše 168–70
Šarruwa 9–10, 39–41, 48, 60–69, 73, 82, 86, 100, 110, 112, 115, 137, 147, 157–62, 164, 177, 190, 227, 281–82
Šarruwanta 160
Šattiwaza 149, 151, 167–68
Šuppiluliuma I 14, 33–36, 41–42, 75, 82, 87, 128, 130, 149–50, 152, 164–69, 171, 176, 220, 282
Šuppiluliuma II 184
Tagib-šarri 168
Tagiya 144
Taguhli 136–39
Taguwa (of Alalah) 136
Taguwa (of Niya) 149, 151–52, 169
Taguya 144
Takuwa *See* Taguwa (of Niya)
Tasi 124–25
Tehiya 137–38
Tette 168
Tiglath-pileser III 251
Tudhaliya (Hittite official) 40
Tudhaliya I 14
Tudhaliya II 251
Tuppiya 137
Tuttu 136, 138, 153–54, 185
Ur-šanabi 119
Urtenu 75, 117, 123, 129, 176
Uštaya 136
Wantaraššura 188
Yarim-Lim 13
Zakkar 70, 205
Zaludi 226
Zimri-Lim 13, 52
Zukraši 226
Zulkiya 150

IV. Toponyms

'Ama 209
Alašiya 206
Aleppo 3, 13, 16, 70, 149, 167, 186–87, 189, 191, 212, 215, 251. *See also* Halab
Alime 144–45
Amae *See* Ama'u
Ama'u 4–6, 40, 70, 172, 209, 218
Ammiya 4–6, 144, 206–8, 217
Amurru 22, 82, 112, 169–70, 195, 207, 210–11, 214, 222, 228, 233, 284
Anaše 207
Arahtu 150–51, 169
Assyria 22, 49, 142, 282
Babylonia 22, 142, 184
Bit-Agusi 251

Byblos 22–23, 112, 190, 197, 207–8, 222, 229, 233, 247, 257, 263
Canaan 4, 70, 72–73, 124, 206–7, 210, 228
Carchemish 22, 123, 125, 255
Casius *See* Hazzi, Mount
Der 52
Drehem 13
Ebla 13, 66, 95, 99, 186, 209
Egypt 22–25, 44, 79, 82, 112, 142, 150, 162, 165, 170, 195
Ekalte 22, 92, 199
Emar 3–4, 6, 22, 34, 58, 65, 69, 71–72, 92–93, 100, 127–28, 130, 143–44, 148, 163, 180–81, 192–93, 200, 202, 207, 219, 222, 241–42, 244, 273
Euphrates 3, 24, 52, 58, 271
Gath 229
Halab 3–4, 6, 13, 69–72, 142, 147, 155, 163, 185–90, 208, 212, 219, 226, 239. *See also* Aleppo
Hamath 205
Haššuwa 250–51
Hatti 7–8, 10–11, 13–15, 17, 23, 33–34, 36–37, 39–41, 44, 48, 51, 68, 71, 74, 76, 78, 82, 98, 101, 115, 123–25, 127, 130–31, 134, 136, 139, 142, 149–52, 160, 162–65, 167–70, 184–85, 187, 190, 207, 216–17, 222, 225–26, 247–53, 257, 260, 270
Hattuša 22, 92, 115, 118, 197, 212, 225
Hayasa 169
Hazor 95, 104, 130, 194
Hazzi, Mount 5, 215, 217
Huluhhan 7, 249
Hurri 6–7, 11, 43–44, 68, 80–81, 122, 129, 131, 221–22, 224, 226–27, 239, 273
Išmirikka 249
Issos 249
I'e 7, 249–52
Jerusalem 112, 197
Kanesh 249
Kasios *See* Hazzi, Mount
Kinanu 124
Kizzuwatna 7, 10, 37–38, 58, 61, 71, 167, 221, 228, 247–49, 251
Larsa 195–96, 256
Mari 13, 45, 49, 52, 56, 65, 148, 187–88, 195–96, 211, 218, 221, 227–28, 231, 241, 246, 250, 254–56, 267–68, 273
Mittani 6, 10–11, 14, 38–39, 43–44, 68, 70–71, 79, 95, 122, 128–29, 131–33, 140, 145–46, 152, 157, 168, 170–72, 176–77, 188–90, 221–22, 247
Moab 49
Mukiš 4–8, 10, 13, 34, 40, 70, 114, 149, 165–69, 171–72, 208–9, 215–16, 218, 247–48, 250–52, 267–68
Nagar 95
Neirab 88
Niya 4–6, 40, 70, 149, 151–52, 156, 165–67, 169–70, 172, 208–9, 218
Nuhašše 162, 164–72, 177–78, 206, 209
Nuzi 22, 59, 92, 145, 197, 221, 273
Orontes 11, 151, 170–73, 208, 217
Paššahe 7, 249
Qaṭna 22, 94–96, 99, 105, 112, 151–52, 156, 164–65, 168–73, 177–78, 194, 266, 273
Ṣapunu, Mount *See* Hazzi, Mount
Saruna 251. *See also* Zaruna
Sis 249
Sision 249
Sissu 249
Siyannu 124–25
Susa 22
Taanach 22, 214
Tamarutla 7, 249
Terqa 221
Tigunanum 212
Ṭubihu 222
Tunip 167, 170, 185, 197, 208
Tyre 217, 233
Ugarit 22–23, 25, 45, 58, 75, 89, 92–93, 95, 107, 111, 117, 119–20, 123–25, 127–30, 141, 150, 165–67, 169, 176, 181, 184–85, 196, 204, 210–11, 214, 217, 219–20, 223, 230, 233, 235–36, 242, 255, 261, 273, 282, 284
Ukulzat 168
Uluzila 7, 249
Ur 11

Uruk 24, 119–20
Yamhad 11, 13, 41, 72, 89, 104, 186–89, 256
Zalaki 160
Zaruna 7, 249–51
Zila 7, 249
Zincirli 96
Zizziya 249

ANCIENT ROOTS, WORDS, AND PHRASES

ʿal 192, 242
* *ʾnh* 131
* *ʿḏr* 184–85
ʿm 234
A$_2$ *See ittu*
A.A *See abu*
abu 91–93, 133
ahu 113–14, 219, 257, 261
ahû 219
akanna 211
alāku 217, 253
(^{d})ALAM *See ṣalmu*
ālu 5, 7–8, 110, 112, 114, 119, 124, 206, 218, 222, 248–52, 258, 269
amāru 209
AN *See šamû*
ana 56, 127, 192, 242, 245–46
ana libbi 205
ana mahar 219
ana muhhi 126–27, 158, 179, 183
ana pāni 219
anāhu 116, 129–31, 219, 227, 234
anāku 266
anamû See anmû
anantu 245–46
anmû 57, 251–52
annīnāti 273
annu 241
annû 149, 241
AN.TA *See eliš*
appūna 75
arāku 211
arki 149
ašarēdu 199
aššu 231
awātu 196
b- 242
balāṭu 285
barû 211
bāštu 253–54
bašû 191, 278
bēlu 89, 207, 284
biātu 205
bīt abi 189, 198
bītu 239–40
būšu 253–55
dagālu 46, 52, 90, 181–82, 198, 200
damāqu 228–29
damqu 228–29
dannu 188, 221, 227, 229
DINGIR *See ilu*
DUB *See ṭuppu*
(^{lu2})DUB.SAR *See ṭupšarru*
DUMU *See māru*
dūru 245
eblu 49, 276
ehelle 134, 145
eliš 244–45
elû 214, 217, 242, 248, 260
EN *See bēlu*
epēšu 128, 214, 260, 272, 278
erēbu 214
ERIN$_2$ *See ṣābu*
erṣetu 275
eṭemmu 89, 284
etēqu 201–2
eṭlu 207
GAL *See rabû* (adj.)
(^{giš})GIGIR *See narkabtu*
(^{lu2})GIR$_3$ 139–40
ġzr 184
habiru 5, 69, 71–73, 147, 207–8, 267
halāqu 280
halqu 191, 192, 194, 239–40
halzuhhuli 188
haniahhe 250
harrānu 139
hasāsu 194–96
hazannu 136, 257
hepû 251–52
hupše 139, 250
hurihtu 202
ibru 116, 256–57, 261
IGI *See pānu*

ilu 271, 279
ina 56, 192, 201–2, 244
inūma 55, 210
(lú₂)IŠ *See kizû*
ištu 203
išû 200
itti 75, 150, 220, 231–34
ittu 232–34, 270
k 55, 210
kakku 257
kalû 246
kânu 268, 271
karābu 90, 183
kīma 262–63, 269
kīma ištēn amīli 218
kīmê 269
kinūnu 238
kispu 68, 107
kizû 143, 145, 201, 203
KUR *See mātu*
kussû 261
l- 192
laqātu 273
leqû 214, 233
libbu 202, 280
LUGAL *See šarru*
madādu 275–77
mahāru 234
mahāṣu 150
māmītu 74, 229, 241
mānahtu 74, 90, 109, 113, 116, 118–31, 147, 176, 179, 182, 220, 226
mannu 196–98
mannu ša 196–97
mannumma See mannummê
mannummê 196–97, 274
maršītu 253, 258
maryannu 62, 133, 135–36, 138–42, 144–46, 148–57, 172, 176, 177, 201
mašālu 6, 9, 244, 261–63
masiktu 61, 69–70, 160, 189–91
mātu 54, 206, 217
mâtu 126
mīnu 197
mn pn 233
**mnḥ* 129
mnḥ(t) 129
MURU₂ *See qablu*
nadû 241
nâhu 129–30, 219
nakāru 149–50, 222–23, 278
NAM.ERIM₂ 229
namkūru 253–55
napāṣu 278
narû 116–20
naṣāru 283
nazāru 273–74
nê'u 219
NINDA₂ *See abu*
niqqu See nīqu
nīqu 238, 271
NISAG *See šakkanakku*
nullû 215–16
**nwḥ* 129
PAD₃ 240
pahāru 210, 253
palāhu 231–34
pānu 191–92
pānû 269
paqādu 106–7, 272
pāqidu 106–7, 176
pašāṭu 278–79
pa'āṣu 278
**pqd* 106
qablu 199
qannu 241
qaqqaru 115, 244
rabû (adj.) 193–94, 221
rabû (v.) 59, 211
rakābu 216
rākib narkabti 145
sakālu 198
sākinnu 140
sebû 212–13
SISKUR₂ *See nīqu*
ṣabātu 240–41, 251
ṣābu 81, 222, 247
ṣābū namê 250
ṣābū piṭṭāti 255
ṣābū tillati 255–56
ṣalmu 45, 51, 63, 66, 88–90, 158, 273, 283
ṣalūlu 251
ṣehru 65
ṣlm 88
šakānu 230
šakkanakku 53, 140, 199
šallatu 253, 258–59
šangû 128, 135–37, 139, 148

šapāru 224, 233
šapiltu 275, 285
šaqû 246
šarru 117, 121, 131, 166, 169, 179, 188, 207, 221, 225, 227, 235, 242
šatam šarri 138–39
šaṭāru 158
šeb'ī *See sebû*
šemû 217
šlm 235
ŠUB *See nadû*
šubtu nēhtu 117, 264–66, 268
šukkallu 136–37, 139
šulmānu 234
šulmu 75, 234–35
šumu 279
tabāku 244–45
tabku 244–45
takālu 46, 52, 90, 182–83, 200
tamû 240
tāpalu 201
tappû 116–17, 256–57, 261
târu 149–50, 213–15, 218, 239–40
tebû 245
tuppallenni 160
TI.LA *See balāṭu*
TUR *See ṣehru*
ṭābu 264–65
ṭehû 216
ṭuppu 51, 63, 100
ṭupšarru 9, 54, 65, 67, 88, 134, 137, 139–40, 158–60, 261, 280–83
ullû 251–52
umma 195
ummānu 81, 222, 247
URU *See ālu*
usandû 212
(*w*)*abālu* 217
(*w*)*arādu* 247, 260
(*w*)*ašābu* 56, 192, 211, 242, 264, 266–68
(*w*)*ašāru* 233
(*w*)*ašbu* 191–92, 194, 211, 217, 242, 253
yr' 233
yṯb 192, 242
zakû 211
zâzu 255, 256

www.ingramcontent.com/pod-product-compliance
Lightning Source LLC
Chambersburg PA
CBHW050856300426
44111CB00010B/1268
* 9 7 8 1 6 2 8 3 7 6 1 3 5 *